Acts

Acts

A New Vision of the People of God
Second Edition

Gerald L. Stevens

PICKWICK *Publications* · Eugene, Oregon

ACTS
A New Vision of the People of God, Second Edition

Pickwick Publications
An Imprint of Wipf and Stock Publishers
199 W. 8th Ave., Suite 3
Eugene, OR 97401

www.wipfandstock.com

PAPERBACK ISBN: 978-1-5326-9324-3
HARDCOVER ISBN: 978-1-5326-9355-7
EBOOK ISBN: 978-1-5326-9356-4

Cataloguing-in-Publication data:

Names: Stevens, Gerald L.

Acts : a new visions of the people of God / Gerald L. Stevens.

Description: Eugene, OR: Pickwick Publications, 2016 | Includes bibliographical references.

Identifiers: ISBN 978-1-5326-9324-3 (paperback) | ISBN 978-1-5326-9355-7 (hardcover) | ISBN 978-1-5326-9356-4 (ebook)

Subjects: LCSH: Bible | N.T. Acts | Commentaries

CLASSIFICATION: BS2625.53 S75 2019 (PRINT) | BS2625.53 (EBOOK)

Manufactured in the U.S.A.   06/12/19

Dedicated to my students
past, present, and future

Credits and Permissions

As I have indicated in other publications, in the pursuit of learning, we never walk alone, and we always stand on others' shoulders. Obvious in these pages will be that I am indebted to the extensive commentary tradition on Acts, as well as special studies. I tried to notate instances of specific debt. Yet, at the same time, I have so reconfigured everything into my own distinctive perspectives that no one is to blame for those ideas but me. In that regard, with the narrative of Acts, I feel a kinship with Paul, who always insisted he got his gospel from no one (Gal 1:12). Especially assisting the production of this volume have been my wife, Jean M. Stevens, and my legal counsel, Joseph W. Looney.

Contents

Figures

Preface to the Second Edition

THE POSITIVE RECEPTION OF the first edition of this study of Acts was a pleasant surprise, since the analysis challenges orthodoxies in the interpretation of Acts and Paul. To be sure, I am a Paulinist through and through, and I never cease to be amazed contemplating Paul's extraordinary impact on the history of the Jewish messianic movement evolving from the story of Jesus. Truth be told, my wife teases that when I pass through the pearly gates, Jesus might be miffed when I thank him for my salvation but then move directly on down to start asking Paul all the pent up questions I never could answer as a professor. So, I admit that Paul is my hero, but I also know that my version of Paul is influenced primarily by Paul himself in reading Paul's own letters.

Yet, Luke has his own version of Paul, and that version certainly is distinct from the impression one gets from reading Paul's own letters. In interpreting Acts, my exegetical goal was to let Luke be Luke and tell his own story. That exegetical quest took me down surprising roads less traveled that Paul simply did not reveal about himself. I tell my students that different perspective is no different than hearing my description of myself as an instructor but then reading student evaluations solicited by the institution that come in at the end of the semester. Sometimes you do wonder if indeed everyone is referring to the same person.

So, what is the main reason for this second edition? New material. Publishing a second edition does offer opportunity for refinement of discussion along the way and corrections of inevitable typographical and other errors. However, the major contribution in this second edition is a whole new chapter at the end. In this epilogue chapter, church traditions post Acts on the death and burial of Paul are explored. Since these church traditions are post Acts and post Paul, I really never had an interest in following them. Then, the recent archeological work by the Vatican unveiling the sarcophagus beneath the altar in the Church of Saint Paul Outside the Walls in Rome, long hallowed as the final resting place of Paul's remains, peaked my curiosity. When the carbon dating of human bones retrieved from within the sarcophagus retuned a first- to second-century date, my interest soared, so I explored. The epilogue represents that exploration, another chapter in a lifetime spent following the life of the apostle Paul, a new voyage of discovery in this never-ending quest to follow in the footsteps of Paul.

Gerald L. Stevens
New Orleans, Louisiana
Easter 2019

Preface to the First Edition

LUKE EXPANDS THE MEANING of gospel originally set out by Mark. He did this by writing Acts. He joins the two volumes with a story of the ascension none of the other Gospels preserve. The other Gospel narratives conclude with cross and resurrection because they are focused on Jesus. Luke's two-volume corpus is focused on the church. He wrote these two volumes because he wanted to refocus what believers meant when they spoke of the "story of Jesus." The ascension will be his lens through which to refract his answer to describing the story of Jesus. For Luke, the story of Jesus became the story of the church. Further, one cannot interpret fully the meaning of Jesus without understanding theologically the mission of the church. The church is messianic Israel. Messianic Israel had a prophetic mission to be "light to the gentiles." As the angels promised Jesus' return to the disciples, they asked why the disciples were "standing gazing into the sky" (Acts 1:11). The angels' question was provocative, not curiosity. The return of Jesus is one continuous theological movement with the ascension. But how? The disciples needed to comprehend that in between ascension and return is the church, and the mission of the church is integral to the function of both ascension and return. The disciples needed a new vision of the people of God to perceive this connection. Such was the vision of Pentecost, and Pentecost would drive the story from Jerusalem to Rome.

The Pentecost story has two parts. The first part is the Holy Spirit empowering messianic Israel (Acts 1–12). Messiah had come to call Israel to her eschatological destiny. To achieve this destiny, Israel had to be renewed because the national Israel that developed after the return from exile was not the Israel God had in mind. National Israel lost her way religiously in an Ezra reform movement that evolved into the Pharisees, a sect so hyper-focused on their own self-serving brand of Torah obedience that they developed spiritual scales on their eyes that rendered them blind and unable to recognize the God of Torah even if he stood before them. National Israel also lost her way politically in the Maccabean revolt that redefined her messianic expectations. Messiah's reimagined role became martial and his solution military force. Such expectations meant that doing miracles was not as important to Israel as driving out the Romans. In the meantime, traditional paradigms of God as king and his people as a kingdom were lost in the perversions of an alien Herodian dynasty usurping the Jewish throne, propped up as a client kingdom of a pagan Roman empire.

Thus, national Israel *had* to be renewed to be God's Israel. God always had promised that in the last days he would bring this renewal. These times of refreshing God did bring through the life, death, and resurrection of Messiah. Messiah's arrival inaugurated messianic Israel, the renewed Israel of God, a story told in Acts 1–5. Israel's full destiny, however, required the spiritual insight of a wing of the Jerusalem church, the messianic Hellenists. Making Hellenists the first "deacons" obliterates Luke's point. They were the core of Israel's eschatological destiny as "light for the gentiles." This destiny is intimated in the most important speech of Acts by the Hellenist Stephen. The two themes of his speech drive the plot of Acts. This Hellenist story is Acts 6–12.

The second part of Luke's Pentecost story is the Holy Spirit empowering messianic Israel's world mission as "light for the gentiles" (Acts 13–28). No Hellenist leader tells this story better for Luke than that of the Pharisee, Saul of Tarsus. Luke tells this story with three missionary journeys in Acts 13–21 and Paul's struggle with God's will in Acts 21–28. Actually, read carefully, Paul's defenses really are not defenses but the story of Paul's catastrophic detour to Jerusalem on his way to God's will in Rome. Luke then concludes Acts with the gospel in Rome preached without hindrance, all barriers overcome in fulfilling the expansion outlined in Acts 1:8. The church's next chapter on the way to the return of Jesus is being written even as you read.

Gerald L. Stevens
New Orleans, Louisiana
Easter 2016

Abbreviations

ANTC	Abingdon New Testament Commentaries
BEC	The Bible Exposition Commentary
BECNT	Baker Exegetical Commentary on the New Testament
BJS	Brown Judaic Studies
BNTC	Black's New Testament Commentaries
BRS	The Biblical Resource Series
CCSNS	Cincinnati Classical Studies, New Series
CIS	Copenhagen International Seminar
CJ	The Classical Journal
ESV	English Standard Version
EGT	The Expositor's Greek Testament
GNT[4]	*Greek New Testament*, 4th Edition
HCSB	Holman Christian Standard Bible
HTS	Harvard Theological Studies
ICC	International Critical Commentary
IDB	*Interpreter's Dictionary of the Bible*
INTF	Institute for New Testament Textual Research
IVPNT	InterVarsity Press New Testament
JBL	Journal of Biblical Literature
JSNT	Journal for the Study of the New Testament
JSNTSup	Journal for the Study of the New Testament Supplement
JSPSS	Journal for the Study of the Pseudepigrapha Supplement Series
KJV	King James Version
LCL	Loeb Classical Library
NASB	New American Standard Bible
NBC21	New Bible Commentary: 21st Century Edition
NCBC	New Century Bible Commentary

NET	New English Translation
NICNT	New International Commentary on the New Testament
NIV	New International Version
NIVAC	The NIV Application Commentary
NJB	New Jerusalem Bible
NKJV	New King James Version
NLT	New Living Translation
NRSV	New Revised Standard Version
NTIC	The New Testament in Context
NTL	New Testament Library
NTM	New Testament Message: Biblical-Theological Commentary
OHE	The Oxford History of England
PBTM	Paternoster Biblical and Theological Monographs
PC	Proclamation Commentaries
PCCS	Paul in Critical Contexts Series
RBS	Resources for Biblical Study
SBG	Studies in Biblical Greek
SBLSS	Society of Biblical Literature Semeia Studies
SBLSymS	Society of Biblical Literature Symposium Series
SHBC	Smyth & Helwys Bible Commentary
SNTSMS	Society for New Testament Studies Monograph Series
SPNT	Studies on Personalities of the New Testament.
TCS	TEAMS Commentary Series
TJ	Trinity Journal
WBC	Word Biblical Commentary
WGRWSS	Writings from the Greco-Roman World Supplement Series

SCRIPTURE

OLD TESTAMENT

Gen	Genesis	1–2 Chr	1–2 Chronicles
Exod	Exodus	Ezra	Ezra
Lev	Leviticus	Neh	Nehemiah
Num	Numbers	Esth	Esther
Deut	Deuteronomy	Job	Job
Josh	Joshua	Ps (*pl.* Pss)	Psalm (Psalms)
Judg	Judges	Prov	Proverbs
Ruth	Ruth	Eccl	Ecclesiastes
1–2 Sam	1–2 Samuel	Song	Song of Solomon
1–2 Kgs	1–2 Kings	Isa	Isaiah

Jer	Jeremiah	Jonah	Jonah
Lam	Lamentations	Mic	Micah
Ezek	Ezekiel	Nah	Nahum
Dan	Daniel	Hab	Habakkuk
Hos	Hosea	Zeph	Zephaniah
Joel	Joel	Hag	Haggai
Amos	Amos	Zech	Zechariah
Obad	Obadiah	Mal	Malachi

New Testament

Matt	Matthew	1–2 Thess	1–2 Thessalonians
Mark	Mark	1–2 Tim	1–2 Timothy
Luke	Luke	Titus	Titus
John	John	Phlm	Philemon
Acts	Acts	Heb	Hebrews
Rom	Romans	Jas	James
1–2 Cor	1–2 Corinthians	1–2 Pet	1–2 Peter
Gal	Galatians	1–2–3 John	1–2–3 John
Eph	Ephesians	Jude	Jude
Phil	Philippians	Rev	Revelation
Col	Colossians		

Apocrypha

2 Macc	2 Maccabees
Tob	Tobit

PSEUDEPIGRAPHA

Jub.	*Jubilees*

OTHER ANCIENT SOURCES

Apocryphal Acts and Martyrologies

Acta Petri	*The Acts of Peter*
Actus Petri	*The Acts of Peter Vercellenses*
APeterPaul	*The Acts of Peter and Paul*
AThomas	*The Acts of Thomas*
HisHApos	*History of the Holy Apostle My Lord Paul*

MPaul	*The Martyrdom of Paul*
MPeterPaul	*The Martyrdom of Peter and Paul*
Pseudo-Ab.	*Pseudo-Abdius Passion of Saint Paul*
Pseudo-Lin.	*Pseudo-Linius Martyrdom of the Blessed Paul*

CHURCH FATHERS

1 Clem.	*1 Clement*
Didache	*The Teaching of the Twelve Apostles*
Diog.	*Epistle to Diognetus*
Mart. Poly.	*Martyrdom of Polycarp*

AUGUSTUS

| *Res Gestae* | *Res Gestae Divi Augusti* |

ARISTIDES

| *To Rome* | *Encomium of Rome* |

ARISTOTLE

| *Rhet.* | *Ars Rhetorica* |

CASSIUS DIO

| *History* | *Historia Romana (Roman History)* |

CICERO

| *Epis. Att.* | *Epistulae ad Atticum* |
| *Epis. Fam.* | *Epistulae ad Familiares* |

CHRYSOSTOM, JOHN

| *St. Ignat.* | *Saint Ignatius* |

EPICTETUS

| *Disc.* | *The Discourses* |

EUSEBIUS

| *H.E.* | *Historia Ecclesiastica (Church History)* |

HERODOTUS

Hist.   *The Histories*

HORACE

Epistles   *Epistularum liber secundus*
Satires   *Satirae (Sermones)*

IGNATIUS

Eph.   *To the Ephesians*
Mag.   *To the Magnesians*

IRENAEUS

Adv. Haer.   *Against Heresies*

JERUSALEM TALMUD

Ta'anit   *Moed Ta'anit*

JOSEPHUS

Ant.   *Jewish Antiquities*
Apion   *Against Apion*
J.W.   *The Jewish War*
Life   *The Life of Josephus*

JUSTIN MARTYR

Apol.   *The First Apology*

LACTANTIUS

Institutes   *Divine Institutes*

LIVY

Livy   *The History of Rome*

MISHNAH

Hagig.   *Hagigah*
Ed.   *Eduyot*
Sukk.   *Sukkah*

Bikk.   *Bikkurim*

PHILO

Dec.   *De Decalogo*
Spec. Leg.   *De Specialibus Legibus*

PLINY THE ELDER

Nat. Hist.   *Natural History*

PLINY THE YOUNGER

Letters   *Epistulae*

POLYBIUS

Hist.   *Histories*

QUINTILLIAN

Inst.   *Institutio Oratoria*

SENECA

Epistulae   *Epistulae morales ad Lucilium*

SIFRE

Piska   *Tannaitic Commentary on Deuteronomy*

STRABO

Geog.   *Geographica*

SUETONIUS

Aug.   *Augustus, De Vita Caesarum*
Tib.   *Tiberius, De Vita Caesarum*
Claud.   *Claudius, De Vita Caesarum*
Nero   *Nero, De Vita Caesarum*
Otho   *Otho, De Vita Caesarum*

TACITUS

Annals   *The Annals of Tacitus*
Histories   *The Histories of Tacitus*

TALMUD

bPes.	*Babylonian Pesaḥim*

TERTULLIAN

Adv. Mar.	*Against Marcion*

THEOPHILUS

Autol.	*The Apology to Autolycus*

THUCYDIDES

War	*History of the Peloponnesian War*

VIRGIL

Ecl.	*Eclogae*

MUSEUMS

AAM	Antalya Archeoloji Müzesi, Antalya, Turkey
AM	Acropolis Museum, Athens, Greece
AMA	Aphrodisias Müzesi, Aphrodisias, Turkey
AMAC	Archeological Museum of Ancient Corinth, Greece
AMD	Archeological Museum of Delphi, Greece
AMR	Archeological Museum of Rhodes, Dodecanese
AMV	Archeological Museum of Veroia (Berea)
ASM	Attalos Stoa Museum, Athens, Greece
ASMK	Ancient Shipwreck Museum, Kyrenia Castle, Girne, Cyprus
BMB	Bergama Müzesi, Bergama, Turkey
BML	British Museum, London, England
CM	Cyprus Museum, Nicosia, Cyprus
DRM	Domus Romana Museum, Rabat, Malta
EMS	Ephesos Müzesi, Selçuk, Turkey
GPMM	Great Palace Mosaic Museum, Istanbul, Turkey
HAM	Hatay Archeoloji Müzesi, Turkey
HAMH	Hierapolis Archeoloji Müzesi, Hierapolis, Turkey
HAMC	Heraklion Archeological Museum of Crete
IAM	Istanbul Archeoloji Müzerleri, Istanbul, Turkey
IAMI	Izmir Archeoloji Müzesi, Izmir, Turkey

IMJ	Israel Museum, Jerusalem, Israel
KAM	Konya Archeoloji Müzesi, Turkey
KMM	Karaman Müze Müdürlügü, Karaman, Turkey
LP	The Louvre, Paris, France
MANRC	Museo Archeologico Nazionale di Reggio Calabria, Italy
MCA	Museo Civico Archeologico, Orvieto, Italy
MCF	Museo Claudio Faina, Orvieto, Italy
MM	Milet Müzesi, Miletus, Turkey
MMM	Manisa Müze, Manisa, Turkey
NAM	Nicosia Archeological Museum, Nicosia, Cyprus
NAMA	National Archeological Museum of Athens, Greece
NMB	National Museum of Bargello, Florence, Italy
NNAM	Naples National Archeological Museum, Italy
OAM	Ostia Antica Museum, Ostia Antica, Italy
PAM	Philippi Archeological Museum, Philippi, Greece
PMB	Pergamon Museum, Berlin, Germany
ROM	Royal Ontario Museum, Toronto, Canada
SMS	Side Müzesi, Side, Turkey
TAM	Thessaloniki Archeological Museum, Greece
TMT	Tarsus Müze, Tarsus, Turkey
YMY	Yalvaç Müze, Yalvaç, Turkey

APPENDIX: VIDEO RESOURCES

Almost two-hundred on-site videos from the author's travels overseas illustrate the story of Acts and a study of its text including images, maps, and museum resources that make the historical, social, and political world of Acts come alive. Content is designed carefully to integrate into the text and enhance major themes. For a description of the content of each video, see https://drkoine.com/paul/ActsVideoCatalog.pdf.

Videos can be linked into study themes. Patron-client relationships and issues of hospitality rituals that surround Paul in his travels could be explored by linking together four videos: (1) the 1MJ video on the Roman villa at Salamis, (2) the 2MJ video on Lydia, the woman dealer in purple at Philippi, (3) the JR video on Valletta: renewing the voyage to Rome at Malta, and (4) the JR video on Aquila and Priscilla in Rome.

Preliminaries

Setting the Stage for Luke's Story

A GOOD BOOK OFTEN WILL start with a good prologue. Luke begins his two-volume work of Luke-Acts with a carefully composed prologue in the first four verses of his Gospel (Luke 1:1–4).[1] Of the numerous pieces of information conveyed in this prologue, two are important for our purposes here. One piece of information is that Luke readily acknowledges he used sources. Even had he not told us, these sources often betray themselves in the style of Greek Luke engages along the way. While his own literary Hellenistic, almost classical, style is clear in the prologue, Luke seems careful to reflect the Greek of his sources. For example, we know he turns to his Gospel of Mark source at the beginning of Luke 3 because the Greek suddenly shifts from the deliberate imitation of Septuagint style indicative of early Judean sources in the infancy narrative of Luke 1–2 to Mark's rough and unpolished Koine style that so dominates Mark's Gospel. On other occasions, Luke's sources are apparent in that the information he shares is otherwise unknown. A good example is the Journey to Jerusalem section of Luke 9:51—19:27. What many readers do not reflect on is

---

[1]We will presume Lukan authorship of both volumes as one work composed at some point after the First Jewish War but in the first century. Silence about Paul's death is no indication whether Paul was alive at the time of composition. The assumption ignores the prevenient question of literary purpose. For introductory critical matters, the student should consult commentaries by Keener (2012), Pervo (2009), Parsons (2008), Walton (2008), Gaventa (2003), Fitzmyer (1998), Dunn (1996), Barrett (1994), Polhill (1992), Bruce (1988), and Haenchen (1971).

that this distinctive, often unique information is true of most of Acts. One obvious stream of unique information about the early church that does not derive from apostolic tradition is the material on the Hellenists that is abruptly introduced in Acts 6 that eventually takes over the entire story by the end of Acts 12. The point is, one should suspect that Luke's main literary purpose for writing Acts is hidden away in this unique Hellenist material.

The other piece of information Luke reveals in his prologue to the Gospel is that some of the evidence he has secured is eyewitness. We would expect this type evidence for the story of Jesus directly, as this type of evidence is the very definition of apostle for Luke (Acts 1:21–22). What Luke does not say at this early stage of the prologue of the Gospel is that he himself will be one of these eyewitnesses. In fact, his own eyewitness information is what helps secure the veracity and legitimacy of the Hellenist story that so dominates Acts as the divinely intended trajectory of the ministry of Jesus.

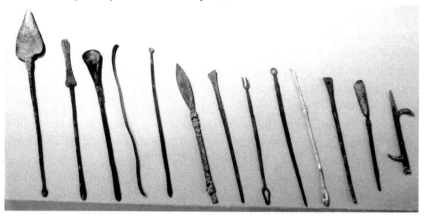

FIGURE P1. First-Century Medical Instruments. Medical equipment in the early empire period had more sophisticated instruments than one might imagine. Pictured are various delicate scalpels and probes. The tradition that Luke was a physician derives from the appellation in Col 4:14. Hobart's old theory (1882) that Luke's medical vocabulary is on display in Acts proving the author was a physician is over-done. The extensive vocabulary simply proves the author is well educated but is not inconsistent with being a physician. See Keener, *Acts*, 1:414–16 (EMS).

We are arguing "Luke" as author at the narrative level about the "we sections." We should use Occam's razor on the issue by arguing that the hypothesis with the fewest assumptions is the more likely explanation of this literary phenomenon. That is, the easiest and least encumbered explanation for a narrative suddenly shifting to first person in a third-person sequence without any rhetorical devices marking the shift is that the author transparently is marking the narrative as eyewitness. The "we sections" are marked eyewitness units of material. Whether this author is Luke the "beloved physician" (Col 4:14) is not the point and not being argued here.

READING STRATEGY

While we are studying Acts, we have a problem on our hands. Luke originally published Acts as part of a two-volume enterprise.[2] This two-volume character means the two volumes really should be read together to "hear" better what the author is saying. Simply put, one is hindered from understanding Acts without its Gospel forerunner, Luke.[3] Why were they separated in the canon? We have to speculate, but the likely reasons seem practical.[4]

Canonical Development

As far back as we can reach with our Greek manuscript copies, early Christian documents circulated as collections, not as individual volumes. One early collection was the Gospels. Further, the genre of Acts was as problematic for the early church as for scholars today. What Luke had done to extend the gospel genre was not understood. As a result, Acts was undervalued and separated from its companion volume. Acts became a canonical orphan. The Gospel of Luke, on the other hand, always was collected with the other three Gospels.

Another early collection was the Pauline epistles. We do not have individual copies of the letters of Paul. We always have them as part of an existing collection. Obvious to all readers is that Acts is about Paul,

---

[2]The typical maximum length of a scroll was about 32 feet, for practical purposes of carrying. The contents of the Gospel of Luke would fill up one scroll. If Luke was not finished writing by the time he got to Luke 24, he invariably would have to publish in two volumes.

[3]For one analysis of narrative flow, see Tannehill, *The Narrative Unity of Luke-Acts.*

[4]Newer reading strategies for biblical material such as Acts move beyond historical-critical interests into literary-narratological, social-historical, and canonical-theological interests. A brief introduction is in Spencer, *Journeying Through Acts*, 21–26.

so Acts could serve as a canonical "bridge" between the two major collections of Gospels and epistles. Three Gospels were very similar in outline and content—Matthew, Mark, and Luke—so these were pulled together, and then John, the maverick Gospel, included at the end. Acts then was placed as a bridge to Paul. This process, however, meant that the Gospel of John separated Acts from its companion volume of Luke. The author's original intention was lost in the canonical shuffle. In this canonical conundrum, one rarely reads Acts thinking, "I need to read the Gospel of Luke to understand this text of Acts fully." But that reading, in fact, richly enhances an understanding of Acts. So, let us overview the narrative flow of Luke better to understand Acts.

Luke's Five Parts

Luke has five parts, distinguishable in the type of Greek used, but also in the material presented. Overviewing these parts helps establish how Luke is pushing the boundaries of what typically was understood as a "gospel," and why we have trouble deciding on the genre of Acts.

1. *Prologue, 1:1–4.* The prologue is about as near to classical style as any part of the New Testament. Luke shows off his best stylistic efforts to indicate he can write this way. The prologue is like his signature coming at the very beginning of the document. Luke gives his statement of purpose for this major production, modeled on the best literary output of the first-century world. Luke thus signals that he can write in a fine Greek style. Thus, when his style changes, this change is intentional. He is reflecting carefully his sources.

In this prologue, Luke begins to tell "The Story of Jesus, Part I: How the Gospel Got Started." Yet, even as he starts this story of Jesus, he coyly speaks of eyewitnesses. By mentioning eyewitnesses, he subtly alludes to his own contribution to the storyline later. The gospel genre traditionally had been associated with the apostles, covering up to the resurrection. Since Luke is not an apostle, his own part of the "gospel" naturally would be "post-apostolic." Luke, however, wants to say that his part of the story, even though admittedly "post-apostolic," is not "post-gospel." Something momentous beyond even resurrection is the essence of what typically had been called a "gospel" for Luke. That momentous event the reader eventually will learn is Luke's unique ascension/Pentecost sequence. The literary trajectory of this sequence eventually will become the Pauline mission. What Luke seems to have

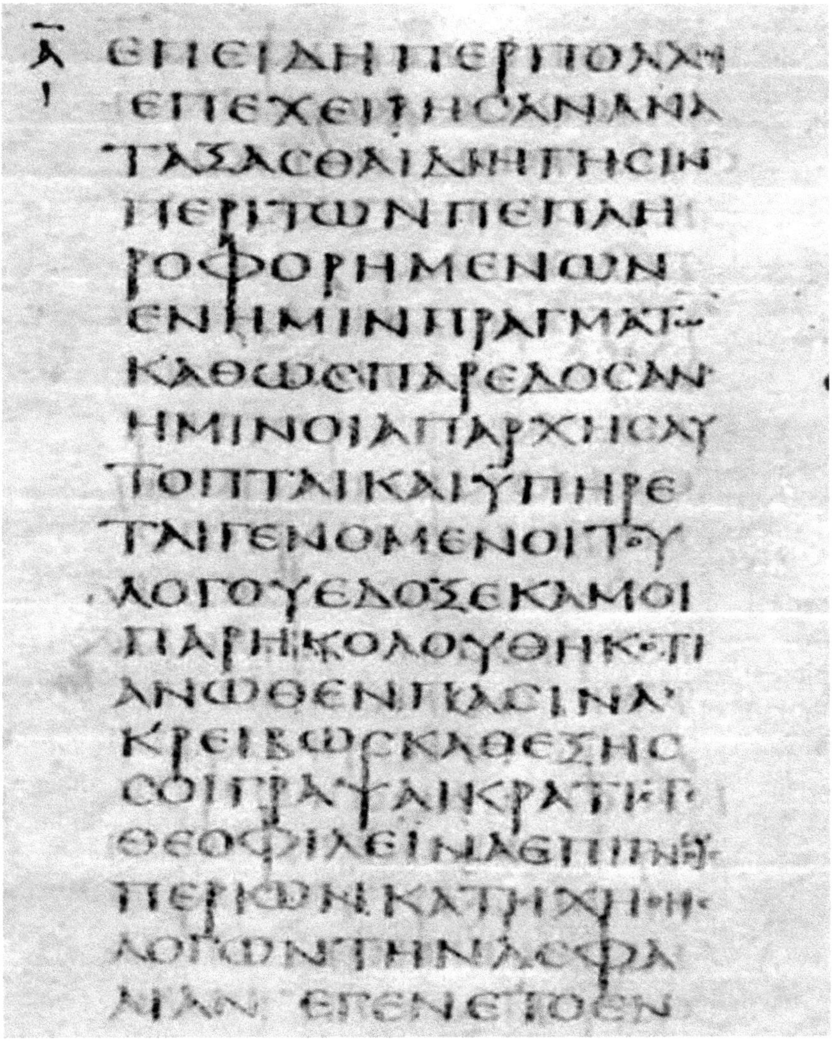

FIGURE P2. Codex Sinaiticus at Luke 1:1–4. This partial column shows the first four verses of Luke's Gospel, typically called the "prologue." The capital uncial script has no punctuation or word divisions. By Permission of Oxford University Press.

grasped about as lucidly as anyone in the early church, even other Gospel writers, is that without the ascension/Pentecost sequence, the resurrection by itself answers few questions that are important to understanding how the church fulfills its mission and destiny, and the mission and destiny of the church is the whole point of the story of Jesus for Luke. So, Luke writes Luke-Acts. This Gospel prologue, then, really is the prologue to both books, and that is why Luke writes a resumptive prologue renaming "Theophilus" again at the beginning of Acts (1:1), clearly tying back to the original prologue of Luke.

FIGURE P3. Jerusalem from the Mount of Olives. This place tells the story of Israel. Her hope was in the coming Messiah, who would transform the very reality of Israel. Early believers proclaimed Jesus to be that long-awaited Messiah.

2. *Infancy Narrative, 1:5—2:52.* Verse five smoothly shifts to a Semitic Greek, evoking the early Jewish sources of the traditions Luke here is working into his presentation; the principals in the drama are pious, loyal, law-abiding, God-fearing people, the Israel of God. Thus, the birth of Jesus is the culmination of the hope of Israel. However, this Messiah will transform the Israel that exists when he arrives on the scene. Politically, Jesus's heritage was not in Zealotism. Jesus comes to save his people, but not according to common political or military expectations. Moreover, this salvation has universal implications from the very beginning. The story of Jesus is "good news" not only for Israel, but also for the world. Such implications are nascent with Simeon's prophecy: "for my eyes have seen your salvation, which you have prepared in the presence of all peoples, a light for revelation to the gentiles and for glory to your people Israel" (Luke 2:32). The Gospel ends with this prophecy unfulfilled. The reader must await Acts 9 and the Damascus Road to begin to see this light for gentiles.

3. *Galilean Ministry, 3:1—9:50.* The Greek shifts significantly to the common, or Koine, style, reflecting sources such as the Gospel of Mark. Since Mark's Gospel has a two-fold sequence of first ministry in Galilee, then ministry in Jerusalem at the end, those writers following Mark reflect those two poles of Jesus's ministry, as does Luke here.

The problem with Galilee as the origin of Jesus is that Galilee was a hotbed of Zealot activity. Further, Jesus died on a Roman cross, an execution for insurrectionists. Some of what Luke wants to show in his post-Jewish War setting is that even though Jesus was condemned as a Zealot from Galilee, such condemnation flies in the face of the facts of his actual ministry, his followers, and his teaching. First, Jesus's sermon in his hometown synagogue (Luke 4) is about his preaching, teaching, healing, helping, and blessing—nothing here about insurrection! The message is that Jesus embodies God's "good news" to Israel and to the world. Second, the kind of disciples Jesus called were honest and hard-working fishermen, even loyal Roman government officials, such as a tax-collector. Such a group is not an army in training. Third, Jesus's training in the Sermon on the Plain clearly indicates his intent that his disciples would be an extension of his own "good news" ministry. His

FIGURE P4. Galilee: The Cliffs of Arbela. These precipitous cliffs held caves that provided hideouts for refugees and rebels alike. Josephus said the Syrian general Bacchides captured Jews who fled and hid here in the Hasmonean period (*Ant.* 12.11.1 [421]); Herod when governor of Galilee fought bandits hiding in these caves in the Herodian period (*Ant.* 14.15.4 [415–17]); Josephus himself fortified the area preparing for the First Jewish War in the procurator period (*J.W.* 2.20.6 [573]). The first recorded Zealot revolt was led by a "Judas of Galilee," opposed to the census by Quirinius to convert Judea into a procuratorship after Archelaus was banished to Gaul by Augustus in AD 6 (*Ant.* 18.1.1 [4]). No wonder Galilee had a reputation as a place spawning insurrection. Gamaliel refers to Judas the Galilean in his warning to the Sanhedrin about opposing the apostles (Acts 5:37).

marching orders to his disciples had nothing to do with insurrection. Fourth, Jesus himself formally commissioned his own disciples to this peaceful, gospel ministry at the end of his ministry. Neither Jesus nor his followers were Zealots, nor did they advocate rebellion. Thus, Christianity is no sponsor of insurrection and so is innocent before Rome. This theme is a hallmark of the Pauline missionary enterprise. Luke shows Paul constantly in favorable interactions with Roman officials throughout much of his work, or has Roman law on his side. Such a theme would be eminently relevant after the First Jewish War, when the Christian sect was well known to have originated in Judea.

4. *Journey to Jerusalem, 9:51—19:27.* The Greek returns to a more refined literary style closer to the prologue, signaling distinctive, even unique material. An important Lukan section with little from Mark, this large unit often is called the "Journey to Jerusalem" because of the unique phrase Luke uses at 9:51: "When the days drew near for him to be taken up, *he set his face [made his resolve] for the purpose of going to Jerusalem*" (αὐτὸς τὸ πρόσωπον ἐστήρισεν τοῦ πορεύεσθαι εἰς Ἰερουσαλήμ). The "set his face" colloquial expression is a determined resolve, a deliberate decision. Jesus already had taught the disciples that he was under a divine commission: "The Son of Man *must [dei*, δεῖ]⁵ undergo great suffering and be rejected by the elders, chief priests, and scribes, and be killed, and on the third day be raised" (Luke 9:22). How should one understand that Jesus was crucified by Romans? Luke says Jesus is in Jerusalem on two counts: (1) he went to Jerusalem by *deliberate choice*; (2) he was in Jerusalem by *divine commission*.

Further, Jesus was innocent. Scripture predicted the false charges against Jesus: "For I tell you, this Scripture must be fulfilled in me, 'And he was counted among the lawless'; and indeed what is written about me is being fulfilled" (Luke 22:37). Ironically, Romans themselves reveal this innocence. The procurator Pilate washed his hands of the blood of an innocent man. The centurion stationed at the cross declared Jesus innocent. Jesus was not a Zealot, but he died a Zealot's death. He died because he was rejected by his own. However, Jesus was not a martyr. He *went* to Jerusalem. Jerusalem was the deliberate choice of Jesus because this destiny was the higher will of God. So while Jesus was not an

---

⁵Luke's special verb for divine necessity, particularly notable for the passion of Jesus and the gentile mission; cf. Squires, *The Plan of God in Luke-Acts*, 167.

unwilling martyr, neither was he another lost Jewish cause. He fulfilled God's eternal purposes of salvation for the whole world.

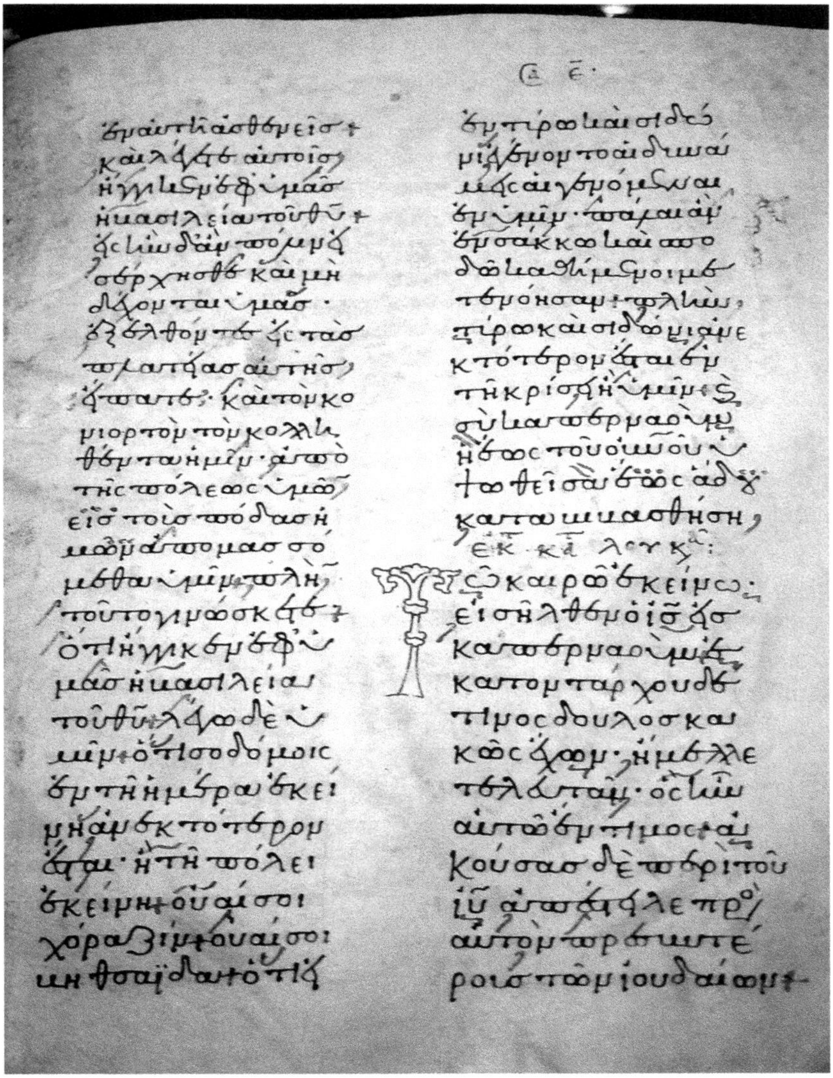

FIGURE P5. Gospel of Luke Lectionary. The text starts at Luke 10:5b–10 but jumps to 7:1–3a at the ornamental "T," including a gloss "in those days" to make the transition. Notice how the lectionary system ignores Luke's narrative flow and the impact of the "Journey to Jerusalem" section and its focus on the divine destiny embraced by Jesus.

Jesus's ministry is as in Galilee, but time and geographical notations are notably imprecise, as in "on his way," "passing along," so this "journey" is theological, a statement about the death of Jesus. Even if the plot of movements of this part of the Gospel looks more like an Etch-A-Sketch screen and not an actual itinerary of going directly to Jerusalem, Jesus inevitably will wind up in Jerusalem, because this city is his destiny. This journey will inaugurate Isaiah's new Exodus for eschatological Israel in Acts.[6]

5. *Passion Narrative, 19:28—24:53.* Having finished his unique "Journey to Jerusalem" section as the story of Jesus embracing God's will and moving to his life's destiny, Luke now returns to his Markan source for the passion narrative, the story of Jesus's death. The Jews opposed Jesus; his death was the result of heavy-handed manipulation of the crowds and of the procurator by the Jewish leaders. He was not any Zealot. His life and his ministry provide ample proof of his work. His trial was a miscarriage of justice, his sentence a crime, his resurrection a total vindication by God overturning the human

FIGURE P6. Church of the Holy Sepulchre. Luke says Jesus went to Jerusalem by choice fulfilling God's will, a destiny that establishes in his death a new Exodus for the Israel of God.

verdict. Volume one of Luke's literary project begins to draw to a close, but Luke now breaks away from the pack of other Gospels. Luke insists Jesus's story does not end with resurrection. The heritage and hope of Israel planted in the hearts of faithful Israelites such as Simeon, Zechariah, and Anna who are encountered in the infancy narrative will blossom in the hearts of Jesus's disciples. That tale would be "The Story of Jesus, Part II: How the Gospel Became the Christian Movement," and awaits to be told. That story is the book of Acts.

---

[6]See Pao, *Acts and the Isaianic New Exodus.*

LUKAN PURPOSE

What does Luke intend by writing Luke-Acts? That the story of Jesus becomes the story of the church. We begin to see this purpose when we overview the content of the Gospel. But we also have what Luke himself said. To this we can add themes Luke develops implicitly.

Luke's Explicit Indication

Luke's prologue to the Gospel is an explicit statement of purpose for the entire production. He writes to provide an authoritative account of the origins of the Christian movement. He dedicates this work to Theophilus, probably the patron paying for the publication.[7] In this effort toward an authoritative account, he researched sources carefully, but not as if the other Gospel writers were not careful. What he implies by writing Acts too is that he researched additional sources that would modulate his "gospel" account into another key, that is, from Jesus to the church. Luke in the prologue then is claiming that the material he adds to the "gospel" on the church is trustworthy. Since Luke traces Paul as the future of the church, that claim to have a trustworthy word on the future might have been hard to swallow for some original readers more enamored with Peter and the Petrine traditions (Matt 16:18) or with John and the Johannine traditions (John 21:21–22). Turned out Luke was right. Peter and John had the privilege of being eyewitnesses to Jesus's ministry to Israel, but Paul had the privilege of being eyewitness to Jesus's mission to the world.

Luke's Implicit Themes

Implicit themes have to be teased out of the narrative by recurring ideas from episode to episode. Many of these could be suggested. Consult the commentaries for excellent suggestions, especially those investigating social dynamics. Our present focus is on those themes that are prominent or integrate well literarily into enhancing Luke's extension of the gospel genre in order to parse out the meaning of the church. Luke especially achieves his goal by using character development as a strategy for his plot development.

---

[7]Similarly, Josephus dedicated his works to a patron, Epaphroditus, also honored as "most excellent," *Life* 76 (430); *Apion* 1.1 (1); 2.1 (1); 2.42 (296); cf. *Ant.* 2 (8).

Defending Christianity

One hidden purpose surfaces in a verse near the end of Acts. Jewish leaders allude to the "bad press" the Jesus movement had received. They indicate that this sect is "everywhere spoken against" (Acts 28:22). This negative reputation concords well with the "perfect pest" characterization of Paul by the lawyer Tertullus (Acts 24:5). Such was the official synagogue and Sanhedrin opinion. What about Roman civic officials? They persistently were pressed with accusations that leaders of the Jesus movement intended public agitation, even insurrection against Rome, as in "turning the world upside down," or in preaching "another king" (Acts 17:6–7). Luke countermands negative opinions by his narrative characterizations. Actual Roman response to Jesus and his followers is positive, as in the centurion at the cross, the proconsul Sergius Paulus on Cyprus, the proconsul Gallio at Corinth, Asiarch friends at Ephesus, and multiple public attestations of Paul's innocence by Felix, Festus, and Agrippa II. Luke clearly is going for an apologetic defense of followers of Jesus, whom Luke eventually called "Christians" at Antioch (Acts 11:26). Though originating in the rebellious province of Judea recently subdued at great cost to the Romans, Christianity is innocent and no insurrectionist threat to Rome.[8]

Defining Messianic Israel

Luke is concerned to anchor the messianic movement of Jesus in the Israel of God. He starts his narrative with Peter insisting that Judas's vacated office among the "twelve" *must* be filled (Acts 1:22). Why must be filled? Surely eleven men could have done whatever job was ahead just about as well as twelve. More, Luke constantly has Jesus followers quoting Jewish Scripture about the last days as fulfilled to Jewish audiences, particularly addressing them as "Israelites" in the process (Acts 2:16–21; 3:12, 22–23; 13:16, 33–35). Luke ends the narrative with Paul insisting he is in chains for the sake of the "hope of Israel" (Acts 28:20). Luke is clear. Messiah is the hope of Israel and has come and is calling out the messianic Israel of God. The present moment of gospel proclamation of Jesus as Messiah fulfills John the Baptist's clarion call to national Israel for repentance to make ready the way of the Lord and Israel's baptism of the Holy Spirit with fire (Luke 3:16). Pentecost

---

[8]On issues of apologetic, see Squires, *The Plan of God in Luke-Acts*, 52–53, n. 83.

already has happened, but amnesty for ignorant actions in murdering the Righteous One of God still is offered. Seizing Israel's eschatological moment of destiny is fleeting away (Acts 3:17–20).

Following Jesus as Messiah, thereby becoming part of messianic Israel, is an opportunity for national Israel now, not tomorrow. The future will bring war with Rome in which national Israel is utterly destroyed. At that point, identifying as an "Israelite" then loses all traditional significance as a nation among nations. The arrival of Messiah is transforming the Israel of God into the reality of the

FIGURE P7. Jerusalem's Western Wall. Reading Scripture at the Western Wall, the one surviving part of the Herodian temple complex destroyed by the Romans in AD 70 in the First Jewish War. Luke wants to make clear what Jesus taught about the Israel of God by defining messianic Israel.

eschatological promise of a messianic Israel in the form anticipated by Isaiah. Luke will show that even Isaiah's anticipation of the restoration of the divided kingdom is captured in the expectation of evangelizing Samaria in Jesus's commission in Acts 1:8 and effected in the story of Philip's ministry to Samaria in Acts 8.[9]

Clarifying the Church

The nature of that messianic transformation of Israel was contested in Luke's day and today as well. The thorny thicket is the "church." The word "church" (*ekklēsia*, ἐκκλησία) never occurs in the Gospel of Luke. In fact, in all the Gospels together, "church" occurs only three times, all three in just two verses of Matthew (Matt 16:18; 18:17). Even in the rest of the New Testament, the word "church" outside of Paul is rare, only six times in all the general epistles combined, but twenty times in Revelation because of the letters to the seven churches.[10] With the dom-

---

[9]On Israel's restoration, see Pao, *Acts and the Isaianic New Exodus*, 122–29.

[10]Twice in Hebrews (but in Old Testament context, Heb 2:12, or heavenly typology, Heb 12:23), once in James (Jas 5:14), three times in 3 John (3 John 6, 9, 10), and twenty

inance of the use of the term "church" today in contemporary parlance for the community associated with the followers of Jesus, one might think that the New Testament evidence for the term would have been much more robust.

FIGURE P8. Apse Mosaic, San Clemente Basilica, Rome. Byzantine arabesque motif embellished with scrolled acanthus tendrils, c 1200. The basilica is dedicated to Clement I of Rome (92–99), the first of the Apostolic Fathers of the church. The present 11th cent. basilica is built on top of a 4th cent. basilica, which itself was modification of a Roman nobleman's home that later served as a church in the 1st cent. Thus, this basilica's history takes us all the way back to the 1st cent. and helps illustrate how early Christians met in homes of wealthy patron sponsors. Use of "church" in that context really was not about a building at all, but a body of believers. For the basilica interior and discovery of its first-century level, see Figures 15.93 and 15.94.

Well, that is the point. We have not talked about Paul yet. The term "church" occurs *sixty-two times* in Pauline literature.[11] One could make a good case for Paul bearing responsibility for imposing this term onto traditional Christian vocabulary. We begin to perceive this significance of Pauline influence in that the word church does not occur in the Gospel of Luke at all but *twenty-three times in Acts.* That lopsidedness makes sense. Acts is all about Paul. We further could consider the distribution of the term "church" in Acts. We have only *one* occurrence

times in Revelation, obviously mostly the seven letters (Rev 1:4, 11, 20; 2:1, 7, 8, 11, 12, 17, 18, 23, 29; 3:1, 6, 7, 13, 14, 22; 22:16).

[11]Pauline here means all the epistles carrying Paul's name, irrespective of authorship questions. The point is simply influence in the Pauline universe.

in all the first five chapters dealing with the early movement in Jerusalem (Acts 5:11). All twenty-two other occurrences of the term are *after* the Hellenists are introduced in Acts 6. When one remembers that the introduction of the Hellenists is the beginning of a major shift in the leadership and geography of messianic Israel, and that that leadership eventually will devolve onto the shoulders of Paul intensively, then we see how Luke with the word "church" is tracking Paul directly with a term Paul innovated for the Israel of God (Gal 6:16), since the church is the "congregation of God" (Gal 1:13) that is "in Messiah" (Gal 1:22). This conceptual cluster means that "church," both for Luke and for Paul, functions like the christological term "messianic Israel."[12] Further, Paul's sense of "church" may derive from countercultural households in the Jesus movement (the politics of patronage, not family).[13]

Nuancing the Kingdom of God[14]

Another theme Luke develops in Acts is the kingdom of God. Explicit kingdom language, while infrequent, prominently is positioned with high literary visibility at the beginning and ending of Acts. Kingdom language also is placed in the mouths of prominent players in the Acts drama, which adds to its significance. Below are the eight occurrences.

- "And to whom he presented himself alive after his passion by many proofs, through forty days appearing to them and talking about the things related to the kingdom of God" (Acts 1:3)

- "When therefore they had gathered together, they were asking him and saying, 'Lord, is this the time you are restoring the kingdom to Israel?'" (Acts 1:6)

---

[12]Of course, any language of "church" in the same breath as "Israel" automatically is labeled "supersessionist," as if we all know precisely what that term means, and that the meaning is exclusively pejorative. I would lean to Wright's admittedly oxymoronic "Jewish supersessionism." Cf. Wright, *Paul and the Faithfulness of God*, 805–10. At least for Paul (perhaps not for his interpreters) with "church" we still are talking about continuity—Israel's election and its fulfillment in the promise to Abraham. Further, whatever these concepts of church and messianic Israel are for Luke and Paul, clear both in Luke and in Paul is that such christological reflection has nothing to do with a national Israel—precisely why Jesus detoured around the disciples' dull-headed question about national Israel after the resurrection (Acts 1:6).

[13]Destro and Pesce, "Fathers and Householders in the Jesus Movement," 212.

[14]This section is derived with only minor changes from Stevens, *Revelation*, 188–92.

- "But when they believed Philip, who was proclaiming the good news about the kingdom of God and the name of Jesus Christ, they were being baptized, both men and women" (Acts 8:12)

- "As they were strengthening the souls of the disciples, they were exhorting them to remain in the faith, and, 'Through many tribulations we must enter the kingdom of God'" (Acts 14:22)

- "And after he entered in the synagogue, he was speaking out plainly over the course of three months, arguing and persuading concerning the kingdom of God" (Acts 19:8)

- "And now, behold, I know that all of you no longer will see my face, among whom I went about preaching the kingdom" (Acts 20:25)

- "Now after they had set a day, they came to him at his residence in great numbers, to whom he was expounding, testifying to the kingdom of God, persuading them concerning Jesus from the law of Moses, and the prophets, from morning until evening" (Acts 28:23)

- "Preaching the kingdom of God and teaching the things concerning the Lord Jesus Christ, with all boldness unhindered" (Acts 28:31)

Kingdom Framing. Two features related to these passages jump out right away. The first is Luke's bracketing of the entire narrative of Acts with kingdom language. The first mention is part of the note about Jesus's teaching for forty days after the resurrection and then the disciples' kingdom question that precipitates a statement of Luke's witness theme of Acts (1:3, 6). The last mention is part of Paul's teaching in Rome, which actually is the last verse of Acts (28:23, 31). So, Luke literarily is "framing" the narrative of Acts itself with kingdom language. The narrative, then, is used to redefine the kingdom of God.

Ecclesiological Pattern. The second feature to note about these references is that, in the Acts narrative, anytime the kingdom of God is mentioned, that reference always is connected directly to mention of Jesus's name or the early church's gospel mission and preaching in that name. In this way, Luke builds his association of kingdom and the nature and mission of the church.

For example, notice that the mention of kingdom language in regard to the evangelist Philip's work immediately is equated with preaching the name of Jesus Christ, followed by a notation of the early

FIGURE P9. Jerusalem Temple Baptismal Pool. Ritual lustrations were common in first-century Judea. This pool was used for ritual cleansing for pilgrims to Jerusalem participating in the three great pilgrim feasts of Passover, Pentecost, and Tabernacles. The Jewish sect living at Qumran also had baptismal pools and rites. Such rituals typically were for cleansing, as even the repentance baptism of John the Baptist (Luke 3:3). Christian baptism as inaugurated by Jesus went beyond that of John. Christian baptism was initiation into messianic Israel by confessing faith in Messiah. This difference between the baptisms of John and Jesus is why the disciples of John the Baptist at Ephesus were baptized "into the name" of the Lord Jesus (Acts 19:2–7).

church rite of baptism. This is an *ecclesiological initiation* emphasis. Notice as Paul and Barnabas are exhorting converts on the first missionary journey to persevere in the faith, they teach that present tribulations are the path into the kingdom. This is an *ecclesiological eschatology* emphasis. Notice that Paul's synagogue preaching to Jews in Ephesus on the third missionary journey incorporates kingdom language, but this language is tied to the life, death, and resurrection of Jesus. Paul's kingdom preaching is reprised in the Miletus speech to the Ephesian elders at the end of the third missionary journey. This is an *ecclesiological mission* emphasis. Finally, Luke concludes the entire narrative of Acts with Paul preaching the kingdom of God both in the synagogue and in general. Luke states that this kingdom preaching of Paul always is "concerning Jesus." By the time we finish Luke's Gospel we already have been appraised that the phrase "concerning Jesus" is about the events directly related to the life, death, and resurrection of Jesus. This Jesus is Messiah who constitutes messianic Israel.

Thus, we conclude that by constructing his kingdom references with this constant *ecclesiological* association, Luke reinterprets Jewish kingdom language, modulating the meaning to a higher ecclesiological key. Luke is careful to make clear by how he has constructed Luke-Acts that the church's gospel mission and preaching about Jesus grew directly out of the mission of Jesus. Further, Luke says this movement of the gospel story from the mission of Jesus to the mission of the church was at Jesus's own direction in the power of the Holy Spirit. Thus, for Luke, the essence of the kingdom of God after the resurrection and ascension of Jesus is in the nature and mission of the church.

Disciples' Question. This ecclesiological pattern of Luke's kingdom language throughout Acts is what provides an exegesis of the disciples' question to Jesus at the beginning of the Acts. Even after forty days of intense post-resurrection training on the kingdom of God (Acts 1:3), the disciples still have trouble getting their minds around Jesus's own messianic consciousness, which, in the storyline in Acts, is going to evolve into the early church and her gospel mission. They ask a question about the kingdom framed in terms of Jewish nationalism: "Lord, is this the time when you will restore the kingdom to Israel?" (Acts 1:6). In this question we learn about the *second* major issue the disciples had to rethink completely about Messiah and his kingdom. The first issue, the identity of Messiah as suffering Son of Man, we learned from Mark. The second issue, that of the nature of the kingdom of God now revealed as the church and her suffering gospel mission, we learn from Luke. If the new wine of Messiah as suffering Son of Man broke all the old wineskins of the disciples' old messianic thinking patterns, the same ever more was true about the kingdom of God. If Messiah radically is redefined as the suffering Son of Man, logically, the kingdom of this same Messiah likewise radically must be redefined as the suffering mission related to this suffering Son of Man. This process of redefining the kingdom Luke begins developing immediately in Acts with Jesus's redirection of this obtuse kingdom question of the disciples.

Jesus's response is curiously ambiguous. He does not say yes, and he does not say no. Instead, he almost puts them off. He tells them they do not know the times or periods of the Father's choosing (Acts 1:7). As Luke will make clear with his contextualization of kingdom language in his narrative development of Acts, this response is another way of saying softly without strong remonstrance that the disciples still misunderstand the very essence of the messianic kingdom. Jesus replaces the disciples' Jewish nationalism with his own concept of expanding waves of global gospel witness empowered by the Holy Spirit. Jesus responds, "Rather, you will receive power after the Holy Spirit has come upon you, and you will be my witnesses, in Jerusalem, and all Judea and Samaria, even until the uttermost places of the earth" (Acts 1:8). This word, "you will be my witnesses," redefines the essence of the kingdom of God. That essence is not Jewish nationalism, but gospel witness. This witness is defined by the church's preaching of Jesus and embracing a global mission that takes the message to the heart of the empire, and from there to propagate to the whole world. In fact, this mission is the very point of Simeon's prophecy about the significance of the child Jesus as a "light for revelation" and the journeys of Paul.[15]

Pentecost Fulfillment. Jesus promised the Spirit to empower this global mission of witness. The Spirit came at Pentecost. Luke parallels the baptism of Jesus, with its descent of the Spirit to empower Jesus for his mission in the world, with the event of Pentecost, with its descent of the Spirit to empower the church for her mission in the world (Luke 3:21–22; Acts 2:1–4). The manifestation of this power was the ability to speak the languages of the world to those pilgrims assembled for the feast from around the world. The miracle meant that everyone could hear and understand the message of "the great deeds of God." In the Gospel context of Luke, these great deeds would be none other than the

---

[15]In all of this about Acts 1:6, we note that Luke's presentation lends no support for a "holy land" theology, nor does the rest of the New Testament for that matter. Obsession with the holy land is prominent in the United States and drives intense political lobbying in zealous support of the secular state of Israel. Burge, *Jesus and the Land: The New Testament Challenge to "Holy Land" Theology*, offers a careful critique of "holy land" theology in a study of Old Testament promises related to Israel and the land carried on through the intertestamental period and into the New Testament. Burge notes, "To fight for holy territory, to defend the land as a divinely appointed duty, is to regress utterly in the most miserable way" (*Jesus and the Land*, 107). Even an eschatological work such as the book of Revelation lends no support to end time scenarios dependent on land. While "land" (*gē*, γῆ) occurs 82 times in Revelation, not even once does the term ever mean the holy land. Thus, Burge concludes, "There is no sense in Revelation that Christians are to invest in or to fight for the restoration or preservation of Jerusalem in the climactic scenario of the Last Days" (*Jesus and the Land*, 106).

essence of the gospel, the death, resurrection, and exaltation of Jesus, which Peter clarifies in his speech explaining the dramatic event to the amazed crowds (Acts 2:22–36). The only reason to speak the languages of the world is if you have a story to tell. Pentecost is the realization of the early church of her mission and destiny that transformed an upper room prayer meeting into global gospel witness.

By these three elements of his kingdom language framing of Acts, his ecclesiological pattern describing that kingdom, and his Pentecost narrative, Luke has made clear the nature and mission of the church. The church in her nature reflects Jesus and the pattern of his life. The church in her mission reflects Jesus and the preaching of his message. Between the ascension and return of Jesus, the kingdom of God is evidenced in the church on earth, where God's will is done as in heaven.

Demonstrating Pentecost Fulfillment

Another theme of Acts is Pentecost fulfillment. Among the Gospel writers, Luke alone describes Pentecost, the only major pilgrim festival unmentioned in the other Gospels. So deemphasized, no wonder some readers of Acts leave Luke's drama of Pentecost in the rearview mirror after Acts 2, never again to reflect on its significance for the rest of Acts. Yet, this annual harvest festival always anticipated Israel's promise of eschatological fulfillment for the people of God, dis-

FIGURE P10. Pentecost Harvest Festival. Celebrated fifty days after Passover, this annual pilgrim festival becomes an epic event in the life of the church that Luke transforms into a thematic motif for the entire narrative of Acts.

tinctively marked by divine forgiveness, harvest bounty, harvest joy, and harvest inclusiveness—all anticipated in the very form of the original festival in the life of Israel. Readers never appreciate that the great symbol of Pentecost fulfillment resides in the character of Barnabas as "Pentecost facilitator" and in the Hellenist movement as the Pentecost destiny, epitomized in the life of its greatest leader, Saul of Tarsus, advancing Cornelius as the paradigmatic Pentecost conversion and Antioch as the paradigmatic Pentecost church. That whole story is the significance of the Jewish Pentecost festival in its ancient setting of

Israel's Exodus and subsequent possession of the promised land. An entire chapter is devoted to developing this crucial theme.[16]

Validating the Hellenist Movement

Another theme that Luke develops in Acts is validating the Hellenist movement in Jerusalem. Luke foresaw that the church's true destiny resided in this Hellenist movement. Further, this movement was no accident of circumstances but, in fact, fulfilled Jesus's original intentions as Messiah in calling out messianic Israel.

FIGURE P11. Stoning of Saint Stephen. Lunette over main entrance of Saint-Étienne-du-Mont Church, Paris, 1863, by Gabriel-Jules Thomas (1824–1905). Credit: Jebulon.

The story will not be easy to tell. Hellenists, after all, have a hard time in Jerusalem. Even when first introduced in Acts 6, their widows are being overlooked in church distributions, which is a hypocrisy as a denial of Pentecost fulfillment. Their premier early leader, Stephen, even though full of the Holy Spirit, is stoned to death after he makes plain the implications of the coming of Messiah for religious institutions of national Israel such as the temple in downtown Jerusalem. No wonder the center of gravity for this movement inevitably must shift from Jerusalem to Antioch, and Antioch will become the paradigmatic church of Pentecost fulfillment, and Saul of Tarsus will resound Stephen's message of messianic Israel to the ends of the earth. Antioch becomes surrogate "mother church" for messianic Israel.[17]

[16]See chapter 1: "Pentecost as Thematic: Luke's Perspective on an Epic Event."
[17]See chapter 2: "Hellenists and Antioch: The Making of a Paradigm."

Knighting the Apostle Paul

Luke nominates Paul for churchman of the year award. The historical exigency is post-war Judea when everyone is searching for their soul. Jews are confronted with the unfathomable horrors of an enslaved population, destroyed country, ruined economy, and stunned religion.[18] Christians, whose movement originated in this Jewish world, added to this national calamity their own disaster of the 60s, which is the loss of almost all the great Christian leaders. Church tradition indicates martyrdom of both Peter and Paul in Nero's persecution after the great fire of Rome in July AD 64.[19] The Jewish high priest, Ananus, instigated the death of the highly respected James the Just of Jerusalem, the brother of Jesus, about AD 66. In such a chaotic, traumatic time when entire ways of life are being destroyed and leadership lost, one easily could wonder what being a Christian should be about in this new, seemingly post-apocalypse world, truly wondering where do we go from here?

Acts is Luke's answer. Luke sees in the passion and vision of Paul, most particularly preserved

FIGURE P12. Apostle Paul Monument, Berea, Macedonia. See Acts 17:10–12.

---

[18]Josephus provides the most detailed information about the despoiling of Judea; cf. temple spoils, *J.W.* 7.5.7 (161); 97,000 carried off as slaves, some to die in theaters around the empire by sword and wild beasts, *J.W.* 6.9.2–3 (418–20); the mass suicide at Masada, *J.W.* 7.9.1 (389–405). The great Colosseum of Rome inaugurated by Vespasian was financed from the spoils of this war, and among the slave builders were 20,000 Jews. Cf. Feldman, "Financing the Colosseum."

[19]On James, cf. Josephus *Ant.* 20.9.1 (200); on the fire of Rome, cf. Tacitus *Annals* 15.44.2–8; Suetonius *Nero* 16.2. On Peter's death, cf. Ferguson, *Backgrounds*, 592 in discussion of the tomb of Peter. On Paul's death, cf. Eusebius *H.E.* 2.25.

in the Damascus Road story, the future mission and destiny of the church until Jesus comes. In all of Luke-Acts, no story is emphasized more than that of Paul's Damascus Road, which Luke repeats three times.[20] The obvious repetition is a clue to Luke's purpose for writing. Luke knew the legacy of Jesus was a new vision of the people of God, and the legacy of Paul was to bring that vision's realization to the ends of the earth. So, Luke wrote Acts to knight the apostle Paul.[21]

HISTORICIAL MATTERS

We covered reading strategy and purpose first, because these matters offer an excellent "quick fix" to orient the reader to how special is this book of the New Testament. For standard introductory matters, students should consult recent critical commentaries.

Authorship and Accuracy

Authorship is argued, but Luke is likely. Common authorship of both Luke and Acts is argued less, as the evidence is pretty overwhelming, though not universally accepted. While external evidence is strong, the internal evidence is even stronger in the common prologues, common language and style, common purpose, and common distinctives. We already have argued the three "we sections" (16:10–17; 20:5—21:18; 27:1—28:16) intend to express eyewitness authority for that content, not alien material in which the "we" inexplicably is retained, nor literary contrivance for participation or entertainment value alone.

Historical accuracy can be defended, but difficulties remain. The mention of Theudas and sequencing of Judas the Galilean in Acts 5:32 is a clear difficulty, as well as the census under Quirinius in Luke 2:2. At the same time, so much that was so questioned is so passé now. The most famous of these claims of Luke's inaccuracy was his use of the

---

[20] Acts 9:1–19; 22:5–16; 26:12–18.

[21] Not to say Luke's portrait of Paul is not tendentious and idealized. Luke, however, is not an obsequious fan. Luke is more honest about Paul's failures than even modern commentators. (See chapter 3, "The Character Saul-Paul: Paul, Jerusalem, and God's Will.") Even idealized, Luke's material on Paul is fundamental to any semblance of piecing together Paul's biography and mission. Bruce observed that Christianity probably became such a western phenomenon when its roots were so eastern because of the eminently successful missionary work of Paul (Bruce, *Acts*, 16).

term "politarch" for the civic leaders at Thessalonica (Acts 17:6). We simply had no evidence of this term whatsoever in any literature of the

ancient world, Greek or Latin, prior to its appearance in Acts, nor in any inscriptions. Such total silence on a term is extremely rare in the ancient world and was a "lock tight" case against Luke. Clearly, Luke invented the term out of thin air. Clearly not. Only in the last century did inscriptions and other artifacts start being found with that very term used for civic officials exactly as Luke used the term in the very provenance suggested by Luke's

FIGURE P13. Politarch Seal. Clay seal mentioning the politarchs of Berea, Macedonia, found on papyrus document (AMV).

text (Macedonia). In contrast, Luke uses the correct civic designation of "praetors" at Philippi as a Roman colony (Acts 16:20). Thus, Luke's accuracy in Roman details is specific even from city to city.

FIGURE P14. Politarch Inscription. Pedestal of a statue that was an offering of a group of politarchs at the end of their term, 200–150 BC (TAM).

Further, Luke's picture of Judean believers is accurate. One could add that his nautical knowledge, while not that of a sailor, is much more enhanced than even the typical passenger regularly plying the waves conducting business. In fact, Luke's description of the voyage to Rome is so detailed that the bay where he shipwrecked arguably can be calculated with some precision.[22] Luke mentions as many islands, cities, provinces, civic officials, geography, topography, roads, and the like in so short a space as to match famous ancient historians.

Speeches in Acts

To write history, ancient authors had to learn to write speeches, because the essence of history is not events but how what happens is to be interpreted. The vehicle of historical interpretation was provided in the speeches historians composed. Speeches were crucial to the task.

The question of the speeches of Acts has been studied intensively. Luke is following the principles of first-century historiography in the style of Thucydides. That is, he summarizes faithfully. Thus, the style and wording is Luke's, but the meaning and content faithfully represents the speaker. Peter's sermon at the temple after healing the lame man is a good example. The reader is told directly that Peter's message lasted several hours, from mid-afternoon to sundown (Acts 3:1; 4:3). Yet, Luke covers the entire message in only fifteen verses (Acts 3:12–26)—clearly a summary.

What about Paul's speeches? These speeches have been the most contentious as to whether Luke misrepresents Paul, or even promotes "un-Pauline" theology (the Areopagus in Athens in Acts 17). No doubt, Luke has his own take on Paul. However, allow for audience analysis and the redactional character of Luke's entire work of Luke-Acts with his distinctive focus on church mission and gentile expansion, then Luke does not distort Paul.[23]

Date

The most likely date range is in the decades after AD 70. Use of Mark, which not only has to circulate but become generally accepted as authoritative, is one factor. The clear political apologetic is another. The exigency of defining the nature and mission of the church and the

---

[22]Smith, *Voyage and Shipwreck*, 125–42; for alternatives, see discussion of Acts 27.

[23]'Tis a moot point, really. What interpreter of Paul does *not* distort Paul?

relationship of Peter and Paul (post-apostolic question) is another. The post AD 100 date so popular in the 1800s was based on faulty assumptions and questionable developmental theories about early Christianity. Late dating resurfaces again in the Acts Seminar of the Westar Institute. Arguments, though updated, have an eerie déjà vu feeling.[24]

The educated style of the prologue suggests a literate audience. The content of Acts suggests Greco-Roman, gentile readers.

LITERARY MATTERS

Western Text

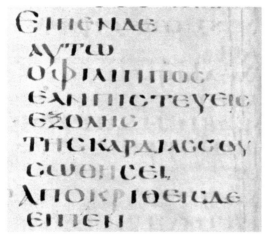

FIGURE P15. Laudian Acts (MS 08). Bilingual Latin and Greek 6th cent. manuscript at Acts 8:37: "And Philip said to him, 'If you believe with all your heart, you will be saved.' And he answered and said . . ."

Our main literary problem is the text of Acts itself. Greek manuscripts include a "Western text" tradition. This tradition is notable for generally longer readings. Such a result often is due to expansions, explanations, and other efforts in the vein of "helps for the reader." The prevailing view among textual critics is that the shorter readings more typical of earlier manuscripts are

---

[24]Parallel to the Jesus Seminar, but attention turned to Acts with similar presuppositions: Acts is not history, not first-century, and not by someone historically working with Paul; "we sections" are literary convention, Homeric-style *mimesis*; the Corinth "bema" did not exist until late first century, so a clear anachronism revealing the later time period of the author; many Acts names are fictional; the context indubitably is second-century because the issues are: order of widows, mention of bishops, presbyters, and deacons, misuse of community funds, and conflicting dogmas, all issues of *1 Clement*, Ignatius, and Justin Martyr; Acts is a reductionist, simplistic, idealized Christianity originating exclusively in Jerusalem among the apostles and their Hebrew Scriptures and moving outward in the triumphalism so notable of early Catholicism; Smith and Tyson, *Acts and Christian Beginnings*. Similarly, Rubén and Penner, *Engaging Early Christian History: Reading Acts in the Second Century*. For a recent solid defense of a first-century setting, cf. Keener, *Acts*, 1:90–257.

more likely original. This "Western text" is understood as second-century editorial work of scribes.

Since the few late Greek manuscripts available for developing an edited text of the New Testament at the time of the work of the King James translators had "Western readings," then one can find these readings in the KJV. One notable example is the addition of an entire verse, Acts 8:37, in the conversation between Philip and the Ethiopian eunuch. The addition reads: "And Philip said to him, 'If you believe with all your heart, you may.' He said in answer, "I believe that Jesus Christ is the Son of God."' This addition is intentional on the part of church scribes. The addition makes the Ethiopian's response to Philip conform to the formulaic confession of faith by baptismal candidates in the later centuries of the church. ("Jesus Christ is the Son of God.") Consult the commentaries for more information on this Western text tradition. The Western text reading often enhances our understanding of issues important to the church in the use of Acts.

The Ending of Acts

The ending of Acts seems abrupt, but not as dramatic as the ending of the Gospel of Mark. The problem is more narrative logic. Paul appeals to Caesar, but we never hear the result, after several chapters following the story. We have no trial account, and no imprisonment outcome. The ending has caused speculation about the reason. Perhaps the author unexpectedly died. Perhaps he planned a third volume to which he would build a transition but never got to the project. Perhaps the ending represents the present time of the author, so the trial outcome is unknown.

One can speculate like this until the cows come home, but such suppositions can go no further than suppositions. More likely, such an ending has literary purpose. The narrative, followed carefully, can be shown to contextualize the ending within a narrative function.

Outline of Acts

Three outlines have become traditional. The geographical follows the gospel expansion of Acts 1:8: Jerusalem (1–7), Judea and Samaria (8–12), Uttermost Parts (13–28). The leadership mission follows Peter and Paul: Peter and the Jewish Mission (1–12), Paul and the gentile Mission

(13–28). The summary extensions follows the six formulaic summary statements: Early Church (1:1—6:7), Palestine Extension (6:8—9:31), Antioch Extension (9:321—12:24), then Asia Minor Extension (12:25—16:5), Europe Extension (16:6—19:20), and Rome Extension (19:21—28:31).[25] All of these are good and emphasize various points of the Acts text. One even can merge all three into a combined outline, with all but the first two of the six summary statements ending units in the outline. Thus, Jerusalem and Judea-Samaria are folded into the Petrine half, and the uttermost parts made equal to the Pauline half.

Earlier we teased out the purposes and major themes of Acts. The outline we are suggesting follows that logic. This approach resonates with Haenchen's simple but crucial observation of how different are the traditions in the Hellenist Cycle that are thrust into the storyline of Acts.[26] Everything is new at Acts 6. We have new terminology for believers ("disciples," *mathētai*, μαθηταί), a new dimension to the social complexion of the Christian community ("Hellenists," *Hellēnistai*, Ἑλ-ληνισταί), new leadership group in the Seven, new negative critique of the temple as a Jewish institution (Stephen's speech), and new directions for the gospel mission inaugurated at Pentecost (Samaritans, Ethiopian eunuch). This new material with such distinctive traditions not found elsewhere in the New Testament and point of insertion has to be core to Luke's plan and structure to the whole narrative. So, we make Acts 6 a major turning point dividing the first half of our outline of Acts.

The major divisions, as many have noted, are two: the first half of Acts 1–12 and the second half of Acts 13–28. If one focuses on personalities, then one thinks of Peter and Paul and the "Jewish mission" and the "gentile mission." But this conceptualization is flawed. These two leaders never worked exclusively in their missions. Peter worked among gentiles (Cornelius), and Paul worked in every synagogue he ever encountered. Acts even ends with Paul addressing the synagogue leaders in Rome. So, really, a so-called "Jewish mission" and a "gentile mission" in Acts is a narrative fiction that obfuscates Luke's picture.

---

[25] As in Acts 6:7: "The word of God continued to spread; the number of disciples increased greatly." Similarly, note 6:7; 9:31; 12:24; 16:5; 19:20; 28:31. Cf. Bruce, *Acts*.

[26] Haenchen, *Acts*, 264–69.

One personality, however, does override both halves of Acts. An outline better would focus on this personality—the Holy Spirit. The theme would be Spirit empowerment. Acts really is not the acts of the apostles. Acts is the acts of the Holy Spirit (like all of Luke-Acts). So, we would do better from a narrative standpoint to call the two halves by the major character: The Spirit Empowers Messianic Israel (1–12), and the Spirit Empowers World Mission (13–28). The outline, then, would subdivide according to this narrative movement. This messianic Israel presented in Acts is Luke's new vision of the people of God.

ACTS: A NEW VISION OF THE PEOPLE OF GOD

I.   THE SPIRIT EMPOWERS MESSIANIC ISRAEL (ACTS 1–12)
   A. *The Spirit Empowers Messianic Israel's Renewal (1–5)*
      1. Renewal Beginnings (1)
      2. Renewal Empowerment (2)
      3. Renewal Witness (3–5)
   B. *The Spirit Empowers Messianic Israel's Hellenists (6–12)*
      1. Hellenist Leaders Emerge (6–7)
      2. Hellenist Mission Advances (8–10)
      3. Hellenist Center Shifts (11–12)

II. THE SPIRIT EMPOWERS WORLD MISSION (13–28)
   A. *The Spirit Empowers World Mission Journeys (13:1—21:17)*
      1. 1MJ: From Cyprus to Conference (13–15)
      2. 2MJ: From Asia to Europe (16–18)
      3. 3MJ: Ephesus (18:23—21:17)
   B. *The Spirit Empowers World Mission Destiny (21:18—28:31)*
      1. Destiny Denied: Jerusalem Disaster (21:18—23:32)
      2. Destiny Delayed: Caesarean Custody (23:33—26:32)
      3. Destiny Achieved: Journey to Rome (27–28)

Integrating Themes and Plot

Of the seven themes we have identified implicitly surfacing in the Acts narrative,[27] the last three (Pentecost, Hellenists, Paul) are essential to

---

[27]Defending Christianity, defining messianic Israel, clarifying the church, nuancing the kingdom of God, demonstrating Pentecost fulfillment, validating the Hellenist movement, and knighting the apostle Paul.

plot development. Luke establishes Pentecost as the theological foundation for the Hellenist movement, and the Hellenist movement as the messianic foundation for the mission of Paul. That is, Paul has proper place in Acts only as one part of the Hellenist movement within early Christianity. Paul and his mission do not stand independently, not, at least, as Luke frames his story.[28] Treatment of the character of Paul in Acts usually leaves him sticking out like a sore thumb, almost as if the first twelve chapters of Acts are a "diversion" to the real story of the so-called "missionary journeys of Paul" in the last half. In truth, without the Hellenists and their core experience symbolically codified in the city of Antioch told in the first half of Acts, Paul's story in the last half simply falls apart without essential narrative exigency.

So, three themes drive the Acts plot across all twenty-eight chapters: Pentecost, Hellenists (Antioch), and Paul. These themes focus the ending of Acts with laser precision as *an eminently powerful conclusion to the Hellenist story*, not to Paul's story. If, at the end of Acts, we are asking questions about Paul, we are asking the wrong questions. These three themes, eminently important to understanding the narrative flow of Acts, either have not received significant attention (Pentecost), or sufficient integration into the plot of Acts (Hellenists, Paul). Thus, part one of our study is establishing thematic foundations for the plot development. Parts two and three reveal the plot that develops on these foundations.

SUMMARY

The prologue to Luke's Gospel actually introduces two volumes, Luke and Acts. In composing these two volumes together, Luke wants to write an accurate account of the origins of the Christian movement. Of many items, the prologue reveals two important aspects of Luke's work. One is that Luke used sources. These sources are discernable just beneath the surface by the nature of the Greek text or the distinctive content not found in any other Gospel. For understanding Acts, the most important source material to recognize and parse out is the Hellenist Cycle beginning in Acts 6.

---

[28]Paul's own perspective, of course, as revealed in his letters is another matter altogether. While Paul is Luke's "hero," Luke makes clear his differing perspectives on this provocative character on more than one occasion in Acts.

The other important aspect revealed in the prologue is the use of eyewitness material. Such documentation makes sense for the story of Jesus, so thoroughly dependent upon apostolic eyewitness. But the prologue also insinuates the function of the "we sections" of Acts in which the narrative without any rhetorical signals suddenly shifts to first person. The author means to indicate that the author is one of the eyewitness sources for some of the material as stated in the prologue.

Canonical developments explain why Acts was orphaned from its first volume sibling. This separation of Acts from Luke, however, from a literary point of view impedes the design and function of the two volumes meant to be read together. In terms of reading strategy, then, one would do well to read and comprehend Luke to understand Acts.

The Gospel of Luke breaks out into five macro units. The first is the prologue, characterized by a fine Greek style. The author seeks to establish that the account to follow is authoritative. That emphasis will be necessary due to the composition itself pushing the boundaries of what might be called a "gospel." No other Gospel writer is only halfway done when the resurrection is narrated. All the other Gospel writers are finished. Luke is not. Crucial to telling the story of Jesus is telling the story of the church, and that formulation requires Acts. Luke will bridge to that second part of the story with his famous ascension/Pentecost sequence.

The second part is the infancy narrative in a Semitic Greek evoking early Judean sources. This unit presents the Israel of God awaiting the arrival of the promised Messiah. Jesus is that Messiah. Elements in the story set a trajectory that will transform the meaning of the Israel of God. Gentiles will figure into that transformation.

The third part is Jesus's Galilean ministry. The Greek shifts to the common Koine Greek, suggesting the Gospel of Mark underneath the material. Though the story is in Galilee, Jesus is not a Zealot, does not teach like a Zealot, does not train like a Zealot, and does not lead like a Zealot. Jesus preaches and embodies "good news." He is no threat to Rome, nor are his disciples who follow him.

The fourth part shifts back to a literary, Hellenistic Greek, suggesting Luke's more direct editing of the material. The shift is for Luke to develop his unique "Journey to Jerusalem" section. Jesus goes to Jerusalem by deliberate choice and divine commission. Jerusalem is his destiny, his journey into God's will to die for the sins of the world. He will set the stage for the new Exodus of the people of God.

The fifth part shifts back to the common Koine Greek, once again picking up with the material in the Gospel of Mark to give the passion narrative of Jesus's death and resurrection common to all the Gospels. Jesus was innocent. He died due to Jewish leadership manipulating the crowds and Roman authorities. God, however, overturned the verdict through resurrection. Yet, Luke insists the story of Jesus does not end with resurrection. A sequel is to follow that will transition the story of Jesus into the story of the church.

Luke's purpose is to show that the story of Jesus becomes the story of the church. In the Gospel's prologue, he expresses his desire to give an authoritative account so that he can substantiate this expansion of the "gospel" genre. Other themes related to this newly-minted "gospel" are a defense of Christianity as innocent before Rome, important in a post-Jewish war setting surrounding this composition. Luke also wants to define messianic Israel in this post-war setting, since the Israel of God already has been transformed by the arrival of Messiah. Israel now can realize her eschatological destiny anticipated by the prophets. National Israel will not agree with this reconfiguration of the meaning of Israel taught by Jesus to his disciples.

Along the way in defining messianic Israel, Luke also canonizes Paul's take on the Israel of God as the church. Luke clarifies what the church is by using the Pauline universe as his frame of reference. This new construct for Israel as the church inevitably radicalizes the concept of the kingdom of God, a traditional symbolic universe in Jewish thought that Luke intends to nuance through his story of Jesus. In contrast to other first-century Jewish voices, this kingdom of God taught by Jesus means political nationalism is out. Christological messianism is in. This kingdom when perceived on earth is embodied in the church and her present mission to the world with the gospel of Jesus as Messiah and Lord, Son of God.

Luke purposes to demonstrate Pentecost fulfillment in this new messianic Israel. The one feast undeveloped by other Gospel writers Luke uses to establish a theme across the entire narrative of Acts. What was anticipated in the historical feast of Pentecost—divine forgiveness, harvest bounty and joy, social inclusiveness—is realized in the church. The fullest realization of the fullness of this promised eschatological

Pentecost is among the messianic Hellenists of Jerusalem. Pentecost's center of gravity will shift in this story from Jerusalem to Antioch, and from Peter to Paul. The Holy Spirit guides this movement all the way.

In the cataclysm otherwise known as first-century Judea, most especially after the disaster of the first Jewish War, the abiding question for many was, Where can one get one's bearings on where to from here? Luke answers with Acts. We find our destiny as the church by following the Damascus Road vision and boarding that good old gospel ship with Paul.

We accept the traditional attestation to Luke, sometime companion to the apostle Paul, who authored a two-volume work, Luke-Acts. The "we sections" intend to convey what is claimed in the prologue that the traditions researched include eyewitness material. Historical clarity has difficulties. Luke's accuracy however, gains increasing support with each archeological discovery. Newer evidence lends significant weight and wisdom to adopting a more neutral "wait and see" attitude on remaining issues rather than unilaterally declaring Lukan accuracy a *de facto* impossibility, which is more presuppositional than evidential.

Ancient historians told history through speeches. The art of writing a speech was much discussed among the ancients. With no CNN worldwide news network, no audio or video recorders, no reporters who have rushed to the developing scene to broadcast live in their satellite-equipped news vans—well, about the best one could do was to interview eyewitnesses, access written official records, and summarize as best as possible. Luke aspired to faithful summary. While expressed in his own words and writing style, inspired by the Holy Spirit, Luke achieved his goal. Everyone finds Paul difficult, candidly admitted by another New Testament author (2 Peter 3:16). Luke was faithful here too; but, as with every interpreter of Paul, we have to allow for Lukan perspective.

Date is first century, not second. The context that best explains all the evidence in the text is in the decades following the First Jewish War, not the early decades of the second-century church. The anticipated audience is literate, Greco-Roman, gentile.

The Western text has informative, sometimes useful, additional information but probably is not as close to the original text as the edited Greek text currently published. Theories trying to connect this tradition to late publication of Acts are interesting but unpersuasive.

The ending of Acts has caused speculation, since the outcome of Paul's appeal to Caesar is unremarked. All such historical speculation is unpersuasive and unnecessary. In fact, not remarking on the outcome of Paul's appeal clearly shows from a narrative point of view that Luke never was focused on Paul's appeal to Caesar in the first place. Narrative considerations adequately can explain the ending of Acts within Luke's literary purposes for composing Luke-Acts.

Acts is a new vision of the people of God. Essential to this vision was the teaching of Jesus. Jesus transformed the national Israel he encountered into the messianic Israel the prophets promised. He thereby renewed Israel into the eschatological people of God, and got them on track into their historic destiny of world mission through the Hellenist movement of the early church in Jerusalem. The passion and powerhouse of this world mission was Saul of Tarsus.

Three crucial themes drive the plot of Acts: Pentecost, Hellenists (Antioch), and Paul. The first part of this narrative study of Acts will be three chapters devoted to establishing these three thematic foundations. The second and third parts of this study will show how these themes define and integrate characters and action and drive the plot that ensues all the way to the ending of Acts. We will start where Luke starts, with Pentecost.

PART 1

Thematic Analysis

Thematic Foundations of Characters and Plot

1

Pentecost as Thematic

Luke's Perspective on an Epic Event

O F THE THREE ANNUAL pilgrim feasts, Passover and Tabernacles are well developed in the Gospels. The absence of Pentecost is a loud silence, save Luke alone.[1] Two basic questions arise: (1) from what historical matrix did Luke derive his emphasis on Pentecost in Acts, and (2) what was he up to at the narrative level by profiling this feast in prominent narrative position as the lead event from which all the following narrative plotline flowed?

HISTORICAL BACKGROUND

The feasts of the Jewish year had two basic components in their historical development. As a rural and agrarian society, Jewish life found its social rhythms in the agricultural seasons. Harvest time was an occasion of joy and thanksgiving. Celebration at harvest was a natural part of the seasonal cycle of the year. Most Jewish feasts can be traced to an original agricultural celebration. The second component of a feast was religious. Jewish history is punctuated with vivid memories of epic

FIGURE 1.1. Pentecost Harvest Festival.

---

[1]Pentecost derives from the Greek numeral *pentēkostos* (πεντήκοστος, "fiftieth").

37

events that became foundational to Jewish identity. These dramatic events became tied to the agricultural feasts to remember them and celebrate their significance for the life of the nation.

Agricultural Origins

Pentecost was used by ancient Jews to refer to one of three annual pilgrim festivals.[2] The sources are mixed on the nature of the original festival: (1) either a celebration of the firstfruits of the wheat harvest,[3] or (2) a celebration of the completion of the barley harvest that had begun three months earlier.[4] The time was set at seven weeks after the beginning of the barley harvest, yielding a week of weeks, hence the name "Feast of Weeks."[5] The time also was calculated as fifty days after Passover, hence, "Pentecost" (Lev 23:16).

The actual festival technically was only a one-day celebration (Lev 23:21), but the practicality of insuring everyone had opportunity to participate expanded the festival into two days. According to Reinhardt, offerings still could be brought for several days after the actual feast.[6] No evidence suggests the number of visitors to Jerusalem was less at the Feast of Weeks than the other festivals.[7] Polhill argued that Pentecost was even more popular than Passover due to better weather travel conditions.[8] The actual calendar date for the celebration is a vexed question, since this date was argued differently among various groups (Sadducees, Pharisees, Essenes and others).[9] Lohse concluded that, though the date for celebration was argued, the Pharisaic calculation (exactly fifty days after the first day of Passover) was followed in Judea prior to AD 70.[10]

---

[2]Tob 2:1; 2 Macc 12:32; Philo, *Dec.* 160; *Spec. Leg.* 2.176; Josephus, *J.W.* 1.11.6; 1.13.3; 2.3.1; 6.5.3; *Ant.* 3.10.6; 13.8.4; 14.13.4; 17.10.2.

[3]Exod 23:16; 34:22; Lev 23:16; Num 28:26.

[4]Deut 16:10; Jer 5:24. So Gaster, *Festivals of the Jewish Year*, 14, 59; Olson, "Pentecost," *ABD* 5:222.

[5]That is, חַג שָׁבֻעוֹת, Deut16:10, 16; Lev 23:15; Num 28:26; 2 Chr 8:13.

[6]Reinhardt, "The Population Size of Jerusalem," 263.

[7]Ibid.

[8]Polhill, *Acts*, 97.

[9]In Mishnaic discussion, note *Hagig.* 2:4; *Ed.* 2:10; Cf. Fitzmyer, *Acts,* 233.

[10]Lohse, "πεντηκοστή," *TDNT* 6:44–53.

Festal Activity

The precise elements of the Feast of Weeks never are explained in any detail. Even information in the Mishnah and Talmud is sparse. While the other two pilgrim feasts, Passover and Tabernacles, have entire tractates dedicated to discussion of them, Pentecost receives only scant mention in the Mishnah and Talmud. These few references are themselves difficult to adjudicate as to tradition lineage back into the first century.

While detailed discussion of Pentecost in the ancient sources is missing, the general sense of the nature of the festival is not hard to estimate. One could say that from within the context of Jewish monotheism, Jewish harvest festivals in general were opportune occasions both to declare God's ownership of the land and to acknowledge his grace to cause that land to bring forth food. Further, any such focus on the land inevitably would provoke remembrance of national events of election, covenant, and exodus and inspire a sense of gratitude to God for that salvation (cf. Deut 26:1–15).[11]

The issue of all Jewish feasts was, in fact, related to the overarching monotheistic thrust of the entire Exodus narrative. For example, the prelude to a discussion of the Jewish feasts in Exod 34 is verses 10–17, a restatement of God's exclusive covenant relationship with Israel. The burden of this restatement is a pointed warning against participation in pagan feasts connected to the worship of pagan gods. Only then does the discussion of the three great pilgrim feasts ensue. Thus, the feasts and their celebration inherently included the confession of God alone as the source and sustainer of life and the rejection of the worship of all other gods.

Related to worship, one element would be some type of liturgy. Falk noted that liturgical prayers and the *Hallel* on festival occasions would have been a common feature.[12] Another liturgical element would be offerings brought by the worshipper to the temple. For the Feast of Weeks, these offerings were either two loaves from the new corn[13] or a

---

[11] Sanders, *Judaism,* 139.

[12] Falk, "Jewish Prayer Literature," 293.

[13] Lev 23:17—leavened bread as a contrast to the unleavened bread of Passover; cf. *Sukk.* 5:7.

freewill offering.[14] A third element would be sacrifices. Both Lev 23:16–20 and Num 28:26–31 prescribe the sacrifices to be offered at the Feast of Weeks. The sacrifices included burnt offerings of seven lambs, a bull, two rams,[15] a grain offering, a drink offering, a sin offering of a goat, and two yearling lambs as a sacrifice of well-being (שְׁלָמִים, Lev 23:19).

One ritual procedure was described by Sanders.[16] He noted that for firstfruits offerings (of any type on any occasion, but including Pentecost), the worshipper brought his basket of firstfruits offering to the priest, reciting the words of Deut 26:2: "I declare this day to the Lord your God that I have come into the land which the Lord swore to your fathers to give us." Then the priest would set the basket before the altar, and the worshipper would continue his avowal by quoting the rest of Deut 26:3–10.

In such a ritual, one can see combined the two themes of God's gift of the land and the Exodus. Gaster pointed out that the idea of collaboration was involved: the farmer collaborates with God in making the land yield produce and the ingathering is the necessary condition of life and prosperity in the coming year.[17] In noting that the feast was a reminder of deliverance from Egypt as the covenanted people of God, Freeman observed, "The ground of acceptance of the offering presupposes the removal of sin and reconciliation with God."[18] This appropriation of God's forgiveness was the ground of joy in the festival. Themes of harvest, God's blessings and promises, life, salvation, and forgiveness all come together to energize a joyous time of Pentecost celebration.

Another ritual element that has received some attention as a likely constituent part of the Pentecost activities is wine. Fitzmyer suggested that the mockery from the crowd, "they have just had too much new wine" (Acts 2:13), possibly could reflect Qumran traditions within the Temple Scroll of a series of three Pentecostal feasts, one of which celebrated new wine (Feast of Weeks, Feast of New Wine, Feast of New

---

[14]Deut 16:10 indicates a "freewill offering" (נְדָבָה) in proportion to the blessings received at the Lord's hand.

[15]Num 28:27 indicates two bulls, one ram.

[16]Sanders, *Judaism*, 154. Bringing firstfruits to the temple is described in *Bikk.* 3.2–4.

[17]Gaster, *Festivals*, 62.

[18]Freeman, "Pentecost," *IBD* 3:1188.

Oil).[19] "Luke may have known such multiple Pentecosts among contemporary Jews and so alluded to the Pentecost of New Wine, when speaking more properly of the Pentecost of New Grain."[20] While this idea can be offered as an interesting speculation on Luke's description, A Qumran connection to Luke's presentation is highly dubious, as Luke generally does not show such a detailed interest in Qumran ritual nor does he use Qumran traditions for narrative development anywhere else in Acts. The suggested allusion is weak at best.

Josephus provides us another piece of information regarding the first-century celebration of Pentecost.

> When a week of weeks has passed over after this sacrifice (which weeks contain forty and nine days), on the fiftieth day, which is Pentecost, but is called by the Hebrews Asartha, which signifies Pentecost, they bring to God a loaf, made of wheat flour, of two tenth deals, with leaven; and for sacrifices they bring two lambs.[21]

Fitzmyer argued that behind Josephus's reference to "is called by the Hebrews Asartha" (ἣν Ἑβραῖοι ἀσαρθὰ καλοῦσι) is an Aramaic expression for "solemn assembly," implying this feast called for an assembly of Judean Jews.[22] This solemn assembly seems confirmed in other references to Pentecost by Josephus.[23]

Social Inclusiveness

Harvest in all agrarian societies is both work and celebration: hard work for getting in the crop, joyous celebration for the life needs thereby supplied. A feast is a common token of that joyous time. The Jewish offering of two loaves of leavened bread symbolized gratitude to God for the plentiful harvest and was a token of the feast celebrated in Jewish homes. This feast was meant to be inclusive. No one in Israel should be in want of food at the celebration of harvest. The exhortation in Deut

[19]Fitzmyer, *Acts*, 234–35.

[20]Ibid., 235.

[21]Josephus, *Ant.* 3.10.6.

[22]Fitzmyer, *Acts*, 232. The phrase identifying where offerings would be brought, "place which the Lord your God will choose" in Deut 26:2, though ambiguous, traditionally in rabbinic Judaism always was understood to be Jerusalem; cf. *Piska* 298, in the *Sifre* Tannaitic commentary.

[23]Cf. *Ant.* 14.13.4; 17.10.2; *J.W.* 1.13.3; 2.3.1.

16 repeatedly echoed in the elaboration of the feasts celebrated by Israel is: "Rejoice before the LORD your God—you and your sons and your daughters, your male and female slaves, the Levites resident in your towns, as well as the strangers, the orphans, and the widows who are among you—at the place that the LORD your God will choose as a dwelling for his name" (Deut 16:11, NRSV). That is, the Pentecost celebration is intended to be inclusive, with specific attention given to those normally vulnerable to life's vicissitudes.

This inclusiveness surrounding the celebration of the Pentecost feast is prominent in the story of Tobit, a fictional presentation from the Intertestamental period of a pious Jew living in Nineveh. At one point in the story, Tobit prepares to celebrate the Pentecost feast in his home. Before he does, though, he is careful to perform those demands in the Torah calling for inclusion in the feast. He commissions his son, Tobiah, to go out and retrieve someone from the pious poor of the exiles in Nineveh to share the Pentecost feast with his family in his home.[24]

Were the pilgrim feasts significant as well for Diaspora Jews? Probably so. We already have noted the story of Tobit. In addition, Barclay argued that the feasts did play an important role for Diaspora Judaism, perhaps even as much or more than for Judean Jews. Of three significant aspects noted by Barclay that bound Jews in the Diaspora together in their religious, social, and financial affairs, one was festival and fast observance. The Jewish festivals were prominent social and religious events. They attracted even non-Jews to participate. The annual feasts were one of the most significant factors contributing to a sense of solidarity for Jews, including the Diaspora.[25] These observa-

---

[24]Tob 2:1–2. In fact, the Pentecost meal is only a foil for proving the extraordinary piety of Tobit in the next few verses of the story (2:3–7). When his son returns with the horrible news of murder in the market and an unburied Jewish corpse, Tobit immediately jumps up from table to perform the pious act of proper burial. He returns to the Pentecost meal, only now to be submerged in sorrow rather than the joy that had been anticipated initially. This causes Tobit to remember the words of the prophet Amos: "Your festivals shall be turned into mourning, and all your songs into lamentation" (Amos 8:10).

[25]Barclay, *Jews In The Mediterranean Diaspora*, 415–16.

tions resonate with Luke's narrative development of the protracted list of those Jews present at Pentecost.[26]

Religious Significance

The religious significance of the Jewish feasts involves association with the historical events of Exodus, wilderness, and settlement religiously interpreted. Some associations are contested, Pentecost no exception. One frequently proposed for Pentecost is a connection to Sinai.

Proposed Sinai Connection

Sinai is metonymic for covenant. Dunn argued that a connection to covenant renewal seems implied in 2 Chr 15:10–12, is probable at Qumran, and is certain in *Jub.* 6.17–21 (*c.* 100 BC).[27] We already have noted that a sense of general covenant connection is evident in Deut 16. But even if this general concept is to be expanded into an actual "covenant renewal ceremony" due to certain Jewish texts such as those at Qumran or *Jubilees*, can such a covenant renewal particularly be related specifically to the Sinai traditions that later Judaism ascribed to Pentecost? Dunn concluded "almost certainly," even though he did acknowledge that no Pentecost/Sinai link actually can be documented before the second century after Jesus.[28] Fitzmyer also was convinced of a Pentecost/Law association. He pointed to certain Qumran texts, as well as a collection of other so-called indirect allusions to the Sinaitic covenant in Luke's Pentecost account.[29] As another example, Wright also seemed persuaded of the Pentecost/Sinai connection.[30]

No doubt, later Judaism did associate Pentecost with the giving of the Law at Sinai.[31] Perhaps such a development could be viewed as near-

---

[26]Acts 2:9–11; most likely Diaspora Jews in Jerusalem specifically for the feast, not resident Jerusalemites, *contra* Haenchen, *Acts*, 168, n. 7. For discussion and bibliography, cf. Barrett, *Acts*, 118, 121–24.

[27]Dunn, "Pentecost," NINNT 2:784.

[28]Ibid.

[29]Fitzmyer, *Acts*, 233–34.

[30]"Not mentioned in this connection in the OT, but clearly a pre-rabbinic tradition, with echoes in the NT"; he then cited *Jub.* 1.5; 6.11, 17; 15.1–24; *bPes.* 68b; Acts 2:1–11; Eph 4:7–10. Wright, *The New Testament and the People of God*, 234, n. 73.

[31]Gaster, *Festivals*, 60–63; cf. *bPes.* 68b. Gaster noted that the Book of Ruth came to be read in the later liturgy for two reasons: (1) the story has a barley harvest back-

ly inevitable. A connection was suggested already just in the general time frame: Both the dated arrival of the Israelites to Sinai three months after Passover and the general time of the barley harvest in the spring of the year were close enough to lend to this association. Polhill tellingly pointed out, though, that the supposed parallels of Luke's account to the Sinai theophany are more apparent than real because much of this language is stock theophany terminology.[32] Neither does Luke make any explicit connection to Torah, whether in the narrative or in Peter's speech that follows.[33] Dunn would agree that, even if Luke probably was aware of an already established Pentecost/Sinai connection, we have no evidence that such a connection was driving his narrative in Acts 2.[34]

Other Proposed Connections

Other Old Testament or Jewish background connections commonly encountered in discussion of Pentecost include Philo, theophanic fire, and the tower of Babel. Philo has a discussion of the Sinai theophany that includes an element of God's voice as a sound turning into fire.[35] This connection at least has an element of fire and voice. A major weakness here, however, is that Philo himself never connected his remarks about the Sinai theophany to the feast of Pentecost. Another suggestion has been God's descent in fire in Exod 19:18. Again, this is in a Sinai context at the foot of the mountain in a revelatory theophany of God to the people of Israel after the Exodus. Yet, fire is one of the most common features of theophanic revelation, so provides nothing distinctive for our understanding of Acts 2. Finally, suggestion has been made that Pentecost is a symbolic reversal of the confusion of tongues in the tower of Babel episode in Gen 11:1–9. While some logical connection has been attempted in this suggestion, once again, the logic is external to Luke's

---

ground itself, and (2) a pagan embraces Israel's faith; these are the two main features of the feast: (1) harvest ingathering, and (2) acceptance of the law, Gaster, *Festivals*, 70.

[32] Polhill, *Acts*, 105, n. 93.

[33] Polhill, *Acts*, 105.

[34] Dunn, "Pentecost," NIDNTT 3:785.

[35] Philo *Dec.* 33: "which by giving form and tension and transforming it to flaming fire, like breath through a trumpet, gave out such a clear voice ..." (ἢ τὸν ἀέρα σχηματίσασα καὶ ἐπιτείνασα καὶ πρὸς πῦρ φλογοειδὲς μεταβαλοῦσα καθάπερ πνεῦμα διὰ σάλπιγγος φωνὴν τοσαύτην ἔαρθρον ἐξήχησεν).

actual narrative of Pentecost itself. This suggestion, in other words, is the weakest of all three at the narrative level.[36]

In short, none of these other background suggestions has persuasive force. The major objection to them all is that Luke never reveals any use of them for his narrative development of Acts. As we see Luke work the elements of plot and character development, other themes becomes much more evident in the construction of his narrative world.

Historical Background Summary

Pentecost was an ancient spring harvest festival celebrating both God's deliverance from oppression in the events of the Exodus and his covenant provision of life for the community of Israel through the abundant produce of the promised land. That is, Pentecost celebrated the concrete realization in the life of the nation of God's covenant promises to be the sole sustenance and life of Israel. Observance of the feast was demonstration of covenant loyalty within an exclusively monotheistic faith. The date was fixed exactly fifty days after Passover, but whether this date always should fall on a Sabbath or variously during the week was argued.

In Jerusalem, a day of solemn assembly was observed for Pentecost. Worship elements at the temple included ritual liturgy, offerings, and sacrifices. Acceptance of the offerings presupposed the removal of sin and reconciliation with God, a spiritual basis for great joy and celebration in the feast. The Jewish feasts were one of the three fundamental factors contributing to Jewish solidarity in the Diaspora, and observance of the feasts, including Pentecost, was as important in the Diaspora as in Judea.

The offering of two loaves of bread was a token of the Pentecost meal celebrated in Jewish homes. This meal was conceived as a table fellowship to be shared by all. The inclusive emphasis of the meal served as a tangible expression of the essence of that fullness of life promised to Israel, for even widows, orphans, poor, strangers, and Levites—those typically disenfranchised in the ancient economy—were invited to participate in the feast.

While covenant relationship is integral to all Jewish feasts, association in particular of the giving of the law with Pentecost is not a produc-

---

[36]Note Barrett's incisive critique, *Acts*, 119.

tive avenue of interpretation for the narrative of Acts. No ancient writer actually did so, and neither did Luke, even if such an association with Pentecost already was in place by the time Luke wrote, or, further still, even if he was aware of that association.

If the typical Pentecost/Sinai connection is not really helpful for understanding the Acts narrative, what does Pentecost mean to Luke? If we probe at the narrative level, the meaning of Pentecost surfaces fairly easily. Overviewing the historical background simply clears the way to see Luke operating from within his own narrative structure.

NARRATIVE DEVELOPMENT

The first and foremost observation to make, acknowledged immediately by all, is that the Pentecost narrative is uniquely Lukan.[37] No other New Testament author mentions or even alludes to the event.[38] Now, this type literary phenomenon usually is taken as a signal that in such material we have to do with elements special or peculiar to that author that give us an inside track into that author's themes and purposes. While we can agree with Barrett that Pentecost is a "special 'founding' gift of the Holy Spirit,"[39] this does not take us very far in analyzing Luke's narrative. At the end of his discussion of Acts 2, Barrett rather blandly observed, "Luke's narratives are by no means always theologically motivated. He had a good deal of plain common sense."[40] Even a commentary focused on sociological perspective simply does nothing with the Pentecost background to Acts 2, much less how the story later

---

[37]We do not need to pursue tradition criticism of Luke's work, such as Fitzmyer's remarks: "may be Luke's historicization of aspects of Christ's resurrection/exaltation, as he did with the Ascension itself" (*Acts*, 232); further, Fitzmyer speculated the date of this first confrontation of Jews with Christian proclamation was in the tradition Luke used; Luke simply dramatized that received tradition with the story of the outpouring of Spirit (*Acts*, 232). Barrett has given a good overview of tradition analysis of Acts 2; *Acts*, 109–10.

[38]Dunn has called John's report of the Spirit in John 20:22 a "Johannine Pentecost," but that simply is to confuscate Luke's contribution. Dunn, "Pentecost," *NIDNTT*, 2:787. Barrett wisely was much more cautious, noting that John's passage "differs markedly" from the account in Acts (*Acts*, 108). Paul assumes the gift of the Spirit as the bedrock of Christian experience (cf. Rom 8:9) and discusses the Spirit-led life often, but nowhere mentions Pentecost in this connection.

[39]Barrett, *Acts*, 108.

[40]Ibid., 112.

is developed in Acts 1–12.[41] Surely Pentecost has more narrative significance than these superficial soundings suggest. For one, Pentecost's prominent position in the Acts narrative alone deserves more attention. We turn, then, to the narrative priority Luke places on Penetecost.

The Narrative Priority of Pentecost

First, we observe at the narrative level that Luke fronts the Pentecost story. That is, Luke launches his narrative with Pentecost. This choice alone already establishes the priority of this episode. This easily made observation is also all too easily passed over. Even Luke's preliminary materials at the end of Luke and the beginning of Acts point ahead to Acts 2. What narrative elements build bridges to Pentecost?

Promise of the Father

Luke gives the necessary preliminary materials in Acts 1 that set the stage for Pentecost in Acts 2. They include a resumptive prologue (1:1–2), a reprise on the ending of the Gospel, including appearances, teaching the disciples, and commission (1:3–8), a second ascension account as a conclusion to the post-resurrection appearances of Jesus (1:9–11), and a reconstitution of the Twelve (1:12–26). The stage now properly set, Pentecost becomes the epoch event transforming the original Twelve and the believing community into a mission of dynamic witness, even as Jesus had commanded (1:8).

Within these preliminary materials in Acts 1, literary signals have displaced the reader's attention forward toward a coming event yet to be narrated. Already this displacement is anticipated at the end of the Gospel. In Luke 24:49 the reader hears Jesus tell the disciples to expect "the promise of my Father" (τὴν ἐπαγγελίαν τοῦ πατρός μου), which will have the certain effect of an extraordinary divine empowerment. The disciples then are charged to remain in Jerusalem to receive this promise. Clearly, the plotline has been extended by the narrator in the last chapter of the Gospel. By reference to this promise of the Father, Luke builds a narrative bridge to Pentecost.

Acts 1:4–5 is resumptive of this Pentecost bridge. As Luke recapitulates the promise of the Father theme, he adds a specific content exposition, "you will be baptized with the Holy Spirit" (ὑμεῖς δὲ ἐν

---

[41]Witherington, *The Acts of the Apostles: A Social-Rhetorical Commentary.*

πνεύματι βαπτισθήσεσθε ἁγίῳ). This addition facilitates the reader's prescience of the narrative that will follow. Luke also adds a specific time element, "not many days hence" (οὐ μετὰ πολλὰς ταύτας ἡμέρας). This brief time frame keeps the reader's expectations primed. The narrative importance of Pentecost could not be expressed more carefully at the end of the Gospel and the beginning of Acts.

That is to say, Luke fronts Pentecost in his narrative not simply because the first apostolic witness to Jerusalem happened to have a coincidental connection to one of the Jewish feasts but because Luke perceived a divine fulfillment integral to that feast. Events surrounding Pentecost comprise the essence of the "promise of my Father" the reader has been directed to expect to happen to the disciples of Jesus in Jerusalem since the end of the Gospel.

Fulfillment Rhetoric

The promise of the Father carries the idea of divine fulfillment. For this reason, Luke is careful to launch the story of Pentecost in Acts 2:1 with the rhetoric of fulfillment: "And when the day of Pentecost was fulfilled" (Καὶ ἐν τῷ συμπληροῦσθαι τὴν ἡμέραν τῆς πεντηκοστῆς). Moessner, for example, has pointed to the similar use of "fulfilled" in Luke 9:51 (ἐν τῷ συμπληροῦσθαι τὰς ἡμέρας) in reference to the divinely ordained days of Jesus being taken up in Jerusalem as the interpretive rubric for Luke's sense of "fulfilled" in Acts 2:1.[42] The common element that makes Moessner's connection highly probable is the divine necessity guiding both narratives. Both narratives at these verses are at crucial turning points in the story. Note how at Luke 9:51, Jesus turns toward his ultimate mission and destiny in Jerusalem. In a similar narrative pattern at Acts 2:1, note how the church turns toward its ultimate mission and destiny in the world.

Our key point here is that this sense of divine guidance that Luke has injected into Acts 2, both by narrative prolepsis and by fulfillment rhetoric, is related to a particular Jewish feast, Pentecost. Pentecost has narrative priority for Luke because Luke finds significance in the feast itself for elements in his narrative development. In terms of narrative

[42]Moessner, *Lord of the Banquet*, 66. That "fulfilled" would be that the total of fifty days from Passover had transpired has little support in the Greek text, for which Luke is careful to use singular, not plural, for "day" (ἡμέραν). Luke is focused on the feast itself, not the time interval from Passover.

strategy then, Luke presents Pentecost in Acts 2 as the controlling narrative event in Acts from which all future plot development flows. The question is, what significance does Luke attach to Pentecost in the narrative?

Pentecost Development in Acts 2

We can establish the narrative significance Luke attaches to Pentecost by starting with the narrative development in Acts 2 itself. We then can see these Pentecost trajectories as they play out in subsequent chapters.

Eschatological Divine Forgiveness

The historical Pentecost celebration included sacrifice as prescribed in the Law. Acceptance of sacrifices by the priests in the temple communicated divine acceptance and forgiveness of sins. This appropriation of God's forgiveness contributed to the sense of festal joy for the Pentecost worshipper. Abundant crops signaled God's blessings and prevenient forgiveness, a positive covenant relationship enacted in sacrificial ritual.

Luke has a characteristic emphasis on forgiveness. This emphasis surfaces, for example, in the way he chooses to epitomize Jesus's final instruction to the disciples in Luke 24:47: "and that repentance for the forgiveness of sins be preached to all the nations, beginning from Jerusalem."[43] Luke's emphasis on forgiveness also shows up in Peter's Pentecost speech. That is, Jesus's charge to preach repentance and forgiveness in Luke 24:47 Peter immediately discharges in his first message in Jerusalem. In his mission speech interpreting the outpouring of the Holy Spirit for the Jerusalem crowds in Acts 2:14–36, Peter establishes the eschatological context of the Pentecost phenomenon from Joel 2:28–32. Peter then exhorts in 2:38: "Each of you repent and be baptized in the name of Jesus Christ for the forgiveness of your sins."[44] For Luke,

---

[43]Greek: καὶ κηρυχθῆναι ἐπὶ τῷ ὀνόματι αὐτοῦ μετάνοιαν εἰς ἄφεσιν ἁμαρτιῶν εἰς πάντα τὰ ἔθνη. ἀρξάμενοι ἀπὸ Ἰερουσαλήμ.

[44]Greek: μετανοήσατε, [φησίν,] καὶ βαπτισθήτω ἕκαστος ὑμῶν ἐπὶ τῷ ὀνόματι Ἰησοῦ Χριστοῦ εἰς ἄφεσιν τῶν ἁμαρτιῶν ὑμῶν. A regular word in Petrine speeches; cf. 5:31; 8:22; and 10:43. The Lukan tendency especially surfaces in formulating Paul's synagogue sermon at Antioch of Pisidia in 13:38: "that through this man forgiveness of sins is being proclaimed to you" (ὅτι διὰ τούτου ὑμῖν ἄφεσις ἁμαρτιῶν καταγγέλλεται); cf. 26:18. In the undisputed Pauline epistles, such forgiveness terminology using the ἄφεσις root is extremely rare: only once in the verbal form in Rom 4:7, and this is

Pentecost is the historic moment of God's offer of eschatological forgiveness to Israel. For our purposes, we note that Luke has placed this divine offer of forgiveness carefully within the festal background of Pentecost. Why? Because forgiveness, while integral to the ritual of the Pentecost feast, is not the most prominent element of that feast.[45] The most prominent element is a harvest meal. The appropriation of God's eschatological forgiveness through Jesus Christ that is offered in this festal setting, then, inherently anticipates a communal celebration of festal joy. Therefore, our attention is drawn to how Luke establishes a theme of eschatological harvest bounty.

Eschatological Harvest Bounty

Luke uses the reality of the Spirit to establish the theme of eschatological harvest bounty. Notice how behind all of Acts 2 is the assumption that the outpoured Spirit is the eschatological dawning of the last days.[46] Peter extends the realization of this eschatological promise of the Holy Spirit to the Jewish audience in 2:39, "for this promise is for you" (ὑμῖν γάρ ἐστιν ἡ ἐπαγγελία). The historical underpinnings for this eschatological perspective reside in the Mosaic traditions revolving around the Exodus story. Particularly pertinent in this regard is how Luke's summary of Peter's exhortation closes with Peter's admonition in 2:40, "With many other arguments he testified and urged them, saying, 'Save yourselves from this corrupt generation.'"[47] This exhortation finds an intertextual echo of Moses's song in Deut 32 warning the Israelites of grievous idolatries in the context of the Exodus redemption.[48] Those who rebel against God after his glorious redemption are castigated in Deut 32:5 as "a crooked and perverse generation" (γενεὰ σκολιὰ καὶ

---

simply a quote of Ps 32:1. Even if we include all the Paulines, we only add the noun form twice in the doublet of Eph 1:7 and Col 1:14.

[45]Neither is the most prominent element the miracle of tongues, which is unconnected to the festival itself. This miracle *does* have narrative significance as the manifestation of the fulfillment of the "promise of the Father," the empowering presence of the Holy Spirit, for which the reader has been primed both at the end of the Gospel and in the preliminary materials in Acts 1.

[46]Dunn, "Pentecost," NIDNTT 2:785.

[47]Greek: ἑτέροις τε λόγοις πλείοσιν διεμαρτύρατο καὶ παρεκάλει αὐτοὺς λέγων· σώθητε ἀπὸ τῆς γενεᾶς τῆς σκολιᾶς ταύτης.

[48]Cf. Fitzmyer, *Acts*, 267.

διεστραμμένη).[49] A rehearsal of Israel's Exodus redemption and wilderness wanderings then is followed by a summary of the realization of God's gift of the land to Israel in 32:13, "he brought them up to the heights of the land, he fed them with the harvest of the fields."[50] The bounteous harvest points toward God's blessings and the faithfulness of God's people.

The reader of Acts further is appraised of this Exodus tradition echoing in Acts 2:40 in Peter's next speech to Jerusalem crowds in Acts 3:22. Here, Peter explicitly refers to Deut 18:18, the tradition of a Prophet like Moses to come, and applies this to Jesus. That is, even in the Mosaic traditions, God's provision for his people through the harvest of the fields is only the penultimate climax of the whole story of the Exodus. Even Moses anticipated One to come who would bring the ultimate prophetic fulfillment to the Exodus journey. Thus, in his own eschatological Pentecost setting for Acts 2–3, Luke has presented the ultimate climax of this Mosaic tradition as realized in Jesus Christ and his followers.

Luke integrates messianic traditions into these Mosaic traditions. Peter also refers to "the times of the restoration of all things" (χρόνων ἀποκαταστάσεως πάντων) at Acts 3:21, which is meant to supplement the previous kingdom phrase in 3:20 of "times of refreshing" (καιροὶ ἀναψύξεως). Such phrases reflect Jewish messianic expectations about messiah's universal reign. While Luke faithfully incorporates messianic language into Peter's speech in Acts 3 from early apostolic preaching, note how Mosaic traditions actually drive Luke's Pentecost setting.[51]

The Jerusalem crowds respond favorably to Peter's exhortation. This response is the beginning of the gospel advance outlined in the

---

[49]Cf. Deut 32:20, LXX.

[50]LXX: ἀνεβίβασεν αὐτοὺς ἐπὶ τὴν ἰσχὺν τῆς γῆς ἐψώμισεν αὐτοὺς γενήματα ἀγρῶν.

[51]The Mosaic traditions perhaps even may serve as the corrective to certain nationalistic strands of messianic expectation. This seems to reflect the spirit of the question of the disciples to Jesus in 1:6, "will you at this time restore the kingdom to Israel?' and the nature of Jesus's ambiguous response. While Jesus neither affirms nor denies this question, he certainly redirects the disciples' focus toward the tangible realities of the promised Holy Spirit as manifestation of that kingdom (1:7–8). That Spirit was Pentecost. Peter's quote of Joel in 2:17–21 in his Pentecost speech expresses an inaugurated eschatology that reflects concord with the spirit of Jesus's teaching in 1:7–8 and sets the larger context for what Peter says in Acts 3.

programmatic Acts 1:8. A significant response to Peter's exhortation is registered. Whatever the actual numbers, Luke's narrative theme is clear: his emphasis is on the fullness of the response.[52] For Luke, the point of this significant response is not evangelistic bragging or proof of the veracity of the message. The response is the beginning of the promised eschatological harvest bounty anticipated annually in the Pentecost festival.

Eschatological Harvest Joy

The most prominent element that Luke develops directly out of the Pentecost festival in his narrative account in Acts 2 is the shared bounty of the harvest signified in the joy of table fellowship. The Pentecost meal fellowship of Jesus's disciples represents the inaugurated eschatological harvest joy anticipated in the Exodus traditions. This characteristic fellowship is portrayed by Luke in the narrative that immediately follows Pentecost describing the life of the early church, Acts 2:41–47. The reader through Luke's smooth transition is thereby given a clear signal that this community experience is to be understood as the direct result of the Pentecost event. Luke's festival connection between the two narratives of the outpouring of the Spirit in the last days at the beginning of Acts 2 and the description of the early life of believers at the end of Acts 2 is clear in his fourfold description.

Luke characterizes this Pentecost community life by four aspects: (1) the apostles' teaching, (2) fellowship, (3) breaking of bread, and (4) prayers. The first aspect, the apostles' teaching, would be an extension of Jesus's kingdom teaching during the days between resurrection and ascension (Acts 1:3). The core of this teaching interprets Jesus's life, death, and resurrection as scriptural fulfillment anticipating God's kingdom (Luke 24:44–47). Eschatological realities already are unfolding in the story of Jesus. At the narrative level this core is highlighted in Peter's Pentecost presentation. Noteworthy in Peter's speech is the christological hermeneutic implicitly identified by Jesus in Luke 24:44 that Peter explicitly applies to the law (2:23), prophets (2:17–21), and writings (2:25–28, 31, 34–35).

---

[52]Luke's statistical accuracy is not essential to our narrative argument. However, for a defense of the accuracy of Luke's numbers here, cf. Reinhardt, "Population Size of Jerusalem," 237–65.

Thus, Luke demonstrates in the inaugural speech of Acts that the kingdom fulfillment theme in the teaching of Jesus is preserved by the Twelve with Peter as spokesman. Luke also shows how this theme has concrete implications for the life of the community of believers. Luke's other three aspects characterizing community life are meant to spell out these kingdom fulfillment implications.

The three specified aspects of community life—fellowship, bread, and prayer—comprise a recognizable group, because these aspects are components of the celebration of the Pentecost feast. In short, Luke is extending the reality of the Pentecost feast. Messianic fulfillment in Jesus transforms the temporal limitations of an annual Jewish pilgrim festival to its eschatological correlate and reality. Peter used a similar eschatological hermeneutic when interpreting the outpouring of the Spirit. That is, this promised Holy Spirit not only energizes apostolic witness, this Spirit also inspires harvest response to Jesus and harvest communion among disciples. God's eschatological joy now is being realized among God's people. Thus, fellowship, bread, and prayer are a perpetual token of that festal fulfillment.

Thus, Luke's emphasis on the fullness of the response to Jesus in Jerusalem is the bounty of the Pentecost harvest modulated into the eschatological key of Jesus. The harvest that the annual festival of Pentecost anticipated in the kingdom of God has arrived, a bountiful harvest, not of sheaves of grain, but of people, a visible harvest with visible results: joyous communion and shared fellowship over a meal. Positively, anytime Luke punctuates his narrative with a word about the church growing bountifully with God's blessings, often used as a way to outline the entire Acts narrative, this is his Pentecost fulfillment theme sprinkled generously throughout the entire narrative to tie all sections back to the original controlling narrative event of Pentecost.[53] Negatively, the breakdown of Pentecostal table fellowship is what gives the issues in Acts 5 and Acts 15 their significance for the church as serious matters of eschatological kingdom fulfillment.

Recognizing this Pentecost fulfillment theme would bring more clarity for commentators into what might otherwise appear to be superfluous parts of Peter's scriptural quotations in his Pentecost speech. For example, in commenting on Peter's speech, Polhill was perplexed that

---

[53] Acts 6:7; 9:31; 12:24; 16:5; 19:20; 28:31.

Peter included in his quotation in Acts 2:25–28, taken from Ps 16:8–11, the words of Ps 16:11, "you have made known to me the paths of life; you will fill me with joy in your presence."[54] Polhill commented, "since it adds nothing to his argument about the resurrection."[55] This assertion simply is not correct. Polhill missed the implications of God's present eschatological harvest in the Pentecost feast context. The joy in God's presence is the eschatological joy of the feast. Narratively, we can note that Peter's quote of Ps 16:11 in Acts 2:28 Luke explicitly plays out in his description of the early community of believers in Acts 2:46: "Day by day, while remaining associated closely and continuously in the temple of one accord, they were breaking bread in each home, sharing their food together with gladness and singleness of heart."[56]

Readers might recognize that at this point this argument would resonate well with that of Moessner.[57] His work in the Gospel of Luke involved an interpretive scheme for Luke's travel narrative beginning in Luke 9:51 using Deuteronomy's land of promise fulfillment theme. Moessner observed that this theme is echoed in the early stages of Acts: in Luke's narrative of Pentecost, in the unity of the community in all things common, in the joy of the harvest as the eschatological joy of the community in the time of fulfillment, and in Ananias and Sapphira as destroying that unity and joy. Further, meal scenes in Luke, especially as transparently laid out as in the climactic Emmaus story (Luke 24:13–32), have their key in recognition of the journeying guest who is revealed at table as Lord, and as host of the banquet in the kingdom of God.[58] Moessner then inferred a connection in Acts with this journeying guest motif of the eschatological banquet in the Lukan travel narrative.[59] Regarding this narrative development by Luke in Acts, Moessner wrote, "The New Exodus of Deuteronomy 30 has been ac-

---

[54] Greek: ἐγνώρισάς μοι ὁδοὺς ζωῆς πληρώσεις με εὐφροσύνης μετὰ τοῦ προσώπου σου.

[55] Polhill, *Acts*, 11.

[56] Greek: καθ᾽ ἡμέραν τε προσκαρτεροῦντες ὁμοθυμαδὸν ἐν τῷ ἱερῷ, κλῶντές τε κατ᾽ οἶκον ἄρτον, μετελάμβανον τροφῆς ἐν ἀγαλλιάσει καὶ ἀφελότητι καρδίας.

[57] Moessner, *Banquet*, 275–76.

[58] Ibid., 184.

[59] Ibid., 185–86.

complished!"[60] This current presentation of Luke's development of Pentecost fulfillment is in concord with this understanding.

Eschatological Harvest Inclusiveness

One feature common to the Jewish festivals preserved in the Law was their intent to be inclusive social events. Those typically disenfranchised economically or by society were to be included intentionally in the festal meal. This inclusive intent clearly comes out in the story of Tobit, for example.[61]

Luke makes clear that this festal inclusiveness is dominant in the character of the meal fellowship of the followers of Jesus. The shared communal life indicated by Luke in 2:44, "they were having all things common" (εἶχον ἅπαντα κοινά), is the concrete realization of the promise of social inclusiveness portrayed in the Pentecost feast. That this realization was not understood to be temporally limited is indicated by the selling of capital goods in order to preserve the ongoing status of Pentecost fulfillment (2:45). The verses then following in 2:46–47 are a perfect encapsulation of the two foci of the Pentecost feast activities in temple and home: "Day by day, persevering in one accord in the temple, breaking bread at home, they were sharing their food with gladness and singleness of heart, praising God and having the goodwill of all the people."[62] The eschatological Pentecost harvest and inclusive meal fellowship are now what we see and hear in Acts 2:41–47. Israel's festal fulfillment anticipated annually in the Pentecost pilgrim festival in Judea and throughout the Diaspora has arrived: abundant harvest, great joy, inclusive communion, sustenance and life, all a reality in the homes of those confessing Jesus as Messiah.

Pentecost Development in Acts 3–12

The promise of eschatological festal fulfillment in the community of believers is thematically carried along both positively and negatively in

---

[60]Ibid., 277.

[61]Tobit, however, did limit his sense of obligation to searching out only particularly pious individuals.

[62]Greek: καθ' ἡμέραν τε προσκαρτεροῦντες ὁμοθυμαδὸν ἐν τῷ ἱερῷ, κλῶντές τε κατ' οἶκον ἄρτον, μετελάμβανον τροφῆς ἐν ἀγαλλιάσει καὶ ἀφελότητι καρδίας αἰνοῦντες τὸν θεὸν καὶ ἔχοντες χάριν πρὸς ὅλον τὸν λαόν.

the chapters that follow the messianic Pentecost revealed in Acts 2. The two characters that Luke immediately uses to develop the theme are Barnabas and the duo of Ananias and Sapphira.

Barnabas as Pentecost Fulfillment

Barnabas is introduced in Acts 4:32–37. Shared communal life is the resonant setting that connects Acts 4:32–37 with the earlier Pentecost fellowship of Acts 2:41–47. This connection is implicit in the close similarity of the two descriptions, selling possessions, bringing the proceeds for distribution, but especially in the verbal echo of the last phrase, "as any one might have need" (καθότι ἄν τις χρείαν εἶχεν):

> 2:45 "and they were selling their possessions and property and distributing the proceeds to all, as any one might have need." (καὶ τὰ κτήματα καὶ τὰς ὑπάρξεις ἐπίπρασκον καὶ διεμέριζον αὐτὰ πᾶσιν καθότι ἄν τις χρείαν εἶχεν.)
>
> 4:34–35 "For not any one among them was needy, for as many as possessed lands or houses, selling them, they were bringing the proceeds of what was sold and laying it at the apostles' feet, and it was distributed to each, as any one might have need." (οὐδὲ γὰρ ἐνδεής τις ἦν ἐν αὐτοῖς· ὅσοι γὰρ κτήτορες χωρίων ἢ οἰκιῶν ὑπῆρχον, πωλοῦντες ἔφερον τὰς τιμὰς τῶν πιπρασκομένων καὶ ἐτίθουν παρὰ τοὺς πόδας τῶν ἀποστόλων, διεδίδετο δὲ ἑκάστῳ καθότι ἄν τις χρείαν εἶχεν.)

This description in 4:34–35 indicates that the eschatological harvest fullness of the people of God epitomized in Acts 2:41–47 has been extended in the narrative plotline. The purpose of this extension is in order to tie the introduction of the character of Barnabas in Acts 4 specifically to the Pentecost festal fulfillment theme of Acts 2.

Further, Luke also specifically characterizes Barnabas as a Levite (4:36, *Leuitēs*, Λευίτης)—the only time in all of Acts this term is used, which especially marks out Barnabas above other characters in Acts. Barnabas is uniquely marked this way as a character in Acts because this characterization resonates with the specific covenant obligation to include the Levite in the Pentecost feast (Deut 16:11). Since this Levite himself is the channel of blessing to the community, rather than the community being a blessing to the Levite, Luke dramatically illustrates how full is the eschatological realization of Pentecost in messianic Israel.

Even more, this character trait of a channel of blessing is codified in Barnabas's surname in 4:36: "Son of Encouragement" (ὅ ἐστιν μεθερμηνευόμενον υἱὸς παρακλήσεως). Commentators have balked at Luke's interpretation of the meaning of Barnabas's name. Clearly, this surname relates to no possible etymological analysis by Luke.[63] What possible narrative connection is Luke making by specifying the surname? The connection is Pentecost fulfillment. This fulfillment actually ties all the way back to the prophet Simeon in the nativity narrative of the Gospel. Simeon the prophet was looking for the "consolation of Israel" (παράκλησιν τοῦ Ἰσραήλ) when he had his revelatory encounter with the baby Jesus in the temple in Luke 2:25. Jesus is the consolation of Israel. This consolation in the church is realized through the Holy Spirit, the eschatological promise of the Father to the followers of Jesus. This eschatological realization is key to Luke's summary statement of the church in Acts 9:31: "The church, therefore, throughout all Judea, Galilee, and Samaria experienced peace, being built up and continuing in the fear of the Lord and in the consolation of the Holy Spirit, it was multiplying."[64] Barnabas is called a "Son of Consolation" because his actions have representative power on behalf of Messiah as an effective channel for the consolation of Israel in the community of believers. This consolation is in the realization of Pentecost fulfillment. In fact, Barnabas becomes the key character who facilitates the realization of the promise of Pentecost fulfillment in each of his significant interactions in the episodes that follow.

The second characterization of Barnabas by Luke is that he was from Cyprus. This location makes him a Diaspora Jew, at least in his affiliation. This affiliation allows Barnabas within the scope of Luke's narrative to represent the broad movement of the gospel beyond Judea, alluded to in Peter's Pentecost speech in 2:39, "for this promise is to

---

[63]Fitzmyer, *Acts*, 320–21, has provided a concise overview of the etymological problems.

[64]Greek: Ἡ μὲν οὖν ἐκκλησία καθ᾽ ὅλης τῆς Ἰουδαίας καὶ Γαλιλαίας καὶ Σαμαρείας εἶχεν εἰρήνην οἰκοδομουμένη καὶ πορευομένη τῷ φόβῳ τοῦ κυρίου καὶ τῇ παρακλήσει τοῦ ἁγίου πνεύματος ἐπληθύνετο.

you, and to your children, and to those who are far off."[65] Further, the connection to the first destination in the itinerary of the first missionary journey is given its foundation.

Ananias and Sapphira as Pentecost Threat

The story of Ananias and Sapphira has been one of the great enigmas of Acts. Note in the narrative, however, that Luke has juxtaposed the story of Ananias and Sapphira immediately against that of Barnabas. Luke intends the reader to compare this couple to Barnabas.

That comparison creates intentional narrative irony, because the contrasts are strong. If Barnabas is the positive image of Pentecost fulfillment, Ananias and Sapphira are the negative. Ananias's actions, along with those of his wife, serve to threaten Pentecost fulfillment in the life of the church. To the harmony of one accord, this couple creates discord; to the strength of shared life, this couple offers a selfish life; to the potential of Pentecostal fullness, this couple brings a short-changed purse. Where Barnabas functions as a "Son of Consolation" and is an effective instrument of the Holy Spirit in the community, Ananias and Sapphira egregiously provoke the Spirit into judgment. The problem they pose is serious, and Peter's quote to the Jerusalem population of Moses's warning about heeding the Prophet to come (Deut 18:19) already sets the stage for this showdown.[66] On the one hand, we have Ananias's duplicity, which will play havoc with the Pentecost harvest fulfillment; on the other hand, we have the Spirit's determination to bring Pentecost to eschatological fulfillment in the church. Ananias is Pentecost fulfillment threatened—a grave lesson for the church Luke will pick up again in Acts 15 with the Jerusalem Conference.

---

[65]Greek: ὑμῖν γάρ ἐστιν ἡ ἐπαγγελία καὶ τοῖς τέκνοις ὑμῶν καὶ πᾶσιν τοῖς εἰς μακράν.

[66]Acts 3:23:"And it shall be that every person who does not obey that Prophet will be utterly cut off from the people" (ἔσται δὲ πᾶσα ψυχὴ ἥτις ἐὰν μὴ ἀκούσῃ τοῦ προφήτου ἐκείνου ἐξολεθρευθήσεται ἐκ τοῦ λαοῦ). The verb translated "he will be utterly cut off" (ἐξολεθρευθήσεται) in Peter's formulation is neither a part of the MT nor the LXX of Deut 18:19. The verb form probably was derived by Peter from the LXX of Lev 23:29, a description of the fast of the Day of Atonement; so Fitzmyer, *Acts*, 289–90; also, Dunn, *Acts*, 47, who added, "it is response to the new Moses which determines membership of the people."

This theme of Pentecost threat communicated in the Ananias and Sapphira story sets the stage for the introduction of the Hellenists in the next chapter (Acts 6). Their widows are being denied in the daily distribution. This denial is no less serious than the lie of Ananias and Sapphira. We just learned that holding back is denial of Pentecost fulfillment, a serious matter, and now the church is holding back from the Hellenist widows their daily distribution *of food*.

The Hellenists as Pentecost Fulfillment

After Barnabas (Acts 4) and Ananias and Sapphira (Acts 5), beginning in Acts 6 we encounter the sudden introduction of unique traditions only Luke in the New Testament provides, that of the Hellenist movement in the early church. The structure of Acts clearly takes an entirely new direction with the Hellenist Cycle (Acts 6–12). The narrative indicators of a change are clear: we have new terminology for believers ("disciples," *mathētai*, μαθηταί), a new dimension to the social complexion of the Christian community ("Hellenists," *Hellēnistai*, Ἑλληνισταί), new leadership group in the Seven, new negative critique of the temple as a Jewish institution (Stephen's speech), and new directions for the mission inaugurated at Pentecost (in the two stories of the Samaritans and the Ethiopian eunuch). Luke moves to this cycle because this material formulates the story of the gospel's first advance after its initial soundings in Jerusalem, the gentile movement that eventually will receive apostolic blessing.

Key to this gentile movement are the "Hellenists." Acts 6 is the beginning of the Hellenist breakthrough to wider witness. Three new characters will carry the weight of the plot development in the early stages of this Hellenist Cycle: Stephen (Acts 6–7), Philip (Acts 8), and Saul (Acts 9). Stephen represents the definitive critique of Jewish resistance to the gospel in Acts 7. Reaction to Stephen plays out the reality of the self-condemned status of the Sanhedrin regarding the preaching of Jesus established in Acts 5. Philip represents the first witness outside Jerusalem in Acts 8. Philip advances the word about Jesus both to those considered "half-Jews" as well as to a non-Semite. Saul is commissioned on the Damascus Road in Acts 9. In due time, this character of Saul will incarnate the philosophy, passion, and powerhouse behind the gentile mission. The weight of the entire narrative of the combined Luke-Acts in the end will be on Saul's shoulders.

After the text Peter quoted to the Sanhedrin in Acts 4 begins to come true in Acts 5,[67] the plotline must take a new, divinely ordained direction for Pentecost fulfillment to continue playing out in the narrative. This Hellenist Cycle will involve social ramifications already inherent in the very nature of the profile of the celebrants in the Pentecost festival called for in Deut 16:11 regarding even "the stranger."[68] The material of the Hellenist Cycle will tell that part of the story, the realization of the full social dimensions of Pentecost's eschatological harvest.

Saul the Pharisee as Pentecost Fulfillment

Saul is commissioned by God in Acts 9:1–31 to proclaim Jesus's name. Sandwiched between the story of Philip's work among the Samaritans and the Ethiopian eunuch and Peter's revelation guiding him into acceptance of gentiles such as Cornelius without circumcision as part of the people of God, Saul's story is given its sense and interpretation as an integral part of the Hellenist Cycle. Philip's work in Acts 8 alludes to the direction of that mission, and Peter's insight in Acts 10 shows the apostolic blessing on that mission. (See Fig. 1.2.)

1–2	3–4	5	6–7	8	9	10	11	12
Pentecost	Lame M.	Ananias	Seven	Samaria	D. Road	Vision	J. Church	Persecu.
Peter	Peter	Peter	Stephen	Philip	Saul	Peter	Peter	Peter

FIGURE 1.2. Acts 1–12: Narrative Flow.

Saul's powerful apologetic in the Damascene synagogues in 9:22, "And Saul grew . . . more powerful and confounded the Jews,"[69] shows that he is taking up Stephen's synagogue mantle characterized by Luke in 6:10, "and they were not able to withstand the wisdom and spirit in which he was speaking."[70] Luke's point is that the Sanhedrin has not prevailed in the murder of Stephen: the voice of the Hellenist martyr speaks again. Note especially the characterization of Saul in 9:29, "He was speaking and arguing with the Hellenists, and they were attempt-

---

[67]The messianic Ps 118:22 in Acts 4:11, "the stone which the builders rejected," ὁ λίθος, ὁ ἐξουθενηθεὶς ὑφ᾽ ὑμῶν τῶν οἰκοδόμων.

[68]Which is גֵּר; LXX = καὶ ὁ προσήλυτος.

[69]Greek: Σαῦλος δὲ μᾶλλον ἐνεδυναμοῦτο καὶ συνέχυννεν [τοὺς] Ἰουδαίους.

[70]Greek: καὶ οὐκ ἴσχυον ἀντιστῆναι τῇ σοφίᾳ καὶ τῷ πνεύματι ᾧ ἐλάλει.

ing to kill him."[71] Saul becomes the character in the narrative embodying the Hellenist Cycle's destiny—an unstoppable voice, an unbeatable apologetic—because God will preserve this witness by both human[72] and divine[73] means. Saul's escape from Damascus begins this preservation motif that will play out numerous times in Acts.

The intervention of Barnabas, however, is required for Saul in Jerusalem. Suspicion greets Saul in his first effort to visit Jerusalem after the Damascus Road. Hesitation among the disciples is understandable: this person is the great persecutor of the church (8:3; 9:26). Such suspicion unabated would be a serious setback for Saul, because the legitimization of Saul's mission from the Twelve is crucial, since their symbolic role in Acts is to represent the heart and intention of Jesus. Barnabas personally mediates Saul's introduction to the apostles in Jerusalem as an advocate for Saul (9:26–27). Once again, Barnabas also plays his characteristic role in Acts, established in the first episode introducing him as a character to the Acts narrative—Pentecost fulfillment facilitator. Saul's acceptance by the Jerusalem apostles in Acts 9 validates for the church Saul's commission from God and places him in an esteemed category similar to that described of Stephen in 6:6, "These men they stood before the apostles, who, after praying, laid their hands on them."[74] Pentecost will find its broader fulfillment in the ongoing story of Jesus through the divinely commissioned Saul, and Barnabas will facilitate all the crucial early stages of that fulfillment in the character of Saul of Tarsus.

Finally, one will observe that Luke has concluded the Damascus Road sequence of narratives with one of his Pentecost summary verses in 9:31. In this summary he specifically points out the comfort of the Holy Spirit. Within the narrative, Barnabas, "Son of Consolation," is the channel of that comfort to a church disquieted by the presence of the former persecutor Saul now claiming a divine commission from God on behalf of Jesus.

---

[71]Greek: ἐλάλει τε καὶ συνεζήτει πρὸς τοὺς Ἑλληνιστάς, οἱ δὲ ἐπεχείρουν ἀνελεῖν αὐτόν.

[72]Acts 9:23–25; 18:12–16; 19:30–31; 20:2–3; 21:30–32; 23:6–10, 12–24; 25:1–5, 9–11.

[73]Acts 14:19–20; 16:23–26; 18:9–10; 27:23–24; 28:3–6.

[74]Greek: οὓς ἔστησαν ἐνώπιον τῶν ἀποστόλων, καὶ προσευξάμενοι ἐπέθηκαν αὐτοῖς τὰς χεῖρας.

Cornelius as Pentecost Fulfillment

Acceptance of the implications of Pentecost harvest among gentiles by the Jerusalem church is going to take more than an initial acknowledgement of Saul by the Twelve. Yet to be worked out, of course, is the story of the status of the law of Moses in this gentile mission, as well as the proper accommodations for table fellowship. Table fellowship is no mere social formality. This fellowship will be a crucial decision for the church, because this issue resides at the very heart of the demonstration of the eschatological Pentecost harvest that inaugurated the entire narrative movement in Acts 2.

In Acts 9:32–43, Luke uses the memories of Peter's seacoast ministry to validate Peter as a reflection of Jesus's own ministry before proceeding to narrate the crucial but controversial episode of Cornelius's conversion. The well-known doublet strategy with which Luke has constructed Acts 10 and 11 serves to highlight this episode at Caesarea as an epoch event in the life of the church.

What usually receives little attention is that Peter's vision is about the divine provision of food. In the story, Peter had become hungry, and food was in the process of being prepared for him when he fell into a trance (10:10–12). In the trance Peter saw a vision of a sheet let down from heaven with food that Peter was commanded to take and eat (10:13). Peter does not get the point, and the scene repeats two more times. The key declaration is in 10:15, "what God has cleansed, do not treat as unclean" (ἃ ὁ θεὸς ἐκαθάρισεν, σὺ μὴ κοίνου). Peter's confusion about the meaning of his unusual vision does not clear up until the interpretation is provided by the messengers from Cornelius and Peter's subsequent witnessing of the Holy Spirit poured out on the gentile Cornelius and his household (10:44–46). After witnessing this outpouring of the Spirit, Peter understands that the vision of God's command to eat means that God has declared gentiles "clean."

But "clean" specifically for what in the narrative? Just as pilgrim worshippers who presented themselves at the feasts in Jerusalem had to purify themselves in order to participate in the rituals, so God has provided access to the great, eschatological Pentecost feast by himself purifying those who come to the celebration through faith in Jesus. Therefore, gentiles such as Cornelius are clean to participate in the eschatological Pentecost feast. Peter may share this feast celebration with Cornelius symbolically by eating in Cornelius's house. Peter's meal fellowship inferred in staying in Cornelius's home symbolically plays out the central characteristic of the early church portrait painted by Luke in the first summary statement at the end of the Pentecost narrative in 2:46. The connection of Peter eating with Cornelius to Pentecost fellowship is clear in Peter's explicit question in 10:47: "Can anyone withhold the water for baptizing these who have received the Holy Spirit just as we did?"[75] Since that Pentecost narrative of 2:1–4 is tied to the closely associated festal meal fellowship of 2:41–47, the eschatological nuance of the festal celebration in Acts 2 is inherent to Peter's question about Cornelius in Acts 10 and provides the rationale for the specific character of Peter's vision in Joppa being *about food*.

A problem arises in Jerusalem when news from Caesarea hits the Jerusalem church. Some Jerusalem believers react negatively, pointing to the need for circumcision and continued social barriers supposedly expressing ritual purity (11:1–3). Such demands, however, are a fundamental failure to grasp the eschatological dimensions and social implications of the Pentecost experience. Peter's testimony to the Jerusalem church about the Cornelius episode is crucial to acceptance of Peter's action on behalf of Cornelius. Peter's rhetorical question in 11:17 encapsulates the new revelation, "If then God gave them the same gift that he gave us when we believed in the Lord Jesus Christ, who was I that I could hinder God?"[76] God was creating a new fulfillment of the Pentecost festival powered by the promised Spirit. Faith in Jesus has transcended the law of Moses in a new Exodus.[77]

However, even though concord on the issue of gentile inclusion seems achieved in Acts 11:18, Luke slips in a revealing note about an undercurrent of problems in 11:19: "Therefore those dispersed by reason of the persecution on Stephen's account went through Phoenicia,

---

[75]Greek: μήτι τὸ ὕδωρ δύναται κωλῦσαί τις τοῦ μὴ βαπτισθῆναι τούτους, οἵτινες τὸ πνεῦμα τὸ ἅγιον ἔλαβον ὡς καὶ ἡμεῖς;

[76]Greek: εἰ οὖν τὴν ἴσην δωρεὰν ἔδωκεν αὐτοῖς ὁ θεὸς ὡς καὶ ἡμῖν πιστεύσασιν ἐπὶ τὸν κύριον Ἰησοῦν Χριστόν, ἐγὼ τίς ἤμην δυνατὸς κωλῦσαι τὸν θεόν;

[77]Luke 9:31, "they were talking about his exodus which was going to be fulfilled in Jerusalem," ἔλεγον τὴν ἔξοδον αὐτοῦ, ἣν ἤμελλεν πληροῦν ἐν Ἰερουσαλήμ. Cf. Moessner, *Lord of the Banquet*, 46.

Cyprus, and Antioch, speaking the word to Jews only."[78] The issue is only silenced in Acts 11, not settled. This alerts the reader not to be surprised when the large influx of gentiles resulting from the success of the first missionary journey means that the issue of gentile inclusion no longer can be ignored. The narrative already hints in 11:19 that the Jerusalem Conference in Acts 15 is inevitable.

In the broader scope of Acts 1–12, given the narrative thrust of Acts 2, the problem raised in Acts 11 by some Jerusalem believers with Cornelius translates into *which* Pentecost feast is to be celebrated, the historical annual pilgrim feast as defined in the law of Moses on the basis of the Exodus redemption, complete with the burden of the law and its social exclusiveness, or the eschatological supratemporal feast as defined in the gospel of Jesus on the basis of his own sacrificial redemption, complete with the gift of the Spirit and a social inclusiveness? Peter is commanded to take and eat from the new feast of God's special provision at this opportune time of eschatological Pentecost fulfillment— and so is the church. God has provided a new redemption in Jesus. God has provided a new harvest festival in the Spirit. Gentiles are cleansed by faith and included in a new festal celebration marked by continuous fellowship in the homes of believers.

Antioch as Pentecost Fulfillment

Even as some of those who were dispersed through the Jerusalem persecution speak to Jews only (11:19), Luke shifts the narrative focus to Antioch, because here the true significance of Pentecost will find fulfillment in the church. Jerusalem no longer will be the center of Pentecost fulfillment, because negative reaction to the action of God in cleansing gentiles such as Cornelius will quench the Spirit of Pentecost in Jerusalem. Luke insinuates this quenching of the Pentecost Spirit in Jerusalem by noting that believers are first called Christians at Antioch.

Luke moves from the Cornelius narrative immediately into its Antioch sequel. The essence of the first light of full Pentecost harvest realization is given in Acts 11:20: "which ones after they came to Antioch were speaking also to the Hellenists and proclaiming the Lord Je-

---

[78]Greek: Οἱ μὲν οὖν διασπαρέντες ἀπὸ τῆς θλίψεως τῆς γενομένης ἐπὶ Στεφάνῳ διῆλθον ἕως Φοινίκης καὶ Κύπρου καὶ Ἀντιοχείας μηδενὶ λαλοῦντες τὸν λόγον εἰ μὴ μόνον Ἰουδαίοις.

sus."[79] Evangelizing Hellenists signals a distinct turn in a new mission agenda. This turn happens in Antioch, not Jerusalem. The Pentecost promise of inclusive harvest is receiving fuller realization, with echoes of the Jerusalem Pentecost harvest in 2:41, since Luke emphasizes that many believed ("a great number," πολύς τε ἀριθμὸς, 11:21).

Once again, Barnabas plays the key role. Jerusalem determined to investigate the activity already taking place in Antioch and sent Barnabas as an apostolic representative (11:22–24). Barnabas rejoiced in what he witnessed at Antioch, which echoes the eschatological joy of the harvest first felt among believers in Jerusalem (2:46). But when Barnabas begins to appreciate the significant size of the response,[80] he realized the need to incorporate Saul into the work and retrieved him from Tarsus for that purpose (11:25–26). Once again, Barnabas is the Pentecost facilitator in the life of Saul. Barnabas originally introduced Saul to Jerusalem, and now he introduces Saul to Antioch.

The work in Antioch was so notable over the course of a year's time that Luke in the same breath draws attention to that specific appellation that would become the historical watermark used for followers of Jesus.[81] Why note believers are called "Christians" first at Antioch? Because Antioch is where the new vision of the people of God born at Pentecost first matured into its more universal ramifications as mission strategy.[82] Because Antioch is where Saul, the one specially called to gentile mission by God, was integrated into that particular fellowship that would become the missionary sending agent for the first missionary journey.[83]

Luke then moved to narrate the famine relief visit of Barnabas and Saul to Jerusalem, beginning in 11:27–30. The narrative of this famine relief visit is "interrupted" by the story of Herod Agrippa I in Acts 12:1–23. In 12:24–25, though, Luke returns to the famine relief visit of Barnabas and Saul. The famine relief visit thus becomes a bracketing device

---

[79]Greek: οἵτινες ἐλθόντες εἰς Ἀντιόχειαν ἐλάλουν καὶ πρὸς τοὺς Ἑλληνιστὰς εὐαγγελιζόμενοι τὸν κύριον Ἰησοῦν.

[80]Indicated in 11:24: "and a large crowd was brought to the Lord," καὶ προσετέθη ὄχλος ἱκανὸς τῷ κυρίῳ.

[81]Whether self-ascribed by believers or used in derision by Jewish or pagan detractors is inconsequential to the narrative significance.

[82]Similarly, Polhill, *Acts*, 273.

[83]Ibid.

used by Luke to surround the story of Herod.[84] At the narrative level this bracketing action should mean that the story of Herod enhances or interprets the famine relief visit. How?

The famine is a threat to Pentecost harvest joy in Jerusalem. God, however, does not stand idly by. Instead, God inspires the prophet Agabus to predict the famine so that the church in Jerusalem may be supplied adequately through the believers in Antioch (11:27–28). This famine threat is a role reversal of Pentecost blessing: instead of from Jerusalem outward, we have a reverse flow inward to Jerusalem. This proactive ministry taking up the Pentecost fulfillment mantle, when coupled with the proactive Hellenist mission already noted, contributes to perceiving the gist of Luke's pointed observation that believers first were called "Christians" at Antioch—Luke's paradigmatic church of Pentecost mission and ministry.

Similar to the threat of famine to the whole church, we have the threat of Herod targeted directly against the apostolic leadership of the church. James, brother of John, is killed, and when Herod perceives the favor of the Jews about this policy, goes after Peter as well (12:2–3).[85] God, however, also deals with Herod as he did with the famine—by divine intervention. Peter miraculously is released from prison (12:7–10), and Herod meets his end at a feast in Caesarea (12:21–23). Luke has interpreted Herod's dramatic and sudden death as God's judgment (12:23: "an angel of the Lord," ἄγγελος κυρίου).

More significant than usually granted is a brief mention by Luke of Herod's relationship with the inhabitants of Tyre and Sidon in 12:20. Why mention this

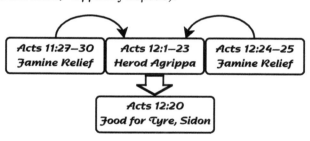

FIGURE 1.3. Herod Agrippa and Food for Tyre and Sidon.

at all? At first, this remark seems an aside contributing little to the

[84]Cf. Polhill, *Acts*, 276–77.

[85]Herod will find his own story haunted by Peter's recent question to his detractors in the church in 11:17: "who was I that I could hinder God?" The question did not occur to Herod apparently.

plotline.[86] However, the bracketing of the Herod narrative with the Jerusalem famine visit of Barnabas and Saul suggests that the connection within the developing plotline of Acts 1–12 is the very nature of Herod's relationship with Tyre and Sidon.

Herod apparently was attempting to strengthen his reign through developing patron-client relationships in neighboring regions.[87] Luke indicated in 12:20 that the relationship with Tyre and Sidon had been on behalf of food supply: "they were asking for peace because their country was supplied with food from that of the king."[88] Herod had attempted to establish himself as the provider of food for Tyre and Sidon. He almost seems positioned as guarantor of the harvest. That role is God's when the background material of Exodus 34 is recalled. Jewish festivals were intended to inculcate that belief that God alone was the source and sustainer of life. Herod's unexpected demise is as much to say he is not much of a guarantor of harvest and provides the reader with the contrast of the insecurity of life supplied from within human resources, and life supplied by God. Even in famine, God can effect a harvest supply for Jerusalem believers. This power of God's provision contrasts that of a frail human king and his client territories, and, translated into an eschatological key, reinforces the sense of the surety of the eschatological Pentecost harvest. God is able to overcome all obstacles to bring about Pentecostal fullness in the church. This ability to overcome obstacles will be an important reassurance when following the narrative of Saul's mission in Acts 13–28.

Finally, the Herod material prepares the reader for subtle but observable shifts in the narrative that set the stage for the second half of Acts. Herod's persecutions in Acts 12 seem to be the catalyst of several leadership transitions: (1) a shift in church leadership from Peter and the Twelve to James and the elders,[89] and (2) a shift in mission lead-

---

[86]Commentators hardly take note, sometimes voicing curiosity over Luke's source here, since Josephus does not relate any word about this arrangement between Herod and these two Phoenician cities; e.g., Barrett, *Acts*, 589; Bock, *Acts*, 430–31; Dunn, *Acts*, 166; Fitzmyer, *Acts*, 490; Pervo, *Acts*, 312–13; Polhill, *Acts*, 284.

[87]So Dunn, *Acts*, 166.

[88]Greek: ἠτοῦντο εἰρήνην διὰ τὸ τρέφεσθαι αὐτῶν τὴν χώραν ἀπὸ τῆς βασιλικῆς.

[89]E.g., note Peter's instruction after his release in 12:17, "tell these things to James and the brothers" (ἀπαγγείλατε Ἰακώβῳ καὶ τοῖς ἀδελφοῖς ταῦτα).

ership from Peter in Acts 1–12 to Saul in Acts 13–28.[90] Finally, a geographical shift also can be perceived in the center of gravity for the gentile mission from Jerusalem to Antioch. With these scene shifts in Acts 12, the reader is prepared for a new mission and a new leader of that mission in the ongoing saga of eschatological Pentecost fulfillment.[91] That Pentecost echoes reverberate with meaning far into the second half of Acts, even for someone who was not there, is seen in Luke's explanation of Paul's haste to pass by Ephesus at the end of the third missionary journey in 20:6: "for he was hurrying, if it might be possible for him, that he be in Jerusalem on the day of Pentecost."[92]

Summary of Narrative Development

The Pentecost narrative of Acts 2 is uniquely Lukan. Luke fronts the narrative for plot development, making Pentecost the controlling narrative event of Acts. Divine fulfillment already is integral to Luke's characterization of the Pentecost experience before he actually narrates the event. The fulfillment theme comes through a "promise of the Father" motif that bridges the end of the Gospel to the beginning of Acts, as well as fulfillment terminology to begin the Pentecost narrative. The promise of the Father is the Spirit. The Spirit inaugurates the eschatological fulfillment of God's promises to Israel derived from Exodus traditions. The historical celebration of Pentecost anticipated a full consummation in a future prophetic figure. The Gospel of Luke has presented Jesus as

---

[90]In 12:17, Peter's departure after so extensive a role in the narrative seems quite anticlimactic, just "going out he went to another place" (ἐξελθὼν ἐπορεύθη εἰς ἕτερον τόπον). Peter does not reappear in the Acts account except for a cameo scene at the Jerusalem Conference in Acts 15 to voice one last time the apostolic validation of Saul-Paul's mission (15:7–11). Note that James actually pronounces the final decision at the conference (15:13). The anticlimactic nature of Peter's stage exit in Acts 12 reinforces the overall narrative impression that Saul has, after all, the premier character role in Acts.

[91]Even a message to pagans does not fail to echo the Pentecost theme. Note that even when explicit christological language falls out, Paul's message to pagans at Lystra still alludes to the Pentecost harvest motif through a focus on the creator God who blesses mankind with seasons, crops, and harvest, and fills the human heart with gladness (14:14–17).

[92]Greek: ἔσπευδεν γὰρ εἰ δυνατὸν εἴη αὐτῷ τὴν ἡμέραν τῆς πεντηκοστῆς γενέσθαι εἰς Ἱεροσόλυμα.

this promised prophet leading Israel into a new Exodus redemption. Pentecost is the next stage in the redemptive story.

On the negative side, Peter's characterization of Israel as "this crooked generation" is a deliberate echo of Moses's warning to Israel in Deut 32. The context of Deut 32 is the Exodus redemption prior to the realization of God's gift of the land with its promise of abundant harvest providing for the ongoing life of Israel. Moses warned Israel that they could fail to realize fulfillment of God's promises through failure to respond faithfully to God's Exodus covenant. As Israel of old, Israel now is confronted with the choice that determines fulfillment of the Pentecost promise, only now, the choice is endowed with eschatological consequences in failure to respond to what God has accomplished for Israel's redemption in Jesus the Messiah.

Historically, Pentecost celebrated the grain harvest. A successful harvest was epitomized in a joyous festal meal in Jewish homes. Luke has modulated this historical festal meal setting into its eschatological fulfillment in the homes of Jesus's disciples in 2:41–47. The believers' shared life is Pentecost's promised fulfillment. Social inclusiveness always has been a key component of this celebration of the Pentecost feast. Social inclusiveness, therefore, is central, a key component to the fulfillment of Pentecost in the church.

The character of the Levite Barnabas conveys the positive side of Pentecost fulfillment in Israel. Barnabas's surname, "Son of Encouragement," obviously is not based on etymology. Rather, this surname has narrative function symbolizing Pentecost fulfillment. Barnabas is the Pentecost fulfillment facilitator.

The characters Ananias and Sapphira, on the other hand, are set in direct contrast to Barnabas. This couple illustrates Pentecost imagery negatively as frustrated fulfillment. That is, their actions threaten Pentecost fulfillment. Their judgment serves as a warning both to the Sanhedrin and to the church about the serious issues involved for God in the fulfillment of Pentecost in Israel.

Luke introduces the Hellenist Cycle in Acts 6 because the material will help develop the social dimensions of Pentecost's eschatological harvest. In this Hellenist Cycle, Saul is commissioned by God as the character who will embody the Hellenist Cycle's destiny in the gentile mission. Barnabas is the facilitator for Saul's realization of this role.

Pentecost fulfillment among gentiles comes through faith and the purifying power of the Holy Spirit. Peter learns this truth in his encounter with Cornelius in Acts 10. God's Spirit has pronounced Cornelius "cleansed," a purification that allows gentile participation in the eschatological harvest festival. However, this gentile development is met with resistance from elements within the Jerusalem church in Acts 11, which is the literary prelude to the crisis of Acts 15.

Disciples first are called Christians at Antioch because the full dimensions of Pentecost fulfillment develop in this church. A distinct turn in mission strategy occurs at Antioch with deliberate preaching to Hellenists, who respond in significant numbers. Barnabas is the Pentecost facilitator in Antioch, as in Jerusalem. Barnabas facilitates Saul's ministry too, once again, by retrieving him from Tarsus for the Hellenist work in Antioch. Jerusalem's new vision of the people of God born in Acts 2 matures into Antioch's inclusive mission strategy in Acts 11. The famine relief visit of Barnabas and Saul to Jerusalem completes the picture of Antioch as the paradigmatic church of Pentecost mission and ministry. Pentecost fulfillment is why Luke notes that believers first are called "Christians" at Antioch.

Luke constructs the story of Herod in Acts 12 to interpret the famine relief visit of Barnabas and Saul to Jerusalem sandwiched on either side (11:27–30; 12:24–25). Famine, naturally, is a direct threat to Pentecost harvest fulfillment. God, however, is able to supply the needs of the Jerusalem church through divine intervention from Antioch. Herod's story provides the stark contrast for Luke's famine relief account of God's harvest provision for Jerusalem. Herod's attempts to force Tyre and Sidon into a patron-client dependency for food supply are undermined by Herod's untimely death. In contrast, against the threat of famine in Jerusalem, God does not fail to provide the surety of the harvest. Further, Antiochene famine relief through Barnabas and Saul in Jerusalem points to the surety of the eschatological harvest through these same characters in future Antiochene mission efforts in the Diaspora. Thus, Acts 12 prepares the reader for a new stage in the story of Pentecost fulfillment among both Jews and gentiles.

In sum, Exodus traditions related to Moses, God's future prophet, and the final Pentecostal consummation of Israel's Exodus journey are compressed by Luke into the story of Pentecost in Acts 2 and the events that flowed from that foundational eschatological event. Pentecost defined the profile of the early church mission and the social parameters of her eschatological life in the world. In the Gospel of Luke, with the journey of Jesus to Jerusalem, a new Exodus had occurred. In Acts, with the Father's outpouring of the Spirit on his people, a new Pentecost is celebrated. The last days have dawned.

CONCLUSIONS

Pentecost is more than a circumstantial time frame surrounding the miracle of languages giving rise to Peter's inaugural mission speech in Acts 2. The narrative development of both the end of the Gospel of Luke and of Acts 1–12 indicates that Luke's strategy evolves out of the significance of the Pentecost feast in the ancient Jewish setting of Israel's Exodus and subsequent possession of the promised land. Luke has translated this dimension of Israel's story into its corresponding eschatological fulfillment in Jesus and the church. Within his narrative strategy, Luke combines Pentecost fulfillment with both the narrative development of the character of Barnabas as Pentecost facilitator and the motif of the church's gentile mission developed in the character of Saul as Pentecost destiny.

2

Hellenists and Antioch

The Making of a Paradigm

T HE 1964 CLASSIC MOVIE *MY FAIR LADY* starring Rex Harrison and
Audrey Hepburn has Harrison playing professor Henry Higgins, an
English phonetics expert who boasts he can determine one's place of
origin to within a few miles on phonetics alone.[1] Hepburn plays Eliza
Doolittle, a low-class Cockney flower girl. One memorable song production in Alan Jay Lerner's musical adaptation is the pub ditty sung by
Eliza's father, Alfred. Alfred is a hard-drinking scoundrel and bachelor.
By the hilarious circumstances of a fortuitous inheritance, Alfred feels
forced to legitimize the social position of his live-in companion, Eliza's
stepmother, by marrying her. Before taking this fateful and dreaded
step, Alfred goes out on the town one last time with his friends. In the
waning hours of his bachelor freedom, drunk Alfred asks his pub companions for one last favor: "Get Me To the Church on Time." He belts
the chorus:

> *I'm getting married in the morning,*
> *Ding dong the bells are gonna chime*
> *Kick up a rumpus, but don't lose the compass*
> *And get me to the church—Get him to the church*
> *For Gawd's sake get me to the church on time.*

Luke characterized the Jerusalem disciples and their leaders as a
community of believers that increasingly, like Eliza Doolittle's father,

---

[1] *My Fair Lady*, Warner Bros. Pictures, 1964.

Alfred, just did not get to church on time for the main event of gospel advance. The Acts narrative documents how Antioch becomes the surrogate "mother church" in terms of the gospel mission in the ever-increasing circles of witness announced in the programmatic Acts 1:8. One can appreciate these points Luke made through applying specific aspects of historical, sociological, and narrative analysis.

ANTIOCH: A MATRIX OF SETTINGS

Historical Setting

After Alexander the Great's death, his general Seleucus I (Nicator) won the decisive battle against Antigonus, fought at Ipsis in 301 BC. While control of Syria after Alexander was contested, its Hellenistic culture never was in doubt. Seleucus settled the region with Greeks. He founded the city of Antioch in Syria with its strategic location on the Orontes River.[2] His city plan incorporated the Hippodamian grid style (city blocks) of the standard Hellenistic design. Seleucus also settled a large number of Jews in Antioch, giving them full citizenship rights that were reaffirmed by later Seleucid and Roman rulers.[3] As a result, Antioch had a significant Jewish presence from its beginnings. With a strong Hellenistic culture and a large Jewish quarter, this city had a distinctive cultural mix among cities in the ancient world.[4]

Even after Pompey's Near East Campaign brought Antioch politically and militarily into Roman orbit in 64 BC, Antioch's deep roots in Hellenism remained unchanged. In fact, despite Rome being three times larger than Antioch, Antioch had the larger Jewish population. Julius Caesar conducted major Hellenistic building projects in Antioch, including a theater, an amphitheater, bathhouses, an aqueduct, and a Kaisareion (dedicated to the Roman cult). Caesar also rebuilt the Pantheon temple. Among other reasons, the large Jewish presence and

[2]One of no less than sixteen cities named after his father, Antiochus.

[3]Josephus *Ant.* 12.3.1.

[4]The classic source, still unsurpassed, for all things Antioch is Downey, *Ancient Antioch*. A good summary is provided by Hood, "A Socio-Anthropological Analysis of Gentile-Jew Relationships in Rome and Antioch."

extensive Hellenistic public works are why Josephus ranked Antioch as the third city of the empire, just behind Rome and Alexandria.[5]

Antioch remained a bastion of Hellenism into New Testament times. Herod the Great contributed a marbled street that ran the entire length of the city north and south, dividing the city in half, according to Josephus.[6] Antioch's total population is estimated anywhere from 200,000 to 300,000.[7] The Jewish population may have been 65,000, perhaps one seventh of the city's population.[8] Thus, the Christian community in Antioch had a more Jewish social mix than even Rome.[9] Antioch played a key role in the First Jewish War as a staging ground for Roman troops under Titus. Tensions ran high against the Jewish population in Antioch, which became acute when parts of Antioch burned in a great fire and Jews were blamed. Though lobbied intensely by the Antiochene populace, the Roman general Titus refused to expel Jews from the city.[10]

Social Setting

Antioch's historical background brings into focus the city's ethnically and culturally diverse populace. This diversity highlights the distinctive social matrix of this ancient city among others of the empire. Hood concluded the social-anthropological description of the Christian community at Antioch evidenced in the late first to early second-century documents as high group and fairly high grid.[11] Boundary maintenance concerns, therefore, were high.[12] The conclusion of Hood was, "Since the community in Antioch was subject to a strong Judaizing influence, and the use of Jewish practices and terminology were [sic] apparent in

---

[5]Josephus *J.W.* 3.2.4. See Longenecker, "Antioch of Syria," 11.

[6]*J.W.* 1.21.11; *Ant.* 16.148. For more on Herod the Great, cf. Richardson, *Herod* (1996); Vermes, *The True Herod* (2014); Marshak, *The Many Faces of Herod* (2015).

[7]See Strabo *Geog.* 16.2.5; cf. John Chrysostom *St. Ignat.* 4.50. Estimating size of ancient cities is notoriously hard because ancient sources vary significantly.

[8]Longenecker, "Antioch of Syria," 15–16.

[9]Which was more gentile; see Hood, 164, 166.

[10]Josephus *J.W.* 7.55–57; 7.96.

[11]Using the social modeling tool derived from the work of Mary Douglas. See Douglas, *Purity and Danger*, 1966; *Natural Symbols*, 1982.

[12]Hood, "Gentile-Jew Relationships," 163, 168.

the community, the group had an increased need to legitimize the existence of the community as a separate entity. Christianity in Antioch, which was predominantly Jewish in form, struggled to define itself especially as distinct from Judaism."[13] The beginnings of some drawing of distinctions already seems implicit in the nature of Luke's reference to the appellation "Christians" in Acts 11:26, a topic that will be discussed in more detail below.

Persons and Their Place

In terms of kinship associations in the ancient world as a social structuring device, one preliminary question to consider is whether significant differences existed between Jewish and non-Jewish families, such that the conceptualization of kinship associations would be affected significantly. Probably not is the conclusion of Ross Kraemer in an important essay on the topic.[14] Kraemer concluded, "The dynamics of Jewish families do not appear appreciably different from those of non-Jews (of similar class and status conditions) in the early imperial Roman period."[15]

Particular interest lies in the connection between persons and their place. In a discussion of the nearby cities of Asia Minor, Bruce Malina has pointed out the organic link in the ancient sociological matrix between persons and their place, that is, their city of origin.[16] City of origin provided identity especially through kinship associations. Since kinship ideas can be broadened to include groups bound by common interests or social interactions, such as *collegia* or guilds, then "Christians" in Acts 11:26 will have its context as a powerful sociological force in the development of early Christianity in terms of identity and unity. That is to say, though Christianity clearly had roots in Jerusalem, Luke had to wrestle with the historical role Antioch played in defining that distinctive kinship of "Christian" known both within and without the church. Luke's use of the term "Christians" in Acts 11:26 will be his tipping the hat to this historical reality. The exegetical responsibility will be to place that usage within its proper context.

[13]Ibid., 189.

[14]Kraemer, "Typical and Atypical Jewish Family Dynamics," 130–56.

[15]Ibid., 155.

[16]Malina, *New Jerusalem*, 41.

"Christians" in the New Testament

Surprisingly, the term "Christian" is quite rare in the New Testament. Acts 11:26 is one of only three times the term "Christian" (*Christianos*, Χριστιανός) is used in the New Testament. These instances can be considered together. The three passages are listed below for reference:

> Acts 11:26
> "And after he found (him) he brought him to Antioch. And it happened that for an entire year they were gathered together with the church and they taught a large crowd. Now, the disciples were called 'Christians' first in Antioch."[17]

> Acts 26:28
> "Then Agrippa said to Paul, 'With so little do you persuade me to make a Christian?'"[18]

> 1 Pet. 4:16
> "Let one not be ashamed as a Christian; but let that person glorify God in this name."[19]

"Christian" in 1 Peter. The use of *Christianos* in 1 Peter can be taken as a forensic setting, but that setting usually has to be nuanced carefully. That is, the term can be understood to echo charges made by authorities, but not suggesting a state-sponsored or empire-wide effort. Those who would date 1 Peter later in the first century, or early second century, would opt for the kind of Roman jurisprudence that is evidenced in Pliny's correspondence from Bithynia (AD 115) with its allusion to those who recanted their faith twenty years earlier (that is,

---

[17]Greek: καὶ εὑρὼν ἤγαγεν εἰς Ἀντιόχειαν. ἐγένετο δὲ αὐτοῖς καὶ ἐνιαυτὸν ὅλον συναχθῆναι ἐν τῇ ἐκκλησίᾳ καὶ διδάξαι ὄχλον ἱκανόν, χρηματίσαι τε πρώτως ἐν Ἀντιοχείᾳ τοὺς μαθητὰς Χριστιανούς. The translation of the infinitive χρηματίσαι admittedly is difficult. Taken as middle, the idea would be Christians making self-reference with the name. Taken as an intransitive active with a passive sense, the meaning would be the name as applied by those outside the group. Most scholars take the second option, as reflected in the translation above. A good summary of the issue is found in Fitzmyer, *Acts*, 478.

[18]Greek: ὁ δὲ Ἀγρίππας πρὸς τὸν Παῦλον· ἐν ὀλίγῳ με πείθεις Χριστιανὸν ποιῆσαι.

[19]Greek: εἰ δὲ ὡς Χριστιανός, μὴ αἰσχυνέσθω, δοξαζέτω δὲ τὸν θεὸν ἐν τῷ ὀνόματι τούτῳ.

during Domitian's reign).[20] Other New Testament literature evokes a similar background. For example, in writing Revelation, John has pitted his community over against his society. "The prophetic work of John might thus have its most far-reaching effect on the church, serving the function of evoking the hearers' commitment to continuing and fortifying the identity of *communitas* over against the *societas*, thus to maintain their uncontrolled allegiance to the God revealed in Christ against both the coercive and seductive drives towards compromise with the imperial world."[21]

Those who would date 1 Peter in the 60s would opt more for a context within the authority of the Sanhedrin and the high priest in Jerusalem or Nero in Rome.[22] The high priest option, in effect, would be a renewed effort of the type of persecution Saul attempted to extend from the high priest's authority in Jerusalem to the synagogues in Damascus (Acts 9:1–2). While the "forensic" setting might be pushing the civic and legal context too much both for 1 Peter and for Acts 9, the persecution aspect, perceived or real, is clear. This persecution setting, then, is evocative of the inevitable direction of the social relationships that will be developing for those identified with the *Christianoi*, and premonitions of that direction happen early.

"Christian" in Acts 26:28. The use of *Christianos* by Herod Agrippa II connects to the earlier Antioch passage as evidence that the term is a reference by those outside the community of faith. Another connection between the two passages (Acts 26:28; 11:26) is Paul himself. Paul is a central character both in this conversation with Agrippa II and in Paul's earlier ministry in Antioch, along with Barnabas and others. The association of the use of the term *Christianos* particularly as due to the influence of Paul and his preaching in Antioch, with Paul's charac-

---

[20]Elliott, *1 Peter*, 138 (between 73–92); Achtemeier, *1 Peter*, 49–50 (likely AD 80–100); Michaels, *1 Peter*, lxvi (later than the Neronian setting, but Peter could have lived longer than church tradition indicates); Best, *1 Peter*, 63 (between AD 80–100).

[21]deSilva, "The Social Setting of the Revelation to John," 301.

[22]Schreiner, *1, 2 Peter, Jude*, 36–37 (AD 62–63 before Nero); Hillyer, *1 and 2 Peter, Jude*, 3 (AD 63); Marshall, *1 Peter*, 23–24 (apostle Peter); Davids, *The First Epistle of Peter*, 10 (AD 64–68, through Silvanus at Peter's direction); Kelly, *The Epistles of Peter and of Jude*, 33 (the apostle Peter, pre-Nero).

teristic emphasis on Christ, lies close at hand.[23] A strong sense of Pauline tradition and kinship is voiced by Ignatius to the Ephesians: "You are fellow initiates with Paul, a man sanctified, of character magnificently attested, and worthy of every felicitation, in whose footsteps I wish to be found."[24] The notion of a distinct *societas* whose boundaries are not permeable is clear, if not earlier, at least by Theophilus, bishop of Antioch (168 to 181), who declared Christians as the only bearers of truth.[25] Herod Agrippa's use in Acts 26:28 also shows that this appellation has reached the elite of society. Thus, even if the term has origins in street slang,[26] which simply cannot be known, the use is beginning to percolate fairly rapidly through various strata of society (as well as geographically).

Herod Agrippa's use of *Christianos* in Acts 26:28 from the perspective of one "outside" the group transitions to the question of the pagan documentation for the term *Christianos*. The most frequently referenced documentary evidence is within Tacitus's discussion of the fire of Rome. Tacitus spoke of those who were "called Christians by the populace."[27] This usage is significant. Though circulating among the common people, the term has become familiar to the political and literary elite of Roman society. This significance would be true even if Tacitus is reading back into the term the more political ramifications of his own day.[28] Dicke noted Blass's conjecture that the correct reading in Tacitus should be *Chrestianos* (notice the "e").[29] The confusion could occur among pagan populations between the Greek designation of the

[23]Noted by Grundmann, "χρίω," 537: "Thus the designation Χριστός was perhaps the dominant one for Jesus in Antioch, and Paul played a decisive part in promoting it. This leads to the use of Χριστιανοί for the μαθηταί, and the term spreads rapidly to other places."

[24]Ignatius *Eph.* 12.3.

[25]Theophilus *Autol.* 2.33.

[26]So Dicke, "Christian," 657, by way of agreeing with Ramsey's earlier assessment. Dicke's article, simply reprinted from the original ISBE edition, probably still is the most succinct and informative overview of the background and use of *Christianoi* and is followed in the main in the discussion above. He lacks, however, sociological analysis, which has been supplemented.

[27]Tacitus *Annals* 15.44: *vulgus Christianos appellabat.*

[28]Thompson, *Revelation: Apocalypse and Empire*, 167.

[29]Dicke, "Christian," 657.

Jewish Messiah, *Christos* (Χριστός), and a common Greek slave name, Chrestos (Χρηστός, "beneficial," "useful").[30] The Roman historian Suetonius does seem to make this mistake when he is reporting Claudius's expulsion of Jews from Rome.[31] By Tacitus giving the correct formulation *Christus* just a few words later in the *Annals* 15.44 reference,[32] Blass conjectured that Tacitus's intent was to reflect, but then immediately correct, the common misunderstanding among the population about the *Christos* name, which is a possibility.[33]

Three other extra-biblical references include Josephus, Suetonius, and Pliny.[34] While the references from Josephus and Suetonius do not add significantly beyond what already can be observed in the Tacitus reference, Pliny's reference requires comment.

Pliny the Younger was the proconsul of Bithynia. He attempted to establish proper legal (and functional) lines of enforcement between *religio* and *superstitio* particularly in dealing with Christians. In terms of Roman provincial administration, *superstitio* is set within a matrix of political loyalty to the state. (The Romans never divested themselves of the equation of *superstitio* and sedition.) Pliny reviewed for the emperor Trajan current procedures for dealing with persons brought before him on the charge of being Christians (*Christiani*). Pliny wrote, "For the moment this is the line I have taken with all persons brought before me

[30]Cf. Cicero *Epis. Fam.* 2.8.1, *et Chresti compilationem*, "of robberies by Chrestus."

[31]Suetonius *Claud.* 25.4, *Iudaeos impulsore Chresto assidue tumultuantis Roma expulit*, "he banished from Rome all the Jews who continuously were making disturbances at the instigation of one called Chrestus." Cf. Acts 18:2.

[32]In a clarifying phrase, *auctor nominis eius Christus*, "Christ, the progenitor from whom the name."

[33]Such a conjectured correction is not too far-fetched. Tacitus is a careful historian and certainly surpasses Suetonius in both research and writing skill. Interestingly, the spelling *Chrestianos* (with the "e") corresponds to all three New Testament occurrences in the uncorrected readings of Codex Sinaiticus (א). See *Novum Testamentum Graece*, textual apparatus.

[34]Josephus *Ant.* 18.64: "still until the present time the tribe of Christians, so named from such one, are not extinct" (εἰς ἔτι τε νῦν τῶν Χριστιανῶν ἀπὸ τοῦδε ὠνομασμένον οὐκ ἐπέλιπε τὸ φῦλον); Suetonius *Nero* 16.2: "he inflicted punishments on Christians" (*afflicti suppliciis Christiani*), rehearsing the same material as covered by Tacitus; Pliny *Letters* 10.96.3: "I personally interrogate them whether they are Christians," (*Interrogavi ipsos an essent Christiani*), using a common cognomen.

on the charge of being Christians."[35] Trajan responded with affirmation and further directives. In doing so, Trajan revealed that no set policy was in place; that cases had to be handled individually; that the central issue was a perceived challenge to the political order; and that such persons were not to be hunted down.[36] The loss of any connection with the synagogue setting of the original Antioch context for *Christianoi* is patent. However, one must be careful not to read the Pliny context back into Acts 11:26.

"Christian" in Acts 11:26.[37] The first observation is linguistic. The inflection *-ianos* is a Greek derivative based on the Latin adjectival form *-ianus*. This adjectival usage occurs in the early empire and is widely distributed; thus, the usage is not exclusive to Italy or even a Latin audience. The suffix typically was used to mark adherents of a person or party.[38] The linguistic likelihood, then, is that the term *Christianoi* had its origins outside the group. If so, who might be the likely candidate?

Would Jews themselves have coined such a term? Probably not. Antiochene Jews probably would not have chosen such a term for disciples of Jesus, not because the inflection is Latin based, but because in so doing they would have conceded the very point of dispute (Messiah). Inasmuch as can be determined from the text of Acts, Jews seemed to prefer other names, such as "sect of the Nazarenes" (Acts 24:5). Thus, the rare term *Christianoi* as used in Acts 11:26 is unlikely to be of Jewish origin. This appellation in 24:5, however, does confirm the sectarian framework of Jewish perceptions about disciples of Jesus, which also

---

[35] Pliny *Letters* 10.96.2, *Interim, iis qui ad me tamquam Christiani deferebantur, hunc sum secutus modum*.

[36] Ibid., 10.96.97.

[37] Our first problem with this occurrence of the term is the Western text tradition in some Greek manuscripts two verses later. The Western reading at 11:28 encodes a "we" style notation evocative of those three famous first-person plural sections in the text of Acts: "and when we had assembled" (συνεστραμμένων δὲ ἡμῶν), the reading in D it^dp (cop^meg) Augustine. The Western text infers Luke was from Antioch, which reflects an ancient tradition in the church. The Western reading at 11:28 might suggest that Luke had personal knowledge of the special use of *Cristianoi* such that the term slips into 11:26 as only a fortuitous, circumstantial note. One does not need to adjudicate whether Luke was from Antioch to be fully persuaded that Luke did not write so circumstantially with such inattention to detail. Later discussion will show Luke's use of *Christianoi* to be integral to his narrative.

[38] As adherents, see the *Herodianoi* of Matt 22:16; Mark 3:6; 12:13.

could prejudice perceptions in the pagan populace as well that these disciples, though distinct, still should be understood within a synagogue context.

The origin of the term *Christianos*, then, more probably was with Antioch's pagan population. Taking the cue from Herod Agrippa's use in 26:28 and the Jewish sectarian framing of the alternate appellation in 24:5, the connotation in 11:26 would be Jewish sectarian. That is, in its earliest use by Antiochenes, the term had its functional force as *a social appellation applied to a perceived Jewish subgroup within Antioch's synagogues*. The general populace probably was able to perceive some type of distinction between this group of *Christianoi* and others within the Jewish synagogues of Antioch who did not associate particularly with this group.[39] This usage would be in a context before the parting of the ways.[40] Luke was saying outsiders noticed a difference between traditional groups in the synagogue and others in the synagogue who confessed Jesus as Messiah. He was, then, insinuating that difference in his characterization of the disciples at Antioch.

"Christian" Among Christians. While the term began as an appellation by outsiders, *Christianos* was taken over by believers themselves and became the definitive name historically for the Jesus movement. Unfortunately, this transition of usage cannot be documented in the first century. After all, the New Testament itself has only three occurrences. However, the usage by the early second century is clear. The earliest documented Christian self-reference outside the New Testament perhaps is *Didache* 12:4.[41] The dating can be argued. In any case, in the Apostolic Fathers, Ignatius frequently uses the term in self-reference as a believer. His most famous statement is, "It is proper, therefore,

---

[39]*Contra* Grundmann, "χρίω," 537: "A reason for coining the term Χριστιανοί is that the Christians in Antioch were now viewed as a separate society rather than as a section of the Jewish synagogue." Nothing concrete actually indicates this kind of institutional schism already has taken place this early in the church. The scattering of Hellenist believers in Acts 8:4 is localized to Jerusalem and is the direct consequence of Stephen's alleged blasphemy before the Sanhedrin.

[40]Alluding to Dunn, *The Partings of the Ways*.

[41]"According to your own judgment decide how, not being idle, he will live among you as a Christian" (κατὰ τὴν σύνεσιν ὑμῶν προνοήσατε πῶς μὴ ἀργὸς μεθ᾽ ὑμῶν ζήσεται χριστιανός); *Apostolic Fathers*, ed. Michael W. Holmes.

not only to be called Christians, but actually that we be Christians."[42] This Ignatian evidence bears some weight. As bishop of Antioch during the reign of Trajan (98–117) and a martyr in Rome in 115, Ignatius is the standard-bearer of Antiochene traditions. The evidence from Ignatius serves to confirm the historical probability of Luke's observation in Acts 11:26 connecting the use of the appellation *Christianos* especially to Antioch.

Polycarp (d. 156) was bishop of Smyrna in Asia Minor and was a colleague of Ignatius, exchanging letters with him. Polycarp provides evidence for the continuing spread of the use of *Christianos*. He proclaimed the term as an identifying self-appellation in *Mart. Poly.* 10.1: "Listen carefully: I am a Christian!"[43] Continuing use of the term in the mid-second century seems to have spread rapidly. Justin Martyr, a leader in Rome (d. 166), already was arguing that the justification for using *Christianos* as a social and religious marker of group identity extended all the way back to Jesus himself, apparently not aware that in making this argument, he tacitly had stumbled into contradicting Luke's own observation in Acts 11:26 that the term first was used in a post-resurrection setting, and not even in Judea itself.[44] Eventually, by the late second century, *Christianos* shows evidence of being in constant use, as illustrated, for example, in the *Epistle to Diognetus*, written by an unknown author.[45]

---

[42]Ignatius *Mag.* 4:1, Πρέπον οὖν ἐστὶν μὴ μόνον καλεῖσθαι Χριστιανούς, ἀλλὰ καὶ εἶναι; *Apostolic Fathers*, ed. Michael W. Holmes.

[43]Greek: μετὰ παρρησίας ἄκουε· Χριστιανός εἰμι; *Apostolic Fathers*, ed. Michael W. Holmes. The story continues that the Asian proconsul's herald proclaimed three times to the stadium crowds in 12.1, "Polycarp declares himself to be a Christian" (Πολύκαρπος ὡμολόγησεν ἑαυτὸν Χριστιανὸν εἶναι). The text in 12.2 further indicates that Polycarp's enemies in Smyrna in demanding his death in the theater used a string of appellations, including "the father of the Christians" (ὁ πατὴρ τῶν Χριστιανῶν). The *Martyrdom* also has the unusual phrase "race of the Christians" in 3.2, "they marveled at the nobility of the God-loving and God-fearing race of the Christians" (θαυμάσαν τὴν γενναιότητα τοῦ θεοφιλοὺς καὶ θεοσεβοὺς γένους τῶν Χριστιανῶν).

[44]Cf. Justin Martyr *Apol.* 12. Justin asserted that the name "Christians" was received from Jesus Christ himself: "Jesus Christ; from whom also we have the name of Christians." He simply could be pointing out the obvious connection, but in context this meaning is less likely, because his argument would have less force.

[45]*Diog.* 1:1; 2:6, 10; 4:6; 5:1; 6:1, 2, 3, 4, 5, 6, 7, 8, 9; since the author is unknown, obviously the date is disputed, but a common assignment is to the late second century; *Apostolic Fathers*, ed. Michael W. Holmes.

Narrative Setting

Ethos as Crucial

Ethos is characterization, and characterization can be a crucial ingredient to understanding a narrative. The element of characterization captured the attention of Greek writers. Take, for example, this self-reflective observation from the Greek historian Polybius:

> What advantage do readers have in describing wars and battles and the besieging and capturing of cities, unless they understand the causes according to which the withstanding or the overthrowing happens in each individual case? For the immediate results of such matters barely interest the hearers, but what follows after the cessation of the hostilities necessarily benefits the students. Above all is the revealing of the management of each part by those who joined in the attack.[46]

In this reflection, the historian is advising writers that action without development of characters, their stratagems, and their motivations is a vain exercise. In so doing, Polybius is avowing the historiographical approach of Isocrates.[47]

Of course, such Greek historians were taking their cues from the great poets, especially Homer. What one remembers most upon finishing the famous *Iliad* are not the battles, though these are portrayed magnificently. Western society forever will memorialize the indelible characterizations of Hector and Achilles, the powerful kings Agamem-

---

[46]Greek: τί γὰρ ὄφελός ἐστι τοῖς ἀναγινώσκουσι διεξιέναι πολέμους καὶ μάχας καὶ πόλεων ἐξανδραποδισμοὺς καὶ πολιορκίας, εἰ μὴ τὰς αἰτίας ἐπιγνώσονται, παρ' ἃς ἐν ἑκάστοις οἱ μὲν κατώρθωσαν, οἱ δ' ἐσφάλησαν. 2 τὰ γὰρ τέλη τῶν πράξεων ψυχαγωγεῖ μόνον τοὺς ἀκούοντας, αἱ δὲ πρόσθεν διαλήψεις τῶν ἐπιβαλλομένων ἐξεταζόμεναι δεόντως ὠφελοῦσι τοὺς φιλομαθοῦντας. 3 μάλιστα δὲ πάντων ὁ κατὰ μέρος χειρισμὸς ἑκάστων ἐπιδεικνύμενος ἐπανορθοῖ τοὺς συνεφιστάνοντας. Polybius *Hist.* 11.19a.

[47]Greek historiography actually had two traditions. One school centered on a hero with a series of dramatic incidents intended to captivate the reader and inspire admiration, expectation, delight, annoyance, fear, etc.—the ancient equivalent to the Hollywood "action" movie. This "Peripatetic" historiography worked to create a sense of ἡδονή ("pleasure") in readers. The other school came from Isocrates, who advocated a goal of διδαχή (instruction) in regard to the reader. Polybius is following the Isocrates tradition. See Leeman, *Orationis Ratio*, 1:174.

non and Priam, and others.[48] Since the Greek historians schooled on these great stories, their minds were set at a young age to pay close attention to characterization, through which the story is insinuated line by line so that the reader almost can declare the result of the engagement before the battle is fought.

For example, Aristotle spoke of the lawyer's training, insisting, "Rather, trustworthiness of character, so to speak, yields almost complete mastery."[49] Aristotle went on to discuss how useful is adapting the character of the speaker to the character of the audience.[50] In the elite training of the rhetor, then, the study of characterization was considered essential. As Leeman observed in speaking of the development of Roman historiography in the early empire period, "Still, no writer of the Empire could or wanted to free himself altogether from the powerful influence of rhetoric."[51] Characterization in its concept, function, and development was one such powerful influence that rhetoric exerted.

Ethos as Insinuated

Auctor ad Herennium contains advice on using figures of "personal representation," that is, how characters should be portrayed. Summarizing this use, Leeman said,

> Character portrayal, *notatio*, (ἠθοποιία),[88] belongs to the same sphere of light dramatization, but may also occur in a *narratiuncula*. It implies not only a straightforward sketch, but also a

---

[48]Pretty much obliterated in the movie starring Brad Pitt (*Troy*, Warner Bros., 2004). Notice in the modern movie how the ancient storyteller's art is turned on its head: instead of unforgettable characters that drive the plot, one encounters the unforgivable absurdity of plot driving the characters. What becomes so important for the director is not Homer's literary genius—the story of character—but making an "action movie," wasting time and energy painting a fantasy fleet of impossible thousands of Greek ships stretching across the entire Aegean horizon. Peripatetic wins out over Isocrates with a vengeance.

[49]Greek: ἀλλὰ σχεδὸν ὡς εἰπεῖν κυριωτάτην ἔχει πίστιν τὸ ἦθος. Aristotle *Rhet.* 1.2.4. Cf. Kennedy's translation: "Character [of the speaker] is almost, so to speak, the controlling factor in persuasion." *On Rhetoric* (1991).

[50]Throughout chapters 12–17 in Book 2 covering topics related to ethos.

[51]Leeman, 256.

story which [sic] characterizes a person indirectly by his behavior in everyday life.[52]

---

[88]*Rhet. Ad Her.* 4.63–65. Not a figure according to Quintilian.

This characterization happens as much implicitly by behavior and actions as by any direct statement. The ancient writer expects the reader-listener to be accumulating a character profile indirectly on the basis of behavior and action characterizations in stories about that person (or city, in the case of corporate ethos, discussed below).

One might wonder whether such literary conventions would be too subtle for the ancient reader. Not really. As Leeman noted about Roman historians,

> I think that the allusive element in Latin literature is generally underestimated. In comparison with modern literature, the Romans had very little direct, naturalistic or realistic description, and they kept equally far from pure fiction and illusion. Theirs was the middle way of allusion, and this 'allusionism' determined not a few of their literary conventions. . . . Tacitus again follows this allusive method in his *Dialogus*, and thus gives indirect expression to his personal experiences.[53]

Ethos as Corporate

Ethos can be applied to groups and institutions, especially cities, as much as to individuals.[54] In fact, the importance of an individual by a stroke of destiny could be tied to a particular city. Quintilian gave this example of the famous Roman general, Scipio, while discussing the art of *antonomasia* (replacing a name with something else): "I should not hesitate to say 'the sacker of Carthage and Numantia' for Scipio."[55]

---

[52]Ibid., 40.

[53]Ibid., 346. As an example, Leeman wrote, "Under a new regime Tacitus begins to speak. But from the beginning he chooses an indirect form of expression: Agricola and Maternus are Tacitus; Vespasian is, in a way, Trajan, Nero perhaps what Tacitus feared in the designate emperor and philhellene Hadrian" (Leeman, 347).

[54]For example, in discussing the *trope* (figurative use of a single word) of *metonymy* (use of one term for another), when Quintilian admitted, "Usage permits 'cities of good character,'" (*bene moratus urbes*), he implicitly was drawing upon the common concept of how cities are characterized. Quintilian *Inst.* 8.6.24.

[55]Quintilian *Inst.* 8.6.30.

Quintilian continued by describing how epithet rhetorically was an "ornament" (actually a technical designation) more for poets than for orators.[56] The epithet builds on the *trope* of *antonomasia* if the noun for which *trope* stands is added, as in adding "Scipio" to "sacker of Carthage and Numantia."[57] Perhaps this type of maneuver is reflected in Luke's pointed designation of "disciples" as "Christians" at Antioch in Acts 11:26.

Thucydides provides another example involving "Hellene." This Greek historian made astute observation of Homer's own transformation of the use of "Hellene" from an individual city into an appellation of an entire people: "On the other hand, neither does he say barbarian, likely, as it seems to me, because the Hellenes had not yet struggled to be set apart unto one name. Even so, therefore, as each Hellenic city acquired the name, in as much as they came to understand one another, then finally all together they were called."[58]

Much later the Smyrnean orator Aelius Aristides (155 AD) seems to echo this Homeric invention noted by Thucydides when the orator addressed the imperial court about Rome, the city, as actually a marker not exclusively for a city, but for a culture and way of life of an entire people developed out of that city:

> But you have sought a citizen body worthy of it, and you have caused the word 'Roman' to belong not to a city, but to the name of a sort of common race, and this not one out of all the races, but a balance to all the remaining ones. . . . You have divided people into Romans and non-Romans. So far you extended the use of the city's name.[59]

Such a conceptualization is paralleled by the golden milestone positioned prominently in the forum of Rome in 20 BC marking distances of all major empire cities to the gates of Rome, supporting the

[56] Ibid., 8.6.40.

[57] Ibid., 8.6.43.

[58] Greek: οὐ μὴν οὐδὲ βαρβάρους εἴρηκε διὰ τὸ μηδὲ Ἕλληνάς πω, ὡς ἐμοὶ δοκεῖ, ἀντίπαλον ἐς ἓν ὄνομα ἀποκεκρίσθαι. οἱ δ' οὖν ὡς ἕκαστοι Ἕλληνες κατὰ πόλεις τε ὅσοι ἀλλήλων ξυνίεσαν καὶ ξύμπαντες ὕστερον κληθέντες. Thucydides *War* 1.3.3–4.

[59] Aristides *To Rome* 63.

timeless myth that Rome was the center of the world (*caput rerum*).[60] According to the fourth-century church father Lactantius, Seneca compared Roman history to the life stages of a person.[61]

Of course, the use of a city as a *trope* or even *figure* (metaphor) is common in biblical writers. One can trace the history of names such as the infamous Sodom and Gomorrah in the Old Testament[62] or the use of Chorazin and Bethsaida in the New Testament.[63] One of the most dramatic New Testament examples is when Jerusalem itself is a place of evil, the dual *trope* of a combined Sodom and Egypt![64] This rhetorical twist startles the readers into reevaluation of their own context at Ephesus, Smyrna, Sardis, Pergamum, Thyatira, Philadelphia, and Laodicea.[65] Our focus will turn to another biblical author, Luke, to observe how he uses "Antioch" and its narratively defined corporate ethos.

Summary of Settings

Antioch of Syria was born a Hellenistic city of the Seleucid dynasty that eventually came under Roman provincial administration by New Testament times. Though thoroughly Greek, the population from the beginning also had one of the more significant Jewish quarters per resident population of ancient cities in the Roman empire. This strong Jewish presence created a distinctive social mix even more notable than that of Rome itself.

Kinship ideas when tied to Antioch as a city of origin would be a strong socializing force shaping the boundaries of social groups along these dominant, often competing, Hellenistic and Jewish elements. Antioch's synagogue Jews, as well as the general populace, would be able to notice the social distinctions generated by disciples of Jesus who were attempting to function within Antioch's synagogues. Initial Jewish

---

[60]Cassius Dio *History* 54.8.4. See Griffin, "Urbs Roma, Plebs, and Princeps," 20.

[61]As indicated by Lactantius *Institutes* 7.15.14, "Seneca therefore not unskillfully divided the times of the Roman city by ages. For he said that at first was its infancy under King Romulus," etc.

[62]Isa 1:9; Jer 23:14; Ezek 16:46.

[63]Matt 11:21 (Luke 10:13).

[64]In Rev 11:2, 8, and 13; probably Sodom for perversion, Egypt for idolatry.

[65]Cf. Futral, "The Rhetorical Value of *City*," 250.

perceptions of these disciples would be sectarian, and the general populace would absorb these sectarian perceptions. The probable setting, then, for the use of the appellation *Christianoi* in Acts 11:26 is external to the group and Jewish sectarian in perception.

The Christian movement in its distinctive Antiochene formulation eventually would come to dominate the history of Christianity. This dominance probably was due to the ministry of one of the brightest stars in the constellation of early Christianity, Antioch's own Paul the apostle. Inevitably, the Jesus movement would experience growing pressure for a title of self-definition within the social matrix of persecution. The choice was "Christian" in the Antiochene sense. This choice is clear by the early second century.

In the ancient world, ethos, or characterization, was an essential feature of writing, both in classical poetry and in historiography, as well as in speaking, that is, rhetorical training. Literary characterization should not be seen as the pedantic exercise of dry, descriptive text. Ethos could be a sophisticated exercise, insinuated subtly through dialogue or astute observations of behavior in everyday life. Such literary sophistication was not felt to be beyond the normal expectations of an ancient reader-listener, nor was ethos the exclusive domain of individuals. Corporate ethos especially included characterizations associated with cities. These associations at the social level were based on ideas of extended kinship. Groups find their identity in their city of origin.

Thus, in making a special notation that disciples first were called "Christians" in Antioch, Luke was doing more than showing extraordinary historical prescience. From a historical perspective, he had the insight to point to the appellation that history would canonize for the Jesus movement. From a literary perspective, though, Luke also defined the profile of this Antiochene church through an insinuated corporate ethos by contrasting churches in Jerusalem and Antioch. He intended to leave a vision of a paradigm to be emulated by any community wishing to identify itself as "Christian." That paradigm was focused more on Antioch than on Jerusalem. Our attention now turns to the narrative features of corporate ethos framed by the Acts account related to the churches in Jerusalem and in Antioch. Our goal is to reveal the meaning of disciples being called "Christians" first at Antioch.

ANTIOCH: ETHOS AND IDENTITY

Luke has generated a carefully composed document in which characterization is a crucial component for understanding the plot movement.[66] In the latter part of Acts, for example, the city of Jerusalem functions as a *topos* integrated into the development of Luke's negative characterization of Saul-Paul.[67] In the early part of Acts, Luke has trained the reader's attention on the *topoi* of two cities, Jerusalem and Antioch, as a way to develop characterization of the early church. Luke will use Jerusalem both to contrast and to highlight Antioch. A brief overview of the basic structure and movement of the plot in Acts 1–12 will reveal the significance of this design.

Literary Structure of Acts

The structure of the story line in Acts falls neatly into two major parts based on the twin ideas of leadership and mission. The first half, Acts 1–12, presents the Jewish mission of the early church in, around, and beyond Jerusalem under the leadership of Peter. The second half, Acts 13–28, presents the gentile mission of the early church moving out into the world under the leadership of Saul-Paul. The internal structure of the first part of Acts, the focus of this discussion of Antioch, can be visualized schematically in the figure given below. Notice the significance of characters that drive the plot, especially the character of Peter "bracketing" the new characters in the dramatic turn at Acts 6.

FIGURE 2.1. Acts 1–12: Characters and Narrative Flow.

The crucial point to make here is that the second half of Acts does not exist without this first half. Actors and actions in the second half almost entirely lose their meaning and significance without the characterizations carefully developed in the first half. Notice, for ex-

---

[66]Shipp, *Paul the Reluctant Witness.*

[67]Compare Shipp's overall outline, *Paul the Reluctant Witness,* 90–92.

ample, at the macro-literary level the six literary subunits centered on Peter "bracketing" the beginning and the end of the material introducing the Hellenist movement in chapters 6–9. This bracketing communicates the representative significance of Peter's character. That is, Peter's character for Luke is the official post-resurrection tie back to the original mission of Jesus in Luke's Gospel. Luke has used Peter's character to "bracket" the Hellenist movement in the early church to justify and legitimate the movement as both having apostolic blessing and representing the intended design of the original mission of Jesus in the Gospel. The Hellenist movement in the early church was no fluke. In fact, God guided that very movement to become the foundation of the church's witness, fulfilling the programmatic Acts 1:8. Thus, one can observe how Luke used various narrative techniques to move his story along. What other techniques did Luke incorporate? Luke developed narrative characterizations of Jerusalem and Antioch. An outline of Jerusalem's ethos sets the stage for understanding Antioch's distinctive profile.

Jerusalem's Ethos in the Gospel

Jerusalem as Positive in Luke

Jerusalem has the preeminence historically. She represents the historic roots of Jewish faith. As a city of origin, she endows any group associated with her with the religious traditions of Jewish faith. To be identified with Jerusalem is to have kinship with Israel as the people of God. For example, characters associated with the city of Jerusalem in Luke's story of Jesus express the ancient hopes and aspirations of Israel at their finest. Zechariah and Elizabeth "were righteous before God, living blamelessly according to all the commandments and regulations of the Lord."[68] Their son, John, is filled with the Holy Spirit even before his birth.[69] Zechariah, though a simple functionary in the temple service, is a prophet of God.[70] Mary is favored of God and is filled with

---

[68]Luke 1:6, ἦσαν δὲ δίκαιοι ἀμφότεροι ἐναντίον τοῦ θεοῦ, πορευόμενοι ἐν πάσαις ταῖς ἐντολαῖς καὶ δικαιώμασιν τοῦ κυρίου ἄμεμπτοι.

[69]Luke 1:15, πνεύματος ἁγίου λησθήσεται ἔτι ἐκ κοιλίας μητρὸς αὐτοῦ.

[70]Luke 1:67, Καὶ Ζαχαρίας ὁ πατὴρ αὐτοῦ ἐπλήσθη πνεύματος ἁγίου καὶ ἐπροφήτευσεν.

God's Spirit (Luke 1:28, 35). Joseph and Mary perform all the legal requirements for their infant and also make the annual trek to Jerusalem for each Passover (Luke 2:22–24, 41). The old prophet Simeon is righteous and devout, looking for the consolation of Israel, endued with the Holy Spirit, and so prophesying about Jesus.[71] Three times in three verses the reader is told that the Spirit controls Simeon and even directs his path (Luke 2:25, 26, 27). This Spirit guided movement will reverberate in Acts in the story of how the Hellenist Philip intersects with the Ethiopian eunuch (Acts 8:26, 39). The prophetess Anna serves to confirm Simeon's prophecy, and thereby satisfies the requirements of the law for two witnesses (Luke 2:36–38). Thus, the emerging story of Jesus is grounded thoroughly in Jerusalem and shares in the kinship of that city of origin in its character as the city encapsulating the hope of Israel.

Jerusalem as Negative in Luke

Jesus's Death. While Jerusalem can encapsulate the hope of Israel, the city also bears a negative characterization. Luke left subtle hints along the way,[72] but the formal inauguration of the negative characterization is Luke 9:51, often taken as the dividing line at the crucial mid-point in the outline of Luke: "Now it happened that the days for his taking up were fulfilled, and he set his face for the purpose of going to Jerusalem."[73] In terms of "fulfilled" in Luke 9:51 and Acts 2:1, both narratives at these verses are at crucial turning points in the story: at Luke 9:51, Jesus turns toward his ultimate mission and destiny in Jerusalem, and, at Acts 2:1, the church turns toward its ultimate mission

---

[71]Luke 1:35, ὁ ἄνθρωπος οὗτος δίκαιος καὶ εὐλαβὴς προσδεχόμενος παράκλησιν τοῦ Ἰσραήλ, καὶ πνεῦμα ἦν ἅγιον ἐπ᾽ αὐτόν.

[72]One example is the episode of the boy Jesus in the temple declaring that he *must* be in his father's house, Luke 2:49 (οὐκ ᾔδειτε ὅτι ἐν τοῖς τοῦ πατρός μου δεῖ εἶναί με;). This "must" (δεῖ) is the well-known, theologically loaded term for Luke that expresses the divine imperative of God's sovereign will. Jerusalem's recently celebrated Passover festival provides the context that insinuates the divine necessity.

[73]Greek: Ἐγένετο δὲ ἐν τῷ συμπληροῦσθαι τὰς ἡμέρας τῆς ἀναλήμψεως αὐτοῦ καὶ αὐτὸς τὸ πρόσωπον ἐστήρισεν τοῦ πορεύεσθαι εἰς Ἰερουσαλήμ. The "taking up" (ἀνάλημψις) is a *hapax legomenon* (singular occurrence in the New Testament), so the exegesis is impeded. In terms of range of meaning, the expression could be an allusion to his impending death or to his ascension. Most commentators opt for the latter meaning, since Luke is the only New Testament author to incorporate a formal ascension story into his text, and twice at that, providing another narrative connecting device between the plotline in the Gospel and that in Acts (Luke 24:50–51; Acts 1:9).

and destiny in the world. The difference between the two story lines, however, is that in 9:51, this word of a turn toward Jerusalem strikes an ominous note in the text. While Jesus deliberately moves to Jerusalem to fulfill his messianic destiny, the story ends in Jesus's death. Jerusalem's own destiny is interlocked with her Messiah and sealed by Jesus's fate. In contrast, the mission of the church is open-ended at the end of the Acts narrative.

Jerusalem's Destiny. Four Lukan passages in the second part of the Gospel are focused on Jerusalem's destiny.[74] These passages work in concert to build a theme of judgment. Each of these passages either enhances or amplifies the reality that Jerusalem is under divine judgment as a consequence of the rejection of Jesus and his own destiny of death in that city. The picture is blunt in Jesus's remonstration, "O Jerusalem, Jerusalem! The one who kills the prophets and stones those sent to her!"[75] Thus, while Jerusalem represents the historic roots of Israel's faith, that city also is where Jesus was rejected and crucified.

Jerusalem's Ethos in Acts

Attention in Acts is delimited to the church. The discussion of ethos is directed to developing profiles of the church in Jerusalem and in Antioch. The crucial focal point will be the ethos of mission impulse. The profile of the Jerusalem church is more developed in order to show distinctively the contrasts with Antioch on this crucial point.

Jerusalem as Positive in Acts

Pentecost Festival. In Acts, Jerusalem is where the church formally is launched on its mission of witness. Jerusalem represents the earliest stages of the Spirit's activity with the nascent church. Using the theme of the "promise of the Father," the end of the Gospel and the beginning of Acts are tied together.[76] This promise is the effluence of the Spirit,

---

[74]Luke 13:33–35; 19:41–44; 21:20–24; and 23:27–31.

[75]Luke 13:34: Ἰερουσαλὴμ Ἰερουσαλήμ, ἡ ἀποκτείνουσα τοὺς προφήτας καὶ λιθοβολοῦσα τοὺς ἀπεσταλμένους πρὸς αὐτήν. "Jerusalem" is *metonymy* (a part for the whole) for the Jewish nation, especially her leaders; one should note, though, the amazing amnesty granted in Acts 3:17 to Jerusalem by Peter: "You acted in ignorance, as also your leaders did" (κατὰ ἄγνοιαν ἐπράξατε ὥσπερ καὶ οἱ ἄρχοντες ὑμῶν).

[76]Luke 24:49; Acts 1:4.

which happens at Pentecost. As the Spirit had guided all developments at the beginning of the story of Jesus and empowered Jesus at the beginning of his public ministry, so the Spirit guides all developments at the beginning of the story of the church and empowers the church at the beginning of her public ministry of witness.[77] In this way, the role of Jerusalem as the mother church in the early stages of the Jesus movement is made clear, inextricably tied to the story of Jesus. The early church finds its initial characterization through kinship with its city of origin, Jerusalem. The eschatological harvest of the people of God to which the original Pentecost annual festival celebration pointed is being realized in Jerusalem in the church.[78]

The story of initial unity and worship appended to the Pentecost event in Acts 2 adds to the characterization of the Jerusalem church. The realization of Pentecost fellowship in home and hearth is represented in the early church's sharing of meals and homes.[79] The harvest celebration was rich in imagery, symbolized by an offering of two loaves of leavened bread, which can be summarized in the following way.

> The Jewish offering of two loaves of leavened bread symbolized gratitude to God for the plentiful harvest and was a token of the feast celebrated in Jewish homes. This feast was meant to be inclusive. No one in Israel should be in want of food at the celebration of harvest. The exhortation in Deut 16 repeatedly echoed in the elaboration of the feasts celebrated by Israel is: "Rejoice before the LORD your God—you and your sons and your daughters, your male and female slaves, the Levites resident in your towns, as well as the strangers, the orphans, and the widows who are among you—at the place that the LORD your God will choose as a dwelling for his name" (Deut 16:11, NRSV). That is, the Pentecost celebration is intended to be inclusive,

---

[77]Luke 3:21–22; Acts 1:5, 8; 2:4. In 1:5, for example: ὅτι Ἰωάννης μὲν ἐβάπτισεν ὕδατι, ὑμεῖς δὲ ἐν πνεύματι βαπτισθήσεσθε ἁγίῳ οὐ μετὰ πολλὰς ταύτας ἡμέρας.

[78]This theme of eschatological harvest is an interpretive narrative superstructure in Acts derived from the story of Israel's movement from wilderness to promised land giving eschatological significance to the historical events taking place in the early church as defined in the seven Petrine speeches in Acts 1–12, 15. See the previous chapter on Pentecost.

[79]Epitomized in the intertestamental literature in the story of Tobit through his command to his son Tobiah to retrieve one of Israel's poor in the streets of Nineveh for their Pentecost festal meal in Tobit's home. Cf. Tob 2:1–2.

with specific attention to those normally vulnerable to life's vicissitudes.[80]

The character of Luke's description of the Jerusalem church in Acts
2:42–43 clearly is meant to be a direct reflection of this Pentecost fellowship. Then, Luke immediately went a step further and modulated
this time-delimited, annual feast celebration, which itself anticipated
the final fulfillment of God's complete and abundant provision for his
people, into a higher key: the extension of the agricultural Pentecost
fulfillment into that timeless church experience of perpetual eschatological fulfillment in Acts 2:44–47.[81]

Apostolic Characters. Luke also characterized the Jerusalem church
corporately through her apostolic leaders. Peter is the premier representative, the heart and soul of the original Jesus movement.[82] Luke
carefully portrayed the life and ministry of Jesus replicated in the life
and ministry of his followers, but especially Peter. As Jesus preaches, so
does Peter.[83] As Jesus heals a lame man, so does Peter.[84] As Jesus raises
a girl back to life, so does Peter.[85]

Even though this preaching and healing receives opposition from
Jewish leaders, the condemnation is transformed into witness. Already
noted is how Antioch responded by the early second century such that
the term "Christian" was transformed into a positive badge, even in
spite of persecution. DeSilva pointed out,

> Suffering for Jesus' sake is even transformed into a badge of
> honor before God. This strategy represents perhaps the strong-
> est tool the minority group has for reversing the effects of
> society's attempts to reign the "deviants" back into line with
> dominant cultural values. The response of the twelve apostles to

[80]Chapter 1, "Pentecost," pp. 41–42.

[81]"They were having all things in common," εἶχον ἄπαντα κοινὰ, Acts 2:44.

[82]Luke 9:20; Acts 2:14.

[83]Luke 11:28; Acts 5:29.

[84]Luke 5:17–26; Acts 3:1–10. Observe the parallel structure: a lame man, a healing
miracle, and a word of forgiveness.

[85]Luke 8:49–56 (Jairus's daughter); Acts 9:36–43 (Tabitha). Observe parallel structure: a young girl, an untimely death, and the close wording of the command (*talitha
koum* vs. *Tabitha koum*). Luke makes a play on the moniker for "little girl" (*talitha*) in
the Gospel episode and the actual name of the girl in the Acts episode (*Tabitha*). Only
one letter separates the two words.

the Sanhedrin's marking them with the whip as deviants requiring correction becomes paradigmatic: "They rejoiced that they
were considered worthy to suffer dishonor for the sake of the
name" (Acts 5:41).[86]

Jerusalem as Negative in Acts

However, though Jerusalem was the mother church, the picture is not
completely rosy. Numerous episodes indicate either a passivity or,
worse, a growing resistance on the part of the Jerusalem church to
God's action through the Spirit, but most acutely in the key issue of the
outward impulse of gospel witness. In terms of outward impulse,
Jerusalem just never gets to church on time, like Eliza Doolittle's father,
Alfred, in *My Fair Lady* in jeopardy of missing the main event because
of his recalcitrant behavior. What narrative elements carry this theme?
This theme shows up in stories such as Ananias and Sapphira, the
constant after-the-fact attempts to "validate" gospel expansion among
unacceptable social groups after the Spirit already has taken the
initiative, the preaching of the gospel exclusively to Jews, and the
Jerusalem Conference.

Ananias and Sapphira. The story of Ananias and Sapphira is the
harbinger (Acts 5:1–11). This episode has been the source of much
confusion in commentaries. Narrative analysis clarifies the meaning.
The episode is bracketed by the two appearances of Peter before the
Sanhedrin. Peter's first appearance in Acts 4:10–12 is an offer of
forgiveness to Israel's leaders for the death of Christ. Peter's second
appearance in Acts 5:40 is the Sanhedrin's public rejection of Peter's
offer. The consequence of that rejection, within the eschatological
context of God's unique offer of forgiveness for the death of Jesus, will
be tragic and fatal (cf. Acts 3:17). The Ananias and Sapphira story
reveals the Sanhedrin's fatal flaw of presuming upon God's Spirit at a
critical juncture in the story of God's people.

The crucial indictment is coded in Gamaliel's warning to the
Sanhedrin in 5:38–39: "So now about these things I tell you, keep away
from these men and leave them alone; because if this counsel and
activity be of human origin, it will be destroyed; but if it is of God, you
will not be able to destroy them—lest even you be found to be God-

---

[86]deSilva, *Honor, Patronage, Kinship and Purity*, 66–67.

fighters!"[87] Bluntly, opposing the Jesus movement is fighting God himself. Ironically, Gamaliel's warning eventually goes unheeded, not only by the Sanhedrin, but also by his best student, Saul of Tarsus. Playing the part of a "God-fighter" becomes a theme in Acts among individuals and groups inside and outside the church. Such was the position of Ananias and Sapphira, and their situation was a harbinger of judgment to come. Significantly, Peter alluded to this "God-fighter" theme when confronted by the Jerusalem church about Cornelius: "Who was I, as if I was able to resist God?"[88]

"Validating" Gospel Advance. Jerusalem is either passive and not involved or remonstrating others when the Spirit moves the gospel outward beyond Jews. Gospel expansion in Acts actually happens in the Hellenist movement, not in Jerusalem. Luke used the story of the daily widow distribution in Acts 6 not to introduce the formal office of deacon but to introduce the main leaders of the Hellenist movement within the early church. Thus begins the Hellenist Cycle in Acts.[89] Luke was forced to access this Hellenist material to tell the story of gospel expansion, because gospel expansion never was the *initiative* of the Jerusalem church. Outside of preaching to Jews themselves in and around Jerusalem, the Jerusalem church never gets to church on time when the issue is gospel expansion. Careful reading in the stories about the Samaritans, the Ethiopian eunuch, Cornelius, and Antioch reveal that Jerusalem representatives either *are not involved at all* or always are sent *after the fact,* as if presuming they could sit in judgment on what the Holy Spirit already had accomplished in moving the gospel outward.

For example, Philip the Hellenist leader, not Jerusalem, evangelizes the Samaritans (8:5). Only *afterward* does Jerusalem send out its own emissaries seeking to verify the Spirit's work (8:14). The Ethiopian eunuch story is the result of the Spirit's initiative through an obedient Hellenist, Philip, not Jerusalem (Acts 8:26, 29, 39). Even Peter himself

---

[87]Greek: καὶ τὰ νῦν λέγω ὑμῖν, ἀπόστητε ἀπὸ τῶν ἀνθρώπων τούτων καὶ ἄφετε αὐτούς· ὅτι ἐὰν ᾖ ἐξ ἀνθρώπων ἡ βουλὴ αὕτη ἢ τὸ ἔργον τοῦτο, καταλυθήσεται, εἰ δὲ ἐκ θεοῦ ἐστιν, οὐ δυνήσεσθε καταλῦσαι αὐτούς, μήποτε καὶ θεομάχοι εὑρεθῆτε.

[88]Acts 11:17, ἐγὼ τίς ἤμην δυνατὸς κωλῦσαι τὸν θεόν;

[89]For a full development of the Hellenist Cycle, see Haenchen, *Acts.*

initially resists God's instructions in the heavenly vision leading up to Cornelius's conversion (10:13–15). Afterwards, circumcised believers in the Jerusalem church dare to *challenge* Peter's actions with Cornelius (11:2–3). Or again, the narrative is clear that those who breach the gentile boundary in Antioch are "some men of Cyprus and Cyrene," *not* Jerusalem (11:20). Only *after* news of the Hellenist evangelization at Antioch hits Jerusalem's ears were they even aware of what the Spirit was doing and felt like they needed to send a representative to check things out.[90] When the issue was gospel preaching to gentiles, the Jerusalem church never got to church on time. The issue came to a climax in the Jerusalem Conference in Acts 15.

Jerusalem Conference. What looks like a tacit agreement about gospel expansion among gentiles reached by the Jerusalem church in 11:18 after Peter refuses to back down about Cornelius in reality is only a flanking action by the circumcision wing of the early church. *The very next verse* reveals the *true* situation: even after Cornelius, Luke makes patently clear, Jerusalem's gospel preaching is "to Jews only."[91] Real feelings explode out in the open again after the first missionary journey brings gentiles into the church in such large numbers they no longer can be ignored (15:1–2).

In playing out the Jerusalem Conference, Luke was building on the earlier Sanhedrin story in Acts 5. That is, the earlier episode of the Sanhedrin's condemnation by God in Acts 5 has reverberations in the narrative for the church itself. Notice that Peter's question to Sapphira in Acts 5:9 about "putting the Spirit of the Lord to the test"[92] has its eerie echo in Acts 15:10 as Peter challenges the Jerusalem Church at the Jerusalem Conference![93] Peter's similarly phrased question in both accounts shows that the demand for gentile circumcision in Acts 15 has put the Jerusalem church on the brink of a judgment disaster just like the Sanhedrin was in Acts 5.

---

[90] Acts 11:22, Ἠκούσθη δὲ ὁ λόγος εἰς τὰ ὦτα τῆς ἐκκλησίας τῆς οὔσης ἐν Ἰερουσαλὴμ περὶ αὐτῶν καὶ ἐξαπέστειλαν Βαρναβᾶν [διελθεῖν] ἕως Ἀντιοχείας.

[91] Acts 11:19, μηδενὶ λαλοῦντες τὸν λόγον εἰ μὴ μόνον Ἰουδαίοις.

[92] Greek: πειράσαι τὸ πνεῦμα κυρίου.

[93] Greek: νῦν οὖν τί πειράζετε τὸν θεὸν.

Antioch's Ethos in Acts

Hellenists in Acts

The story of Antioch is the story of the Hellenists. Of the seven leading Hellenists chosen to assist in the distribution to widows in Acts 6:5, only the first and last are given additional description along with their names. Stephen, the first on the list, further is described as "a man full of faith and of the Holy Spirit."[94] Stephen is highlighted because he will bring the definitive critique of the Jerusalem temple in his speech in the next chapter. Nicolaus, last on the list, further is described as "a proselyte of Antioch."[95] Nicolaus is highlighted to allow Luke's penchant for name-dropping in anticipation of developments later in the narrative.[96] In addition, in this quick stroke, Luke has characterized Nicolaus two ways: by indicating his religious status as a proselyte[97] and by indicating his social status through his city of origin. In this description Luke deftly provides in a nutshell the two principal and defining characteristics of gospel expansion in the early church: notably, successful among gentiles, notably centered on Antioch. Through this story of conflict and prejudicial treatment within the ranks of Jerusalem's church, Luke already was hinting that Jerusalem Hellenists would not flourish in Jerusalem. The Hellenist movement will have to find a more hospitable city of origin.

The next time Antioch is mentioned in Luke's narrative, the story has arrived at a crucial text that bluntly reveals that responsibility for gospel expansion is among Hellenist leaders. The reader explicitly and unambiguously is told in 11:19–20, "Now those who were dispersed because of the persecution that happened due to Stephen went through

[94] Acts 6:5, ἄνδρα πλήρης πίστεως καὶ πνεύματος ἁγίου.

[95] Acts 6:5, προσήλυτον Ἀντιοχέα.

[96] In this case, the name of a city, i.e., Antioch. Of many examples of Luke's name-dropping, one can illustrate with the introduction of Barnabas in 4:26 because of his later crucial role in the early days of Paul's ministry (introducing Saul to the Jerusalem leaders, 9:27; getting Saul from Tarsus to work in Antioch, 11:25; taking the famine relief funds to Jerusalem, 11:30; leading the first missionary journey, 13:2). Saul himself is another example, subtly introduced at the end of the stoning of Stephen in 7:58 before the dramatic Damascus Road in Acts 9.

[97] A rare term in the New Testament, προσήλυτος occurs only four times, three in Acts (Matt 23:15; Acts 2:11; 6:5; 13:43). The general consensus is that the term refers to a convert to Judaism subscribing to the whole law, including circumcision.

Phoenicia, Cyprus, and Antioch, speaking the word to no one but Jews alone. *But certain ones of them, men of Cyprus and Cyrene, when they came to Antioch were speaking to the Hellenists also*, proclaiming the Lord Jesus."[98]

For those involved in this novel phase of missionary impulse, the place of origin is specified particularly: these men are of Cyprus and Cyrene. Luke is clear that *these evangelists' identity is not grounded in Jerusalem's ethos*. Identifying Nicolaus as a "proselyte of Antioch" in 6:3 now becomes clear as an interpretive marker for understanding the Antiochene audience of 11:20. Preaching the gospel to Hellenists was a synagogue breakthrough, especially made possible in Antioch because that is where these Hellenists[99] would have been found in significant numbers due to Antioch's large Jewish population and numerous synagogues, and due to a basic overall compatibility with Antioch's strong Hellenistic social environment historically.

Passive Versus Responsive Ethos

Jerusalem, as usual, misses the initiative in this Hellenist impulse and gospel advance. Yet, Jerusalem still feels compelled to send Barnabas to check things out after the fact (11:22). Barnabas, ever true as an Acts character to his suname,[100] is encouraged by these developments in Antioch and gets Saul from Tarsus to help (11:26). An obvious question arises: Why did Barnabas not think of getting someone from Jerusalem?[101] In any case, Barnabas and Saul work together in Antioch for a year. This success implicitly is based upon the notation in 11:20; that is, when evangelized, Hellenists in Antioch's synagogues responded in significant numbers. This unhindered evangelism and significant response is one reason Luke specifies that the disciples first were called Christians at Antioch. In part, what Luke means by this observation is

[98]Emphasis added.

[99]Both full proselytes like Nicolaus in Jerusalem and "God-fearers" like Cornelius in Caesarea (10:2, εὐσεβὴς καὶ φοβούμενος τὸν θεὸν).

[100]Clearly, this surname relates to no possible etymological analysis by Luke. For a concise overview of the etymological problems, see Fitzmyer, *Acts*, 320–21.

[101]Curiously, Barnabas also has his kinship of origin in Cyprus, just like these evangelists making this bold move to preach to Hellenists in Antioch. This Cyprus connection possibly may explain why Luke was careful to note Barnabas's home territory of Cyprus when he first introduced this character into the narrative (4:36).

a subtle critique of the Jerusalem church: Jerusalem was simply out of the game completely in this Hellenist mission impulse. After all, what is the meaning of the Jerusalem delegation to Antioch? Just what did the Jerusalem church think they were going to do in the first place if their delegation brought back a critical report of Hellenist developments at Antioch? Would they have attempted to coerce some type of Jerusalem conformity, as the Sanhedrin had attempted to do in Damascus through Saul? We need to remember that the Jerusalem Conference itself was one such attempt on the part of certain elements of the Jerusalem church to enforce Jerusalem ethos that failed.

Antioch, on the other hand, in notable contrast to Jerusalem, is responsive. At the time Barnabas and Saul are working in Antioch, Jerusalem prophets come to Antioch and warn of a great famine for Judea (11:27).[102] Antioch responds to the famine warning with an offering (11:28). This famine aid will comprise another key distinguishing mark of the Antioch church: responsiveness and social benevolence outside their own municipal boundaries. Their assistance is delivered by Barnabas and Saul (11:29). This type of social action even may be another visible form of expressing kinship ideas.[103] In any case, Barnabas and Saul deliver the collection to Jerusalem and return to Antioch (12:25).

Note at this point that the Antiochene collection was not given to the apostles. The "elders" formally received the gift (11:30).[104] With this reference to "elders," Luke was name-dropping again. He already was insinuating the leadership base at Jerusalem was shifting away from the early dominance by the apostles. The Cornelius episode continues to haunt the church, as the reader has the first insinuation by the Acts author that Peter no longer is the principal spokesman for the Jerusalem

---

[102]The translation "over all the world" for ἐφ᾽ ὅλην τὴν οἰκουμένην in 11:29 is common (cf. KJV, ASV, NASB, NRSV). However, the broad semantic domain for οἰκουμένη simply means that "over the entire region" is perfectly adequate; the province of Judea seems the main intent, which is the reason the prophets are identified as from Jerusalem. That the church in Antioch understood Judea as the object of the prophecy is clear in sending the gift to Jerusalem only, not other parts of the world. For a contrary view, see Winter, "Acts and Food Shortages," 59–78.

[103]deSilva, *Honor, Patronage, Kinship, and Purity*, 216. As to prophets and prophecy, the reader will learn that Antioch itself is no slouch in spiritual giftedness; Antioch also has its prophets (13:1).

[104]Greek: ἀποστείλαντες πρὸς τοὺς πρεσβυτέρους.

church.[105] Whereas James and the elders do work with the apostles in the Jerusalem Conference,[106] by the time Paul arrives in Jerusalem at the end of the third missionary journey, James and the elders alone meet with him (21:18). At this point, the silence on the apostles is deafening after the incredibly crucial leadership role they play at the beginning of the story.

Summary of Ethos Development

Luke has structured Acts such that characterization is an important ingredient to the development of the plot, in terms of characterizing both individuals and groups. The first half of Acts is focused on Peter and the Jewish mission. The second half is focused on Saul-Paul and the gentile mission. The gentile mission is built upon the foundation of the mission of the Jerusalem church, but Antioch is a crucial component to that story. Luke has set up the characterization of the Jerusalem church as a foil for presenting the difference in Antioch's ethos that shifts the center of gravity for the gospel's mission impulse from its early origins in Jerusalem to Antioch.

Jerusalem's ethos is both positive and negative in the Gospel and in Acts. In the Gospel, she represents the heritage of the faith of Israel. The characters in the early part of the story are faithful and righteous Israelites. Jesus is born to those who in their humility represent the best of Israel's hopes and aspirations. Yet, even with such a promising beginning, the story turns dark, and Jerusalem becomes central to that darker part of the story. Jesus's message was rejected, and eventually he was crucified in Jerusalem. As a result, absent any intervention, Jerusalem's destiny is judgment.

In Acts, the discussion here is focused on the church. Jerusalem's positive ethos is as the place of the church's formal launch on her mission of witness. The Pentecost event that opens up the Acts narrative after preliminaries in chapter 1 shows God fulfilling the eschatological

---

[105]This reality is explicit in Luke's statement at the Jerusalem Conference in Acts 15:22 that the decision of the conference was sent out by the "elders and the apostles" (τοῖς ἀποστόλοις καὶ τοῖς πρεσβυτέροις).

[106]Acts 15:2, 4, 6; careful reading, however, reveals that James, not Peter, is the one who summarizes and concludes the discussion, makes the definitive pronouncement of the conference decision, and authorizes the notification letter to be sent out with Jerusalem representatives (15:13–21).

promise for God's people to which the annual Pentecost feast pointed. The Jerusalem church is the center of that fulfillment. As interpreter of this fulfillment, Peter is the premier example of the original heart and mind of Jesus's life and ministry in Peter's preaching and healing.

Jerusalem's negative ethos is revealed several ways, but primarily in the infamous story of Ananias and Sapphira, the constant after-the-fact attempts to "validate" gospel expansion among unacceptable social groups after the Spirit already has taken the initiative, preaching the gospel exclusively to Jews, and the Jerusalem Conference. Ananias and Sapphira illustrate the seriousness of opposing God, both within the church and for the Sanhedrin. In the Acts narrative, Jerusalem never initiates gospel expansion to non-Jews. The typical Jerusalem response when the Spirit moves the gospel to non-Jews is either passivity or remonstrance. In fact, Peter's action with Cornelius, for which he was censured by Jerusalem, is the beginning of the slow erosion of apostolic authority in the inner leadership circles of the church in Jerusalem. A new group of "elders" appears in the Jerusalem church exerting a controlling influence. The Jerusalem Conference is the crisis of the Jerusalem church's resistance to the Spirit's actions in moving the gospel outward to non-Jews, a judgment disaster with echoes of Ananias and Sapphira, but barely averted.

Luke basically has identified Antioch's ethos with the Hellenist movement in the early church. This movement is the key point at which the gospel moves outward to non-Jews led by Hellenist leaders such as Philip, Stephen, and Saul of Tarsus. The nerve center of this movement never was Jerusalem. Antioch would become the surrogate home base for this movement after men of Cyprus and Cyrene began reaching the Hellenist populations in Antioch's synagogues in significant numbers. Barnabas, a native of Cyprus, is a key figure providing a Jerusalem connection to this ministry. Finally, positive characteristics are evoked in the narrative about the Antiochene church. Not only does the text highlight that disciples first were called Christians at Antioch, but also that the Antioch church reveals a distinctive responsiveness and social benevolence in reaction to a prophetic announcement of a famine crisis in Judea.

ANTIOCH: ETHOS AS PARADIGM

The discussion in the previous sections has attempted to lay the foundation for understanding that Luke intended to present the church at Antioch as a paradigm, the intratextual hermeneutic of being labeled "Christian." Regardless whether the epitaph was pejorative originally, Luke assigned an ethos to the term "Christian" that was tied to the ethos of a city and, more particularly, to the ethos of the developing church in that city. The purpose for this section is to provide a descriptive silhouette of the Antiochene church profile generated from the previous sections. Such a project could be difficult, because the nuances of Luke's narrative are complex and can be viewed from any number of angles. The delimited interest here, though, is to tease out characteristics in the ethos of the Antiochene church.

Three characteristics stand out in the narrative for this purpose: (1) discipleship emphasis, (2) mission initiative, and (3) social inclusiveness.[107] For Luke the key issue in Antioch's spiritual identity is in the dynamic balance among these three through the energizing role of the Spirit.

Discipleship Emphasis

Core relationships within the community of faith include discipleship and conflict management. The narrative that develops discipleship as an Antioch characteristic can be traced in the call of Saul of Tarsus and the subsequent threading together of this story with the existing story of Barnabas. Basically, without Barnabas, Saul's story would have been dramatically different.

Barnabas is first met at the conclusion to the story of Pentecost. This feast setting interprets the outpouring of God's Spirit as the fulfillment of the promise of Joel related to the last days and Jewish traditions surrounding the agricultural harvest festival (2:16–21). Pentecost was a celebration of God's deliverance of Israel from Egypt and the subsequent entry into the promise land with its abundant harvest. In Luke's narrative in Acts, Barnabas becomes the symbolic bearer of Pentecost's promise fulfilled. That is, Barnabas's character is developed as Pentecost facilitator in Israel. He sells his property and

---

[107]Others could be listed, of course, but these three seem to be fairly dominant.

makes a gracious contribution to the church in Jerusalem to enact Pentecost harvest abundance (4:34–37).

The full harvest to come, however, is not restricted to Israel. The Pentecost harvest includes the nations. Barnabas facilitates the key figure in that story, Saul of Tarsus, by introducing Saul to the Jerusalem church just when that church was about to reject the very one who was chosen by God (9:26–28). Saul would be the central character for implementing the light to the nations theme of Simeon's prophecy about the Christ child out of Luke's nativity narrative in the Gospel (Luke 2:30–32).

With regard to this light to the nations theme in Acts that establishes the profile of Barnabas's relationship to Saul, one can observe that any group or individual that aligns against God in this matter will induce God to act in judgment. That is, one crucial opposition God will not abide and that reveals a lack of Spirit vitality is the intent to limit the full preaching of the gospel to the nations. Indeed, a "full gospel" in Acts has nothing to do with the residual effects of the Spirit, such as speaking in tongues. In Acts, a "full gospel" is one that is preached without delimitation to any group—tongues or no tongues. Any church that hides a subtle racism or would exclude socially any group from the church's responsibility to engage the world and to apply the gospel in redemptive action is not a healthy church, no matter how large the church budget or how many multiple worship services are proffered for tickling the fancy of a preferred worship modality.

Barnabas later becomes Pentecost facilitator outside Jerusalem in his ambassadorial role in Antioch after the Spirit has begun moving there among gentiles. Barnabas retrieves Saul from Cilicia for the work of discipleship in Antioch for an entire year (11:25–26). Once again, in the impetus to mission activity, the Spirit singles out Barnabas and Saul for what commonly is called the first missionary journey (13:2). Barnabas is the leader of this team, at least at the beginning, even though this status does seem to change after Cyprus.[108]

That is, Luke has indicated that the first order of business for the spiritually vivacious church is a solid discipleship foundation that has a

---

[108]In customary usage in the ancient world, the leader of the group always is named first, accommodating proper social conventions. Notice that the team is referred to as just Paul and his companions by 13:13.

clear focus on the nations. Before presenting any of the missionary work of the Antioch church, Luke has woven the story of Saul into the story of Barnabas, who is Pentecost facilitator. In Saul's case, this facilitating role meant engaging a discipleship that developed a missionary leader who would become the paragon of Simeon's light to the gentiles (Luke 2:32). From this observation one could infer that mission is a derivative *outflow* of discipleship—hence, the first missionary journey comes *after* the year of discipleship among gentiles in Antioch.

Luke did not indicate the specific nature of this discipleship between Barnabas and Saul. Whether the exact profile of the Jerusalem pattern given in Acts 2:42–47 should be inferred at Antioch is possible but debatable. This description of the early Jerusalem church in Acts 2 has broad Pentecost allusions and resonates again in Acts 4:32–37. The second passage is set up in order to introduce the key figure of Barnabas. Since Barnabas also is the central figure in the early period of the church in Antioch, one might speculate that the Jerusalem pattern would be repeated at Antioch. Although the narrative is not clear about the matter, the assumption has a few difficulties.

One difficulty is the absence in Antioch of the Jerusalem temple setting, which is crucial to the Jerusalem context, along with a related Pentecost festival. This temple setting is precisely the one component that renders the Jerusalem scene distinctive, if not unique—and certainly completely Jewish.[109] The early church had not yet made the break with the temple-centric focus of traditional Judaism for which Stephen, a Hellenist leader, lost his life by criticizing.[110] Antioch simply did not

---

[109]The early church's focus is centered on temple activity. Cf. Acts 2:36; 3:1; 5:20, 42. The summary in 5:42 is key: "Every day, both in the temple and at home they did not cease teaching and proclaiming Jesus as the Messiah," πᾶσάν τε ἡμέραν ἐν τῷ ἱερῷ καὶ κατ᾽ οἶκον οὐκ ἐπαύοντο διδάσκοντες καὶ εὐαγγελιζόμενοι τὸν χριστὸν Ἰησοῦν.

[110]A fervent temple movement is witnessed even today in Jerusalem. The Temple Institute, established in 1988 by Rabbi Israel Ariel, has produced a beautiful, richly illustrated publication with large folios on the temple and its service, personnel, and ritual. The introduction has these remarks: "A huge number of thoroughly researched paintings and scaled-to-size gold and silver reproductions of temple vessels, instruments and vestments are on display at the Temple Institute in Jerusalem, and may be viewed by the public. These amazing works of art have been fashioned by accomplished, contemporary craftsmen. They patiently await the day when priests will take them and ascend the Temple Mount to perform the sacred service in the Holy Temple of God, as in days of old." Ariel and Richman, *Holy Temple*, v.

have the centering force of one singular institution like the Jewish temple in Jerusalem religiously or socially, and the impact of the removal of this factor from the religious/social matrix at Antioch is hard to calculate. Antioch gave rise to a more Hellenized Judaism.[111] The synagogue was the primary centering institution for the Jewish population at Antioch—precisely the reason for the immediate outward thrust of the gospel to the gentiles in Antioch due to their strong presence in the Antiochene synagogues.

A second difficulty is whether the shared-life experience in the earliest Jewish church could be sustained outside Jerusalem, or even over time in Jerusalem. No indication exists in Acts that the shared life of the early Jerusalem church was emulated anywhere else, whether by the Petrine or Pauline missions. Luke's point, however, was still made. With this shared life, the symbol of Pentecost fulfilled was established, and that symbolism is all the mileage Luke probably intended to get out of the description in 2:42–47 and 4:32–37 in his narrative. Further, we should keep in mind that the shared-life experience was in association with the disciples still gathering and worshipping in the temple.

A third difficulty for assuming Jerusalem's religious experience and its style of discipleship simply would be replicated in Antioch is the pre-Jerusalem Conference setting of this "all things in common"[112] description that is so overplayed in attempts to provide a critique of the contemporary church. Such a critique depends upon caricature, an over-idealized, superficial description of the Jerusalem church that today's church should emulate or be shamed against. "All things in common"—indeed—as long as one was a Jew! We should not doubt that the meals shared in Jerusalem's homes at that time were completely kosher—gentiles not invited. Even Peter himself had to have a heavenly vision repeated *no less than three times* about this very issue before he was shaken up enough to be ready to accept an invitation into Corne-

---

[111]Not to say that Jerusalem did not have its own Hellenizing influences, just that the degree of Hellenization in Antioch was greater. We should note the "synagogue of the Freedmen," ἐκ τῆς συναγωγῆς τῆς λεγομένης Λιβερτίνων, in Acts 6:9. See Hengel, *Judaism and Hellenism*, 1:236–37; Ferguson, *Backgrounds*, 550–51.

[112]Acts 2:44, εἶχον ἅπαντα κοινά.

lius's home (Acts 10:9–16).[113] The evidence provided in previous discussion of the discomfort of the Jerusalem church with Peter's actions should be kept in mind.

Mission Initiative

The inevitable outflow of discipleship is mission, and Antioch is the premier paradigm of mission in Acts. Luke makes a decided point to say that the first time any church launches on a specific mission effort, this impetus is centered at Antioch, not Jerusalem. This mission locus in the Antioch church is in stark contrast to the total lack of any such mission from the Jerusalem church. Antioch seemed predisposed to mission as a result of its distinct social and cultural mix as a city in the Roman empire. Thus, those identified with the ethos of this city more easily grasped the significance of the prophetic theme of light to the gentiles from Isaiah. This theme is announced early in the Gospel of Luke by the prophet Simeon with the baby Jesus in his hands: "a light of revelation to the gentiles."[114] God's desire to take the gospel to the nations on the basis of faith in Christ alone found a quicker hearing among the Hellenists in Antioch. The first missionary journey Luke uses to play out this reality in the life of the Antioch church.

An important ingredient to this development of mission in the Antioch church is at the leadership of the Spirit. Luke makes this point rather explicitly in Acts 13:2: "While they were worshiping the Lord and fasting, the Holy Spirit said, 'Set apart for me Barnabas and Saul for the work to which I have called them.'"[115] This word of commission by the Spirit has been working among the Hellenists for quite some time in Acts, ever since Philip was sent off on the road to Gaza to meet the Ethiopian eunuch (Acts 8:26). Luke seems to suggest that once the Hellenist movement was forced out of Jerusalem due to the persecution following Stephen's martyrdom and reached Antioch, the movement had found its home, its ethos. So, in Antioch the movement took root,

---

[113] Although not a part of the Acts text, one almost cannot help but here to think about the serious problem Peter presented to Paul by withdrawing table fellowship from gentiles believers after "men from James" came to Antioch. Cf. Gal 2:11–21.

[114] Luke 2:32, φῶς εἰς ἀποκάλυψιν ἐθνῶν. Resonates with Isa 42:6; 49:6.

[115] Greek: Λειτουργούντων δὲ αὐτῶν τῷ κυρίῳ καὶ νηστευόντων εἶπεν τὸ πνεῦμα τὸ ἅγιον· ἀφορίσατε δή μοι τὸν Βαρναβᾶν καὶ Σαῦλον εἰς τὸ ἔργον ὃ προσκέκλημαι αὐτούς.

strengthened in its discipleship by famous teachers such as Barnabas, Saul, Simeon, Lucius, and Manaen (Acts 8:4; 13:1). For Luke, Antioch is a fork in the road.

Social Inclusiveness

The mission initiative was founded on another prominent part of the Antiochene profile, social inclusiveness. After all, the Hellenist leader Philip was the one willing to take the gospel to Samaria to preach the Messiah to the despised Samaritans, not any of the other leaders from Jerusalem (Acts 8:5). Philip also was the leader willing to baptize an Ethiopian eunuch (Acts 8:38). These episodes are described by Luke precisely because they are his initial narrative soundings that build up implicitly the Hellenist ethos of social inclusiveness. Add to this narrative characterization the dramatic story of Saul on the road to Damascus and learn that he is commissioned by Jesus himself "to bring my name before gentiles" (Acts 9:15), then the Hellenist profile of social inclusiveness is all but a done deal for the reader of Acts.

The reason for this social profile is, again, probably the result of the history of Antioch. This city always was intended as a bastion of Hellenism, settled with Greeks by Seleucus I and strategically located on the Orontes river. This character was not lost even when Rome eventually enveloped the city into its empire system. Jews early in this history also settled here, and their synagogues were infused with this strong cultural and social mix. Primed and ready, the city was a fertile place for Hellenists preaching a gospel unhindered by ethnic distinctions and social exclusiveness.

Summary of Ethos Development

Luke's characterization of Antioch as an ethos of discipleship is built upon the narrative development of the relationship of Barnabas as Pentecost facilitator and Saul of Tarsus. Further, Saul's discipleship by Barnabas in the long run is in service of reaching the nations. This overarching "light for the gentiles" theme in carried all the way from the beginning of Luke on into Acts. While Luke infers that mission is the natural outflow of this discipleship, he does not provide the details of its content. The Jerusalem pattern, however, is not replicated in the more Hellenized and less temple-centric Jesus movement in Antioch.

Thus, Antioch, not Jerusalem, is where this story of mission inevitably was to be told. Luke's point about Antioch's ethos is that the Hellenist movement in the early church, which took root in Antioch, not in Jerusalem per se, brought light to the gentiles. This mission initiative then is played out in the narrative by the Hellenist leaders, Barnabas and Saul, who are commissioned by the Spirit on the first missionary journey, and the rest is history.

Another crucial profile to the Antioch ethos is social inclusiveness. This characteristic comports with the very essence of Antioch from its foundation as a Hellenistic city by the Hellenizing generals that followed upon the empire built by Alexander the Great. Settled by Greeks with a strong Jewish incursion early on, the city grew to one of the great cities of the Roman empire and distinguished itself as a social melting pot. Because the Hellenist movement in early Christianity took root here, the city also became a vibrant center of Christianity. Some of our great post-apostolic writers, such as the famous martyr Ignatius, hailed from Antioch.

CONCLUSION

Antioch's history shows the familiar profile of a typical Hellenistic city of the ancient world, but this history also has distinctive elements that shaped the development of early Christianity. As a dynamic city intersecting multiple trade routes with extensive trade contacts, Antioch always provided a bustling market with significant commercial diversity as well as a strong social identity as a city of origin. Another distinctive element of Antioch's profile was the strong Jewish presence from the very inception of the city. The large Jewish quarter meant that Antioch's pagan population would have significant and continual exposure to the Jewish religion and the Jewish way of life. This exposure would have its greatest impact through the institution of the synagogue. Gentiles either strongly attracted to the Jewish faith ("God-fearers") or else converted to the Jewish faith (proselytes) would have had a background in worship and Scripture upon which Antiochene leaders such as Barnabas, Saul, Simeon, Lucius, and Manaen could convert the converts. These disciples would have continued to attempt to function within the synagogue setting, and the pagan population, at least initially, would have understood them as another Jewish sect under the synagogue umbrella. Historical developments, however, rapidly would have driven those disciples into a status disassociated with the synagogue, perhaps within a few decades. The social matrix of persecution would have become a dominant factor impacting these developments.

Luke used insinuated corporate ethos in his narrative to define Antioch as a city of origin for believers as distinct from Jerusalem. Luke achieved this ethos by way of contrast. He showed Jerusalem's ethos with both positive and negative elements that were targeted for putting into bold relief the profile at Antioch. Luke particularly used the negative elements of Jerusalem's ethos for this contrast. The stories that build this negative Jerusalem ethos include Ananias and Sapphira, attempts to "validate" gospel expansion to non-Jews after the Spirit already has moved preemptively to achieve gospel expansion, preaching exclusively to Jews only, and the Jerusalem Conference.

The positive ethos in this contrast is the creation of the profile of Antioch. The Hellenist movement in the early church was forced out of Jerusalem but took root in Antioch. The movement's full ethos on display in Antioch encapsulates this profile. A discipleship that leads to mission is fundamental, pervaded by a social inclusiveness that is as natural as breathing air. Within this movement no internal struggle ever was witnessed in opposition to the outward thrust of the gospel to gentiles. Further, Antioch was ground zero when the Spirit moved to initiate intentional missionary impulse. For this reason, disciples first were called "Christians" at Antioch. Their city was their identity.

All the principal characters on the stage, all the epoch events in the drama, and all the significant actions in the plot are in concord with this ethos. Further, this entire narrative of the Hellenist movement and its characters is prefaced, provoked, and prospered by the Spirit. As far as the construction of the narrative in Acts, the future of the church is in Antioch, not Jerusalem. We should avoid singing the song of poor Alfred in *My Fair Lady*—not getting to church on time. Antioch, for Luke, is "getting to the church on time," the making of a paradigm of the early Hellenist movement.

3

The Character Saul-Paul

Paul, Jerusalem, and God's Will

COMMENTATORS ON ACTS NORMALLY assume that Luke presented Paul's last visit to Jerusalem as God's will.[1] Literary and narrative analysis, however, can show that this assumption is wrong. We have to be aware of Luke's narrative strategy long before getting to the key texts in Acts 19–21 in order to see how Luke proceeds. Luke's story of Paul's last trip to Jerusalem actually evolves out of two previous narratives: (1) Stephen's speech in Acts 7, and (2) the opening scenes of the second missionary journey in Acts 15:35—16:10. Thus, before ever getting to Acts 19:21, we first must explore the themes of the Stephen speech and then read closely how Luke describes the beginning of the second missionary journey. Our target is how Luke characterizes Paul. These characterizations later will become pertinent to this plotline of the last visit to Jerusalem. After this preliminary research, we are ready for a brief exegetical analysis of the six key passages related to Paul's last visit to Jerusalem and the issue of God's will.[2] Finally, implications of the study for Luke's portrait of Paul will be suggested.

[1] As representative, cf. Haenchen, *Acts,* 591; Bruce, *Acts,* 371, n. 43; Tannehill, *Narrative Unity,* 2:239; Dunn, *Act,* 262; Kee, *To Every Nation Under Heaven,* 233; Fitzmyer, *Acts,* 677; Witherington, III, *Acts,* 588; Bock, *Acts,* 605; Pervo, *Acts,* 482; Keener, *Acts,* 4:3448–49.

[2] Acts 19:21; 20:22–23; 21:4, 11–12; 22:17–21; 23:11.

STEPHEN SPEECH THEMES

The themes of the Stephen speech in Acts 7 provide a nice starting point on a note of agreement. Scholars have shown a fair consensus on the themes of this speech.[3] The length of the speech alone indicates the narrative weight Luke has given to this speech.[4] In content the speech is an overview of Jewish history from the call of Abraham up to Solomon's temple. The purpose is apologetic: to answer the charges brought against Stephen in the Sanhedrin of speaking against Moses and the temple and against God. Verses 7:2–19 set up the themes. The overview of the patriarchal age (7:2–8) introduces the theme of God active outside the Promised Land. This theme in Stephen's narrative summary is played out with God speaking to Abram in Ur, to Joseph in Egypt, and to Moses in Arabia. Stephen thus deftly is able to tease out another "story within the story," an unnoticed gentile narrative that shadows Israel's own: God as active in gentile territory always has been part of Israel's own story. A monotheistic faith inherently proclaims God's claim on all humans. The overview of Israel in Egypt (7:9–19) introduces the theme of God's people opposing God's plans. The theme in Stephen's narrative summary is played out in the rejection of Joseph by his brothers, the rejection of Moses by his fellow Hebrews, and the rejection of Yahweh by the idolatrous Israelites in the desert. In short, this speech provides the profile of the plot for Acts. One can review the narrative development and observe the themes of the Stephen speech being played out all the way through Acts. An overview of the episodes in Acts 1–12 will be provided to illustrate the significance of the Stephen speech themes for plot development.

[3]While expressed variously, the themes are given their clearest portrayal in Bruce, *Acts*, 130–31. Bruce's approach and outline to the speech are followed here.

[4]Luke probably follows the Isocrates tradition of historiography, in which action without interpretation is meaningless. Thus, speeches are important "interpretation" provided by the ancient author to give meaning to the action. Ancient audiences perked up for the speeches. Modern audiences, in stark contrast, go dull in dialogue, thoroughly trained in Hollywood's Peripatetic tradition going for "pleasure," giving action all preeminence. Speeches put us to sleep. All we crave is car chases, explosions, fight scenes (in which the law of gravity no longer applies), and incredible pyrotechnics. Forget the dialogue. You even can have the main character almost never say a full sentence, as for Arnold Schwarzenegger in the classic *Terminator* series. Note that the television mini-series entitled, "A.D.: The Bible Continues," that NBC premiered in 2015 entirely cut out almost all the speeches of Acts. See p. 85, n. 48.

Theme 1: God Active

The positive side of the story line is God's activity outside of the land of promise on behalf of gentiles. This positive, or "bright" side of the plot, is established early in the narrative of Acts in the episodes of prayer and Pentecost in Acts 1–2. Here, a new vision of the people of God of eschatological fulfillment begins to develop within the scriptural reflection of the earliest community of Jesus's disciples. That this new vision of the people of God will involve God's activity outside the land of promise on behalf of gentiles is what we could call the "gentile movement" of the plot. This movement in Acts already is prefigured at least two ways in Acts 1–2. One way is the programmatic command of Jesus in Acts 1:8. This command involves a mission whose outreach proceeds in ever-enlarging circles that inevitably include gentile territories ("and unto the uttermost parts of the earth"). Another way is Pentecost itself, and that in two ways. First, supernatural ability to speak the languages of the world inherently infers a mission to that world as the *raison d'etre* of the miracle. Second, the movement outward also is inferred in Peter's declaration in his Pentecost speech to the Jerusalem inhabitants. Peter indicated that the intended target of eschatological fulfillment of the prophetic word is "and to all those who are far off" (2:39). In the plot development, this statement is proleptic of the plot outward to the gentiles, even if Peter himself is not fully cognizant at Pentecost of the *gentile* implications of this promise.[5]

Ironically, the preparatory stages in Jerusalem foundational to a gentile movement are not within internal developments in the earliest days of the Jerusalem church or its leadership. The Hellenist cycle[6] has to be brought in by Luke at Acts 6 to launch this new stage of the plot.[7] Historically, the Hellenist leadership introduced in the disgruntlement over table service is key to this gentile movement, not the Jerusalem apostles. The Hellenist Stephen provides the controlling themes that drive the plot of Acts in his speech, but he is martyred. The narrative

[5]We allude to the burden for Peter of the Cornelius cycle in Acts 10–11. Even the infancy narrative at the beginning of the Gospel already hints at this element of the plot in Simeon's prophecy: "a light of revelation for the gentiles" (Luke 2:32).

[6]Haenchen, *Acts*, 234.

[7]See the previous chapter for full development of the Hellenist movement.

moves to the Hellenist Philip in Acts 8, whose activity with a Jewish proselyte infers the broadening circle of the church's mission.

The story of Saul then is introduced between narratives of Philip and Peter, involving a proselyte on the one hand and a gentile on the other, as Luke frequently anticipates a major plot character by early introduction, as with Saul, present at Stephen's martyrdom. The story of Saul will embody the very essence of the gentile movement of the plot, as noted in the divine word to Ananias about Saul (9:15: "to bear my name before gentiles"). Literary soundings also echo in the eunuch's question to Philip in 8:37, "what hinders me from being baptized?" and Peter's question to circumcised believers about Cornelius's household in 10:47, "Is anyone able to withhold water from them?" Most importantly, the Damascus Road experience is told precisely in ways that allow the reader to establish parallels with the themes of the Stephen speech. A new vision of the people of God is announced in the message about Jesus, but the zealous Pharisee Saul opposes God's activity violently (cf. 22:3). Saul's opposition is the dark side of the story. Just outside Damascus (that is, outside the Promised Land), however, this zealous Saul has an encounter with the Lord, similar to Abram in Ur, Joseph in Egypt, or Moses in Arabia, that changes the destiny of God's people. Here, close to Damascus in gentile territory is where Saul finds God active, not in Jerusalem (nor the Sanhedrin). The blinding light on the Damascus road is the illuminating light of gentile mission. This aspect is the bright side of the story.

Since Saul and his mission later will be points of controversy for the Jerusalem church, Luke will mold the reader's orientation to Saul by relating the Cornelius episode in Acts 10–11 before launching out on the story of the Pauline mission. In this Cornelius story at the narrative level, Peter's response is twofold to illustrate the two themes of the Stephen speech. Peter's initial response is resistance to God's will (a heavenly voice giving a direct command) concerning what should be counted as "unclean." Peter eventually acquiesces. Peter's dual response sustains within his own character development the two thematic points of the Stephen speech—God active, God resisted. For the God active theme, two points are made. First, Peter's entrance into the home of a gentile is one small step for an Israelite, but one giant leap for Israel. Second, Peter's positive response to the heavenly vision by extension in the narrative plotline provides the apostolic blessing on Saul's mission.

This blessing assures the reader that the burden of Saul's call and career plays out the heart of Jesus's own intentions in calling the original twelve disciples. Luke's gentile movement involves the divine will, and Saul will become the key figure in that movement.

Theme 2: God Resisted

The sequence of events and speeches in the lame man at the temple episode in Acts 3–4 sets the stage for the eventual rejection of the good news by Jerusalem's leaders, which is the dark theme of God's people resisting God's plans. The church, however, is not immune to this resistance phenomenon, which is played out in microcosm in the story of Ananias and Sapphira. This episode has proven somewhat obscure to interpreters of Acts. At the narrative level, however, the purpose is transparent: this story is intercalated into the events transpiring with the Sanhedrin's rejection of early apostolic preaching of Jesus in Jerusalem. The Sanhedrin has warned Peter not to speak in the name of Jesus (4:21), a warning Peter ignores, which precipitates the Sanhedrin's formal, public rejection of the apostolic message, sealed with a flogging (5:40). The resistance of the Jerusalem religious establishment to God's new activity in Jesus on behalf of God's people is clear. The stoning of Stephen and the persecution by Saul of Tarsus incarnates the Sanhedrin's rejection of the gospel in the narrative (7:57–59; 8:1–3). Saul, brandishing official Sanhedrin letters of seizure, even seeks to extend this resistance to the Diaspora setting of Damascus (9:1–2).

The dark narrative theme actually is explicit in Gamaliel's counsel to the Sanhedrin: "lest we also be found God-fighters" (5:39). This counsel to the council, of course, is loaded with irony. Luke, however, has used the Sanhedrin resistance as foil to present the church's own resistance to God. Precisely for this reason, then, Luke has intercalated the Ananias and Sapphira story about resisting (testing) the Spirit of God (5:9: "to test the Spirit of the Lord") right in the very heart of the Sanhedrin's rejection of Peter's preaching; Luke thus illustrates that not even the church is immune to resisting God. This ominous note will become true not only for the church, but for her most illustrious apostle to the gentiles, Saul of Tarsus. The double irony of Gamaliel's advice (and quite clever on Luke's part) is that Saul did not follow the advice of his own teacher (Acts 22:3), not as a Pharisee fighting the followers of the Way at the beginning of his story in Acts as "Saul," nor as an apostle fighting the will of God toward the end of his story as "Paul."

The reader of Acts is appraised fully of God's will that gentiles be included into the people of God by the end of the Cornelius cycle in Acts 10–11. The doublet nature of the Cornelius story being told two times—once *about* Peter (Acts 10) and once *by* Peter (Acts 11)—itself shows Luke's emphasis and the importance of this gentile movement to plot development.[8] Curious for the reader, then, is the hesitation of some Jerusalem disciples to accept these developments (11:3: "Why do you go to uncircumcised men and eat with them?"). This hesitation, however, is allusive of future plot strategy related to Christian resistance to God's plans.

What is shocking in the conclusion to the Cornelius narrative is the stark juxtaposition by Luke of both a formal statement by the church acknowledging the divine will to include gentiles into the people of God but then blatant disobedience to that very will. In Acts 11:18 the Jerusalem church concludes: "So, therefore, God also has granted repentance unto life unto gentiles." This is clear, and the reader knows the statement conforms not only to the view of the narrator but to the authoritative divine voice of God himself. What more confidence does the reader need? Yet, in the *very next verse*, Luke indicates that those dispersed by the persecution precipitated by Stephen's speech went as far as Phoenicia, Cyprus, and Antioch, but were "not speaking the word to anyone except Jews only" (11:19)! For the reader, after two chapters of hammering home the will of God for gentiles in the Cornelius cycle, this forthright statement is nothing if not blunt and shocking. God's will is known clearly, but violated impudently. Such a juxtaposition of known divine will and blatant disobedience to that will is not the last time Luke will use this narrative strategy in Acts—intimations of Paul insisting on going to Jerusalem.

---

[8]Luke designed the Petrine speeches in Acts to trace this development. From the initial offer of forgiveness at Pentecost alluding to "those who are far off," to this climactic speech to the church on gentile inclusion as the definitive statement of God's will (rephrased in the Jerusalem Conference as a warning, 15:7–11), the reader can mark the successive stages of this narrative development. James's ratification of that will in the Jerusalem Conference (15:19), then, the reader perceives as both anticlimactic and dilatory.

Thus, the reader of Acts by this point in the narrative perceives that the leadership for the gentile mission will have to come from somewhere else besides Jerusalem. So, as is his narrative habit, Luke drops in the geographical notation about "Antioch" in 11:19 preparatory to shifting the center of gravity of the story of God active in the gentile mission from Jerusalem to Antioch. Here in Antioch, "some" among the group of dispersed believers, who are from Cyprus and Cyrene Luke is careful to point out (i.e., not Jerusalem), also preach to the Hellenists (11:20). God's blessings on this effort are emphasized immediately (11:21: "and the hand of the Lord was with them, and a great number believed and turned to the Lord"). The story of the new vision of the people of God will shift from Jerusalem to Antioch for the crucial moments that were to become definitive for the future history of the church. Antioch is where the church's story intersects decisively with Saul's story and the two plots merge into one.

Before Luke proceeds with merging those plots, he has to finish the narrative business regarding target audiences for the message of Jesus in Jerusalem. Jerusalem's crowds have been offered opportunity to respond to the message of Jesus (2:41; 5:14; 6:7). Already decided by now is that the religious leadership represented in the Sanhedrin has definitively rejected the message of Jesus (5:40). What of the political arena? That sphere also will show resistance to God's new activity in Jesus. God is calling forth the people of God to respond to the new vision of the eschatological fulfillment of God's promises to Israel in Jesus. Crucial for catching the narrative significance of the Agrippa story in Acts 12 is the historical background. Many configurations of Jewish expectations for the coming of the kingdom of God in the first century were fundamentally political in character. Even the disciples of Jesus show a rather incredible obtuseness to this issue in their question to the resurrected Jesus at the beginning of Acts in 1:6: "Lord, will you at this time restore the kingdom to Israel?" Jesus's answer, while not explicitly rejecting the formulation, redirects the presuppositions to the question.[9] This political kingdom configuration crops up in Gamaliel's

[9]The kingdom of God not as a political power exerted externally but as a spiritual power exerted internally through the presence of the Spirit within believers generating a witness to the world.

observations to the Sanhedrin about recent disasters with messianic pretenders such as Judas and Theudas (5:36–37).[10]

Herod Agrippa represents the top levels of Jewish society and the authoritative voice of the political sphere in Jerusalem. The story of Agrippa's move against the church in Acts 12, a move intended to kill the sect by decapitating its leadership, was used by Luke to complete the story of the rejection of Jesus within significant strata of Jerusalem's society. The responsibility of witness to Jerusalem at all levels of society and in every arena of power has been fulfilled faithfully by the church by the end of Acts 12. The narrative burden now is to thrust the plot forward in the ever-increasing circles of witness according to reader expectation set up by Acts 1:8.

Below is a graphic depicting the plot development outlined above. Notice the chiasm binding the dark side of the plot development related to issues surrounding Jerusalem's inhabitants and leaders and the Jerusalem church and its leaders.

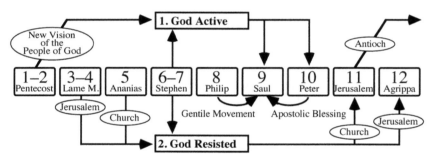

FIGURE 3.1. Acts 1–12: Stephen Speech Themes Driving Plot.

SECOND MISSIONARY JOURNEY

The themes of Luke's Stephen speech in Acts 7 promote plot development in Acts and contribute to the context of Paul's last journey to Jerusalem. Another narrative development in Acts that contextualizes Paul's last trip to Jerusalem is the peculiar beginning to the second

---

[10]At the narrative level, the historical problems of the Theudas reference do not impact plot development, in so far as the illustrative point of false messianic pretenders moves the speech along.

missionary journey. The peculiar nature is partly due to the contrast to the narrative of the beginning of the first missionary journey.

At Antioch, harmony and unity prevail within the church's leadership, and the church flourishes. Saul and Barnabas have worked in Antioch among gentiles successfully for a year (11:26). After this discipleship period, the Spirit then inaugurates the gentile mission as an intentional geographical advance further into the Diaspora through these two leaders. Luke redundantly points out the Spirit's initiative twice within the space of three verses (13:2: "the Holy Spirit said"; 13:4: "having been sent out by the Holy Spirit"). This intentional redundancy makes clear the divine will in the matter for the reader.[11]

The difference between this description of the beginning of the first missionary journey with Luke's description of the beginning of the (so-called) second missionary journey could not be more obvious. First, at the beginning of the (so-called) second missionary journey, the initiative patently is Paul's, not the Spirit (15:36: "Paul said to Barnabas"). Second, the mission team has lost harmony and concord over the issue of John Mark. Paul obviously has interpreted John Mark's departure at Perga on the first missionary journey as an unforgivable defection, quite differently than did Barnabas (15:37–38). Then, Luke is clear, the mission team fragments over this argument, rendering the possibility of the Spirit's blessing remote: "and a fierce disagreement arose so that they separated from one another" (15:39). Notice that in terms of the posture of the Antiochene church, Luke says deftly only that Paul and Silas were "committed to the grace of the Lord by the brothers" (15:40). Such a statement is not anywhere near the ringing divine endorsement of this (so-called) mission as with the sendoff of the first missionary journey. Antioch is noticeably passive this time. What the reader should not miss about Luke's description of the beginning of the (so-called) second missionary journey are multiple narrative motifs about Paul: Paul's initiative, Paul's stubbornness, and Paul's damage by splitting the Antiochene mission team.

That Paul actually is fighting the Spirit is evident in the way Luke characterizes the launching of this new initiative. The major difference

---

[11]In terms of narrative strategy, observe that when Luke wants the reader to understand his reference is to the Spirit in a critical passage, he usually is explicit with the adjective "Holy."

with the first missionary journey is the absence of explicit divine will: Paul simply moves through Syria and Cilicia on his own recognizance. To be sure, Luke indicates Paul's passing through "strengthens" these churches, but this strengthening is because the Jerusalem Conference's positive and affirming decrees are delivered, not anything Paul himself actually is doing mission wise. We must add "so-called" as a descriptor to this second missionary journey because, in fact, no mission strategy is evident, and no divine necessity is guiding the way.

The geography of this part of the trip itself is humorous for the attentive reader. What really happens on this "journey" is that the Spirit *restrains* Paul in almost every direction. First, Paul apparently decides Asia (probably Ephesus) would be a good mission destination. That plan is vetoed by the Spirit explicitly (16:6: "being hindered by the Holy Spirit from speaking the word to Asia").[12] Well, if southwest will not do, Paul conjectures, how about northeast? That is, forbidden by the Spirit to head over to Asia, Paul has another idea, the opposite direction of Bithynia: "they were attempting to enter into Bithynia, but the Spirit of Jesus would not permit them" (16:7).[13] Paul is all over the map, but the Spirit refuses to go along for the ride.

Two points need to be observed about the wording at 16:7. One is the verb tense. The other is an unusual, even unique, phrase. First, the verb "they were attempting" in the Greek is imperfect (*epeirazon*, ἐπείραζον), so the action is durative, which means over and over. What is the inference? Paul is *having an argument with the Spirit over a period of time*, not having a momentary passing thought and then flitting on to something else like a butterfly over a garden. Second, we encounter a most unusual phrase for Luke: instead of the normal "the Holy Spirit," the reader hears "the Spirit of Jesus." This phrasing is unique to the entire corpus of Luke-Acts, and surely should grab the reader's attention. In Paul's story, this name "Jesus" is preeminent for the moment of revelation on the Damascus Road: "I am Jesus whom you are persecuting" (9:5). This personal encounter is significant for the dramatic intensity of Saul's experience; Luke repeats the phrase in both

---

[12]Again, note that Luke makes the matter clear for the reader, using the adjective "Holy" with the noun "Spirit." Clearly, this is God's Spirit, not Paul's inner spirit.

[13]Greek: ἐπείραζον εἰς τὴν Βιθυνίαν πορευθῆναι, καὶ οὐκ εἴασεν αὐτοὺς τὸ πνεῦμα Ἰησοῦ.

of the other accounts of the Damascus Road (22:8; 26:15). Thus, to specify here that the Spirit that Paul is resisting on the (so-called) second missionary journey is not simply the Holy Spirit, but more personally and directly, the *Spirit of Jesus*, suggests that Paul's irreconcilability with Barnabas fracturing the mission team and his ongoing stubbornness now with the Spirit about the direction he should go is at the point of damaging God's very purposes for Paul's call on the Damascus Road ("I am Jesus, whom you are persecuting," 9:5). Suddenly, the advice of Paul's own Pharisaic teacher, Gamaliel, echoes hauntingly across the chapters of Acts: "lest we be found to be God-fighters" (5:39).

Already having completed southern Galatia behind, then denied entrance into Asia, then denied entrance into Bithynia, where can he go? Hemmed in on the left, hemmed in on the right, finished behind, he can go nowhere but follow his nose, meandering forward through

Mysia to Troas between the two "no's" of the Spirit. A song from a long-distant era echoes in the mind for any Beatles fan that seems perfectly descriptive: "He's a real nowhere man, sitting in his nowhere land, making all his nowhere plans for nobody."[14]

FIGURE 3.2. The Second Missionary Journey.

Fortunately, each time Paul gets off track on God's will in Acts, God graciously sends along a vision to pick him back up, dust him off, and send him on his way toward the divine will for his life. Paul's visions in Acts, that is, regularly are rehabilitative. Earlier in the story, while Paul was fighting the disciples of Jesus, the rehabilitative vision was the Damascus Road that redirected Saul toward the gentile mission. Here, as Paul is fighting the Spirit of Jesus about the direction of that gentile mission, the new rehabilitative vision is the Macedonian at Troas redirecting Paul toward the European mission (16:9–10).[15] The Troas vision is when we finally actually begin the second missionary journey in earnest with the Spirit's approval.

[14]John Lennon and Paul McCartney, *Nowhere Man* (London: Capitol Records, 1965).

[15]Significantly, the beginning of the first "we" section in Acts.

We must be sure to note here that Paul *does* get to go to Asia as he had wanted to at this time. He spends nearly three years at Ephesus on the third missionary journey. At that point in the narrative Paul is back on track with the divine will. Luke presents Ephesus as the crown jewel of the Pauline missionary enterprise among the gentiles. That picture of success is no accident. Lukan literary strategy is in play. When the reader learns that the Ephesian mission implodes suddenly, unexpectedly, and catastrophically, the reader should be dying to know why, because everything was so good. This awkward beginning to the second missionary journey with a stubborn Paul is the smoking gun.

PAUL, JERUSALEM, AND GOD'S WILL

The exegetical burden of Luke's perspective on Paul's last journey to Jerusalem is borne by six key texts: Acts 19:21; 20:22–23; 21:4, 11–12; 22:17–21; 23:11. Our purpose is to review these texts in the light of the narrative context provided by the themes of the Stephen speech and the peculiar nature of the beginning of the second missionary journey. Luke moves into this sensitive presentation of Paul's last visit to Jerusalem by carefully setting up the immediate literary context. The narrative antithesis of the Jerusalem disaster is in the outstanding success of the Ephesian mission immediately prior to this trip.

The Ephesian mission is presented by Luke as the crown jewel of the Pauline missionary enterprise. Nowhere else is Paul presented as directly laying on hands with the consequent reception of the Spirit (disciples of John the Baptist, 19:6). Nowhere else does Paul spend so much time or have such a reputation in the surrounding region (19:10). Nowhere else does Luke so emphasize the miracles that Paul personally accomplished that even his very clothing and work cloths are imbued with power (19:11–12). Nowhere else does the world of evil so publicly acknowledge the reputation of Paul as on a level with Jesus: "but the evil spirit answered them, 'I know Jesus, and I know Paul, but who are you?'" (19:15). Nowhere else is such a gospel impact brought to bear that those practicing magical arts foreswear their arts and even burn their textbooks at great economic loss personally (19:19). Then, to slam dunk the point, Luke summarizes: "In this way the word of the Lord with power grew and was strengthened" (19:20). Even an entire guild of artisans is affected by Paul in Ephesus (the reaction of Demetrius and the silversmiths).

Without any doubt, Paul in Ephesus is back on track with the divine will. Luke presents Ephesus as the spiritual apex of the Pauline mission among the gentiles. This presentation is no accident of the Lukan literary strategy. The contrast with what happens in Jerusalem simply could not be more obvious. The question is, how do you fall so rapidly, dizzily spinning down from the heights of such preeminent success to the depths of miserable chaos, confusion, and life-threatening disaster? You make a poor decision contrary to the will of God and stubbornly insist on following through against all the cumulative wisdom of prophets and believers everywhere, including the narrator of the story. You make decisions that make the advice of your own teacher a warning that comes home to roost in your own rafters: "lest we be found to be God-fighters" (5:39). Let us trace this tragic story.

Ephesus: Paul Announces Plans (19:21)

Luke records carefully in Acts 19:21 Paul's announcement of his mission plans. Here is what Luke says from the original Greek text.

> Now after these things had been accomplished, Paul made up his mind to go through Macedonia and Achaia, and then to go on to Jerusalem. He said, "After I have been there, I must also see Rome."

Two observations need to be made. One is bad translation. The other is Luke's style for indicating divine necessity.

Bad Translation Decision

Bad translation has to do first with a grammar issue and then an issue of idiomatic Greek. First, the grammar is significant. The verb that is translated as "resolved" (NRSV, HCSBS), or "purposed" (KJV, NASB), or "decided" (NIV) is *etheto* (ἔθετο), and is *middle voice*. English does not have middle voice, just active and passive. The Greek middle voice is the voice of personal interest. As a work-a-round translation, we can use a reflexive pronoun to get the middle voice idea across in English: Paul resolved "for himself" to go to Jerusalem. With this middle voice, Luke already begins isolating the decision made here as Paul's own.

Second, the idiomatic usage is significant. While the verb's voice already is a clue to Luke's meaning, the entire phrase including "in the spirit" is idiomatic. Louw and Nida indicate that the construction of placing this verb in middle voice followed by the prepositional phrase "in the spirit" is an idiom for "to make up one's mind."[16] Thus, with both (1) middle voice grammar and (2) idiomatic phrasing, Luke has made clear that the decision maker is Paul. The Holy Spirit simply has nothing to do with the decision to go to Jerusalem.

Third, the original Greek text does not distinguish capital and small letters, meaning all the letters are the same. Thus, the decision whether in English translation to capitalize *pneuma* (πνεῦμα) as in "Spirit" or leave in small case as "spirit" *is the decision of the translator.* Yet, rendering the Greek phrase Luke constructs (ἔθετο ὁ Παῦλος ἐν τῷ πνεύματι) as "Paul resolved in the Spirit," violates the idiomatic expression Luke has composed, especially noting the middle voice.

Fourth, not only does this translation violate the idiomatic Greek used here, this translation violates the known style of the author when he wants to indicate the Holy Spirit's involvement. Luke is very clear to indicate the Spirit's involvement carefully in context when needed.[17]

Fifth, the entire weight of the whole narrative in Acts 19–23 is against capitalizing "spirit" in 19:21.[18] Thus, we conclude that English translations that capitalize "Spirit" in Acts 19:21 *prejudice the reader's perspective without grammatical or narrative warrant.* This one truly

---

[16]Louw and Nida, *Greek English Lexicon,* 1:359 (30.76). Louw and Nida inexplicably then add that 19:21 could be reference to the Holy Spirit (1:360), but see next note.

[17]Luke regularly clarifies the divine Spirit's involvement *in strategic mission directives* by adding "Holy"; cf. Acts 13:2, 4. Note that the KJV translators were clear about the sense of 19:21; they left the word "spirit" in small case. Both RSV and NRSV, however, have "Paul resolved in the Spirit" with no note. NEB has "Paul made up his mind," giving due weight to the Greek idiom, but then compromises the clarity of the grammar with the note, "*Or* Paul, led by the Spirit, resolved . . ." NASB has "Paul purposed in the spirit," and a note "Or, *Spirit.*" Both NIV and NET have "Paul decided" with no note. While some English translations, that is, want to suggest Lukan ambiguity on the role of "spirit" in this passage, *the verb's middle voice grammar and the known Greek idiom on decision making are not ambiguous.* Keener's "grammar cannot settle the question either way" is too cautious (*Acts,* 3:2861). Even the venerable Lightfoot concluded the rendering "spirit" (small case), "seems necessary" (*Acts of the Apostles,* 251). Further, later passages on the divine will are clear and warrant the conclusion that Luke judges the 19:21 decision to be Paul's own, without divine approbation (cf. 21:12 with 21:4).

[18]We will indicate this narrative flow shortly.

bad translation decision here sets off track, even destroys, Luke's entire narrative intention about Jerusalem and God's will for Paul.

Luke's Style for Divine Necessity

Second, Luke has a style for indicating divine necessity. His idiomatic verb of divine necessity is *dei* (δεῖ), "it is necessary" or "must." By the time one works though the Gospel and Acts, one sees that Luke uses this verb intentionally at crucial narrative moments to indicate divine necessity. The point here at 19:21 is that *Luke carefully limits the "divine necessity" verb δεῖ to seeing Rome, not going to Jerusalem:* "it is necessary (δεῖ) for me to see Rome also." Luke makes clear the divine necessity is Rome, not Jerusalem. Luke does not use "it is necessary" with the verb that expresses "to go to Jerusalem." Luke is dropping another hint, this time stylistic, about the human nature of the decision to go to Jerusalem.

The absence of the use of the divine necessity verb δεῖ in connection to Jerusalem should red flag commentators that Luke is *not* setting up this trip to Jerusalem by Paul on par with, or even literarily parallel to, the mission of Jesus to Jerusalem. This supposed parallel commentators seem uncontrollably compelled to force upon Luke's narrative.[19] What is ignored here is that Jesus's own decision to go to Jerusalem *is* introduced with the divine necessity verb "it is necessary," but Paul's trip to Jerusalem decidedly is *not*. Jesus moves to his destiny, a Journey to Jerusalem motif of the Gospel at Luke 9:51. Paul's journey to Jerusalem is actually the *narrative antithesis* of Jesus's journey to Jerusalem, that is, *not* God's will.

Miletus: Sermon to Ephesians (20:22–23)

The Ephesian ministry implodes in the very next episode of the silversmiths' riot narrated after Paul announces his mission plans in 19:21. Paul is forced out of Ephesus, so loses his mission base. He winters in Corinth, then moves overland back through Macedonia on his way to Jerusalem. The second "we section" picks up at Philippi and continues

---

[19]*Contra* Parsons, *Acts*, 273–74; Pervo, *Acts*, 482; Dunn, *Acts*, 265; Polhill, *Acts*, 394; Tannehill, *Narrative Unity of Luke-Acts*, 2:239. Other major dissimilarities that have been pointed out include the lack of a death scene for Paul, which is huge, and that the narrative moves on beyond Jerusalem to Rome, which is inexplicable. The narrative continuing on to Rome already is a signal clue that Jerusalem is *not* divine destiny.

all the way to Jerusalem (20:5—21:18), so Luke is eyewitness to this journey and Paul's words and behavior. At the port of Miletus, Paul addresses the Ephesian elders who have come down to him at his request. Here is what Luke says from the original Greek text.

> And now behold, having been bound in the spirit, I am going to Jerusalem, not knowing the things in it that will happen to me, except that the Holy Spirit testifies to me in every city that bonds and tribulations are waiting for me (Acts 20:22–23).

In these words, Paul reiterates his plans for Jerusalem. Again, this passage needs to be read carefully. We make three observations. First, Luke here has another opportunity, if he had so desired, to use the divine necessity verb, "it is necessary," with this expression "to go to Jerusalem," to indicate that the trip to Jerusalem is the divine will. He explicitly does not. This feature is in stark contrast to Luke's persistent use of "it is necessary" whenever Rome is mentioned (19:21; 23:11).

Second, other passages will make clear that Paul's expression, "I have been bound in the spirit," Luke intends as *double entendre*. Several elements indicate this double meaning. One element is style: Luke does *not* use "Holy" to clarify for the reader that the Holy Spirit is meant in Paul's words.[20] In other words, "I have been bound in the spirit" is Paul's own stubborn self-determination that will entangle him in his own yarn like a cat that does not know when to quit. God will have to "tie" Paul up to control him (the irony in the Agabus prophecy). This characterization of Paul parallels the narrative developments at the beginning of the second missionary journey when the Spirit had to hem Paul in geographically, refusing to allow Paul to go where he stubbornly wanted to go. That stubbornness, though significant, was a time from which Paul's purposes could be recovered by the Spirit (Troas vision); more significantly, Luke could use that episode as an ominous sign for future plot developments, as here. Paul's stubbornness now is fatal to Paul's purposes. A final element is narrative: Luke will indicate clearly in the voice of the church (21:4) and of God himself (22:21) that Paul's insistence on going to Jerusalem is against the explicit, communicated will of God to Paul.

---

[20]For this stylistic observation, see notes 11 and 17 and the discussion to follow on 21:4.

Third, at other critical and dangerous junctures of the Pauline mission, Paul has received divine protection. On the first missionary journey he is stoned and left for dead at Lystra, but life returns back to his body, to the amazement of the disciples (14:19–20). On the second missionary journey an earthquake springs Paul and Silas from prison (16:26). Then, in Corinth, a vision of the Lord gave Paul a promise of divine protection for the difficult work in Corinth right before he has to appear before the proconsul Gallio (18:9–10). Notice on this trip to Jerusalem that, instead of divine protection, as on the first and second missionary journeys, and instead of divinely empowered witness with a regional reputation, as at Ephesus on the third missionary journey, Paul now is promised by the Spirit[21] only that "bonds and afflictions" await him, and Paul hears this everywhere ("in every city").

These words of affliction, of course, could be read as the faithful Paul who has a powerful witness, which, Luke points out, is actually Paul's own take on the matter (cf. 20:24). Paul's own characterization of coming events is adopted without question in the commentaries to interpret the Lukan significance of Paul's last trip to Jerusalem. Luke's point, however, is to contradict Paul with explicit statements by the Holy Spirit that Paul is not to go to Jerusalem. Reading Paul's words in 20:24 as an expression of the *divine* perspective is too superficial at the narrative level. Chaos and confusion is more the picture Luke actually presents of future events in Jerusalem, not powerful witness.[22]

Commentators, perhaps misdirected by their reading of 20:24, do not observe that in the entire episode of the disaster in Jerusalem not one story of coming to faith as a result of Paul's words or deeds in Jerusalem is given by Luke. If Paul in Jerusalem is to be characterized as a powerful witness on behalf of the mission to the gentiles in this story, his positive impact in Jerusalem on behalf of that mission at the narrative level is practically zero: no laying on of hands with dramatic reception of the Spirit, no evidentiary miracles of numinous powers, no sounding forth of reputation to surrounding regions, no direct comparisons with Jesus from the lips of the forces of evil, no expensive

[21] Again, Luke is careful when the context could be ambiguous: as Paul's own opinion, just "in the spirit"; for the divine will explicit to and acknowledged by Paul, the addition of the adjective, "the Holy Spirit." Even Paul himself acknowledged the reality of his own spirit in the midst of spiritual activity; as one example, cf. 1 Cor. 14:14.

[22] *Contra* Polhill, *Acts*, 433, n. 105.

book burnings, no threat to entire guilds of local artisans dependent upon idolatrous pagan worship for their livelihoods.

Paul perhaps sincerely *desired* to witness in Jerusalem, almost as if he could bend the city into obedience to Christ by the sheer force of his own will. Yet, the actual description of Paul in 20:24 eerily recalls Saul of Tarsus, zealous Pharisee, stubbornly hunting down believers in Jerusalem, all the while assured for himself he is doing God's will. At Miletus, Luke again emphasizes Paul's own recalcitrance through the admission out of Paul's own mouth: "in every city." Inferred is that Paul is confronted by God over and over, every place he sets foot, but Paul the apostle stubbornly pushes ahead to Jerusalem just as much as did Saul the Pharisee pushing on to Damascus.

Thus, this character in Acts has two names, Saul-Paul, because this character is a complex mix of two antithetical sides: fighting God with profound stubbornness (Saul the Pharisee) and serving God with inspiring commitment (Paul the apostle). What most forget that Luke does not is that, even after the Damascus Road, Paul never stopped having the potential to be Saul. In any case, the narrator himself is not ambiguous on this issue of some supposed Jerusalem ministry of Paul as Paul seems to have envisioned himself having here in the speech at Miletus: Jerusalem (what actually happened when Paul got there) is *not* Ephesus—not even by a long shot, Luke will insist as he describes the disaster that unfolds after Paul arrives in Jerusalem. So, from the point of view of the *whole* narrative of Acts, Paul's opinions in 20:24 clearly have to be taken with a grain of salt.

Tyre: The Spirit's "No" (21:4)

With this passage, all interpretive ambiguity about Jerusalem as God's will is eliminated absolutely. The Spirit directly told Paul *not* to go to Jerusalem. With this divine directive so explicit, any impression that Jerusalem is God's will by a misreading of 19:21 or 20:22–23 has to be abandoned altogether and rethought completely. Here is what Luke writes about the disciples at Tyre warning Paul in 21:4.

> We looked up the disciples and stayed there for seven days.
> Which ones through the Spirit told Paul not to go to Jerusalem.

The text simply could not be more simple, straightforward, or unambiguous. The stumbling of commentators down the stairwell of exegesis here is awkward. This text is unambiguous: the Spirit said "no" to Paul's desire to go to Jerusalem. While the point is clear even in English translation, we are forced to emphasize several points of exegesis because commentators simply stick their fingers in their ears here.

First, note Luke's grammar. The verb "they were saying" (*elegon*, ἔλεγον) has a *plural* subject and *imperfect* tense. This plural subject makes absolutely clear that the singular "through the Spirit" is the Holy Spirit, not an individual person's own human spirit, a grammatical clarity obviating any need for the adjective "Holy," as is Luke's normal literary pattern to indicate God's Spirit when the sense of "spirit" might be ambiguous in the context. On the imperfect tense, imperfect action is durative. Durative action implies a successive sequence of multiple statements, or on multiple occasions. The disciples were having to try to communicate this divine will *over and over*. The inference? Someone must disagree. That someone? Paul, of course.

Second, the "not to go" is the unambiguous divine command to Paul and is *left uncorrected by the narrator*. Thus, the 21:4 narrative positions Paul's intransigent insistence on going to Jerusalem not only as stubborn, but clearly rebellious and out of God's will. Further, the verb itself is vivid and forceful, more like "not set foot in,"[23] making the point even more transparent. The text is plain. Commentators are not.

The problem is whether 19:21 or 21:4 is the crux of this matter. Which is the tail and which is the dog? Commentators encountering 19:21 first and misreading as the Spirit's directive to Jerusalem simply cannot abide the incredibly explicit indication in 21:4 to the contrary. Bruce is startlingly blunt:

> It should not be concluded that his determination to go on was disobedience to the guidance of the Spirit of God; it was under constraint of that Spirit that he was bound for Jerusalem with such determination (19:21; 20:22). It was natural that his friends who by the prophetic spirit were able to foresee his tribulation and imprisonment should try to dissuade him from going on . . .[24]

To begin with, these comments by Bruce have nothing to do with the narrative Luke actually wrote. Bruce would urge the reader to understand these prophets as Paul's "friends" would "dissuade" Paul—*so the*

[23]Noted by Lightfoot, *Acts of the Apostles*, 269.
[24]Bruce, *Acts*, 398. Keener, *Acts*, 3:2861, similarly is controlled by 19:21, not 21:4.

supposed prophecy is not true prophecy, just an attempt at psychological manipulation. Such dissimulation would be narratively incongruous (out of character) for prophets and prophecy in Luke-Acts.[25] Further, Bruce confuscates what the text plainly says the prophets actually foresaw: *not* Bruce's disingenuous gloss ("tribulation and imprisonment") of which *this* text says nothing, but precisely that Paul should "not go to Jerusalem." Clearly, Bruce is fighting the plain sense of the text with such tendentious comments totally extraneous to the actual narrative.

Fitzmyer is simply contradictory on the matter. Commenting on 19:21, he wrote: "'put (it) in his spirit/mind,' which uses the middle voice of *tithenai* to indicate that it is a question of Paul's own *pneuma*. It does not mean, 'he purposed in the Spirit,' as Bruce (*Acts*, 393) renders it; nor does it mean that Paul decides 'under guidance of the Spirit,' *pace* Marshall (*Acts*, 312)."[26] Contradicting this insistence that the decision to go to Jerusalem is Paul's at 19:21, however, Fitzmyer later wrote concerning 20:22: "'bound in the spirit,' which could mean 'constrained in (my own) spirit,' but more likely means 'influenced by the (Holy) Spirit,' because elsewhere Luke has described Paul's missionary activity as guided by God's Spirit (13:2, 4, 9; 16:6–7; 19:21). Now Paul views his journey toward his city of destiny, Jerusalem, as imposed by God's Spirit."[27] Such remarks are just plain contradictory statements. Further, at the crux verse under discussion here, 21:4, Fitzmyer, like Bruce, dissimulates the literal message of the Tyrian prophets to Paul as about "his coming troubles"; but such a remark completely obfuscates the actual message of the Spirit-filled Tyrian disciples: In truth, they warned Paul *not* about his "troubles" but *explicitly* "not to go" to Jerusalem![28]

This obfuscating approach to the clear message of 21:4 is the chosen tactic of other commentators. One also sees such an approach in Kee, for example, in his comments at this crucial verse; note as well that pointing to coming troubles in Jerusalem is Keener's tactic too.[29]

More forthright with the text is Dunn. Dunn, however, is just as confused because of misreading 19:21.

[25]Polhill also took this psychologizing "natural reaction" approach, *Acts*, 433.

[26]Fitzmyer, *Acts*, 652.

[27]Ibid., 677.

[28]Ibid., 688.

[29]Kee, *To Every Nation Under Heaven*, 246; Keener, *Acts*, 3:3083.

One of the most striking features of the section is the confusion within the narrative as to what God's will for Paul actually was. Somewhat surprisingly, Luke has no hesitation in ascribing the prophecy telling Paul not to go to Jerusalem (21.4) to the Spirit, and apparently no qualms in presenting Paul as one who disregarded a clear-cut command of the Spirit (21.13–14; contrast 16.6–7)! Whether Luke saw any tension or even contradiction with 19.21 we cannot tell, although it could be significant that he does not repeat the reassurance of 19.21 at 21.13. On the other hand, *Luke surely cannot have thought or intended his readers to understand that Paul went on up to Jerusalem in defiance of the Spirit!*[30]

But really, *why not*? Even Tannehill observed, "Nevertheless, it is interesting that the narrator has allowed to surface at least a superficial contradiction in the divine guidance that Paul is receiving."[31] A true curiosity to ask is, Why are interpreters of Acts so reticent to admit what Luke's narrative so plainly indicates?[32] In going to Jerusalem, Paul stubbornly disobeyed the will of the Spirit! Acts 19:21 versus 21:4 thus becomes the great stumbling block of commentators that derails grasping the whole point of Acts 20–28 and the narrative exigency of detailing the voyage to Rome—few pondering even for a moment why Luke would spend nearly two whole chapters on this one voyage.

Note that Luke's characterization of Paul at 21:4 is entirely consistent. Saul-Paul's stubbornness is a clear character trait. Characterization even *begins* with stubborn Saul, persecutor of the church. After the Damascus Road we *still* have stubborn Paul of the opening scenes of the second missionary journey. He fights Barnabas. He fractures the mission team. He fights the Spirit over where to go. The Spirit has to tie him up, hem him in geographically at Troas. A rehabilitative vision relaunches the Spirit-led gentile mission. So, development of the Saul-Paul character sets the stage for development of the plot in Acts 19–23. As at Troas, Paul's stubborn insistence on going to Jerusalem will require another rehabilitative vision in Jerusalem (23:11).

[30]Dunn, *Acts*, 280–81; emphasis added. So also Keener, *Acts*, 3:3081–83.

[31]Tannehill, *The Narrative Unity of Luke-Acts*, 2:263. Tannehill must circumscribe his comment with "at least a superficial" because he already has decided that 19:21 is an indication the trip to Jerusalem is the Spirit's will, not Paul's decision.

[32]Centuries of aggrandizement as *the* apostle to gentiles? Or, Paul is untouchable to criticize since Scripture derives from his pen? Pure speculation, but one wonders.

Witherington offered three possibilities for understanding Luke in this passage: (1) that *dia*, δία, could be used in an occasional sense (on an occasion of prophesying, some offered their opinion Paul should not go); (2) that Luke was attempting to conform prophecies about Paul to the pattern of earlier prophecies about Jesus; (3) that New Testament prophecy was distinct from the "Thus, says the Lord" definitive, absolute nature of Old Testament prophecy, in that New Testament prophecy was of a character as to require Christians to sift through even the prophecies of true prophets.[33] After supplying reasons for passing on the first two, Witherington opted for the third. However, this option will not do. The option simply begs the question. Even if we grant Witherington's characterization of the nature of New Testament prophecy, what *explicit narrative indication* do we have here, before, or after this passage that Luke wanted his readers to conclude that these Tyrian prophets, while true Christian prophets, were *wrong* in this case? No other Christian prophecy in the entire narrative of Acts was falsified by the narrative! Why should the reader suddenly jump to that conclusion here? That option simply is nonsense within the narrative of Acts.

Caesarea: Agabus's Prophecy (21:11–12)

Paul and company have sailed down to Caesarea, the city where prophecy is strong (the point about Philip's four daughters, 21:9). They stay at Philip's house, one of the Seven Hellenist leaders, Luke says pointedly (21:8). These leaders were introduced in Acts 6, which is the beginning of the entire Hellenist cycle in Acts, which encapsulates the movement to gentiles. The Hellenist movement has run full circle. Luke is asking the attentive reader to think about the whole point of Acts since Acts 6. Paul's insistence on going to Jerusalem will jeopardize that point.

A prophet speaks a prophecy to Paul. Not just any prophet. Old Agabus himself, the prophet who was so correct that he possibly saved the Jerusalem church from starvation due to famine (11:28). This guy has a proven track record, and Paul himself was a part of a delegation faithfully responding to his prophecy about famine (11:30). Paul had better listen again this time. Here is what Agabus did and said.

[33]Witherington, *Acts*, 630–31.

> And coming to us and taking Paul's belt, after binding his own feet and hands with it, he said, "Thus says the Holy Spirit, 'The man whose belt this is, thusly the Jews in Jerusalem will bind and will deliver him over to the hands of the gentiles.'"

This is the text in which the "we" participant personally becomes involved in the business of discouraging Paul's trip to Jerusalem. This first-person involvement is an important narrative signal; whatever the source of the "we section" materials, they have authoritative function in the narrative.[34] At the rhetorical level, Witherington captured the significance: "What is striking about the entire section is that Luke is perfectly willing to portray a deep difference of opinion between equally sincere Christian groups (even between 'we' and Paul or more notably between 'we' and God's will) on an important matter."[35]

In this text the prophet Agabus reiterates the Spirit's warning. Four observations need to be made. First, the expression "Thus says" is a deliberate Septuagintalism, that is, echoing the Greek Old Testament language read by most Jews of the first century, including Paul. The allusion is to prophetic *judgment* contexts, usually negative. This judgment context can be seen in many passages.[36]

Second, Agabus's use of the impersonal form of address in "The man" is *confrontational* in prophetic contexts. The most obvious illustration is Nathan's daring confrontation of David: "You are the man!" (2 Sam 12:7, LXX). This mode of address emphasizes the hubris that has set human behavior off course from God's will. Observe how this

---

[34]Portraying the "we sections" as simply bringing verisimilitude and drama to the narrative ignores the literary function of the claims made by the author in the prologue (Luke 1:1–4). Also, asserting that the "we" narrator is not omniscient and shares the limited insight of Paul's companions (Tannehill, *The Narrative Unity of Luke-Acts*, 264, n. 5) begs the point: *the narrator does not have to be omniscient to be authoritative*; this too ignores the literary function of asseveration of accuracy of the sources used in composing the document.

[35]Witherington, *Acts*, 631, n. 291.

[36]This phrasing is the traditional *tade legei* (τάδε λέγει), "thus says" to introduce a word of the Lord. Examples include Judg 2:1; 6:8; Exod 4:22; 5:1, 10; 7:17; 2 Sam 12:7 (Nathan's daring public exposure of David, "You are the man!"); 1 Kgs 21:19 (bold judgment of Ahab); Amos, *passim*; Mic 2:3; Obad 1:1; Hag 2:6; Zech 1:4 and throughout; Isa 1:24; Jer 4:27; Ezek 2:4 (note the problem concerns being "impudent" and "stubborn"); 3:11 (specifically note the vacillation of "hear" or "refuse to hear") and throughout the text.

mode of address distances the character so addressed from honorable messenger status or divinely commissioned act.

Third, the statement, "But as we heard these things, we and the people there begged him not to go up to Jerusalem" (21:12) is positively loaded with narrative freight. Numerous points set the significance. One point is that the narrator resurfaces in the first-person style, a device which catches the reader's attention to provide authoritative weight to the opinion expressed. Another point is the rhetoric: rather than subordinated participles, two indicative verbs and a compound subject together serve to intensify the exhortation to Paul. No ambiguity or vacillation adheres to the opinion given or to lessen the narrative impact. A final point ignored by many commentators is that the opinion given by the narrator himself *lines up with the express will of the Spirit in 21:4* through deliberate repetition of the wording of the Spirit's command, "that he should not go to Jerusalem." When Luke wants to emphasize, he will repeat. Since this is a "we section" of the narrative, the text is clear: Luke himself[37] argued with Paul *against* going to Jerusalem. Would the narrator align himself so openly and blatantly against the Holy Spirit by arguing that Paul *not* go to Jerusalem if the Spirit had actually intended that Paul go to Jerusalem?

Finally, one cannot help but to hear in the response of those in Caesarea an echo of the response of Antiochene believers frustrated, even bewildered, by Paul's stubborn spirit against Barnabas at the beginning of the second missionary journey, when all the Antiochenes could do after the fracture of the mission team was to commend Paul and his group to the grace of the Lord (15:40: "being commended to the grace of the Lord by the brothers"). A haunting pathos is heard in the final words by disciples at Caesarea, including Luke and Paul's many other companions, when confronted by the same stubbornness: "May the grace of the Lord be with you!" (21:14). Luke here deliberately evokes the beginning of the second missionary journey, because the Pauline characterizations of stubbornness are parallel.

Jerusalem: Paul's Temple Vision (22:17–21)

This passage bears the same narrative weight of the explicit, unequivocal divine "no" to Paul at Tyre in 21:4. Paul now is in Jerusalem. The

---

[37]Or the "we" narrator; the point is the same.

only result is disaster for James and the Jerusalem church and for Paul and the gentile mission. No one gets saved. No sermons are preached. No miracles are performed. No jails are miraculously opened. No demons are exorcised. No magicians have a bonfire of their magical books. Instead, we have chaos, confusion, riot, and murderous mobs. How's that for a mission trip? Jerusalem—what a fall from Ephesus!

In the midst of addressing the murderous mob in Jerusalem, Paul admits to having a vision in the Jerusalem temple itself. The reader of Acts never has heard of this vision before now, even though the vision happened to Paul many years ago immediately after the Damascus Road vision. Paul actually had had two visions in a row. Why did Luke delay revealing that Paul had had this second vision after the Damascus Road while in the Jerusalem temple? Cool narrative strategy. Great writer. Here is Paul's own account from his own lips.

> "After I had returned to Jerusalem and while I was praying in the temple, I fell into a trance and saw Jesus saying to me, 'Make haste and get out of Jerusalem quickly, because they will not accept your testimony about me.' And I said, 'Lord, they themselves know that in every synagogue I imprisoned and beat those who believed in you. And while the blood of your witness Stephen was shed, I myself was standing by, approving and keeping the coats of those who killed him.' Then he said to me, 'Go, for I will send you far away to the gentiles.'"

Luke uses intentional narrative delay for dramatic impact. This is Saul's vision in the temple in Jerusalem close on the heels of the Damascus Road experience. Now, in Acts 22, the reader learns that the Spirit *already had communicated to Saul* that his witness would not be accepted in Jerusalem, so his presence in that city would be nothing but problematic, so consistently undesirable in terms of mission strategy. Luke does not narrate the vision until now during this last trip of Paul to Jerusalem to provide sharp narrative relief to the words of the Spirit to Saul at that time that would interpret decisively the Spirit's counsel to Saul about Saul's relationship to Jerusalem. Saul's reaction at that time, stubbornness about the revelation, is parallel to Paul's reaction now, stubbornness about the Spirit's revelation.

In that temple vision years ago, God's word to Saul was: "Make haste and get out quickly from Jerusalem!" God's reason is blunt and forthright: "because they will not receive your testimony concerning me." Luke time-delays telling the vision as a brilliant narrative move: a way to tell the reader that God's word to Saul *then*, in fact is God's word to Paul *now*. Paul had that word directly from God already in a vision long ago. The reason never changed. That temple vision means that *all his ministry Paul knew that God did not want him in Jerusalem*. Thus, insisting on going to Jerusalem from Ephesus is a deliberate act of rebellion by Paul—even without the express command not to go from the Tyrian disciples in 21:4. Paul *already knew* he was not supposed to go to Jerusalem. Instead, we find him stubbornly insisting he knows better than God what is good for his ministry.

Significantly, Luke's characterization of Saul-Paul never changes. In that earlier episode with God in the temple, Saul argued with God (!) that the value of his testimony had been underestimated by God, since his testimony was so dramatic: "Lord, they themselves know that in every synagogue I imprisoned and beat those who believed in you. And while the blood of your witness Stephen was shed, I myself was standing by, approving and keeping the coats of those who killed him" (22:19–20). God, however, remains unimpressed by this argument born of a stubborn spirit, and still commands unequivocally: "Go!" This "Go!" is God's definitive word to Paul about Jerusalem in Acts.

Brilliantly situated within this later literary setting, this vision's stark irony is apparent in the reason God gave then: "for I will send you far away to the gentiles" (22:21). Luke brings home the narrative value of mysteriously restricting the divine necessity "it is necessary" to Rome back at 19:21. The narrative value of God's will for Paul invested in the words "far away to the gentiles" in the temple vision long ago now is cashed in by the reader for its equivalent narrative currency—Rome—producing extraordinary dramatic tension in the narrative. The tension exists because the reader knows Paul should not be in Jerusalem, and is out of God's will by stubbornly insisting on going, for whatever reasons Paul himself may have thought justified his fighting the Spirit on this. Paul should be in Rome, not Jerusalem. Saul-Paul's character does not change: he argues with God. He argued with God about the "heretical" followers of Jesus before the Damascus Road; he argued with God about the command to leave Jerusalem that he received in the temple vision soon after the Damascus Road; he argued with God about the direction of the mission at the beginning of the second missionary journey; and now, completely in character, he argued with God about going to Jerusalem, to the point of total meltdown of his ministry.

Jerusalem: Paul's Antonia Vision (23:11)

Luke takes another opportunity to make clear what is God's will for Paul. That will would be Rome. Paul's divine date with destiny always has been Rome, not Jerusalem. The reader of Acts can take this observation to the bank: Every time Paul has a vision in Acts except the two that affirm his safety, Paul is off track from the divine will (think Damascus Road, temple vision, Troas vision). Like the Troas vision got Paul back on track on the second missionary journey after the fight with Barnabas, this Antonia vision reported in one verse assures Paul of his destiny in Rome, in spite of the present circumstances.

> That very night the Lord stood near him and said, "Keep up your courage! For as you have testified for me in Jerusalem, so you must bear witness also in Rome."

In this text God speaks a word of grace to Paul. Paul needs this word of grace because Paul is off track again. This word, therefore, functions in a manner parallel to the Troas vision during the crisis of mission (mis)direction at the beginning of the (so-called) second missionary journey. Back then, Paul was seriously off course from God's will because of his fight with Barnabas. The literary pattern then is parallel to the literary pattern now in the Jerusalem crisis. Paul in Jerusalem is seriously off course from God's will.

Once again, Luke is keen to the irony of the divine word: "for as you have testified the things concerning me." This expression rhetorically is tongue-in-cheek. God does not say "you have testified." He says, "as you have testified." The "as" indicates the *condition* in which Paul has testified, not the *fact* that Paul has testified. What condition is this? Chains. Imprisonment. That is how Paul will testify in Rome. In Roman custody. In other words, *God will not intervene* like he did at Philippi on the second missionary journey causing an earthquake that opens the prison in which Paul and Silas are locked away. *God will not intervene* like he did at Corinth causing the governor of the province to throw the case out of court. In stark contrast to Corinth, Felix, the governor of Judea, will detain Paul in custody for *two years*. Luke will be contrasting this two years in Caesarea with the two years in Ephesus for the attentive reader (19:10).

The irony of "as you have testified" also leans on the word "testified." Testified? That is a joke. All Paul has done is created a riot! The Jerusalem context is total chaos. Again, be careful to note that no one gets saved, no miracles are performed, and Paul's reputation does not resound in all the surrounding districts as at Ephesus: "so that all the inhabitants in Asia heard the word of the Lord Jesus, both Jews and Greeks" (19:10). Again, we do not hear anything of a reputation like in Ephesus on the order of: "and fear fell on them all, and the name of the Lord Jesus was magnified" (19:17). In other words, the contrast with Ephesus—the Pauline missionary crown jewel that imploded on him when this ill-advised trip to Jerusalem at Paul's behest was announced (19:21)—could not be more stark.

After this classic double entendre of "as you have testified," Luke for the second time then gives the divine necessity over Paul's life that God will accomplish by his sovereign power: "so you must bear witness also in Rome." This is where Paul should be now. He is not, but he will be. God will get Paul to Rome in spite of Paul. Thus, Luke repeats the divine mission destiny of Rome clearly spelled out in 19:21 in the Antonia vision briefly reported in 23:11. The plot, though, has thickened extraordinarily due to the extraordinary stubbornness of the apostle to the gentiles. How God will get Paul out of this pickle is a story still to be told in Acts.

The very nature of Paul's complex character in Acts is thematic because this character illustrates *both* themes of the Stephen speech at the same time in one person: God active, God resisted. Indeed, this Saul-Paul character drives the plot in the second half of Acts precisely because his own ministry fulfills the themes of the Stephen speech.

CONCLUSIONS

We draw conclusions of this narrative analysis by way of summarizing the discussion. We then venture to suggest Luke's narrative strategy.

- Luke is blunt that Jerusalem was *not* God's will for Paul. The evidence of 21:4 on this issue is unimpeachable.

- Any explicit statement that Jerusalem is God's will is only from the mouth of Paul himself—and Paul continually is contradicted on this point by the Spirit all the way to Jerusalem ("in every city," 20:23), even by Luke himself (21:12).

- Luke's divine necessity verb, "it is necessary," Luke never used with Jerusalem, only with Rome (19:21; 23:11).

- Luke carefully balances Paul's insistence ("determined," 19:21) with the determined opposition of the Spirit ("they were saying," 21:4).

- What the Spirit *does* explicitly say about Jerusalem to Paul always is negative, even including a prophetic judgment, with no immediate promise of protection, rather of bonds and affliction.

- In a brilliant literary move, Luke shows the reader Paul's earlier temple vision in time-delayed sequence to be unambiguous about where the problem with Paul in Jerusalem always will lie—Paul's own stubborn will against a hardened audience, a sure guarantee of a tender box ready for conflagration.

- The point of documenting Paul's troubles at the beginning of the second missionary journey is Luke's literary anticipation of the plot to develop in the Jerusalem fiasco, for the Pauline characterizations are exactly the same.

- The themes of the Stephen speech find their most stunning yet tragic illustration in all of Acts in the life of Paul himself, the dark side most poignantly in this last trip to Jerusalem.

- Luke never indicates *why* Paul is going to Jerusalem.

We have intentionally restricted our comments to the narrative in Acts, not using Pauline correspondence. Our desire was to focus on Luke's narrative strategy and plot development, which is not advanced by appeal to Paul. Appealing to the Pauline correspondence is tempting because some of the material closely dovetails this material at the historical level.

However, if we do allow ourselves to shift to the historical level to include Paul's own indications, especially the Corinthian and Roman correspondence, we might venture to speculate why Luke is so persistently silent on ever giving the reason why Paul is going to Jerusalem, outside of one oblique reference in terms of Felix's corruption looking for a bribe from Paul in 24:17. Paul in Acts is driven so incessantly, even against all advice and the Spirit's instruction, that he simply bulls his way past everyone, God included, on his way to Jerusalem. But *why* is he going to Jerusalem?

To deliver the collection we learn from his correspondence (Rom 15:16, 25–28). Paul's correspondence makes clear that he has attached huge symbolic significance to the collection for Jerusalem that he has pulled together over some time from all his gentile churches. He invests this collection with the entire meaning of his mission to the gentiles and Jerusalem's full acceptance of that law-free mission and those churches.

In fact, the company of Paul's entourage on this trip to Jerusalem absolutely explodes without any explanation in Acts 20:4: "And he was accompanied by Sopater of Berea, the son of Pyrrhus, and by Aristarchus and Secundus of the Thessalonians, and Gaius of Derbe, and Timothy, and Tychicus and Trophimus of Asia." No more room is left to cram one more person onto the elevator going down to Jerusalem. An inquisitive mind asks, "Who are all these people and why are they suddenly going with Paul to Jerusalem?" Luke does not say a word. If we analyze the list, we notice representatives from all three missionary journey locales, yet Luke leaves not a clue why they are now on board. An obvious conclusion lying close at hand is that these individuals are representatives of the Pauline churches that comprise the collection offering Paul intends to deliver with symbolic fanfare to Jerusalem.

With this historical curiosity of the collection so prominently pushed by Paul in his letters and so persistently unmentioned by Luke in Acts in mind, we might venture to synthesize Luke and Paul. So, Paul is going to Jerusalem because he insists on accompanying the collection to Jerusalem personally. When we keep in mind that this unit of material is a "we section" in Acts in which Luke is an eyewitness, then Luke's different perspective on the matter is instructive. Along these lines, Luke appears to have drawn two conclusions about Paul's last trip to Jerusalem. For Luke this trip by Paul was:

- an *unintended detour* in the divine itinerary west to Rome from Ephesus

- an *unfortunate decision* in the matter of the collection on Paul's part that destroyed its intended symbolic impact

That is, by the deft handling of this last trip to Jerusalem, with its dual perspectives in the will of Paul and the will of the Spirit, Luke wanted to shield as best he could Paul's most brilliant idea, the collection, from the shame of Paul's most baneful idea, that he personally should deliver that collection to Jerusalem. The end result of that insistence on Paul's part was an unmitigated disaster for Paul and for the church. In terms of narrative strategy, Luke wanted to present Paul not only as "hero" but also as the preeminent paradigm of the Stephen speech themes: while God always has been active outside the land of promise on behalf of gentiles, the story of Paul's mission to gentiles, God's people characteristically have resisted God's plans, the story of Paul's misery in Jerusalem. This negative, dark side to the story of the early church and its Hellenist movement, even with its most illustrious apostle, Luke does not avoid telling.[38]

The longest speech in Acts by the Hellenist Stephen in Acts 7 justifies its protracted length because this speech provides the profile for this tragic plot development with Paul toward the end of Acts. The reader of Acts never should forget that the main character throughout the narrative is really the consistent and complex layering of a two-fold reality. He is Saul-Paul.[39]

[38]The argument of this chapter totally rejects the fundamental mischaracterization of Rapsky, *Paul in Roman Custody*, 403–11. Rapsky's collective comments on the six crucial texts discussed above demonstrate he misses entirely Luke's narrative character development of Paul. Patently obvious is his plea-bargaining against the clear evidence of Acts 21:4. Rapsky completely *reverses* what the text literally says, showing he would rather impugn the character of the Tyrian disciples than that of Paul. He suggests that these Tyrian disciples either (1) misunderstood the Spirit's communication, or (2) actually dared to counsel disobedience on Paul's part (p. 408)! Those are astonishing comments, simply because the actual text Luke wrote in 21:4 *explicitly says the opposite: the Tyrian disciples spoke through the Spirit, and Paul disobeyed.*

[39]Parallel to the distinctive dual character of the entire composition as Luke-Acts.

PART 2

Narrative Analysis 1

The Spirit Empowers Messianic Israel
(Acts 1–12)

4

Renewal Beginnings

Messiah and His Disciples (Acts 1)

T HE LITERARY DESIGN OF LUKE'S WORK shows in its macro structure
parallels between the life of Jesus and the life of the early church.
The overarching rubric is the kingdom of God, but reinterpreted in
light of the new revelation Jesus brings as Israel's promised Messiah. In
the large scheme, the Gospel of Luke is what Jesus began to do, the story

FIGURE 4.1. Literary Design of Luke's Two-Volume Work.

of Jesus, part one, his life and ministry. Luke's infancy narrative shows the nurturing activity of the Holy Spirit initiating and empowering this story from within the heart of Jewish faith and its expectation of a coming Messiah, the hope of Israel. One can note how the public ministry of Jesus is launched by a descent of the Holy Spirit at his baptism. This ministry will send Jesus to Jerusalem, where he fulfills his divine destiny and dies for the forgiveness of sins. The Gospel of Luke ends with Jesus being resurrected and ascending to heaven.

FIGURE 4.2. The Descent of the Spirit. Luke parallels the life of Jesus and the life of the early church.

In fact, though, this last chapter of the Gospel is not the end of Luke's literary design. Luke writes to extend the gospel genre. He continues his story into another volume. Thus, the book of Acts is what Jesus continued to do, the story of Jesus, part two, the church and its mission. A brief upper room vignette, in parallel to the story of Jesus, part one, again will show the Holy Spirit initiating and empowering this new stage of the story from within the very heart of Jesus's faithful followers. This upper room group is messianic Israel waiting on its cue.

Again, parallel to the life of Jesus, the church's public ministry is launched by its own empowering baptism of the Holy Spirit. This Spirit baptism John the Baptist had anticipated Israel would need to become the eschatological people of God. From this crucial experience, the church's ministry will send the church out into world mission, and on to Rome, where, as Luke tells the story, the church will fulfill its divine destiny, as did Jesus in Jerusalem.

Thus, when we jump into the text of Acts, we already are in the middle of a story. Even had we not read the Gospel of Luke first, we would know immediately we were in the middle of a story at the beginning of Acts, because the prologue to this new volume we had just picked up is resumptive. We already have suggested this prologue ties back to the Gospel of Luke. A resumptive prologue thus infers literary purposes and narrative themes carry over from Luke to Acts, even on the grand scale of the literary macro structure as outlined above.

PROLOGUE

In the brief prologue to Acts, Luke capitalizes on his gains in the first part known as the Gospel of Luke. His Acts prologue builds a bridge backwards to the earlier volume and forward to this new volume.

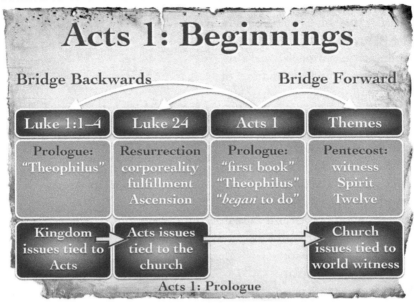

FIGURE 4.3. Acts Prologue: Building Bridges.

Bridge Backwards

Bridge Backwards to the Beginning (Luke 1–2)

Luke builds a bridge backwards to the beginning of the Gospel of Luke in its prologue and infancy narrative because he insists the Christian movement is sourced in Jewish faith and Scripture. Luke builds a literary bridge back to the prologue with multiple connections. He mentions his patron again, Theophilus. He also alludes to his "first book," meaning he intended Acts the moment he wrote the first verse of Luke. He expresses his Greek carefully by nuancing the verb tense "all that Jesus *began* to do," which clearly infers the story of Jesus is not finished. What he relates in Acts is what Jesus continued to do.

Luke builds a bridge backwards to the infancy narrative with kingdom issues. The kingdom issues at the beginning of Luke in the infancy narrative are tied to Acts. So, when mention is made in Luke 1:32 of the "throne of his father, David," that issue is still on the table. These are kingdom issues and arguments about legitimate Jewish roots of Christian faith. The issue will be whether to capitulate to national Israel's re-definition of the look and feel of that kingdom when eschatological. Indeed, is this kingdom like the kingdoms of this world—military, armies, wars, conquest? Is Messiah of the end times another Judas Maccabees of our times?

FIGURE 4.4. Antiochus IV Coin. Zeus seated, holding Nike and scepter. Judas Maccabees successfully revolted against the Syrian king Antiochus IV (HAM).

Kingdom issues also raise questions of politics. The Jews just had fought a bitter war with Rome, one of the worst rebellions the Romans ever had to put down. If Luke is so adamant that this new Christian movement has its origins in Jewish faith, then he has a political hot potato in his hands in a post-AD 70 environment. He will have to defuse the issue by showing that while the Christians have "another king, Jesus,"[1] their faith is innocent of in-

FIGURE 4.5. Arch of Titus Relief. Temple items paraded in Rome after defeating the Jews in a bitter, costly war.

surrection designs. Thus, Acts has a pervasive political apologetic in the way Luke portrays interaction with Roman officials. Paul will convert a Roman proconsul on the island of Cyprus, and the proconsul at Corinth summarily will throw his case out of court.

---

[1] As Paul was charged at Thessalonica (Acts 17:7).

One way to litmus test eschatological kingdom ideas in Israel is to mention gentiles.[2] The prophetic spirit included gentiles integrally in messianic Israel. That spirit is why emphasis is placed on Simeon's Spirit-inspired word of prophecy about the impact of the child Jesus: "light for revelation to the gentiles" (Luke 2:32). This prophecy for Luke meant the inevitability of the gentile mission. The Spirit was going to work with that part of messianic Israel ready to strike out on the road to gentiles. That road will be Saul's storyline.

Bridge Backwards to the Ending (Luke 24)

Luke also bridges back to the ending of the Gospel in Luke 24. The post-resurrection setting allows Jesus to demonstrate his corporeality, an important part of conceptualizing resurrection doctrine. Luke also emphasizes fulfillment of Jewish Scripture and concludes with a story no other Gospel preserves, the ascension.

Scriptural fulfillment circulates around several ideas when Acts 1 and Luke 24 are read together. One idea is the meaning of Jesus's death as forgiveness, seen in Luke 24:25–27, 44–46 and Acts 1:3. Another idea is repentance, seen in Luke 24:47 and Acts 1:5. Luke summarizes these two together: "And that repentance and forgiveness of sins is to be proclaimed in his name to all nations, beginning from Jerusalem" (Luke 24:47). Another idea is Spirit-filled witness, seen in Luke 24:48–49 and Acts 1:4–8. This idea is expressed as a promise of future power: "You are witnesses of these things. And see, I am sending upon you what my Father promised; so stay here in the city until you have been clothed with power from on high" (Luke 24:48–49). Thus, Scripture fulfillment is not just about the life and ministry of Jesus only but will continue to play out in the band of followers of Jesus, which ecourages disciples to interpret community events with Scripture. Jesus's own summarizing words of Scripture fulfillment are clear in Luke 24:44–46:

> Then he said to them, "These are my words that I spoke to you while I was still with you—that everything written about me in the law of Moses, the prophets, and the psalms must be fulfilled." Then he opened their minds to understand the Scriptures, and he said to them, "Thus it is written that the Messiah is to sufffer and to rise from the dead on the third day."

[2] The moment Paul did so in Jerusalem, he incited a riot (Acts 22:21–23).

Bridge Forwards

Acts 1 not only is a bridge backwards to the beginning and end of the Gospel, this chapter also is a bridge forwards to Acts itself. Luke builds his story in chapter 1 with themes of witness, Spirit, and the Twelve.

Witness Theme

The witness theme builds the case for the church's commission. This commission is what the church is charged with doing post ascension. The job description is transparent. The Gospel already had concluded with the declaration, "You are witnesses of these things" (Luke 24:48). The famous Acts 1:8 passage ties the bow on this theme for Acts.

Spirit Theme

The Spirit theme is ministry empowerment. This empowerment is the effective enabling of the witness commission. Jesus had promised, "And see, I am sending upon you what my Father promised; so stay here in the city until you have been clothed with power from on high" (Luke 24:49). This promise is repeated in Acts 1:4–8. Waiting on the fulfillment of this promise is Pentecost preparation.

Often observed is that the central character of all of Luke-Acts is God. The entire narrative across both books is both initiated and driven by God. While true, the Spirit is God manifest. Luke's language, then, defaults to Spirit when God's presence is perceived in a powerful way. Thus, while Pentecost is understood as the Spirit descending, this language simply is Luke's way of speaking of God's personal, powerful presence. Only Jesus's resurrection and ascension releases such a transforming presence into human experience. This divine power belongs to Messiah alone. Never before in the history of God's people had such a corporate power ever been available from heaven. Pentecostal power is what vivifies and identifies the messianic people of God.

The Twelve Theme

The Twelve theme is Israel's destiny. This destiny is to realize messianic Israel. Messiah's job is to transform Israel. Through death, resurrection, ascension, and Pentecost, Messiah is renewing Israel. Those baptized into Messiah are baptized into messianic Israel. They live by the power of the Spirit.

Historically, Israel always has been identified with the number twelve. This identification is the natural result of the patriarch Israel having twelve sons. These sons established the traditional twelve tribes who occupied the land of promise and became a nation. Thus, when Judas is described as having been "allotted" his part in Acts 1:17 (*lanchanō*, λαγχάνω), this verb alludes to receiving a special place, taking an office. Since Judas abandons his "ministry and apostleship" (Acts 1:25), this vacated position cannot be ignored. Something symbolic is lost. What is lost is the sign of the Israel of God. That sign requires the symbolic number of twelve. Thus, his place must be taken by another, particularly an eyewitness. This election to the Twelve is Acts 1:14–26.

The story of the replacement of Judas is not told in any other Gospel. However, the story is crucial for Luke. Among Gospel writers, only Luke purposes to show that the story of Jesus becomes the story of the church. Since Jesus is Messiah, and confessed to be so in the Christian rite of baptism, then the question of what group do the followers of Jesus constitute, Luke gives the definitive answer in the replacement of Judas episode—the Israel of God renewed by God's Messiah into the eschatological, messianic Israel, the Israel the prophets anticipated for the future kingdom of God. This messianic Israel is, for Luke, a new vision of the people of God. We always wondered what exactly the prophets were speaking about. Now we know.

MESSIAH

After the brief resumptive prologue in Acts 1:1–2, which bridges together Luke and Acts and their symbiotic themes, Luke then moves to situate the reader's understanding of Jesus as the Messiah. If the Jews themselves had trouble understanding Messiah with their own Scriptures as background, then the task for the typical Greco-Roman reader is formidable. One key marker to identify about this group is that this novel Jewish sect is a messianic movement. Thus, after the prologue, Luke immediately turns attention to the person of Jesus the Messiah. Then, he will shift gears smoothly to the band of Messiah's followers.

Forty Days (1:3)

The significance of the forty days is the reconstitution of Israel as the Israel defined by Messiah. Jesus interprets Scripture, not the Pharisees with their oral traditions confuscating Moses, or the Sadducees with their collusion with Rome that has perverted Israel as a nation. The passion and resurrection define the salvation of Israel for which the prophet Simeon had waited in Jerusalem (Luke 2:30). Luke is making clear that kingdom issues are in the process of being transformed by Messiah. The full implications of this transformation will not be immediately apparent. Even after the forty days, the disciples will insist on asking about Israel framed in nationalistic terms (Acts 1:6). Those nationalistic terms would be the default understanding of a Greco-Roman reader as well in the post-AD 70 years.

The corporeality of resurrection is important to Luke. We see him emphasizing this matter both at the end of his Gospel (the Emmaus disciples, Luke 24:39–43) and again at the beginning of Acts (Acts 1:3). This doctrine is foundational to Christian belief, and integral to the story of Acts. Resurrection is core to Saul's experience and his message. When Saul asked who was addressing him on the Damascus Road and

FIGURE 4.6. Jewish Ossuary from Jerusalem. After a body has desiccated, the bones are placed into an ossuary (burial box). This practice was popular in Judea from about 40 BC–AD 135.

was told, "I am Jesus" (Acts 9:5), his hard drive crashed. Resurrection was an end times event in Jewish thinking. Resurrection as part of the now times turns this worldview upside down. Further, Paul refuses to surrender this corporeal doctrine to Greek philosophical sensibilities, such as in speaking to the Athenians, and claims that he is on trial for this doctrine in the Sanhedrin.[3]

Regarding resurrection, the corporeality of Jesus is given ample demonstration ("presented himself alive to them by many convincing proofs"). These proofs will set up an understanding of the doctrine of resurrection that will pervade the speeches of Acts. Resurrection doctrine presented multiple times in the Acts narrative will differentiate theologically the followers of Jesus from other major philosophies of the first-century world.

[3] Athenian philosophers (Areopagus), Acts 17:32; Sanhedrin, 24:21.

Commission (1:4-8)

This passage emphasizes Spirit, kingdom, and witness. Witness is the commission of the church. Spirit is the power of that commission. Finally, how this commission relates to the kingdom of God has to be negotiated, because kingdom language would be a sore spot for many who experienced or were impacted by the Judean war with Rome.

The Spirit

The early Christian movement did not have as clear a hierarchy as in Roman military and provincial systems. A Greco-Roman reader might wonder how such an organization got on with its mission. How did anything get accomplished? Who set the agenda? Luke wants his readers to understand that this movement is Spirit directed and Spirit driven. Oddly enough, in this community, one suddenly could find oneself traveling down a desert road to Gaza not knowing the intended destination or duty. Such stories communicate how dynamic is this organization. Whence this dynamism?

Luke answers with the promise of the Father. This promise Luke repeats in this unit from the ending of the Gospel. In the very next chapter, we learn that this promise is the effluence of the Spirit. This Spirit outpouring will transform messianic Israel into an altogether different corporate reality than the Israel identified by Sanhedrin and synagogue as the people of God. This reality is the eschatological "baptism" promised by John the Baptist and now coming soon (Luke 3:16; Acts 1:5). The power of the Jesus movement is not in its leaders; the power is in its Spirit. Wherever the Spirit is, there is Messiah's Israel.

The Kingdom

Kingdom issues relate to the fog of confusion that continued to swirl around the minds of the disciples even after the resurrection and the forty days of teaching on the kingdom by Jesus. When one grows up with a particular understanding thoroughly reinforced by society and its institutions, being disabused of that (mis)understanding takes time. The major perversion of kingdom the disciples had to grapple is the equation of national interests with God's, an equation that took centuries to put in place after the exile, and an equation that drove Judea to rebel. The Maccabean revolt and subsequent Hasmonean and Herodian dynasties permanently perverted understanding the relationship of kingdom and Israel. Israel was conceived primarily as a national entity tied to temple as an institution and land as a birthright. Even when Jesus drew near Jerusalem, his disciples thought the kingdom of God magically would appear (Luke 19:11). Asking about "restoring the kingdom to Israel" is still presuming rather obtusely this post-exilic, pre-passion national Israel was the Israel God had in mind. Jesus, however, brings the messianic Israel God always intended.

The Commission

In the text, Jesus responds to the disciples question about Israel and the kingdom with a commission, almost as if he did not hear the question. In his answer, Jesus's silence on national Israel is deafening. The problem with the disciples' question is, the presumption is wrong. God *is* restoring the kingdom to Israel. What constitutes the Israel for which Messiah died and the kingdom this Israel is to realize on earth is gospel witness and advance to the "uttermost parts of the earth." "Uttermost parts of the earth" pretty much sounds like a kingdom if you just think about the idea for a moment. The present corporate manifestation of this gospel kingdom is the church. In a way, Jesus told Israel to get with the program, and the program is Acts 1:8.

Gospel witness long had been anticipated by Jesus far back in his ministry. In Luke's "Journey to Jerusalem" section, Jesus already had promised his disciples, "When they bring you before the synagogues, the rulers, and the authorities, do not worry about how you are to defend yourselves or what you are to say; for the Holy Spirit will teach you at that very hour what you ought to say" (Luke 12:11–12). This promise is not as much anticipating something in the life of disciples at that moment as anticipating the story in Acts. This promise in Luke 12 anticipates Peter and John being hauled before the Sanhedrin after healing the lame man in Acts 5, or Stephen defending Jesus before the Sanhedrin in Acts 7, or Saul before the Sanhedrin in the fateful return to Jerusalem in Acts 23, or Paul standing in Gallio's tribunal at Corinth in Acts 18, or before Felix, or Festus, or Agrippa II in Caesarea, or even potentially before Caesar himself in Rome at the end of Acts. In all these powerful stories of gospel witness and advance, the kingdom is being restored to Israel—the kingdom Messiah died to establish. Whatever else the kingdom of God involves is not the prerogative of disciples to know. The commission is clear, definitive, and exclusive.

Ascension (1:9–11)

The ascension is told as a doublet in both Luke 24:51 and Acts 1:9. What is the literary function of this doublet? The Gospel ascension story links back in that narrative context to the resurrection. The Acts ascension story links forward in that narrative context to the Pentecost event. In this creative narrative structure of a doublet, the ascension theologically joins in one seamless movement the resurrection and the outpouring of the Spirit. Without the resurrection and ascension of Jesus, no full outpouring of the Spirit would be possible. The doublet ascension stories together communicate that both resurrection and ascension are essential to what takes place at Pentecost. Thus, with the close sequence of resurrection, ascension, and Pentecost, something has happened in Israel regarding the Spirit that never had been possible for Israel before. In this unique process, Pentecost

FIGURE 4.7. Ascension of Jesus. No matter how an artist might conceive the ascension, for Luke the theological implications for the church are crucial to grasp.

post resurrection will transform the Israel of God. Messiah is renewing Israel by the promise of the Father, another transfiguration miracle in the story of Jesus, only this time corporate—messianic Israel.

The ascension is told as a theophany, with the standard feature of a cloud as a visible token of divinity. The ascension formally marks the end of the incarnation. That end is important. Limitations upon Jesus such as space and time are transcended. In his incarnation, Jesus could be in only one place at one time. Such a limitation no longer applies, a crucial consequence for empowerment of world mission.

This ascension also circumscribes the witness commission just delivered to certify that Jesus's commission is a heavenly mandate, not just a suggestion to consider possibly doing. The ascension ties church witness to the process of Jesus's glorification, so the ascension is only a *beginning stage* of Jesus's glorification. Believers might miss the Lukan connection between ascension and Pentecost. The role of the church is involved. If Jesus ascends to heaven to be in his glorified state, but his Spirit then descends from heaven onto the church at Pentecost, then the church becomes the locus of the present glorification of Jesus. That is to say, Jesus's glory in heaven is tied to the church's action on earth. Thus, if the church's destiny is world mission, that mission and Jesus's glory are one and the same. By reason of the ascension, Jesus is omnipresent to the church along the roads to Gaza, Damascus, Antioch, or Rome, and also glorified along those very roads. In effect, Luke sets up three stages of glorification, one in the Gospel (transfiguration, Luke 9:28–36), one in Acts (ascension), and one anticipated (Jesus's return, Acts 1:11). The return of Jesus, however, in as much as Luke has integrated that return into the stories of ascension and Pentecost, is the proper punctuation mark concluding the present glorification of Jesus through gospel witness. In between ascension and return is the church, and they all work together. Ascension, church, return: here is the kingdom of God for those who are looking. Whereas kingdom issues are tied to Acts, Luke will continue to hammer home by way of building literary bridges that Acts issues are tied to the church.

DISCIPLES

After presenting Messiah's post-resurrection activity, which is getting his disciples ready for transformation into messianic Israel, Luke turns attention to Messiah's disciples themselves, specifically their preparation for Pentecost. Pentecost preparation involves upper room prayer and the replacement of Judas.

Upper Room (1:12–14)

The upper room is a brief narrative that plays out Luke's emphasis on prayer. The setting is preparatory to Pentecost. Three groups are indicated: Jesus's disciples, Jesus's family, and the women. These groups are the core of the early Christian movement in Jerusalem, and they will be the bearers of Pentecost power. They relate directly to the ministry of Jesus. Within this group is the hope of Israel.

About one hundred twenty persons is a significant number. This number probably includes more than just the males of the group, in the traditional Jewish manner of counting, since women are identified. Luke shows a characteristic interest in numbers. He summarizes the conversions not only at Pentecost but at other times. He specifically numbered all those saved in the shipwreck on the way to Rome as two hundred seventy-six (Acts 27:37). Like the shipwreck number, this upper room number has no symbolic significance. (Luke never develops any narrative point from the number.)

FIGURE 4.8. The Cenacle of Jerusalem. "Cena" means dinner in Latin. This site is the traditional location associated with numerous Gospel events, including the washing of the disciples' feet (John 13:4–11), the last supper (Luke 22:12–13), resurrection appearances (John 20:19), the upper room and selection of Matthias (Acts 1:13), and Pentecost (Acts 2:1–4). The surviving Gothic-style structure has six rib-vaulted bays.

Those in this group are devoted to prayer. Until the "promise of the Father" arrives, this action is well chosen for a group not yet clear what will happen when the promise is realized. Luke's notable emphasis on prayer in the life of Jesus and his followers suggests that he sees this activity as one of the most characteristic activities of the church. Prayer and power are spiritual twins in the Lukan spiritual universe. Notice in the Acts narrative how mighty events always follow on mention of prayer. One excellent example is Cornelius, the centurion "God-fearer" in Caesarea. Though a Roman centurion, he especially is characterized as a person that "always prayed to God" (Acts 10:2). Then, Cornelius is told by an angel in a vision, "Your prayers and your acts of charity have come up as a memorial offering before God" (Acts 10:4). Peter comes to his house, and the whole household is saved.

Replacement of Judas (1:15–26)

In the story of Judas's replacement, we note Peter's early leadership, because this will change. Peter is the unquestioned spokesperson now. The Jerusalem church will reveal social dynamics that begin to make Peter's position less and less tenable as the gentile ramifications of his teaching about the gospel become more and more clear.

Replacement warrant is given through Scripture. Peter here uses Ps 69:25 and Ps 109:8. The first passage is, "May their camp be a desolation; let no one live in their tents." Desolation alludes to judgment. Being cut off from the camp is to be in mortal danger. Thus, Judas's action is judged. The second quote makes a different point: "May his days be few; may another seize his position." Judas did not jeopardize just Messiah. Judas jeopardized the renewal of Israel Messiah is inaugurating. Israel's destiny resides in the symbolic significance of the body of Jesus's specially called disciples as numbering twelve. They are Israel of the end times, eschatological Israel, the Israel of Messiah. By using Scripture, Peter is applying what Jesus had taught during the forty days of teaching after the resurrection. Jesus had shown how Scripture is the key to understanding this new day and this new vision of the people of God transformed by Messiah.

Replacement qualifications are straightforward: an associate of Jesus from the time of John the Baptist to the ascension, and a witness to the resurrection (meaning, appearances of Jesus). This framework is recognizable as the basic literary structure of the "gospel" form established by Mark. These qualifications become the classic definition of the twelve apostles. Apostle is used in this way in the prologue: "giving instructions though the Holy Spirit to the apostles whom he had chosen" (Acts 1:2). The apostle role will be absolutely imperative for Luke. This role is what he means by "eyewitnesses" in the prologue to the Gospel. By defining apostle here in this narrative on the replacement of Judas, Luke has made clear that everything that defines the essence of Christianity is rooted in this apostolic identity: apostolic practice, apostolic witness, apostolic writings, apostolic teaching, apostolic doctrine. The church finally produced the "Apostles' Creed" out of this apostolic reality of the original historical core of messianic Israel.

The method for choosing Judas's replacement is by lots, a traditional Jewish procedure for making decisions. The lot fell to Matthias. Luke says, "and he was added to the eleven apostles." The number of

Israel is returned to full symbolic strength as the Twelve. Bathed in prayer in the upper room, here awaits eschatological Israel, formed by Messiah, primed and ready for the epic event of Pentecost. This upper room creates the latent messianic Israel ready to burst forth in power upon Jerusalem. This Israel will begin immediately to embody Messiah's mission once empowered by the Holy Spirit the Father had promised—the presence of Jesus himself in the church. Jesus's presence and power will launch Messiah's world mission.

Interestingly enough, by these very requirements given by Luke here for apostle, Paul does not qualify. So why did he become known universally as the "apostle" Paul? Because Paul claimed the title for himself in his letters. Luke hardly calls him that title anywhere in Acts with only one exception, which exception has its own delimitations.[4]

SUMMARY

That Luke wrote both the Gospel and Acts together shows up even in the macro structure of the two literary volumes. Preparatory stage, descent of the Spirit to empower public ministry, and impulse of the Spirit to drive outward toward a divine destiny are all part of the story of Jesus and the story of the early church. Thus, when we jump into Acts, we already are in the middle of a grand literary scheme. That is why the prologue to Acts is resumptive.

We may conveniently divide the first chapter of Acts into three units: the opening prologue (Acts 1:1–2), material on the resurrected Messiah (Acts 1:3–8), and a focus on Messiah's disciples (Acts 1:9–21) in a preparation stage. These units set the stage for the second half of the story of Jesus.

The prologue builds literary bridges. The bridge backwards is to the previous volume of Luke. The Christian movement is sourced in Jewish faith and the expectation of a Messiah redeemer, who is Jesus. He establishes a kingdom unlike any worldly kingdom, so neither Jewish kingdom ideas nor Roman can comprehend Jesus's kingdom. This

---

[4]Acts 14:4, 6 implicitly, 14:14 explicitly. Luke here probably is referencing not the permanent office of the Twelve, but those specifically authorized and commissioned in a missionary thrust of the Antioch church at the behest of the Spirit. After the Jerusalem Conference in Acts 15 and one reference to the decision made by the Twelve at this conference in Acts 16:4, the word "apostle" never appears again in Acts.

kingdom will reach the uttermost parts of the earth, so inevitably will include gentiles. This Messiah and the profile of his unearthly kingdom on earth is predicted in Jewish Scripture. He brings good news. He redeems. He forgives sin. He is proclaimed.

The bridge forward builds on themes of witness, Spirit, and the Twelve. Witness is the kingdom commission. Spirit is the kingdom power. The Twelve are this kingdom's manifestation and destiny.

The material on the resurrected Messiah shows Messiah getting the disciples ready for their transformation into messianic Israel. This material first establishes corporeality of the resurrection, essential for understanding the doctrine that was core to Christian preaching and never surrendered. The resurrected Messiah begins to resurrect Israel from the dust of post-exilic identity distortions by the Pharisees and Sadducees, among others.

Messiah also gives a commission to his followers. The Spirit will empower that commission and direct its paths. The process will not be easy or automatic. Kingdom issues will confuse the understanding. The Spirit's direction will transform these confusions into the clarity of the eschatological Israel of the prophets, messianic Israel, tasked with a witness to the world. The program is Acts 1:8, but this program Jesus had been preparing the disciples for long before the forty days training when he spoke during his ministry of their testimony before synagogues, rulers, and authorities that the Spirit would guide at the needed hour. Whatever else is involved in the future kingdom of God can represent a distraction from focus on the commission, or worse, failure to fulfill that commission in this day. The commission is clear, definitive, and exclusive.

The ascension doublet units link resurrection and Pentecost. The trifecta series of resurrection, ascension, and Pentecost creates an unparalled reality in the history of Israel that transforms the very essence of the Israel of God, a transfiguration into messianic Israel. This Israel has both unbelievable corporate power for witness and the universal, personal presence of Jesus unlimited by space and time to accompany the journey of any disciple on mission for Messiah. This mission is the ongoing glorification of Jesus. Ascension, church, and return: here is the kingdom of God for those who are looking.

The third part of the introductory material in Acts 1 involves the disciples of Messiah in a preparatory status awaiting the promise of the

Father. Pentecost preparation involves the upper room prayer and the replacement of Judas. The prayer mentioned here, though covered but briefly, is supported by all the narratives in the Gospel about Jesus in prayer or teaching his disciples how to pray. Prayer for Luke is a premier Christian virtue and activity. Notice in the Acts narrative how mighty events always follow on mention of prayer.

The replacement of Judas reconstitutes the apostles as representative of the Israel of God. Replacement warrant is given in Scripture. Replacement qualifications inherently define the special role of one called an "apostle" in the early Christian movement. An apostle is witness to the story of Jesus from John's baptism to ascension. So, apostolic is what Luke means in his prologue about "eyewitnesses." The apostles formed the original historical core of Christian faith and messianic Israel.

5

Renewal Empowerment

Pentecost as Thematic (Acts 2)

LUKE ALONE TELLS THE STORY of Pentecost, the only festival ignored by the other Gospel writers of the three great pilgrim festivals of Passover, Pentecost, and Tabernacles in the annual Jewish calendar. Luke builds on the historical background of Pentecost and constructs not just an event in Acts 2 but a thematic force driving the entire Acts narrative. Many episodes often found confusing or obscure in Acts, such as Barnabas' unexplained generosity in Acts 4, or the tragic story of Ananias and Sapphira in Acts 5, or ignoring the Hellenist widows in Acts 6, or the famine predicted by Agabus and the famine relief visit of Barnabas and Saul in Acts 11, or the small detail about Herod's agreement with the inhabitants of Sidon for food in Acts 12, all these find their hermeneutic in Luke's Pentecost theme.

In the life of Israel, the Pentecost celebration followed Passover fifty days later with the religious significance of escape from slavery to promised land provision of abundant crops and food, life and security at the hands of a gracious God and his gracious gift of land. The land makes Israel's life even possible. Thus, a harvest offering at the temple of two loaves of bread when accepted by the priest was a sign of God's forgiveness and partook of the reality of the Pentecost meal in Jewish homes. The waving of the barley sheaf at Passover was in anticipation of the harvesting of the barley crop fifty days later in the first part of the dry season. As a religious festival, pilgrims to Jerusalem celebrated covenant fulfillment and covenant blessing. Yet the problem was the exile. Israel had failed covenant obligations and lost the land meant for crops and harvest blessing. Even after return from exile, Israel's situation was hardly better. The nation already was on its second non-Davidic dynasty (Hasmonean, Herodian), and everyone kept trying to redefine Israel.

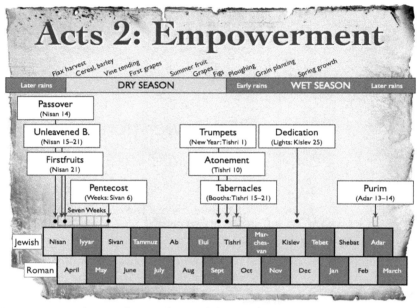

FIGURE 5.1. Jewish Festival Year. The Jewish festivals followed the agricultural calendar of the dry and wet seasons and crops and harvest. Over the course of time, religious significance was attached to these observances that followed the story of Israel's salvation. All festivals point to eschatological fulfillment in Messiah. The one pilgrim festival not developed by other Gospel writers is Pentecost.

Pharisees were trying to redefine Israel. Pharisee synagogue efforts to push priestly observance prescribed in the law onto everyone had at best mixed results. Pharisees were respected among the common folk, but their meticulous observance and purity rituals were not followed. Worse, the oral traditions that the Pharisees developed to accomplish this purity program in the life of Israel actually backfired by providing a pretense and subterfuge whose real purpose was to *violate* the law.[1]

As a result of this history and these problems, Israel after exile had failed to enter into the Pentecost fullness God originally had intended. That fullness would require a renewed Israel yet to be realized on earth, an Israel full of the Spirit, empowered to enter into spiritual Pentecost abundance. Only Messiah could effect such an Israel. What would such

[1]See Jesus's rebuke of the oral law called "Corban" (*korban*, κορβᾶν) in Mark 7:11.

Pentecostal fullness look like? The historical Pentecost feast Israel had celebrated for centuries sets up the profile of the eschatological fulfillment those awaiting the future kingdom of God could expect. That historical profile clearly has a harvest abundance theme—abundance of divine provision, divine forgiveness, harvest joy in fulfilling God's will, shared food, shared fellowship, and social inclusiveness.

A defining characteristic of historical Pentecost encoded into the very law that established the feast is social inclusiveness, another way to signal God's fullest blessings on Israel. Whom to invite to share the festal meal? Not only your sons and daughters, your kin. Instead, for this feast, invite even those normally vulnerable to life's vicissitudes, male and female slaves, resident Levites (think Barnabas)—even strangers, orphans, and widows. These too were to be included intentionally into this distinctive harvest celebration in Jewish homes (Deut 16:11). Divine forgiveness, harvest bounty and joy, social inclusiveness, these are the signal features of Pentecost in Israel. These are the very features Luke particularly emphasizes in Acts 2.

Luke's narrative strategy in Acts evolves out of the significance of the Pentecost feast in the ancient Jewish setting of Israel's Exodus and subsequent possession of the promised land. Luke has translated this dimension of Israel's story into its corresponding eschatological fulfillment in Jesus and the church. Within this narrative strategy, Luke combines Pentecost fulfillment with both the narrative development of the character of Barnabas, who will become "Pentecost facilitator," and the motif of gentile mission developed in the Hellenist movement and preeminently represented in the character of Saul. Whereas the "promise of the Father" Jesus directed the church to anticipate is a baptism of the Spirit, the reason for this Spirit baptism is to fulfill Pentecost in Israel in that eschatological fullness God always intended for messianic Israel to which the annual feast pointed every year. After the descent of the Spirit, Pentecost reality in Israel is permanent.[2]

PENTECOST EVENT

Luke is well prepared to expound on this epic event in the life of Israel, so he dives right in. The action is narrated, but the ancients were not

---

[2]See chapter 1, "Pentecost as Thematic: Luke's Perspective on an Epic Event," for a detailed development of this crucial narrative strategy for understanding Acts.

enthralled with action as is the modern American public so trained by Hollywood to salivate like Pavlov's dogs at the sound of a crashing car. What the ancients wanted was a speech to interpret the action, which Peter obligingly supplies.

Descent of the Spirit (2:1–4)

Luke says, "when Pentecost arrived." He is subtle. He writes with double entendre. He means more than the annual festival. He means the moment of eschatological fullness for which Messiah had been preparing Israel during his entire ministry on earth, including that intense period of training for his disciples after the resurrection for forty days, as well as an extended upper room prayer meeting. This "arrived" at one level is the annual pilgrim festival, but at a deeper level is the moment of messianic Israel's empowerment.

The "strong rushing wind" easily is identified as a signifier of the Spirit of God. Ancient Jews long had associated "wind" and "Spirit" because the word in Hebrew is the same.[3] Combined with the "fiery tongues," no one would have any doubt the experience is an epiphanic event—God manifest. All the commotion commands undivided attention. Then, "tongues of fire" distribute indiscriminately. In terms of manifestations of God, the burning bush of Moses at Mount Sinai can be suggested. More important than echoes or associations in the Old Testament are the words of John the Baptist himself, who will put the eschatological spin on the event as prophetic fulfillment: "he will baptize you with the Holy Spirit and fire" (Luke 3:16–17). Since we have the fire, the rushing wind has to be the Spirit John meant.

The miracle of Pentecost is not tongues, but speech. All spoke "as the Spirit gave them utterance." Two key parameters should be kept in mind about the nature of this miracle. First, the Spirit controls, not the individual. Second, the manifestation is communal, not personal.

The narrative parallel is Jesus's own baptism in Luke. Empowerment for mission is the point, both for Jesus and for the church, and the experience formally launches the public ministry of each (as illustrated in Fig. 4.1, p. 147).

---

[3]The noun רוח (*ruach*) can be translated "breath," "wind," or "spirit" depending on context. Elijah anticipated God might be in the "mighty wind," and then the "fire" that followed, but God did not manifest himself as expected (1 Kgs 19:11–12).

Crowd's Amazement (2:5–13)

FIGURE 5.2. Pentecost Nations and Territories. Luke develops an extensive list not simply for curiosity's sake. He has a crucial theological truth to establish about the nature of Messiah's kingdom fullness and the meaning of Israel's return from exile.

List of Nations (2:5–11)

Luke focuses on the countries represented. His list intends to convey a vast expanse.

- East of the Euphrates: Parthia, Media, Elam, and Mesopotamia. In these areas we have the Jewish populations of the exile that resulted from deportations by Assyria and Babylonia. They returned to Judea speaking Aramaic.

- Judea: Luke's exact meaning is unclear. Naturally, scribes of Greek manuscripts tried to emend to clarify. Does Luke mean Jerusalemites? Or, does he mean Samaria? Or, Samaria and Galilee together as a broader unit?

- Asia Minor: Cappadocia, Pontus, Asia, Phrygia, and Pamphylia. All these areas have large Jewish populations and later would become the focal point of Pauline mission work.

- North Africa: Egypt and Libya. Again, these territories would have large Jewish populations. The famous Philo of Alexandria would hail from this region, as well as Simon of Cyrene who carried the cross for Jesus (cf. Mark 15:21).

- Italy: represented through Rome. This notation of Rome infers the early beginnings of Christianity in Rome long before any apostle arrived. From a literary point of view, Rome is mentioned by way of *inclusio*. The text of Acts will end in Rome. This movement is by design, promised already in the programmatic Acts 1:8. In fact, Rome will become a narrative focal point from Acts 19:21 on.

- Cretans: the island of Crete. Mentioned to include even the islands in the list. Crete will become famous as the source of the storm that overtook Paul's ship on the way to Rome (Acts 27:7–15). The extended corpus of Pauline letters will include a letter to Titus, who ostensibly is on Crete.

- Arabs: the other half of the story of Abraham, if the sons of Ishmael are meant. Some have suggested perhaps the Nabatean kingdom is meant. If so, Saul will encounter Nabatean jurisdiction in Damascus after the Damascus Road. The Nabatean king, Aretus IV, had a governor ruling Damascus when Saul's life was threatened. Saul escaped the city over the wall in a basket in Acts 9:25.[4]

What is the point of this broad list that encompasses the general extent of the Roman empire? Certainly not the reversal of the tower of Babel. Luke has no interest in the tower of Babel, nor does he develop any theme based on the flood account in Genesis. The point of the list is the actual account in Acts itself: Pentecost is the reversal of the exile, God's people called from among all the nations.[5] What is significant about how the return from exile has been configured is the new day of eschatological fulfillment in Messiah, and this fulfillment requires calculating the point of the ascension into the equation of meaning for

---

[4]When combined with the information in 2 Cor 11:32. Incidentally, this Nabatean king's daughter was the first wife of Herod Antipas. Antipas divorced the Nabatean princess in order to marry Herodias, wife of his brother Philip. King Aretas IV was enraged. This divorce received the public rebuke of John the Baptist (Luke 3:19–20).

[5]"Save us, O God of our salvation, and gather and rescue us from among the nations" (1 Chr 16:35; cf. Ps 106:47). "I shall save my people from the east country and from the west country" (Zech 8:7). "And all the nations shall stream to [the mountain of the Lord's house]" (Isa 2:2). "He will raise a signal for the nations, and will assemble the outcasts of Israel, and gather the dispersed of Judah from the four corners of the earth" (Isa 11:12). "I will give you [my servant] as a light to the nations, that my salvation shall reach to the ends of the earth" (Isa 49:6). "I am coming to gather all nations and tongues; and they shall come and shall see my glory" (Isa 66:18).

Pentecost, both stories only Luke preserves, and both already seamed together in the narrative sequence of Luke 24 flowing immediately into Acts 1–2. Luke tells the ascension twice because the event has theological import. With the list of Pentecost pilgrims, Luke hits theological pay dirt: *Promised return from exile happens in a way that does not require occupation of a land or physical return to a land if Messiah is omnipresent in any land by reason of the ascension.*[6] This truth will become vital to the message of the church in the post-AD 70 world after the Jewish nation is lost, temple destroyed, and land becomes meaningless by default.

Thus, the commission to go "to the uttermost parts of the earth" represents a *spiritual* possession by Messiah, not a *national* kingdom dispossessing other nations of their boundaries by force and conquest like the Roman empire. In this way, Christianity *does* preach "another king" but is *no threat* to the conquest designs of imperial Rome, unless the emperor is converted—which Paul, given the opportunity, would have attempted to do. After all, he did convert a Roman proconsul, only one step down from the emperor in imperial status.[7]

Another implication of the Pentecost miracle is the multicultural diversity of the early church from inception. Not even the earliest days of the Christian movement were restricted to Judea alone or even to Judean inhabitants. The Jerusalem church just took a while to figure out the full implications of this messianic Israel for the Mosaic law and the Sadducean temple. In fact, the Hellenists, a movement only Luke details in the New Testament, had to lead the way to this realization, which underscores the importance of Luke's Hellenist Cycle beginning in Acts 6.

Notice that the result of these tongues is immediate access to the story of Jesus ("speaking the magnificent acts of God in our own languages," 2:11). These "magnificent acts" would include Jesus's miracles, death and resurrection, appearances, ascension. A final implication of the Pentecost miracle is that speaking the languages of the world has only one real *raison d'etre*: if you have a story to tell. The early church had a story to tell, the story of Jesus. The very nature of the Pentecost

---

[6] One among many lessons Saul learned on the Damascus Road.

[7] Sergius Paulus on the island of Cyprus, a senatorial province, according to most interpretations of the meaning of Acts 13:12.

miracle impels messianic Israel toward accomplishment of the commission announced in Acts 1:8. The miracle is about the mission.

Speaking in Tongues

FIGURE 5.3. Tongues: Pentecost Versus Corinth. Exegetical differences are substantial between these two contexts that wrongly are assumed equivalent.

A careful Bible student will note the substantial differences between the "speaking in tongues" at Pentecost and tongues at Corinth (the *only* Pauline community ever known to manifest this behavior in the New Testament). For example, the tongues at Pentecost are unique. (One does not get baptized every Sunday.) The phenomenon at Corinth is repeatable. The tongues at Pentecost have corporate manifestation with observable other effects, such as "fiery." Corinth tongues are individual, private, never attended with obvious physical effects such as "fiery," and usually a part of personal prayer. Tongues at Pentecost do *not* require interpretation as known human languages, but tongues at Corinth *require* interpretation as fundamentally unknown utterances, basically nonsense sounds. The content of tongues at Pentecost is the known facts of the gospel. The content of the tongues at Corinth is unknown, esoteric information, ecstatic prophecy. Finally, the tongues at Pentecost have tremendous contextual significance for the development of the narrative of Acts. (One does not launch the same corporate enterprise every week, or have grand openings every month.) The tongues at Corinth, in stark contrast, have no contextual significance. If Corinth tongues had *not* caused trouble for worship order, we never would have known the phenomenon even existed. Tongues at Corinth *did* cause trouble, which forced Paul to have to regulate them in the only known locale of the phenomenon in a Pauline church.[8]

---

[8]Converted pagans could have brought their Bacchanalian frenzy rites as supposed spiritual depth through being seized by the deity to their worship at Corinth.

Diverse Reaction (2:12–13)

The crowds, obviously, are confused and ask, "What does this mean?" For some, the occasion is one that prompts derision. "Filled with new wine" would be intoxication. The early morning hour makes that supposition highly unlikely, which observation Peter will seize upon.

The point of the extensive list of Pentecost pilgrims itemized by Luke is that those who are experiencing this fresh outpouring of God's Spirit on Israel represent the entire width and breadth of Diaspora Judaism. World Judaism will hear the message about Messiah at one time. As these Pentecost pilgrims from around the world return home, the gospel in principle instantly has reached the "uttermost parts of the earth." In principle, Acts 1:8 is fulfilled in the second chapter of Acts. What the apostles will have to do is to establish on the Spirit's foundation the messianic Israel Messiah has empowered at Pentecost. That work will depend on the apostles coming to understand that to establish this Israel of God, they must move out of Jerusalem and into the world. Surprisingly, that movement is not automatic, as the story happens to unfold.

PETER'S SERMON (2:14–40)

All Israel from around the world will hear this sermon. These pilgrims are representatives of world Judaism in exile. Crowd confusion predicates why Peter must speak. He works to bring order to the general disorder that prevents people from perceiving the true point of the miracle, which is Messiah has come, has redeemed, has been raised and glorified, and now calls. He answers the question and deflects the ridicule. He uses as a transition their observation of the "magnificent acts" of God to parse out what these acts mean for Israel. The bottom line will be a call for personal decision about Jesus as Messiah.

Apostolic Preaching Form

Luke constructs the message with the formed structure of apostolic preaching that surfaces in multiple ways in the New Testament that eventually provided the literary structure of the gospel genre itself, as in the Gospel of Mark.[9] The basic outline of Peter's message is:

[9]Pointed out many years ago by C. H. Dodd, *Apostolic Preaching*.

- Announcing the age of fulfillment (2:16–21)

    resurrection inaugurates the last days

    outpouring of God's Spirit is evidence

- Telling the story of Jesus (2:22–24)

- Citing scriptural support (2:25–36)

    showing Jesus as fulfillment (in this case, the psalm could not be about David; he saw corruption in the grave; only Jesus did not see corruption in the grave)

    usually quoting the LXX form

- Calling to repentance (2:37–40)

One will observe a very similar structure to Peter's message to Cornelius and his household in Acts 10:36–43.

Peter's Seven Sermons as Thematic

Peter's Sermons
The Church's Movement from Jews to Gentiles

Sermon	Audience	Significance
1. Acts 2	Jerusalem's pilgrims	Church empowered
2. Acts 3	Jerusalem's people	Forgiveness offered
3. Acts 4	Jerusalem's leaders	Forgiveness offered
4. Acts 5	Jerusalem's leaders	Forgiveness rejected
5. Acts 10	Cornelius's house	Gentile plan unfolds
6. Acts 11	Circumcision party	Gentile plan resisted
7. Acts 15	Church leaders	Gentile plan settled

FIGURE 5.4. Peter's Thematic Sermons. Peter's speeches work together in Acts.

Another observation to make about this sermon (or speech from the ancient historian's point of view) is that this speech is the first of seven in Acts that Luke gives to Peter. Viewed together as a corpus, one can see how Peter's speeches work as a literary unit to establish the church's movement from Jews to gentiles as a divinely superintended development. Peter's character in Acts functions as an apostolic "stamp of approval" in this process as part of Luke's program of Luke-Acts as the story of Jesus. With Peter's speeches, Luke shows that the movement to gentiles was not just a fluke of circumstances in the early church. Gentile inclusion was at the heart of Jesus's intentions all along. Peter is the connection back to the ministry of Jesus himself.

Significant Points

Critical commentaries can provide helpful verse-by-verse exegesis. For our purposes, we emphasize significant points for the narrative flow.

Eschatological Prophecy

Peter's "spoken by Joel" (2:16) is a reference to Joel's prophecy about the last days, the so-called, "end times." In effect, Peter says, "this is that." The prophetic last days have dawned. Strangely, one will hear well-meaning believers ask, "Do you think we are in the last days?" as if we are not. Peter includes Joel's use of the language of the sun turning to darkness and the moon to blood to interpret the Pentecost event. Yet, Luke described only a mighty rushing wind and tongues of fire. Clearly, these prophetic heavenly portents in Joel are interpreted symbolically by Peter in relation to Pentecost. What we have in Peter's quote of Joel is a fine example of the New Testament's inaugurated eschatology. Are we in the last days? Yes. Have been ever since Pentecost.

One of the signals of the last days is what Joel made clear: the Spirit. Joel had said you would know the last days because you would see God's Spirit manifested in every aspect of messianic Israel. No longer would Spirit-inspired knowledge of God's will for God's people be restricted to a school of prophets—one over in this village, and another far down to the south. In Israel of the last days, everyone would be having dreams like Daniel and seeing visions like Isaiah, as in being knocked off a horse on the way to Damascus (Acts 9:4), or seeing a Macedonian calling to come help (Acts 16:9). Further this outpouring of the Spirit will be absolutely indiscriminate: sons, daughters, young men, old men, men slaves, women slaves. Indeed, "all flesh" will participate, which is, by definition, this Pentecost event. The outpoured Spirit at Pentecost is the event that convinced early believers such as Luke and others that the last days had arrived. "Wonders and signs" (2:22) would include Jesus's own healings and exorcisms, and his resurrection and ascension, but also miracles in the on-going story of Jesus in the church, Pentecost tongues, causing the lame to walk, healing the sick.

Eschatological Crisis

Further, Peter's choice of eschatological prophecy to interpret Pentecost means that the Israel of God has come to her denouement in history. The eschatological moment is Messiah. All decisions national Israel makes from this point on have judgment written all over them, with eschatological consequences. This point derives directly out of Joel's prophecy itself. Joel concluded his prophecy by declaring God's own word that, "Then everyone who calls on the name of the Lord shall be saved" (Acts 2:21). "Then" means when that unique moment in history has arrived. "Then" those who call will "be saved."

Israel had been looking for salvation for centuries. Simeon, a righteous and devout prophet in Jerusalem, had been waiting all his life for the salvation of the Lord, the consolation of Israel (Luke 2:25). The Holy Spirit had promised Simeon he would not see death before he would see the Lord's Messiah (Luke 2:26). When Simeon sees the child Jesus being presented by his parents in the temple, the Spirit inspires him to proclaim, "My eyes have seen your salvation" (Luke 2:30). Simeon's response is what Pentecost requires. Jesus is to be confessed as Messiah. Thus, Joel's prophecy is about a now or never proposition, a historic moment for Israel and all those calling themselves Israelites.[10]

Eschatological Call

Thus, the proper conclusion to this message of eschatological crisis at this unique moment in Israel's history would be a call to decision. Peter does so: "repent and be baptized" (2:38). Peter echoes John the Baptist (Luke 3:3). However, Peter's call is not a simple reprise of John. Two new Jewish elements distinguish Peter's Pentecost call. One is that the baptism is "in Jesus's name" (2:38). This baptism is not John's. Messiah now has a name. His name is Jesus. This baptism is incorporation into a renewed Israel, not the present Israel of the Pharisees and Sadducees, but the Israel of Messiah, the messianic Israel formed by resurrected

---

[10] Luke 2 seems intentionally designed to interpret Acts 2.

power outpoured at Pentecost. The second new Jewish element is that this baptism has eschatological power John's never did. Pentecost gives the gift of the Holy Spirit. John's baptism never accomplished that eschatological miracle.

Target Audience

The target audience ostensibly is Jewish. Those present are Jews of Jerusalem, Judea, and the uttermost parts of the earth. Peter mentions not only those Pentecost pilgrims present, but that the gospel call is "to those who are far off" (2:39). Now, at this particular moment in time, Peter means Diaspora Jews not attending the Pentecost feast this year, not gentiles. The narrative reveals this, because Peter still has a cloudy understanding of what in messianic Israel makes for clean and unclean. That issue is the whole point of the Cornelius story and Peter's Joppa vision (10:14–16). Eventually, Peter will figure out the full implications of the presence of the Holy Spirit. Wherever the Holy Spirit is, there is ritual cleansing. The eschatological outpouring of the Spirit is replacing the priestly rituals of the temple and its service. Another dot Peter has yet to connect is that if the priests and their temple rituals for declaring clean and unclean in Israel no longer are needed, neither is the temple.

So when Peter concludes, "everyone God calls" (2:39), for the moment he is thinking of Jews. The trajectory of Simeon's prophecy about "light for revelation to the gentiles" (Luke 2:31) has yet to become clear to the nascent messianic community. As we trace Peter's sermons and his own experience, however, we will see this gentile movement coming into clearer focus in the Acts narrative.

MESSIANIC COMMUNITY (2:41–47)

Pentecost is not about tongues. Pentecost is about Israel's renewal as the people of God. Two characteristics of the annual festival of Pentecost now determine the shape of the following narrative: Pentecost as a Jewish festival (1) celebrated abundance and (2) enacted this abundance in shared community, most notably in a festal meal to which all were invited. Luke now plays out these Pentecost festival themes. He means to say that the eschatological fulfillment to which the annual celebration of Pentecost historically pointed is now reality. These are the last days.

Pentecost Abundance

The point of numbers is not the numbers. The point of numbers is to show eschatological Pentecost realized. Pentecost was the promise of harvest abundance. Jesus himself had said, "the harvest is plentiful, but the laborers are few; therefore ask the Lord of the harvest to send out laborers into the harvest" (Luke 10:2). We started in Acts 1 with one hundred twenty in the upper room. The ranks now explode into the thousands. That type of growth pretty much sounds like harvest abundance any way you wave the sheaf. Indeed, with such a response, more laborers for the harvest most truly are needed.

About three thousand are added (2:41).[11] The number includes both permanently resident Jerusalemites and disaspora pilgrims. The salient point is that many non-resident festival attendees will return home. In contrast to all other Pentecost treks to Jerusalem, this year pilgrims will be returning to their own countries across the Roman empire with this good news about Jesus the Messiah and the "magnificent acts" of God.

Pentecost Community

Luke provides a quick overview of the matrix of early messianic Israel, the renewed Israel of God. He starts with the core, the apostles.

Apostles' Teaching

The apostles' teaching is foundational eyewitness testimony from the original followers of Jesus validating authoritative church teaching, as Luke indicated in the Gospel prologue. These disciples were with Jesus from the baptism of John

FIGURE 5.5. Apostles' Teaching. The selection of Matthias shows the importance of remembrance.

through the ascension. Their teaching is the fount of Christianity.

As time goes on, however, social dynamics in Jerusalem become intense prior to the war with Rome. Jewish groups more and more are

---

[11]Charging Luke with embellishing the numbers simply misses the narrative point.

forced to posture for or against revolt, as if these positions meant one was for or against "Israel." These politics will include attitudes to gentiles as supposed wind vanes of attitudes to Israel. Church acceptance of gentiles without requiring circumcision nor the obligation of the law of Moses would be highly suspect to the interests of national Israel in the opinion of many Jews. Attitudes to the church and the apostles in these conditions would deteriorate rapidly.

Fellowship

Having "all things common" marks a major shift in social identity. This new identity creates an intimate, fictive family. This intimate social identity would be similar to the Jewish community at Qumran. In this environment, referring to other disciples as "brothers" or "sisters" would become natural and soon would become commonplace and traditional among those called Christians.

Bread

Bread is metonymy for the Pentecost meal. This annual festival now finds fruition in a messianic fulfillment long anticipated by the prophets. The annual festal meal now becomes perpetual. Shared bread is another sign of eschatological

FIGURE 5.6. Breaking Bread. The annual shared Pentecost meal becomes a shared life in perpetuity.

Pentecost abundance. The shared meal becomes a shared life in perpetuity. Allusion to growing observance of the Lord's supper is possible.[12] The festival connection is stronger and supported by the blessing of the dinner guest, "Blessed is anyone who will eat bread in the kingdom of God!" (Luke 14:15) spoken about the destiny of Jesus in Luke's Journey to Jerusalem section.

[12]Because bread is a constituent part of the supper (Luke 22:19). This ritual connection also is suggested for the breaking bread and recognizing Jesus in the Emmaus disciples' story (Luke 24:30, 35). Less likely is an answer to the request for daily bread in the Lord's prayer, but this prayer instruction has no banquet context (Luke 11:3).

Prayers

Offering prayers is Luke's literary "bowtie" on his Pentecost unit. Prayers form an *inclusio* with the upper room prayers. The upper room prayers for clarity, identity, and direction for this fledgling messianic community huddled around the Twelve have been answered.

Signs and Wonders

Signs and wonders offer proof of the gospel message for those who need such proof. The point will be the close connection between the *nature* of these signs and wonders and the *message* of the gospel. A sick person healed confirms the gospel message that Messiah indeed has come as promised and desires God's goodness and wholeness for all, as even Jesus preached in his inaugural sermon in his hometown of Nazareth, quoting Isaiah (Luke 4:18–19). A person raised from the dead confirms the promise of restored life in the gospel and proleptically anticipates the final resurrection to eternal life. All such signs and wonders are proofs of the gospel message that a new age truly has dawned in Jesus the Messiah, a new age inspiring a new vision of the people of God. Further, the ongoing signs and wonders means Jesus is present in his community just as he was present in his ministry. The ascension is the theological word of the power of divine presence in the church.

FIGURE 5.7. Jerusalem Temple Model. The early Jerusalem church was temple centric. The radical implications of the gospel were not apparent immediately (IMJ).

Temple Centric

Luke makes clear that the earliest form of messianic Israel, at least the community in Jerusalem, was temple centric. The community has a strong Jewish identity and extremely Jewish focus. Three features reveal this Jewish focus still centered on Jerusalem and its temple. First, the community is hovering around the temple all the time. The temple compound is where they teach and preach, encounter the lame to heal, and return to preach after being imprisoned. Second, this community still has no missionary impulse. Lack of missionary impulse could be fatal to messianic Israel, given the command in Acts 1:8. In fact, concerning missionary initiative, the Jerusalem church never gets to church on time! In Luke's version of Christianity, missionary impulse will be absolutely essential to the future of the church, hence the importance of Antioch to Luke.[13] Third, even after the persecution following the martyrdom of Stephen that scatters the church, Luke explicitly points out that "they spoke the word to no one except Jews" (11:19).

Thus, several radical implications of the gospel of Jesus are not yet clear to the earliest followers in Jerusalem. One is the gentile complexion of the church. Another is that the ritual institutions of Mosaic Israel are defunct. Messiah has come suddenly to his temple only to find the building a den of thieves (Luke 19:46). Eschatological judgment falls, preeminently signified in the cleansing of the temple (Luke 19:44–46). What use is the law of Moses if the very means of its propitiation, the temple and its ritual, is eliminated in judgment? Worse still, what if instead of a place of forgiveness the temple has become a provocation to idolatry? Is that even possible? Stephen's speech is still to come.

SUMMARY

Luke's narrative strategy in Acts evolves out of the significance of the Pentecost feast in the ancient Jewish setting of Israel's Exodus and subsequent possession of the promised land. Luke has translated this dimension of Israel's story into its corresponding eschatological fulfillment in Jesus and the church. The reason for the Spirit baptism is to fulfill Pentecost in Israel with that eschatological fullness God always intended and to which the annual feast pointed every year. After the descent of the Spirit, Pentecost is a permanent reality in messianic Israel in the abundance of divine forgiveness, harvest bounty and joy, and social inclusiveness.

[13]See chapter 2, "Hellenists and Antioch: The Making of a Paradigm."

The narrative parallel of Pentecost is Jesus's own baptism. Both Jordan and Pentecost empower and formally launch public ministry. This miraculous manifestation of the Spirit is not controlled by any one person and is not a private experience. The miracle in Acts is speech, not tongues. The exegetical differences from tongues at Corinth render impossible the equation of the two. In the Acts narrative, Pentecost is unique, not repeatable, corporate, not individual, and consists of known languages, not nonsense sounds. Pentecost content is the known facts of the gospel, not esoteric mysteries privy to one person. Pentecost is contextually significant. In contrast, tongues at Corinth simply are a problem to be solved and have no contextual significance.

The expansive list of Pentecost pilgrims and their countries is to evoke a sense of Diaspora Judaism, which evokes a secondary sense of the exile that created Diaspora Judaism in the first place. Diaspora pilgrims return to the promise land to discover that a true return from exile is in Messiah and his ascended power and glory. By reason of his resurrection and ascension, this Messiah can be known and experienced anywhere in the world. His kingdom through the Spirit already extends to the uttermost parts of the earth.

Speaking the languages of the world has only one reason, which is, one has a story to tell. This story is the Jesus story, the gospel, the magnificent acts of God in Jesus the Messiah. Pentecost empowers the ability to fulfill Acts 1:8. The miracle of tongues is about mission. In figurative potential, all Diaspora Judaism and Jerusalem hears the story of Jesus at one time at Pentecost, so Acts 1:8 already is on the road to fulfillment by the second chapter of Acts.

Peter's Pentecost sermon reveals that standard outline of early apostolic preaching. As a unit, all Peter's sermons taken together also communicate the church's movement from Jews to gentiles. The essence of his Pentecost message is bringing Israel into eschatological judgment. Messiah has come. The last days have dawned. The proof is the indiscriminate outpouring of the Spirit, just as Joel predicted. The salvation for which Israel had been waiting for centuries has arrived. Eschatological judgment means crisis. A personal decision has to be made. Peter's call to decision calls for baptism into Messiah's name to become part of the Israel that Messiah is renewing and to receive the power of the new age, the gift of the Spirit that Messiah by reason of his ascension now is able to pour out to actualize his presence in his community everywhere, all the time. Peter's original focus in this message was on Jewish recipients of this promise. Over time he will learn the broader implications of Pentecost for gentiles.

Pentecost is about Israel's renewal as the people of God. The signature of the festival is abundance, harvest joy, and shared community. That festival signature shapes the profile of messianic Israel. This community will derive its core teaching and identity from the apostles. This social identity will generate a sense of fellowship so intimate that a sense of fictive family relationships will evolve naturally. Pentecost harvest bread no longer is an annual celebration but a daily reality. All this Pentecost bounty began with a prayer meeting, and the practice of prayer always will define messianic Israel in forever gratitude. The ongoing signs and wonders means Jesus is present in his community just as he was present in his ministry. These signs and wonders of healings, exorcisms, and raisings individually and together point to the realities promised in the gospel message: Jesus is Messiah. Faith in Messiah facilitates forgiveness that brings harvest-abundant life and joy, here and hereafter. Jesus creates the renewed Israel always promised by the prophets for the last days—Pentecost fulfilled.

6

Renewal Witness

Messiah Appeals to Israel (Acts 3–5)

CHAPTERS 1–5 OF ACTS DOCUMENT the Spirit empowering messianic Israel's renewal. Luke has described the very beginnings of that renewal in the preparatory post-resurrection days of teaching on God's kingdom, commissioning to a task, and expectantly waiting in upper room prayer. He then moved on to describe the epic event of empowerment, Pentecost, that publicly launched the witness mission of the church and established its profile as an eschatological community of Messiah. Luke now moves to show messianic Israel in witness to national Israel and her leaders. This witness is that God is doing a new work in the last days to which they are called to respond. We can see the progression of Messiah's appeal in the series of Peter's sermons.

The first step of this appeal to national Israel was to empower the church for this witness task. This empowerment is Pentecost. Tongues at Pentecost involved announcing to all Israelites from all around the world the "magnificent acts" of God. God sent Jesus as Messiah. Jesus died for the forgiveness of sins. God raised Jesus from the dead, and Jesus ascended to heaven to pour out his Spirit as a permanent power for his people. Jesus is the time of God's decisive action in the last days for Israel's salvation, just as the prophet Joel had predicted. The promised life that the celebration of Pentecost every year anticipated now is realized. This renewal of Israel and the launching of messianic Israel is revealed in Peter's sermon at Pentecost.

Once God's decisive action in Jesus the Messiah is announced, the time is set for the formal offer of forgiveness to all Israel. Messiah appeals to national Israel, both people and leaders, to accept God's offer of eschatological renewal of Israel Joel had prophesied. One only has to accept the forgiveness offered by Messiah through his death and be baptized into the name of Messiah to become part of this renewed Israel, this magnificent act of God—messianic Israel of the last days.

TEMPLE HEALING

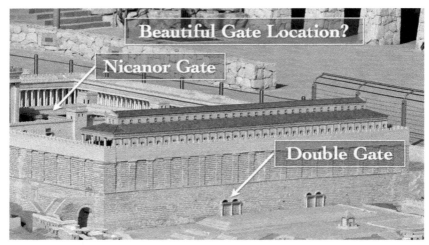

FIGURE 6.1. The Beautiful Gate. The exact identity of the "Beautiful Gate" of Acts 3:2 is unclear; no gate in the temple complex formally was called by that name (IMJ).

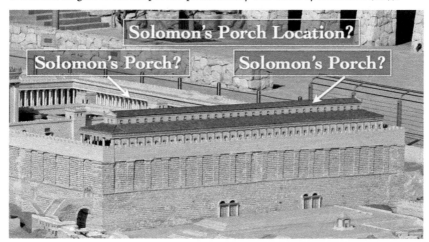

FIGURE 6.2. Solomon's Porch. The exact identity of "Solomon's Porch" of Acts 3:11 is unclear. In any case, the common area allowed for a large crowd to assemble (IMJ).

Peter and John heal a lame man sitting at the "Beautiful Gate" (3:2). Its exact identity is unclear, since no gate of the temple complex by formal name was called "Beautiful Gate." The Nicanor Gate within the temple compound is described as beautiful in Jewish sources. Another possibility is the Double Gate on the south wall, because this gate was one of the main access points into the entire temple complex. Peter will preach to the crowd that assembles at a place called "Solomon's Porch" (3:11). Once again, the exact identity of this nomenclature also is unclear, often identified with the structure on the south side of the temple complex, but sometimes identified with the structure associated with the eastern wall (see Fig. 6.2 above).

Bruce pointed out that Luke gave the healing of the lame man at the temple by way of providing one example of the summary of apostolic activity in Acts 2:43 that "many signs and wonders were done through the apostles."[1] This sign in particular is chosen perhaps as the most obvious fulfillment of Isa 35:6 that "then the lame shall leap like a deer."

Another feature often pointed out is how this story illustrates the ministry parallels between Jesus and the disciples. The episode in Luke 5:17–26 of Jesus healing a lame man at Capernaum has the same three basic components of a known lame man, a healing miracle, and a word of forgiveness. Once again, we see Luke working his Luke-Acts theme of Luke as the story of Jesus, part one, and Acts as the story of Jesus, part two.

Temple Sermon (3:12–26)

Peter's temple sermon in Acts 3 is the eschatological offer of forgiveness to the general population of Jerusalem for those who participated in the crucifixion of Jesus. A chance is offered for repentance. The moment of the revelation of divine grace in the message is 3:17, "you acted in ignorance." These words are an incredible offer of amnesty. The effect is to place ultimate accountability for the death of Jesus on Jewish leaders. Still, the crowds called for Jesus to be crucified, and now they learn God has raised him from the dead. The resurrection is God's veto of their verdict, and they now find themselves having acted directly against God himself.

[1] Bruce, *Acts*, 76–77.

Peter's Sermons
The Church's Movement from Jews to Gentiles

Sermon	Audience	Significance
1. Acts 2	Jerusalem's pilgrims	Church empowered
2. Acts 3	Jerusalem's people	Forgiveness offered
3. Acts 4	Jerusalem's leaders	Forgiveness offered
4. Acts 5	Jerusalem's leaders	Forgiveness rejected
5. Acts 10	Cornelius's house	Gentile plan unfolds
6. Acts 11	Circumcision party	Gentile plan resisted
7. Acts 15	Church leaders	Gentile plan settled

FIGURE 6.3. Peter's Sermons: Acts 3. After the call of messianic Israel at Pentecost, Messiah makes appeal to national Israel, offering forgiveness, first to the people.

Peter's call is a direct appeal to "repent" in order to have their "sins wiped out" (3:19). The narrative context for this declaration is crucial. This message of sins being "wiped out" is preached in the temple itself— a significant claim in the context of Jewish tradition! The temple was the Jewish center of ritual expiation. The claim being made is that the entire ritual system of the Jewish temple is realized in Jesus. Thus, Jesus becomes the place of expiation, not the temple.[2] In essence, the present temple ritual and the function of the high priest are declared defunct. This present central system of ritual forgiveness is transcended and its central figure, the high priest, who has murder on his hands, declared corrupt. Caiaphas is being given his pink slip.

Acceptance of this call for eschatological decision is characterized as "times of refreshing" (3:19).[3] In the narrative shadow of Pentecost

---

[2] An idea theologically resonating with Rom 3:25.

[3] A rare term, *kairoi anapsyxeōs*, καιροὶ ἀναψύξεως. In the Bible, this ἀναψύξεως elsewhere is only in Exod 8:15 in the sense of respite from judgment. Linguistic data alone suggests not to make much of the expression—as if a technical term of Jewish messianic eschatology, which clearly is begging the question, because the term is not. This passage often wrongly is connected to a (mis)interpretation of Acts 1:6 assuming a national Israel is the divine program; contra Bock, *A Theology of Luke and Acts*; cf. Stevens, *Review Article: A Theology of Luke and Acts*. Ignored in many schemes of the "last days" is that the usage here could be just as general as a good night's rest for all we

and the shared community described as its fulfillment in Acts 2, then times of refreshing in context infers what Jerusalemites can see before their very eyes already described in the Acts narrative: the present joy and shared abundance of the community of believers in Jerusalem. What God desires is that this joy of messianic Israel become universal, or the "times of restoration of all things"[4] for which Jesus remains in heaven in order to effect by continuing to pour out the Spirit.[5]

Rejection, on the other hand, is cataclysmic. Rejection will mean eschatological judgment. That dark consequence is clear in all the prophets. Speaking of the prophet like Moses to come, Moses himself had warned, "anyone who will not hear that prophet will be cut off from the people" (Deut 18:19). Being cut off from the people means having no part of Israel. All the prophets from Samuel on confirm that such a crisis will ensue upon rejection of God's Messiah.[6]

The call is personalized to the hearers in 3:25. Peter reinforces this prophetic warning with "you are the children of the prophets." By this word he invokes the significance of the Abrahamic covenant, to which the prophets appealed by underlining the core of being Israel, which is a call. Israel has a destiny. That destiny is to bless all the families of the

really know exegetically. Texts that refer to return from exile (such as Isa 40:9–11; Jer 32:42–44; Ezek 37:21–28; Hos 11:9–11; 14:4–7; Amos 9:11–15) were fulfilled historically. They must not be taken out of their original context to apply to a so-called "end times." What was *not* fulfilled historically after the exile was the other part of the equation and the whole point of the land, a *spiritual* return to God. That part of the return never really happened despite all Ezra's efforts; otherwise, national Israel never would have crucified the Lord of glory (1 Cor 2:8). Israel to be consummated does not require land. Israel requires a heart for God (Jer 31:31–34), which is, by definition, messianic Israel.

[4]Again, another rare term, *chronōn apokatastaseōs pantōn*, χρόνων ἀποκαταστάσε-ως (3:21). The root of "restoration" here is the same as in the disciples question in Acts 1:6. Luke clearly broadens the disciples' interest exclusively in national Israel in the original Acts 1:6 question to "all things" here, which subtly corrects the original question's errant assumption that national Israel is the focus of the kingdom of God.

[5]We should avoid suggesting that in heaven Jesus is just twiddling his thumbs, waiting on some arbitrary ticking of a cosmic clock before he can jump off the sidelines of history and get back in the game of establishing the kingdom of God. Luke has made clear that Jesus ascended in order for the Spirit to descend and be active in the church. That movement is the whole point of the unique ascension-Pentecost literary interlock by Luke. The Spirit at work in the church is the signature of the enthroned Jesus accomplishing the purpose of his ascension.

[6]Perhaps this understanding about "all the prophets from Samuel on" was part of the teaching for forty days by Jesus after the resurrection (Acts 1:3).

earth, one of the core responsibilities of the covenant of Abraham (Gen 12:3). Messiah is actualizing this blessing through messianic Israel. He starts in Jerusalem. He builds outward from that point. That blessing is spiritual: "by turning each of you from your wicked ways" (Acts 3:26). For one, that would mean if Jesus came again, you would not crucify him.

The Pentecost abundance theme is integral to this message by Peter as well. Later on, we find out about five thousand responded to this offer of amnesty (4:4). Israel as a nation was at a fork in the road. This response, of course, sounds promising. One does wonder what could have been. However, the response of the temple leaders that will determine the fate of the nation is yet to come.

Sanhedrin Sermon (4:1–22)

Peter's Sermons
The Church's Movement from Jews to Gentiles

Sermon	Audience	Significance
1. Acts 2	Jerusalem's pilgrims	Church empowered
2. Acts 3	Jerusalem's people	Forgiveness offered
3. Acts 4	Jerusalem's leaders	Forgiveness offered
4. Acts 5	Jerusalem's leaders	Forgiveness rejected
5. Acts 10	Cornelius's house	Gentile plan unfolds
6. Acts 11	Circumcision party	Gentile plan resisted
7. Acts 15	Church leaders	Gentile plan settled

FIGURE 6.4. Peter's Sermons: Acts 4. Jesus is confronting Israel for her sin of rejecting Messiah. He offers forgiveness to all responsible, both people and leaders.

We have a new chapter division (4:1), but not really a new story. The division here is poor, because the division breaks up what is one continuous narrative. We still are playing out the consequences of the healing of the lame man by Peter and John. This narrative is a story of grace and forgiveness for Jerusalem, first for the population at large, then for the leaders who conspired to have Jesus killed. Messiah's offer of forgiveness to Jerusalem is a crisis with eschatological consequences for national Israel. The response of the leaders to Messiah will determine the rest of the story. Rejection once is ignorance. Rejection twice, in the face of resurrection, is obstinacy and hard-heartedness. "The priests, the captain of the temple, and Sadducees came to them" (4:1). Cue the ominous tones from the orchestra.

Annas ruled as high priest from AD 6–15. He was appointed by the Roman legate, Quirinius, in Damascus as the Romans converted Judea into a procuratorship.[7] When he took power, Annas reformed the Sanhedrin to give Sadducees control when formerly the Pharisaic sect dominated. He established a high priestly dynasty that controlled the office of high priest for decades through five of his sons and one son-in-law holding that office after him. The son-in-law was Caiaphas, appointed by the prefect Gratus. Caiaphas ruled from AD 18–36, so was the one who condemned Jesus to death. Caiaphas cast his lot with the Romans, and his collusion with Rome was a sore spot for Jews ready to revolt to be rid of the despised overlords of their country.

Caiaphas's most notable act was to move the financial exchange market from the Mount of Olives opposite Jerusalem across the Kidron Valley into the temple compound itself. Most coins had the imprint of a pagan ruler's visage, so were interpreted as graven images prohibited by the law. Jesus used this coin image from a denarius to teach about paying taxes to Caesar (Luke 20:22–25). To purchase the appropriate sacrificial offering for the temple ritual, a coin without a ruler's image had to be used. As with any financial operation, a charge was

FIGURE 6.5. Denarius of Tiberius (14–37). The coin produced for Jesus in his temple encounter about paying taxes (ASM).

incurred for the exchange. By relocating the Mount of Olives market to their temple precincts, Sadducees enabled adding their cut to the charge and were lining their own pockets. They were profiting, becoming even richer, with temple business. Caiaphas moving the exchange market

---

[7]Quirinius is mentioned by Luke in Luke 2:2. Herod's son, Archelaus, ruled Judea so corruptly that Augustus exiled Archelaus to Gaul in AD 6.

and related animal pens into the temple itself for mercenary Sadducean interests is the direct target of Jesus actions in cleansing the temple by overturning the tables of the money changers (Luke 19:45–46). This same Caiaphas also was the high priest who only a few weeks earlier had led the council to accuse Jesus of blasphemy and lobbied Pilate to have Jesus crucified (Luke 22:66–71).

Thus, the temple was the special domain of the priests and Sadducees, and Jesus already had caused trouble there. Now one of his own followers is back again, teaching and stirring up another crowd. Peter is "on their turf," so to speak. Luke mentions the Sadducees to make clear why they were "much annoyed" (4:2). Sadducees did not believe in the resurrection. What Peter was preaching about Jesus confounded their doctrine.

The leader who had Jesus crucified now confronts Peter. Caiaphas and the Sanhedrin challenge apostolic authority to speak on religious matters, most particularly forgiveness of sins, in the very precincts of the temple, which was the exclusive domain of forgiveness of sins in Israel. Peter is blunt: "Let it be known to all of you, and to all the people of Israel, that this man is standing before you in good health by the name of Jesus Christ of Nazareth, whom you crucified, whom God raised from the dead" (Acts 4:10). Peter is face to face with murderous Caiaphas, yet challenges him right back with truth Caiaphas cannot deny: "whom you crucified, whom God raised from the dead." That punch line would put a dagger in a Sadducee's theological heart. Peter is contradicting Sadducean doctrine with the Easter reality of only a few weeks before and about which Jesus had taught for forty days before the ascension. Peter also is contradicting Sadducean authority, implicitly rejecting their leadership of Israel, and accusing the high priest of sin of a high hand, hence, being corrupt and illegitimate. With an illegitimate high priest, the offerings of the Day of Atonement for Israel are meaningless. Peter brings the Day of Atonement disaster for Israel into bold relief when he declares unequivocally, "Salvation is in no one else, for no other name under heaven given among humans exists by which we must be saved" (4:12). "No other name under heaven" means "not even you, Caiaphas!" So when the next day of Atonement rolls around in a few months, Israel will be destitute of forgiveness.

What is clear to Peter in this moment of Sanhedrin challenge and obstinacy is the fulfillment of Ps 118:22, which was given Christian messianic exegesis: "the stone which was rejected by you, the builders, has become the cornerstone" (4:11). The prophet Isaiah provides the early church with this type of stone imagery. The idea of a stumbling stone in Isa 8:14–15 was used by Jesus to confront the scribes and chief priests in Luke 20:17–18. The idea of a cornerstone being laid in Jerusalem by God himself in Isa 28:16 resonates in multiple New Testament texts.[8] Even though the builders (the scribes, chief priests, Pharisees) rejected the stone as suitable for construction of the Israel of God, repentance still is possible. This time of being presented with the facts of the resurrection and of the power of the Spirit poured out on the church is a time pregnant with historical consequences for national Israel. The nation is at a watershed moment. After Peter's absolutely clear declaration, rejection of Jesus no longer will be taken as "ignorance" but hard-heartedness. Destiny is in the balance.

FIGURE 6.6. Herod's Temple Stones. In the southeast, southwest corners of Herod's temple foundation in Jerusalem today can be seen over eighty-ton, solid limestone blocks sixteen feet thick, the largest known foundation stones of the ancient world.

Israel's leadership makes a fateful decision. They recognize the boldness of these quite ordinary men when anyone else would have

[8] Rom 9:33; Eph 2:20; 1 Pet 2:6.

been shaking in their boots. They put two and two together that these men were companions of Jesus. Finally, the cured man standing right beside them was irrefutable proof of apostolic preaching (the power of Jesus's name) and apostolic doctrine (resurrection). Conclusion? "They had nothing to say in opposition" (4:14). All they can do is to try to restrict the spread of this movement, even though all Jerusalem has a miracle buzz in the streets, and even though, in regard to the matter, they confess to themselves, "we cannot deny" (4:16). All they can do is to try to threaten and intimidate. They command the apostles "not to speak or teach at all in the name of Jesus" (4:18). Good luck with that.

Peter's response is classic. When confronted by a high court with listening to God (in the sense of obeying) or listening to human authority that contradicts God, no choice really is being offered (4:19–20). The refusal to be compliant by the apostles calls the bluff of the Sanhedrin. All they can do is repeat the threat, and then release the disciples, for the man healed was forty years old and known to everybody, since he had for years stationed himself at one of the busy gates of the Jerusalem temple. Even Jewish pilgrims not resident in Jerusalem coming to the feasts probably would recognize this former lame man and be confronted with his miraculous healing (4:21–22).

The die is cast. A fateful decision is being made, only to be sealed the next time. An act of ignorance becomes an act of rebellion. God's amnesty offer will be rejected, and Israel's national destiny decided.

Church Response (4:23–31)

Messianic Israel quotes a messianic psalm to interpret the Sanhedrin showdown. "Why did the nations rage?" (4:25) comes from Psalm 2, long used in the nation's history as part of coronation rituals installing a new king on the Davidic throne. The topic of this psalm is the Lord's anointed and his rule, already read messianically in Jewish tradition by the time of the first century. The application moves through a contextual inversion. In the original context, the nations raging are Israel's national enemies. The present Israel defined by the Sanhedrin and her leaders is now aligned in collusion with pagan Rome. Caiaphas and Pilate had worked *together* to have Jesus crucified. So this Israel of Caiaphas, the scribes, chief priests, Sadducees and Pharisees now plays the role of "raging nations" along with pagans that were the original target of the psalm. So, Herod, Pontius Pilate, gentiles, and the peoples of Israel are all confederate in raging against the Lord and against his Messiah in the voice of the Sanhedrin's threat (4:27).

Sadducees have tied Israel's fate to pagan Rome. They will lose everything in the bargain in only a few decades with the First Jewish War. They lose their temple, their place, even their very existence—ironically, within the lifespan of the lame man who was healed on this day in Israel's history. After this point of the Sanhedrin's response to the healing of the lame man, is "Israel" really Israel?

The church prays for boldness in speaking God's word, which would be the story of Jesus (4:29). The Sanhedrin threat falls impotent. The church prays that God would stretch out his hand to heal and do signs and wonders that silence the raging nations (4:30). The divine response to messianic Israel is strong affirmation. The place of prayer and praise is shaken. The prayer of the church is answered immediately: "they were all filled with the Holy Spirit and spoke the word of God with boldness" (4:31). The reader is to presume that the healing of the lame man was just one example of what Jerusalem saw and heard in those days of messianic Israel's witness.

ISRAEL'S DESTINY

The logic of the narrative continues to evolve out of the healing of the lame man. This particular miracle of the many signs and wonders performed by the apostles was different. Luke chose to tell this miracle, because response to this miracle tells the story of Israel. Whereas the game has to be played on out, already the chess master can see that the pieces are lining up for checkmate.

Pentecost Israel (4:32–35)

First, Luke wants to demonstrate the destiny that could have been. This destiny would have been Pentecost Israel. Pentecost Israel is Israel of the last days, Israel of festival fulfillment, Israel of great abundance—messianic Israel. This Israel is the kingdom of God realized on earth, the story of Jesus, part two, the church and her mission.

We noted that Pentecost as a pilgrim festival concluded with an inclusive communal meal to which the poor, Levite, and stranger were invited. Luke already has suggested this communal meal is part of the early community of followers of Jesus in his post-Pentecost description of the social life of the church in Acts 2:42–47. This description is placed immediately prior to the story of the healing of the lame man. Luke now resumes that story of communal life. One way to see the connection is the precise literary echo of the exact same wording, "as anyone might have need" both at 2:45 and 4:35 (as shown on p. 56).

The communal experience has grown deeper. The whole group is "one heart and soul" and even to the point that "no one claimed private ownership of any possessions" (4:32).[9] The point is the very promise of Pentecost abundance has been transcended. This experience is totally unmarked territory even in Israel's long journey. Nothing in the life of the patriarchs, the tribes occupying the promised land, the kingdom period, or even after exile comes close to "all things common." A needy person was not to be found.[10] The Lord's prayer for daily bread is answered (Luke 11:3). Israel cares for the poor, Levite, and stranger. This Israel, obedient to God, is close to heaven on earth.[11]

During this extraordinary period of communal abundance, the apostles show great power in preaching. Their testimony to the resurrection resounded throughout Jerusalem. The efforts of the Sanhedrin to quarantine this message have been vain. No wonder Luke could summarize that "great grace was upon them all" (4:33). Efficacious prayer is part of the story of this power, signaled by the upper room set piece at the beginning of the narrative and the prayer in 4:31.

Barnabas, "Son of Consolation" (4:36–37)

Joseph is introduced with three descriptors: clan, country, and surname. Each has a point. First, Joseph is a Levite (*Leuitēs*, Λευίτης). No other time in all of Acts is this term used, making Joseph a unique

[9]This action is voluntary, not enforced, inspired by God's Spirit, not humanistic, so clearly not even in the ballpark of a socialist state or political communism.

[10]Let the thought simmer. Imagine any modern city without a single beggar with a coin cup extended, and not a single homeless person on the streets at night.

[11]Land and homes being sold does not sound like good, long-term fiscal policy, and rightly so. However, our critique should not be hasty. This financial activity probably should be contextualized around the expectation of the return of Jesus. The angels promised at the ascension that Jesus "will come in the same way as you have seen him go into heaven" (1:11). What would keep them from thinking anything other than that the "you" meant them?

character. Levite integrates this character into Luke's Pentecost theme. In fact, Joseph will turn the Pentecost theme inside out. The Levite is one of the categories of those especially to include in the Pentecost invitation (Deut 16:11). Yet, in messianic Israel, Pentecost abundance is so extraordinary, *the Levite himself is making contribution* to the needs of others (4:37).[12] This action is Pentecost in reverse, Pentecost transcended.

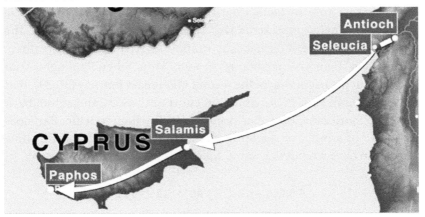

FIGURE 6.7. Cyprus on the 1MJ. Cyprus, the Antioch mission team's first stop, is Barnabas's home territory and where the conversion of Sergius Paulus takes place.

Second, Joseph is from Cyprus. This country of origin connects two ways in the narrative. First, Cyprus puts Joseph in the category of Diaspora Israel. He serves as representative of the broader categories of Israel beyond localization in the promised land, even though he does have relatives in Jerusalem (12:12).[13] Second, Cyprus will become significant as the first stop of the first missionary journey and where the proconsul Sergius Paulus is converted at Paphos (13:12), one of the mission team's most socially elite conversions.

Third, Joseph is surnamed "Barnabas" by the apostles. Luke gives the meaning as "Son of Encouragement" or as "Son of Consolation" (4:36). No known etymology[14] for this term means the meaning lies at the narrative level for Luke. This idea of consolation resonates with the

---

[12]Ostensibly, Levites were not supposed to own land (Num 18:20, 24; Deut 10:9; 18:1–2. Yet, Jeremiah, a priest, did (Jer 32:6–15), as well as Josephus (*Life* 433).

[13]John Mark's mother lived in Jerusalem. For John Mark as cousin, cf. Col 4:10.

[14]See Fitzmyer, *Acts*, 320–21.

infancy narrative. The prophet Simeon is described as looking for the "consolation of Israel" (Luke 2:25). Jesus is the consolation of Israel, and Jesus has poured out his Spirit to bring about Pentecost fullness in the church. Barnabas is a "Son of Consolation" because he channels the consolation of Israel that comes through Messiah to the church. Further, Barnabas will be the one person who facilitates every major step of the early part of Saul's career after the Damascus Road. Thus, Barnabas will have a direct role in facilitating the fruition of the Hellenist Cycle through its major representative, Saul of Tarsus. By virtue of the representative value of Barnabas at multiple levels of the narrative, then, Barnabas is "Pentecost facilitator" in Acts. Thus, when Paul fights with Barnabas at the beginning of the second missionary journey (15:39), that fight will derail Paul's entire mission effort until God can get him back on track. Spiritually, Barnabas is no one with whom to trifle. Barnabas has more of a mind of the Spirit than does Paul. Saul-Paul will show himself to have a tendency not to follow his mentors appropriately.

Ananias and Sapphira (5:1–11)

The chapter division, again, is unfortunate. The break generates the wrong impression a new story begins. However, the story of Ananias and Sapphira continues the story of Pentecost Israel. That recognition is what will liberate the exegesis to make sense of what has caused so much trouble for commentators. The problem is, the punishment of death does not seem anywhere near the crime, so the story assaults a sense of the justice of God, that is, minus Luke's macro context.

The first point will be to note how the story of Barnabas "fronts" the story of Ananias and Sapphira. Barnabas and Ananias are set as reverse literary images. The macro context still is flowing out of the Pen-

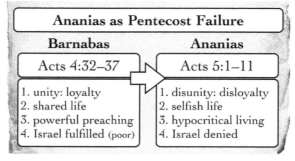

FIGURE 6.8. Barnabas and Ananias. Ananias is the literary foil to the character of Barnabas on the Pentecost theme.

tecost event. In this overarching context, their actions are contrasted directly to emphasize the importance of Pentecost fulfillment.

Ananias and Sapphira formulate a conspiracy against messianic Israel. When Ananias conspires to defraud the church, he becomes the foil to Barnabas, since Barnabas, even as a Levite who was supposed to receive the Pentecost blessing, is himself amazingly generous to all. If Barnabas is Pentecost facilitator, then Ananias is Pentecost failure. The threat is failure of eschatological fulfillment of the prophets and the word of God about the Pentecost fullness of messianic Israel, not simply the poor who need financial support. This fullness is divine proof to Jerusalem that God has raised Jesus, and the ascended Jesus has poured out his Spirit on the church. Ananias is antithetical to Pentecost fulfillment and, unchecked, threatens the core witness of the church to Jerusalem in these crucial early days after the resurrection.

Both Ananias and Sapphira are judged immediately. Why they are judged is revealed in Peter's question to Sapphira, which question is the whole point of this story—a plot revealer later for the story of the Jerusalem Conference in Acts 15. Peter asks Sapphira,

> How is it that you have agreed together to put the Spirit of the Lord to the test? (Acts 5:9)

Putting the Spirit of the Lord to the test is a famous wilderness theme from the Exodus story, which is an important context to support the Exodus-Pentecost theme in the Acts narrative. When the children of Israel camped at Rephidim, in other traditions known as Massah, but had no water to drink, they quarreled with Moses, who asked, "Why do you quarrel with me? Why do you test the Lord?" (Exod 17:2). The law encodes this wilderness experience as prototypical of idolatry, a behavior that would arouse the wrath of God.

> Do not follow other gods, any of the gods of the peoples who are all around you, because the Lord your God, who is present with you, is a jealous God. The anger of the Lord your God would be kindled against you, and he would destroy you from the face of the earth. Do not put the Lord your God to the test, as you tested him at Massah (Deut 6:14–16, NRSV).

This "Do not put the Lord your God to the test" of Deut 6:16 is quoted by Jesus in his own wilderness temptation (Luke 4:12), which sets the trajectory straight for Ananias and Sapphira. Ananias's fraud put God to the test by threatening messianic Israel. The couple revealed that, in fact, they were idolaters, wanting their personal cut, valuing money more than God. And just what were the Sadducees doing moving the Mount of Olives financial exchange to the temple? More connection between Annas and Ananias than first appears. Compare Peter's harsh words to Simon for his sorcery for financial gain in Samaria.

> Peter answered: "May your silver perish with you, because you thought God's gift was for sale. You have no part or share in this ministry, because your heart is not right before God. Repent therefore of your wickedness. Pray to the Lord that, if possible, your heart's intent might be forgiven to you. For I see that you are filled to the brim with bitterness and the chains of wickedness" (Acts 8:20–23).

Ananias becomes a judgment paradigm. His character and his fate anticipate two future judgment crises, one in the story of Acts, and one beyond the story. In the story in Acts is the ecclesial crisis, the Jerusalem Conference (Acts 15). Leaders representing major parts of the church convene to discuss circumcision and gentiles. In the debate, Peter asks of the church the question he asked of Sapphira about testing God (15:10). Notice that the summary "great fear seized the whole church" (5:11) is the first time "church" occurs in Acts. Use here may be to link Peter's testing the Spirit

FIGURE 6.9. Ananias as Judgment Paradigm. Ananias serves as a judgment paradigm for both the church and for Jerusalem.

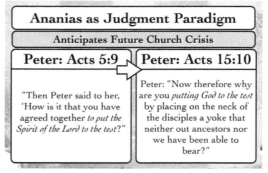

FIGURE 6.10. Peter's Question to Sapphira. Peter's question in Acts 5:9 becomes the motif of judgment that sets the stakes for the Jerusalem Conference.

warning in Acts 15 to a church on the precipice of judgment disaster. Luke's use of "church" is Pauline. "Church" is Paul's characteristic word for messianic Israel in his letters, a term he bequeaths to Christianity.

National crisis will come only a few decades after these events recorded in Acts. Judea will revolt against Rome in a disastrous war that ends the nation in AD 66–70. The reader needs to remember that this tragic war is the result of the watershed moment in Israel's history with which Luke is dealing at this point in the narrative of Acts as Messiah appeals to Israel with all the proofs of his messiahship before them (resurrection life, Pentecostal abundance).

Putting God to the test is the key thought in Acts 5. Luke chooses this incident in the early life of the church in order to prepare the way for understanding how God was going to perceive the persistent obstinacy of Israel's leaders, particularly the Sadducees and the Sanhedrin, for opposing the gospel. For Luke, the motives of Annas and Ananias are parallel. Sadducees were putting God to the test, and God would bring judgment on this Sadducean syndicate in Jerusalem and their prized institution of the temple just forty-seven years later.

Sanhedrin Threat (5:12–42)

Pentecost Continues (5:12–16)

These verses indicate that signs of Pentecost abundance in messianic Israel continue. The witness in Jerusalem is exploding. The apostles continue to work signs and wonders and to assemble in Solomon's Porch, apparently to teach the people. Great numbers continue to be added to the church. The renown is so public that the sick are laid out along the street hoping to catch Peter's shadow, and even surrounding villages are getting the word of messianic Israel in Jerusalem, bringing their sick and tormented. The real kick in the pants for the Sanhedrin is Luke's summary, "and they were all cured" (5:16). No charlatans in this group! The Sanhedrin either cannot cognize or else will not admit that Messiah has brought such Pentecost abundance to Israel.

Sanhedrin Responds (5:17–33)

The high priest took action. He is Caiaphas, the one who had Jesus killed as a false messiah, but is vexed by the truth that Jesus is Messiah. The apostles are imprisoned, all of them this time, not just Peter and

John. Imprisonment did not work before. What is wrong with Caiaphas? He is desperate. The story signals that the high court opposition is going to harden into outright rebellion against God. The matter is beginning to look like an attempt to repeat the action with Jesus.

An angel releases the apostles, and commands they continue to preach in the temple "all the words of this life" (5:20).[15] This "life" is messianic Israel in Pentecost abundance. The direction to place themselves "in the temple" is intentionally provocative, and evokes Jesus in the temple overturning tables of Sadducean money changers. This deliberate action is a direct challenge to the Sadducees, since this temple is the domain of their authority in Jerusalem. Once again, we see how Luke weaves the narrative of the disciples to reflect that of Jesus, fulfilling the Luke-Acts design of telling the story of Jesus in two parts.

When the Sanhedrin learns of the apostles' apparent escape without any signs of a forced exit, they are confounded (5:22–24). Either they have been hit with an inside job, a grave option, since that would mean they are a house seriously divided, or God himself has intervened, in which case they publicly are humiliated, shown to be wrong about Jesus. Their situation has grown even worse in less than twenty-four hours. All they know to do is to put out another summons for an appearance before the high court.[16] The apostles hold the high ground, having the favor of the people, so they go peaceably, which is the only "good news" the Sanhedrin will get in this day.

In this second Sanhedrin appearance of the apostles, the high court has no viable option. The scene would be comical were the matter not tragic. All they can do is repeat their impotent threats from the last session and reiterate the silence edict (5:27–28). Reiteration indicates Sanhedrin recalcitrance. Their action is culpable for two reasons. First, they admit apostolic success ("filled Jerusalem"), so they understand the messianic claims of the apostles' preaching as proven. Second, they tacitly admit blood guilt responsibility in having Jesus crucified ("this man's blood"), so they are in the state of sin of a high hand.

We now encounter the fourth sermon in the Petrine series. This sermon shows that God's forgiveness to Israel is rejected (5:29–32). In

---

[15]Release from imprisonment has literary resonance with the resurrection of Jesus.

[16]I always think at this point in the narrative that the temple guards must be getting tired constantly retrieving these guys from the temple precincts.

this sermon, Luke summarizes the crux of the issue of the resurrection of Jesus and apostolic testimony to Messiah.

> "The God of our fathers raised up Jesus, whom you had killed by hanging him on a tree. This one God exalted to his right hand as Prince and Savior in order to give repentance to Israel and forgiveness of sins. And we are witnesses regarding these words, and the Holy Spirit whom God gave to those who obey him" (5:30–32).

This statement is loaded with key phrases that summarize the essence of the matter.

- "God of our fathers": the issue of messianic Israel, God's purposes
- "whom you had killed": the Sanhedrin's wrong verdict
- "God exalted": the divine veto on the Sanhedrin verdict
- "Prince": the true king leading Israel to repentance (*not* Herod)
- "Savior": the true forgiveness of sins (*not* Caiaphas)
- "we are witness": the core commission of Messiah
- "Holy Spirit": the fountainhead of all Pentecost power, abundance

"We are witnesses" means viable proof has been given in a court of law. Two witnesses are required, yet the apostles form a group of twelve! In the face of the trial of Jesus, the whole situation is full of great irony.[17] Mention of the Holy Spirit clearly is an accusation that the Sanhedrin's business at this very moment has nothing to do with God. The dig made by Peter is that this Spirit is given "to those who obey him"—like the Sanhedrin is not and has not ever since Messiah showed up in Israel.

With these words of Peter's sermon, the high priest's office and function are declared null and void, and the Sanhedrin's claim to be the high court of the land completely bankrupt as an institution of national Israel's own making after the exile, self-serving the worst national sins, not even capable of rendering the most rudimentary sense of justice in

---

[17]The matter is ironic, since not even two witnesses who agreed could be produced against Jesus at his mock trial before this same judicial body, and what false witnesses were produced did not even agree (Matt 26:20; Mark 14:55–59). Judicially, the case should have been thrown out of court immediately.

the land. The word "Savior" and "forgiveness" is spoken directly in the face of the high priest Caiaphas only weeks after having Jesus sentenced to die on a cross. The high priest is responsible for atoning the sins of the nation on the Day of Atonement. Opposition to Jesus is opposition to God himself. Thus, the real question is, Who is on trial here? The Sanhedrin! The tables are turned.

Peter's Sermons
The Church's Movement from Jews to Gentiles

Sermon	Audience	Significance
1. Acts 2	Jerusalem's pilgrims	Church empowered
2. Acts 3	Jerusalem's people	Forgiveness offered
3. Acts 4	Jerusalem's leaders	Forgiveness offered
4. Acts 5	Jerusalem's leaders	Forgiveness rejected
5. Acts 10	Cornelius's house	Gentile plan unfolds
6. Acts 11	Circumcision party	Gentile plan resisted
7. Acts 15	Church leaders	Gentile plan settled

FIGURE 6.11. Peter's Sermons: Acts 5. This fourth sermon seals the deal of rejection of divine forgiveness on the part of temple leaders.

The words of the Sanhedrin's response are dramatic: "They were enraged and wanted to kill them" (5:33). This situation parallels that of Jesus. With their murderous hearts, they would have tried to do the same now as then, but the apostles are so many and the crowds so behind them; the Sanhedrin is locked up, not the apostles. We have progressed in response from the first appearance of Peter and John before the Sanhedrin with its "ordered them not to speak or teach at all in the name of Jesus" (4:18) to this second appearance by all the apostles and "enraged and wanted to kill them" (5:33). Given all the evidence presented—not in this vain hearing but all over Jerusalem and the surrounding villages for weeks—this response reads every way as climactic, final, and irrevocable. Had not a wise Pharisee been in this crowd of Sadducees, they might have tried anyway. Peter's quote of the psalm in the original hearing about the "stone which the builders rejected" now comes true (4:11).

Gamaliel's Advice (5:34–42)

This part could be entitled, "Saved by a Pharisee," although the Sadducees would not have been amused. The Pharisees arose as a sect among
the Jews following the days of the Maccabean Revolt a few centuries
before Jesus was born. At one time they controlled the Sanhedrin, but
they were pushed to the sidelines as a minority party in the reforms of
Annas, Caiaphas's father-in-law, in AD 6. Yet, with their widespread
system of synagogues throughout the land, Pharisees wielded popular
power in the people's high opinion. Thus, Pharisee presence in the
Sanhedrin was imperative to gain popular support for high court decisions. Pharisaic beliefs are operative assumptions in Gamaliel's advice,
particularly resurrection doctrine and belief in the sovereignty of God.

Gamaliel's logic is practical. If God is involved, you cannot resist
God in the first place. If God is not involved, any rebel cause will fail
anyway without you lifting a finger, because Rome will not suffer insurrection. So, you need not waste effort trying to do Rome's job. His
two examples are recent revolts in memory of Theudas and Judas the
Galilean; both Rome destroyed.[18]

Gamaliel's premier word of wisdom is going to become a bedrock
theme for Luke explaining the entire sweep of the plot of Acts, but most
particularly the story of Saul of Tarsus. This theme will become quite
ironic, given that, in the narrative of Acts, Saul will be a self-described
student of Gamaliel (22:3). The advice is summarized:

> "So, in the matter presently before us, I tell you, leave off from
> these men and let them alone, because if their cause or plot be
> of human origin, it will fail; but if their cause is from God, you
> will not be able to overthrow them; otherwise, you only will
> distinguish yourselves as God-fighters!" (Acts 5:38–39).

---

[18]The only known Theudas is a messianic pretender Josephus dates during the procurator Fadus (*Ant.* 20.5.1 [97–98]), later than Judas the Galilean. Gamaliel, however,
implies a time *before* Judas. Archelaus was deposed by Augustus in AD 6 and Judea
converted to a procuratorship. Judas the Galilean revolted but was defeated. The later
Zealot movement may derive from this failed revolt in Galilee. These failed revolts show
Luke's need to interpret the Jesus movement as no threat to Rome, since their leader
was condemned as an insurrectionist from Galilee. History again would illustrate
Gamaliel's wisdom in the rebellion of the Second Jewish War of AD 133–35 under the
messianic pretender, Simon bar Kokhba. The most famous rabbi of that day, Akiba, had
hailed Bar Kokhba as messiah; Jerusalem Talmud, *Ta'anit* 4:6 (68d–69a); cf. Gruber,
Rabbi Akiba's Messiah. The Romans destroyed that rebellion as well.

Carefully note that the noun "God-fighters" (*theomachoi*, θεομάχοι) occurs only here in all of biblical Greek.[19] The motif of being a "God-fighter" will drive Luke's plot and character development. He is using Gamaliel to reinforce in advance one of the two major themes of the Stephen speech that guide plot development in Acts.

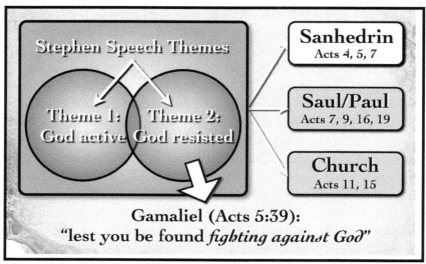

FIGURE 6.12. Gamaliel's "Fighting Against God," Acts 5:39. This word to the Sanhedrin reinforces a major plot and character dynamic in all of Acts.

Gamaliel leads the Pharisees, and their opinion has to be heeded. Otherwise, the Sanhedrin is a house dangerously divided. The apostles still are flogged for their disobedience of a direct command of the high court, and the command is repeated for the third time. This repetition for the third time of so ignored a command is a supreme signal of the Sanhedrin's impotence. Flogging is such a trauma to the human body that one could die from the punishment. The gravity of what happened here to the apostles must not be trivialized or ignored. This flogging fulfills Jesus's prediction during his ministry of persecution for his followers, yet Spirit-empowered witness.[20]

Thus, the apostles' public witness continues unabated (5:41–42). They counted themselves fortunate to be counted "worthy to suffer dishonor for the Name" (5:41). They spend every day in the temple. They totally won the temple turf war. The power of Messiah has bro-

---

[19]The cognate verb occurs only once in 2 Macc 7:19.

[20]Luke 12:11–12; 21:12–19.

ken the power of the Sanhedrin. Note that this entire movement began in the temple in Acts 3 and concludes in the temple in Acts 5. This literary design forms a grand *inclusio* over the whole structure. The temple is where the story started with the healing of the lame man at the Beautiful Gate by Peter and John, followed by Peter's preaching to the Jerusalemites in the temple complex. Now, Peter's temple preaching continues despite all efforts of the Sanhedrin. So, the apostles continue to preach "that Jesus is the Messiah" (5:42).

FIGURE 6.13. Temple Literary *Inclusio*. All of Acts 3–5 is one literary movement in which Messiah makes earnest appeal to Jerusalem's people and her leaders.

In Acts 3–5, Messiah makes earnest appeal to Israel. Willingness of his followers to be flogged is a measure of the gravity of that appeal. National Israel has been given every chance to be renewed by Messiah to become part of a new day and a new vision of the people of God, messianic Israel of the prophetic last days. Jesus is a climactic moment of decision for Israel, witnessed centuries before in Moses, who spoke of a prophet like himself to come (Deut 18:18). God had warned about this coming prophet, "Anyone who does not heed the words that the prophet shall speak in my name, I myself will hold accountable" (Deut 18:19). Jesus as the climactic moment of decision for Israel also is witnessed in John the Baptist, whom Jesus declared the Elijah forerunner of Messiah of the last days (Luke 1:17). John had warned, "Even now the axe is lying at the root of the trees; every tree therefore that does not bear good fruit is cut down and thrown into the fire" (Luke 3:9). Checkmate for the Sanhedrin, the Sadducees, and the family of Annas.

The post-resurrection mission to Jerusalem is complete. Advance beyond Jerusalem, however, will require new leadership to emerge— the story of the Hellenists.

SUMMARY

Acts 3–5 is one continuous narrative. Messiah appeals to Israel. This appeal will be the formal offer of forgiveness to all Israel for culpability in the death of Messiah so that all Israel can participate in the eschatological renewal Joel predicted and integrate into messianic Israel of the last days suffused with Pentecost abundance.

The healing of the lame man is one example of the "many signs and wonders" worked by the apostles. This healing illustrates how the life of the disciples parallels the life of Jesus, so Acts is simply the story of Jesus, part two. This one in particular, however, instigates a series of decisive interactions with the people of Jerusalem and the leaders of the temple and the gospel call for decision about Messiah. These interactions can be summarized in three sermons of Peter. The first sermon to the people offers divine forgiveness for their "ignorance" in the death of Jesus. The second sermon to the Sanhedrin offers divine forgiveness for conspiracy to have an innocent man crucified, but the temple leadership balks. The third sermon offers a final chance to the Sanhedrin to accept divine forgiveness by admitting blood guilt, but is a revelation of rank rebellion against God. Thus, the initial positive response of the people in great numbers shows great promise, but the promise will go unrealized as temple leadership torpedoes the future of messianic Israel in Jerusalem. Peter declares the high priest office null and void, and the Sanhedrin a bankrupt judicial institution. All of the effort by Annas, his family, and the Sadducees since AD 6 to control the judicial function of Judea through their Sanhedrin and the religious function of the nation through their temple and its business will come to naught in AD 70. After the Sanhedrin response to the lame man incident, their "Israel" no longer is God's Israel of the last days.

Luke continues to develop his Pentecost theme. This theme plays out positively and negatively in the characters of Barnabas and Ananias. Barnabas as a Levite shows Pentecost transcended. His character in Acts becomes "Pentecost facilitator." He functions as a channel of Pentecost fulfillment and is essential to the story of Saul of Tarsus. Ananias, in contrast, is Pentecost denied, a threat to the fulfillment of Pentecost in Israel. He and Sapphira test God and provoke his anger, reprising the wilderness experience of Israel at Rephidim, used in Deuteronomy to illustrate prototypical idolatry. Ananias and Sapphira act together as a judgment paradigm. Their story of holding back God's money as their own anticipates the story of the Sadducees and the temple business, which Jesus already had condemned. The judgment of Ananias, then, interprets the decision of Annas's Sanhedrin to reject Jesus as Messiah. The root problem is idolatry in the temple and its lucrative business. The future tragedy is, national Israel is in jeopardy with the rejection of Messiah by Jerusalem's leaders. The Ananias and Sapphira episode also anticipates the grave danger of "testing the Spirit of God" for the church in Acts 15, revealed in the parallels of Peter's words in both.

Besides Barnabas and Ananias, the third important character in Acts 3–5 who helps advance important motifs of Acts is Gamaliel. His word of advice to the Sanhedrin provides Luke with one of the most potent thoughts guiding plot development in Acts: "fighting against God." This paradigmatic idea will resurface as one of the two premier themes of the Stephen speech that undergirds not only the entire plot of Acts but also the complex development of the most important character of all, Saul-Paul.

Messiah's post-resurrection appeal to Israel in Jerusalem and her spiritual leaders is complete. In order to show gospel advance beyond Jerusalem, however, the story will take a sharp turn in Acts 6. To envision this development, here is a reminder of our outline of Acts.

ACTS: A NEW VISION OF THE PEOPLE OF GOD

I. THE SPIRIT EMPOWERS MESSIANIC ISRAEL (ACTS 1–12)
   A. *The Spirit Empowers Messianic Israel's Renewal (1–5)*
      1. Renewal Beginnings (1)
      2. Renewal Empowerment (2)
      3. Renewal Witness (3–5)
   B. *The Spirit Empowers Messianic Israel's Hellenists (6–12)*
      1. Hellenist Leaders Emerge (6–7)
      2. Hellenist Mission Advances (8–10)
      3. Hellenist Center Shifts (11–12)

II. THE SPIRIT EMPOWERS WORLD MISSION (13–28)
   A. *The Spirit Empowers World Mission Journeys (13:1—21:17)*
      1. 1MJ: From Cyprus to Conference (13–15)
      2. 2MJ: From Asia to Europe (16–18)
      3. 3MJ: Ephesus (18:23—21:17)

7

Hellenist Leaders Emerge

The Foundation of Stephen (Acts 6–7)

SPEECHES ARE EVERYTHING TO the ancient historian. A speech reveals the undercurrents driving the surface plot, the real story behind the story. The longest speech given to any character in Acts is not to Peter or Paul, no matter how important these names are to later Christianity. The longest speech in all of Acts is Stephen's speech. Length alone should tell us what is important to Luke. Its very length tells us Stephen's speech is the holy grail of Acts exegesis.

Haenchen made the crucial observation how different is the tradition with which Luke now worked.[1] One can add the content beginning in Acts 6 also is suddenly different. Everything is new: new terminology for believers ("disciples," *mathētai*, μαθηταί), new social matrix of the believers ("Hellenists," *Hellēnistai*, Ἑλληνισταί), new leadership group (the Seven), new critique of the temple (Stephen's speech), new location for the preaching activity (synagogue), and new directions for gospel mission (Samaritans, the Ethiopian eunuch). This new material reveals distinctive tradition otherwise either unknown or unremarked in other sources of early Christianity, so clearly a standout Lukan source, which infers a distinctively Lukan purpose and point for inclusion—similar to the attention that needs to be paid to the distinctive Lukan material in the "Journey to Jerusalem" section of the Gospel. Thus, making Acts 6:1 a major turning point in an Acts outline seems imminently logical.

[1] Haenchen, *Acts*, 264–69.

What is the point? Everything in Acts will drive to Stephen, and everything will flow from Stephen. The surprise here is that Stephen is not part of the Twelve. He is a Hellenist leader outside the authorized Twelve. If everything Christian is apostolic, what is Stephen doing in the mix in this pivotal role in Acts? Stephen is the story of the Hellenist movement that Luke wants to tell.

Luke's new source material derives from the Hellenist movement in the Jerusalem church. Stephen was the premier spokesperson of this movement. This movement came to define the essence of gospel mission. Was this definition just historical happenstance or approved by the Spirit? Luke answers, not only approved—guided! The Hellenists will pick up the new and radical direction Messiah eventually will take messianic Israel faster and more perceptively than even the Twelve. In fact, in terms of outward mission, one could say the Jerusalem church never really got to church on time. Hellenists are like an inoculated subgroup, not susceptible to socially exclusive, religiously Mosaic, or nationally patriotic interpretations circumscribing what Israel must look like. For the gospel to go to the world, traditional Jewish social, religious, and national boundaries no longer define Israel and must be crossed. Hellenists crossed those boundaries, forcing the early church to see transparently that Pentecost is more than a fading event moving down the stream of history out of view only to be forgotten before the next generation of believers comes of age. Pentecost is everything to making Israel the Israel of God. Hellenists tell us unambiguously that the eschatological Spirit poured out inevitably defines social identity, redefines clean and unclean, and reimages covenant loyalty. Those who come to understand this Hellenist message that crosses such boundaries can get on board the messianic Israel Jesus always intended by pouring out the Spirit at Pentecost.[2] Luke the historian is on his way to defining the essence of Christianity for all time.

These are the boundaries that Luke crossed. Thus, Christianity for Luke requires the apostles; yet, ironically, Luke also is saying, to be truly apostolic requires the Hellenists. Only then does the gospel get to Rome in the way God intended. That is the story Luke now begins to tell.[3]

[2]Nothing less than what Paul said in Rom 8:9.

[3]Squires compared Luke's historiography with Hellenistic writers, especially their common emphasis on the providence of God. He concluded that no matter how complex the issue of the purpose(s) of Luke-Acts, the two features that inevitably surface in

HELLENISTS INTRODUCED

The Hellenist Cycle that is introduced in Acts 6:1 is the breakthrough to wider witness. The grand movement of the Acts storyline is the movement to gentiles. The origins of that movement are the Hellenist leaders we meet here. This cycle of traditions Luke is working into Acts will comprise Acts 6–12. The way Luke chooses to transition to this grand cycle of material is by way of introducing the Seven.

Among the Seven Hellenist leaders, the ones Luke singles out for plot development in Acts are Stephen, Philip, and Saul. Stephen represents the definitive critique of Jewish resistance to the gospel. Philip represents definitive witness expansion effecting the first witness outside Jerusalem, as well as the first witness to a non-Semite. Saul represents the philosophy, passion, and powerhouse behind the gospel mission's destiny.

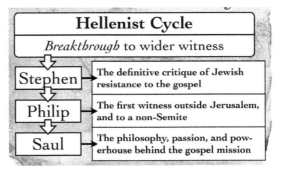

FIGURE 7.1. Hellenist Leaders. Three Hellenist leaders in particular represent breakthrough to wider witness.

Appointing the Seven (6:1–7)

Luke documents the launching of the gentile mission by telling of the appointment of the Seven. Not only are new leaders introduced here, a new center of gravity for the gospel mission also arises. By the time the narrative reaches Acts 12, the shift of locale from Jerusalem to Antioch will be achieved.

The story of the Hellenists starts with social distress and never improves. The Hellenist movement never was an easy one. Their first challenge is a threat to Pentecost fulfillment, which basically threatens the integrity and purpose of the church. Hellenist widows are being denied in a daily distribution. This action renders the Pentecost promise an unexpected hypocrisy within the church itself, but not due to

the narrative are the Jewishness of Christianity and the Hellenization of Christianity; Squires, *The Plan of God in Luke-Acts*, 190.

avarice as was the case in the early story of Ananias and Sapphira. The incident with this duplicitous couple reveals those inherent social and religious tensions in the early church that already bespeak the reason why outward gospel thrust is not going to be an intuitive idea for the Jerusalem church.

Hellenist widows are being distinguished from Hebrew widows. Why? That they are Diaspora Jews or that their synagogue worship was in Greek, not Aramaic, simply would not be pertinent. Diaspora Judaism had been around for centuries. Likely, the problem is not really racial in these terms. As Haenchen long ago suggested, the problem more likely resides in the religious arena in Hellenist perspectives on the implications of Pentecost for the law of Moses and the temple.[4]

The apostles solve the problem by allowing leaders among the Hellenists a role in the distribution decisions. What most preaching today completely ignores about this passage is, that the apostles even had to take this action is no compliment to the Jerusalem church.[5] However, the story allows for introducing the Seven leaders, Luke's whole point for getting the Hellenist names in front of the readers.

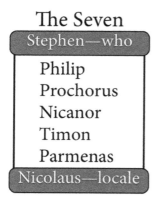

FIGURE 7.2. Hellenist Seven.

The seven are Stephen, Philip, Prochorus, Nicanor, Timon, Parmenas, and Nicolaus. The list is distinguished in that the first and last names are the only ones with extra description attached. This literary device is as a marker. The list's first name, Stephen, is marked because he will provide the key speech of Acts. The last name, Nicolaus, is marked because he is linked with the key city in Acts, Antioch. So, between the key speech on the temple by Stephen and the key city of Antioch for Nicolaus, Luke creates a literary *inclusio* indicating the two key data points of this Hellenist Cycle: *who* is most important among the Hellenists, and *what locale* will most identify the Hellenist base.

---

[4]"This persecution can have but *one* possible cause: that the teaching which this group attempted to disseminate by its mission contained some element which to many Jews went beyond the bounds of the tolerable." Haenchen, *Acts*, 267.

[5]This passage has absolutely nothing to do with establishing the later office of deacon, the almost ubiquitous manner of approaching this text homiletically.

Progress Report (6:7)

Luke gives the first of the six formulaic progress reports in Acts (6:7).[6] These reports do not so much as give a grand outline of Acts as they indicate more minor narrative moments that keep advancing the story, such as here in the solving of a problem of Pentecost fulfillment. Naturally, with Pentecost in the background, the emphasis is on the resulting growth in maturity and numbers that was facilitated, enhancing the standard Pentecost fulfillment theme throughout Acts. What is distinctive about this first progress report is the additional information that "many priests" were coming to the faith. The Sanhedrin and the Sadducees lost their gambit in flogging the apostles. The early church continues to chip away at the foundations of the Sanhedrin authority, even now challenging them over control of their own. This challenge will set the stage for the showdown with Stephen in which Gamaliel's sound and practical advice will go completely unheeded.

THE HELLENIST STEPHEN

Stephen's Ministry (6:8–15)

Introducing the Hellenists is in order to introduce Stephen into the narrative. Stephen lays the foundation for the rest of Acts.

Stephen's Divine Certification

Stephen evidences all the signs of an apostle, though not being one. He performs great "signs and wonders." He is popular with the people. Notice that in his description of Stephen's ministry, Luke repeatedly characterizes this Hellenist leader with spiritual authority.

- "full of faith and the Holy Spirit" (6:5)

- "full of grace and power" (6:8)

- "the face of an angel" (6:15)

Luke clearly is pushing a point, because he needs to. Stephen's temple critique to come will be radical, sweeping, and provocative, the probable reason why these Hellenist widows were being ignored in the daily distribution. So, by these characterizations, Luke wants to assure the

[6]Acts 6:7; 9:31; 12:24; 16:5; 19:20; 28:31.

reader the Hellenist message is divinely sanctioned. "Full of the Holy Spirit" in Acts signifies Pentecost certification. This expression translates to mean Stephen's message to the Sanhedrin is the message of Jesus. Now that Messiah through Peter formally has offered forgiveness to the Sanhedrin (Acts 4), and that offer definitively has been rejected (Acts 5), Messiah through Stephen will speak the eschatological word of judgment on that leadership and its premier institution.

Stephen's Synagogue Context (6:8–10)

What numerous commentators seem to ignore is the decided change in the stage with Stephen. The locale shifts. The whole story has been temple centric from day one. Suddenly, with Stephen, the reader is thrust into the synagogue. We simply have not been here before. That locale change should catch our attention. In the long run, this stage shift puts us on a trajectory for Saul of Tarsus.

FIGURE 7.3. Capernaum Synagogue. Capernaum was a focus of Jesus's activity in Galilee, including its synagogue (Mark 1:21–28). This construction dates to the 4th to 5th cent., but a basalt foundation underneath is believed to be 1st cent.

Stephen preaches in a new context, the synagogue, but runs into trouble. In the synagogue of the Freedmen he is confronted by the Cyrenians, Alexandrians, and those of Cilicia and Asia. This mention of synagogue activity on the part of a follower of Jesus is the first time in Acts Luke has recorded any preaching of Jesus in the synagogue. In fact, synagogue activity simply is never associated with the apostles in Acts. Thus, mention of the synagogue is virgin territory for the story.

FIGURE 7.4. Sardis Synagogue. The synagogue at Sardis is the largest Diaspora synagogue ever found. The worship assembly area measures 197 x 59 feet, with an estimated standing capacity of one thousand people. Pictured is the outside vestibule.

This synagogue as an institution in Israel belonged exclusively to the Pharisees. Its origins are obscure, either during the exile or soon after the exile, but by the time of Jesus, its dominance as an institution in the life of Israel and its power with the people was unchallenged. In the synagogue, Pharisees promoted their vision of the Israel of God, which was Moses. Mention Pharisees, and Moses suddenly becomes everything. For a Pharisee, Moses was the greatest prophet God ever had, and all of life hung in the balance on Moses's words, the law. Over time, Moses has to be interpreted for a new generation, especially after Jews engaged Hellenism. This interpretive tradition was passed on orally by the Pharisees and became as authoritative as the law itself.

Thus, in effect, by preaching Jesus in the synagogue, Stephen had made the synagogue a new turf war for gospel mission. What he had to say about Jesus countermanded the oral law, even as Jesus already had done. The synagogue already had been invaded by Jesus (Luke 4:44). Jesus even had healed a synagogue leader's dying daughter (Jairus, Luke 8:41–42). Jesus's message in the synagogue was blunt, as he spoke a word of warning to Pharisees who loved their seats of honor in the synagogue (Luke 11:43). Jesus also anticipated that his followers would be active in synagogues, opposed, and persecuted (Luke 12:11; 21:12). The trajectory of this word in the Gospel drives straight to this Stephen incident in Acts. Further, the trajectory of Jesus's insight into the future of his mission in the synagogue is consummated by the mission work of Saul. *Thus, Stephen's synagogue setting explains why the Pharisee Saul of Tarsus now will begin to shadow this story of Stephen.*

Stephen's Synagogue Trouble (6:11–15)

Two charges are leveled. First, Stephen is accused of "speaking against Moses and God" (6:11). "Against Moses" is because of some perceived abrogation of the law; in the synagogue context, "law" probably means the Pharisees' oral law. "Against God" is because of a perceived attack on the temple, which would be equated with an attack on God. Note that such charges had not been leveled at Peter or the other apostles. Perhaps Stephen was not as "politically correct" as Peter. To be sure, we have not heard of Peter attacking the institution of the law or of the temple, and we see Peter joining early believers faithfully convening in the temple's porticos and plazas. Stephen's preaching apparently is more pointed about the meaning of Pentecost and the implications of the story of Jesus for the institutions of law and temple in Israel. His problem, then, is that he makes the radical implications of the gospel message rather too plain. That type of preaching is why people have become agitated, a note not heard about the apostles' public preaching. (Sadducean leadership reacted, but more on preaching of Jesus's resurrection, a doctrine they did not hold.) Hellenist preaching brings trouble not only for their widows in the daily distribution within the church, but also trouble for their mission within the synagogues where they missionize.

They (synagogue opponents, scribes, elders) seized Stephen and dragged him before the Sanhedrin (6:12). Well, the previous narrative in Acts 4–5 already has shown us where *this* plot is going. We've already poured the gasoline. All we need to do now is strike a match.

The Sanhedrin charge is specifically about the temple (6:13–14). They use the animosity of the Sanhedrin to their mortal enemy, "Jesus of Nazareth." This identification Peter has memorialized as a typical feature of his sermons.[7] Importantly here though, the Nazareth synagogue is premiered by Luke as the inaugural sermon of Jesus. In that sermon, Jesus said that even though Isaiah's prophecy of an anointed Servant was speaking of him, those positively impacted in Israel by Messiah's coming would be as few as the one widow in Israel in the days of Elijah and the draught, or of all the lepers in Israel, the one non-Israelite pagan, Naaman the Syrian, cleansed by Elisha (4:25–27). In response to Jesus's sermon, Luke notes, "all in the synagogue were filled with rage," and they tried to hurl Jesus off a cliff (Luke 4:28–30). In the reaction to the inaugural sermon of Jesus in the synagogue at Nazareth we have premonitions of what Stephen can expect.

The charge is that Jesus said he would destroy "this place," meaning the temple, and "change the customs Moses handed down to us" (6:14). Concerning the first charge, Jesus is being misquoted. He had spoken metaphorically of the temple of his body; these false charges were brought against Jesus at his mock trial.[8] The slanderous charge is recapitulated, though royally falsified in the resurrection. The second charge about Moses might have more bite, particularly if by "customs handed down to us" is meant the customs of the oral law taken by Pharisees as authoritative as the actual law of Moses itself.

The problem with the temple was not so much the temple itself as idolatry inspired by false ideas of the temple. Jews had centuries of relationship with David's temple in Jerusalem. While this edifice was David's idea, Solomon built this monument to the Davidic monarchy, since David's life was marked by military violence (1 Chr 22:8). David took the initiative to place the ark of the covenant in this building, and then he appropriated rituals of the law meant for the tabernacle for his own temple (2 Chr 5:2–14). We even are told fire from heaven consumed Solomon's dedicatory sacrifices at the temple inaugural, apparently meant as divine approval (2 Chr 7:1).[9]

---

[7] Acts 2:22; 3:6; 4:10.

[8] Matt 26:61; 27:40; Mark 14:58; 15:29. The resurrection after three days already had proven that Jesus, understood correctly, not only was speaking literally about three days, but also was absolutely correct. He was literal about the time, but metaphorical about the place. He was not prophesying that he himself would stir up insurrection and destroy the temple in Jerusalem.

[9] The Chronicler's Davidic aggrandizement should be kept in perspective. He makes no reference to David's intense conflicts with Saul, made clear in 1 Sam 16–20, nor that

FIGURE 7.5. Jerusalem Temple and Courtyards. Scale model of Herod's Jerusalem temple showing the inner sanctuary and surrounding courtyards (IMJ).

In all the time the temple stood in Jerusalem, however, God never promised its permanence. Yet, somehow, Jews developed the idea that the temple was God's most prized possession in all the earth, that his glory never would depart its precincts, and that the artifice itself was inviolable. A good example of these attitudes in the centuries before Jesus was born is the strong assertion of the high priest, Onias III, during a crisis of Judea with Syria in 170 BC.

> And he said that it was utterly impossible that wrong should be done to those people who had trusted in the holiness of the place and in the sanctity and inviolability of the temple that is honored throughout the whole world (2 Macc 3:12).

Even early Jewish believers in Jesus as Messiah continued to assemble in the temple. Thus, the reader should keep in mind that Stephen's law and temple critique originates, not with the apostles, but in the Hellenist wing of messianic Israel. This Hellenist critique and reaction to its implications as Luke tells the story insinuates that the church's shift from Jerusalem to Rome not only is inevitable but divinely superintended. That concept will be a hard pill to swallow for everyone in Jerusalem, for the synagogue, for the Sanhedrin, and even for the early church. The Stephen speech insinuates all the future elements of the plot of Acts.

David's kingdom was torn in strife in its early days (2 Sam 1–5). Then, of David's son, the Chronicler completely omits the report of Solomon's idolatry in 1 Kgs 11.

So, Stephen faces trumped up charges. What is his disposition in all this? "The face of an angel" is the account (6:15). This countenance is not meant to evoke the cherub, plump-faced baby with wings. This word is not "sweetness." This word is like Michael poised with his sword ready to do battle for God. The meaning is direct: God will be at work in judgment on the Sanhedrin in the words of Stephen.

Stephen's Speech (7:2–53)

The most insightful analysis of the Stephen speech that sets the lines of development for the whole plot of Acts is from Bruce's commentary on Acts (1988), which is followed directly here. Stephen's strategy is to use Israel's own history to answer the charges. The speech outline is simple. Stephen introduces the major themes, then answers the two charges of speaking against Moses and God and speaking against the temple. For the first theme, Stephen focuses on the patriarchal age using the idea "our father, Abraham" to note that even in the patriarchal narratives, one sees how God always has been active outside the land of promise revealing himself particularly to gentiles. In truth, God never needed a promised land to go after gentiles. Further, God's call should create an inclusive people, not exclusive. For the second theme, Stephen focuses on the Egyptian sojourn using the idea "our nation Israel" to note that even in the story of Israel's redemption, one sees how God's people always have resisted God's plans, even when he is trying to save them. Stephen spends most of his time answering the first charge. He dispatches the second with a quick volley on the tabernacle, Solomon's edifice, and Isaiah's word.

STEPHEN'S SPEECH

I.   INTRODUCING MAJOR THEMES (7:2–19)
   A. *Theme 1—God active: patriarchal age (7:2–8)*
   B. *Theme 2—God resisted: Egyptian sojourn (7:9–19)*

II.   ANSWERING CHARGE #1 (7:20–43)
   A. *Moses's early days (7:20–29)*
   B. *Moses's call (7:30–34)*
   C. *Wilderness wanderings (7:35–43)*

III.   ANSWERING CHARGE #2 (7:44–53)

Stephen's Strategy: Use Israel's History to Answer Charges		
I. Introducing Major Themes	II. Answering Charge #1	III. Answering Charge #2
7:2–19	7:20–43	7:44–53
A. God Active	Against Moses/G	Against Temple
Patriarchs (2–8)	Moses (20–29)	Taber. (44–45)
B. God Resisted	Call (30–34)	Solomon (46–47)
Sojourn (9–19)	Wilder. (35–43)	Isaiah (48–53)

FIGURE 7.6. Stephen's Speech Outline. Stephen's strategy is to use Israel's history to answer the trumped up charges against him on Moses, God, and the temple.

The high priest likely is Caiaphas again, so this appearance by Stephen resonates with the trial of Jesus. The episode illustrates the tragic, permanent opposition to the gospel in the Sanhedrin, especially under the control of the Sadducean majority. The Pharisee Gamaliel's wise counsel to "leave these men alone" will prove to have had only a temporary impact.

Introducing the Themes (7:2–19)

God active (7:2–8). The patriarchal narratives show that in some of the most epic moments of Israel's history, when God is observed active, he is active outside of the promise land, and his activity is with gentiles, not Israel. Where was Abraham when God first spoke? Mesopotamia. Where was Joseph when God gave dreams? Egypt. Where was even famous Moses, so beloved in the synagogue? Arabia. God is interested in the whole earth and all peoples, not one, small, time-share condominium and one ethnic destiny.

God resisted (7:9–19). If one studies the history of Israel, the most characteristic feature of God's people is that they are defined more by their rebellion than by their obedience. God's people characteristically always resist God's plans, most especially in times when God is working to save. This storyline is true even before Israel is Israel the nation. God chooses Joseph, but who opposes Joseph? Joseph's own brothers.

Answering Charge #1 (7:20–43)

Moses's story illustrates both themes. The sojourn in Egypt illustrates God resisted in Moses's early days (7:20–29). God's people always are resisting God's plan. Moses was chosen to help Israel in Egypt. The Israelite slaves, however, rejected Moses as their "deliverer." Echoes of the story of Jesus are strong. Then, in the story of Moses's call, God is seen active outside the land of promise (7:30–34). Moses is called at the burning bush, and is told, "the place where you stand is holy ground." Strange, since that ground was Arabia, not the promised land.

The wilderness experience is not too impressive for Israel's reputation as the people of God (7:35–43). All the time God is active in redemption, Israel is rebelling. God gives Israel the covenant of law, but in that very moment at the foot of

Wilderness Experience	
Promise	Reality
(1) Moses as leader	(1) Moses' authority rejected
(2) Yahweh's own assembly	(2) Yahweh's assembly ruined
(3) Angel of the Presence	(3) Divine Presence sacrilege
(4) Living oracles guidance	(4) Living oracles ignored
Fullness of God without need of promised land or holy city	Israel's history more defined by idolatry than faithfulness

FIGURE 7.7. Wilderness Experience. Stephen points out Israel's wilderness experience should not be idealized. Promise and reality are two different matters altogether.

Mount Sinai, Israel has made a golden calf. Later in the wilderness, idolatries continue to mock the covenant with God in the worship of Moloch and Rephan, traceable backward to Babylonian star worship and forward to the Roman Saturnalia.[10] Israel's real history is defined more by her idolatry than by her faithfulness. From the very beginning and consistently throughout, Israel worshipped foreign gods, from Sinai (golden calf), through the wilderness (Moloch and Rephan), and on into the kingship (2 Kgs 21:3). Israel's sins from the very beginning ripened into the reason for exile, which is the reason for Stephen's quote of Amos 5:25 (7:42–43).

[10] Worship of Moloch involved child sacrifice by immolation. The star god Rephan is Babylonian; later the Roman Saturnalia festival, a carnival of inverted social norms.

FIGURE 7.8. Tel Be'er Sheva. Tel Be'er Sheva sits on the southern frontier of Israel on the edge of the desert wilderness. The ancient tel is believed to be biblical Beersheba. Beersheba often is named in the Bible as the southern border of the land of Israel (Judg 20:1; 1 Sam 3:20; 1 Kgs 4:25; 1 Chr 21:2; 2 Chr 30:5).

Answering Charge #2 (7:44–50)

Answering charge number two about the temple requires immediately going to the heart of the matter: the tabernacle is what God actually commanded, not the Davidic temple in Jerusalem. The points are simple. The tabernacle is the divine command, not the temple (7:44–45). The temple only is divinely allowed, not commanded (7:46–47). These are really moot points anyway: God does not live in houses made with human hands in the first place (7:48–50). Isaiah is quite clear on this (Isa 66:1–2), and Jesus the Messiah already pronounced judgment on the institution of the temple (Luke 19:45–46).

Stephen's Countercharge (7:51–53)

Stephen turns the tables. The Sanhedrin had placed him in the dock. Now, he places the Sanhedrin in God's dock. Stephen does not mince his words: "You stiff-necked people" (7:51) is no way to win friends and influence people—but judgment is not about winning friends and influencing people. With "stiff-necked," Stephen has charged the Sanhedrin with being the wilderness generation redux, rank idolatry all over again. Their spiritual problem is in "uncircumcised hearts," which makes appeal to Moses meaningless.[11] Being stiff-necked is a problem, but the real problem is lack of repentance. Stephen gets after this issue: "always resisting the Holy Spirit," which is what Caiaphas and the Sanhedrin have been doing since having Jesus crucified, then Peter flogged, and soon ready to stone Stephen. Testing the Spirit is shades of old Ananias—a wilderness theme preserved in the law—and the Ananias episode was prelude to the second appearance of Peter and John before the Sanhedrin when they were ordered flogged.

FIGURE 7.9. Temple Shofar Inscription. This top stone was discovered in the temple mount's southwest corner. The inscription, "to the place of trumpeting," probably was instruction for original placement. From this corner of the temple the priests would blow the shofar horn to signal the beginning of Shabbat and festival days.

Stephen pushes further with the provocative question, "Which of the prophets did your ancestors not persecute?" (7:52). So, the "Israel" represented by the Sanhedrin is not the Israel nostalgically idealized in the synagogue every Sabbath as faithful to Moses and to God. That "Israel" of synagogue memory really is non-existent in history. No, synagogue and Sanhedrin represent the Israel persecuting the prophets, now reprised in the present generation. Stephen here puts himself in the category of a prophet. Remember at the beginning of this address

[11]Precisely the spirit of Paul's argument in Rom 2:23–29.

he had "the face of an angel," which is as a messenger from God. Jewish ancestors killed the prophets who foretold the coming of Messiah, the "Righteous One." This "Righteous One" appellation is a resurrection slap in the face over the verdict passed on Jesus only recently. The resurrection reveals that "you have become his betrayers and murderers." They are betrayers because the Sanhedrin misled the people into such a heinous crime, so have betrayed their own nation, when they were supposed to recognize and lead the people to Messiah. They are murderers in the death of Jesus, and will relive that role in the stoning of Stephen. Indeed, they are like a "brood of vipers," even as John the Baptist had warned to flee the wrath to come (Luke 3:7).

FIGURE 7.10. Temple Western Wall. The only surviving portion of the Herodian temple construction after its destruction by the Romans in AD 70 is this southwest corner of the western wall. The area is a holy site of Jewish prayers and bar mitzvah rituals.

So what of the two charges? On speaking against Moses and the law, Stephen brashly throws that one back in their face. They received the law as so spiritual that they preserved Jewish traditions that its giving was "ordained by angels" (7:53),[12] yet here is one with the "face of an angel" bringing God's word to them, and they plug their ears. So

---

[12]Also alluded to by Paul (Gal 3:19) and in Hebrews (Heb 2:2).

ironic that supposedly they would receive from angels as God's word the law of Moses but reject God's word from the superior agency of the divine Son and his own representatives. The stinger? "And yet you have not kept it." Stephen actually *reverses* the charge on him. He now charges the Sanhedrin with the same! What messianic Israel can see is that the law of Moses points to Jesus (Deut 18:15), but the Sanhedrin rejected and killed Jesus. Killing Jesus is not keeping the law of Moses.

The second charge about the temple in a way is accepted. Jesus did not destroy the edifice physically, but he did render its purpose moot spiritually. Killing Jesus reveals temple idolatry. Killing Jesus shows Israel would rather cling to a building built by David as a monument to his monarchy than to the Messiah who transcends that monarchy. Patriarchs, prophets, and the Scriptures affirm this truth. Truth be told, worship of the golden calf, Moloch, and Rephan still can be witnessed in Israel. Rejection of Messiah is idolatry. Whereas God is active, God is resisted, and his own people offer the stiffest resistance.

Stephen's Martyrdom (7:54–60)

The Sanhedrin is enraged (7:54). Stephen is enraptured (7:55–56). We are told two items about his experience. First, Stephen is "filled with the Holy Spirit," which means the speech is validated by God. God just told the Sanhedrin what he thinks of their high council. Second, Stephen witnesses Jesus enthroned. The only way Stephen here was able to speak with such power, courage, and truth in this intense encounter is because Jesus has ascended in order to be able to empower his church through the Spirit. No ascension, no Spirit, no power—and Stephen never could have said what he said.

In Stephen's experience before the Sanhedrin, two prophecies of Jesus are fulfilled. Jesus promised those confronted by authorities and powers in defense of the gospel would find Spirit-filled words to say (Luke 12:11). Jesus also promised Caiaphas and the Sanhedrin at his trial that they would witness the Son of Man at God's right hand: "But from now on the Son of Man will be seated at the right hand of the power of God" (Luke 22:69).

Stephen is stoned. Stoning is a brutal death by blunt force trauma. Whether this action should be interpreted as a formal sentence enacted by the Sanhedrin or the tragic consequence of mob violence is not clear.[13] In any case, in this stoning, Gamaliel's advice is being ignored, not only by the Sanhedrin, but also by Gamaliel's most promising student. Saul is introduced as complicit in the act (7:57–58). Luke has a tendency to drop names prior to their major introduction into the narrative.

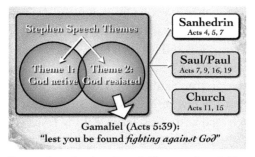

FIGURE 7.11. Stephen Speech Themes: Acts 7. The plot of Acts will play out these themes, both in groups and in individuals.

We already know about Barnabas in this manner. Soon, Barnabas will become absolutely crucial to Saul. Now, Luke drops the name of Saul to introduce this key character. Why now? For two plot reasons. One, the Stephen speech inaugurates the church's mission destiny. This speech represents a decided break from the Jerusalem leadership, striking out independently. This action becomes the point of breakthrough to wider witness in the gentile mission of the church. Two, Saul will become the key figure in the Hellenist movement, and the entire last half of Acts follows him exclusively. So, the great irony of this moment at the stoning of Stephen is that Saul eventually will spend the rest of his life living the truth of the witness Stephen gave here with his life. Here was Saul, student of Gamaliel,[14] not reflecting his own teacher's wisdom. Gamaliel the teacher had practical insight. Saul the student had only blinding zeal. In persecuting the church, the next story in Acts, Saul actually dishonors his own teacher. He does not follow Gamaliel's Pharisaic wisdom. Saul is the worst kind of Pharisee: He is a zealot.[15]

During this stoning, two expressions by Stephen parallel those by Jesus at Jesus's death. Stephen prayed, "Lord Jesus, receive my spirit" (7:59), and then cried out, "Lord, do not hold this sin against them" (7:60). The point of these intentional echoes of Jesus seems to be that Stephen died for similar reasons. He died for sayings regarding the temple and for sayings about Jesus as the glorified Son of Man. The faithful disciple is following his master.

---

[13]More likely seems to be informal crowd violence unhindered by the Sanhedrin.

[14]In the narrative (Acts 22:3).

[15]Self-confessed by Saul-Paul in Acts (Acts 22:3) and in his own letters (Rom 10:2).

SUMMARY

Acts 6:1 is a major turning point in the Acts narrative. The Hellenist material suddenly introduced brings in new elements not seen in Acts before. The reason is the Hellenist Stephen. All Acts roads, including the Damascus Road, lead to Stephen and depart from Stephen. Hellenists in the early church crossed the socially exclusive, religiously Mosaic, and nationally patriotic boundaries of the Jerusalem church in their breakthrough to wider witness. Pentecost is their theology. The poured out Spirit creates a new family, new cleanness, and a new covenant that transcends the old. Stephen gives the definitive Hellenist critique, which is his speech. Philip is the definitive Hellenist witness expansion, which is the Samaritans and the Ethiopian. Saul is the definitive Hellenist destiny, which is Rome. By the way the list of Hellenist leaders is produced, we learn that the premier leader in the early period is going to be Stephen, and the premier locale of this movement will be Antioch.

Hellenist widows are ignored in the daily distribution, a shocking violation of Pentecost abundance that is supposed to characterize the church's witness that Jesus really is Messiah who has inaugurated the realities of Joel's last days in Israel. The nature of Hellenist preaching is the likely cause, not racial prejudice. The apostles solve the problem, so a progress report infers Pentecost abundance is renewed.

Stephen's introduction is to make absolutely clear he is divinely certified. His radical message on law and temple will require this certification. Stephen's synagogue locale is new in Acts and puts him head on with Pharisees. Stephen simply is following the lead Jesus already had established in his own ministry. Stephen's synagogue setting explains why Saul of Tarsus will become part of the story.

Stephen is dragged before the Sanhedrin charged with speaking against Moses and God and against the temple. These charges represent Pharisee concerns (law) and Sadducean interests (temple) smartly combined, so well poised to capture the attention of everyone in the council guaranteeing everyone will have an issue with Stephen. Notably, none of the apostles ever are charged this way, so their preaching has been politically correct enough not to arouse this type of agitation.

To respond, Stephen uses Israel's history. He uses the patriarchal period to show that when God is active in decisive moments of the patriarchal story, he is active outside the land of promise and among gentiles. So God has interest in more than the promise land and more than an exclusive group of people. Stephen next uses the Egyptian sojourn to show that when God is active, he is resisted by his own people, even when God is working to save them. Stephen then plays out the God active and God resisted themes in the story of Moses and the wilderness wanderings. Israel is more defined by her idolatry than her faithfulness. So much for speaking against Moses and God. The Sanhedrin certainly is not speaking for Moses and God in their rejection of Jesus as Messiah. As for the temple, that institution was David's anyway, not God's. God's institution was the tabernacle.

So the Sanhedrin is a stiff-necked people like Israel of the wilderness. They identify with those who persecuted the prophets. In their treatment of Jesus the Messiah, they are betrayers and murderers. The Sanhedrin fulfills this characterization by murdering Stephen. Stephen witnesses Jesus enthroned. Stephen's vision tells the reader that what he had spoken to the Sanhedrin is the intention of Jesus. Stephen died echoing the words of Jesus in his own death. The Hellenist message is Pentecost unleashed in all its power.

Stephen has laid the foundation for the rest of Acts. His speech sets up the two themes that drive the Acts plot, both at the macro and micro levels, both groups and individuals—God active, God resisted. His Hellenist tradition sets up the church's breakthrough to gentile mission and the entire story of Saul of Tarsus. This Stephen moment is the mother lode for Acts exegesis.

8

Hellenist Mission Advances

Breakthrough and Validation (8–10)

STEPHEN CAUSES THE GENTILE MISSION in the early church to reach critical mass. The chain reaction now has been released, and nothing will stop the resulting gospel explosion onto the Mediterranean world. Most of the time, readers of Acts trace this explosion to the apostle Paul, but that is not really how Luke tells the story. Saul's story, like everything else in the rest of Acts, is just a reaction to Stephen. When we first see Saul in action, he is exhausting himself on the effort to rid Israel of Stephen's teaching. Reaction to Stephen changes everything for Saul. Reaction to Stephen also changes everything for the church.

HELLENIST BREAKTHROUGH

The gospel will have a breakthrough to the Samaritans. The path will be Hellenist persecution. The Spirit will control all.

Hellenist Persecution (8:1–4)

A general persecution following Stephen is a new experience for the church. Persecution changes the church's social structure, geography, and enemy. Socially, the church in Jerusalem becomes decidedly more Hebrew. The problem of the Hellenist widows goes away naturally. A secondary reaction is the beginning of a leadership shift away from the apostles. Once favored by the people of Jerusalem, messianic Israel now is targeted. This targeting is the hidden signal of Stephen's martyrdom.

Eventually, after the catastrophe of the First Jewish War, the Jerusalem church simply fades into history with hardly a trace.[1]

Persecution changes geography. "All except the apostles" (8:1) are scattered, which probably means the other Hellenists leaders surviving Stephen—Philip, Prochorus, Nicanor, Timon, Parmenas, Nicolaus—in particular are targeted. These persecuted Hellenists begin to fulfill the programmatic expansion of Acts 1:8 because of the persecution. They continue faithfully to "proclaim the word" (8:4). That "word" would be the word of Stephen putting the law and temple in its eschatological place by arguing for the radical results of Jesus's death and resurrection that creates messianic Israel through an outpoured Spirit. The dispersion regions are Judea and Samaria, explaining the Hellenist activity in these regions. The Hellenist wing of the church is in exile already, which corresponds to the nature of their journey in Acts, which never is easy. The Spirit turns this negative into a great positive, since Hellenists are comfortable preaching the gospel to all and are dependent on the Spirit and the power of Pentecost.

Persecution changes the enemy. The opposition shifts from the Sanhedrin to Saul. He is a Pharisee, and he is an intense advocate of the integrity of the synagogue's teaching office and vision of Israel. Stephen not only has invaded his home turf, challenging his authority, but Saul intuits that Stephen's preaching represents the most serious threat that the synagogue's vision of Israel has seen since its inception after the exile. Thus, Saul agreed with Stephen's death (8:1), and he is driven to hunt out these Hellenists to bring them to trial, as with their leader Stephen, and bring down on these apostates the full force of Israel's high court of judgment (8:3). In this way, Saul acts as a true zealot for his

---

[1]Eusebius, desperate in the heretical wars of the church to prove the historical line of succession of the church's traditions as a "chaste and pure virgin," tries to prove complete historical continuity for Jerusalem after the war. He asserts that after the death of James, the Lord's brother, the Jerusalem church fled to Pella before the war (*H.E.* 3.5.3). Thus, the church survives the Jewish war. After the war, the apostles reconvened to appoint Jesus's cousin, Symeon, (asserted) son of Clopas, (supposed) brother of Joseph, to rule the Jerusalem church (*H.E.* 4.22.4). Symeon was followed in succession by fifteen Hebrew appointees to the post, which would take the succession to the time of Hadrian (*H.E.* 4.5.1–4). The only other note about the relatives of Jesus is Eusebius, reporting Hegesippus, recording that two grandsons of Jesus's brother Judas, were hauled before Domitian, but no action was taken (*H.E.* 3.19.1–20.7). Most of this, especially the long and pure (dynastic almost) Jerusalem succession after the war, is dubious.

ancestral traditions. He is not aware that his ancestral traditions are really more following post-exile Ezra traditions than Moses.

Samaritans (8:5–8)

Samaritan history is predicated already in Israel's blessing of Judah: "adversaries" are insinuated, portending prescient knowledge of a later divided kingdom (Deut 33:7). During Jewish monarchy, the kingdom of Israel did split into north and south. Attempts were made to reunite the kingdom. Hezekiah tried to reunite the royal houses (2 Chr 30:1–11), and Josiah as well (2 Kgs 23:21–23). In 722 BC, this northern kingdom finally vanished historically as a dis-

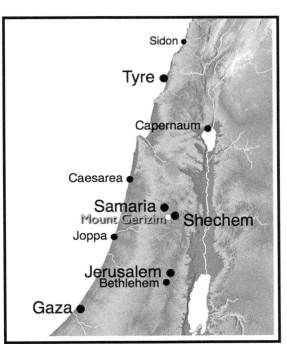

FIGURE 8.1. Samaria. The divided kingdom of David and Solomon left its fingerprint in history in the story of the Samaritans north of Jerusalem.

tinct political entity in the Assyrian captivity. Individual Jews did survive, however, in the northern areas. Their claim to maintain the purity of their religious heritage and worship of God was rejected by their former enemies to the south. However, this southern kingdom of Judah also succumbed to Babylonian captivity in 586 BC. Unlike the northern kingdom, though, the Babylonian captives had the good fortune of a return decreed by Cyrus for the purpose of rebuilding the temple in Jerusalem. Surviving northern Jews in Samaria offered to help rebuild this Jerusalem temple, but the southern Jews balked over issues of intermarriage, religious syncretism, and loss of true worship of God. This rebuffed effort was the only time restoration of a divided kingdom was a genuine possibility in history. Thus, the northern Jews were left with no option but to establish their own sanctuary for the worship of God on a holy site of the patriarchal period, Mount Gerizim. They retained Zadokite priests from Jerusalem for their high priestly office, maintaining the priestly tradition of the united kingdom under David. So they became the Samaritans, claiming their own worship center and worship of the God of Israel according to the law of Moses, which they preserved in their own Scripture, the five books of Moses, or the Samaritan Pentateuch.

The Samaritans had their own holocaust at the hands of southern Jews. The Hasmonean king, John Hyrcanus I, in a bid to rid the region of any competing Jewish cultus, without provocation took his army up to Samaria and destroyed the capital city of Samaria in a surprise attack in 128 BC. He razed the Gerizim temple to the ground. The Samaritans never recovered from this devastating atrocity. Even though the Roman general Pompey restored their worship on Mount Gerizim, the Samaritans never had the strength or resources to rebuild their Jewish temple. Samaritans and Jews always had a rocky relationship, though political survival or economic realities could dictate alliances at various times through the centuries.[2] They regularly were opposed and suppressed by Judea, and these former brothers often endured mutual animosity.

That animosity is why Jesus told the parable of the good Samaritan, preserved only in Luke, in response to the question about what to do to inherit eternal life in the Journey to Jerusalem section of the Gospel (Luke 10:25–37). In Jewish eyes, no "good" Samaritan existed. That the hero in the story taking care of the abused traveler, fulfilling the basic law of human kindness, thus, all the law of Moses, would not be a Jerusalem priest, but a despised Samaritan, was the lowest blow Jesus could strike at incorrigible Jewish animosity. Luke further pointed out that of ten lepers healed, the only one who returned to thank Jesus was a Samaritan (Luke 17:16). Jesus, tongue in cheek, calls the healed Samaritan leper a "foreigner" or "stranger" (*allogenēs*, ἀλλογενής, Luke 17:18). Interesting that one of the categories in the law specially directed to receive an invitation to the Pentecost feast is the "stranger."[3] That "stranger" will be receiving that invitation soon. Luke will be presenting

---

[2] See Reinhard Pummer, *The Samaritans: A Profile.*

[3] Or, resident alien (*prosēlytos*, προσήλυτος, Deut 16:14).

the eschatological expectation of a united Israel. Messianic Israel will reunite Jerusalem and Samaria.

Fortunately for Samaritans, early followers of Jesus already used Deut 18:15–19, Moses's promise of a prophet like Moses to come, as part of the prophetic testimony of the Scriptures to Jesus as Messiah. We already saw this text used by Peter in his message to the general population of Jerusalem after the healing of the lame man (Acts 3:22). Because Samaritan Scripture comprised the law of Moses, they well knew this expectation, except they simply called this eschatological prophet the "Taheb."[4] Thus, preaching Jesus as the Mosaic prophet to come was perfectly compatible with existing Samaritan eschatology. As fate would decree, Samaritans were more ready to receive Israel's Messiah than their southern compatriots, who actually crucified their own promised son of David.[5]

Samaritans, part 1, is Philip's ministry in a new territory of gospel expansion. Part 2 will be Peter's apostolic seal of approval. The typical signs attend: miracles, conversions. What is described is *not* any so-called "Samaritan Pentecost." The context is different. Pentecost is a grand opening of the

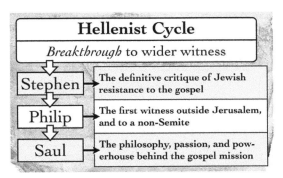

FIGURE 8.2. Hellenist Leaders: Philip. Philip is the breakthrough to the first witness outside of Jerusalem proper and the first witness to a non-Semite.

church preceded by the upper room prayer and witnessed by all Israel including from the Diaspora. The effects are different. Pentecost is a premier experience of fire and wind. The experience is different. Samaria involves two distinct stages. The procedure is different. Samaria involved the laying on of hands. The result is different. Pentecost results in speaking the known languages of the world in order to proclaim

---

[4]For documentation in Samaritan sources, see Stevens, "The Literary Background and Theological Significance of ΟΡΓΗ ΘΕΟΥ in the Pauline Epistles," 83–85.

[5]"Son of David" is an important messianic theme for Luke's presentation of Jesus. See Luke 1:32, 69; 2:4; 18:38; 19:38; 20:41–44; Acts 13:34; 15:16. This theme Luke has to extricate from its nationalistic associations for the proper eschatological reality.

the "magnificent acts" of God in Jesus. Why this emphasis on the difference? So as not to confuse the two events and thus dilute the unique experience Pentecost represents in the Lukan universe. Pentecost is the validation of the gospel that Jesus is raised, ascended, and has poured out the eschatological Spirit to empower the messianic Israel of God. Samaria is validation of the salvation this gospel brings.

The events at Samaria are not intended as a "second Pentecost" but rather *to illustrate the Stephen speech just presented.* Samaria illustrates the first theme of God active, particularly among peoples not assumed part of the promise but who are the ultimate focus of the promise God made to Abraham to be a blessing to all the families of the earth. Samaria also will portray that a united kingdom of Israel fi-nally is achieved through the work of the only true royal son of David, Jesus, and his messianic Israel of the last days.

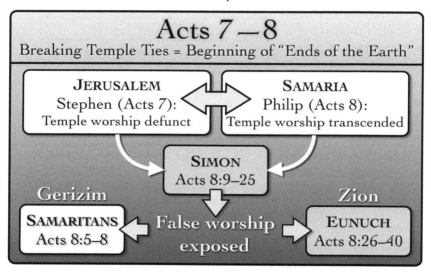

FIGURE 8.3. True Worship in Acts 7–8: Samaritans. On the basis of Stephen, three episodes critique true worship: Samaritans, Simon, and the eunuch.

All worship is critiqued in the series of Acts 7–8. On the basis of Stephen, this critique is communicated through the interweaving of three stories: Samaritans, Simon, and the eunuch. The message will be that Messiah transforms all worship, whether of northern or southern Israel, or of an insincere charlatans like Simon. In the end, Gerizim or Jerusalem is a moot point. Messiah shows no partiality. True worship is receiving the eschatological Spirit of the last days prophesied by Joel.

For the Samaritans, Luke has declared the true Taheb is Jesus the Messiah (8:5). For Simon, this Messiah exposes the secrets of the heart.

Samaritans witness miracles by Philip, as well as possessed and paralyzed being cured (8:6–7). Samaritans are converted and baptized (presumably by Philip and those with him). Luke summarizes with, "So there was great joy in that city" (8:8). Joy is a standard Pentecost theme established in Acts 2. Samaritan conversions are Pentecost fullness spreading beyond Jerusalem and surrounding villages.

Simon (8:9–25)

Simon's Conversion (8:9–13)

Simon is a sorcerer, basically, a shyster. What he wanted out of the gullible was only that they think "he was someone great" (8:9). Simon believes and is baptized by Philip. While his conversion and its sincerity might be disputed, Luke's dual literary strategy is to demonstrate gospel power over magic and illustrate the problem of insincere faith. Philip is horning in on Simon's territory, ruining his racket. The more Samaritans are baptized, the more Simon is losing his "magic touch." Rather laconically Luke writes, "Even Simon himself was believing" (8:13). The reader is left unsure what to make of this type of "belief." The Greek tense seems to suggest durative action, which might leave room for a change (a present condition now, but subject to change).[6]

Spirit's Validation (8:14–17)

Jerusalem suddenly feels the need to "certify" conversions reported here with the Samaritans. Why? Of the thousands of conversions documented in Acts, not even one has been questioned, nor Jerusalem felt the need to certify. Two reasons loom large from the narrative. First, the Samaritans are converted by Hellenist preaching, which is suspect due to the public relations disaster with Stephen. Second, to be blunt, they are Samaritans. The disciples James and John at one time urged Jesus to rain down fire from heaven on a Samaritan village that refused to welcome Jesus since he was on his way to Jerusalem (Luke 9:52–55). These racial prejudices and attitudes endemic to Jews and Samaritans

---

[6]While Samaritan conversions are described with aorist tense, Simon's is described with the imperfect (*episteusen*, ἐπίστευσεν). Cf. Acts 13:12, Sergius Paulus, p. 306.

had prevailed for two centuries—the early church not exempted. Samaritans accepting Jesus as Messiah? Something probably is amiss is the inference some easily could make.

Luke now begins to build a narrative profile that Jerusalem never initiated any mission thrust in the early church. They always were two steps behind what the Spirit was doing, as here at Samaria. Yet, they always felt obligated to "certify" what the Spirit already had done.[7] Jerusalem's typical, default inertia against mission expansion across non-Jewish lines will be a narrative undercurrent showing why the gentile mission *had* to arise out of the Hellenist movement.

The reason for the delay in the reception of the Holy Spirit by the Samaritans has been debated by commentators. Jerusalem, however, cannot argue Spirit reception, because they know what that reality is. The delay seems to be on purpose by the Spirit in order *to confirm for the apostles that the Hellenist Samaritan mission is a genuine operation of the Messiah and an authorized integration into messianic Israel.* To be sure, the Hellenist Philip had no trouble with their conversion, but the apostles in Jerusalem apparently do. So, Peter and John are sent to check things out up there in Samaria (8:14).

When Peter and John lay their hands on the Samaritan believers and they receive the Spirit, the reality of Pentecost is proven before their very eyes (8:15–17). The process described here is not normative in the New Testament precisely because this situation is not normal. What the Spirit is making clear is that the Spirit will drive fulfillment of Acts 1:8 if Jerusalem will not. The Spirit certifies Samaritan inclusion, not Jerusalem. Thus, reception of the Spirit in this delayed fashion at Samaria was not some problem with Philip's mission. Luke is careful to describe the Samaritans as "believers" before the apostles ever arrive. Samaritan salvation is not in doubt. The apostles' acceptance of them is. The Spirit's delaying tactic was especially for the Jerusalem apostles, who "never could get to church on time." Witnessing the reception of the Holy Spirit, the apostles are forced to confess that the Samaritans had become a legitimate part of messianic Israel. That message is what they took back to Jerusalem. Jerusalem had no vote in the matter. The restored, reunited kingdom of David in messianic Israel is now an eschatological reality of the last days.

---

[7]Somewhat odd, when one keeps in mind their own Pentecost experience.

Simon's Hypocrisy (8:18–24)

The ancient world had a full complement of religious charlatans. Simon was one of them. Simon reduces Christian faith to gaining magic power. He sees opportunity in this unusual apostolic operation of laying on of hands and Spirit reception. Simon barters his money for this Christian "magic." Apparently, he is "Simon the Great" but not great enough. Peter puts the "hex" on him for his wickedness, bitterness, and sin.[8] That curse is a potent magical spell for Simon. Only Peter could break the spell. The judgment result is left ambiguous in the text, so Simon's legacy is ambiguous in later Christian traditions.[9]

The triad of episodes in Acts 8 communicates what the coming of Messiah reveals about the nature of true worship, not only for Israel, but for the whole world. Simon puts the spotlight on both Jerusalem and Samaria and their Zion and Gerizim temple systems. Once Messiah has arrived, these traditional Jewish worship systems are made obsolete or transcended. Continuing to cling to them after God has sent his Son is as false a worship as Simon himself revealed.

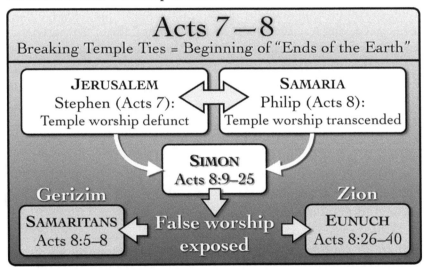

FIGURE 8.4. True Worship in Acts 7–8: Simon. Simon is used to convey false worship exposed, even of those insincerely taking advantage of others. Messiah is not fooled.

[8]Down in south Louisiana with our Marie Laveaux voodoo traditions, "hex" is the way Peter's "curse" would be understood instantly.

[9]Sometimes pictured as a Christian, and other times as a foe of Christianity.

Peter's Itinerary (8:25)

Peter proclaims the word of the Lord going back to Jerusalem. Normally, a Jew would go out of the way to avoid Samaria in going to Jerusalem. Galilean pilgrims to Jerusalem for the feasts would pass through Perea to the east of the Jordon, bypassing Samaria, because Perea also was ruled by their king, Herod Antipas of Galilee. Quite noticeably, Peter's itinerary did not make any bypass. He preached in "many villages of the Samaritans." This preaching illustrates Peter's approval of Samaritan inclusion into messianic Israel. Luke has been transparently clear, however, that Peter did not *initiate* this mission to the Samaritans. This mission is the first major expansion of the church beyond Jerusalem. Luke's point about this first major mission thrust is that *gospel expansion is a Hellenist movement.*

Ethiopian Eunuch (8:26–40)

Philip Commissioned (8:26–27)

Philip is commissioned by the Spirit to travel down the southern road to Gaza. Leaving Jerusalem, one always is going "down," because Jerusalem is in the hill country. The "desert" area borders the Negev. The point of these directions is to indicate not even close to Jerusalem. The angel guidance is crucial, as the angel functions to show the divine initiative in the story and that Philip is not out on a lark. Once again, Hellenist leadership is key to church expansion as presented in Acts 8, as Luke continues making his point about the breakthrough to wider witness for the church.

FIGURE 8.5. Desert Road to Gaza. Leaving Jerusalem toward Gaza, one travels down from the mountains into the Shephelah foothills on to the coastal plain.

The Ethiopian is introduced as a court official of the Ethiopian queen.[10] This

---

[10] "Candace" (*Kandakés*, Κανδάκης) is not a personal name but the dynastic title of the Ethiopian queen as head of government. Another Ethiopian eunuch in Scripture, Ebed-melech ("servant of the king"), rescued Jeremiah out of the well (Jer 38:7–13).

eunuch is in charge of the national treasury. We are told this to indicate his high social status. This person is intelligent (governmental office), educated (literate), wealthy (riding in a chariot; personal copy of Scripture), and honored. That he had "gone to Jerusalem to worship" means he falls into the category of a "God-fearer."[11] Attracted to Jewish religion, he never could be a full participant. The law of Moses disbarred

FIGURE 8.6. Miletus "God-Fearers" Inscription. This inscription in the theater at Miletus reserves a seat for Jewish "God-fearers" who attended events there.

eunuchs from temple entry (Deut 23:1). Further, eunuchs were disqualified from full proselytism. This eunuch endured a religious "no-man's-land," fully acceptable to no one.

Witness Prelude (8:28–31)

The eunuch is reading from the scroll of Isaiah. That he has his own personal copy is incredibly rare in the ancient world. Philip "heard" him reading because all ancient reading was out loud. Philip asks him if he understands what he is reading. The hermeneutical problem is that Messiah's arrival was not as expected, and Messiah's mission was not as envisioned. What the Ethiopian needs is the Messiah's interpretation of these matters, which is available to the apostles through the forty days training by Jesus at the beginning of Acts.

Witness Provided (8:32–35)

The text is from the famous "Servant songs" of Isaiah, a series of passages about God's special Servant accomplishing the eschatological

---

[11]Luke's distinctive term for non-proselyte synagogue sympathizers (*phoboumenos ton theon*, φοβούμενος τὸν θεόν). An Aphrodisias "God fearer" inscription published in 1987 may illustrate Lukan usage (Reynolds and Tannenbaum, *Jews and God-fearers at Aphrodisias*), but note dating issues (Chaniotis, "Jews of Aphrodisias"). For Luke's usage as distinct, non-Jewish, religious, cf. Levinskaya, "The Problem of God-Fearers."

realization of all God intended in Israel and for Israel. This particular Servant song excerpt is from Isa 53:7–8 (NRSV):

> Like a sheep he was led to the slaughter,
>   and like a lamb silent before its shearer,
>   so he does not open his mouth.
> In his humiliation justice was denied him.
>   Who can describe his generation?
>   For his life is taken away from the earth.

These type passages had become famous in early Christian *testimonia* to Jesus. The likely source of the use of such passages and their interpretation is Jesus's own teachings.[12]

The Ethiopian asks the standard questions all the rabbis asked of this enigmatic passage: Is this about the prophet Isaiah himself, or someone else (8:34)? The messianic answer is "the good news about Jesus" (8:35). The reason this Servant song tradition from Isaiah might be personal for the eunuch is that Isaiah had promised that in the future congregation of Israel, the eunuch would be included (Isa 56:3–5). True future worship, then, will result from the Servant's sacrifice that makes all acceptable to God.

Ethiopian Baptized (8:36–40)

The eunuch apparently believes, because he asked Philip to be baptized (8:36).[13] "What prevents me?" is intentional phrasing, because, as a eunuch, he permanently was prevented both from the temple and from being a full proselyte according to the law of Moses, which he apparently well knew, and Jewish tradition. The formerly excluded is included. Denied temple access becomes a moot point. His baptism is inclusion into messianic Israel. The meaning is clear: Messianic Israel transcends Mosaic Israel. The eunuch has been transformed by a new vision of the people of God.

Philip is snatched away by the Spirit (8:39). We see the Spirit's initiative all the way in this entire encounter from start to finish. The Spirit is defining messianic Israel, and his willing servants are the Hel-

---

[12]Luke 24:27, 44–49; Acts 1:3.

[13]The Western text adds an entire verse (8:37) to put the traditional third or fourth-century confessional formula of the later church on the lips of the Ethiopian. See the image of Laudian Acts MS 08 and discussion in the opening chapter, "Preliminaries," pp. 26–27.

lenists who cooperate in the fulfillment of the destiny of Isaiah's
Servant. Philip's itinerary moves
from Gaza, to Azotus (Ashdod),
and finally to Caesarea, where he
apparently settles on the coast.
Luke notes that Paul's host at the
end of the third missionary journey in Caesarea is this Philip and
his four daughters (21:8), which
brings the Hellenist cycle full circle using Philip as bookends, an
inclusio framing that shows Paul

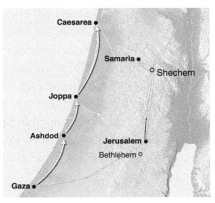

FIGURE 8.7. Philip's Itinerary. Philip
eventually settles in Caesarea.

in his missionary journeys fulfilling the Hellenist movement that breaks
ethnic boundaries, as with this Ethiopian.

Caesarea will be an important city in the story of Acts. Caesarea is
the place of the conversion of Cornelius by Peter in Acts 10, made
paradigmatic by Luke for Paul's gentile converts in the synagogue.
Cornelius was a "God-fearer" like the Ethiopian eunuch. Herod the
Great's grandson, Agrippa I, ruled as king of Judea from AD 41–44 and
lived in Caesarea. He killed John and imprisoned Peter but died in the
theater at Caesarea.

The Ethiopian eu-
nuch finishes out the
third of the three epi-
sodes in Acts 8 used to
expose false worship of
every kind through the
coming of Messiah. The
only union for the true
worship of Israel's God
by a united kingdom of
David is not Jerusalem

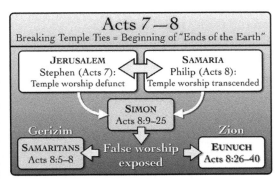

FIGURE 8.8. True Worship in Acts 7–8: Ethiopian.

and its defunct temple or Gerizim and its transcended temple but
messianic Israel with its Spirit-infused life. Now that Messiah has come,
the Lord's Servant, then any insistence on Jerusalem or Gerizim is as
false a worship as with Simon the sorcerer.

Finally, we can note how episodes in Acts 8 illustrate the themes of Stephen's speech. First, God active is seen in the preaching of the scattered Hellenists (8:4), the believing faith of the despised Samaritans (8:12), and the disqualified eunuch being baptized (8:36). Second, God resisted plays out the characterization "fighting against God" of Gamaliel's words (5:39). Resistance is seen in the persecution of the Jerusalem church (8:1), Saul's ravaging of believers (8:3), the hesitance of apostles to accept Samaritan results of Hellenist preaching (8:14), and shortly to come, the high priest's willingness to extend this hunt outward to Damascus (9:2).

DAMASCUS ROAD

Of the three great Hellenist leaders in Acts, Saul is the philosophy, passion, and powerhouse behind the gospel mission of the Hellenist movement. That distinction is why Saul's story is bounded on both sides by Philip and Peter as Luke's heuristic device to interpret the significance

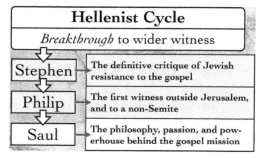

FIGURE 8.9. Hellenist Leaders: Saul. Saul will be the key figure in the Hellenist movement.

of Saul. If Philip represents the Hellenist breakthrough to wider witness for the gospel, Saul will be the key figure who catapults that movement into a world mission. Further, this movement's gentile emphasis will receive apostolic validation due to the apostle Peter and his experience with the centurion Cornelius in Caesarea, especially when Peter defends his actions with Cornelius to the defensive Jerusalem church. So both the stories of Philip and of Peter are used by Luke as bounding stories on behalf of contextualizing the story of Saul.

The literary importance of the Damascus Road is hard to overstate. Its thematic significance is obvious in its repetition three times, the only story so emphasized.[14] This story will complete the Hellenist Cycle in the movement to gentiles. This story illustrates perfectly both

---

[14] Acts 9:1–31; 22:3–21; 26:2–23.

themes of the Stephen speech. This story prepares for the entire last half of Acts. This story begins the transition from a focus on Peter in Acts 1–12 to an exclusive focus on Paul in Acts 13–28. This story launches messianic Israel on her destiny to Rome. This story puts us on the road to consummating all of Luke-Acts.

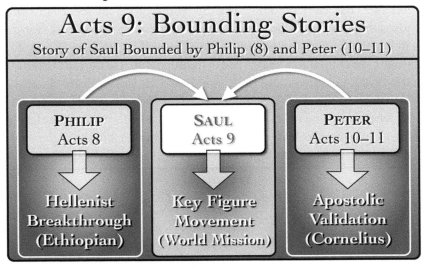

FIGURE 8.10. Acts 9 Bounding Stories. Philip (Acts 8) and Peter (Acts 10–11) are bounding stories that set the interpretation of the significance of the Damascus Road.

The character here is complex. From a literary point of view, while he is one character, he really has dual characteristics. He is Saul-Paul. These names represent the two sides of this person refracted from the perspective of the Ste-

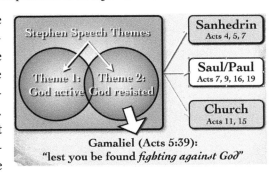

FIGURE 8.11. Stephen Speech Themes: Acts 9.

phen speech themes. Saul is stubborn resistance, God resisted. Paul is sacrificial service, God active. Often missed by readers of Acts is that this characterization does not change, true before *and after* the Damascus Road. Further, Luke builds this characterization into the plot.[15]

[15]As presented in chapter 3, "The Character Saul-Paul."

Saul on the Road (9:1–9)

Fighting God (9:1–2)

First of all, Saul is ignoring Gamaliel's advice. As Gamaliel's student (so 22:3), this action sets up a pattern from the very beginning when we meet this character: We know that he ignores good advice, even from those closest to him who have his best interests at heart. This feature will become crucial to the story of Paul, Jerusalem, and God's will. He ravages the church as a zealot. He is fighting God. He obtains letters of extradition, Roman judicial rights granted to the Hasmoneans since 142 BC that Julius Caesar later transferred to the high priests. Thus, Jerusalem refugees fleeing to Damascus are caught in Saul's reach. So he leaves Jerusalem bound for Damascus with a commission from the high priest. The journey is about six days.

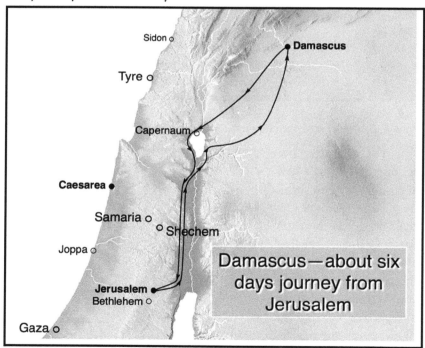

FIGURE 8.12. Damascus Road Map. This journey normally took about six days.

Seeing Jesus (9:3–9)

Was Saul's experience conversion or commission? Typical characteristics of conversion include a different commitment and a change of re-

ligion. The problem here is that if you asked Saul if he "changed religions" on the Damascus Road, he definitely would respond, "No!" He
always considered himself an Israelite of the Jewish faith in God. He
confessed Jesus as Messiah—nothing more Jewish than looking for and
believing in Messiah! Saul himself probably would describe his experience as a commission like other commissioning stories in biblical narratives.[16] The classic example would be Isaiah. Isaiah received a renewed
commitment, not a different commitment. His experience no doubt
was life changing, but not religion changing. Our purpose here is limited to noting specific scene details about this commission to indicate
briefly their literary function:

- vision: fulfills Joel 2:28–32 (Peter's quote at Pentecost, 2:16–18)

- light: signals an epiphany from heaven (Christophany)

- "persecute me": foundation of Pauline unity with Christ concept

- "Lord": more than "master"; divinity assumed in context, both with
  the famous "I am" construction echoing the divine name in Exodus
  (Exod 3:14) as well as Ananias's interpretation supplied (Acts 9:17)

- companions: authenticators of the experience

- blindness: parabolic of the content of Saul's commission, including
  Luke's prophetic light/darkness theme already appearing in both
  infancy narratives for John the Baptist (Luke 1:79) and Jesus (Luke
  2:32); anticipates gentile mission and experience (2 Cor 4:6)

- location: near Damascus, which fulfills the Stephen speech theme of
  God active outside the land of promise on behalf of gentiles; in the
  epoch making events of Israel's history, the voice of God is heard
  outside the boundaries of the promised land

Saul in Damascus (9:10–25)

Ananias's Vision (9:10–16)

Ananias is commissioned to assist Saul in interpreting his encounter.
The main word to alleviate Ananias's apprehension about going to the

---

[16]Moses (Exod 3:4–10); Jacob (Gen 46:2–4); Abraham (Gen 22:1–2); Isaiah (Isa 6:1–
13). Saul's experience was a "revelation," just like Isaiah's description (Gal 1:12, 16).

notorious Saul is that Saul is a "chosen instrument," which speaks to the divine initiative, and "carry my Name," which speaks to the divine commission being realized. This "carry my Name" theme is prophetic in that this theme is the realization of Israel's original vocation[17] and fulfills Jesus's words in Luke 12:11–12 that his disciples would be speaking in synagogues and before rulers and authorities, all of which Saul did. This carrying of the Name in a witness setting is:

- "rulers": Sergius Paulus, Gallio, Felix, Festus

- "kings": Agrippa II, Caesar

- "authorities": Philippi, Thessalonica, Sanhedrin

- "gentiles": 1MJ, 2MJ, 3MJ

- "synagogues": Damascus, Jerusalem, 1MJ, 2MJ, 3MJ, Rome

In these words to Ananias we have an indication of two settings that indicate the nature of this call. One setting is that of witness. Saul will be a witness. Acts 1:8, then, points to the story of Saul. The other setting is forensic, which anticipates the defensive posture Paul will be in throughout the last eight chapters of Luke's narrative in Acts 21–28. Thus, in the carrying of the Name, this witness "must suffer," another element to the forensic setting of carrying that Name. This must suffer theme in a witness setting is seen many ways in the Acts narrative:

- murderous plots and mob action: Damascus, Jerusalem, Ephesus, Corinth, Caesarea

- synagogue rejection: Damascus, Jerusalem, Pisidian Antioch, Thessalonica, Corinth, Ephesus

- stoning: Lystra

- rods, imprisonment: Philippi, Jerusalem, Rome

- shipwreck, snake bite: journey to Rome

Ananias's Ministry (9:17–19)

Ananias is faithful. He goes to Saul to give Saul God's word of revelation that will revolutionize Saul's life. The specifics indicate how Ana-

---

[17]As in, for example, Num 6:27; Isa 65:1.

nias made clear that what was happening to Saul was the reality of messianic Israel of the last days:

- "brother": messianic Israel's fictive kinship and sense of family
- "Lord Jesus": messianic Israel's confession
- "see again": messianic Israel's destiny with the gentiles
- "baptized": incorporation into messianic Israel's community

Functionally, all of this is direct repudiation of the chief priest's commission in 9:1–2, when Saul had asked the chief priest for letters to the synagogues in Damascus. Saul left Jerusalem with a commission from the chief priest. He arrived in Damascus with a new commission from the Lord Jesus.

Saul Preaches Jesus (9:20–22)

Saul began preaching "immediately," which indicates immediate, obedient acceptance of the new commission from Jesus. How could Paul flip-flop so instantly like this? Resurrection. As a Pharisee, he already believed in the resurrection. He simply had to witness its truth, which is the Damascus Road in a nutshell. Saul's message, therefore, is compatible with the messianic belief already in place in his worldview. His message is of messianic Israel. That his interpretation of the Damascus Road is messianic is revealed in Paul's two descriptors of Jesus within a synagogue setting. Saul identified Jesus as the "Son of God." This title derives from the royal enthronement language of Psalm 2. Jews long had used Psalm 2 to speak of God's adoption of Israel's king in their enthronement ceremonies conducted in the Davidic kingdom. These royal enthronement overtones over time accrued messianic sense. Saul clearly is operating within this messianic enthronement ritual context of the title.[18] The other title is even more direct: "Jesus is Messiah." In this title we see that Saul has integrated his thinking into the new vision of the people of God as messianic Israel renewed. The eschaton has arrived. The Spirit is poured out. The prophecies are fulfilled.

As Saul preaches Jesus in this way, he is preaching the message of the Hellenist cycle. He is taking up the mantle of the martyred Ste-

---

[18]As in Gal 1:16; Rom 1:1–4.

phen.[19] The description is that he "grew more powerful." The martyr Stephen speaks again.[20] Thus, Stephen's martyrdom has not been in vain. The enthroned Jesus did receive Stephen's spirit and honored his death. After its launch with Stephen and Philip, the responsibility for fulfilling the Hellenist cycle's destiny will fall upon the shoulders of Saul, the destiny of an unstoppable voice and an unbeatable argument.

Saul Escapes Damascus (9:23–25)

Here is where Saul becomes a basket case. The story also is mentioned by Paul in 2 Cor 11:32–33. Damascus was controlled by the Nabatean king Aretas IV (9 BC–AD 40). This Aretas had an ethnarch in Damascus. We are not told the dynamics behind the story, that is, why Aretas would have had Saul in the crosshairs; various reasons have been speculated, but we just do not know. What Luke wants

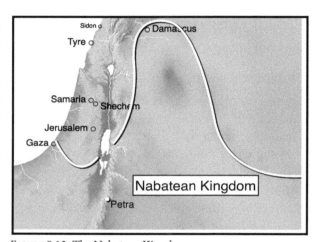

FIGURE 8.13. The Nabatean Kingdom.

to convey is a narrative inversion in which the hunter becomes the hunted. The inversion is an important early illustration for Luke of God's sovereignty over Saul's story. Even when Saul is in the crosshairs, God will accomplish his own purposes.

Saul in Jerusalem (9:26–31)

Saul returns to Jerusalem after escaping Damascus. Why he thought that was a good idea is not clear. His participation in the stoning of Stephen and his zealot-like ravaging of the church in persecution of believers would be a reputation and trauma no one could forget.

---

[19]As in the description in Acts 6:8–10.

[20]Compare Acts 6:9 and 9:29.

Barnabas's Advocacy (9:26–27)

Saul is rejected by a highly suspicious Jerusalem church. They simply did not believe him. Barnabas, however, does, which begins a fruitful relationship of several years. Why Barnabas trusted Saul never is explained, but his character role established by his first appearance in Acts is as Pentecost facilitator. To bring about Pentecost fullness of gentiles in messianic Israel, Barnabas plays a crucial role.

Note that Barnabas facilitates all of Saul's important connections in his ministry, particularly in Jerusalem and Antioch. The Jerusalem connection here is that Barnabas introduces Saul to the "apostles," which would include Peter. Thus, through Barnabas, Saul gains apostolic validity in unbroken continuity with Jesus. How Barnabas knew the details of Saul's Damascus Road experience to explain to the others is not explained, but the result is apostolic acceptance, as with Stephen (6:6). This acceptance will be important for the future legitimacy of the gentile mission. Barnabas later will facilitate Saul's introduction to the Antioch ministry (11:25–26), and then facilitate the first missionary journey (13:2). All of this effort by Barnabas on Saul's behalf will explain why Saul's later fight with Barnabas at the beginning of the (so-called) second missionary journey is catastrophic for Saul (15:36–40). In narrative terms, the die is cast for resisting the Pentecost facilitator.

Saul the Hellenist (9:28–30)

This final part of the Damascus Road narrative is meant to bring the reader full circle back to Stephen's ministry. Saul's story is anchored in Stephen's story. Even though Saul was complicit in Stephen's death, which illustrates the theme of God resisted, here is Saul in Jerusalem doing exactly what Stephen was doing, speaking boldly of behalf of Jesus. Saul continues Stephen's debate with the Hellenist Jews, presumably in the synagogue of the Freedmen (9:29). This verse completes the picture of Saul picking up Stephen's mantle. Stephen was martyred, but his voice lives on in Saul. Thus, the Hellenist movement of the Jerusalem church as represented by Stephen in a Diaspora synagogue becomes the inevitable destiny of Saul's ministry. Saul will be preaching in the world's Diaspora synagogues and reaching Greek populations, the "God-fearers," like the Ethiopian eunuch, in those synagogues. From the original list of the Seven, if Stephen, first on the list gives the key speech about the temple, and Nicolaus, last on the list, gives the key city of Antioch, in between the two is Saul, who is the key character that merges the key speech and key city into his own story and fulfills the Hellenist movement.

Persecution will be a constant is Saul's story, as with the Hellenists in general. He has death threats in Damascus (9:23–25). He has death threats in Jerusalem (9:29–30). He will have more death threats in his ministry (14:19; 20:3; 23:12). Saul the persecutor becomes Saul the persecuted. This persecution context is exactly as promised on the Damascus Road. Often noted is that the narrative movement of the Damascus Road story can be seen as a chiasm in six scenes.[21]

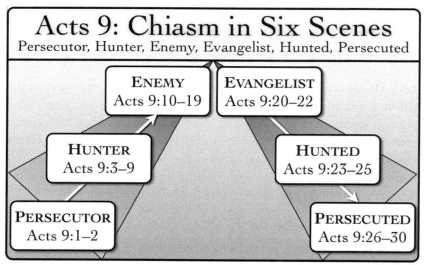

FIGURE 8.14. Damascus Road Chiasm. Six scenes set the development chiastically.

Paul is sent to his hometown of Tarsus in Cilicia as a safe house (9:30). This move probably is because he has relatives there. Tarsus is where Barnabas will come to retrieve Saul for work in Antioch (11:25). The story in Acts will provide two more narratives before launching Saul into orbit: Peter and Agrippa I. A return to Peter is to validate the gentile mission Saul will engage through the story of the conversion of Cornelius (Acts 10–11). The final account in the first half of Acts is Herod Agrippa I's persecution of the Jerusalem church, targeting the apostles like the earlier persecution did not (8:1). Agrippa's attack on the apostles, along with a growing disfavor of the church, is the final

---

[21]As one example among several, consult the analysis by Parsons, *Acts*, 125–34.

death knell of the Pentecost renewal in Jerusalem and will explain why messianic Israel's center of gravity will shift inevitably from Jerusalem to Antioch.

Progress Report (9:31)

This report is the second of six that punctuate the Acts narrative. This note is the bow on the initial development of Saul of Tarsus, who will become the hero of the Acts narrative. Why Saul as hero? The story naturally fell to him. Stephen laid the foundation. Saul now builds on that ministry. Luke makes Saul the hero of Acts because Saul's life forces the issues of the Stephen speech like no other Luke can find. Those issues are God active outside the boundaries of the promise land seeking lost gentiles. This saving God, however, also is resisted, sometimes the most by his own people. Luke uses Saul to say that the person with the genuine faith of Abraham running in the veins will find in Stephen's speech the very voice of God himself—if only that person can meet Jesus personally.

The description of the church in this progress report is noteworthy in terms of locale. The church no longer is just in Jerusalem. The church now is described as "throughout Judea, Galilee, and Samaria." In other words, this church is the church that is arising because of Hellenist leaders. We have followed the story about one in particular as Luke's paradigmatic example, Philip of the Seven. Messianic Israel is beginning to be transformed into the church of the gentile mission. This church had peace, was strengthened, grew in numbers, and lived in the fear of the Lord—encouraged by the Holy Spirit. Yes, indeed. Every single step down every dusty road. Acts 1:8 being fulfilled.

CORNELIUS

Coastal Prelude (9:32–43)

Peter's coastal ministry is a prelude to the Cornelius story. Two stories of healing are told. Their significance is their geography and prior linkage before Luke incorporated them. First, the healings take place in two coastal towns that have increasingly gentile populations. Gentiles is the direction of Acts now. Second, they probably were linked in tradition prior to Luke's use. Personal names, rare use of "saints," and the common "arise" command seem to indicate the linkage. They have distinct use of personal names, when most healing stories are anonymous, such as the lame man in Acts 3, whose name we never know, or the many Samaritans healed in Acts 8. Both of these stories have the rare use of the term "saints," an uncommon term for believers. Finally, both stories also have the same "arise" command. Already linked in tradition probably means these stories were pulled together to use healing and raising from the dead as "signs" to serve the preaching of Jesus as the resurrection and the life.

Luke now finds them useful for his purpose. Luke wants to show the parallel in ministry between Jesus and Peter. This parallel is seen in the story of Jesus's healing of Jairus's daughter in Luke 8:49–56. With both healing stories by Jesus and by Peter

Jesus (Luke 8:49–56)	Peter (Acts 9:36–43)
Jairus's daughter	Tabitha
"Talitha, koum!"	"Tabitha, koum!"
"Little girl, arise!"	"Tabitha, arise!"

FIGURE 8.15. Ministry Parallel: Jesus and Peter. The central command shows intentional ministry parallel.

we have a significant person with an untimely death and a similarity of the central command. In the grand scheme of Luke-Acts, once again we have the Gospel as the story of Jesus, part one, and Acts as the story of Jesus, part two.

Finally, this coastal ministry of Peter is non-missional. Two elements in Luke's description make this non-missional character clear. First, the movement is without strategy. Peter simply moves "here and there" (9:32). Second, the movement targets believers only, as Luke specifically indicates: "among . . . believers." While Peter does have a ministry, his ministry does not yet show the defining features of the Hellenist breakthrough to wider witness. Cornelius will change that.

The first healing is in Lydda. Aeneas had been paralyzed for eight years. Since Peter and John healed the lame man at the temple who had been lame for forty years, this healing does not seem as notable. Peter heals him. Aeneas's healing does generate conversions. The second healing is more toward the coast in Joppa. Tabitha has died. Her name is Dorcas in Greek. She was a disciple of praiseworthy social standing by her acts of charity in making clothing and tunics. Charitable acts had been a standard definition of piety for Pharisees. Tabitha has been prepared for her burial, so the situation at Joppa is much more serious than in Lydda. After hearing that Peter is nearby in Lydda, he is retrieved to help at Joppa. He raises Tabitha from the dead. Her healing generates conversions as well. Luke has incorporated traditions of a seacoast ministry to reaffirm Peter as a

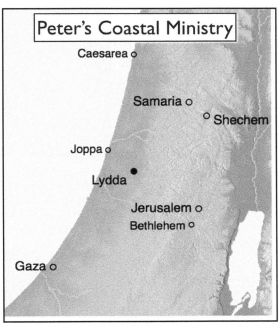

FIGURE 8.16. Peter's Coastal Ministry. Luke uses Peter's healings on the coast to validate Peter as extending the ministry of Jesus before telling the Cornelius story.

reflection of Jesus's own ministry before Luke moves on to tell the crucial but controversial story of Cornelius's conversion.

Cornelius Paradigm (10:1–48)

The literary signal for the importance of this story to Luke is that the story is told twice, once as the story unfolds in real time to Peter, and again as Peter retells the story in his defense to the Jerusalem church. The story provides: (1) apostolic validation of the Hellenist movement to gentiles, and (2) the prototypical conversion for Saul's ministry.

Cornelius's Vision (10:1–8)

Cornelius is a Caesarean centurion of the Italian cohort. The centurion, while not the highest military rank in the Roman army, was one of the most respected men of the entire military system. He was "boots on the ground." He fought hand-to-hand with the legionnaires he commanded. He never commanded what he did not himself do. The centurion, then, was one of the most trusted military officers as a result. His unit was a "century" of about a hundred men. Commanding the centurions were the tribunes,[22] and over the tribunes was the legate.[23]

FIGURE 8.17. Centurion Inscription. Latin inscription 2nd cent. AD; rare documentation of presence of Roman military on the island of Cyprus. "Erected in memory of the centurion Caius Decimius, son of Titus, from the tribe of Stellatina" (CM).

What is unusual of this centurion at Caesarea is that he is a "God-fearer." He is a devout man, fears God, and performs the preeminent marks of Pharisaic piety in almsgiving and prayers. Also, as a "God-fearer," he attends Sabbath services in the synagogue. While such activity would be unusual for a Roman officer, centurions always are pictured positively in the ministry of Jesus. So, Jesus heals a centurion's servant (Luke 7:2–6), and a centurion confesses Jesus' innocence at the cross (Luke 23:47). The centurion Julius was kind to Paul on the journey to Rome (27:3). This "God-

FIGURE 8.18. Centurion Tomb Monument Relief. A tomb monument in military style from 1st cent. BC on tomb of Tiberius Flavius Miccaulus, who was prefect and priest. Shown is centurion with gladius sword leading his troops from his horse (IAM).

fearer" gentile of the synagogue profiles the typical Pauline convert.

---

[22]In Acts 21–22, a tribune in Jerusalem is prominent in the story and is about to have Paul scourged when he learns from one of his centurions that the prisoner is a Roman citizen (Acts 22:27).

[23]We meet the legate of Syria, Quirinius, in Luke 2:2.

God hears Cornelius's prayers. The Roman centurion receives a life-changing vision from God that fulfills the "God active" theme of the Stephen speech on the pattern of Abraham in Mesopotamia (7:2). The God of Abraham has "glorified his servant Jesus" Peter declared to the Jerusalem crowds (3:13). Peter also noted God gave Abraham a covenant that in his descendants "all the families of the earth shall be blessed" (3:25). Cornelius and his family will be one of those receiving this Abrahamic blessing. Like Abram, Cornelius is obedient to the divine command. Thus, Luke presents Cornelius as the paradigmatic gentile prospect for Hellenist preaching and the paradigmatic convert for gentile mission, anticipating the story to unfold with Saul-Paul.

Peter's Vision (10:9–16)

Peter is conflicted with the law. He receives a heavenly command to eat. The command as from heaven would be assumed as the voice of God (10:13). Yet, what God is saying "makes no sense." So, Peter refuses the divine command based on Mosaic law (10:14). New messianic law is given: "What God has made clean, you must not call profane" (10:15). Peter is now learning the full significance of Pentecost. The outpoured Spirit is a cleansing more effective than any Mosaic law ritual. The outpoured Spirit is the new eschaton and a new vision of the people of God. The Spirit is definitive of messianic Israel, not Moses. Peter's refusal of the divine voice persists three times. This repetition reflects how entrenched is the law of Moses in national Israel. Once again, themes of Stephen's speech kick in: When God is active, God is resisted.

Peter's Visitors (10:17–22)

Cornelius's delegation arrives. The timing is crucial for Peter to make the connection to his vision. The Spirit confirms the connection: "for I have sent them" (10:20). Clean and unclean is about gentiles and messianic Israel. Cornelius's reputation is repeated (10:22). While he is a Roman, and a centurion at that, he has strong synagogue connections, indicated in the word that he is "upright" and "God-fearing." That Cornelius is "well spoken of by the whole Jewish nation" means that his spiritual piety and sincerity even would pass muster with the Pharisees. So, pious and sincere Cornelius has been obedient to the divine command. Notice the irony: Cornelius has been more immediately obedient to direct divine command than has Peter!

Peter's Reception (10:23–33)

Peter is received as a divine agent. He is given due honor and respect like an angel from God. This description indicates receptivity to hear the divine word. This gentile receptivity indicates the typical Pauline synagogue convert later in the missionary journeys of the second half of Acts. A crowd has assembled of relatives and close friends.

Peter now interprets his Joppa vision. He begins to make a transition from Mosaic regulations that has been needed since day one. He asserts the law makes "unlawful for a Jew to associate with or to visit a gentile." Well, not really. A little overstated. Jews were not prevented from visiting gentiles in the law. Rituals of clean and unclean simply had to be observed. Pharisaic interpretations had built in "safeguards" in their oral law just to make double sure that clean and unclean never was violated. These oral regulations simply circumscribed association with gentiles as totally off limits. Jesus met these Pharisaic traditions in his own ministry, and he was criticized by Pharisees for socializing with gentile "sinners" (Luke 5:30).[24] Thus, Peter's understanding of the "law" was more Pharisaic tradition than actual Mosaic regulation. Peter now has come to Cornelius without objection because of the strange invitation he has received from his unexpected visitors to Joppa, yet he still is a little unclear of his mission! He still has to ask why they sent for him (10:29).

Peter's question allows Cornelius to repeat his vision (10:30–33). The repetition is a literary technique that affords Luke opportunity to emphasize Cornelius's character once more and the significance of the event. Cornelius is a gentile primed and ready to hear the gospel.

Peter's Sermon (10:34–44)

The point of the whole sermon is summarized at the very beginning in Peter's new realization that "God shows no partiality" because anyone "in every nation" who fears God and does what is right (i.e., like Cornelius) is acceptable to God (10:35). Peter's message here follows the standard apostolic outline of the story of Jesus seen already in Peter's Pentecost sermon.[25] Peter begins with the ministry of John the Baptist, establishes scriptural fulfillment, shows empowerment, then moves on

[24]Cf. Luke 7:34; 7:37–39; 15:2; 19:7.
[25]See pp. 173–74.

to death and resurrection, and finishes with commission. The crucial moment is the outpouring of the Spirit at the end even as Peter still is speaking (10:44), since reception of the Spirit defines messianic Israel. Mosaic regulations are fulfilled by the Spirit. The Spirit's manifestation among gentiles assembled in Cornelius's house is the equivalent of Mosaic cleansing rituals. In effect, Peter just has experienced the radical nature and full implications of Stephen's Sanhedrin message, for which, we need to remember, Stephen was stoned.

Peter's Sermons
The Church's Movement from Jews to Gentiles

Sermon	Audience	Significance
1. Acts 2	Jerusalem's pilgrims	Church empowered
2. Acts 3	Jerusalem's people	Forgiveness offered
3. Acts 4	Jerusalem's leaders	Forgiveness offered
4. Acts 5	Jerusalem's leaders	Forgiveness rejected
5. Acts 10	Cornelius's house	Gentile plan unfolds
6. Acts 11	Circumcision party	Gentile plan resisted
7. Acts 15	Church leaders	Gentile plan settled

FIGURE 8.19. Peter's Sermons: Acts 10. This fifth sermon shows God's plan for gentile inclusion through the Spirit into messianic Israel beginning to unfold.

Circumcised Surprise (10:45–46)

Circumcised believers are surprised. This surprise is a surprise. This surprise speaks to the issue that the Jerusalem church simply did not grasp the full implications of the teaching of Jesus or the meaning of the outpoured Spirit at Pentecost as eschatological harvest abundance from all the nations. Just like they wrongly conflated post-exilic ideas about national Israel with the messianic Israel of the last days (Acts 1:6), the Jerusalem church from the beginning wrongly conflated post-exilic ideas about Mosaic law with salvation in Jesus.

That problem with trying to integrate Mosaic law into messianic Israel is now exposed in raw form: The gift of the Spirit is "even on gentiles." "Even" is the problem. This reaction among the circumcised shows

Jerusalem really did not "get it" from the beginning, suggests why Jerusalem never initiated any mission thrust among those already "known" to be "excluded" from "Israel" (Samaritans, gentiles), and also ominously forecasts the future crisis the Jerusalem church inevitably will have with the Pauline mission, otherwise known as the Jerusalem Conference of Acts 15, after Antioch's first missionary journey. Intimations of this Jerusalem problem will occur shortly.

Peter's Validation (10:47–48)

Peter certifies these gentiles. Their faith is acknowledged in baptism. Gentiles are incorporated into messianic Israel. Peter's action involves only one gentile family. As long as they sit on the back pew, keep quiet, and do not expect to hold any positions of responsibility, the situation, while not desirable, is tolerable. Have them coming in droves thinking they are full members with all the rights, responsibilities, and privileges pertaining thereunto, and we have a real crisis.

For this reason, Peter's authorization is crucial. Peter is the apostolic stamp of approval. Peter is the historical connection to the ministry of Jesus himself. The Cornelius conversion is an epoch event for the church. That Peter accepts the offer of hospitality from Cornelius and agrees to lodge with him is one small step for a Jew, one giant leap for Israel. While the clean and unclean issue here seems to be new to Peter in terms of his grasp of what is meant, this message actually plays out Jesus's own teaching during his ministry.[26] Thus, Peter's multiple refusals to be obedient to the command of the heavenly voice falls in line with the Stephen speech theme of God resisted.

Cornelius himself is a picture of piety. His prayer and almsgiving are emphasized. He conforms to the standard norms of Jewish piety learned in the synagogue from Pharisees. This piety, then, serves to set the synagogue context of this gentile. The synagogue is what makes him fertile ground ready for the gospel seed to be sown. Cornelius is the explanation for why Saul goes to every synagogue he gets a chance. He is not ignoring his call to gentiles. He is taking advantage of his best shot for success among gentiles. Plus, he has the further advantage also of being able to speak to kinsmen, fellow Israelites.[27]

---

[26]Especially Mark 7:14–23.

[27]His great grief in their rejection of the gospel is intense in Rom 9:1–4.

Jerusalem's issues will be over circumcision and table fellowship. The question will be whether circumcision is necessary for salvation. Must one become a "full" Jew before truly being saved? Cornelius was a "God-fearer" only, not circumcised, so not a full Jew. How can one be part of Israel without being a circumcised Jew? Further, what happens to Jewish kosher laws if Jews start consorting with gentiles at the table? For both questions of circumcision and fellowship, the answers are inherent in the Cornelius story. First, the Spirit's blessing is the crucial proof of eschatological realities of salvation. Second, Peter's lodging with Cornelius shows crucial acceptance of table fellowship. Clean and unclean radically have been redefined down to one's own table at home.

Thus, Cornelius is the highpoint to this point in the story of Hellenist expansion. The repetitious style in telling the story is the importance of the event. Cornelius's vision is told four times in Acts 10–11. Peter's own vision itself is told two times. Finally, Acts 11:3–17 will summarize all of Acts 10 all over again! But why is Peter the focus and not one of the Seven Hellenist leaders? The experience *has* to happen with Peter because Peter represents the original ministry of Jesus. That Cornelius is a legitimate part of the story of Jesus is a paramount point to make in Luke's narrative strategy. Peter makes this point. Hellenists did not have any reservations about the operation of the Spirit for establishing anyone in messianic Israel.

Jerusalem Problem (11:1–18)

The Jerusalem problem that has been brewing under the surface since Pentecost, until now only whispered in private conversations, erupts in open conflict. The Jerusalem church picture is not very flattering. News from Caesarea about a "Cornelius affair" hits Jerusalem newsstands.

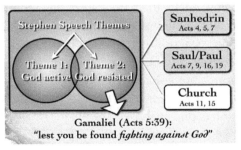

FIGURE 8.20. Stephen Speech Themes: Acts 11. God resisted even applies to the church.

Circumcised believers react predictably and negatively. Peter is challenged in Jerusalem. (Think about that for a moment.)

Circumcision Challenge (11:1–3)

Circumcised believers raise a two-fold challenge: (1) salvation: "uncircumcised men," and (2) table fellowship: "ate with them." Here is the Stephen speech theme two, God resisted, in spades. This challenge indicates that the Jerusalem church still is troubled how to handle Moses. The meaning of Pentecost for messianic Israel is still unclear.

Peter's Sermons
The Church's Movement from Jews to Gentiles

Sermon	Audience	Significance
1. Acts 2	Jerusalem's pilgrims	Church empowered
2. Acts 3	Jerusalem's people	Forgiveness offered
3. Acts 4	Jerusalem's leaders	Forgiveness offered
4. Acts 5	Jerusalem's leaders	Forgiveness rejected
5. Acts 10	Cornelius's house	Gentile plan unfolds
6. Acts 11	Circumcision party	Gentile plan resisted
7. Acts 15	Church leaders	Gentile plan settled

FIGURE 8.21. Peter's Sermons: Acts 11. God's gentile plan is resisted in Jerusalem.

Peter's Defense (11:4–17)

Peter retells the whole story, which allows literary emphasis. He first offers a rehearsal of events (11:4–14). He then presents the reality of the Spirit's action (11:15–16). This reality will resonate with the story of Pentecost (Acts 2) and the Samaritans (Acts 8). He finally concludes with a theological deduction (11:17).

Peter's conclusion is one of those real ringer stingers: "Who was I to think I could *oppose God?*" This idea resonates with so much in the previous Acts narrative about opposing or fighting God:

Gamaliel — Sanhedrin	Peter — Church
5:39: "you will only find yourselves fighting against God"	11:17: "Who was I to think I could oppose God?"

FIGURE 8.22. Gamaliel and Peter. The theme of fighting God parallels the Sanhedrin's reaction with the church.

- Ananias and Sapphira: the question this same Peter asked about "testing" the Spirit (5:9)

- Gamaliel: Gamaliel's dire warning to the Sanhedrin about "fighting God" (5:39)

- Stephen: "stiff-necked people" (7:51); note this charge is made to the *circumcised*, further observing that "uncircumcised in heart and ears, you are forever opposing the Holy Spirit"

- Saul: "Jesus, whom you are persecuting" (9:5)

Jerusalem's Response (11:18)

We have to read this response carefully. Luke's meaning is subtle, and one should not think naively that all is rosy. Otherwise, the crisis that arises after Antioch's first missionary journey that provokes the need for the Jerusalem Conference simply will make no sense whatsoever.

The response of the Jerusalem church actually is ambiguous. In fact, Luke communicates a *dual* response, and he means two different groups with back-to-back "they" occurrences. First, Luke says, "they were silenced." Who is silenced? This "they" obviously has to be the circumcision party that made the complaint in the first place.

Then, Luke says, "they praised God." Who is this "they"? The circumcision party? Probably not, since that group only moments before had to be "silenced." This "they" praising God more likely is the non-circumcision party who agree with Peter's baptism of Cornelius and confess God's initiative in gentile inclusion into messianic Israel ("God has given"). They also agree that gentiles are saved without circumcision in using the words "repentance" and "life."

Two matters about gentiles coming into messianic Israel remain unresolved. Unmentioned at all here in this response of the Jerusalem church is the issue of table fellowship. That issue still will need to be addressed. Further, the circumcision issue is unresolved. The circumcision group is only "silenced." That the issue still lurks dangerously just under the surface is the story of the Jerusalem Conference, when the issue reappears with a vengeance in Acts 15.

So what does this negative Jerusalem action portend? For the perceptive reader, Luke is providing a premonition that the future center of gravity for the Hellenist movement and the future of the church inevitably will have to shift. That shift will be from Jerusalem to Antioch.

Peter's Shifting Roles

Also shifting are Peter's two important roles. In his church role Peter faces growing marginalization. He will pay dearly for the Cornelius affair. Though he is an apostle, his Jerusalem leadership is weakening. That he was challenged in this way about what went down in Caesarea is only one indicator. Leadership in the Jerusalem church shifts almost imperceptibly to James, the brother of Jesus. He is well known, even to Josephus the historian, and has a conservative reputation. By the time of the Jerusalem Conference in Acts 15, even though most notable leaders of the early church are present, including apostles, James is the one who draws the discussion to a conclusion, enunciates the final decision, and then composes a letter communicating the conference decision for distribution to Diaspora churches.

Peter's mission role also is changing. Here too, marginalization is taking place. Mission impetus never had been a part of the Jerusalem church legacy. The center of gravity for mission will shift to Antioch. With this shift comes a shift to the mission leadership of Saul. At first, Barnabas takes the lead outside Jerusalem, but eventually Barnabas will transition to Saul, even though by way of a serious disagreement.

Thus, Peter's church role sees a shift from Peter to James. Peter's mission role also sees a shift from Peter to Saul. These shifting roles are what create in a natural, almost inevitable way the two halves of the Acts narrative in Acts 1–12 and Acts 13–28.

SUMMARY

The three episodes in Acts 8 (Samaritans, Simon, and the Ethiopian) are used by Luke to critique false worship. Messiah changes everything in the religious equation. He breaks Jewish temple ties of both Zion and Gerizim, which breaks any territorial or institutional limitations to the gospel going to the ends of the earth. Messiah exposes false worship in Simon the sorcerer, but Simon is simply a sign of the futility of all systems that fail to confess true faith in Jesus. Acts 8 also continues to illustrate the two major themes of the Stephen speech of God active and God resisted.

After Solomon, the Davidic kingdom divided into the northern kingdom of Israel and the southern kingdom of Judah. Efforts to reunite the kingdoms failed. Samaritans were the surviving Jews of the northern kingdom of Israel lost as a nation in the Assyrian captivity. Northern Jews were despised and rejected by returning Babylonian captives of the southern kingdom. Thus, Northern and southern Jews had competing cultic centers on Gerizim and Zion until John Hyrcanus I destroyed the capital of Samaria and the temple on Gerizim to insure no competing Jewish cultus interfered with Hasmonean dynastic aspirations. Animosity between Jews and Samaritans became entrenched.

Then, Messiah came, redefining Israel. Persecution after Stephen's temple critique sent Hellenists into their own exile from Jerusalem. The Spirit, however, used the Hellenist preaching of Philip to bring the gospel to Samaria, and the Samaritans were united into messianic Israel. The kingdom of David was reunited by David's Son.

Simon was a Samaritan magician "converted" by Philip, but the nature of his "believing" is thrown into doubt in the narrative by his attempt to buy magical power from Peter, as if gospel preachers were operating another charlatan scam of the people. The outcome of this curse on Simon Luke never specifies, but Simon's wicked heart and his hypocrisy are made clear.

Jerusalem sends Peter and John up to Samaria to certify the conversions. Jerusalem has difficulty considering Samaritans as believers. These conversions had two strikes against them: (1) they were the result of Hellenist preaching, and (2) they concerned Samaritans, after all. For the sake of proof for the apostles, the Spirit delays obvious signs of his presence among the Samaritans until Peter and John lay their hands on them. In terms of gospel mission, Jerusalem just never gets to church on time. Jerusalem never sponsors even one missionary journey in Acts, although they always feel obligated to check things out after a revival already has broken out somewhere. Gospel mission breaking territorial boundaries is tied firmly to the Hellenist movement in Acts, not Jerusalem.

Philip is sent by the Spirit to witness to the Ethiopian eunuch, who is reading the prophet Isaiah. Isaiah had indicated that even those excluded from the congregation of Israel in the law would be included in Messiah. The eunuch had gone to the temple in Jerusalem to worship, even though he could stand only outside its gates. As he returns to his gentile homeland, however, he finds true worship in his chariot on a dusty road going down to Gaza. Messianic Israel with its Spirit-infused life is breaking all old barriers of approach to God.

The Damascus Road is the consummate episode in Acts, told three times, the first time being interpreted by stories about Philip and Peter on either side. The full trajectory of Simeon's prophecy of "light for the gentiles" lands on this Damascus road, fulfilled by a light that blinds but then reveals the truth about Jesus the Messiah. This truth energizes a life destiny, that of Saul-Paul, whose story also will play out the themes of the Stephen speech—God active, God resisted. Saul on the road is ignoring Gamaliel's advice, fighting God. Yet, God will have his way with this reluctant witness. The witness theme of Acts 1:8 points to Saul, and this witness is attended by suffering on behalf of the Name. So Saul leaves Jerusalem with a commission from the high priest, and arrives in Damascus with a replacement commission from the Messiah.

Saul preaches Jesus in the synagogues of Damascus, taking up the mantle of Stephen. Saul is the greatest of the Hellenist leaders. His life in danger, Saul escapes Damascus, indicating a sovereign overshadowing of his life. He goes to Jerusalem, but is not welcome there—and he never will be. This status of "unwelcome in Jerusalem" will figure prominently at the end of the third missionary journey when Paul insists on going to Jerusalem against all advice, even the Holy Spirit. Barnabas, Pentecost facilitator, is Saul's mediator to the apostles in Jerusalem. As always, Barnabas facilitates Pentecost harvest abundance in the Hellenist movement by his relationship to Saul. Not only does Barnabas introduce Saul to Jerusalem here, he will introduce Saul to the ministry at Antioch, and he will help Saul launch Antioch's first missionary journey. The progress report at 9:31 makes due note that the church has spread past Jerusalem. The narrative is clear this Pentecost abundance is the result of the Hellenist movement of Stephen, Philip, and Saul.

The story of Cornelius shows the paradigmatic gentile and the paradigmatic conversion of a "God-fearer" of the synagogue that will be typical of the ministry of Saul. In a coastal ministry prelude, Peter is shown as a reprise of the ministry of Jesus, showing Acts is the story of Jesus, part two. Peter's vision of the unclean animals is the lesson that the Spirit cleanses in messianic Israel, not Moses. Peter's fifth sermon in Acts 10 to Cornelius's house shows God's plan for gentiles unfolding.

Conservative elements of the Jerusalem church who are circumcised Jews are not pleased with Peter when news of the Cornelius affair hits Jerusalem. They call Peter to account. Even the church can be found in the Gamaliel analysis of "fighting against God." Peter's sixth sermon in Acts 11 to this circumcision party shows God's plans for gentiles being resisted. Peter makes clear the Spirit was at work in Caesarea, so, given the revelation of the Joppa vision, he was not going to oppose God in the matter. Messianic Israel is defined by the Spirit, not Moses. Luke describes with deliberate ambiguity for the attentive reader Jerusalem's response to Peter's sermon. The circumcision party is only silenced for the time being. This Jerusalem problem is a foreboding of a future crisis that will erupt when the first missionary journey has gentiles coming into the church in droves.

While Peter's sermon wins the day for the time being in Jerusalem, he pays a heavy price for the Cornelius affair. Some of this price is seen in two significant shifts that begin to take place at this point for Peter, almost unnoticed, like continental drift. Peter's leadership roles will be changing. First, leadership in the Jerusalem church will shift to James. Second, leadership in the preaching mission of the church will shift to Saul. After Acts 12, Peter makes one cameo appearance at the Jerusalem Conference in Acts 15 for his last sermon that completes the story of the church's movement to gentile mission. Peter then drops off the radar completely for the rest of Acts. Peter's story, while crucial for the early stages of the Jesus movement after the resurrection, cannot bear the weight of the story yet to be told in the Hellenist movement that is the future of the church. Another character will have to take up that narrative mantle and bear its burden to the end of Acts.

9

Hellenist Center Shifts

From Jerusalem to Antioch (11–12)

A S READERS OF ACTS MOVE into the second half of chapter 11, they are rounding the corner to the finish line of the first half of Acts. Acts 11:19 should begin a new chapter, because this verse begins the development moving the entire narrative to Antioch. This transition is imperative to lay the foundation for the second half of Acts.

ANTIOCH EMERGENCE

Preaching to Greeks (11:19–21)

Antioch is the result of the original preaching from the scattering due to the persecution related to Stephen. Those scattered move ever outward, expanding the circle of gospel proclamation into Phoenicia, Cyprus, and Antioch. Expansion into Phoenicia establishes churches along the coastal cities of Tyre and Sidon. On the voyage to Rome, the centurion Julius allowed Paul "to go to his friends to be cared for" at the port of Sidon (27:3). Believers were there probably because of this push here. However, not all is well in the story.

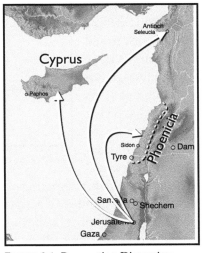

FIGURE 9.1. Persecution Dispersion.

Luke makes one important note about the target audience of this preaching, usually not emphasized in commentaries. Luke is very clear that they preached "to Jews only" (11:19). This preaching is still hung up either on table fellowship or on integrating Moses into messianic Israel. "Jews only" is the probable original sense of Peter's "to those who are far off" at Pentecost (2:39). He likely was thinking Diaspora *Jews*, not gentiles. Only *after* Peter had the revolutionary Joppa vision, confirmed by the Cornelius conversion, could he make this transition. Simply put, circumcised Jews simply were not on board the Cornelius cruise line. Through stories of the Samaritans, the Ethiopian eunuch, and Cornelius, the reader already knows that the Spirit is not in a "to Jews only" frame of mind. Pentecost abundance is not there.

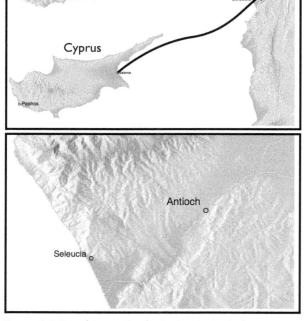

The key transition to where the Spirit is going will be centered in Antioch. The pivotal shift happens as particular disciples from Cyprus and Cyrene arrive in Antioch targeting a new audience, as they preach specifically "to Hellenists also," which would be gentiles (11:20). Their message is a preaching of Jesus as "Lord." Whether this title is to be taken as in distinction to "Messiah"

FIGURE 9.2. Preaching to Greeks Arrives in Antioch.

is debated. With this targeting of Greeks, the Pentecost Spirit breaks out again: "a great number of people believed" (11:21). We have not heard about a "great number" believing for a while. This note is the Pentecost abundance theme with which Acts opened. One interesting note is that this preaching to the Greeks at Antioch first arrives from Cyprus. Yet,

almost ironic is that Cyprus is the first destination of the first missionary journey. One would think someone already had the bases covered
at Cyprus before Saul and Barnabas arrived.

FIGURE 9.3. Valley into Antakya (Ancient Antioch).

FIGURE 9.4. Minaret of Antakya. The dominant faith of modern Turkey is Muslim.

FIGURE 9.5. Roman *Sōtēria* Mosaic. The Hatay Archeological Museum in Antakya holds the most extensive and best preserved collection of Roman mosaics from the ancient world. This mosaic depicts *Sōtēria*, or the goddess Salvation (HAM).

Jerusalem Investigation (11:22–24)

As usual, Jerusalem never gets to church on time. They get wind of the wind blowing in Antioch and send Barnabas to check things out. Note here that Peter and John were sent by Jerusalem to check out matters in Samaria, but Peter distinctly is *not* sent to check out matters in Antioch. The Antioch delegation will be the first time Peter has not led in a significant concern of the Jerusalem church. His quiet absence here is significant, another indication that his role is in transition. He seems still to be hamstrung by the Cornelius affair. In any case, the plot is the same: the Spirit working, Jerusalem investigating. So, the ethos of the Jerusalem church in Acts by now is clear. Jerusalem never initiates any outward mission thrust. Jerusalem also seems to have a persistent problem with social inclusiveness. Those failures will be precisely why Jerusalem never will be the church's future.

The historical problem for Luke with this Jerusalem profile is that this church is the mother church, the church of the Twelve, the direct connection to the ministry of Jesus. Thus, even if the church tries to be fashionably late to every party, the historical grounding in Jerusalem is important to Luke's story in Luke-Acts and cannot be ignored. So, even without Peter, the story presses on with the one figure who has had absolutely nothing but a positive ethos to his character development—Barnabas. As the undisputed champion of Pentecost fulfillment in Acts, but without the baggage of the Cornelius affair, Barnabas is a good compromise to represent Jerusalem, and he is propitious for Luke. Barnabas already has proven himself to Jerusalem as skilled in sensitive matters, able to persuade the hesitant apostles to meet with the suspicious Saul after the Damascus Road.

Barnabas arrives in Antioch, and Mr. Pentecost rejoices with that Pentecost joy. He endorses and encourages believers in Antioch. This positive reaction seals the deal of Jerusalem's acceptance of Antioch. As Luke says of Barnabas, "he was a good man, full of the Holy Spirit and faith" (11:24). That character is good news for the church all the way around, Jerusalem and Antioch. What this Spirit movement in Antioch infers, however, is that Antioch has become the new center of the Spirit's work, and Barnabas still continues his role of Pentecost fulfillment, even outside of Jerusalem. Considering actions that Barnabas will take later in this chapter and then in the next, major points of this character development in Acts are:

- Pentecost sharing in abundance (church, Acts 5)
- Pentecost facilitator with grace (Saul, Acts 9, 11)
- Pentecost expansion in Antioch (teaching ministry, Acts 11)
- Pentecost feeding in Judea (famine relief, Acts 11)
- Pentecost world mission (1MJ, Acts 13)

Finally, notice that this development of the Spirit moving in Antioch happens immediately after the Jerusalem church has challenged Peter about accepting gentiles into messianic Israel. God did not take that challenge lightly. He took his bat and ball to play on another field.

Barnabas Facilitates (11:25–26)

Gentiles respond so significantly, Antioch puts out a "Help Wanted" sign. Barnabas says, "I know just the guy." He knows this because he knows Saul's story and the essence of his call to the gentiles. In this way, Barnabas now integrates the Damascus Road into Antioch, and the two stories grow together as in a divine appointment. Luke will develop the character of Saul as central to

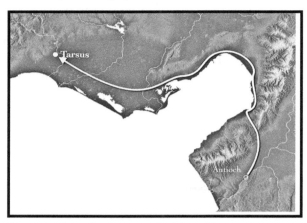

FIGURE 9.6. Barnabas Retrieves Saul from Tarsus.

the gentile mission of the church. Further, the teaching absorbed by Antioch's believers now will reflect Saul. That Barnabas and Saul are devoted to this ministry over an entire year represents a decided impact on Antioch for Saul.

FIGURE 9.7. Ancient Roman Road in Tarsus. Discovered during city construction in 1993, this 23 foot wide Roman road points straight into the heart of ancient Tarsus and has been dated to the early Roman period, potentially when Saul was in Tarsus.

FIGURE 9.8. Saint Paul's Well, Tarsus. While this well probably does not have anything to do with Paul, excavations did reveal that the well does date to the Roman period and is in the heart of the market area of ancient Tarsus.

Luke now uses the term "Christian" (*Christianos*, Χριστιανός) for the first time in Acts.[1] The term likely originated outside the group of Christians in Antioch's pagan population as a social marker applied to a perceived Jewish subgroup within Antioch's synagogues. That outsiders could perceive a distinction within the synagogue itself is a clue to the distinctive profile of Hellenists believers in Antioch. This term later was appropriated by believers themselves to become the definitive name historically for the Jesus movement. Thus, the Hellenist movement that Luke makes crucial to Acts gave Christians their very name.

What does Luke mean narratively by this notification about the name "Christian"? First, Luke intends the timing of the term's usage to reflect the presence and activity of Saul in Antioch. Saul is the powerhouse behind the significance of this name. Second, by the use of this term now, Luke intends to present Antioch as the model church. This paradigm church has two premier characteristics: ethnic diversity and mission impulse. Antioch reflects this ethnic diversity and mission impulse better than any other group in the early Christian movement. On this score, Antioch is everything Jerusalem is not.

Thus, they first were called Christians at Antioch. Antioch for Luke is where the new vision of the people of God matures. Antioch

---

[1]For an analysis of this rare term and the sociological setting of its use, see chapter 2, "Hellenists and Antioch: The Making of a Paradigm," 77–84.

will represent the future of the church in her ethnic diversity and missionary impulse. Saul will become the key figure of that profile in the story in Acts. Thus, Antioch is the consummation of the original Hellenist movement beginning with Stephen, and Saul will consummate this new vision in Acts.

ANTIOCH TRANSITION

The story turns dark. The plot is dominated by famine and persecution. Both developments are used by Luke to show the transition from Jerusalem to Antioch for the future of the Christian movement.

Once again, we are confronted with an extremely poor chapter division. The division between the end of Acts 11 and the following material in Acts 12 destroys the *inclusio* technique Luke has built into the literary structure here to serve as a heuristic device for the narrative. The actions of Herod Agrippa I are bounded by the famine story. In this movement, the famine story is begun, then the Herod story is told, then the famine story is finished. Luke infers Herod Agrippa I is to be understood in those terms of the famine story. But what is famine? Famine is Pentecost abundance denied. Agrippa I, then, is part of *that* story. The theological story behind the story is one of Pentecost promise, Pentecost threat, and Pentecost fulfillment. More than food threatens the fulfillment of Pentecost in messianic Israel.

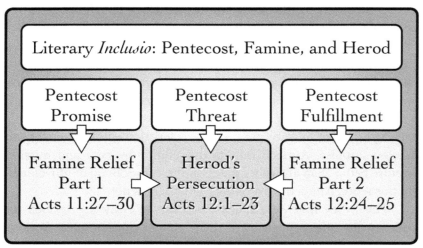

FIGURE 9.9. Literary *Inclusio*: Pentecost, Famine, and Herod.

Pentecost Promise (11:27–30)

The story of famine relief is the story of Pentecost promise. God prepares the church by raising up the prophet Agabus to predict a famine. This Agabus will have a positive and a negative interaction with Saul in Acts. Here with the famine prediction is positive. The negative interaction is the "binding" prophecy at the end of the third missionary journey as Paul insists on going to Jerusalem (21:10–11). A broad famine did occur during the reign of emperor Claudius (41–54) due to successive years of crop failure. The economy is threatened easily because tenant farmers live on the edge of financial ruin from year to year already.

FIGURE 9.10. Marble Bust: Claudius (IAM).

Antioch responds magnanimously. They send relief to Jerusalem. This relief is "Pentecost in reverse." Instead of Jerusalem being a blessing of abundance to others, others are a blessing to Jerusalem. A delegation of Barnabas and Saul are sent to the "elders" (11:30). Not the Twelve? No; not anymore. Jerusalem is in transition. From the apostles in Acts 6 in clear leadership in Jerusalem we now see "elders" in Acts 11. These elders represent an increasingly Jewish profile there in Jerusalem. Matters in Jerusalem seem to be moving in the oppo-

FIGURE 9.11. Claudius Inscription. The name of Claudius is in the third line: ΚΛΑΥΔΙΟΝ, KLAUDION (AMA).

site direction that the Spirit is moving. Internally, the matter of the gentiles probably continues to agitate the community, still debating proper entrance into messianic Israel. Externally, Judea is beginning to experience that slow burn that eventually will break out into the fires of armed conflict with Rome. National politics will begin to put increasing pressure on the church to identify with Jewish patriotism. If gentiles are the enemy of Israel, consorting with them is traitorous.

Even though we have increasing evidence of Peter's decreasing role in Jerusalem, his role in Acts is not in doubt. Peter connects to Jesus and validates gentiles. Peter is that historical link to the original Jesus movement. Peter is the validation of the gentile movement as the original intent of Jesus and its advocate to the conservative circumcision party in Jerusalem. Still, Peter does evince a gentile mission shortfall. We do not see Peter in any concerted gentile mission after the Cornelius affair. That shortfall is why Luke simply cannot follow Peter from this point on. Luke must follow another to tell the story of the gospel going to gentiles. The Hellenists' role in Acts is to tell the gentile story. They are the first group to catch a full vision of the messianic people of God. Their adopted city of Antioch after the push out of Jerusalem becomes the first church to embody that full vision of the people of God corporately.

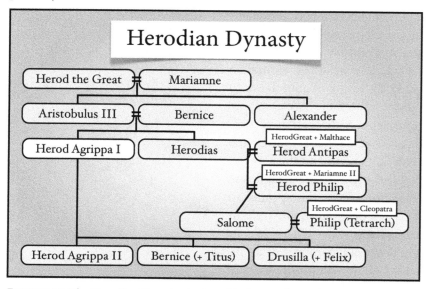

FIGURE 9.12. The Herodian Dynasty. Agrippa I is the grandson of Herod the Great.

Pentecost Threat (12:1–23)

The plot thickens. Agrippa I attacks the apostles. Agrippa I is the grandson of Herod the Great. Agrippa I had a steady rise to power under the emperors Caligula and Claudius. He had schooled in Rome with Caligula, and his friendship gave him promotion to the status of king in AD 37, jumping over tetrarch and ethnarch roles. He gained the territories of the Decapolis, a conglomerate of ten important cities, and Philip's Transjordan tetrarchy. Two years later in 39 Caligula added Antipas's Galilee and Perea after Antipas was banished to Gaul.

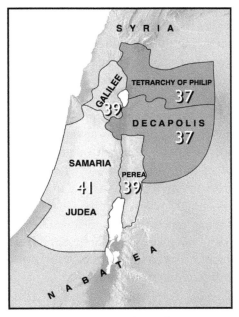

FIGURE 9.13. Territories of Herod Agrippa I.

Agrippa I finished his rise to power when the next emperor, Claudius, gave him Judea and Samaria in AD 41.[2]

Herod's Attack (12:1–5)

Herod Agrippa I's reign was a matter of a precarious balance. His friendship with the emperor Caligula would seem to be a plus, but Caligula's reign was as unstable as Caligula himself. Agrippa's relationship with the Jews was even more difficult. The Achilles heel of all the Herods was the loyalty of their Jewish subjects. Many Jews considered all Herodians as Idumean usurpers to the Jewish throne of David. The Herodians constantly needed to curry favor with their Jewish subjects as a result. Conservative Jewish elements in Judea would be putting constant pressure on the Herodian throne, in a similar context to the apostles themselves. Herod Agrippa could curry favor with these conservative forces by going after the now disfavored apostles, which is

---

[2]Judea had been a Roman procuratorship for thirty-five years ever since Augustus was forced to ban the ethnarch Archelaus to Gaul in AD 6.

exactly what he did. The apostles come into Agrippa's line of fire precisely because the church's favored status in Jerusalem is lost, which leaves the church vulnerable. The attack will be the last dramatic event involving the apostles in the story of Acts. The setting propitiously is Passover again, evocative of the persecution of Jesus himself. Agrippa kills the apostle James, the brother of John, putting him to the sword. Peter is imprisoned awaiting a similar fate after Passover (12:4).

Luke has his own perspective to Agrippa's attack on the apostles. He contextualizes this action not only as persecution, but as resisting what God was doing through Agabus the prophet in providing famine relief to Jerusalem. That perspective is why he uses the famine relief story to envelop the Agrippa story. Agrippa was not just persecuting the apostles, he was disrupting God's Pentecost provision of food. This food connection is the reason for Luke's insertion of Herod's food dispute with Phoenicia, which at first appears to be a totally extraneous piece of data unrelated to the "real" plot of persecution (12:20). Not at all. The real plot in Acts is Pentecost.

Peter's Deliverance (12:6–19)

Peter is under heavy guard. Perhaps word had gotten around the city that the apostles already had given the Sanhedrin a huge embarrassment in a slip from jail (5:19). Agrippa is securing the prisoner due to Passover delay. Peter has a miraculous release and goes to the house of Mary, the mother of John Mark, who will appear later in the story as part of the mission team on the first missionary journey (12:12). The story has a nice touch of comic relief when Peter, the escaped prisoner still exposed on the streets of Jerusalem, is left outside by Rhoda in her haste to tell the others in the house (12:14). One can just hear Peter pounding on the door outside wondering where in the world Rhoda has gone (12:16: "But Peter kept on knocking").[3]

Peter, after finally being let in, gives the lowdown of the release, and says to "tell James and the brothers about this" (12:17). This instruction is another indicator of shifting leadership in Jerusalem. That Peter goes to "another place" probably means a safe house for hiding

---

[3]One of my favorite lines in all of Acts. Luke has other touches of humor that show he is a good storyteller. On the art of storytelling, I agree with Pervo Acts can be read as literary entertainment, but keeping a keener eye on Luke's narrative purposes.

somewhere in the city. The tragic part of the story is that the prison guards are executed for dereliction of duty (12:19). In the ancient world, such a sentence would be imposed upon any escape of prisoners. That consequence is why the guard at Philippi was about to commit suicide after the earthquake compromised prison security (16:27), and why the Roman soldiers on the voyage to Rome intended to kill Paul and the other prisoners during the shipwreck on Malta (27:42).

Taking Jerusalem now too dangerous, Peter changed his address permanently to Caesarea ("stayed there," 12:19). Perhaps he was hosted by Cornelius until he was able to make his own arrangements. After this notation about Caesarea, the last we hear of Peter in Acts is when he is present for the Jerusalem Conference in Acts 15.

FIGURE 9.14. Theater at Caesarea. Seating capacity is about 3,500.

Herod's Judgment (12:20–23)

Arrayed in a resplendent silver robe in the theater at Caesarea, Herod so impressed the crowd they were awestruck. Shouted flatteries turned into divinity accolades that Herod's hubris did not reject. Herod took suddenly ill and died, a divine judgment ("angel of the Lord," 12:23).[4]

[4]The account in Josephus is similar, but has more details; *Ant.* 19.18.2 (343–61).

However, before Luke describes this stunning death, he includes a seemingly extraneous notation about Herod's anger with Phoenicia. The Phoenicians of Tyre and Sidon sue for peace to insure their food supply (12:20). Food distribution was a royal responsibility in ancient times. This information is not extraneous detail. This vignette shows Herod's jealous and aggressive protection of food supply lines during the famine. *This story sets the context for the famine relief visit from Antioch.* Herod could have interpreted the Antioch famine relief effort as a serious breach of royal protocol and a direct challenge to his sovereignty over Judea. Yet, by attacking church leadership and probably threatening the famine relief effort, Herod was jeopardizing God's work to insure Pentecost fullness in the church in Jerusalem. When Herod accepted divinity status in the theater, the divine forbearance over all his actions was at an end.

Pentecost Fulfillment (12:24–25)

These verses are the second part of the famine relief visit that envelops the Herod Agrippa story. Luke gives another progress report and then concludes the famine relief narrative.

Progress Report (12:24)

We now have the third progress report. Once again, this progress is related to the Pentecost theme. Food supply for Jerusalem had been jeopardized but now is guaranteed. The church prospers. In this way, the word of God increased and spread as a result of this Pentecost abundance God provided.

Even so, the times are changing. The church may prosper, but her political status has taken a nose dive. The church in Jerusalem now is in the crosshairs, and the apostles are in constant danger. Peter even has to change his address permanently. The church is under increasing political pressure from without and driven more and more by conservative pressure from within. Cue the lights. As Jerusalem fades out, Antioch fades in. That transition is finalized in the next verse.

Famine Relief Conclusion (12:25)

Barnabas and Saul complete their mission to Jerusalem. Thus, Herod's attempts both to cripple church leadership and to frustrate the famine relief fail. What the famine relief visit from Antioch means in the Acts storyline is that the new center of Pentecost fulfillment is Antioch, to which Barnabas and Saul now return.[5] The gradual transition from Jerusalem to Antioch toward which Luke has been driving ever since introducing the Hellenists into the narrative in Acts 6 now is complete.

So, Luke constructs the famine relief story in two parts, thereby integrating the Herod Agrippa story into the famine relief story. The Herod plot is only a subplot. The poor chapter division at Acts 12:1 makes the Herod story look like a main plot, but this impression only confounds exegesis. The real plot is Pentecost fulfillment, and Pentecost fulfillment has moved to Antioch. The reader now is ready for the second half of Acts. If Pentecost fulfillment is Antioch, then Saul of Tarsus is its unrivaled engine. That story is Acts 13–28.

SUMMARY

Antioch is Luke's premier church in Acts, the new epicenter of Pentecost abundance. Social inclusiveness and mission initiative are defining characteristics. Antioch is the consummation of the Hellenist movement that began in Acts 6. By the end of Acts 12, the center of gravity for messianic Israel has shifted from Jerusalem to Antioch.

Many of those scattered by persecution from Jerusalem preach "only to Jews." The Spirit is not blowing that way. The pivotal shift is when Greeks become the target audience in Antioch. Pentecost abundance breaks out. Now the wind is blowing. Jerusalem never gets to church on time. They investigate, but not with Peter. Peter's role is shifting. Barnabas, Mr. Pentecost, is sent to check out the scene and gives approval. One could wonder really what would have happened if

[5]Compare your English translations. The ambiguous placement of a Greek preposition meaning "to" or "unto" (*eis*, εἰς) *between* two verbs ("returned" and "fulfilled") confuses the reader with which verb to read the prepositional phrase "to Jerusalem." Some scribes apparently assuming the prepositional phrase *must* be read with the *prior* verb, "returned," changed the preposition "to" to "from" for a more logical "returned *from* Jerusalem," since the last we know of Barnabas and Saul from 11:30 is that they are in Jerusalem. The preposition "to," however, is the likely original reading. The best solution is syntactical. Reading the preposition "to" with the subsequent verb, "fulfilled," produces the translation "when they fulfilled this ministry to Jerusalem, they returned." This option is logical, but leaves the assumed city of return, Antioch, not explicitly stated. See Bock, *Acts*, 434–35, for an excellent summary of the issue and the reasonableness of this syntactical solution.

Barnabas had gone back to Jerusalem with a negative report. Fortunately, Barnabas even decided to stay and minister there.

Gentiles respond in numbers in Antioch, and Barnabas retrieves Saul from Tarsus to help. Barnabas knows that Saul's call perfectly fits this Antioch development, so he puts two and two together. Right at this point when Saul is introduced into the equation at Antioch, Luke drops the note that disciples of Jesus first are called "Christians" at Antioch. The definitive name of the movement is associated with the definitive voice of its message. The place where this happens also is definitive—Antioch. With its social inclusiveness and mission initiative, the church at Antioch becomes Luke's paradigm of what calling messianic Israel "the church" is all about. He follows his hero Saul in this terminology. The new vision of the people of God launched by Messiah in the outpoured Spirit at Pentecost reaches maturity in the church at Antioch. Antioch is the future of messianic Israel.

The story turns dark with famine and persecution, both threatening Pentecost fulfillment. The new center of Pentecost fulfillment begins to surface in the famine relief visit organized by Antioch. The delegation contacts the "elders," not the Twelve, another revelation of the leadership shift taking place in Jerusalem. Peter will phase out but not be forgotten. He was the original connection to Jesus and validation of the gentile movement of the church.

Agrippa I attacks the apostles. James, brother of John, is killed, and Peter imprisoned to await the same fate after Passover. God intervenes, just as with the famine threat, and Peter is released. He moves to Caesarea. The story of Herod's dispute with Phoenicia over food supply sets the context for the famine relief visit. Famine relief is told in three panels. Part one is Pentecost promise: famine relief from Antioch. Part two is Pentecost threat: Herod Agrippa I's royal hubris and attempt to control food supplies. Part three is Pentecost fulfilled: divine judgment on Herod and the return of Barnabas and Saul to Antioch, successful in their famine relief visit to Jerusalem. The third progress report indicates the Jerusalem church prospers, even though times are changing, with increasing pressure without and within.

The new center of Pentecost fulfillment is Antioch. The new center of Pentecost preaching is Saul, now poised to take the stage in the second half of Acts, the Holy Spirit empowers messianic Israel's world mission. Here is our outline as a reminder of this narrative flow.

ACTS: A NEW VISION OF THE PEOPLE OF GOD

I. THE SPIRIT EMPOWERS MESSIANIC ISRAEL (ACTS 1–12)
- A. *The Spirit Empowers Messianic Israel's Renewal (1–5)*
  1. Renewal Beginnings (1)
  2. Renewal Empowerment (2)
  3. Renewal Witness (3–5)
- B. *The Spirit Empowers Messianic Israel's Hellenists (6–12)*
  1. Hellenist Leaders Emerge (6–7)
  2. Hellenist Mission Advances (8–10)
  3. Hellenist Center Shifts (11–12)

II. THE SPIRIT EMPOWERS WORLD MISSION (13–28)
- A. *The Spirit Empowers World Mission Journeys (13:1—21:17)*
  1. 1MJ: From Cyprus to Conference (13–15)
  2. 2MJ: From Asia to Europe (16–18)
  3. 3MJ: Ephesus (18:23—21:17)
- B. *The Spirit Empowers World Mission Destiny (21:18—28:31)*
  1. Destiny Denied: Jerusalem Disaster (21:18—23:32)
  2. Destiny Delayed: Caesarean Custody (23:33—26:32)
  3. Destiny Achieved: Journey to Rome (27–28)

Part 3

Narrative Analysis 2

The Spirit Empowers World Mission
(Acts 13–28)

10

First Missionary Journey

From Cyprus to Conference (Acts 13–15)

MISSION INITIATIVE IS A DEFINING characteristic of a healthy church. Antioch will be the paradigm of this characteristic in Acts. The task is daunting: world mission. Such a task would buckle the knees of almost anyone—except Saul of Tarsus. This task is the second half of Luke's portrayal of the early church.

FIGURE 10.1. Acts in Two Parts. After the Spirit empowers messianic Israel, he then empowers messianic Israel on world mission, where Messiah always has been going.

1MJ STATISTICS

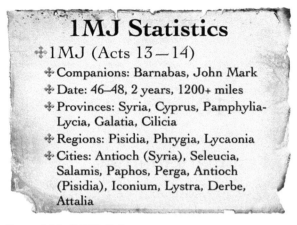

1MJ Statistics

✢ 1MJ (Acts 13—14)

  ✢ Companions: Barnabas, John Mark

  ✢ Date: 46–48, 2 years, 1200+ miles

  ✢ Provinces: Syria, Cyprus, Pamphylia-Lycia, Galatia, Cilicia

  ✢ Regions: Pisidia, Phrygia, Lycaonia

  ✢ Cities: Antioch (Syria), Seleucia, Salamis, Paphos, Perga, Antioch (Pisidia), Iconium, Lystra, Derbe, Attalia

FIGURE 10.2. 1MJ Statistics.

Giving statistics is a way of emphasizing exactly what Saul accomplished. When one thinks that traveling these byways takes weeks on modern roads at significant speed, the admiration for the work redounds. Saul, one thinks, is indefatigable. At the same time, his letters do indicate he grew weary and worn from the toil of his endeavors.

The first missionary journey (1MJ) targeted the island of Cyprus and South Galatia, covering twelve hundred plus miles over a two year period, from about AD 46–48. Since men from Cyprus already had brought the gospel to Antioch (11:20), one might wonder why the team went to Cyprus. Barnabas was from Cyprus (4:36), so may have had family and connections on the island to assist with hospitality and lodging.

1MJ SUMMARY

Spirit's Initiative (13:1–3)

Luke identifies prophets and teachers at Antioch (13:1). Yet, besides Barnabas and Saul, none are known in later tradition nor mentioned again in Acts.[1] Worshipping and fasting indicate spiritual receptivity. Luke makes clear the initiative of the Holy Spirit: "Set apart for me Barnabas and Saul for the work to which I have called them" (13:2). This notation will have huge significance for Luke's report about how

---

[1]These are Simeon (Niger), Lucius of Cyrene, and Manaen, a member of Herod's court. If by "Herod" Luke means Agrippa I, then Agrippa's untimely and unexpected death at Caesarea could have changed Manaen's status and locale. Lucius may have been part of the contingent of "men from Cyrene" who first began preaching to the Greeks at Antioch (11:20).

the (so-called) second missionary journey (2MJ) began, because the Spirit was not involved at all, and that would be Luke's point about Paul's suggestion to Barnabas at that time.

More fasting and praying indicates spiritual preparation for the assignment (13:3). The church lays hands on them and sends them off. Had Antioch already not had the characteristic receptivity to mission endeavor, the Spirit would not have had a foundation upon which to initiate a missionary enterprise. One can notice distinctly that this type of communication from the Spirit never happened in Jerusalem.

Cyprus (13:4–20)

Luke emphasizes the point of the Spirit's initiative a second time in only two verses: "So, being sent out by the Holy Spirit" (13:4). Luke is hammering the initiative of the Holy Spirit for this 1MJ now to set up the contrast for Paul's later suggestion to Barnabas that they consider returning to the 1MJ areas (15:36), which did not come from the Spirit and caused a fight and serious rupture in the mission team. Paul would pay a price for that untoward fight with Barnabas.

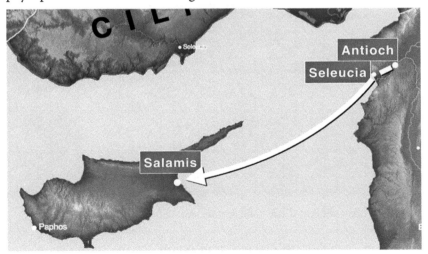

FIGURE 10.3. 1MJ—Cyprus: Salamis. The first stop was the port city of Salamis.

The Antioch team goes down to Seleucia, the seaport serving Antioch inland up the Orontes River. From there, they sail to Cyprus. The mission is on.

1MJ: Salamis (13:5)

FIGURE 10.4. Salamis Breakwaters. The breakwaters of the ancient port where Barnabas and Saul landed at Salamis. The modern city skyline is in the background.

FIGURE 10.5. Salamis Port Road. Main avenue leading from ancient port into the market area.

Luke uses each stop to make certain points for the narrative, sometimes about mission strategy, sometimes important events or developments. Salamis is to introduce the synagogue strategy of the Pauline missionary enterprise. That they go to the Jewish synagogue is in concord with the entire Hellenist movement, whose origins are in Stephen's preaching in the synagogue of the Freedmen in Jerusalem (6:9).

FIGURE 10.6. Salamis Fish Market. Ancient fish market with very rare holding pools used to keep the day's catch live and fresh when purchased.

FIGURE 10.7. Salamis Roman Forum. The Roman forum at Salamis would have been the center of city life, with governmental and market buildings surrounding the square.

Saul never quit being a Pharisee. His "turf" always was the synagogue. That context is why he had fought Stephen and the Hellenists so vigorously in the first place. Further, the gentile breakout at Antioch was in the synagogues. Finally, Acts 10 has made clear Cornelius is Saul's target, the pious, devoted, "God-fearing" gentile already attending Sabbath services every week, absorbing Pharisaic interpretations of the Israel of God, praying and giving alms to the poor.

FIGURE 10.8. Salamis Roman Baths. The Roman baths often were located near the forum or the stadium. The daily ritual was an important facet of social interaction.

FIGURE 10.9. Salamis Theater. Reconstructed theater holds 15,000. Theaters held about one tenth of the population, so the ancient population of Salamis was about 150,000.

At the same time, going to the synagogue also is going to national Israel to proclaim Messiah and his new vision of the people of God. World mission now extends tongues at Pentecost to Diaspora Jews around the world to the gospel. Messiah is bringing that message back home directly to the synagogues around the world represented in that original crowd of Pentecost pilgrims in Jerusalem.[2] Saul probably con-

---

[2]Note Paul's stated mission strategy: "to the Jew first, then to the Greeks" (Rom 1:16).

FIGURE 10.10. Salamis Roman Villa. Roman villas were country homes of the elite of a city, usually located to catch natural sea breezes, as was this one. Perhaps the team went to Cyprus because, as Barnabas's native country, he might have known contacts who could have served for hosting traveling guests, as did Lydia at Philippi (16:15) and Jason at Thessalonica (17:5).

FIGURE 10.11. Salamis Coins. Coins from Salamis representing the two great periods of ancient Salamis history. Left: Alexander the Great (336–323 BC) silver coin. Right: Roman emperor Tiberius (AD 14–37) silver coin (NAM).

siders that he is taking on the mantle of Isaiah's Servant destiny as "light for the gentiles" (Simeon's prophecy, Luke 2:32) due to the very nature of his Damascus Road call as a light on the road.

We do not know the type of travel arrangements Barnabas and Saul had for food and lodging. The modern reader must be careful not to import ideas of easy travel at the drop of a hat to run down fast Interstates in no time at all with lots of signage and mileage indicators, and Marriott hotels and quick MacDonald's hamburgers waiting upon arrival. An ancient inn was no safe place at all, infested with bugs and varmints, and scouted out by robbers. Jesus's parable of the Good Samaritan with a poor traveler who is beaten, robbed, and left to die alongside the road is a typical example of the dangers that travelers faced (Luke 10:30–35). So, one often stayed in private homes, and for this purpose, letters of recommendation were composed to hosts not personally known to the traveler but known to one of the traveler's business associates, or family, or friends. We know that Paul took advantage of the offer of wealthy patrons as often as he could, as he did with Lydia at Philippi (16:15), Jason at Thessalonica (17:5), and Gaius at Corinth (Rom 16:23). Such relationships often were the basis of house churches.

FIGURE 10.12. Salamis Benefactor Inscription. This 1st cent. AD inscription may have been standing when Barnabas and Saul visited the city. Dedicated by Kratis son of Asklepiades in honor of Servius Sulpicius Pancles Veranianus, a citizen of Salamis who also became a Roman citizen, as the Sulpicius family name indicates. Other Salamis inscriptions witness his exceptional benefactions to the city: the gymnasium, theatre, and stadium, organization of festivals and games at his own expense, and many other events. His will included funds for dedicatory monuments such as this one in his memory. The inscription reads: "To Servius Sulpicius Pancles Veranianus; Krates, son of Asklepiades, [erected this monument] according to the will." The ancient world fully was dependent on the benefactions of patrons large and small for civic and daily life (NAM).

From its earliest days, Salamis was a major port city. The large population, perhaps as many as 150,000 in the first century, probably would mean multiple synagogues were needed to service the Jewish community. Even though Luke does not indicate the duration of the stay at Salamis, one would imagine at least several Sabbaths would be required for Barnabas and Saul to make the rounds through these syn-

agogues. Luke does not indicate the general
reception, but if other synagogue experiences indicated in Acts are to be assumed
typical, the results among Jews in Salamis
probably were meager.

FIGURE 10.13. Salamis Synagogue Inscription. This
column stood in one of the synagogues of Salamis.
The bottom inscription refers to a major restoration
project: "Joses the elder with his son Synesios restored
the whole building of this synagogue" (NAM).

Behind the last line of the Salamis visit lurks a future crisis for the
mission team: "And they had John also to assist them" (13:5). This John
is the John Mark whose mother Mary had the house to which Peter fled
after escaping prison (12:12). John Mark leaves the Antioch team after
Cyprus (13:13). This departure becomes a point of contention between
Barnabas and Paul (15:37–39).

The trip to Paphos transverses the island. If on foot, as they likely
were at this point in the journey, this movement would have taken
several weeks to complete. Barnabas and Saul would have needed to
plan stops along the way. One of these stops likely would have been the
city of Kourion along the coast about halfway. Kourion long had been

a favorite coastal city of the Romans for its constant sea breezes on the steep cliffs. North of Kourion on the opposite side of the island is the modern city of Girne (ancient Kyrenia). One of the most important ancient shipwrecks ever recovered is in a museum there.

FIGURE 10.14. Kyrenia Shipwreck. The Ancient Shipwreck Museum in Kyrenia Castle, Cyprus preserves a Greek merchant ship of the time of Alexander the Great and later. After her long voyage from the island of Samos loaded with cargo bound for Cyprus, she sank in a storm less than a mile from final harbor. Sea travel was by no means safe in ancient times. Pictured is Owen Gander, an original expedition diver. For the expedition, see Katzev, "Last Harbor," *National Geographic* 146 (1974): 618–25 (ASMK).

FIGURE 10.15. Cliffs of Kourion. The ancient city of Kourion in the middle of the south side of Cyprus holds important Roman remains and mosaics. Barnabas and Saul likely lodged in such cites on their way to Paphos.

FIGURE 10.16. Kourion Bathhouse. The Roman bathhouse at Kourion has one of the best displays of the engineering required for designing the subterranean system of heating and distribution channels for bathhouses.

FIGURE 10.17. Kourion Creation and Gladiator Mosaics. The goddess of creation, Ktisis, graced the floor of this aristocratic Roman home in Kourion. The mosaic was part of the dining area. Preaching the monotheistic faith of Judaism was a great challenge for both Jews and Christians. The gladiator was a common motif in mosaics of Roman villas. Gladiators were famous, and, if successful and survived, rich. They were followed and revered by a fan base much like modern Hollywood stars or professional athletes. Humility was considered cowardice, antithetical to Christian preaching of the cross.

So, if Luke does not say anything about Barnabas and Saul staying at Kourion, why even mention this major city at the time Barnabas and Saul were visiting Cyprus? What is the point? *That the reader recognize Luke did not write Acts intending an exhaustive account of Paul.* He does not write exhaustively of the particular itineraries he covers, and, even more, he does not write exhaustively of the whole ministry of the apostle Paul. Recognizing Luke writes particularly only what accomplishes his literary purposes is an important realization for several reasons.

First, Luke's account is compressed and selective. Of the work on Cyprus, he says only, "They traveled through the whole island" (13:6).[3] Those five words in Greek compress weeks of time, several overnight lodgings along the way, and numerous experiences day to day. They hardly tell us anything of all that, except that the journey was on land rather than by boat from the port at Salamis to the port at Paphos. Luke also is selective. Of Cyprus, he mentions only Salamis and Paphos in particular. Therefore, what itinerary Luke does mention either seams units together or has some other narrative purpose.

FIGURE 10.18. Provinces of the Roman Empire. The Roman province of Illyricum is the eastern shore of the Adriatic Sea across from Italy and north of Macedonia.

Second, Luke does not intend to be exhaustive about the whole life of the apostle Paul. Luke stays with his main goal of presenting the Spirit empowering Messiah's world mission against all obstacles. So,

[3]*Dielthontes de olēn tēn nēson,* Διελθόντες δὲ ὅλην τὴν νῆσον.

when Paul mentions an area of gospel mission that we do not have a clue about from Acts, we should not be surprised. For example, in Rom 15:19, Paul mentions having worked in the province of Illyricum. This province is directly east of Italy across the Adriatic Sea. Of this work we know nothing from Acts. As another example, Paul indicates he was in mortal danger and actually thought he was going to die at some point while he was in Asia.[4] Luke simply says nothing about this grave danger during his description of Paul's Ephesian ministry.[5]

If Luke is compressed at times, selective at others, and does not pretend to give the whole life of Paul, then he is working the material at a narrative level, not strictly biographical. Narrative study, then, is quite useful for reading Luke-Acts, even though Luke does have an extensive amount of historical material. For example, Luke's narrative of the journey to Jerusalem at the end of the third missionary journey distinctly suppresses ever mentioning *why* Paul is going to Jerusalem, quite the curiosity, since Paul is so absolutely insistent on going. Only by reading Paul's letters that dovetail with this period (1–2 Cor, Rom) do we get an idea, because Paul makes absolutely clear in his letters exactly why he is going to Jerusalem. The question would be: Why does Luke completely suppress this information? The answer is Luke's perspective on Paul.[6]

As another example, a study of Luke's use of narrative time can be useful for exegesis. When he summarizes two weeks in only five words, as here at Cyprus, and then consumes an entire chapter to expand blow by blow another two week period, as with the voyage and shipwreck of Acts 27, then we have a clue to Lukan literary significance. The voyage and shipwreck has *narrative* significance, which we can perceive as we see Luke slowing narrative time to a crawl at that point. Thus, reading the voyage and shipwreck story as simply entertainment purely for the delight of the reader is a superficial reading.[7]

Mentioning Kourion, then, as a major city on the south side of the island of Cyprus is quite helpful for making this point: that Luke writes

[4] 2 Cor 1:8: "for we were so utterly, unbearably crushed that we despaired of life itself." Unfortunately for inquiring minds, Paul did not specify exactly what happened.

[5] The silversmiths' riot does not qualify. Paul himself was not in personal danger. The crowd did not even know where he was or why they had assembled (19:28–34).

[6] This character development is outlined in depth in chapter 3, "The Character Saul-Paul: Paul, Jerusalem, and God's Will."

[7] We shall suggest what that narrative significance might be at that point.

FIGURE 10.19. Paphos Archeological Site. The ancient port lay on the point of the west promontory of the island. The modern city is to the north in the far background.

FIGURE 10.20. House of Aion Mosaic. Paphos was the capitol of the province and residence of the proconsul. Wealthy Romans had stunning mosaic floors in their homes.

FIGURE 10.21. Paphos Asklepion. The asklepion healing center was named after the god of healing, Asklepios. Ancient magicians often portrayed themselves as healers. Elymas the magician probably associated himself with this asklepion at Paphos.

with narrative purpose, not to offer a biography of Paul. We might wish he would have addressed certain matters more fully to help us better understand the context of the apostle, but he did not. So, as we move through these so-called "missionary journeys" of the apostle Paul, we must wrestle with the literary reality that even though Paul is Luke's hero, Messiah is Luke's point. Thus, calling them "missionary journeys of Paul" might be misleading for understanding Acts in and of itself by introducing non-Lukan ideas about Paul's role in these missions that impede understanding either Paul or Acts, but especially Paul in Acts.

The "missionary journeys of Paul" better might be understood not as about Paul as about the Spirit empowering messianic Israel to world mission in order to bring Pentecost reality to "the uttermost parts of the earth." We simply never should forget how Luke starts this so-called "first missionary journey of Paul." Luke actually does not describe the journey that way. Notably, the main character of these journeys is the Holy Spirit, not Paul. Luke is clear: "the Holy Spirit said, 'Set apart for me Barnabas and Saul for the work to which I have called them'" (13:2). The character of Saul-Paul was simply Luke's best plot device for that story of the Holy Spirit moving the church into world mission. Thus, the better hermeneutical frame for reading this mission part of the Acts narrative is not "journeys of Paul," which leaves many questions unanswered, as much as "world mission journeys of the Spirit on behalf of the gospel of Messiah," which opens up the ending of Acts to be read the way Luke intended. We do not hear the eventual outcome of Paul's appearance before Caesar precisely because Paul is not Luke's point at that part of the narrative in the first place. Rome is Luke's point.

1MJ: Paphos (13:6–12)

The story of Paphos is Elymas the magician. Luke wanted to make a major point about magic in the narrative of Acts.

We already encountered Simon the magician in Acts 8. Now we meet Elymas. Who are these guys? Magicians are about harnessing and controlling powers that control life, both personal (gods and goddesses) and impersonal (daemons and the forces of fate and darkness).[8] In

---

[8]Modern fantasy and science fiction films live on "borrowed" ideas. "May the force be with you," "it's your destiny," "come over to the dark side" all could have been spoken as easily by Simon or Elymas as by any character in the Star Wars series. Yoda wielding his light saber is just another magician harnessing "magical" powers.

this way, many magicians claimed to be healers, because sickness often was interpreted as a curse some god had instituted for some perceived affront. In addition, magicians and soothsayers often were associated together. To control the powers is to have access to future knowledge, which can impact present decisions. Almost every Roman government

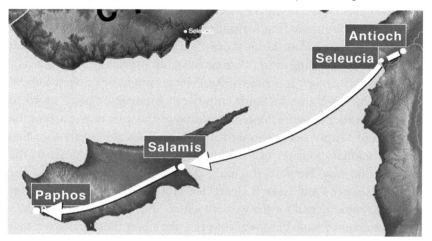

FIGURE 10.22. 1MJ—Cyprus: Paphos. Luke has compressed the record of the itinerary.

FIGURE 10.23. Paulus Inscription. The Paulus family was connected politically in Rome, known well to the emperor, so had many appointments in the provinces. This inscription from Antioch of Pisidia identifies the Paulus family that is related to the Sergius Paulus proconsul of Cyprus met by Barnabas and Saul on the 1MJ (YMY).

official had a magician or soothsayer in his cabinet of ministers advising him as a result. (Who would not want someone with ability to feign the future as their political advisor?) Thus, Elymas (Bar-Jesus) closely is associated with the provincial proconsul, Sergius Paulus.

Luke further identifies Elymas as a "Jewish false prophet" (13:6). That line is the key for understanding the severity of a curse as Saul's response. Elymas was masquerading under the name of a prophet of

FIGURE 10.24. Paphos: Theseus Mosaic. Gorgeous Theseus mosaic, giving the residence its name. This private and governmental office complex was the residence of the proconsul in Paphos. Sergius Paulus would have entertained Saul in this complex.

FIGURE 10.25. Paphos: Theseus House. This apse was the governor's receiving area for visitors. Saul would have waited here for his audience with Sergius Paulus.

Israel. By pretending to represent the God of Israel to the Roman pro-consul, Elymas was blaspheming God and perverting the proconsul's ability to understand the truth of God. In preaching the gospel of the Messiah of Israel, Saul exposed the lies of this false prophet of Israel.

In Saul's preaching of the truth of the gospel that was attracting Sergius Paulus, Elymas immediately saw a threat to his position and power with the governor. Elymas opposed Saul and tried to turn away the proconsul. Saul crushed Elymas with the power of a gospel curse, specifically chosen because curse was the only language a magician could understand as power over power. The titles Saul used were titles appropriate to a false prophet of Israel: "You son of the devil, enemy of all righteousness, full of all deceit and villainy, will you not stop making crooked the straight paths of the Lord?" (13:10). So much for a career advising the governor. The curse's nature is paradigmatic for Luke. Elymas is blinded. Blindness is a metaphor for the paganism and false belief and religious practices Elymas represents. His blindness is sug-gestive of Saul's task according to the Damascus Road revelation: "light for the gentiles." The curse of darkness for Elymas's world was the light of revelation for Sergius Paulus's world.

When the proconsul saw what happened, Luke states, "he was be-lieving" (13:12).[9] Some have argued whether this means the proconsul became a believer or simply was impressed at Saul's magic. Luke's entire narrative point is Saul's witness to the proconsul. Elymas just is an obstructionist to the story. What the proconsul is amazed about is the "teaching of the Lord." This "teaching" in the context of Acts would be the gospel facts about Jesus as in the apostolic outline evidenced in the messages of Peter at Pentecost and at Caesarea that Luke already has established. The more likely interpretation of "was believing" is that the proconsul became a Christian. Otherwise, this story loses its point in the context of mission. The point of the conversion of Sergius Paulus is that Christianity is no threat to Rome, on the order of the centurion confessing, "surely this man was innocent" (Luke 23:47). Another im-portant point about the conversion of Sergius Paulus is that the gospel penetrates all levels of society, from lowest to highest. The proconsul

---

[9]The tense is imperfect (*episteusen*, ἐπίστευσεν), which syntactically is unusual. One might have expected the aorist. This imperfect tense for the state of believing also was used of Simon the magician in 8:13 (see p. 237). Meaning is contextual in each case.

was the closest friend of the emperor, second in status to the most elite of the elite of Roman society.

So, formerly we had Peter and Simon in Acts 8; now we have the equivalent story in Saul and Elymas in Acts 13.[10] Luke is using Paphos to show the gospel's power over other powers in the ancient world (Elymas) and its social reach and lack of threat to Rome (Sergius Paulus).

One last matter about Paphos is a name change: Saul becomes Paul (13:9). The name Saul for this character is not heard again, except in the two further accounts of the Damascus Road.[11] From here on out, the name exclusively used is Paul. The name change has nothing to do with the similar name of the proconsul, or that Saul with the conversion of Sergius Paulus now is operating in the gentile world so should find reference with his gentile name. Rather, we should note that the name change happens in the context of the dual-name for the magician. Luke first introduced the magician as "Bar-Jesus." He then says that name being translated means "Elymas" (13:8). At the beginning of the very next verse, *Luke makes the exact same move with the name of Saul* that he has used exclusively in Acts to this point: "Then Saul, who also was called Paul" (13:9a). In the context of giving the dual name of the magician as a way of translating the meaning of the name, Luke is saying Saul "being translated" means Paul. What is this?

First, this dual-name notation is an unintentional allusion to the letters of Paul. While his Hebrew name is "Saul,"[12] this Saul exclusively called himself "Paul" in his letters. In fact, if all we had were his letters, we never would have suspected Paul had an original Hebrew name.[13] Yet, a subtle tip-off to the letters of Paul is not the purpose of this dual-name notation of Saul-Paul at Acts 13:9.

Second, the dual-name notation is an intentional narrative device for character development. Luke is reminding readers that the "Paul" of later letter fame is the "Saul" of the early church in Jerusalem, the zealous Pharisee ravaging the church in persecution in his zealousness

---

[10] Paul also will square off with magicians at Ephesus (19:19).

[11] Acts 22:7, 13; 26:14.

[12] The Grecized form is *Saulos*, Σαῦλος, but the original Hebrew is *Sauol*, Σαούλ.

[13] Interestingly, Peter has three names: "Simon," "Cephas," and "Peter" (John 1:42). Paul is greatly habited to using the Hebrew name "Cephas" (1 Cor 1:12; 3:22; 9:5; 15:5; Gal 1:18; 2:9, 11, 14) rather than "Peter" (Gal 2:7, 8).

for God. This zealousness, *in terms of understanding the will of God*, is just as much a problem *after* the Damascus Road as before. The dual-name device indicates that this character never changes his colors in Acts. Paul always should be understood as Saul: on the one hand, the indefatigable voice of the gospel, yet, on the other, sometimes the worst thing that could happen to a group of innocent people.

One more narrative shift happens after Paphos. Up to this point, the team leadership has belonged to Barnabas. His leadership also is true throughout the story of Saul. Barnabas is the one introducing Saul to suspicious Jerusalem (9:27); Barnabas is the one getting Saul from Tarsus to work with Greeks in Antioch (11:25–26); Barnabas is the leader of the Antiochene mission team: "Set apart for me Barnabas and Saul" (13:2).[14] However, not long after introducing Saul as Paul, a subtle shift happens in referring to the team from Antioch. Luke now says "Paul and his companions" (13:13). Abruptly, with no explanation from Luke, leadership of the mission team shifts away from Barnabas over to Paul. More telling,

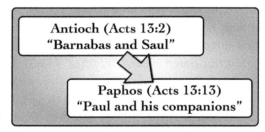

FIGURE 10.26. Mission Team Leadership Shift.

from this point on, Barnabas never is referenced in a way that infers he is the leader of the group again. While the shift in reference might seem almost imperceptible, that would be so only if you were not Barnabas.

Why did the mission leadership take this right turn toward Paul and Barnabas begin to fade? We do not know. Barnabas was crucial as "Son of Encouragement," the Pentecost facilitator, both for Jerusalem and for Saul. No matter how crucial Barnabas was, though, like Peter, after the Jerusalem Conference in Acts 15, his name suddenly drops off a cliff, never to be heard again in Acts. One could wonder if this shift to Paul is possible background for why John Mark left the mission team at Perga immediately after the mission on Cyprus, especially if Saul had said or done something presumptuous, inappropriate, or insulting during that time in regard to Barnabas and the team's leadership.[15]

---

[14]Customarily in the ancient world, the first name listed is the leader of the pack.

[15]Mark as cousin of Barnabas would complicate these social dynamics (Col 4:10).

Southern Galatia (13:13—14:26)

Perga is in Pamphylia on the coast, and Derbe is in Cilicia, but most of this part of the journey is spent in southern Galatia. This work sets up the possibility of Galatians being the earliest known letter of Paul.

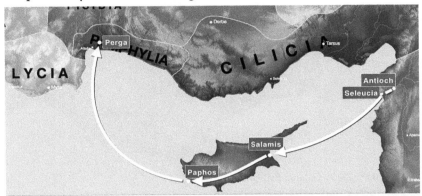

FIGURE 10.27. 1MJ—Pamphylia: Perge.

1MJ: Perga (13:13)

The team left Cyprus by boat to the port of Perga in Pamphylia. Perga was a bustling city because of its port serving the interior of the mainland. Perga's port rival was nearby Attalia to the west.

John Mark left the team at Perga to return to Jerusalem. We are not told why. Later we learn Saul interpreted this departure as a defection and was unforgiving. Barnabas tried to reach reconciliation unsuccessfully. The disagreement between Barnabas and Paul over John Mark split the mission team. Perga also is the point when the reference to team leadership changes to "Paul and his companions," not Barnabus.

FIGURE 10.28. Perge Site. Stadium, theater, nymphaeum (fountain), which fed a center channel of the main avenue with cascading pools of live fish—most unusual.

1MJ: Antioch of Pisidia (13:14–52)

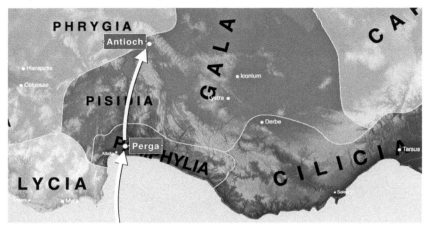

FIGURE 10.29. 1MJ—Galatia: Antioch of Pisidia.

FIGURE 10.30. Snow-capped Mountains of Antioch of Pisidia.

The journey from the lowlands of coastal Perga to the highlands of Antioch's snow-covered mountains would require negotiating steep mountain passes, switchback trails, and circuitous routes around the shorelines of large, inland lakes—in other words, slow and arduous. The destination would be a thriving Roman city overviewing beautiful highland vistas, refreshed by the chilled waters of snowmelt streams carried along miles of Roman aqueducts. Antioch boasted an imperial temple, a rare honor that had to be granted by the emperor himself, dedicated to Augustus, carved into bedrock at the city's highest point.

FIGURE 10.31. Antioch of Pisidia Aqueduct. This aqueduct carried snowmelt water from the nearby mountains over several miles into the city's nymphaeums.

FIGURE 10.32. Antioch of Pisidia: Temple of Augustus. At the highest point of the city sat this magnificent temple to Augustus carved into the bedrock. Paul would have seen this imperial temple and its ongoing rituals while he was in the city.

Luke develops Antioch for two reasons. First, Luke uses Paul's synagogue sermon at Antioch as one of three "example" sermons, one on each missionary journey, illustrating Paul's three typical audiences: Jewish, gentile, and Christian.[16] Second, Luke develops Antioch's dual response to Paul's message to set the theme of the missionary pattern Paul will face everywhere: synagogue resistance but gentile response.

[16]Polhill, *Acts*, 44, noting sermon content changes significantly per audience.

Paul's Paradigm Sermons			
MJ	*Place*	*Context*	*Audience*
1MJ	Antioch	Synagogue	Jewish
2MJ	Athens	Market	Gentile
3MJ	Miletus	Church	Christian

FIGURE 10.33. Paul's Paradigm Sermons: Jewish. Paul's three sermons over three missionary journeys illustrate his three typical audiences: Jewish, gentile, Christian.

So, Antioch of Pisidia is narrated for the synagogue sermon. The theme is from the history of a chosen nation to the history of a chosen Son, from one solitary nation to one solitary life. Paul moves through the Old Testament kerygma, the Israelite confession. He steps through the traditional stages rehearsed among Jews, first with Abraham as the period of the chosen patriarchs (13:17a), then Exodus as the redeemed descendants (13:17b–18), then Canaan as the promised land (13:19–20), and finally David as the choice of kingship (13:21–22). At this point, Paul could have gone on, but David becomes Paul's springboard for proclaiming Christ. The royal house of David has unfulfilled promises. These promises point to Jesus as Messiah, who fulfills the Davidic role.

From David, Paul next moves through the New Testament kerygma, the messianic confession of Jesus. Here, his outline sounds similar to the apostolic outline revealed in Peter's messages that became fairly fixed in the oral tradition of the early church. Paul's form here is:

- Announcing the age of fulfillment (13:23)

   Resurrection inaugurates the last days

   Outpouring of God's Spirit

- Telling the story of Jesus (13:24–32)

- Citing Old Testament texts (13:33–37)

   Showing Jesus as fulfillment

Usually in LXX form

- Call to repentance (13:38–41)

Paul's synagogue sermon conclusion is an appeal to the prophet Habakkuk. The appeal is strategic and appropriately pertinent. Paul sees the present historical situation for Jews in the synagogue in Antioch as parallel to the historical situation faced by the Jews under Habakkuk. Habakkuk's words in Hab 1:5 were spoken on the eve of Babylonian rise to world power (Acts 13:41):

> Look, you scoffers!
> Be amazed and perish!
> For I am doing a work in your days
>   a work that you never would believe even if someone told
>   you.

Great as were the disasters that overtook Jerusalem through this Babylonian world power in the days of Habakkuk's warnings, greater still the disasters that await the nation if the prophetic word about Jesus in the gospel is ignored now at this crucial messianic moment in Israel's history.

The Antioch of Syria mission team is invited to speak to the Antioch of Pisidia synagogue again the next Sabbath, which means, in a way, they are being put off. Still, many Jews and devout converts (gentile proselytes) do respond. The problem is success, because, the next Sabbath, "almost the whole city gathered to hear the word of the Lord" (13:44), which means the number of gentiles swelled. Jealously kicks in over this huge attraction, and synagogue Jews blaspheme (Jesus) and contradict what Paul preached (resurrection). Since they reject the gospel, they have "judged themselves unworthy of eternal life" (13:46). The team announces: "we are now turning to the gentiles" (13:46). This turn is not an announcement of not ever preaching in any synagogues again or to any more Jews for the rest of Acts. This turn is for this local context at Antioch of Pisidia. This synagogue has rejected Jesus. Therefore, further efforts in this city will focus on the gentiles.

The vehement rejection in the synagogue at Antioch arouses a sense among Paul and Barnabas of the Servant's role in Isaiah that authorizes their turning to gentiles. The passage quoted is Isa 49:6, the mission of the Servant individual who fulfills Servant Israel's role. Isaiah's Servant individual Christians interpreted as Jesus. The Servant's role was to be a light for the gentiles. Disciples of Jesus then felt the burden of that role on themselves. As quoted in Acts 13:47,

> I have set you to be a light for the gentiles
> so that you may bring salvation to the ends of the earth.

Israel's Servant profile as given by Isaiah is her intended destiny. Israel is to be a witness to the nations. That Servant profile is interpreted as fulfilled in Jesus, becomes thematic in apostolic preaching, and drives the missionary impulse in the early church. Luke has picked up this Servant theme, signified by "light for the gentiles," and punctuated his narrative with this idea throughout Luke-Acts:

- Simeon's prophecy about the child Jesus (Luke 2:32; Isa 42:6)

- Philip's Ethiopian eunuch encounter (Acts 8:32; Isa 53:7–8)

- Saul's Damascus Road experience (Acts 9:3)

- Jesus's commission to Saul (Acts 9:15)

- Paul's synagogue sermon (Acts 13:47; Isa 49:6; cf. Acts 26:23)

A "light for gentiles" theme from Isaiah's Servant is programmatic for Luke for the gentile mission of the journeys of Paul: first, to synagogue, then to gentiles. In such a strategy, the Cornelius conversion is seen now as Luke's paradigm in Paul's ministry. As a mission strategy,

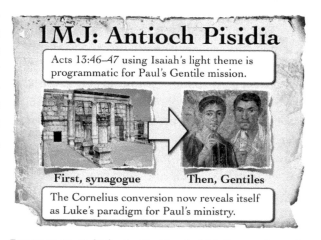

FIGURE 10.34. Light for the Gentiles. Isaiah's Servant theme is programmatic for Luke for Paul's gentile mission.

what Luke presents in Acts comports with what Paul himself indicated in Romans (Rom 1:16).

Gentiles hearing this "light for gentiles" message of Paul rejoice, respond, and spread the word throughout the region (13:48–49). Jews, however, incite high-standing women and leading men to stir up persecution for Paul and Barnabas and their team. The social categories indicated by Luke represent the power brokers in society, the patrons and patronesses holding the purse strings in Antioch of Pisidia of all the beneficent community projects and municipal works, such as the aqueducts and the temple of Augustus. The patron-client relationship that is so integral to ancient society would generate an immediate response from obligated clients, the regular population of the city, expressing the opinions their patrons required. Money always talks no matter how popular the preacher. The Jews drove them out of the region (13:50).

So the team shakes the dust off their feet (13:51), a typical Jewish act of scorn for gentile territory. Returning from travel overseas to the promised land, Jews would perform this ritual.[17] The implications of Paul and Barnabas taking such action is theologically striking. They thereby reveal they consider the rejection of Jesus a category shifting action: Jews of the synagogue now identify themselves as in no better condition than pagan gentiles. Even though driven out of Antioch of Pisidia, they had had moderate success among Jews and eminent success among gentiles. They had much for which to be thankful. So, they "were filled with joy and with the Holy Spirit" (13:52). This word is Luke's characteristic phrasing for Pentecost abundance. The initial Pentecost experience of Acts 2 continues to reverberate throughout the Acts narrative as the Spirit empowers world mission journeys.

So, Antioch serves for Luke to set out an example sermon of Paul to a synagogue audience. Antioch also serves for Luke to give the characteristic synagogue reaction to Paul: rejection by Jews, acceptance by gentiles. This synagogue response pattern will dog Paul for the rest of his mission work.

Another wrinkle also is added related to this typical synagogue response. The gentiles not only respond, they respond in significant numbers. In fact, this response by gentiles is so noticeable, Paul even will use that phenomenon as a distinctive way to summarize the entire 1MJ mission endeavor to the sponsoring church back in Antioch of Syria: "they began to report all things that God had done with them and how he had opened a door of faith to the gentiles" (14:27).

---

[17]Based on scriptural traditions, as when Moses is told to take off his sandals at the burning bush (Exod 3:4–5). Jewish tradition considered the promised land to be holy inherently due to God's presence throughout and the cultic function of the temple.

Now, this significant gentile response might sound good, but in reality presents a problem. As long as gentile presence in the church was a minority, then the Jerusalem church could be kept at bay. The unexpectedly large gentile response on the 1MJ, however, apparently even by Antioch's standards, is predictably problematic. The gentile results of the 1MJ are actually what precipitate a crisis in the church and the need for the subsequent Jerusalem Conference. That connection is why Acts 15 really is still part of the story of the 1MJ.

1MJ: Iconium (14:1–6)

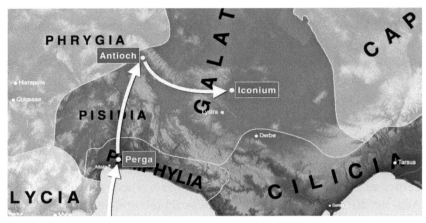

FIGURE 10.35. 1MJ—Galatia: Iconium. Persecuted out of Antioch, the team goes along the main Roman highway to the next major city of Iconium, modern Konya.

FIGURE 10.36. Modern Konya (Ancient Iconium). The modern industrial city of Konya is built right on top of ancient Iconium, so no ancient remains survive. Thus, besides literary, inscriptions are our only evidence of ancient Iconium's existence.

FIGURE 10.37. Iconium Inscription. Outside of literary evidence, inscriptions are our only documentation of the existence of ancient Iconium. This inscription is one of the rare pieces of evidence bearing the actual name of the city of Iconium, in the form IKONIEŌN, **IKONIEΩN** (KAM).

The pattern of synagogue resistance and gentile response continues to develop here at Iconium. This pattern is what Luke means by saying, "The same thing occurred in Iconium" (14:1).

As is now apparent, the team's strategy is to preach in the synagogue first, which they do here, and they have success among Jews and Greeks, but then, predictably, "unbelieving Jews stirred up the gentiles and poisoned their minds against the brothers" (14:2). The stay this time seems to be longer than typical (14:3).[18] Luke even indicates the signs of apostolic confirmation: "granting signs and wonders to be done through them" (14:3). The city is divided between the Jews and the "apostles" (14:4). This reference to apostles here and the one in 14:14 are the only two times in all of Acts that anyone other than the Twelve are called apostles. Since Luke is clear that the definition of an apostle is one who directly witnessed the life of Jesus from baptism to ascension

---

[18]Luke indicates "they remained for a long time." Ambiguous, but relatively longer, apparently, than at other stops (Salamis, Paphos, Perga, Antioch).

(1:21–22), then Paul clearly does not qualify. Further, since others in the church disputed Paul's claim to be an apostle, then the usage here probably betrays Luke's incorporation of some type of tradition from the Pauline perspective for this part of the 1MJ report.

FIGURE 10.38. Roman Sarcophagus. This sarcophagus of the 3rd or 4th cent. has garland sides and lion-head top ribs. The form is typical of the Pamphylia area. The Konya Archeoloji Müzesi has some of the finest Roman sarcophagi preserved (KAM).

Persecution eventually bubbles up again, but this time escalated, including even "their rulers" (14:5), which probably means local civic officials of the municipality. Such rulers were the city elite, wealthy patrons who left beautiful sarcophagi as one testimony to their status and reputation. Iconium opponents attempted a stoning, which is why they had to get the local rulers involved. They were evaded as the team fled to Lystra and on to Derbe and "surrounding countryside" (14:6), which means laying low. Paul and Barnabas are "on the lam."

1MJ: Lystra (14:6–20)

Lystra was a small military outpost established by Augustus that never amounted to much, a "country town" off the beaten track, not even on the main highway system. While some locals spoke Greek, the greater part of the population used only the native Lycaonian tongue. Neither did the town have a synagogue, so was without ten male Jews in the population. No synagogue and off the beaten track means the mission team temporarily has abandoned their overall strategy of main highways, main cities, and main synagogues.

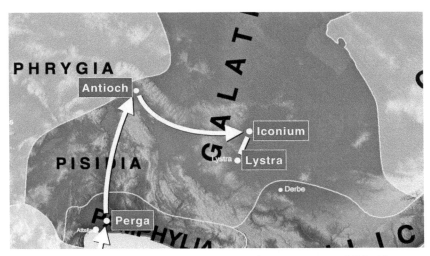

FIGURE 10.39. 1MJ—Galatia: Lystra. Lystra was a military garrison established by Augustus that never amounted to much. Off the main Roman highway system and speaking mostly Lycaonian, this city was a departure for the Antioch team from their typical mission strategy.

FIGURE 10.40. Lystra Tel. The mound representing the occupation layers of ancient Lystra rises up from the valley plain, never excavated to reveal its secrets.

The Antioch team may have abandoned their mission strategy, but they did not abandon their mission. Luke indicates that even on the back roads and in the country, the team went about proclaiming the "good news" (14:7). This proclamation would be in Greek, which was Paul's native tongue. Without an interpreter, this proclamation would be limited in reach. In the market place, however, one would encounter

Greek speaking individuals, since most typical business was conducted in Koine Greek among various populations.

The lame man probably was in the market area in order to seek alms, since he was listening to Paul (14:8–9). Paul saw he had faith to be healed and told the man to stand up. Luke's notation of crippled from birth is important. This status means the cripple's condition was

FIGURE 10.41. Lystra Inscription. Rare inscriptional evidence for the ancient city of Lystra. The city name is in the second line (KAM).

well known to the community, so the event people had witnessed was not a scam by itinerant charlatans, but a genuine miracle of healing.

FIGURE 10.42. Priests in Sacrificial Processional. Frieze from the theater at Perge showing priests in sacrificial processional leading the sacrificial animals, probably dedicatory rites for the theater (AAM).

FIGURE 10.43. Bull and Garland. Bull and garland reliefs signifying sacrificial rituals were common in ancient monuments and sarcophagi. This part of the base to the temple to Domitian at Ephesus was related to Domitian and the Parthians (EMS).

The local crowds interpret the incident as a divine epiphany, exclaiming, "the gods have come down to us in human form" (14:11).[19] Zeus and Hermes often were associated together, so if Paul is doing the talking, he must be Hermes, which leaves Zeus the role Barnabas must have (14:12). A Zeus temple was just outside the city gate, and the priest began sacrificial preparations of oxen and garland. The "apostles" Barnabas and Paul get wind of what really is going on and react in typical Jewish fashion when confronted with blasphemy by tearing their clothes.[20] Here is the second of only two times in Acts "apostles" is used in a non-Lukan manner to refer other than to the Twelve.

Paul responds with basic Jewish theology without quoting Scripture. His first move is monotheism and creation theology: "God who made the heaven and the earth and the sea and all that is in them" (14:15). He then quickly moves to basic human error: "allowed all the nations to follow their own ways" (14:16). He next asserts accountability: "he has not left himself without a witness in doing good" (14:17). He illustrates the divine witness of doing good with the gracious provision for basic human needs: rains, seasons, crops, harvest, food, joy (14:17). Notice that this last point is based on Pentecost motifs. Thus, Pentecost even figures in to preaching to pagans. They restrained the crowd from sacrificing only barely (14:18).

Jews from Antioch and Iconium show up (14:19). The timing is unclear whether at this moment of rebuffed sacrifice, or in days, or even weeks later. The outside agitators won over the crowds at Lystra, perhaps because the pagans had been affronted by the rejection of their offer of sacrifices. Paul is stoned, dragged outside the city, and left for dead, so in terrible trauma. Amazingly, when the disciples surrounded him, Paul got up and returned into the city (14:20a). Paul's description of believed dead at Lystra echoes that of Eutychus at Troas (20:9–10).

Paul directly alludes to this stoning incident at Lystra in his own letters. In listing a litany of his sufferings for the Corinthians, he says, "once I was stoned" (2 Cor 11:25). Another possible allusion is his un-

---

[19]Commentators often note that local Phrygian legend told of mistreatment of the gods in a previous visitation with subsequent punishment of the population, so the locals were not going to make the same mistake again. Often missed, however, is the very form of the exclamation resembles the basic form of the opening of the Christ hymn of Phil 2:5–11. Paul may have been speaking in these terms.

[20]So the high priest with his vestments at the trial of Jesus (Matt 26:65).

usual expression that he had the "brand marks" of Jesus in his body (Gal 6:17). Stoning is brutal, blunt force trauma. Bones are broken. and internal organs can receive severe damage. Often, the skull is crushed as the coup de grâce. Paul even may have been disfigured permanently by the experience in various ways.

The Lystra healing story has various parallels. One parallel is the temple healing by Peter and John. One can compare: (1) the wording: "a certain man lame form his mother's womb" (3:2; 14:8), (2) the significance: extension of the original ministry of Jesus into the mission of the church, and (3) the setting: as prelude to opposition of Jewish leaders. The story also has parallels regarding Jewish opposition. In Jerusalem, the Sadducees of the Sanhedrin had murderous hearts, toward Peter implicitly (4:2, 18; 5:17, 33), and toward Stephen explicitly (7:58). Out in Diaspora synagogues, Pharisees show similar murderous hearts toward Paul (14:19). Finally, the story has parallels to Saul's Damascus apologetics, which, echoing Stephen, has the character of an unstoppable voice and an unbeatable argument.

The Lystra story also serves Luke's apologetic. Christianity is no threat to Rome. Luke explains carefully exactly why everywhere Paul goes, disturbances ensue. The problem is not Paul. In general, people actually flock to his preaching. Paul, however, has a synagogue nemesis, just as Saul once was to Stephen. Luke labors to show that public disturbances related to Paul are not actually Paul but rather Jewish jealousy and Jewish synagogue agitation.

1MJ: Derbe (14:20–21)

Derbe is our turn around point. Functionally, this city is the end of the 1MJ. After a night in Lystra, Paul and Barnabas go on to Derbe. This route means they are back on the main road. Derbe was on the western edge of the province of Cilicia, the same province of Paul's home in Tarsus. Derbe commanded a broad plain along intersecting routes moving east to Cilicia and beyond and west to Iconium and Ephesus.

Luke here is brief. The Antioch team preaches the "good news" and made "many disciples" (14:21). Derbe likely did not have a synagogue. One possible convert is Gaius, whom we meet at Ephesus. He is a Macedonian (19:29), but from Derbe (20:4). Precious few inscriptions ever mention Derbe. A fourth-century inscription identifies a Michael, bishop of Derbe, with rare mention of the city of Derbe.

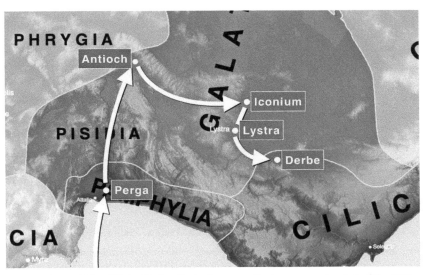

FIGURE 10.44. 1MJ—Cilicia: Derbe. Derbe becomes the turn around point of the 1MJ.

FIGURE 10.45. 1MJ—Derbe Michael Inscription. Rare 4th cent. inscription mentioning the city of Derbe in reference to a Michael, who was bishop of Derbe (KMM).

FIGURE 10.46. Derbe Tel. Based on inscriptional evidence, the ancient site of Derbe has been identified with this mound known as Kerti Hüyük about 14 miles north to northeast of Karaman, Turkey.

FIGURE 10.47. Marker on Top of Derbe Tel. This column marks the official record of the site of Derbe. In the distance beyond the plateau of the plains are the mountain passes leading to Tarsus of Cilicia.

1MJ: Return (14:21–26)

At this point in Derbe, Paul did have the option of continuing on east from Derbe along the Roman highway that went across the wide plateau and on to Tarsus. Instead, the team apparently decided rather to turn around and retrace their steps—a bold move, since that meant returning through a city where Paul had been stoned, and he probably

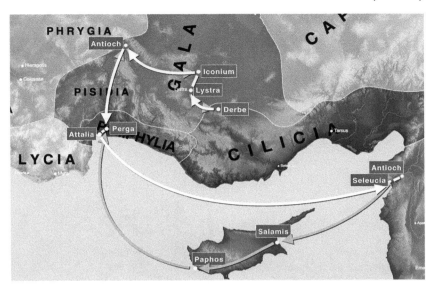

FIGURE 10.48. 1MJ: Return. Look carefully. Something odd happens on the return.

still was recovering from his injuries. The reason for the return is not stated directly, but seems to be inferred by what they did along the way, as Luke describes the matter. First, they wanted to strengthen the disciples, recognizing that, even as Paul had witnessed himself in Lystra, "It is through many tribulations that we must enter the kingdom of God" (14:22).[21] Second, they appointed elders "in each church" (14:23). This "elder" structure is Jewish and reflects the synagogue, which is not surprising given the synagogue emphasis of the mission strategy. Appointing elders evidences concern for future growth and development. This action, however, should not be interpreted as an intended replacement of the synagogue as an institution. One would imagine Paul would have continued worshipping in the synagogue had the response been a confession of Jesus as Messiah rather than stoning.

The team goes back through Lystra, Iconium, and Antioch, then back down out of the highlands to the port at Perga, then a short jog over to the twin port at Attalia (Antalya), which they had not visited on the way inland. Then, something odd happens on this return trip. They completely bypass Cyprus. Why? If the purpose of the return trip was given as to strengthen disciples and appoint elders "in every church,"

[21]For the significance of kingdom of God language here, see "Preliminaries," 15–20.

FIGURE 10.49. Antalya Harbor Panorama. Beautiful Antalya harbor (ancient Attalia).

FIGURE 10.50. Antalya Harbor Mountains. The mountain range comes right up to the edge of the coastline.

FIGURE 10.51. Hadrian's Gate. The only remnant of the Roman empire in Antalya.

then they missed the entire first part of the journey! Add to this return itinerary mystery about Cyprus that John Mark left the mission team immediately after Cyprus, and we never are told why, then something begins to smell fishy about Cyprus. Luke is suppressing information, similar to never mentioning *why* Paul insisted on going to Jerusalem at the end of the 3MJ. Note how Barnabas takes John Mark with him and returns to Cyprus after Paul fractures the Antioch mission team the Spirit had commissioned over the issue of John Mark (15:36–39).

Antioch Report (14:27–28)

The team reports to the sponsoring church at Antioch. They describe all that God had done, "and how he had opened a door of faith for the gentiles" (14:27). That surprising gentile response is Luke's last word about the 1MJ and the lasting impression he wanted to leave, because this result actually sets up the problem that develops. Paul and Barnabas remain in Antioch "for some time" (14:28). While ambiguous, the time frame only needs to suggest that enough time passes for Antioch's crisis with Jerusalem to spill out into open conflict. A regional council of leadership of all constituencies has to be called.

Paul's letter to the Galatians could be written at any time after the 1MJ. If written soon after, then Galatians would be the earliest known letter of Paul. Otherwise, our 1 Thess probably is the first letter. However, Galatians could be written much later in Paul's letter history, since dating is contested. A problem for Galatians in the study of Acts is how to reconcile the sequence of his visits to Jerusalem Paul itemizes in Gal 2 with the vis-

Acts	Letter	From	Date
JC	Galatians	?	?
2MJ	1 Thess 2 Thess	Corinth	50
3MJ	"Previous Letter" 1 Corinthians "Harsh Letter" 2 Corinthians Romans	Ephesus Ephesus Ephesus Macedonia Corinth	55 55 56 56 57
Rome	Colossians Philemon Ephesians Philippians	Rome Rome Rome Rome	60 60 60 62

FIGURE 10.52. Pauline Correspondence: Galatians.

its to Jerusalem precipitated out of the Acts narrative: Acts 9 (post-Damascus), Acts 11 (famine relief), and Acts 15 (conference).

JERUSALEM CONFERENCE

Conference Crisis (15:1–12)

Important to understand is that the Jerusalem Conference is an escha-tological crisis of biblical proportions. Lest this perspective seem an overstatement, consider the context. Messiah's coming created crisis. Crisis for everyone. Period. The prophets always had warned that in the last days, the Lord suddenly would come to his temple and judgment would fall on Israel.[22] The preacher of Ecclesiastes spoke the paradig-matic warning,

> For no one can anticipate the time of disaster. Like fish taken in a cruel net, and like birds caught in a snare, so mortals are snared at a time of calamity, when it suddenly falls upon them (Eccl 9:12, NRSV).

So, first, Messiah's coming creates crisis, crisis for national Israel, and crisis for messianic Israel. Each has a date with destiny. No one escapes crisis in the presence of the Christ. Second, each crisis has a

Eschatological Crisis	Precipitating Event	Leadership Choice
National Israel	Lame Man (Acts 3)	Sanhedrin (Acts 4—5)
Messianic Israel	Gentile Converts (Acts 13—14)	Apostles, Elders (Acts 15)

FIGURE 10.53. Messiah as Eschatological Crisis.

precipitating event. For national Israel, the precipitating event was the healing of the lame man in Acts 3, which is why Luke fronts this heal-ing above all others performed in Jerusalem in those days. For messi-anic Israel, the precipitating event is the saving of "blind" gentiles on the 1MJ in Acts 13–14. Third, each crisis also has a crucial leadership choice. For national Israel, the choice was by the Sanhedrin in Acts 4–5. For messianic Israel, the choice is by the apostles and elders here in Acts 15. National Israel's crisis with Messiah led to national destruc-tion. What should the church expect? At the Jerusalem Conference in

[22]An allusion to Mal 3:1. Cf. Isa 47:11; Jer 4:20; 6:26.

the insistence of Pharisee believers that gentile believers must observe the law of Moses to be part of messianic Israel, the church was walking dangerously close to the edge of divine tolerance.

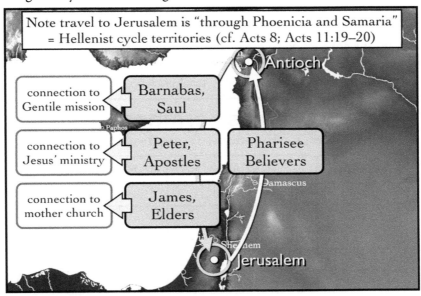

FIGURE 10.54. Pharisee Believers Contradict Antioch's Message.

Pharisee believers in Judea[23] delegated themselves to Antioch as teachers to straighten out the mess Paul and Barnabas had made with Israel. Their issue was salvation. Their covenant was Moses. Their point was circumcision. Their operating definition of Israel was that nothing happened in Messiah to mitigate the Mosaic covenant. Israel after Messiah is the same as Israel before Messiah. They forgot eschatology, that Messiah brought the eschaton, Joel's last days of prophetic hope, and cut a new covenant to inaugurate its fulfillment. They ignored the cross as a covenant event and forgot about resurrection, ascension, and Pentecost as the empowerment of messianic Israel. They were not captivated and energized by a new vision of the people of God. In so doing, they brought the church to the brink of a judgment disaster.

In essence, they wanted to destroy the results of the 1MJ. That intent is precisely why they went to Antioch. Now, since the Spirit had

[23]Likely Jerusalem; the expression "down from" is travel from Mount Zion, the city of Jerusalem, in the hill country of Judea. That they are believers and Pharisees is indicated in 15:5.

inspired this Antiochene mission, where does that put these teachers? Ironically, they reprise the role of Saul of Tarsus.

The issue is the very destiny of the church. Leaders representing the constituencies of the early church convene. Barnabas and Saul are the connection to the gentile mission of Antioch. Peter and the apostles are the connection to the original ministry of Jesus. James and the elders are the connection to the mother church in Jerusalem. They are responsible to hold accountable the teachers who have raised the issue.

Peter's Sermons
The Church's Movement from Jews to Gentiles

Sermon	Audience	Significance
1. Acts 2	Jerusalem's pilgrims	Church empowered
2. Acts 3	Jerusalem's people	Forgiveness offered
3. Acts 4	Jerusalem's leaders	Forgiveness offered
4. Acts 5	Jerusalem's leaders	Forgiveness rejected
5. Acts 10	Cornelius's house	Gentile plan unfolds
6. Acts 11	Circumcision party	Gentile plan resisted
7. Acts 15	Church leaders	Gentile plan settled

FIGURE 10.55. Peter's Sermons: Acts 15.

Peter wins the day on behalf of Antioch. The issue is the same as when the Jerusalem church challenged Peter about Cornelius, and Peter here will make his last speech in Acts defending again his move with Cornelius and the Antiochene mission too. Temple ritual no longer cleanses. God gives the Spirit and cleanses hearts by faith (15:8–9). One can hear the echo of

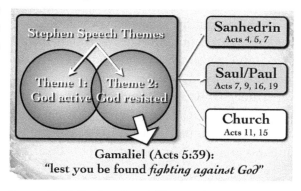

FIGURE 10.56. Stephen Speech Themes: Acts 15.

Gamaliel's advice and Peter's own words from previous narrative. The echo of Peter's question to Sapphira in his conference question to the church means the Ananias and Sapphira incident not only is about the Sanhedrin rejection sequence that envelops that incident, but also does double duty literarily by pointing to this conference. Narrative interrogations and statements carry the theme. First up is Peter's penetrating question to Sapphira: "How could you agree *to test (peirazō) the Spirit of the Lord*" (5:9)? Then comes Gamaliel's prescient advice to the Sanhedrin: "you will only find yourselves *fighting against God*" (5:39). Peter next responds to Jerusalem: "who was I to think *that I could oppose God*" (11:17)? Finally comes Peter's conference challenge: "why do you try *to test (peirazō) God*" (15:10)? Judgment is ready to fall!

Conference Issues (15:13–18)

From a Jewish perspective, conference issues boil down to two questions. One question is salvation. That question is about Jewish proselyte requirements. What establishes the covenant community? The answer to covenant community is the Spirit. The Spirit sanctifies by faith. The new age of Pentecost Spirit renders circumcision a matter of heritage, not holiness. One has to come to an understanding of the new messianic covenant as transcending the old Mosaic covenant. Mosaic Israel is no more. Messianic Israel is here to stay.

The other question is social. The social question is about purity requirements. What establishes table fellowship? The answer to table fellowship is the decrees. The decrees set guidance for gentiles in their Jewish relationships to be sensitive to minimum purity rituals to be gracious about social conscience and tradition. One has to come to an understanding of the new messianic society as the reality of Jew and gentile together. Gracious compromise is required. Thus, salvation is by the Spirit. Social relationships are by Jewish sensitivity.

James speaks the central concept of God's people for Luke. The key word is a "people" (*laos*, λαός, 15:14) that God is taking for himself. The focus is gentiles, as James declares God's intention "to take from among the gentiles a people to his name" (15:14).[24] This "people" created from gentiles is precisely the mission of the Antioch church.

---

[24]E.g., *labein ex ethnōn laon tōi onomati autou*, λαβεῖν ἐξ ἐθνῶν λαὸν τῷ ὀνόματι αὐτοῦ. The quote depends on the LXX reading, but James addresses a broad audience.

FIGURE 10.57. Jerusalem Conference Issues. Questions involve salvation and social relationships. Salvation is by the Spirit, and social relationships are by sensitivity to Jewish tradition.

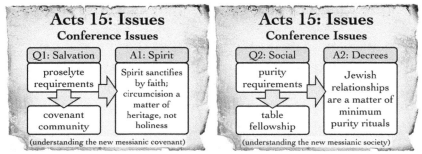

This reality of what God is doing in the Antioch mission through Paul and Barnabas is confirmed, James says, in another last days prophet like Joel, that is, Amos (Amos 9:11–12; Acts 15:16–18):

> After this I will return,
>   and I will rebuild the dwelling of David, which has fallen;
>   from its ruins I will rebuild it,
>   and I will set it up,
>   so that all other peoples may seek the Lord—
>   even all the gentiles over whom my name has been
>   called.
>   Thus says the Lord, who has been making these
>   things known from long ago (NRSV).

This quote is one of the premier pieces of Old Testament *testimonia* from the early church to summarize what Messiah did to create one people in messianic Israel. David's "house" is his royal line. Davidic kingship and the royal line had been utterly crushed, annihilated by exile. David's house was fallen, the royal line now barren. So, how could Amos be fulfilled? To create something from nothing would take a miracle. Precisely. God worked that miracle in Messiah. Messiah in his resurrection resurrects the house of David eternally. All those now incorporated into Messiah in these last days of prophetic fulfillment are incorporated into the new house of David. Messiah's new royal line melds together Jew and gentile into one "people." The concept James presents here is Luke's new vision of the people of God in a nutshell.

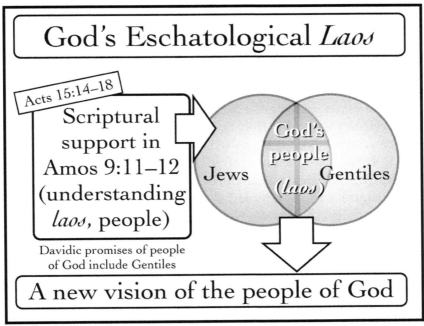

FIGURE 10.58 God's Eschatological *Laos*. James's quote of Amos 9:11–12 becomes for Luke the very definition of what God is doing in Messiah to create messianic Israel.

Conference Conclusion (15:19–35)

James calls the conference to a conclusion. His people had caused the confusion, so his leadership was the point of the spear for the Pharisee believers in Jerusalem, the one they had to follow. Yet, one does notice how Jerusalem decisions are just not what they used to be, for we no longer have the Twelve ruling exclusively over all matters of contention, as with the complaint of the Hellenist widows (6:1–4).

James intends to propagate the decision among the churches that were the target of the dispute to ease the tensions and bring harmony back to the entire community. He composes a letter that validates, accommodates, and personalizes. First, James validates the legitimacy of Antioch's gentile inclusion and of Paul's mission mandate. Then, James accommodates Jewish sensitivities by honoring the Jewish historical role as the people of God in minimal requirements for inoffensive social interaction. Finally, James personalizes the letter's validation function by sending his Jerusalem representatives to disperse the letter. At the same time, sending representatives is a shrewd move on James's part, since hosting these Jewish representatives from Jerusalem will require gentile churches in the Antioch orbit of activity immediately to begin to learn proper social graces with Jewish guests to fulfill the guidance of the conference decision.

Luke makes specific reference to the Holy Spirit in outlining the words of James detailing the conference decision in the letter: "For it has seemed good to the Holy Spirit and to us" (15:28). This type of reference to the Spirit is Luke's stylistic pattern for making clear when the Holy Spirit is or is not involved. If context is unclear, Luke will be explicit. Luke desires to be careful because the Spirit's empowerment is essential to his whole story in Luke-Acts. Thus, the Spirit's role normally he states explicitly. He leaves the Spirit's role implicit only if the context is unambiguous. Why make this point about Luke's stylistic habit in reference to the Spirit? Noting this Lukan style is crucial for interpreting Paul in Acts. The matter of the Spirit becomes imperative for understanding the truly strange beginning of the (so-called) 2MJ that is just around the corner. The matter also is imperative for understanding the end of the 3MJ as Paul bull-headedly insists on going to Jerusalem against all advice from everyone, including the Spirit. We never should forget in reading Acts that Luke's character Paul is Saul-Paul. Regardless the Renaissance portraits picturing Paul with a halo, readers of Acts need to remember Paul is, after all, a human being.

Luke name drops again, as he did with both Barnabas and Saul before their main roles. This time is Silas, Paul's future companion on the 2MJ. After Barnabas falls out with Paul over John Mark, Paul needs a Jerusalem church connection to shore up his work among the gentiles. Silas serves that purpose and becomes a major 2MJ associate.[25]

---

[25] An entire verse, Acts 15:34 in the KJV, is excluded from all modern translations. The reading, which has little support in Greek manuscripts, was an obvious scribal attempt to "solve" the problem of Silas leaving Antioch in 15:33, but suddenly and mysteriously back in Antioch for Paul to choose him as a partner for the 2MJ in 15:40.

The Debate about Acts 15

What is not covered in this narrative analysis presented above is the attempt to integrate Luke's Acts into Paul's letters. Those relationships are a difficult and debated conundrum. Relationship of this Jerusalem Conference, for example, to the "Antioch incident" that Paul details in Gal 2:11–14 is unclear at many points. What Paul reports in Galatians is that Peter changed behavior in Antioch under influence from Judea that caused Peter eventually to abandon table fellowship with gentiles. Peter's hypocrisy was a significant blow to Paul, not only for the truth of the gospel, but also because other Jewish Christians followed Peter's example, even including Barnabas. The timing and nature, and social, religious, and political dynamics about this "Antioch incident" are all much discussed. Even the date of Galatians is much discussed, both of the absolute dating, but even of the relative dating in sequence with this conference. Further, the interrelationship of Gal 2 to Acts 9, 11, and 15 complicates matters even more. All such issues are argued among commentaries without too much general consensus. When one adds to this discussion debated matters of historicity, then even achieving some sense of a historical frame seems pretty illusive.[26]

SUMMARY

Presenting highlights of the 1MJ as bullet points might be helpful. We rehearse some significance features about this journey by locality.

(1) Holy Spirit's initiative
- 1MJ is the initiative of the Holy Spirit (13:2)
- 2MJ is the initiative of Paul (15:36)

(2) Salamis sets the synagogue strategy
- Missionary pattern: synagogue first, if present
- Most viable first gentile converts here as well

(3) Paphos illustrates the gospel's power
- Social elite: conversion of Sergius Paulus
- Magic's rejection: blinding of Elymas

(4) Paphos reveals narrative shifts
- Shift in main character's name: Saul to Paul
- Shift in team leadership: Barnabas to Paul

---

[26]For a judicious but brief overview, the student might consult Bock, *Acts*, 486–93.

(5)   Perga shows John Mark's departure
  • Paul will interpret as defection
  • Paul will fracture mission team later over issue
(6)   Antioch of Pisidia shows an example Pauline sermon
  • Three journeys, three sermons, three audiences
  • This sermon illustrates synagogue context, Jewish audience
(7)   1MJ precipitates the Jerusalem Conference
  • Unexpectedly large gentile response
  • Exposes the Jerusalem church's identity crisis
    –Confusion about messianic Israel, like kingdom of God (1:6)
    –Confusion about gentile incorporation
(8)   1MJ begins integration of Pauline correspondence
  • Galatians possible any time after 1MJ
  • Dating Galatians contested

Luke presents the Jerusalem Conference as much a crisis of eschatological judgment for messianic Israel as was the apostles' confrontation with the Sanhedrin earlier was for national Israel. The 1MJ and its significant gentile result was the precipitating event. Pharisee believers from Jerusalem advocating circumcision for salvation put themselves in the role of fighting against God like Saul before the Damascus Road. Peter reaffirms gentile cleansing though the Spirit in his last of seven sermons in Acts, which settles the gentile issue. His conference challenge, "why do you try to test God?" in 15:10 is a direct allusion to this same question Peter asked of Sapphira, "How could you agree to test the Spirit of the Lord?" in 5:9. The judgment of Ananias and Sapphira looms on the church's horizon. The conference decides salvation is by the Spirit and social relationships are by Jewish sensitivity.

James's words on the people of God based on the eschatological prophet Amos Luke makes foundational to a new vision of the people of God. God has raised up David's house in Messiah. All those in Christ inherit a new royal line, Jew and gentile. James concludes the conference by declaring its decisions and writing a letter to inform Antiochene churches involved. James on behalf of Jerusalem thus affirms Antioch's gentile inclusion and Paul's mission mandate fulfill Amos's prophecy and represents Messiah's vision of the people of God of the last days.

11

Second Missionary Journey

From Asia to Europe (Acts 16–18)

GENTILE INCLUSION NOW settled by the Jerusalem Conference, the rest of story should be set. We all know that history proves that Antioch's gentile mission turned out an incredible success. So, Luke should be done, right? Not really. Depends on the story being told. We only *think* the story was successful. Luke might want to suggest otherwise—not what was, but what *could* have been. The story is not really about Antioch or Paul. The story is about the Spirit empowering messianic Israel to world mission in order to bring Pentecost reality to the *uttermost parts of the earth* (1:8). Luke never describes these journeys as the "journeys of Paul." They are journeys of the Spirit.

This distinction is critical. The beginning of the (so-called) 2MJ simply cannot be understood in a Lukan sense without this important distinction bearing down on our reading of the narrative Luke actually composed. As we have stated before, Paul is Luke's hero, but Messiah is Luke's point.

AIMLESS IN ASIA

We have inserted a parenthetical "so-called" in front of references to the 2MJ for a simple reason. At the beginning, no "journey" exists any way one wants to cut the cake. No Holy Spirit. No corporate commissioning. No laying on of hands. The story is Paul derailing his mission mandate, with no one to blame but himself.

Paul's Fight with Barnabas (15:36–40)

The event is triggered with Paul's suggestion of a return visit to congregations established on the 1MJ. Here are Luke's carefully measured out words in Acts 15:36:

> Sometime later Paul said to Barnabas, "Let us go back and visit the brothers in all the towns where we preached the word of the Lord and see how they are doing."

First, note *who* makes the suggestion: "Paul said." Bluntly, *the initiative is Paul's*, not the Holy Spirit. The Spirit distinctly does not inspire this suggestion. Such a description is miles apart from that of the beginning of the 1MJ ("The Holy Spirit said," 13:2). Second, note *what* is suggested: "go back and visit." Going back is not going forward. Such a suggestion frankly has nothing to do with a new mission endeavor. Third, note *where* is suggested: "in *all* the towns." That "all" can mean none other than including churches in Cyprus. Suddenly, Paul wants to put Cyprus back on the map, as if nothing happened? Remember bypassing Cyprus at the end of the 1MJ? Barnabas does too. Cyprus believers were orphaned by the mission team on the return trip to Antioch. They were not encouraged nor had elders appointed, as in all Galatian churches. Further, John Mark had left after Cyprus, and Paul had had a harsh reaction to that departure. Paul interpreted that post-Cyprus development as a defection and remained unforgiving on the matter. Thus, in multiple ways, Paul's suggestion exposes unresolved issues of Cyprus and John Mark that Barnabas simply cannot ignore.

Barnabas immediately makes these unresolved issues clear. He goes straight to the heart of the matter. Paul's attitude to John Mark is not right, and Barnabas, true to his character in Acts, is trying to be the encourager and Pentecost facilitator, in other words, only to do for John Mark exactly what he had done for Saul when Jerusalem likewise was unforgiving to Saul after he showed up unexpectedly knocking on the apostles' door in Jerusalem after the Damascus Road (9:26–27). So, Barnabas is seeking Paul's reconciliation with John Mark. We must keep in mind with whom Paul is dealing here. Barnabas is Pentecost abundance in the church in Jerusalem and Jerusalem facilitator of the Hellenist movement in Antioch. In fact, Barnabas is the very reason Paul is in Antioch in the first place. Not only did he introduce Saul to Jerusalem, he also introduced Saul to Antioch (11:25–26). Thus, no surprise, "Barnabas wanted to take John, also called Mark, with them" (15:37). Given Barnabas's track record in Paul's life and reputation in Jerusalem, *Paul should not ignore Barnabas's wisdom.* He would not be recommending reconciliation with John Mark on a lark. Yet, if this is Saul-Paul, we should *expect* this character to ignore good advice. Is not ignoring good advice precisely how we first encounter this character in the Acts narrative? He holds the cloaks of those stoning Stephen, deliberately ignoring his teacher Gamaliel's Sanhedrin advice (7:58).

Paul directly refused Barnabas's wisdom (15:38). Pretty brash to respond to Mr. Pentecost facilitator that way. The harsh truth is, Paul here refuses to forgive John Mark. Why? *What Paul is suggesting is not even a new mission endeavor.* For *this* purpose, he simply has *no reason to refuse to reconcile* with John Mark if John Mark were willing to go, which he was (15:39). Saul-Paul's character flaw begins to show. Even *after* the Damascus Road, he still is as much Saul as Paul. As the character Saul, he can show himself aggressively obstinate against all advice. While presenting only a serious problem now, this aggressive obstinacy will become a *fatal* flaw at the end of the 3MJ.

A serious schism in the Antioch mission team ensues. Luke is quite direct and to the point: "They had such a sharp disagreement that they parted company" (15:39). The word translated as "sharp disagreement" (*paroxysmos*, παροξυσμός) is graphic. This word describes a severe fit as with a disease or an attack of fever at its highest point of producing convulsions, hence a state of extreme exasperation or irritation. Our word paroxysm comes directly from this Greek word. If we get the impression matters have grown completely out of control, that would be Luke's point. One would be surprised if this behavior really was Barnabas, not when remembering the description of Saul "ravaging" the church in his pre-Damascus days, even going door to door, "dragging off both men and women" (8:3). We never hear anything close to that type of fury regarding Barnabas in Acts.

This Antioch mission team was not created by Paul and did not belong to Paul and was not his to manage. This team personally was designated by the Holy Spirit (13:2). Thus, if Paul *thought* he had a problem with Barnabas, he actually is not thinking this issue through very clearly. He now has a much more serious problem on his hands—the Holy Spirit. When Paul fractures the Antioch mission team, he winds up accomplishing what the entire Jerusalem Conference had worked so hard to avoid, schism in the church.[1] What strict Pharisee believers could not do in the preceding episode of the Jerusalem Conference—that is, split the church—Paul single-handedly now has done by himself. Paul destroys the original Antioch mission team the Holy Spirit had constituted. This moment of schism generated by Paul himself is precisely where the story begins to turn down a different track from the story that *could* have been told. Now, we never will know.

For his part, and to his credit, Barnabas is insistent upon cleaning up Paul's unfinished business from the 1MJ. Barnabas returns to Cyprus. He takes John Mark with him. We are to assume they encourage believers and appoint elders. After all, Barnabas is Pentecost facilitator in Acts. Barnabas now drops out of the Acts picture, but Luke clearly infers he never should have. Paul's obstinance already is beginning to show—a theme Luke will develop in time into a major crisis for the Pauline mission.

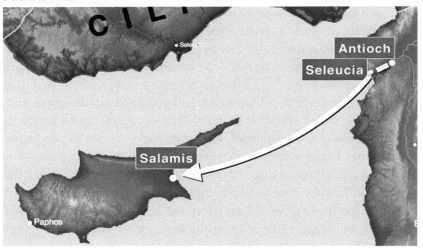

FIGURE 11.1. Barnabas and John Mark. The original Antioch mission team finally returns to Cyprus to clean up Paul's unfinished business from the 1MJ.

So, Paul loses Barnabas. Barnabas is a significant loss for Paul. Paul loses his Damascus Road facilitator. He loses his Jerusalem church connection. He finds his replacement in Silas, the emissary of James's letter. All the Antioch church knows to do is to commend them "to the grace of the Lord" (15:40). Antioch hardly could be happy the mission team

[1]What is ironic is that Paul will excoriate schismatic Corinthians in a later letter.

has fractured. Commending someone to the Lord is not a mission send off and has no sense of a mission assignment.

Paul has nowhere to go, but he hardly can stay. Paul not only loses Barnabas, he also loses his Antioch mission base. Antioch is the key church as a ministry paradigm (famine visit). Antioch is the key church as a mission paradigm (gentiles). Paul loses all this. The motif of his entire ministry is supposed to be a mission mandate. From this point on, however, he is wandering. He officially is "aimless in Asia." Thus begins the (so-called) 2MJ. Unlike the 1MJ, whatever is going on now is no "missionary journey," which is a misnomer, to say the least, because Paul has no Holy Spirit initiative. His real problem is the Holy Spirit, who will not tolerate what Paul has done to the Antioch mission effort. Paul has opposed the Spirit, so the Spirit will oppose Paul. These long trips are not the so-called "missionary journeys of Paul." They are the world mission journeys of the Spirit. The Spirit will control all this business. He will bring Paul back in line by saying "no" until Paul has nowhere to go except wait on a mission mandate from the Spirit. That mandate finally will come in a vision. Notice that most of the time in Acts, if Paul has to have a vision, he is off track from God's will. That pattern already is set by the Damascus Road.

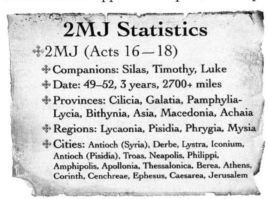

2MJ Statistics

✣2MJ (Acts 16—18)

✣ Companions: Silas, Timothy, Luke
✣ Date: 49–52, 3 years, 2700+ miles
✣ Provinces: Cilicia, Galatia, Pamphylia-Lycia, Bithynia, Asia, Macedonia, Achaia
✣ Regions: Lycaonia, Pisidia, Phrygia, Mysia
✣ Cities: Antioch (Syria), Derbe, Lystra, Iconium, Antioch (Pisidia), Troas, Neapolis, Philippi, Amphipolis, Apollonia, Thessalonica, Berea, Athens, Corinth, Cenchreae, Ephesus, Caesarea, Jerusalem

FIGURE 11.2. 2MJ Statistics.

Paul's Fight with the Spirit (15:41—16:8)

Movement Without Mission (15:41—16:5)

No mission mandate means any route will get you there. Thus, Paul just rehearses the good old times and wanders through regions already missionized. From Antioch Paul went through the province of Syria, then west into the province of Cilicia (15:41). Ironically, this route into Cilicia would have been the same road Barnabas traveled down to retrieve Paul in Tarsus for the work in Antioch (11:25–26). Paul is described as "strengthening the churches." Cyprus could have used some of that. The point is, such work, while useful to the church, is not a mission mandate. We still do not have a "missionary journey."

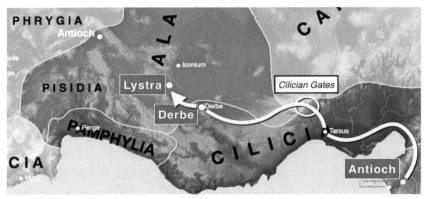

FIGURE 11.3. 2MJ: Syria, Cilicia, Galatia. In these movements, no "missionary journey" actually is taking place. Paul is just revisiting old areas.

Paul probably passed through his home of Tarsus in order to reach the Cilician Gates, a mountain pass out of Cilicia that gave access to the broad Anatolian Plateau and the main Roman road heading westward connecting the surrounding provinces of Cappadocia and Galatia. Conquering armies for millennia marched through this famous pass cutting through the Taurus mountain range. Once through the Cilician Gates, the Roman road turned west to Derbe. This highway Paul could have used from Derbe on the 1MJ to return back to Antioch. Instead, they retraced their steps to strengthen disciples and appoint elders.

FIGURE 11.4. Modern City of Tarsus. Lush orchards in the rolling hills just outside the modern city of Tarsus in the background.

FIGURE 11.5. Cilician Gates (Gülek Pass). The modern highway passes over the old Roman road through this narrow gorge of the Gökoluk River used for millennia.

FIGURE 11.6. Taurus Mountain Range. The towering, snow-capped mountains cut by the Cilician Pass leading into the Anatolian Plateau.

From Derbe Paul goes to Lystra, where he meets Timothy. Timothy's mother is a Jewish believer married to a Greek husband. Since his father was Greek, Timothy was not circumcised.[2] Timothy had a solid resume among believers in the area (16:2). Paul wanted Timothy to join him as a missionary associate. Through Timothy, God already is moving to compensate the damage to the original mission team Paul has

---

[2]The Greeks considered the procedure rather barbaric and a defacing of nature.

self-inflicted, but Paul not yet is aware of how God is moving the chess pieces. God already had positioned Silas, an official emissary of James's letter, to be available to Paul. As a Jerusalem representative already known and respected by James, Silas can replace the loss of Barnabas. God now does similarly with Timothy in regard to John Mark. Timothy functionally becomes John Mark's replacement. Now, to become a genuine missionary journey, all we need is for Paul to get straight with the Spirit and get a mission mandate. That reclamation will take a little Spirit prodding. So the new mission team is in place—Paul, Silas, and Timothy—but they are yet to have a purpose.

In the meantime, Paul had Timothy circumcised "because of the Jews who were in those places, for they all knew that his father was a Greek" (16:3). Is this action a compromise the "real" Paul never would have made? Is not the real Paul the one who wished those performing the ritual would "castrate themselves" (Gal 5:12)? The problem is not so clean cut. We have this same Paul insisting elsewhere that, "To the Jews I became as a Jew, in order to win Jews" (1 Cor 9:20). Given the context of the just concluded Jerusalem Conference and its agreement to reflect Jewish sensitivities, then circumcising Timothy is consistent with Acts and not inconsistent with Paul. *Since Timothy already is described as a believer in context in Acts, the issue of salvation is not even on the table.* Acts 16:3 in context then very much appears to be the Paul of 1 Cor 9:20. Thus, one use of Timothy is for Luke to show that "Paul" is still "Saul" as an observant Pharisee understanding Jewish religious sensibilities without salvation implications.

Luke also uses Timothy, along with two other 2MJ characters, Lydia and the Philippian jailor, to illustrate Jerusalem Conference decrees in action. Timothy illustrates the question of salvation, that is, how proselyte requirements work in messianic Israel as heritage, not holiness. Both Lydia and the Philippian jailer hosting the mission team in their

FIGURE 11.7. Jerusalem Conference in Action. Using 2MJ characters to illustrate the Jerusalem Conference in action.

homes and feeding them illustrates how all purity requirements in messianic Israel reduce down to a few specific guidelines for gentiles on how to be gracious and not give social offense.

Paul, Silas, and Timothy move through the region, delivering the decisions of the conference (16:4). The wise counsel of the conference brings unity and harmony to the church corporate and thus functions as the foundation for the fourth progress report of strengthening in the faith and increasing in numbers daily (16:5). This progress report is placed strategically to show the Jerusalem Conference has been a success, signaled by reiteration of the theme of Pentecost abundance.

Opposition of the Spirit (16:6–8)

These verses will make clear that Paul misfires multiple times on God's will. Paul first misfires on Asia (16:6). Luke says, "having been forbidden by the Holy Spirit to speak the word in Asia" (16:6). With the gospel needing to go to the "uttermost parts of the earth," one would not think the Spirit would be too stingy about where. That is the point. The Spirit is not stingy about where, but *who* is the deal. The Spirit says no to Asia, not because Asia does not need the gospel, but because Asia does not need Paul—at least, not with his present frame of mind and attitude after splitting the Spirit's Antioch mission team.

Paul then misfires on Bithynia (16:7). Two matters make this misfire really stand out exegetically. First, on Paul's part, the Greek tense for the verb "was trying" is imperfect (*epeirazon*, ἐπείραζον). The action is depicted as happening again and again, not just once, that is, "trying over and over again." So Paul kept trying, and the Spirit kept saying no. Point? Paul is not listening. He is arguing, lobbying, giving reasons why Bithynia is a great idea. Reasons perhaps like, "after all, Bithynia is densely populated with many Jews and synagogues." We can suspect this type of argumentative conversation with the Spirit, because that kind of conversation is exactly what Luke indicates when he drops the bombshell announcement on the reader in Acts 22 that *Paul actually had two visions of Jesus related to the Damascus Road.* One was on the Damascus Road. The other was immediately after the Damascus Road in Jerusalem's temple. In the temple vision, Jesus told Paul in no uncertain terms to "get out" of Jerusalem. Yet, Paul had the audacity even with this direct command from Jesus to argue back why he ought to stay in Jerusalem. After all, he countered, he did have such a great testimony that Jerusalem would have to listen to him![3]

The second exegetical point is to notice the most curious phrasing Luke uses, which he never has used before in all of Luke-Acts, and he never uses again. Luke does not just say, "but the Spirit did not allow." Luke is quite specific; he writes, "but the Spirit *of Jesus* did not allow." Now, that qualifier "of Jesus" being unique in Luke-Acts ought to make one sit up and notice. This "Spirit of Jesus" wording is Luke's way of evoking the Damascus Road—*another time Saul was fighting God.*

> "Who are you, Lord?" Saul asked. "I am Jesus, whom you are persecuting," he replied (Acts 9:5–6).

Luke adds a notable qualifier "of Jesus" to remind the reader that the last time Saul heard directly from Jesus in a vision, he was fighting God. Acts 16:7 is one more verse that continues to build the profile of the character who,

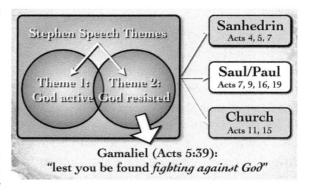

FIGURE 11.8. Stephen Speech Themes: Acts 16.

even at the moment he seems firmly convinced he is doing right, could be found, in truth, fighting against God.

So, look at a map. If Paul already has covered the territory behind him (Galatia), and he wants to go left (Asia) but the Spirit says no, and he wants to go right (Bithynia) but the Spirit says no, then his only option is follow his nose on the no's and drift westward. He drifts past Asia, then Mysia, to the port of Troas on the west coast of Asia (16:8). Hitting the ocean, they literally have nowhere to go. They are dead in their tracks. The Spirit has painted them into a corner. If the Spirit does not do anything, Paul is finished. The Spirit now has made clear to Paul that these world mission journeys are his sovereign control, not Paul's. In these two verses (16:6–7) Luke makes abundantly clear the Spirit's

[3]Read for yourself: Acts 22:17–21.

decided opposition to Paul. The schism with Barnabas is unresolved but not forgotten. Paul left Antioch really going nowhere, without a mission mandate, and that is where his trail has ended up: Nowheresville on the ocean's edge. The Spirit has shut him down and made a point, just like the Spirit will do again at the end of the 3MJ in Jerusalem, as Agabus predicted (21:10–11). The "second missionary journey" is "so-called" because this journey really has yet even to start.

Think about this startling observation: Paul now has logged 830 miles from Antioch to Troas (as in Selma, Ala. to Washington D.C.). The silence is deafening. During all these miles in this Asian saga, Paul preaches nowhere, no synagogues are visited, no one becomes a believer, no miracles are performed, and no churches are established.

FIGURE 11.9. Troas: The Holy Spirit Hems Paul In. Paul cannot go back, because Galatia is where he already has been. He cannot go left to Asia nor right to Bithynia, so he wanders straight ahead until boxed in at water's edge. The Spirit has tied him up.

EUROPEAN MISSION

The Troas Vision (16:9–10)

We encounter the first of three "we sections" in this material that runs from Troas over to Philippi (16:10–17). The narrative suddenly shifts

FIGURE 11.10. Archeology at Troas. Ancient Troas is known as Alexandrian Troas, a few kilometers inland from the beaches of modern Dalyan. Top left: arches of Herod Atticus leading into the baths. Top right: fallen columns and lintel laid out on ground. Bottom left: exposed subterranean archway. Bottom right: vaulted passageway leading into the 100 BC stadium recently discovered by German archeologists.

FIGURE 11.11. Troas Architecture. Troas long was an important port city. Constantine even considered making Troas capital of his Roman empire. The site lay in ruins until German archeologists began working only recently in the twenty-first century.

without any notice from third person (he, she, it, they) to first person plural, "we." Luke is an eyewitness to the Troas vision. This piece of information is important. Luke personally is vouching for the validity and veracity of Paul's Troas vision. Luke is the objective substantiation of the Macedonian mission mandate. Luke affirms the Spirit really was at work in this vision to get Paul back on track, in close parallel to the function of the Damascus Road vision for Saul of Tarsus. The second "we section" at the end of the 3MJ likewise comes precisely at a point in the narrative when the issue of Paul and God's will is at stake, only, this second time around, Luke will make perfectly clear that he absolutely *disagreed* with Paul about going to Jerusalem. *Luke personally testifying on the issue of Paul and God's will at three crucial junctures in the Pauline mission is the essential literary function of the three "we sections" in Acts.* The Acts "we sections" substantiate the Gospel prologue's claim about eyewitnesses in Luke 1:1–4 (emphasis added):

> Since many have undertaken to set down an orderly account of the events that have been fulfilled among us, just as they were handed on to us by those who from the beginning *were eyewitnesses and servants of the word*, I too decided, after investigating everything carefully form the very first, to write an orderly account for you, most excellent Theophilus, so that you may know the truth concerning the things about which you have been instructed.

The Troas vision functions as a call. The vision is styled this way, often labeled, "the Macedonian call." The story is concise, and Luke's concurrence immediate with a juxtaposed "we section" (emphasis added):

> During the night a vision appeared to Paul, a certain Macedonian man who was standing, urging him and saying, "Cross over to Macedonia. Help us!" When *he saw* the vision, immediately *we sought* to depart to Macedonia, being convinced that God *had called us* to evangelize them (16:9–10).

This call is *God's initiative*, not Paul's, as with Paul's earlier suggestion to Barnabas that they revisit the churches of the 1MJ (15:36). This call finally puts the 2MJ on track here at Troas. The Troas vision is key to the 2MJ, because *Paul's vision at Troas is God's gracious renewal of the Damascus Road.* Paul often receives visions when he is fighting God, unwittingly fulfilling Gamaliel's warning. Each vision is bad news, good news: "Paul, the bad news is, you are out of God's will. The good news is, God is gracious!" Thus, this Macedonian vision moves the story across continents, from Asia to Europe, from fighting God to mission mandate. The Spirit empowers these world mission journeys. Paul is humbled and put in his place, but now ready to be the voice of the gospel and an instrument of God's grace. Let the games begin.

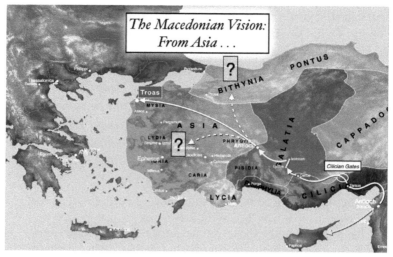

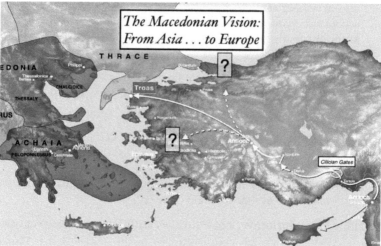

FIGURE 11.12. Macedonian Vision: From Asia to Europe. A vision of a Macedonian calling to come help finally gives Paul a mission mandate. *Now* begins the real 2MJ.

Macedonia (16:11—17:14)

Neapolis (16:11)

Macedonia was a province of Rome immediately north of the province of Achaia (Greece). The mission team had to take passage on a ship to reach their new destination. Luke records leaving Troas by boat and passing by the island of Samothrace on the way to Neapolis.

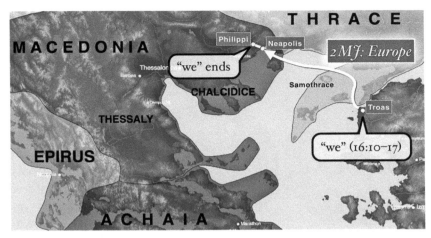

FIGURE 11.13. 2MJ—Macedonia: Philippi. Neapolis (Kavalla) is port serving Philippi.

FIGURE 11.14. Modern Kavala. Modern Kavala is still a thriving port with fishing industry and tourist beaches.

Philippi (16:12–40)

Philippi had rich Greek and Roman history. Philip of Macedon, father of Alexander the Great (fourth century BC), conquered the Thracian city and renamed the place for himself. Philip was able to control the gold mining in the area, which made his kingdom very rich. Macedonian women historically had more power and freedom, including even business activity, than typical of women in general in ancient Greek or Roman society. This part of Macedonian culture continued through time. Different social status of Macedonian women is why we will meet Lydia, a business woman and dealer in the exclusive and lucrative purple dye, on this 2MJ. She had the financial capability and the necessary Roman villa in Philippi to host the mission team in her home. The prominence of women at the Philippi church is seen

FIGURE 11.15. Silver Tetradrachm, Philip II (359–336 BC). Head of Zeus, laurel wreath; rider, palm branch (PAM).

FIGURE 11.16. Gold Diadem, Philippi, 2nd Cent. BC (PAM).

FIGURE 11.17. Philippi Boundary Inscription. Declaration of Philippi's boundaries by Alexander the Great (PAM).

in Paul's later letter to the Philippians, and inscriptional evidence also indicates the activity of deaconesses into later centuries, but their exact duties are unknown.

Romans controlled Philippi from 168 BC on. The famous battle of Philippi engaged in 42 BC was the struggle of pairs of Roman generals, Cassius and Brutus against Antony and Octavian, after the triumvirate collapsed with the murder of Julius Caesar. Octavian eventually came out on top and granted Philippi colony status, a highly coveted civic privilege granting political independence to that city in the province (a "little Rome"). He then settled Roman veterans in Philippi as a reward. Thus, heavily steeped in Macedonian culture, the city was thoroughly Roman as well, and was deeply loyal to the empire. Philippi had a minimal Jewish presence, not even enough male Jews to establish a synagogue. As a result, Paul had to go outside the city gates to a riverside place of prayer on the Sabbath (16:13). More common in Philippi would have been the pagan worship of gods and goddesses, such as the worship of Mithras, the slayer of the bull, a cult popular among

FIGURE 11.18. Philippi Funerary Inscription. Female deaconess Agatha (3rd/4th lines) and Ioannis, a municipal cashier and trader in linen (PAM).

FIGURE 11.19. Drioziges Inscription. Military heroic commander killed at the side of King Riskoupores, who was an ally in the battle of Philippi in 42 BC (PAM).

Roman soldiers, as well as the perennial Egyptian cults, popular across the Roman empire, such as the worship of Isis.

The origins of the church at Philippi are in the story of Lydia and the women at the place of prayer down by the riverside. Lydia became a believer, then offered Paul and team her home. This offer was the official establishment of a patroness/client relationship so typical of ones Paul would engage on behalf of his churches. The church at Philippi will become one of Paul's most loyal supporters in his later ministry. They will provide him with substantial assistance, particularly in both money and personnel.

FIGURE 11.20. Egyptian Goddess Isis. Identified by characteristic center knot of tunic, 2nd cent. AD (PAM).

Lydia's narrative role is twofold. She shows the gospel penetrating all levels of society, both men and women, elite and nonelite. She also is used by Luke to play out the reality of the conference decrees by showing sensitivity to table fellowship issues between Jews and Greeks. One would presume in her role as the hostess to the mission team that, if not already, she would become aware of the necessary accommodations for Silas and others. This very same role will be reprised by the Philippian jailor as he also

FIGURE 11.21. Bust of Priest of Isis from Philippi. His name was L. Titonus Primus, ca. AD 120–130 (TAM).

hosted the prisoners in his own home (16:34). The jailor also shows the gospel reaching all levels of society, like Cornelius in Caesarea.

Paul's encounter with the slave girl with a python spirit (pythoness) rehearses the issues of magic and spirit powers, shades of Elymas the magician at Paphos. Societal issues are similar, with Roman superstitions and pagan beliefs hindering gospel truth Paul was preaching.

Conference in Action

Q1: Salvation	Q2: Social
proselyte requirements: heritage, not holiness	purity requirements: minimum ritual no offense
⇩	⇩
Lystra: Timothy	Philippi: Lydia, Jailer

FIGURE 11.22. Cornelius Grave Stele. Monument to a Roman centurion buried in Philippi, named, coincidentally, Cornelius (PAM).

FIGURE 11.23. Jerusalem Conference in Action. Luke uses Lydia and the Philippian jailor to illustrate the Jerusalem Conference in action. They demonstrate hospitality to the mission team, including food, which is not refused.

So, the exclamations of the pythoness were not only annoying. They did damage. Paul's exorcism of the slave girl's spirit, unfortunately, impacted her owners' business in loss of revenue. A complaint to civic officials gets attention due to the colony status of Philippi. Civic leaders would have different designations in this city than elsewhere, noted correctly by Luke. These two-fold titles are, first, the "magistrates"

FIGURE 11.24. Philippi Funerary Relief. This 1st cent. AD relief depicts a customary funeral supper. Woman on left sits on a *difros* (backless seat), while three male figures sit on couch behind round table filled with fruits. On lower right, a child reaches for fruit, as in lower left a girl holds a vase (PAM).

(*stratēgoi*, στρατηγοί, in Latin, *duuviri*), and, second, the "officers" (*rabdouchoi*, ῥαβδοῦχοι, in Latin, *lictors*; 16:35). The charges are calculated to punch Roman political hot buttons: (1) "Jews" is prejudicial; (2) "uproar" targets Roman law and order; and (3) "customs unlawful for Romans" broadly targets proscribed societies and insinuates alien or socially repugnant customs.

FIGURE 11.25. Philippi Archeological Site. Top left: traditional site of the baptism of Lydia at Krinides Stream. Top right: unusual underground latrine area. Middle left: the Via Egnatia road down which Paul traveled connecting Philippi to Thessalonica. Middle right: the ancient wall leading up to the theater. Bottom left: artist depiction of theater in 1st cent. AD. Bottom right: Roman forum of Philippi. Above: theater of Philippi overlooking the ancient forum and surrounding mountain range.

Paul and Silas are beaten with rods (by the *rabdouchoi*), a severe punishment, whose open wounds could become infected (16:23). Why Paul did not call on his Roman citizenship to avoid this Roman penalty as he did immediately in Jerusalem is a mystery.[4] The earthquake is divine assistance and miraculous release, like for the apostles (5:19) and for Peter (12:7). Philippi release will contrast the absence of divine intervention when Paul is in prison in Jerusalem at the end of the 3MJ. The shame and social stigma of imprisonment threatens the mission, but Paul uses honor-shame rituals to turn the tables on the authorities, forcing them publicly to apologize because they had broken Roman law by punishing Roman citizens with rods and imprisonment (16:35–39). Lukan apologetics here show Christianity is not a threat to Rome, similar to the previous interaction with the proconsul Sergius Paulus at Paphos on the 1MJ and the coming interaction with the proconsul Gallio in Corinth. Apparently, Luke was not involved at this point.[5]

Amphipolis and Apollonia (17:1a)

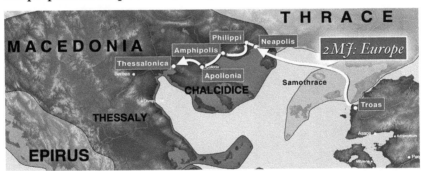

FIGURE 11.26. 2MJ—Macedonia: Thessalonica. Paul moves down the Via Egnatia highway connecting Philippi to Thessalonica through Amphipolis and Apollonia.

Paul is on the Roman superhighway, the Via Egnatia, that the Romans had built in the second century BC across the provinces of Illyricum, Macedonia, and Thrace to connect Dyrrachium on the Adriatic Sea all the way to what later would be Constantinople, a distance of 696 miles. The twenty-foot wide Via Egnatia paved with polygonal stones carried Roman legions across the empire to respond to all border threats.

[4]Acts 22:25. Citizenship is invoked only *after* beating and imprisonment (16:37).

[5]The "we section" ends somewhere along the way of the pythoness exorcism, so we apparently lose Luke's involvement before this beating and imprisonment.

FIGURE 11.28. Lion of Amphipolis. This tomb monument, rediscovered prior to WWI, is thought to have been constructed to honor Laomedon of Mytilene, who was an admiral of Alexander the Great.

FIGURE 11.27. Via Egnatia Milestone. Found near the Gallikos River, this milestone mentions the governor of Macedonia, Gnaius Egnatius, who built this part of the road (TAM).

Thessalonica (17:1b–9)

Paul entered Thessalonica along the Via Egnatia from Philippi in a direction that today the Galerius Arch guards. This famous Macedonian city had Greek and Roman heritage, at one time the second largest, wealthiest city in the later Byzantine empire. Free city status was granted in 41 BC, and then capital of the province. Like Philippi, Thessalonica had high loyalty to Rome. Unlike Philippi, Thessalonica had a synagogue,

FIGURE 11.29. Galerius Arch (299–303). Commemorative arch built over the Via Egnatia entering ancient Thessalonica celebrating Roman victory over the Sassanid Persians.

so, naturally, Paul went there first. His converts include Jews, devout Greeks (as in the Cornelius paradigm), "and not a few of the leading women" (17:4). These women are socially, politically connected, perhaps even a few business women like Lydia. Once again, Macedonian culture surfaces, in which women are held in higher esteem than in the rest of the empire and culturally have more freedom. Paul's preaching about AD 50–51 created the predictable disturbance after only a few weeks. Apparently, his patron and host, similar to Lydia, was Jason, whose house was the search target (17:5), but Paul could not be found, so Jason and a few believers made suitable substitutes as sympathizers. Like Philippi, charges were calculated to punch political hot buttons. "Turning the world upside down" is disturbance of the peace and law and order, which Rome aggressively put down (17:6). The exact reference of the second charge of "acting contrary to the decrees of Caesar" is unclear, but, coupled together with the further accusation of preaching "another king, Jesus," the clear inference is political sedition (17:7). Such slander charges were serious, especially since all emperors from Augustus on were pretty antsy about insurrection. The reference possibly could be to the recent edict of emperor Claudius (41–54) in AD 49 expelling Jews from Rome due to synagogue disturbances over "Chrestus," or possibly Messiah.[6] This edict would have been just prior to Paul's arrival in Thessalonica. Note Luke specifically indicates that Paul was preaching Jesus as Messiah (17:3). On the other hand, the reference could be more general, not specific. Ever since Augustus, emperors had issued decrees prohibiting predictions of a change of ruler or "soothsaying" a future death. Such declarations could be false prophecy as political sedition to foment rebellion or encourage a military coup. Municipalities, as a result, regularly were keen to show their fealty to the emperor in civic inscriptions and oaths.[7]

FIGURE 11.30. Claudius Sardonyx Cameo. Ejected Jews from Rome in AD 49 (BML).

FIGURE 11.31. Claudius Inscription, Berea. Inscription honoring Claudius (AD 41–54) by the citizens of Berea, Macedonia. Berea (ΒΕΡΟΙΑΙΩΝ) appears in the first line of the enlargement, and Claudius (ΚΛΑΥΔΙΟΥ) in the second. Names of city leaders are on the bottom left (AMV).

The bottom line was, Paul was forced to leave, because his host Jason received a peace bond injunction from the authorities (17:8–9). The believers secreted Paul and Silas out of the city that very night (17:10). Paul's sudden departure from Thessalonica after only a few weeks of mission work, that is, the very nature of this brief time in Thessalonica, naturally will set up the issues for Thessalonian

---

[6]Suetonius *Claudius* 25. Widely thought a Latin misspelling by the Roman historian of the Jewish word "Messiah" in its Greek form "Christos" (Christ), that is, the likely controversial preaching of Jesus as Messiah in synagogues in Rome.

[7]For helpful examples, see Arnold, *Acts*, 2:381.

believers with which Paul will have to deal in his later correspondence to them.

Like his accuracy in referring to the civic leaders of Philippi in terms of Philippi officially having the status of a Roman colony, Luke also is extremely specific in his reference to civic leaders at Thessaloni-

FIGURE 11.32. Politarch Inscription, Berea. The word politarch is found at the end of the third line of this inscription from Berea (AMV). Credit: Jean M. Stevens.

ca. He calls them "politarchs" (*politarchai*, πολιτάρχαι, 17:8). The only problem was, we had no evidence of the term anywhere in the first century or before, so Luke was charged with being anachronistic in that he was reading a second-century term familiar to him back into the first-century context, but in error. However, at least seventy inscriptions with the designation "politarch" have been catalogued now, three-fourths deriving from Macedonia, and half of those from Thessalonica itself, some as early as the third century BC.[8] Luke was not just right. He was precisely right. Luke knew a special term true in Thessalonica, but not even true in Philippi only a hundred miles back down the road.[9]

Thessalonica's ancient Roman forum was discovered accidentally in 1962 upon construction for a new courthouse right in the middle of the downtown area. The odeon is the best preserved of the remains, a small theater for performances and orations. The document archive preserving vital family records was to the right of the odeon. Citizens visited the porticos and the square for business and to audition public speakers, such as orators and philosophers. The southern wing contained various shops and offices, as well as the gymnasium and baths. Thessalonica had its own mint under the auspices of the Capitoline

[8] Arnold, *Acts*, 2:382.

[9] For more politarch images (seal and inscription), see p. 24.

trinity of Jupiter, Juno, and Minerva, a sign of great honor and loyalty to the emperor.

FIGURE 11.33. Aerial of Thessalonica Roman Forum. Odeon is to the left, shops along the top (TAM).

FIGURE 11.34. Thessalonica Roman Forum. Top left: odeon. Middle left: market shops. Bottom left: remnants of beautiful floor mosaic of winning chariot racing team. Above: statue of Augustus that stood in the forum (TAM).

Berea (17:10–14)

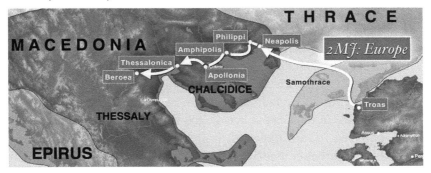

FIGURE 11.35. 2MJ—Macedonia: Berea. Paul's 45 mile journey from Thessalonica to Berea departed from the Via Egnatia main highway (like going to Lystra on the 1MJ).

FIGURE 11.36. Berea Valley. Berea sits on the hillside at the foot of Mount Bermius across from Thessalonica through a wide valley plain, a relatively easy journey.

The believers sent Paul and Silas over to Berea on a secondary feeder road off the Via Egnatia. Reception in the synagogue at Berea was distinctly more open, "more noble" in Luke's words (17:11). Once again, as regularly Luke has noted throughout Macedonia, Greek women of high standing respond (17:12).

FIGURE 11.37. Berea Roman Road. Portions of the ancient Roman road are preserved right in the middle of downtown Veroia.

By departing from the Via Egnatia and going to Berea, perhaps Paul meant to lay low off the Thessalonian radar. If so, the strategy did not work. Thessalonian Jews got wind of Paul's work in nearby Berea and went there to "incite the crowds" (17:13). The irony here is strong. The Thessalonian agitators come over to Berea and do exactly what they falsely charged Paul with doing in Thessalonica—disturbing the peace. That irony is set up by Luke's specific note of the irenic reception of Paul's message in the Berean synagogue before Thessalonian trouble-makers arrived. Luke's apologetic is at work again. He is making clear any public disturbance associated with gospel preaching is not Paul but synagogue agitators.

Once again, Paul is sent away "to the coast." Silas and Timothy "remained behind" (17:14). Luke's narrative here is a little vague. Paul eventually will wind up in Athens, but the route is unclear, whether by land or sea. All Luke says is, "brought him as far as Athens" (17:15). A companion at the end of the 3MJ named Sopater is from Berea (20:4).

Berea never forgot Paul's visit. Today, a plaza in Paul's honor with beautiful mosaics memorializes his visit and the creation of the first Christian community in that city on that 2MJ. Interestingly, one key mosaic is Paul's Macedonian vision at Troas, the mission mandate from the Spirit that resurrected a languishing mission effort and was the reason for Paul's eventual arrival in Berea.

FIGURE 11.38. Saint Paul Monument, Berea. The beautiful plaza and its mosaics honoring the original visit of Paul to Berea on the 2MJ. The Greek Othrodox Church uses the plaza for festivals and conducting high mass.

FIGURE 11.39. Macedonian Vision Mosaic. This Saint Paul Monument mosaic shows Paul, reclining, receiving the vision of the Macedonian calling to come over to help.

FIGURE 11.40. Berean Preaching Mosaic. This Saint Paul Monument mosaic shows Paul preaching to the Bereans, who are listening respectfully. The unrolled scroll in Paul's right hand curiously displays the Greek text of 1 Thess 4:1. One might have expected some part of the Acts 17 record of the Berean visit. The set piece, anacronistically, is depicted in medieval dress and architecture.

FIGURE 11.41. Greek Orthodox Mass. The celebration of mass has just concluded at the Saint Paul Monument in Berea.

FIGURE 11.42. Saint Paul Mosaic. The center apse of the Saint Paul Monument in Berea features this outstanding mosaic of the apostle Paul.

Greece (17:15—18:17)

Athens (17:15–34)

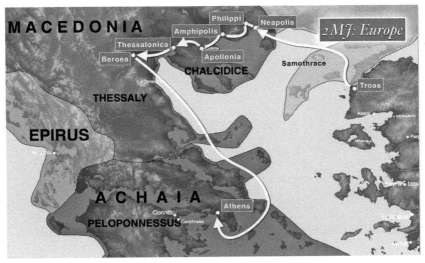

FIGURE 11.43. 2MJ—Greece: Athens. Luke is unclear whether Paul went by boat or on land. "To the coast" (17:14) seems to suggest a possible port access and sea voyage.

Paul was escorted by the Bereans to Athens (17:15). Athens is in the province of Achaia (Greece). Paul sent word back with the escorts who were returning to Berea to have Silas and Timothy reunite with him when possible, since they had been left in Berea (17:14). Paul is alone.

Not often reflected on at this point by readers of Acts is that Paul has left the province of Macedonia, but not of his own will. He had been run out of every town. He has been able to stay hardly more than a few weeks, on occasion possibly a month or two, in any one place. The question legitimately could be asked, What of the Macedonian vision? That vision had been a vision of a *Macedonian* calling to come help. What now? He is not even in Macedonia anymore. Is the 2MJ in trouble once again? Luke gives no indication of Paul fighting the Spirit, so this development seems within the purview of the Spirit's intention.

Athens long ago had lost its empire dominance in world history by the time Paul visited on the 2MJ, but its cultural dominance is forever. Athens is the cradle of democracy and western civilization. Greeks gave us our politics, our philosophy, our city grid plans, our architecture, and our cultural values. When one society can so dominate later societies, they have earned an eternal place in history's hall of fame. They can afford to be a little snooty about a "seed-picker" babbling in their marketplace, like a cat toying with its prey.

FIGURE 11.44. Athens Skyline. The city of Athens, viewed here from the top of the Acropolis scanning the ocean on the horizon, is the cradle of western civilization.

FIGURE 11.45. Parthenon. Built to house a grand statue of Athena by Pericles in the golden age of Athens (447–438 BC), the Parthenon widely is considered the most architecturally perfect building in the world, and one of the world's greatest cultural monuments, even though today the edifice is only a shell of its former glory. For visual perspective, the columns actually are not spaced evenly; the ones on the corners are closer together. The columns also are wider at the bottom than at the top. Further, the floor is convex, not straight. Had the long run of the floor been straight, the appearance visually would have been concave to the human eye.

FIGURE 11.46. Parthenon Lioness. Lioness savaging a bull, right wing of pediment of earliest acropolis building (570 BC) (AM).

FIGURE 11.47. Kore Statue. Gently flowing garments, lavishly decorated, earrings, diadem, with highly elaborate, waved hairdo, a masterpiece of ancient Greek skill (520–510 BC) (AM).

FIGURE 11.48. Acropolis Odeon. Donated in AD 161 by famed patron of Athens, Herod Atticus, the three-story odeon once was covered with cedar of Lebanon timber. The theater is used in modern times, including the Miss Universe 1973 pageant and musical performances.

FIGURE 11.49. Greek Wrestlers. One face of an Athens funerary base that stood over the grave of an athlete. Pictures a palestra scene of athletes practicing skills and techniques for a pentathlon, five events in one day—the long jump, javelin throw, discus throw, stadion (foot race), and wrestling. Pentathletes were the most highly trained, whose skills were so highly prized that this athletic training was considered part of military training with skills useful in battle. Left is a long jumper ready to spring. Right is another athlete preparing the sand pit for the wrestlers. The modern Olympic movement, inspired by Greece, has revived pentathlon competition (NAMA).

FIGURE 11.50. Ancient Agora of Athens. The marketplace is where Paul would have spoken his philosophy of life, filled with temples and altars, even an altar to an unknown god. The temple of Hephaestus in the background Paul would have seen.

FIGURE 11.51. Temple of Hephaestus. Hephaestus was the god of metal working, whose artisans in this area honored their patron. Begun in 449 BC, this project was delayed by the Parthenon. The Doric peripteral style building was not dedicated until 416–415 BC. The temple is situated on top of the Agoraios Kolonos hill overlooking the ancient Agora of Athens. When Athens was made capital of modern Greece in 1834, the royal edict was announced from this temple.

FIGURE 11.52. Stoa of Attalos. The covered walkway originally donated by Attalos II of Pergamon (159–138 BC) to adorn one end of the ancient Agora of Athens was reconstructed faithfully by American architects in the 1950s. The original structure would have been viewed by Paul as he taught in the marketplace.

FIGURE 11.53. Parthenon Acropolis from the Areopagus. The Areopagus was a council of Athenian elders, somewhat like the Jewish Sanhedrin or the Roman senate, before the classical age. The meeting site of this council was associated with a hill northwest of the Acropolis given this same name. Romans referred to this hill as "Mars Hill" after Mars, their god of war. The Areopagus has a stunning view of the Parthenon.

*Sermon Background (17:16–21).*The whole point of Athens is the Areopagus sermon to the philosophers after attracting attention in the market area. The gospel here will encounter the ingrained prejudices of Greek philosophy, most especially as represented by the Epicureans and the Stoics. Athenian philosophers sought to discover the most desired life to live though nurturing the most desired virtue. Epicurus (340–270 BC) taught the greatest virtue was pleasure through tranquility. His goal was to live life free from fears, passion, and pain. He was neutral on the question of the gods' existence, but insisted, if they ex-

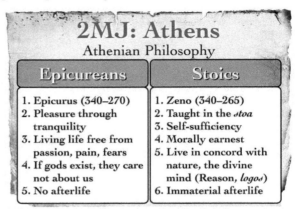

FIGURE 11.54. Greek Philosophy: Epicureans and Stoics. Greek philosophy was a great challenge for the gospel.

isted, they cared not about human existence. Epicurus also taught no afterlife, because no evidence at all could be adduced for its existence. So, live this life well, as this life is all one has. Stoics derived from Zeno (340–265), who was habited to teaching in the *stoa*, or columned porticos. For Zeno, life's greatest virtue was self-sufficiency, best achieved through moral earnestness in relationships and concord with nature. Nature could be abstracted as the divine mind that gave consistency to all operations of the world, even capitalized as Reason, or the *logos*. Any afterlife would be immaterial. So, the Epicureans said God was nowhere in nothing, while the Stoics said God was everywhere in everything. Such a quick summary shows how these philosophies would provide quick points of minimal contact with the gospel, but, as well, significant points of fundamental disagreement.

The philosophers easily could conflate Paul's language with their own and misunderstand his meaning. They thought he was proclaiming "foreign divinities," which Luke explains as the preaching about "Jesus" and the "resurrection" (17:18). Preaching "Jesus" could be confused with a god Paul seemed to call "Healing," since Jesus in Greek would sound similar to the word for healing, and similarly with the word for resurrection.[10] So, their curiosity gets the best of them, and the Athenians invite Paul to expound further. Then comes another one of Luke's little humorous quips: "Now all the Athenians and the foreigners living there would spend their time in nothing but telling or hearing something new" (17:21). In other words, Paul was little more than the diversion for the day, which some already had insinuated by calling him a "seed-picker," that is, like a bird picking up little seeds as scraps off the ground, here is a poor, unsophisticated soul picking up discarded scraps of discredited philosophies as if he truly understands anything of substance for the public good (17:18).[11]

Paul's sermon on the Areopagus in Acts 17 is the second of three paradigm sermons Luke provides on each missionary journey. This sermon illustrates the nature of Paul's preaching to a gentile audience.

Paul's Paradigm Sermons			
MJ	Place	Context	Audience
1MJ	Antioch	Synagogue	Jewish
2MJ	Athens	Market	Gentile
3MJ	Miletus	Church	Christian

FIGURE 11.55. Paul's Paradigm Sermons: Gentiles. The Athens Areopagus illustrates Paul's preaching to gentiles.

Notice how Scripture is not quoted, the story of Israel is not elaborated, and messianic language is not used. However, fundamental themes of Jewish theology undergird the basic assumptions and points that Paul attempts to make, such as monotheism, creation theology, human accountability, and judgment eschatology. Paul cannot give up the resurrection, even though he probably well knew he would lose his Greek philosophical audience right there. The idea of physical resurrection was antithetical to the Greek goal of a higher, spiritual existence unencumbered by the material flesh. Inability to be "politically correct" by avoiding a reference to resurrection shows how this doctrine is an indispensable datum of Paul's Christian theology.

[10]Jesus is *Iēsous* (Ἰησοῦς), which could be confused with *Iasi*, or healing. Likewise, resurrection, *anastasis* (ἀνάστασις) could sound like a second deity's name.

[11]The Greek word is *spermologos* (σπερμολόγος), which literally means "seed-picker" from birds picking up small seeds off the ground. Sometimes translated "babbler."

The sermon has Hellenist foundations. One foundation is Peter's insight about gentile inclusion into messianic Israel, outlined in the seven sermons Peter preaches. Peter's words to Cornelius are particularly pertinent: "I truly understand that God shows no partiality, but in every nation anyone who fears him and does what is right is accept-able to him" (10:34–35). Another Hellenist foundation is Stephen's in-sight into man-made temples, which ought to be particularly relevant to Athens: "Yet the Most High does not dwell in houses made with human hands" (7:48). One could compare this statement by Stephen with the statement by Paul in the Areopagus: "does not live in shrines made by human hands" (17:24). Another Hellenist foundation is its implicit theology on two concepts that are fundamental to Paul's rhetorical strategy. One concept is monotheism—that crucial, core belief in a personal God who, in particular, is creator, so, logically, universal. The other key concept is revelation, which makes God accessible, humans accountable, and judgment inevitable. Thusly, the Hellenist movement of the early church confronts the Hellenist world of Athenian philosophers.

Sermon Presentation (17:22–31). While Paul does not quote Scripture, scriptural principles pervade his points. Paul uses monotheism as a foundation for his introduction. He then uses divine revelation as a foundation for development of his points. He begins his address with the standard rhetorical advice of building rapport with the audience on the basis of what he has seen as a first-time visitor to one of the most famous cities of the ancient world.

Introduction (17:22–23). Athenian religiosity is duly noted (17:22). Paul mentions objects of worship he has observed in the marketplace, which would include the temple of Hephaestus overlooking the entire agora area, among numerous other religious monuments. The famous Parthenon would have stood prominently and gloriously as the back-drop to the Areopagus vista as he spoke. He makes his transition using one particular altar he had observed, an altar to an "unknown god" (17:23). He intends to proclaim to them that "god."[12]

---

[12]Unusual in this declaration, often unnoted, is that the Athenians would have been aware fully of the Jewish God. Athens had had Jewish synagogues for quite some time by this point, so Jewish preaching would be no secret to Athenian philosophers. Paul's reference here may infer the person of Jesus himself more than is recognized. This perspective would correspond to the Holy Spirit earlier in the narrative being referred to as the "Spirit of Jesus" in 16:7.

More than meets the eye may be calculated into this reference to an altar to an "unknown god." The allusion is calculated to connect to the figure of Epimenides, whom Paul will quote shortly. Epimenides famously saved Athens from pestilence. Already legendary in Greece as a favorite of Zeus, Epimenides was bidden from his home on the island of Crete to Athens to help rescue the city from scourge. Since the source of divine offense was unknown, his remedy was unusual. Epimenides took sheep to the Areopagus and released them to roam freely through the city. He instructed they be followed and wherever each laid down to rest, the place be marked for offering sacrifice to the unknown local divinity. Athenians did so, and the plague was stayed. Thereafter, altars could be found across Attica with no inscribed name as memorials of this atonement.[13] So Paul's reference to an altar to an "unknown god" in Athens likely would be associated by the Athenians with this famous story related to Epimenides. Paul probably is setting up his quote of the person with whom such altars were associated in one of the famous legends in the history of Athens.[14]

Revelation: God the Creator (17:24–29). Paul moves to revelation doctrine to build his case. God is creator, and as creator has creative purpose. One purpose is boundaries. Unclear is whether Paul's sense of boundaries relates to the seasons or to the nations.

Paul then quotes from Greek literature to substantiate his point that God is creator, so is not "in everything" as Stoics taught, and has easily perceived purpose, such as boundaries, so is not aloof from the creation or disinterested, as Epicureans asserted. The first quote, "in him we live and move and have our being," is a line from Epimenides (600 BC).[15] This quote would resonate with an Athenian audience for whom Epimenides famously was connected in the city's history.

[13]The story is preserved in Diogenes Laertius, *Lives of Eminent Philosophers* 1.110.

[14]This connection, though original to this author, actually was noted years ago; cf. Hastings, "Notes of Recent Exposition," *The Expository Times* (Dec 1906): 98.

[15]Bruce, *Acts*, 339, gives the text of the stanza of the poem with this line. We actually do not have any copies of Epimenides. Rendel Harris reconstructed the lines at the turn of the twentieth century when Harris found a portion of the original lines from Epimenides's *Minos and Rhadamanthus* quoted in Syriac (both in a Syrian lectionary on Acts, *Garden of Delights*, and in a commentary on Acts by Isho'dad of Merv, ca. AD 850, both dependent on a now lost work of Theodore of Mopsuestia, ca. AD 400). Harris took the Syriac back into Greek and discovered a balanced Greek hexameter poetic pattern. Harris, "Cretans Always Liars." Also, see Lawlor, "St. Paul's Quotations

The second quote, "We are his offspring," is from the Greek poet Aratus (310 BC).[16] His work, *Phaenomena*, details the order of the constellations in their quadrants in the sky, celestial observations, and weather lore in forecasting. All of these phenomena together (and hence, the title of the work) are the foundation of human welfare because of predictability. The quoted words are the fifth line at the very beginning of the work in which Aratus celebrates Zeus, who in his kindness to humans, reveals exactly when to sow and when to harvest by signs in the heavens. As a result, all things grow unfailingly, thereby giving harvest and life. Such thoughts by Aratus echo the Pentecost harvest theme with which Luke launched the text of Acts in order to tell the story of messianic Israel. Thus, the Aratus quote may have more in its use here than just the words themselves but the context in Aratus that surrounds those words. Again, we already heard Paul using the theme of seasons, crops, and harvest with the pagans at Lystra (14:17). Paul seems to be working a similar angle here with the pagans at Athens.

Paul's specific point in using Aratus is the foolishness of idolatry. Humans build idolatrous icons of wood, stone, and metal as if these inert objects are gods. Yet, if what Aratus said is true, that humans come from God—but humans are alive—then God himself has to be alive. Even their own poet tacitly shows that the reality of God cannot possibly be in an inert statue made of human hands. Greek thought and Greek religion are inherently contradictory.

So God's first creative purpose is to reveal his reality and his goodness through ordering of the world in ways that benefit human life. His second creative purpose is to establish the accountability of humans to him. Humans show this accountability in the universal desire to connect with God. Indeed, humans always are seen "groping" for God as if possibly they might "find" him (17:27).[17] That groping is Paul's char-

---

from Epimenides." The *Acts Seminar Report* labels this quote a "probable allusion" to Epimenides, even while labeling Paul's visit to Athens as completely fictitious (Kindle loc. 3852).

[16]*Phaenomena* 5. Aratus, like Paul, was a native of Cilicia (whether Soli or Tarsus is unclear).

[17]Paul's verbs carefully are expressed in the optative mood, which means possibility of fulfillment is only remote at best. "Reach out," "touch," or "grope" is the first aorist optative *psēlaphēseian* (ψηλαφήσειαν). "Find" is the present optative *heuroien* (εὕροιεν). Basically, Paul is not actually allowing for the success of the venture.

acterization of the temples and altars he already has referenced at the beginning of his address. Yet, while not successful, the groping effort itself is instructive, because the idolatry that is the inevitable result at least shows an innate sense of accountability.

Revelation: God the Judge (17:30–31). The first revelation of the "unknown god" Paul now is unveiling to the Athenians is that God is creator. This revelation has a dual thrust by indicating that God has creative purpose and humans thereby are rendered accountable. The second revelation of the "unknown god" Paul is proclaiming is that God is judge. God has overlooked "times of human ignorance," such as thinking Epimenides really was the hero of Athens who staved off the plague with his mindless ritual of meandering sheep or that God could be slandered as having the unholy characteristics of a Zeus who populates Mount Olympus with his erotic encounters, so calling him "father" would be incumbent on many in a most literal way. This "unknown god" no longer is unknown. Ignorance no longer is bliss. This God now "commands all people everywhere to repent" of such ignorance, which would include Athenian philosophers (17:30). Since ignorance is the cardinal Greek sin, the call for repentance presses the hot button of Greek conscience.

Paul then declares that the God who is judge and calls for repentance has "fixed a day" (17:31). An appointed end conceptualizes time as linear. Philosophically, such an idea would be incompatible with a Greek worldview. Greeks thought of time as cyclical.[18] So, the first strike against Paul here at the end is the concept of time he is presenting. While the contrary philosophy of time would be difficult enough for the Athenians to stay with Paul's argument, the torpedo blowing up the whole speech is resurrection. God has proven this fixed point in time and its related judgment by raising from the dead "a man whom he has appointed" (17:31).[19] Mention of resurrection would have been either repugnant or simply inconceivable to the Greeks in his audience, most certainly undesirable. Greeks so separated soul and body dichotomously that they had to invoke a dualistic philosophy of anthropology to

[18]The basis of their term "age" or "eon." One age simply cycles into another. Time does not end.

[19]Paul is oddly oblique in his expression, "a man whom he has appointed." One might have expected actual reference to "Jesus" here. Jesus is the fundamental core of the gospel story, which is not about an idea but a person.

sustain the construct, when even basic human consciousness by default is antithetical to dualism. (Notice how with the use of "I" any person is making internal reference to just one reality at one time.)

Sermon Result (17:32–34). Some of his listeners scoffed immediately, while others put him off to later, which might not have been much better (17:32). Luke concludes this dramatic scene with a notably short, anticlimactic, "Paul left them" (17:33). The sum total of the mission effort in Athens was meager. First, we have the synagogue. Paul initially had argued in the synagogue, as was his custom (17:17). This effort probably met with little success. Luke is habited to pointing out Paul's synagogue successes, but says not a word at Athens. Paul also spoke in the market too, but we hear no report of any conversions. The import seems to be that Paul was having trouble getting traction anywhere in Athens. Results of the Areopagus address likewise are quite meager: Dionysius the Areopagite, a woman Damaris, and a few others (17:34). Basically, Athens was a tough nut to crack. While Paul did not "shake the dust off his sandals" as at Antioch of Pisidia (13:51), still, bluntly, "after this Paul left Athens" (18:1). No known church was established.

FIGURE 11.56. Athens Academy Mural: Paul's Areopagus Speech. Results in Athens were meager at best. Pictured are Dionysius the Areopagite, Damaris, and a few more.

Corinth (18:1–17)

Paul left Athens and went to Corinth. This movement is before Silas and Timothy have been able to rejoin him from Berea.

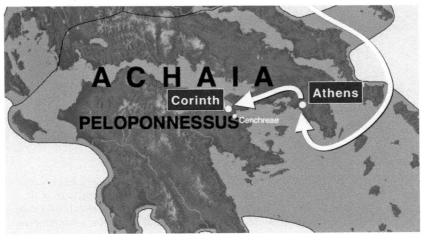

FIGURE 11.57. 2MJ—Greece: Corinth. Paul arrives in Corinth alone after Athens.

FIGURE 11.58. Gulf of Corinth from the Theater. Corinth was situated on an isthmus connecting mainland Greece with the Peloponnesus peninsula. Corinth was the harbor for maritime shipping between the Gulf of Corinth servicing the Ionian Sea on the west to the Aegean Sea on the east. The method was portage across the isthmus. Ships were unloaded on one side, hoisted out of the water, dragged along rolling beams to the other side, hoisted back into the water, and cargo reloaded.

FIGURE 11.59. Corinth Theater. The theater at Corinth is in a poor state of preservation. The Acrocorinth is in the background. The sunken cavea (seating area) of the theater is center right. The street accessing the theater paved with funds provided by the patron Erastus, the city treasurer, is in the foreground. The Erastus inscription is between the two poles.

FIGURE 11.60. Erastus Inscription. The name Erastus who paid for paving the street leading to the theater is in the top line: ERASTVS-PRO-AEDILIT[at]E, "Erastus, Pro-aedile." The aedile supervised public works and oversaw organization of festivals and games (cf. Dio *History* 49.43). Career-minded politicians sought the office. Of the three New Testament references to an Erastus (Acts 19:22; Rom 16:23; 2 Tim 4:20), one sends greetings to Rome as the "city treasurer" (Rom 16:23), but Paul uses the term *oikonomos*. Romans likely is written from Corinth on the 3MJ. The inscription is pre-AD 50 (Shear, "Excavations," 525), so connection of the inscription to the Erastus of Rom 16:23 is quite possible, but debated. For a judicious summary with open possibilities, cf. Clarke, *Secular and Christian Leadership in Corinth*, 47–56.

FIGURE 11.61. Meat Market Inscription. This inscription is the building of the Roman meat and fish market (macellum) at Corinth by one of the most prestigious families of Rome, the Cornelii family, between 27 BC to AD 14. Paul deals with the problem of meat sacrificed to idols in 1 Cor 8:1–13 and 10:27–29 (AMAC).

FIGURE 11.62. Synagogues in Corinth. The inscription above identifies a "synagogue of the Hebrews" at Corinth. The relief at right shows the seven-branched lampstand modeled on the pure gold tabernacle menorah of Moses later put in the temple, one of the most ancient symbols of Judaism (AMAC).

FIGURE 11.63. Apollo Temple at Corinth. One of the oldest temples of Greece, the Apollo temple had been standing five centuries by the time Paul visited Corinth. Built around 540 BC, the Doric columns are monolithic, cut from single pieces of limestone. The temple stands on the highest terrace of the city with a commanding view.

FIGURE 11.64. Periene Fountain. Artist's depiction of the famous fountain built over a natural spring still flowing today and at the end of the Laechean Road running into ancient Corinth from the port.

FIGURE 11.65. Laechean Road. This road was the main avenue into ancient Corinth from the Laechean port servicing the Gulf of Corinth. The road leads directly into the Roman forum and the bema area. The Acrocorinth citadel is in the background.

FIGURE 11.66. The Bema at Corinth. The bema is a rostrum area for addressing an assembly. If this construction is middle first century, this area would have been where Paul appeared before Gallio the proconsul in Acts 18:12.

FIGURE 11.67. Corinth Odeon. An odeon is a theater for smaller venues and more intimate performances. According to Philostratus, the odeon at Corinth was built by the same Herod Atticus who built the odeon on the Acropolis at Athens.

FIGURE 11.68. West Shops of Corinth. This row of shops located west of the west forum temples had a broad central staircase leading up from the forum level framed on both sides by six piece Corinthian colonnades. This construction dates to the third quarter of the first century AD, about the time Paul was in Corinth.

FIGURE 11.69. Dionysius Mosaic. Exquisite Roman mosaic that adorned the home of a second-century AD Roman villa in Corinth (AMAC).

FIGURE 11.70. South Stoa of Corinth. This two story office and shop complex was remodeled under Augustus into a major urban area including baths and latrines. One suggestion is that officials had office space in the South Stoa, including duovirs, the aediles (like Erastus), the Senate, and an official of the Isthmian Games. The road (left) Paul took to Cenchreae led out of the South Stoa.

FIGURE 11.71. Gallio Inscription. An inscription found at the temple of Apollo in Delphi, Greece records a letter from emperor Claudius to the proconsul Gallio and is preserved in nine fragments. The dated inscription provides a frame for dating Gallio's proconsulship, and, hence, the time of Paul's appearance before Gallio's tribunal in Corinth in Acts 18:12–17. The name of Gallio, ΓΑΛΛΙΩ, is shown in the enlargement (AMD).

FIGURE 11.72. Bronze Mirror. This bronze mirror dating to 475–450 BC shows the use of polished bronze as mirrors for centuries in the ancient world. As one of the great trade cities situated strategically on important trade routes both east and west, Corinth long was famous for its pottery and bronze works, but particularly for its polished bronze mirrors. Due to its favorable location and its own skilled craftsmen, Corinth became a trade and commercial powerhouse that distinguished this city almost uniquely in the ancient world. Paul refers to looking into a bronze mirror in his comments to the Corinthians in 1 Cor 13:12 (NAMA).

History (18:1–3). Corinth's history is defined by its location. The city was located strategically commercially and militarily. The city was a crossroads to important trade routes. From north to south were the Peloponnese land routes connecting the Peloponnese to the central and northern mainland, linking the important cities of Sparta, Corinth, Athens and Delphi. East and west were the major sea routes through two ports, one at Lechaeum on the Gulf of Corinth to the Ionian Sea, and the other at Cenchreae on the Saronic Gulf to the Aegean Sea. Situated fortuitously, Corinth naturally became a commercial and trade power-house. Her most famous products through the centuries were pottery and bronze, but pride of place went to the Corinthian bronze mirrors.

One almost could say this commercial profile was so strong at Corinth as to create a distinctive social profile, because Corinth had a disproportionate number of businessmen and craftsmen in its population. Workshops and guilds dominated the social structure of the city, creating a near "middle class" unlike almost anywhere else in the empire. Corinth's distinctive business climate sets the stage for Aquila and Priscilla migrating over to Corinth to set up shop after the edict of

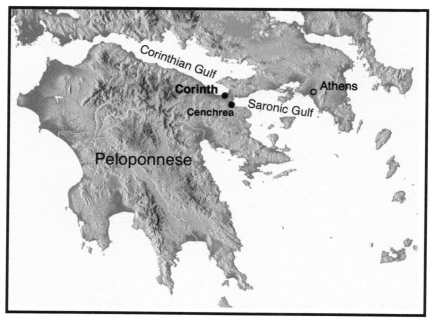

FIGURE 11.73. Corinth's Strategic Commercial Location. Corinth was well situated for both land and seafaring trade.

Claudius had forced them from Rome. Likely, Aquila and Priscilla both were Jewish believers in Jesus as Messiah in one of the synagogues in Rome. Recently arrived in Corinth, they encountered another craftsman of the same trade and a Christian as well, whose name was Paul. They formed a business partnership (18:2–3). A typical place for them to have rented space would have been in the West Shops. Here, they would have had regular contact with the inhabitants of the city that would have afforded opportunity for sharing the gospel in an informal setting of daily life.

FIGURE 11.74. Gold Coin of Claudius (41–54). The emperor ejected Jews from Rome in AD 49 due to synagogue disturbances related to one called "Chrestus" (PMB).

Corinth's military history was defined by its location as well. The city was a rival of Athens in politics, commerce, and as a naval power.

Corinth's defining moment, however, came not with Athens but with Rome. Corinth, with other powerful Greek city states, participated in the disastrous revolt against Rome by the Achaean League. In 146 BC, the Roman general Mummius finally leveled the city to the ground, slaughtered all Greek males, and sold Greek women and children into slavery. Corinth lay in destruction, uninhabited, for a century.

However, the strategic character of its location caused Julius Caesar to decide to revive the city back from its ruins in 44 BC. Caesar Romanized Corinth. He gave the city Roman colony status and resettled the area with freedmen from Italy, so gave Corinth Roman culture and society. The city soon regained its former importance and status and began to reassert itself as a commercial powerhouse by once again controlling land and sea trade. This commerce gave Corinth an unusually robust market economy, but also generated an atypical social structure of almost a "middle class" of artisans and merchants almost unparalleled in ancient cities. Since business attracts people, oriental and Greek immigrants moved in, generating a social melting pot of multiple languages and religions. Religious excess was not uncom-

FIGURE 11.75. Julius Caesar (49–44 BC). Restored Corinth and her good fortunes as a city (AMAC).

mon, including Bacchic frenzy rites with their mantic behavior, convulsive seizures, and babbling supposedly marking possession by the god for those spiritually capable. Corinth became notorious for sexual license due to cultic prostitution, especially at the shrine of Aphrodite. Corinth was named capital of the province of Achaia in 27 BC, only seventeen years after coming back from total destruction.

Corinth's unusual social structure changed typical social dynamics of ancient society. Patron-client relationships that were so dominant and controlling elsewhere were not as dominant in Corinth. Power was redistributed away from individuals and more toward special-interest groups, such as merchant guilds. Such groups advance self-interests at the expense of others, potentially fostering factionalism and disunity. These are the social dynamics Paul will have to negotiate at Corinth.

So Paul practiced his trade at Corinth like a good rabbi.[20] His rabbinic heritage expresses itself in the idea that a good rabbi did not charge the congregation. He would be self-employed. Paul's practicing a trade, however, was problematic in his Hellenistic setting. Worthy philosophers (for so he would be understood in a Greco-Roman context)[21] had financial sponsors. A patron was willing to invest in a phi-

losopher who was worthy to be heard. In contrast, a working philosopher was not really a worthy philosopher. Fortunately, he had refugees from Rome to join with him as co-laborers. So Paul worked in the market in one of the shops, which was a mission habit.[22]

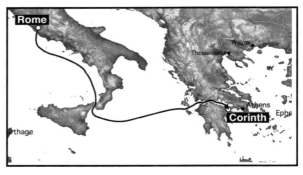

FIGURE 11.76. Aquila and Priscilla: Rome to Corinth. Forced out of Rome by the edict of Claudius in AD 49, this couple sets up shop in Corinth, where they meet Paul.

Paul's Synagogue Activity (18:4–8). Another mission habit is synagogue first, if present. Jesus as Messiah is a synagogue message (18:4). Only Jews were expecting an eschatological figure called "Messiah." At the same time, the synagogue is where gentile "God-fearers" could be found. So, the synagogue also affords Paul opportunity to express a call as "a light for revelation to the gentiles." The synagogue pattern holds as true here in Corinth as anywhere: Gentiles respond, Jews resist. Synagogue opposition causes Paul to pronounce an "anathema" judgment, after which he shift focus to gentiles. This judgment corresponds to the

[20]Paul's trade is unclear. The term Luke uses in 18:3, *skēnopoios* (σκηνοποιός), has no qualifier in the Greek text, so is indeterminate. Etymologically, the meaning is clear. The term means "maker of stage properties," as in theatrical productions. That sense, however, seems indecorous for a Jew, given Jewish attitudes to the theatrical stage. So, efforts to explain the term substitute anything that skirts around the clear etymological sense. Thus, in fact, the "tentmaker" and "leatherworker" traditions in modern English translations have little basis and disguise serious problems. Consult the BDAG lexicon.

[21]Agreeing with Wright, *Paul and the Faithfulness of God*, 1359–62.

[22]Acts 20:34; 1 Cor 9:3–8; 2 Cor 11:7; 1 Thess 2:9; 2 Thess 3:8.

action of shaking the dust off their sandals at Antioch of Pisidia (13:51). That is, the anathema is a pronouncement locally on the Corinth synagogue, not a universal indictment and abandonment of further Jewish preaching in any synagogue. Paul did speak of blood guilt for those who resisted the gospel with his dire warning: "Your blood be

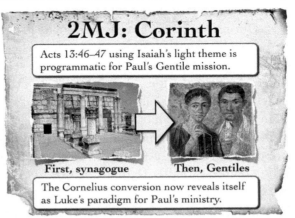

FIGURE 11.77. Light for the Gentiles: Corinth.

on your own heads" (18:6)! This theme echoes the implicit confession of the Sanhedrin to Peter: "You intend to bring this man's blood upon us" (5:28). The fact is, Jesus died. His blood is on someone's hands. The issue is eschatological. This decision about the death of Jesus impacts the future. As Paul had told the Athenians: "God has fixed a day in which he will judge the world in righteousness by a man whom he has appointed" (17:31). Ironically, Paul moves to the house of Titius Justus, a "God-fearer," who apparently lived right next door to the synagogue (18:7). Specifically pointed out as a "God-fearer," Titius Justice would be the Cornelius paradigm that Luke has established, a role Lydia also fulfilled in Philippi.

One distinctive of the synagogue experience at Corinth is that Paul gains significant synagogue leadership. Crispus, the synagogue ruler (*archisunagōgos*, ἀρχισυνάγωγος), and all of his household became believers (18:8). They all were baptized.[23] One would presume that this Crispus was followed in succession by Sosthenes, since Sosthenes later was the synagogue ruler attacked by the Corinthian crowd after the failed attempt to accuse Paul before Gallio (18:17). However, since a

---

[23]But only Crispus, Gaius, and the household of Stephanas by Paul himself (1 Cor 1:14–16).

synagogue could have multiple rulers, Sosthenes already might have been in this position along with Crispus.[24]

During this time of Paul's synagogue preaching, Silas and Timothy arrived from Macedonia (18:5). Last we heard, they were in Berea (17:14). Apparently they had instructions to retrace their steps back to other Macedonian cities, and that movement is why Luke says more generally "Macedonia" in 18:5 and not specifically "Berea."[25] Paul had been forced out of Philippi, Thessalonica, and Berea after only brief visits, so he had left these associates behind to minister. One would presume this return activity in Macedonia would be similar to the action on the 1MJ after Derbe. The stays in each of these cities of both missionary journeys really had not been long due to persecution and synagogue resistance, so the stability of these new churches probably would be tenuous.

If we allow a bit of Pauline correspondence into the Acts storyline, Timothy's return to Paul in Corinth at this time brings good news from Macedonia (1 Thess 3:6). Paul first had brought good news to Thessalonica, so now, he gets good news in return. So, good news can be a two-way street. The

Acts	Letter	From	Date
JC	Galatians	?	?
2MJ	1 Thess 2 Thess	Corinth	50
3MJ	"Previous Letter" 1 Corinthians "Harsh Letter" 2 Corinthians Romans	Ephesus Ephesus Ephesus Macedonia Corinth	55 55 56 56 57
Rome	Colossians Philemon Ephesians Philippians	Rome Rome Rome Rome	60 60 60 62

FIGURE 11.78. Pauline Correspondence: 1–2 Thessalonians.

church at Thessalonica not only is surviving, they are thriving (1 Thess 1:7). Paul responds to Timothy's report with 1 Thessalonians.

[24]Curiously, a Sosthenes is coauthor of 1 Corinthians with Paul (1 Cor 1:1), written from Ephesus on the 3MJ. We cannot ascertain connection with the Sosthenes of Acts 18:17, but probably should leave open the possibility.

[25]Information in 1 Thess 3:1–2 indicates Timothy's activity back in Thessalonica. Silas we do not know about, but, potentially, he could have returned to Philippi while Timothy was in Thessalonica.

Paul's Corinth Vision (18:9–11). We have been wondering about the Macedonian experience all the way. The sum total of this 2MJ is persecution and forced departures everywhere, and even laughed out of Athens. Wondering whether a vision had been interpreted correctly would be natural at this point. Paul's Corinth vision has two purposes.

First, the Corinth vision reassures Paul of divine protection. God had used an earthquake to get Paul out of prison in Philippi, so God is not unaware of Paul's circumstances and difficulties. These difficulties have purpose in the divine will. In fact, God will bless Paul's stay at Corinth with longevity, of which Paul sorely is short on this 2MJ. Paul is told to speak and not be silent, to be bold and courageous, because "no one will lay a hand on you to harm you" (18:10), an allusion to the beating with rods at Philippi and an anticipation of the Gallio tribunal to come shortly. The very next verse indicates that Paul "stayed there a year and six months" (18:11). This eighteen-month stay in Corinth is Paul's longest residence to date in Acts, even longer than the original twelve months with Barnabas in Antioch (11:26).

Second, the Corinth vision is a reaffirmation of the Troas vision. Thus, Philippi: run out; Thessalonica: run out; Berea: run out; Athens: laughed out; so, Corinth is what? We have a sense of Paul's thinking, because he admits in his own correspondence to them that he arrived in Corinth in trepidation (1 Cor 2:3). What of the Troas vision? Has the Macedonian call been aborted? Macedonia was such a brief and problematic time, and that province already is history. What could he expect now in Corinth? If Paul entertained any doubts of the Troas vision due to the adverse circumstances since then, God now lays those to rest. He assures Paul that he has "many in this city who are my people" (18:10). Thus, either many Corinthian believers already are in the city to be gathered and taught, or Paul will have many converts.

Paul's Corinth vision is fulfilled two ways. First, Paul has the longest ministry in Corinth than he has had anywhere else. Second, Gallio immediately dismisses the case brought against Paul. By now in the text in Acts we can observe that Luke is using Paul's visions to show fulfillment of Joel's last days prophecy as quoted by Peter at Pentecost: "and your young men shall see visions" (2:17). Remember that when Luke first introduced Saul into the narrative of Acts, he characterizes him as a "young man" ("and the witnesses laid their coats at the feet of a young man named Saul," 7:58).

So, was the Macedonian call a "wash out"? No, not if one takes a long view. Philippi became one of Paul's most beloved churches, generous to him in both money and personnel throughout his ministry, even at the end. Thessalonica became Paul's most aggressively evangelistic church. Berea celebrates Paul's Macedonian vision to this very day. Corinth became one of Paul's most dynamically gifted churches, spiritually eclipsing by far and away its perennial rival Athens.

Paul Before Gallio (18:12–17). The Gallio inscription from Delphi is dated in Claudius's twenty-sixth acclamation, which was January to July, AD 52. This inscrip-

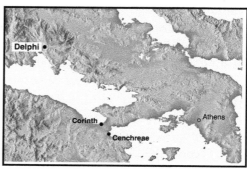

tion mentions Gallio, the proconsul of Achaia, so interlocks with Paul's appearance before Gallio relative to the time of Gallio's accession to his office. Luke will use this appearance as an apologetic. Gallio's elite status and imperial connections in Rome will mean

FIGURE 11.79. Delphi, Greece.

his decision with Paul here at Corinth will set precedent for other proconsuls across the empire. Gallio was a member of a famous family

in Rome. His own father was Seneca the Elder, famous rhetorician, and his brother also was a famous Stoic philosopher, Seneca the Younger. Due to his inherited social status, Gallio's forceful decision will be

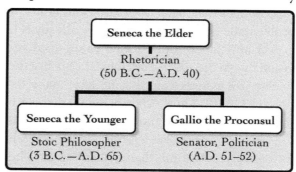

FIGURE 11.80. Gallio's Famous Family in Rome.

vital to Paul's future mission across the empire.

The charge against Paul is propagating a new religion. If Gallio took the bait, Paul would lose legality for his mission in Roman eyes. Gallio, however, was no proconsul with whom to trifle. He recognized the subterfuge in the charge immediately, and dismissed the case on the spot as no Roman matter at all. (Contrast Felix in Caesarea!) Since the source of the complaint was the synagogue, Gallio determined instantly the matter was an internal Jewish affair, and flatly told them so. Once again, social disruption from Christian preaching Luke shows is synagogue instigated and not native to the Christian message.

Sosthenes, the synagogue ruler, was beaten by the crowd in mob reaction. Unclear is whether this action is also an internal Jewish affair among Jews humiliated publicly at Gallio's quick remonstrance, and taking out their embarrassment and frustration on their own synagogue ruler, or the gentile crowd assembled at the bema reading the proconsul's signals of negative Jewish attitude and responding accordingly—conveniently overlooked by Gallio.

Gallio's positive decision on Paul's behalf finally overcomes the stigma of the charges at Philippi of preaching "customs not legal for Romans to adopt or practice" (16:21) and at Thessalonica of preaching "against the decrees of Caesar" (17:7). In this important judicial action, Gallio completely absolves Paul such that Paul regains his own honor in Roman society. The final results of Gallio's tribunal are four-fold.

- *Christian mission:* high positive impact, setting precedent for other Roman provinces

- *Mission charges:* charges at Philippi and Thessalonica decisively rejected and the Pauline mission exonerated

- *Political apologetic:* synagogue agitators are the culprit of public disturbances; Christianity no real threat to Rome

- *Paul's appeal:* the positive response from Gallio at Corinth might set the stage for Paul's willingness later to appeal to Caesar (Bruce)

2MJ Conclusion (18:18–22)

Cenchreae Vow (18:18)

After eighteen months, Paul leaves Corinth with Priscilla and Aquila.[26] They depart Corinth through the South Stoa, which is cut by the road leading southeast to Cenchreae. Taking Priscilla and Aquila along with him as Paul departs Corinth means that their fortuitous business deal

---

[26]Priscilla is mentioned first, which implies a leadership role.

that initially had motivated the relationship quietly has transformed into a relationship of trusted mission associates.[27]

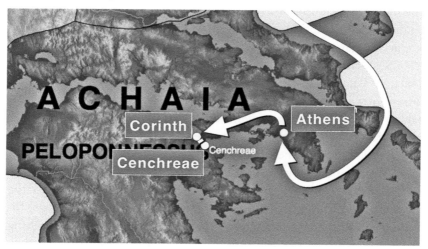

FIGURE 11.81. 2MJ—Return: Cenchreae. The Aegean port connected to Corinth.

At Cenchreae, Paul shaves his hair. Some unknown private vow of a Jewish nature has been fulfilled.[28] While Luke is not specific about the exact nature of the vow, his narrative purpose for mentioning the vow is clear. With this Jewish vow, Luke intends to form a narrative *inclusio* over the entire 2MJ using the decrees of the Jerusalem Conference. *The 2MJ has lived out the conference decrees.* Thus, Paul has not required gentiles to become observant Jews to be saved, nor has he asked observant Jews to become gentiles to be social. So, Paul affirms that Jewishness is a matter of heritage not holiness, and "gentileness" is a matter of sensitivity, not separation. Luke attests to Paul's agreement with the conference decrees *and* continuing Jewishness both at the beginning of the 2MJ in having Timothy circumcised at Lystra (16:3) and at the end in Paul's own Jewish vow at Cenchreae (18:18).

---

[27]Although the exact sequence is unknowable, apparently Priscilla and Aquila wind up back in Rome. One could assume this movement would be facilitated by the death of Claudius, since all imperial decrees are rescinded at the death of the emperor. Being back in Rome seems to be indicated in Paul's greetings to Prisca and Aquila at the end of his letter to the Romans; in those greetings, Paul calls them, "my fellow-workers in Messiah Jesus" (Rom 16:3).

[28]The vow possibly could be related to a covenant with God as a result of the Corinth vision after the vision's fulfillment in the Gallio tribunal.

Ephesus Preparation (18:19–21)

Paul winds up in Ephesus where he wanted to go at the beginning of the 2MJ journey, but was blocked by the Spirit (16:6).[29] Ephesus was the capital of the province of Asia with a large Jewish population. That Paul would want to go there is perfectly reasonable.

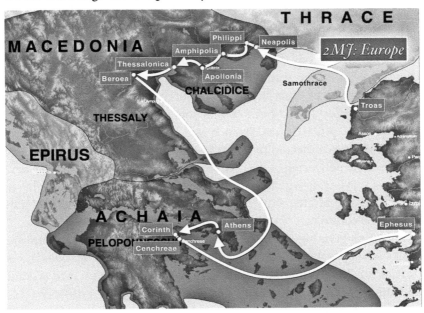

FIGURE 11.82. 2MJ—Return: Ephesus. Paul is back to where he first wanted to go.

Leaving Priscilla and Aquila behind is another signal of his original intentions for Ephesus at the beginning of the 2MJ. Priscilla and Aquila do advance work to prepare for an anticipated visit by Paul. He makes an initial foray into the synagogue (18:19). They ask him to stay longer. He declines (18:20). He indicates a desire to return; however, this time around, in stark contrast to the beginning of the 2MJ, Paul is forthright. He rightly concedes, "if God wills" (18:21). This condition is a key signal of Paul's change in attitude since the beginning of the 2MJ. Paul has learned his lesson: Mission with no mandate is no mission. With this word on God's will, Luke has shown that Paul has submitted to the will of God on the timing for Ephesus. In a way, the 2MJ was as

---

[29]The text at 16:6 indicates more generally simply "Asia," but the high likelihood of the intention is being expressed now by this present stopover by Paul in Ephesus.

much a spiritual journey into God's will for Paul as into the Roman provinces of Europe. Stay tuned for the journey to Rome!

Greeting Jerusalem (18:22–23)

Luke is very brief, compressing much time, so moving the narrative on. Paul finally reaches his last stops. He disembarks at Caesarea, the chief Mediterranean port of Judea, and then goes up to Jerusalem to greet the church there, then finally "down" to Antioch.

This greeting of the Jerusalem church is a new wrinkle, because the Antioch mission team did not report to Jerusalem at the end of the 1MJ, but rather to their sponsoring church of Antioch (14:26). Paul, however, has lost his Antioch connection over his fight with Barnabas. He no longer officially has Antioch as a sponsor. His only connection is Silas, who is connected to James in Jerusalem. Paul's last assignment had been the delivering of the conference decrees to Antioch, Syria, and Cilicia (15:22–23), which he had performed (16:4), and now he is reporting. The hidden story is Paul has no sponsorship. That problem is why the coming story of Ephesus will mean everything to Paul.

In this greeting of the Jerusalem church, Luke wants to indicate Paul's solidarity with Jerusalem, one of his clear literary agendas in his portrait of Paul. While others might have painted the picture of Paul and the Jerusalem church with different shades or even different colors (including Paul himself), Luke wants to say when the heat cools and the dust settles, more unity was present in these days than all the admitted contrariness between Paul and others otherwise would have suggested. Luke's main reason for thinking this is not because he unintelligently misunderstood or deliberately misrepresented Paul, or even was naively oblivious. Luke thinks this because, for Luke, the story of the church never was about James and Jerusalem, Barnabas and Antioch, or Paul and the gentiles. The story of the church was about the Spirit. Without the Spirit, neither James, nor Barnabas, nor Paul, nor even messianic Israel would have mattered in the least. The church's story always was about the Spirit taking the gospel to the uttermost parts of the earth, not James, or Barnabas, or Paul. That story is more in spite of everyone and everything than because of anyone or anything. In *that* story, Paul greeting Jerusalem is Luke's way of driving home a *divine perspective on the whole matter*, not human. God was more at work at the time than even the principals involved may have been aware.

We now know why when Luke reports that Paul spends time in Antioch, the ending is so decidedly anticlimactic. Nothing productive actually is reported. The whole atmosphere is so unlike the conclusion to the 1MJ (14:27). Luke drops the subtle hint that the winds in Antioch are changing. We can note that from this point, Paul simply goes "from place to place" (18:23). As at the beginning of the 2MJ after the fight with Barnabas, we are minus any official commissioning or send-off by laying on of hands. The relationship with Antioch quietly has changed. Paul's mission, in fact, is now missing a home base. Paul still suffers the consequences of the fight with Barnabas, even though the Holy Spirit is working with him. Yet, without a home base, the entire missionary enterprise is threatened.

SUMMARY

Once again, journey highlights are summarized as bullet points. The following are significant features of the 2MJ.

(1) Pauline fight
- Paul's fracture of the Antioch mission team
- Paul loses his Jerusalem connection and Antioch base
- Paul acquires a new Jerusalem connection through Silas
- Paul's efforts out of God's will
- Spirit opposes, boxes Paul in ("aimless in Asia")
- Sets up later issues with Paul's Jerusalem itinerary (3MJ)

(2) Decrees fulfillment
- Delivering the decrees through James's letter
- Fulfilling the decrees in 2MJ characters and actions
- Timothy joins at Lystra and is circumcised

(3) Troas vision
- Crucial for launching the real 2MJ
- Puts Paul back on track with God's will
- Gracious renewal of Damascus Road mandate
- Continental shift: Macedonian call to European mission
- First "we section" of Acts confirms Paul's vision as God's will

(4) Synagogue agitation
- Constantly dogs Paul's efforts among synagogue Jews
- Israel fails to fulfill Servant mission ("light for gentiles")
- Apologetic that public disturbance not caused by Paul

(5) Athens sermon
- Luke's second of three example sermons of Paul
- How Paul preaches to gentiles

(6) Edict of Claudius (AD 49)
- Thessalonica: background to "decrees of Caesar" charge?
- Corinth: explains presence of Aquila and Priscilla in Corinth

(7) "God-fearers" in Acts
- Core to Paul's gentile success, with Cornelius as paradigm
- At Philippi, Lydia; at Corinth, Titius Justus

(8) Corinth vision
- Reassures of divine protection, anticipating Gallio's tribunal
- Reaffirms the Troas vision

(9) Gallio's tribunal (AD 51–52)
- Gallio inscription at Delphi crucial for Pauline chronology
- Exoneration of slander at Philippi and at Thessalonica
- Christianity no threat to Rome

(10) Pauline churches
- Macedonia: Philippi, Thessalonica, Berea
- Greece: Corinth; Athens is questionable

(11) Pauline correspondence
- Corinth: 1–2 Thessalonians
- Timothy brings news from Macedonia
- Paul's interrupted mission work sets up context of letters

12

Third Missionary Journey

Ephesus (Acts 18–21)

Ephesus is the crown jewel of the Pauline missionary enterprise. No other mission station Paul ever attempted achieves the success and outstanding reputation and acclaim of Ephesus. Paul was firing on all pistons. Even surrounding areas were impacted as Paul's associates fanned out into the cities of the Lycus valley. The empowering Spirit was abundantly manifest in a plethora of miracles. Luke clearly has framed up Ephesus as the promise of Pentecost fulfilled, the prospect of Paul's new mission base, and the power of messianic Israel finally fulfilling Isaiah's Servant role of "light for revelation to the gentiles." Sound like a fairy tale? Almost. Never fear, Saul-Paul will reappear.

3MJ STATISTICS

Observations

The big secret about Paul that Luke suppresses in his account of the 3MJ is insinuated right in the list of statistics. A few other matters of curiosity also are aroused. One of these curiosities is Silas. Where is he? He has simply dropped out of the narrative completely, never to be heard from again. All through the 2MJ is the recurring "Paul and Silas" almost every step of the way from Antioch to Corinth. Then, at Corinth, the last little tidbit we get on Silas is his rejoining Paul in Corinth from Macedonia (18:5). After that mention, nothing. We do not even know if Silas actually left Corinth with Paul on the way to Ephesus. When and where he drops out we do not actually know, but Silas no longer is with Paul at the beginning of this 3MJ. So, we take due narrative notice about Paul's companions, just Timothy. (Luke joins in only after Ephesus on Paul's journey to Jerusalem at Philippi in 20:6). So, Barnabas served as the 1MJ connection to Jerusalem. Silas served as the 2MJ connection to Jerusalem. So, who is the 3MJ connection to Jerusalem?

3MJ Statistics

✤3MJ (Acts 18—21)
  ✤ Companions: Timothy, Luke, Others
  ✤ Date: 53–57, 4–5 years, 2500+ miles
  ✤ Provinces: Cilicia, Galatia, Asia, Macedonia, Achaia, Lycia, Cyprus
  ✤ Regions: Lycaonia, Pisidia, Phrygia, Lydia, Mysia, Judea
  ✤ Islands: Lesbos, Chios, Samos, Cos, Rhodes
  ✤ Cities: Ephesus, Corinth

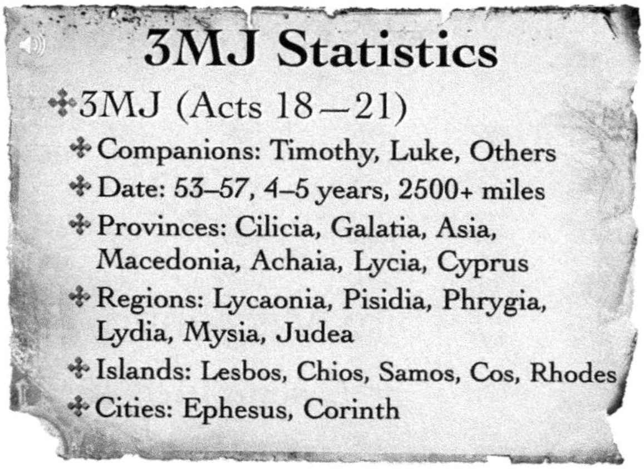

FIGURE 12.1. 3MJ Statistics.

We do not have one. Paul, so the matter seems, is without any connections at all. He has no connection to Jerusalem. He has no connection to Antioch. In a connection-structured, patron-client world, Paul is in a most precarious position for his mission. Luke, however, does drop a hint. Paul *does* have a connection. Paul left Corinth "accompanied by Priscilla and Aquila" (18:18). When he got to Ephesus, he "left them there" (18:19). So, we have Priscilla and Aquila doing preparatory work in Ephesus. But just what is their connection? Luke told us when he introduced them—Rome. Stay tuned.

Another item to notice about the companions is "others." What is this? This is a total mystery, at least in the Acts narrative itself. They are specified in 20:4: "He was accompanied by Sopater, son of Pyrrhus from Berea, by Aristarchus and Secundus from Thessalonica, by Gaius from Derbe, and by Timothy, as well as by Tychicus and Trophimus from Asia." The list here explodes with names. Paul never has had that many people with him ever. What in the world is this large entourage all about? Luke never says—and that is narratively significant. He acknowledges their presence, but never their purpose.

Finally, listing "cities" as Ephesus and Corinth, we are compressing. Ephesus actually is where Paul is almost all this time, nearly three years. So why do we call this a "journey"? He does go to Greece for the winter at the end, then heads to Jerusalem on a long trek, but one needs to be clear that most of this 3MJ is really just Ephesus. Along the way, Luke mentions in passing other cities, such as Antioch, Philippi, Troas, Assos, Mitylene, Miletus, Patara, Tyre, Ptolemais, Caesarea, and Jerusalem. His catalog of geographical details is impressive.

Mute Points

These 3MJ statistics raise questions both internal and external to the narrative. Some questions admittedly are provoked by an "insider's perspective." We are aware of what Paul himself reveals about this same period through his letters, particularly 1–2 Corinthians and Romans. This perspective shows four mute points in Luke's account. One of these will be significant to understanding Luke's story of Ephesus.

- *Corinthian crisis Paul endured.*[1] Paul is corresponding significantly with the church in Corinth during his time in Ephesus. We know of at least four letters he wrote during this time, two of them we have, two he mentions in the two we have. For example, Paul wrote, "For even if I made you sorry with my letter, I do not regret it (though I did regret it, for I see that I grieved you with that letter, though only briefly" (2 Cor 7:8). This letter, apparently written after 1 Cor but before 2 Cor, has been called the "sorrowful" or "painful letter." When all this information is put together, the impression Paul almost loses the Corinthian congregation at this time is hard to avoid, although he was the one who founded the church. They re-

Acts	Letter	From	Date
JC	Galatians	?	?
2MJ	1 Thess 2 Thess	Corinth	50
3MJ	"Previous Letter" 1 Corinthians "Harsh Letter" 2 Corinthians Romans	Ephesus Ephesus Ephesus Macedonia Corinth	55 55 56 56 57
Rome	Colossians Philemon Ephesians Philippians	Rome Rome Rome Rome	60 60 60 62

FIGURE 12.2. Pauline Correspondence: 1 Corinthians.

---

[1] 1 Cor 5:9; 7:1; 16:12; 2 Cor 2:1–13; 7:8; 12:14.

ject his authority and leadership even to the point in some way of publicly humiliating him. Luke says not a word of all this.

- *Extent of dangers Paul faced.*[2] The language could be purely metaphorical, but one wonders about Paul's ambiguous remark, "If with merely human hopes I fought with wild animals at Ephesus, what would I have gained by it? If the dead are not raised, 'Let us eat and drink, for tomorrow we die'" (1 Cor 15:32). More pressing, however, are the following comments, which do not seem metaphorical at all.

    > We do not want you to be unaware, brothers and sisters, of the affliction we experienced in Asia; for we were so utterly, unbearably crushed that we despaired of life itself. Indeed, we felt that we had received the sentence of death so that we would rely not on ourselves but on God who raises the dead. He who rescued us from so deadly a peril will continue to rescue us (2 Cor 1:8–11).

    Of these dangers, Luke says not a word.

- *Symbolic collection Paul gathered.*[3] During his time at Ephesus, Paul was gathering a collection from his churches for Jerusalem. "Now concerning the collection for the saints; you should follow the directions I gave to the churches of Galatia" (1 Cor 16:1). After he finally reconciled with the Corinthian congregation, Paul wrote two chapters trying to motivate them to catch up on their part in this collection effort, which had fallen behind (2 Cor 8–9). By the time of Romans, the collection was complete, and Paul was just about on his way to Jerusalem to make delivery: "So, when I have completed this, and have delivered to them what has been collected" (Rom 15:28). So important for Paul, yet Luke says not a word about the collection.

- *Spanish mission Paul planned.* When Paul wrote Romans, he shared major plans for a new mission thrust into Spain. Delivering the collection to Jerusalem was all that hindered him from this mission. Paul announced, "So, when I have completed this [the collection], and I have delivered to them what has been collected, I will set out by way of you to Spain" (Rom 15:28). Again, Luke says not a word.

[2] 1 Cor 15:32; 2 Cor 1:8–11.
[3] 1 Cor 16:1–4; 2 Cor 8–9; Rom 15:25–28.

EPHESIAN CROWN JEWEL

Paul moves through the "regions of Galatia and Phrygia" (18:23). One would presume this movement would be retracing the basic cities of the 1MJ where Paul would have connections, and then pushing on into the province of Asia from Antioch of Pisidia through the Phrygian region. The typical route would have taken him through the Lycus valley and into Ephesus. From Antioch, the distance was about 685 miles. He finally arrives in Ephesus, where he has wanted to go for quite some time (16:6) and had left Priscilla and Aquila (18:19). Odd that the tradition has been to call this a "missionary journey," since once Paul reaches Ephesus, he shows no intention of going anywhere else. Ephesus seems to become something of a permanent residence for Paul.

FIGURE 12.3. 3MJ—Asia: Ephesus. Luke does not mention specific cities, only that Paul went through the "regions of Galatia and Phrygia" (Acts 18:23).

Luke intends to leave the impression that Ephesus is the epitome of Paul's gentile mission work. In terms of sponsorship, Paul operates rather independently from the impression given by earlier narratives. He has no Jerusalem representative, as with Barnabas (1MJ) or Silas (2MJ), so he seems to be functioning on his own, almost like "Paul, incorporated." In terms of preaching, Paul is presented at the height of his

FIGURE 12.4. Ephesus: Curetes Street. The main marbled and colonnaded avenue leading from the upper city to the lower city and the Library of Celsus.

FIGURE 12.5. Ephesus: Library of Celsus. Façade of the library built as a mausoleum for the Roman senator Tiberius Julius Celsus Polemaeanus in AD 135 by his son, Gaius Julius Aquila, who was consul in AD 110. The library was built to hold 12,000 scrolls. A crypt below the library still holds the remains of Celsus.

persuasion and power. Ephesus is the antithesis of Athens. The extent of miracles performed is unparalleled. The extent of mission impact is

FIGURE 12.6. Ephesus: Terrace Homes. Palatial Roman villas spilled down the hillside onto Curetes Street. This view shows a peristyle courtyard with frescoed walls, mosaic floors, and marble columns. Ephesus was one of the wealthiest cities of the Roman empire, but suffered numerous earthquakes and river silting.

FIGURE 12.7. Ephesus: Horizon of Harbor Marshland. The Ephesian harbor had to be dredged due to silting of the river. Today the seacoast is several miles away.

unparalleled too, both locally and regionally. Even his associates apparently establish churches in the nearby Lycus valley area.[4] No other mission is described the way Luke describes Ephesus. Luke is setting up a dramatic narrative turn. Since Ephesus was one of the major cities of the Roman empire, the capital of the province competing with Smyrna

---

[4]Such as Epaphras; cf. Col 1:7; 4:12; Phlm 23.

FIGURE 12.8. Harbor Street of Ephesus. Ephesus was one of only three cities in the ancient world to have a lighted avenue with 50 huge street lamps, behind only Rome and Antioch. Harbor Street was 580 yards long, 12 yards wide, colonnaded all the way, lined with shops and statues of famous patrons, benefactors, and others. The street's western termination indicates the ancient shoreline of the Ephesian harbor.

FIGURE 12.9. Pollio Aqueduct of Ephesus. Built by one of the greatest patron families of Ephesus, the Pollio aqueduct supplied the main fountains of the city, financed by C. Sextilius Pollio, his wife Ofillia Bassa, and his son-in-law C. Offilius Proculus. The aqueduct was built during the reign of Augustus, so served the city during Paul's stay.

and Pergamum as the glory of Asia, renowned in her wealth, prestige, power, and influence, then Paul's preeminent and unparalleled success in this city was supposed to indicate the future of his gentile mission, had not the sticky matter of obstinate human will gotten in the way.

Ephesus Narratives

Luke will tell the story of Ephesian success with six narrative vignettes.

He first introduces Ephesus with his vignette on Apollos. In a quick succession he then relates five episodes on the topics of the Spirit, preaching, miracles, reputation, and impact to demonstrate the theme of how truly extraordinary was Paul's Ephesian mission. The stories

Ephesus Narratives		
Introductory	Apologetics	Apollos (18:24–28)
Episodic Narratives Theme: Extraordianry	Spirit	Disciples (19:1–7)
	Preaching	Tyrannus (19:8–10)
	Miracles	Diseases (19:11–12)
	Reputation	Seven Sons (19:13–17)
	Impact	Burning (19:18–20)

FIGURE 12.10. Ephesus Narratives. An introduction plus five episodic narratives tell how extraordinary was Paul's Ephesian ministry, the crown jewel of his gentile mission.

cumulatively make the point that Luke intends to present this Ephesian ministry as the crown jewel of the Pauline gentile mission in Acts.

Apollos: Apologetics (18:24–28)

Luke indicates that he is using the Apollos story to launch the Ephesian saga because he links Paul's arrival in Ephesus with the ministry of this Apollos in Corinth after Priscilla and Aquila developed Apollos and commissioned him to Corinth (19:1). This temporal link is the literary clue that the Apollos vignette introduces Paul in Ephesus.

Apollos is a Jew from Alexandria, so probably Hellenistic in outlook, and "taught accurately the things concerning Jesus" (18:25), but he knew only John's baptism. The "baptism of John" makes him pre-Pentecost. He speaks in the synagogue, Paul's venue, which is where Priscilla and Aquila hear him. The couple have to explain "the Way of God more accurately to him" (18:26). So how can one understand the things of Jesus accurately but still need the way of God explained even "more accurately"? Apollo's knowledge is pre-Pentecost, so he knows about Jesus and the resurrection, but not Jesus and the Spirit that creates and empowers messianic Israel. That he is instructed further by Priscilla and Aquila not only means that he gets a view of Pentecost and Jesus and the Spirit, but he also gets the Pauline perspective on Pentecost, which is the voice of the Hellenist movement best represented in

Stephen's preaching, followed by Philip's missionizing, climaxing in the Damascus Road. After ministering for a year and a half with Paul in Corinth, Priscilla and Aquila are well versed in the Pauline gospel that epitomizes the Hellenist movement. This relationship probably is part of the reason for Paul's positive reception when he gets to Rome.

Apollos wanted to go to Achaia, perhaps at the encouragement of Priscilla and Aquila, because he winds up in Corinth (19:1). He greatly helps believers there, arriving with a letter of recommendation from the believers in Ephesus. He powerfully refutes Jews "in public," probably meaning not in the synagogue. Paul already himself had had to move to the home of Titius Justus (18:7).

Why introduce Ephesus with this Apollos prequel? Luke wants to indicate his awareness of other notable preachers of the church. Apollos has skill, rhetorical eloquence, scriptural knowledge, and powerful apologetics arguing for the Christian faith. Luke knows Paul is not the only preacher in the church. Indeed, other preachers have stories full of power and purpose. Their stories, however, do not tell the story Luke is telling. Luke does not follow Apollos because Apollos does not tell the story of the Hellenist movement. Paul is the fulfillment of the Hellenist movement. This movement defined the future of Christianity for Luke ("they first were called Christians at Antioch") because this movement facilitated messianic Israel's role as Isaiah's Servant to bring "a light for revelation to the gentiles" as Simeon had prophesied to Jesus's parents (Luke 2:32).

Paul is not the only early apologist, but he is the preeminent trailblazer of the gentile mission, and without need of special instruction. Apollos had great learning, as Paul, and great ability to confute opponents, as Paul, but Apollo's story is not the story of "light for the Gentiles." In the early church, Paul's mission best tells that story for Luke.

Disciples: Spirit (19:1–7)

Luke uses the John the Baptist disciples to indicate the *extraordinary Spirit* that accompanied Paul in Ephesus. The John the Baptist disciples had made ready for the coming of Messiah with John's baptism of repentance, but John's baptism was only preparatory. Jesus's baptism is the empowering Spirit, so the difference between John and Jesus is Pentecost. Paul instructs these disciples, pointing out their deficiency regarding baptism, parallel to Priscilla and Aquila instructing Apollos more fully. Paul lays on hands, which shows he independently acts like the apostles (6:6), Peter and John (8:17), Ananias (9:12), and even the church at Antioch (13:3). The recipients speak in tongues, which is an intratextual echo of Pentecost (2:3) to show that the power working in Paul is the original Spirit of Pentecost that launched messianic Israel on her world mission. Speaking in tongues also reimages significant points of advance in the Hellenist movement, as with the Cornelius household (10:46). Pentecost waves keep undulating to the outer shorelines of Acts. That Paul's recipients also receive the gift of prophecy is targeted to amplify the Pentecost theme, because Joel had said that one of the signs of the last days would be the prophetic spirit poured out upon all (2:18). So, these prophets now in Ephesus will fulfill roles helpful to the church and her ministry on the pattern of Agabus predicting famine to allow Antioch to prepare and send famine relief funds to help out believers in Judea (11:28).

With the these Baptist disciples, Paul functions in ways that show all the standard manifestations of the presence and power of the Spirit. He is doing in one person what Peter, John, Agabus, and others were doing all combined together. Paul in Ephesus is a Spirit dynamo in full concord with the work of the Spirit in world mission advance.

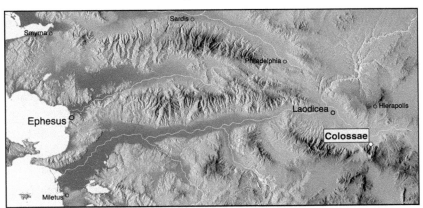

FIGURE 12.11. Colossae Map. The church at Colossae likely was established by Epaphras, one of Paul's associates of the Ephesian campaign (cf. Col 1:7; 4:12; Phlm 23).

Tyrannus: Preaching (19:8–10)

Luke uses the lecture hall of Tyrannus work to show the *extraordinary preaching* of Paul in Ephesus. Paul proves himself as one of the greatest

FIGURE 12.12. Colossae Tel. Colossae sat at the foot of Mount Cadmus, supplied by cool and refreshing snowmelt waters.

FIGURE 12.13. Colossae Excavation. Colossae never has been excavated. Artifacts, pottery, even an inscription, lie exposed on the surface. Credit: Jean M. Stevens.

evangelists. Luke's indication of the results after two years of preaching is astounding: "so that all those in Asia heard the word of the Lord Jesus" (19:10). The Tyrannus lecture hall is the antithesis of the Areopagus. No being laughed out of town in Ephesus! Also note the difference from the story in Macedonia—no constantly being run out of town like an imperial renegade on the lam. The tribunal of Gallio saw to that. Further, Paul is reaching more than a city. Through Ephesus, Paul is reaching an entire province, probably through associates such as Epaphras.

Paul does not even have to move for the gospel to penetrate entire regions. Hold that thought.

Diseases: Miracles (19:11–12)

Luke uses the cure of diseases and other wonderful deeds to show the *extraordinary miracles* of Paul in Ephesus. Miracles and exorcisms, plentiful and marvelous, more than with any other person, cause Paul to stand out in bold relief against other characters of Acts in his work at Ephesus. Paul undeniably has incredible access to the miracle-working power of God. Would Simon the Samaritan ever be envious!

Seven Sons: Reputation (19:13–17)

Luke uses the seven sons of Sceva to show the *extraordinary reputation* of Paul in Ephesus. Seven sons of a purported Jewish high priest, Sceva, are imposing their charlatan cheap tricks on the Ephesian population. The story echoes with Simon in Samaria. They attempt to add another "power name" to their incantation rituals by invoking the "Jesus whom Paul preaches" for an exorcism. First, that the pretenders would think to add this name of Jesus to their bucket list shows how Paul's reputation has grown in Ephesus more than anywhere else he ever has worked. Second, Luke brings in the humor. The evil spirit responds to these seven sons, "Jesus I know, and Paul I know, but who are you?" (19:15). Classic. Then the spirit supercharges the possessed person to overpower all seven sons, with the final humiliating line, "they fled out of the house naked and wounded" (19:16). After the reader finishes chuckling at the scene just described, suddenly a stunning thought floods in: *Paul here receives acknowledgement by the forces of evil on par with Jesus.* That kind of respect on the part of the world of evil for the work of Paul is incredible. No other disciple in Acts ever is accorded that kind of spiritual status. The glory went to Jesus: "When this became known to the Jews and Greeks living in Ephesus, they were all seized with fear, and the name of the Lord Jesus was held in high honor" (19:17).

Book Burning: Impact (19:18–20)

Luke uses the burning of the magical books to show the *extraordinary impact* of Paul in Ephesus. The episode here is the direct result of the seven sons of Sceva fiasco, which implicated all charlatans in Ephesus that their false practices would become public humiliation. Magic is renounced in mass, wholesale. A magic books bonfire sees the equivalent of 50,000 silver pieces rising up in smoke.[5] Any type of event like this would stun any community of the ancient world. Paul has had a truly devastating impact on belief in magic power. This impact is on another scale altogether from that indicated in Peter's

FIGURE 12.14. Tetradrachma Stash. Part of a hoard of 2,484 silver Ptolemaic tatradrachmas found below a mosaic floor in the House of Dionysius at ancient Paphos, Cyprus. The tetradrachma is one-fourth of a drachma (NAM).

encounter with the magician Simon Magus in Samaria (8:17–24).

A fifth progress report seals the deal (19:20). Ephesus is Pentecost abundance, the apex of gentile mission. Six narratives drive home that Ephesus is the crown jewel of the Pauline missionary enterprise, unsurpassed in success, without peer in comparison. Ephesus is where gentile mission was heading until Paul himself got in the way. Paul represents both Stephen speech themes: God active, God resisted.

EPHESIAN COLLAPSE

The Ephesian mission implodes catastrophically. Luke has a delicate balancing act to perform in telling this story. Paul is Luke's hero, no doubt. Paul also is his own worst enemy, and Luke knows this. Luke knows this because he personally experienced firsthand as an eyewitness one of the most devastating blows to Paul's career that Paul ever

---

[5]The term used for silver is *arguros* (ἄργυρος), which was a drachma, or the equivalent of a day's wage for an average worker. "Books" here is used loosely, of course. The reference probably is to rolled papyrus texts with incantations, special instructions, and rituals normally carried on the person in some type of small cylinder or locket. Larger scrolls likely also were involved. The practice of magic was so common in the city of Ephesus that written magical formulas even were named for the city as *Ephesia grammata.* Cf. Keener, *IVP Bible Backgrounds Commentary: New Testament*, 379.

endured. Luke is an accurate historian, so he does intend to present an honest appraisal of the situation that developed now in Ephesus, but still maintain the sense that God was in control because the Pauline mission reached its goal. The following is an abbreviation of this story that already has been discussed in detail in chapter 3, "The Character Saul-Paul: Paul, Jerusalem, and God's Will." You may want to review that chapter to recall the complete narrative argument incorporating themes of the Stephen speech as well as those important narrative characterizations at the beginning of the 2MJ that set the stage for the carefully nuanced development Luke engages here beginning with the riot by the silversmiths at the end of the 3MJ.

The silversmiths' riot brings the Ephesian ministry to sudden collapse, forcing Paul to abandon the mission. The question few readers ask is, why? Literally nothing has stood in Paul's way in Ephesus. That message is as loud as the roar of a jet engine through the episodic narratives of 18:24—19:20. The key verse marking the change is Acts 19:21. The problem is not the silversmiths. The problem is Paul—again.

Crisis of Paul's Plans (19:21–22)

The crisis is Paul's plans, stated in 19:21. Here is the text.[6]

> Paul resolved in the spirit that after passing through Macedonia and Achaia, he would proceed on to Jerusalem, explaining, "After I have been there, I must also see Rome."

Luke writes carefully. We detail a few crucial items about this verse.

"Resolved" is Middle Voice

First notice that Luke puts the verb "resolved" or "decided" in Greek middle voice (*etheto*, ἔθετο). English does not have middle voice, so an English translator cannot bring out the force of the middle voice in the first place. Middle voice here means, "resolved for himself." The middle voice means that the true origin of the Jerusalem destination is Paul himself, *not* the Spirit. This decision compares exactly to Paul suggesting to Barnabas an itinerary revisiting churches of the 1MJ (15:36).

---

[6]Greek: Ὡς δὲ ἐπληρώθη ταῦτα, ἔθετο ὁ Παῦλος ἐν τῷ πνεύματι διελθὼν τὴν Μακεδονίαν καὶ Ἀχαΐαν πορεύεσθαι εἰς Ἱεροσόλυμα εἰπὼν ὅτι μετὰ τὸ γενέσθαι με ἐκεῖ δεῖ με καὶ Ῥώμην ἰδεῖν.

"Spirit" is not Capitalized

But wait a minute, you say. Does not the text say, "Resolved *in the Spirit*"? No, the text does *not* say that. Who capitalized Spirit? Your translator. Ancient Greek uncial script does *not* distinguish small and capital letters. So, *translators* have to decide whether to translate as "spirit" or "Spirit." Now, the reader needs to know that Luke does speak of Paul's own spirit in distinction from the Holy Spirit. Such a distinction is the case in 17:16, "While Paul was waiting for them in Athens, *his spirit was troubled within him* when he saw that the city was full of idols." So, Luke does speak of Paul's own spirit. Further, the reader needs to note that the King James translators nailed the matter rightly by translating "in the spirit," indicating Paul's spirit (small letter), not the Holy Spirit. So, this translation is not a new innovation.

The use of "spirit" in 19:21 is nuanced carefully on purpose. Luke is separating the Rome itinerary from the Jerusalem itinerary. Whereas the Rome itinerary is God's plan, the Jerusalem itinerary is not. While nuanced subtly in 19:21, Luke will make absolutely clear in later passages that the Holy Spirit had nothing to do with Paul's decision to go to Jerusalem. As a sneak peek, consult the blunt and unequivocal command by the Spirit in 21:4. The disciples at Tyre tell Paul *through the Spirit not to go to Jerusalem.* Finally, at the narrative level, notice that Luke throws his hat into the ring in the second "we section" of Acts in 21:12 when Luke includes *himself* in telling Paul *not to go* to Jerusalem. Remember that the function of the "we sections" in Acts is to clarify the will of God regarding Paul's plans.[7]

"Must" is Rome

The third item to note is Lukan style. Luke's verb of divine necessity, "must" (*dei*, δεῖ), *is used of the divine destiny of Rome, not Jerusalem.* Luke uses "must" in contexts of divine destiny, as in Jesus's journey to Jerusalem.[8] The "must" verb in 19:21, however, is not about Jerusalem.

---

[7] The first "we section" confirms the Troas Macedonian vision as God's will (16:10).

[8] Luke 9:51; 13:33; 17:25. Trying to force parallels between Jesus and Paul on a "journey to Jerusalem" motif often drives misreading Acts 19:21 so badly among commentators; cf. Keener (*Acts*, 3:3082). Note Tàrrech, "Les Voyages à Jérusalem," who along the way mistranslates Acts 19:21, ignores the counter evidence of Acts 21:4, and strains too hard to find narrative parallels between Luke 9 and Acts 19. Read in context with all applicable verses, Luke makes clear Jesus went to Jerusalem by God's will, Paul did not.

Riot is the Result

Paul sends Timothy and Erastus into Macedonia, apparently in advance of his own announced itinerary to both Macedonia and Achaia (19:22). Luke never says why Paul should go to Macedonia and Greece in order to go to Jerusalem. Those provinces, in fact, are the *opposite* direction to Jerusalem. We would know what that circuitous itinerary was about only by reading Paul's letters. Then, we could surmise that Paul has reconciled finally with the Corinthian church, plans to visit them, and is putting together the final contributions of his churches in Macedonia and Greece for the Jerusalem collection that he personally plans to deliver. Of all this collection project work, Luke says not a word.

Meanwhile, back at the ranch, Paul lingers in Ephesus. Now, "about that time," Luke writes deftly, "no little disturbance broke out concerning the Way" (19:23). A disturbance broke out? What? After five dramatic narratives have made clear that Paul's Ephesian ministry was this stunning display of Spirit power and miracle manifestations, even unto all Asia? Kidding, right? "No, not kidding," Luke responds. Well, what happened? That question is why Luke writes, "About that time." What time? Timothy and Erastus in Macedonia? Yes, and that movement is directly connected to Paul's announced plans to go to Jerusalem in the previous two verses. So, "about that time" means about the time Paul made the decision to go to Jerusalem. Paul's decision to go to Jerusalem causes an implosion of the Ephesian ministry. That implosion is the message of the sudden, unexpected silversmiths' riot. That implosion the Spirit in his sovereignty allowed. The Spirit did not want Paul in Jerusalem, but Paul has insisted on going regardless. Now, Paul is in the same predicament he was at the beginning of the 2MJ. He is fighting God, and the Spirit

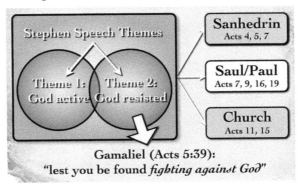

FIGURE 12.15. Stephen Speech Themes: Acts 19.

is opposing him. Once again, we have in the character of Saul-Paul both themes of the Stephen speech. Ephesus the crown jewel is God active.

Paul insisting on going to Jerusalem is God resisted. When Paul made the Jerusalem decision, God took his hand of power off Paul's mission. Why would God do that? Why would God be so adamant about Paul *not* being in Jerusalem. Hang tight. Luke will make that clear in due time as the story of going to Jerusalem unfolds from port to port.

So then, what is Jerusalem? Jerusalem is an unintended detour of God's will. Jerusalem is Paul's own decision that precipitates the catastrophic collapse of the Ephesian mission. Paul, however, did not simply lose the crown jewel of his gentile mission, nor even his home base for future mission. Paul lost a sense of God's will. He is nowhere again, just like being aimless in Asia on the 2MJ. This time, unfortunately, the consequences are more serious and destiny changing. For one, this time will take longer from which to recover. For two, and even more serious, this time will affect the realization of the commission "to the uttermost parts of the earth" that God had in mind at the beginning of Acts. That story of what *could* have been is the hidden, unwritten story of Acts.

Crisis of Silversmiths' Riot (19:23–40)

FIGURE 12.16. Artemis Temple Column. The area of the Artemis temple in Ephesus is now a swamp. All that is left of the original temple complex is a lone column erected by archeologists to suggest the original temple.

FIGURE 12.17. Artemis Statue. The mother goddess worshipped in all of Asia (EM).

The temple of Artemis in Ephesus was one of the seven wonders of the ancient world. Artemis in Asia was worshipped as the mother goddess. The manufacture and sale of miniature statues of the goddess for use in home altars was a significant business.

FIGURE 12.18. Ephesus Theater. Holding 25,000, largest in Anatolia, this theater had a three-story skene (stage), nearly sixty feet high, elaborately decorated.

FIGURE 12.19. Ephesus Market. Market area directly across from the theater with Harbor Street to the right. Demetrius the silversmith had his shop in this market area.

Demetrius Instigates Riot (19:23–29)

Demetrius led the silversmith guild in Ephesus, so was a powerful person in his society. He was upset at the loss of financial revenue in his business of selling Artemis figures. He appeals to religious and civic pride in stirring up a mob to bring mob justice to his nemesis, Paul, whose preaching he had attributed to his loss of income. Paul could not be found immediately by the mob, so they seized two of Paul's associates, Gaius and Aristarchus. They drug them down the Marble Way into the theater, which was immediately across the street. The Ephesian theater could hold about twenty-five thousand people. General confusion, however, reigned in the theater, since the source of the ruckus was unknown. As Luke indicated, "Most of the people did not even know why they were there" (19:32).

Paul's Foolish Attempt (19:30–32)

Paul responds brashly and foolishly. He desires to speak to an unruly gentile mob when he himself is the target of the commotion. Wanting to address the theater crowd was rejected by multiple constituencies. Not only did Paul's own disciples reject the idea as foolish, but even the Ephesian Asiarchs (the city leaders) also rejected Paul's unwise notion to attempt to address the crowd. Luke writes, "Paul wanted to appear before the crowd, but the disciples would not let him. Even some of the Asiarchs, friends of Paul, sent him a message begging him not to venture into the theater" (19:30–31). This wise advice to Paul from multiple groups Luke uses to put in bold relief that Paul's decision making capabilities are poor at this point. This unwise idea here of addressing a riotous mob reflects back poorly on Paul's insistence on going to Jerusalem when God had indicated clearly he was supposed to go to Rome instead (19:21). Paul more and more is beginning to sound and act like the character at the beginning of the 2MJ. Paul more and more will be slipping out of God's will. Every step he takes toward Jerusalem and away from Rome will be a step out of God's will. Further, Luke is signaling that Paul is beginning not to heed good advice. Not heeding good advice on Paul's part becomes a crucial problem on the way to Jerusalem, especially in light of 21:4 where the disciples of Tyre explicitly tell Paul through the Spirit not to go to Jerusalem, and then in 21:12 when Luke himself agrees that Jerusalem is not God's will for Paul.

Paul's stubbornness becomes a theme for several chapters that defines his actions. He refuses the advice of the Spirit about Jerusalem. He tries to refuse the advice of his companions and civic leaders about going into the Ephesian theater. Similarly, along the way to Jerusalem, he constantly will be refusing the advice of fellow believers and the Spirit himself about not going to Jerusalem. This obstinance all begins here in Ephesus with the decision to go to Jerusalem. Notice that Paul unwisely seeks again to address an unruly mob when he actually gets to Jerusalem. Predictably, another riot ensues, and he asks the tribune to be able to address a riotous mob (21:39). The only problem in Jerusalem was, Paul now was alone with no one there to attempt to dissuade him. Therefore, when the tribune gives him permission, Paul foolishly goes ahead to try to address the murderous mob. The result? Another riot ensues. Notice the stark contrast of this Paul constantly causing nothing but riots with the Paul of the earlier Ephesian mission who could do no harm and could even have magicians burning their incantations with no riotous reaction. The point is obvious: After Paul makes the decision to go to Jerusalem, all Hades breaks loose. Publicly, nothing but riots ensue every time he tries to speak. Luke's narrative contrast before and after Paul's Jerusalem decision could not be more stark.

Alexander's Abortive Attempt (19:33–34)

The Jews wanted to exculpate themselves from responsibility for riot. So they put forward a Jewish leader named Alexander to try to make a defense (19:33–34). The crowd cut him short when they realized he was a Jew, and knew that Jews did not believe in their great god, Artemis. So they chanted for two hours in unison, "Great is Artemis of the Ephesians" (19:34). Luke uses the crowd reaction to Alexander to insinuate Paul's own foolishness, because Paul would have fared no better and probably worse.

City Clerk's Pacification (19:35–40)

The city clerk pacifies the crowd through civic responsibility in relation to the Romans. He points out that, regardless the reason, public assembly in the theater was in riotous chaos, and that reason alone was enough to expect the full wrath of Rome. Almost nothing was as anathema to Rome as disturbing the peace. He points out they were shouting only what everyone knew already (the greatness of Artemis) and that the men brought into the theater had not been accused of one single crime. Therefore, by default, the Ephesians themselves were violating Roman law. Even more, if some charge was to be brought in the first place, the city theater most certainly was not the proper Roman venue for making formal charges. Romans had legal courts, and the proconsul of Asia held tribunal right there in Ephesus. Demetrius could bring his charge directly to the proconsul (19:35–38). The clerk's blunt conclusion brings the Ephesians to their senses: "For we are in danger of being charged with rioting today, since there is no cause that we can give to justify this commotion" (19:40). The mob finally quelled.

Crisis of Mission Collapse (20:1–3)

Paul's Necessary Departure (20:1)

Luke makes patently clear that Paul had to abandon Ephesus because of the silversmiths' riot, because he ties these two events directly together: "After the uproar had ceased . . . he left for Macedonia" (20:1). After such a riot of the entire city that came within an inch of bringing down the wrath of Rome, Paul's reputation was ruined and the cause of Christ seriously damaged. Paul's Ephesian mission had collapsed suddenly and catastrophically. Yet, that loss is not the really bad news. The really bad news is, until he gets his act back together again, Paul officially now is in rebellion against God. The second of the Stephen speech themes takes over the narrative development of this character. Even though Paul will be able to encourage believers individually or in already established congregations (20:2), he no longer has a viable mission, because he unilaterally has rewritten on his own terms the mission to Rome as divinely given to him at Ephesus by insisting on going to Jerusalem first, an itinerary post-Ephesus the Spirit did not inspire (19:21). Notice in all Paul's effort to get to Jerusalem, he does not evangelize publicly. He establishes no churches. He does not lay on hands. No one speaks in tongues. He does no miracles.[9] No evil force acknowledges his name. Fundamentally, the gentile mission has stalled completely.

---

[9]The passage about Eutychus falling out of the window at Troas from drowsiness while Paul speaks long into the night is ambiguous (20:9–11). He is picked up "dead," but Luke's meaning could be "as dead," since all Paul does is investigate himself and announce that "his life is in him" (20:10)—in other words, not really dead. Miracles are attended by a note of crowd amazement, of which this episode is totally absent.

Macedonian Movement (20:1–2)

Another signal that Paul has stalled is Luke's brevity. Travel though all of Macedonia and on down into Greece is only one verse (20:2). Even when Paul gets to Greece and spends three months there, again, all that time is compressed into only one quarter of one verse (20:3). If all we read is the Acts narrative, during all this time after Ephesus, Paul says and does almost nothing. He encourages believers. Encouragement is Luke's only note about Paul at this time. The silence is over-whelming and pregnant with innuendo about the absence of mission.

Since Luke's coverage of this period is so bare, we are dependent on biographical information in Paul's Corinthian correspondence for piecing together a little more about Paul's movements after this point of Paul's sudden departure from Ephesus. For example, a stop at Troas does show up on the correspondence radar in 2 Cor 2:12. Paul has a preaching opportunity in Troas, but he is too distracted in his anxiety, especially in attempting to rendezvous with Titus, who had delivered the "harsh letter" to Corinth but had not returned to Paul to indicate the Corinthian response to his final ultimatum.

FIGURE 12.20. Paul's Movements After Ephesus—Troas. We are dependent on Pauline correspondence to gain a better sense of Paul's movements after Ephesus.

FIGURE 12.21. Paul's Movements After Ephesus—Macedonia. Paul finally meets up with Titus to receive good news of Corinth's reconciliation (2 Cor 2:13; 7:5–6).

Another development is that Paul finally does rendezvous with Titus somewhere in "Macedonia" (2 Cor 7:5–6). The cities identified for Macedonia are assumed from the 2MJ. Titus brings Paul good news of reconciliation with the Corinthian congregation. Paul is relieved. He writes 2 Corinthians to express his joy and to send Titus back to Corinth soon. He wants the Corinthians to get back on the collection for Jerusalem that has languished during the time of their dispute (2 Cor 8:6).

Acts	Letter	From	Date
JC	Galatians	?	?
2MJ	1 Thess 2 Thess	Corinth	50
3MJ	"Previous Letter" 1 Corinthians "Harsh Letter" 2 Corinthians Romans	Ephesus Ephesus Ephesus Macedonia Corinth	55 55 56 56 57
Rome	Colossians Philemon Ephesians Philippians	Rome Rome Rome Rome	60 60 60 62

FIGURE 12.22. Pauline Correspondence: 2 Corinthians.

Right at this point we should consider the detail Paul provides in the letter to the Romans written after he arrives in Corinth. Paul says he had worked in Illyricum (Rom 15:19). This province is north of

Macedonia.[10] Conceivably, work in Illyricum could have been conducted at this time on the way to Corinth. Luke is silent about Illyricum.

Greece for Three Months (20:2–3)

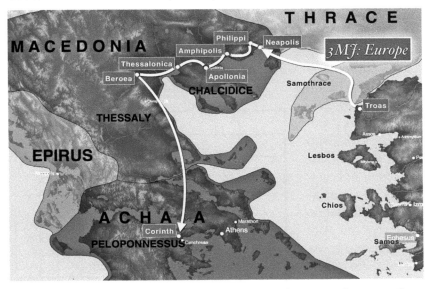

FIGURE 12.23. 3MJ—Greece (Corinth). Luke is mysteriously quiet on the reasons for all this movement by Paul after Ephesus. Paul was supposed to be going to Jerusalem.

All Luke says is, "he came to Greece and stayed three months"—eight words in Greek (20:2b–3a).[11] Where did Paul actually stay? What did he do? Why was he there? Whom did he see? What experiences did he have? Why is Luke so ambiguous on the *reason* for all this post-Ephesus movement? Paul said he was going to Jerusalem in 19:21, but ever since that announcement, *he has been everywhere but Jerusalem*—very strange. Luke's three months in "Greece" we learn from Paul himself is Corinth. To be sure, Paul could have sailed directly from Ephesus to Corinth. Why go through Macedonia in the first place? Luke never says. He never says why Paul went through Macedonia, and he never says why Paul went on down to Greece.

Paul does say. Paul says he is trying to rendezvous with Titus about the Corinthian crisis and to gather together the contributions of his

[10]For a map situating the province, see Fig. 10.18, p. 300.

[11]Greek: ἦλθεν εἰς τὴν Ἑλλάδα ποιήσας τε μῆνας τρεῖς.

Macedonian churches for Jerusalem. So, the itinerary of both Macedonia and Greece—all of Paul's post-Ephesus movement so mysteriously reported by Luke without any explanation—is all about the collection, but Luke never admits this purpose. Because Luke has made this part of the 3MJ such a mystery, we have to go to Paul's letters at this time to get the inside scoop of what is going on. Yet, for Luke's part, he clearly is suppressing any information on Paul's collection. We will surmise Luke's purpose later with more of his narrative in view.

During his time in Corinth, Paul writes Romans. This sequence is established by combining Paul's 2 Corinthians comments about finishing the collection and comments in Romans that this collection is ready, and Paul immediately is on his way to Jerusalem with the offering (Rom 15:25–28). So, Romans is written during this time in Corinth toward the end of the 3MJ as Paul contemplates his Jerusalem itinerary before going to Rome.

Acts	Letter	From	Date
JC	Galatians	?	?
2MJ	1 Thess 2 Thess	Corinth	50
3MJ	"Previous Letter" 1 Corinthians "Harsh Letter" 2 Corinthians Romans	Ephesus Ephesus Ephesus Macedonia Corinth	55 55 56 56 57
Rome	Colossians Philemon Ephesians Philippians	Rome Rome Rome Rome	60 60 60 62

FIGURE 12.24. Pauline Correspondence: Romans.

Crisis of Jerusalem Journey (20:3–21:17)

After all this Macedonia and Greece movement after Ephesus, totally unexplained by Luke, Paul is ready to sail to Jerusalem. He plans to go straight to Syria, perhaps visiting Antioch, then catch coasting vessels on down to Judea's principal port at Caesarea and then the last jog by land to Jerusalem.

Jewish Plot (20:3)

A plot on his life radically changes matters and prevents a sea voyage directly back to Syria and Judea (20:3). A plot on a seafaring voyage would be easy to pull off. Paul would be a sitting duck confined on a boat. The meaning of the Jewish plot on his life is, Paul is now on the run. His difficulties, however, from here on out are of his own making. He is like Jonah, at least in terms of stubbornly going the opposite direction of the divinely ordained destination, and constantly running into storms as a result. He no longer channels that divine power that protected him for years in Ephesus. Paul will not escape the downward spiral his gentile mission now is taking. Almost every move he makes is a bad one, and drives him more deeply downward until the circulation of the volitional vortex finally spits him up on a beach on some island, dazed, but a repentant prophet finally back on track on doing God's will. At that point, the attentive reader should notice how power and miracles suddenly begin manifesting again.

Paul is forced to change his cruise itinerary, and instead takes the safer route overland back through Macedonia. The cities indicated are presumed from the 2MJ.

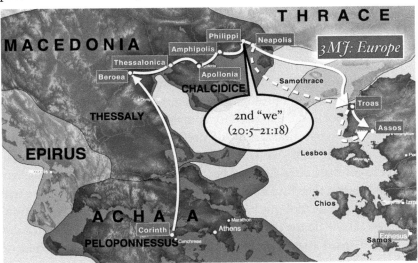

FIGURE 12.25. 3MJ—Return: Macedonia. A plot forces Paul to travel by land. The second "we section" begins at Philippi. Then, the group has a split itinerary twice.

Paul's Companions (20:4)

The list of Paul's companions explodes in 20:4 and is unexplained by Luke. The greatest likelihood is that these individuals are the regional representatives for the Jerusalem collection that Paul has gathered but

Luke has suppressed. From Galatia of the 1MJ are Gaius of Derbe and Timothy of Lystra. From Macedonia of the 2MJ are Aristarchus and Secundus of Thessalonica and Sopater of Berea. From Asia of the 3MJ are Tychicus and Trophimus of Ephesus. This unexpected list suddenly popping up here represents one of the notable mute points in Luke's story about Ephesus. Luke is strangely silent about the Jerusalem collection Paul worked tirelessly to put together among his main mission churches and was so vocal about in his letters. Luke never actually says that the reason Paul insists on going to Jerusalem (19:21) is to deliver this collection personally and that that is why so many people suddenly now accompany Paul on his journey.

Second "We Section" (20:5)

The second "we section" of Acts begins at Philippi on this return trip to Jerusalem. Oddly, Philippi is precisely where the first "we section" had trailed off on the 2MJ, sometime during the episode of the pythoness exorcism and the consequent imprisonment. The second "we section" implies that Luke rejoins Paul's party at Philippi.

Two narrative elements of the "we section" come into play again. First, Luke officially serves as an eyewitness to the matters now being reported about Paul's journey to Jerusalem. That eyewitness function was insinuated in the prologue as a reference not just to the apostles and others, but to Luke himself for some parts of the story he has to tell. Second, the "we sections" show up precisely when the issue is Paul and God's will. The first "we section" on the 2MJ popped up at Troas in order to confirm, after Paul had been aimless in Asia because of his fight with Barnabas, that Paul's Troas vision was indeed God's will and a true mission mandate that put Paul back on track. The second "we section" on the 3MJ will do the opposite. The second "we section" will contradict Paul and insist that Jerusalem was *not* God's will and Paul had no mission mandate for this destination. Everything else in the Jerusalem story consequently follows on a stubborn Paul out of God's will not only damaging his gentile mission but endangering both himself and innocent people around him, including Luke.

Philippi Passover (20:5–6)

The Philippi departure happens in two groups, because some wanted to tarry in Philippi for Passover (dotted line on map). The composition of the two groups is unknown. At least three constituents are involved: Paul and constant companions,[12] collection companions,[13] and Luke himself. Of these, we cannot determine the mix involved in "we" and "they" in the narrative.[14] The "we" group stays in Philippi for Passover. The "they" group went on to Troas. Five days later, Luke and his "we" group joins back up with "they" at Troas and stay for a week (20:6).

Eutychus Incident (20:7–12)

Two descriptors might give the impression the assembly was gathered formally for worship. The first is "first day of the week." While the timing of when Christians began worshipping on Sunday cannot be determined, the possibility exists this tradition began fairly early in the movement. Thus, a "first day" assembly might suggest a Sunday worship event. The second descriptor is "to break bread." Again, this type of expression might have Eucharistic overtones, or perhaps at least invoke the experience of the Emmaus disciples, which also was on the first day of the week.[15]

Such intertextual echoes are possible, but probably the stronger echo is intratextual, that is, within Acts itself. Narrative symbolism might be in play in an *inclusio* with the location, Troas. Placing Paul in Troas where he received the vision that put the gentile mission back into gear after being aimless in Asia will now have a strong element of pathos. Here Paul is, back again in Troas, but now back out of God's will. He should be moving to Rome, but he stubbornly is moving to Jerusalem. The gentile mission has derailed again. God is ready for Rome, but Paul is on a detour.

Paul speaks too long, and Eutychus falls asleep, falling out of the window into which he probably has wedged himself for fresh air.[16] They are three floors up, so the fall is significant. Luke says simply, "he was picked up dead" (20:9). Now, dead could be really dead, or only "mostly

---

[12]Potentially, for example, Titus, presumed from the Corinthian correspondence.

[13]Including Timothy, by Luke's reckoning.

[14]We know Luke is part of the "we" group, but does "we" include Paul, or is Paul part of the "they"? Are the collection companions part of the "we" group or part of the "they" group? Or, is this a completely haphazard mix? And so forth.

[15]Cf. the sequence in Luke 24:1, 13, 30–31.

[16]Luke specifically notes that "many lamps were in the room," which would have increased heat and decreased available oxygen.

FIGURE 12.26. Bronze Lamp. Votive oil lamp from Pompeii, AD 79 (LP).

dead."[17] He could have had the breath knocked out of him and have suffered a mild concussion, so, naturally, not breathing and unresponsive. Some have argued that since Passover is a part of the previous context in Philippi and a "first day of the week" resurrection day assembly is part of the immediate context, this incident is meant to evoke resurrection, so Paul would be understood as having raised the young man back to life miraculously.

While this reading has some context to recommend itself to the reader, one narrative element speaks decisively against such an understanding: Luke makes absolutely nothing of the matter. First, all Paul announces is, "his life is in him," which is not a known resurrection formula for provoking a resurrection miracle. Second, Luke presents zero crowd reaction, and crowd reaction is the most potent part of any miracle story and the whole point for telling them, that is, to speak of the crowd's amazement. Astounding people is the essence of the work of miracle workers in the ancient world, the very *modus operandi* of Simon the Magician in Samaria (8:11). In Troas, in stark contrast, no one exclaims anything and no one is amazed among any of those in the assembly about the incident. Third, the subsequent action is all out of whack if the child actually had died right there on the street: Paul goes back upstairs to eat as if nothing happened (20:11). Of course, since they had thought the young man dead, but he was not really, then naturally they "were not a little comforted," but this expression is much more like the relief that an awful fate one might have imagined actually turned out not true. The very way Luke describes the incident and the lack of reaction to the event argues decisively that he does not take the incident as a miracle of the giving of life but of realizing a life was not actually taken away. Remembering that Luke is not picturing Paul in this part of Acts as firing on all pistons, then the likelihood is that the Eutychus incident should be read as relief of recovery, not a miracle. In fact, the incident echoes directly Paul at Lystra (14:19–20).

[17]You know, "The Princess Bride" kind of dead.

Assos (20:13–14)

FIGURE 12.27. Cliffs of Assos. Panorama from the steep cliffs leading down to the port of Assos. Troas would be up the coast to the right.

FIGURE 12.28. Assos Harbor. View of the modern harbor from the cliffs above, whose breakwater is built on the same semicircle as the ancient breakwater.

FIGURE 12.29. Temple of Athena, Assos. Doric columns of the 530 BC temple of Athena on top of the Assos acropolis with the island of Lesbos in the background.

FIGURE 12.30. Assos Theater. The Assos theater, dating to the 3rd cent. BC and seating 5,000, has a spectacular view of the ocean and the island of Lesbos off the coast.

FIGURE 12.31. Roman Road, Assos. The modern highway runs parallel to the ancient Roman road from Troas to Assos. This road Paul traveled down in his trek apparently on foot by himself to meet up with his traveling companions at the port in Assos.

After a week, the group leaves Troas in two parties again like Philippi, but for unspecified reasons (dotted line on map). Luke and his group leaves Troas by boat ("we set sail for Assos," 20:13), sailing around Cape Lectum, but Paul goes by land on foot down the Roman road to the port of Assos, about thirty-one miles, so likely a two-day journey. At Assos, Paul boards the ship on which Luke and the rest of the company already have been traveling.

Miletus (20:15–38)

The vessel they are on makes scheduled stops on an island hopping journey down to the famous double port at Miletus. These ships are coasting vessels; they are not made for the open waters but to ply up and down coastlines delivering their trade goods and supplies to various ports. The first stop is at the port of Mitylene on the island of Lesbos, not that far from Assos. From Mitylene a day later they run opposite the island of Chios. One more day sailing and they make a quick stop at the busy island of Samos, known for world trade in fine wine, loaded into amphorae. Bypassing the port of Ephesus, they arrive at the Lion Harbor of Miletus on the fourth day. Favorable prevailing winds have produced a quick journey.

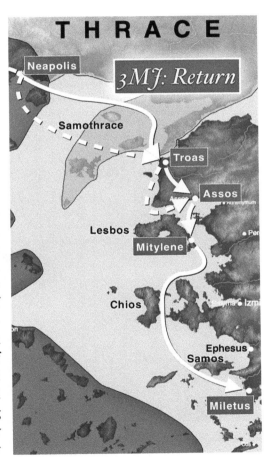

FIGURE 12.32. 3MJ—Return: Miletus. Favorable winds bring the group quickly to Miletus. From there, Paul calls for the elders at Ephesus to visit with him.

FIGURE 12.33. Miletus Lion Harbor Model. Miletus was one of the busiest harbors on the eastern Aegean, actually having two harbors, Theater Harbor and Lion Harbor. Lion Harbor leads directly to the markets of Miletus. The famous Miletus Market Gate is at the center top of this picture (PMB).

FIGURE 12.34. Miletus Lion Monument. Two lion statues guarded the Lion Harbor entrance, mentioned often by ancient writers. Marsh almost has covered up the one remaining lion, weather worn.

Paul sailed past Ephesus, ostensibly "so that he might not have to spend time in Asia" (20:16). Given the recent silversmiths' riot, this action seems a little obvious. Luke tinges the comment with irony: "he

FIGURE 12.35. Poseidon Monument. Trident relief of the Poseidon Monument in Lion Harbor celebrating Pompey's victory over pirates in the Mediterranean, who seriously were hindering the shipping and trade interests of Rome's new business class.

FIGURE 12.36. Miletus North Market. The Lion Harbor led to the North Market that itself led to the South Market. Like Ephesus, the Miletus harbor suffered constant silting, such that today much of the site is marsh and the actual seacoast is miles away. The North Market was completed in AD 50, only a few years before Paul's visit, so Paul would have seen these columns as he proceeded from the harbor into the city.

was eager to be in Jerusalem, if possible, on the day of Pentecost." The note of Pentecost now connects Paul's journey to Jerusalem with the premier theme of Acts that launches the entire narrative. Pentecost is the eschatological harvest abundance of the gentiles in the kingdom of God. Paul wants to take his collection to Jerusalem as a sign of this es-

FIGURE 12.37. Miletus Market Gate. Market Gate led into the North Market area. This gate was removed to the Pergamon Museum in Berlin and reconstructed (PMB).

FIGURE 12.38. Market Gate Drawing. An artist's conceptualization of the Market Gate about second century AD (MM).

chatological harvest fulfilled. Thus, Luke infers Paul's thinking about the collection without specifically mentioning the collection. The note might seem subtle, but think for a moment: Pentecost is not a subtle theme in Acts. So, mentioning Paul's desire to time his arrival in Jerusa-

FIGURE 12.39. Miletus Theater. The grand theater at Miletus held 25,000. For the "God-fearer" inscription carved into a seat in this theater, see Fig. 8.6, p. 241.

FIGURE 12.40. Miletus Roman Mosaic. Floor of a Roman dining room (PMB).

lem with the celebration of the Pentecost festival is not fortuitous, not given Paul's reason for going to Jerusalem, loaded as he is with his offering from his gentile churches and their seven representatives.[18]

At Miletus, Paul calls upon the Ephesian elders to meet with him in Miletus, which is almost a fifty-mile trek one way (20:17). That distance is a minimum two to three day journey one way, so messengers going to Ephesus and elders coming to Miletus would consume almost a week's time under the best of weather and road conditions. Seems a

[18]Paul actually says something very close to this in Romans, written from Corinth just prior to this journey to Jerusalem (cf. Rom 15:9–12, 16, 25–28).

little self-defeating to bypass Ephesus in order to "not have to spend time in Asia" in one verse (20:16), and then in the very next verse spend an entire week in Asia waiting on elders to arrive from the place you bypassed (20:17).[19] In any case, their arrival to Miletus affords Luke the opportunity to use Paul's long farewell speech at Miletus as the third of Luke's strategic "example" sermons, one given on each missionary journey, in order to illustrate how Paul preached to three major audiences in

Paul's Paradigm Sermons			
MJ	Place	Context	Audience
1MJ	Antioch	Synagogue	Jewish
2MJ	Athens	Market	Gentile
3MJ	Miletus	Church	Christian

FIGURE 12.41. Paul's Paradigm Sermons: Christian.

his mission work. The sermon has four topical parts: retrospect, prospect, charge, and admonition. Luke then concludes with a vignette on parting.

Retrospect (20:18–21). Paul reviews his ministry in Asia. He emphasizes humble service, open proclamation, and inclusive witness. He alludes to "trials . . . through the plots of the Jews" (20:19). Actually, we do not hear of any such plots at the hands of Jews in Asia. All we get from Luke is the silversmiths' riot. This allusion by Paul is another one of those "mute points" in Luke's account of Ephesus. The dangers of which Paul spoke in his own letters, particularly the one in which Paul despaired for his life, are not presented by Luke.

Prospect (20:22–24). The prospect is Jerusalem and is one of foreboding. This passage has to be read carefully. Of utmost importance is to note is that these words are *Paul's perspective* on Jerusalem. Luke will use Paul's words with *double entendre.* Paul asserts, "And now, behold, having been bound by the Spirit, I am going to Jerusalem" (20:22).[20] Paul still is asserting Jerusalem is God's will. Luke soon will make clear most assuredly that Jerusalem is *not* God's will. Luke still reports these words of Paul because they ironically are true. God *will* have to tie Paul

[19]Calling the elders down to Miletus makes bypassing Ephesus for time's sake seem like just a ruse for laying low from recent trouble only a few months before.

[20]Greek: Καὶ νῦν ἰδοὺ δεδεμένος ἐγὼ τῷ πνεύματι πορεύομαι εἰς Ἰερουσαλήμ.

up to control him. That constriction will come in the form of a prophecy pronounced by Agabus in Caesarea. Paul is bound by the Spirit,
indeed, but not in the way he thinks. The "binding" of which he speaks
is metaphorical, but his "binding" will become rather literal when the
Holy Spirit allows him to be shackled in Roman chains in Jerusalem to
restrain him from any further movement on his own.

What is taking place right now is Paul behaving badly, just as he
did on the 2MJ as he was trying over and over to go into Bithynia but
constantly was being opposed by the Spirit (16:7).[21] At that time, the
Spirit boxed in Paul at Troas with nowhere to go. The Spirit will do the
same in this current situation by imprisoning Paul in Jerusalem. Soon,
Paul definitely will be "bound by the Spirit." So, Paul asserts Jerusalem
is God's will, but Luke will indicate otherwise shortly.

The *double entendre* in Paul's own words is when he acknowledges
that the Holy Spirit "is testifying to me in every city, saying that imprisonment and tribulations are awaiting me" (20:23).[22] Luke actually has
not reported any of these warnings. Apparently, friends and acquaint-
ances already are advising Paul of the realities in Jerusalem. Paul paints
himself as the righteous martyr. He is not. For another time in his life,
Paul does not cognize his own recalcitrance. Note what will be missing
entirely from the Jerusalem story is divine intervention. In Jerusalem,
God will not spring Paul from prison as he did at Philippi (16:26). In
Jerusalem, God will not offer a vision promising security and success
on the eve of a proconsul tribunal as he did at Corinth (18:9–10). Instead, the Holy Spirit promises only that Paul will endure bonds and
affliction with no purpose and no positive result. In Jerusalem, no one
gets saved. No miracles are performed. No prison doors spring open.

Charge (20:25–31). Paul charges the Ephesian elders. Luke intends
to globalize this charge to the Ephesian elders to the church universal.
The "made you overseers to shepherd the church of God" is directed at
Paul's heritage (20:28). An overseer function presciently anticipates
false teachers, but Paul has plenty of experience already with distortions
to the gospel, as in the Jerusalem Conference in which he participated.
He sees future challenges for the gentile thrust of the Hellenist movement. Paul describes future problems graphically: "savage wolves will

---

[21]The verb is imperfect: "was trying (over and over) to go into Bithynia."

[22]Greek: κατὰ πόλιν διαμαρτύρεταί μοι λέγον ὅτι δεσμὰ καὶ θλίψεις με μένουσιν.

come in among you, not sparing the flock; some men will arise even from among you" (20:29–30). He anticipates false teachers at Ephesus. In fact, these very problems are on plain display in the New Testament both in the Pastoral Epistles and in the Apocalypse. In the Pastorals we have Hymenaeus and Alexander (1 Tim 1:19–20); the latter days will be characterized by a general falling away (1 Tim 4:1–3); the talk of Hymenaeus and Philetus will spread like gangrene (2 Tim 2:17–18); the last days will be a precarious time for the faithful (2 Tim 3:1–9). Later, in the Apocalypse, one has the letter to Ephesus that reveals a decided effort by the Ephesians to resist false doctrine (Rev 2:1–7).

As for himself in his own discharge of his shepherding responsibility, Paul indicates blood innocence (20:26). The divine mandate has been discharged. This word of blood innocence is comparable to that of Peter before the Sanhedrin (5:28). The point is that shepherding of the church is a responsibility not to take lightly. One has to keep in mind that God obtained this church "with the blood of his own Son" (20:28). Thus, Luke is placing serious weight on gospel accountability as he globalizes this task to the church universal.

One statement of curiosity in this charge to the church section is that Paul tells the elders that they will "see my face no more" (20:25). The interpretation is ambiguous. The tone may be ominous. If so, is this Luke's subtle notation of the final result of Paul's trial in Rome? If not meant as ominous, is such an expression just Paul's anticipation that his mission work will take him so far away as not to be much in contact with former congregations?[23] The allusion is not easy to decipher at this point, but Luke will clarify soon in the elders' reaction.

Admonition (20:32–35). This section functions as Pauline apologetic. The controlling thought is personal integrity. The emphasis is twofold: fiduciary responsibility and ministerial conduct. When Paul insists that he "coveted no one's silver or gold" (20:33), we have a probable allusion to the collection, and a possible allusion to charges of embezzlement.[24] When Paul explains he "worked with my own hands" (20:34–35), we consider such a statement as honorable. Not in Paul's

---

[23]In Romans, Paul indicated that he planned to make his next mission endeavor the remote province of Spain (Rom 15:24).

[24]Which seems insinuated in the Corinthian correspondence; cf. 2 Cor 7:2; 8:20; 9:5; 12:17–18.

world. This statement would be a philosopher's disrepute in ancient society. A philosopher that had to work was not worth his words. Yet, though such activity casts a dishonorable shadow over Paul's mission, working was Paul's gospel choice so as not to burden a church.[25] Paul quotes an independent Jesus *logion* to support such a countercultural choice ("more blessed to give than to receive," 20:35). The *logion* refocuses calculating cost on the basis of being able to count non-financial return.[26]

Parting (20:36–38). Here is where the darker musical tones of this Jerusalem journey begin to arise from the orchestra pit. Deep concern for Paul is expressed, in terms of "much weeping" (*hikanos de klauthmos,* ἱκανὸς δὲ κλαυθμός, 20:37). Nothing in the narrative, however, has prepared the reader for this strong, emotional outburst; the vocabulary is quite dramatic.[27] The response seems out of all proportion to the situation. Paul going to Jerusalem is just another bend in the road of his Pauline mission that would not of itself be anywhere near the justification for such deep and openly-expressed feelings. Only if the nuance of Paul's

FIGURE 12.42. Grave Stele Relief. Krito mourns the death of her mother, Timaresta (AMR).

previous word of "see my face no more" is taken in a desperate and cataclysmic way would the emotional outburst have any reasonable

---

[25]He specifically tells the Corinthians he made precisely this choice when he was at Corinth (2 Cor 11:7–9).

[26]Paul's quote of a saying of Jesus without any narrative context around the saying illustrates how sayings of Jesus could have circulated as a collection of one saying after another without narrative contexts.

[27]The noun for weeping (*klauthmos,* κλαυθμός) occurs only twice in Luke-Acts, but the cognate verb (*klaiō,* κλαίω) is used almost exclusively in contexts of death and mourning or eschatological judgment. For the noun, cf. Luke 13:28; Acts 20:37. For the verb, cf. Luke 6:21, 25; 7:13, 32, 38; 8:52; 19:41; 22:62; 23:28; Acts 9:39; 21:13.

context. The weeping in 20:7 suggests that the meaning given by Paul to "see my face no more" could be death. The possible death anticipated, however, is not any subtle allusion by Luke to the outcome of Paul's trial in Rome. Rather, this anticipation is Paul's own for his Jerusalem destination. The tone of Jerusalem foreboding begins.[28]

FIGURE 12.43. Temple of Aphrodite, Rhodes. One of the islands Paul and company passed by is Rhodes, whose city of Rhodes has one of the oldest temples dedicated exclusively to the goddess Aphrodite.

FIGURE 12.44. Roman Mosaic Floor, Rhodes. One of the largest, intact Roman mosaics is this exquisite, circle and square geometric scene that is only part of the entire floor decoration of a Roman governmental complex (AMR).

[28]This nuance corresponds exactly to what Paul expressed when he petitioned the Romans for their prayers: "Pray that I may be rescued from the unbelievers in Judea, that the gift I am bringing to Jerusalem may be acceptable to the saints" (Rom 15:31).

Tyre (21:1–6)

The ship continues its island hopping routine. Luke mentions passing by Cos and Rhodes on the way to Patara, a mainland port in the province of Lycia, not far from another port at Myra where they later will pick up an Alexandrian grain ship bound for Rome (27:5). At Patara, they pick up another ship bound for Tyre on the Phoenician coast (21:2). They come within sight of Cyprus, passing that island on their left, which means an open seas shot straight to the port of Tyre, where the Patara ship was to unload its cargo (21:3).

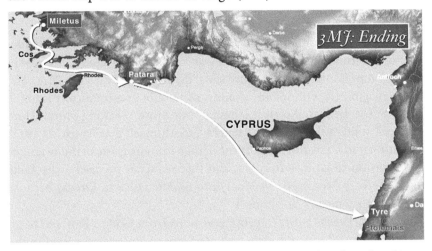

FIGURE 12.45. 3MJ—Return: Patara to Tyre. Paul and his group board another ship at Patara bound for the Phoenician coast. They pass by Cyprus and land at Tyre.

Tyre is absolutely crucial to understanding Paul and God's will. Tyre offers unimpeachable evidence of God's will regarding Paul and Jerusalem in Luke's account. That their stay is an entire week ("seven days," 21:4), becomes an important note of time (because of the tense of the following verb). Here is this absolutely fundamental verse.[29]

> Which ones were saying to Paul through the Spirit, "Do not go to Jerusalem!"

We note two important grammatical items about "they were saying." First, the verb is plural. Plural number means the following "Spirit" in the singular has to be the Holy Spirit. Absolutely no ambiguity at all is

---

[29]Greek: οἵτινες τῷ Παύλῳ ἔλεγον διὰ τοῦ πνεύματος μὴ ἐπιβαίνειν εἰς Ἱεροσό-λυμα. The ἐπιβαίνειν is taken as a discourse infinitive.

involved in Luke's reference to "Spirit." Second, the verb is imperfect, therefore, the action is durative ("were saying," not "said"). This tense is *exactly the same tense Luke used to speak of the effort to go into Bithynia* that the "Spirit of Jesus" would not allow during Paul's time of being aimless in Asia (16:7). The meaning is the same here as then. Someone disagrees. In this case that someone would be none other than Paul himself. His refusal to acknowledge that this exhortation comes directly from the Holy Spirit requires giving the word over and over—hence, the significance of Luke's time notation of the seven-day stay in Tyre. Paul was hearing this command over multiple days, yet stubbornly refusing to comply.

Now, if any ambiguity at all still might be attached by the reader to the question whether Jerusalem was Paul's idea or God's, the reader has to contend with the unequivocal, "through the Spirit" in 21:4. The reference in 21:4 without any shadow of a doubt grammatically is to the Holy Spirit, because Spirit is singular, but those speaking plural. Here is a rock solid indication in the text by Luke himself that "spirit" in 19:21 is *Paul's spirit*, not the Holy Spirit. Paul's human spirit is the origin of his decision to go to Jerusalem, and that reality is precisely why Luke puts the verb "resolved" in 19:21 into *middle* voice in Greek, because middle voice means "for himself."

Thus, Tyre is a direct, prophetic word from God to Paul *not* to go to Jerusalem. This prophetic word confirms what Paul admitted to the Ephesian elders he has been hearing all along from the Holy Spirit in his travel from city to city (20:23). The Spirit's word of imprisonment and tribulations waiting for Paul in Jerusalem is not a "Keep Calm and Carry On" poster for a bombing blitz. Rather, given the clarity of 21:4, the Spirit in previous prophetic words to Paul has been warning Paul that *God will take his divine mandate for mission off of Paul if he insists on going to Jerusalem.*

So, Acts 21:4 becomes a key verse for exegesis of all the coming chapters on Paul and Jerusalem. God's will was explicit, "Paul, do not go to Jerusalem!" Therefore, all other remarks by Paul himself about Jerusalem now must be reevaluated in the light of the indisputable evidence of 21:4. Thus, what Paul claimed during his time in Ephesus (19:21) and what he claimed later to the same Ephesian elders in his speech at Miletus (20:22) have to be reframed as *Paul's perspective*, not

God's. Further, with clear communications from the Holy Spirit telling Paul *not* to go (repeatedly), then Paul's obstinate insistence on going to Jerusalem is a flagrant act of a knowing disobedience. Paul is back to square one: fighting

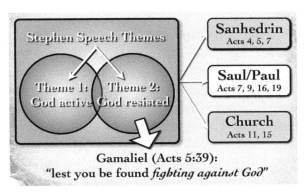

FIGURE 12.46. Stephen Speech Themes: Acts 21.

God, just like he was on his way to Damascus. Paul never quit being Saul-Paul, and Luke was honest about that characterization. The Holy Spirit's clear communication in 21:4 establishes not only the correct exegesis of previous passages, such as 19:21 and 20:22, but also the following prophecy by Agabus. Escorted to the beach by entire families, a serious farewell, they kneel, pray, say goodbye, and depart (21:5–6).

Caesarea (21:7–14)

The jaunt from Tyre to Ptolemais is a short hop. Their one-day stay with believers, probably on the ship's own schedule, echoes back to the coming of the gospel to Phoenicia from the Stephen persecution (11:19), as well as Paul and Barnabas on their way to the Jerusalem Conference going through the area reporting on the conversion of gentiles that generates great joy (15:3). One more day, and they arrive in the port of Caesarea. Luke is specific about their host.

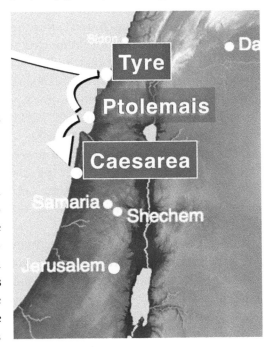

FIGURE 12.47. 3MJ—Return: Caesarea.

Philip the Host (21:8–9). Luke says that they were hosted by Philip "the evangelist," and adds "one of the seven" (20:8). Here at Caesarea is the first time Philip has been called "the evangelist" in Acts.[30] His evangelization of the Samaritans and subsequent Spirit-led encounter with the Ethiopian eunuch on the Gaza road have become his defining moment in history; they are now a permanent fixture of his reputation and secure him a permanent place in the lore of the Hellenist movement to became inscribed into the pages of Acts. So, he is now not simply Philip, but "Philip the evangelist"—you know, the famous one.

Luke deftly adds, "one of the seven." These seven are the famous heptad of leaders of the original Hellenist movement that catapulted the church into its gentile mission (6:1). Luke's deliberate wording of "one of the seven" intentionally has brought the reader back full circle to the Hellenist Cycle beginnings. Why do this? Luke's narrative strategy is *to establish what is at stake in Paul's current insistence on going to Jerusalem against God's will.* The Hellenist movement is at stake. Paul is the passion, powerhouse, and voice of that movement, its premier leader. Paul's fate is the movement's fate. Yet, Paul in one of his more obtuse moments is about to ravage the Hellenist movement, in eerie parallel to what he was doing to the church before the Damascus Road (8:3)—both times, ironically, assured within himself he was doing God's will.

Luke next mentions that Philip "had four unmarried daughters who had the gift of prophecy" (21:9). Why bring in this detail? His points will cascade. How many women prophets do we hear about in Jerusalem? Indeed. One point here for Luke is that the fullest expression of Joel's last days prophecy ("your sons *and your daughters* shall prophesy," 2:17) is in the Hellenist movement. The next point is that one of the most potent places of the spirit of prophecy in messianic Israel within the Hellenist movement is in Caesarea. The Spirit is strong in Caesarea. Paul better had heed the prophetic word in this place of all places.

Agabus the Prophet (21:10–14). Agabus is from Jerusalem (11:27). He is the prophet who predicted the famine in Judea to which Antioch responded by sending Barnabas and Paul to Jerusalem with a famine relief offering (11:29–30). That is, Agabus has a proven track record. Now, this same Agabus on mission from God comes to Caesarea to let

---

[30]Acts 6:5; 8:5, 6, 12, 13, 26, 29, 30, 31, 34, 35, 38, 39, 40.

Paul know God's response to Paul's recalcitrance after Paul refused the Spirit's direct command at Tyre not to go to Jerusalem. Agabus takes Paul's belt, binds his own hands and feet in parabolic action like a Jeremiah or Isaiah, and declares, "Thus says the Holy Spirit, 'The man whose belt this is thusly the Jews in Jerusalem will bind and will deliver over into the hands of gentiles'" (21:11).[31] Several matters need to be noted about the very expression of this prophecy that make clear the context is negative, not positive, and punitive, not protective.

First, "Thus says" is the famous beginning of prophetic speech from the LXX translation evoking Old Testament *judgment oracles*. The contexts typically are *negative* judgments against the person so addressed by the prophet, and often the person is being impudent and stubborn and refusing to hear.[32] Second, the address, "the man" (*ton andra*, τὸν ἄνδρα) is impersonal and, therefore, rhetorically harsh in such judgment contexts. This blunt rhetoric is precisely that of Nathan confronting David over Bathsheba: "You are the man!" (2 Sam 12:7). This rhetoric emphasizes that human hubris is the core problem, evidenced in a rebellious posture toward God. Note that Nathan then asks David, "Why have you despised the word of the Lord?" (2 Sam 12:9). Nathan's question to David is now God's question to Paul after the disciples of Tyre spoke so clearly and consistently over a period of days.

The binding parable is what God will have to do to Paul to keep him from doing further damage to the gentile mission. Agabus's prophecy is the death knell to Paul's mission mandate. After Tyre, God had had enough and drew the line. Instead of "light for the gentiles," Paul now is darkness. In great irony, instead of freeing gentiles from darkness to light, he will be imprisoned by gentiles from light to darkness.

Now, the whole point of the second "we section," which Luke consistently has written in since Philippi, comes to bear. Luke throws his own hat into the ring against Paul. Luke uses the "we sections" to speak

---

[31]Greek: τάδε λέγει τὸ πνεῦμα τὸ ἅγιον· τὸν ἄνδρα οὗ ἐστιν ἡ ζώνη αὕτη, οὕτως δήσουσιν ἐν Ἰερουσαλὴμ οἱ Ἰουδαῖοι καὶ παραδώσουσιν εἰς χεῖρας ἐθνῶν.

[32]This phrasing is the traditional *Tade legei* (Τάδε λέγει), "thus says" to introduce a word of the Lord. Examples include Judg 2:1; 6:8; Exod 4:22; 5:1, 10; 7:17; 2 Sam 12:7 (Nathan's daring public exposure of David, "You are the man!"); 1 Kgs 21:19 (bold judgment of Ahab); Amos, *passim*; Mic 2:3; Obad 1:1; Hag 2:6; Zech 1:4 and *passim*; Isa 1:24; Jer 4:27; Ezek 2:4 (note the problem is being "impudent" and "stubborn"); 3:11 (specifically note the vacillation of "hear" or "refuse to hear") and *passim*.

to the issue of Paul and God's will. At Troas on the 2MJ, the first "we section" confirmed the Macedonian vision as God's will. Now, in stark contrast, the second "we section" will disconfirm Jerusalem as God's will: "Now, when we heard these things, both we and the local inhabitants strongly urged him not to go up to Jerusalem" (21:12). Luke could not be more blunt or forthright. He includes *himself* in those against Paul's decision. The expression is emphatic in the Greek text.[33] Now, the full weight of claiming eyewitness testimony for the material Luke is providing for Theophilus all the way from the Gospel prologue comes home to roost (Luke 1:2–3). "Not to go" advice Luke and others give here at Caesarea exactly repeats the divine prohibition at Tyre (21:4).

Everyone concurs with Agabus save Paul alone. He now makes a promise he will not keep. Luke and others were "weeping" (21:13) the same dramatic verb used for the elders saying farewell at Miletus. Again, the tone is ominous. Danger is near. Paul declares, "For I am ready not only to be bound but even to die in Jerusalem for the name of the Lord Jesus" (21:13). Not really. The moment he actually has this chance in Jerusalem, he hides behind the skirt of an appeal to Caesar (25:10). This appeal will be the nadir of Paul's descent out of God's will. He depends on another lord.

The conclusion is resignation: "The Lord's will be done" (21:14). This response echoes the resigned response of the Antioch church to the split of the mission team by Saul after his fight with Barnabas ("commended to the grace of the Lord by the brothers," 15:40). Of course, the statement actually has double entendre, because God's will has been the whole point since 19:21! Luke has confidence in the sovereignty of God. God's will most certainly *will* be done. God will get Paul to Rome. Paul might arrive in chains, but God will get him there. Paul now officially is off-track, He is fighting God. So, we now have a déjà vu of the beginning of the Hellenist movement with Saul holding the cloaks of those stoning Stephen, as well as the beginning of the 2MJ with Paul splitting the mission team in his fight with Barnabas over John Mark. Saul-Paul always is the same character in Acts. Agabus prophesies that Paul will be bound by God if Paul insists on going to

---

[33]Greek: ὡς δὲ ἠκούσαμεν ταῦτα, παρεκαλοῦμεν ἡμεῖς τε καὶ οἱ ἐντόπιοι τοῦ μὴ ἀναβαίνειν αὐτὸν εἰς Ἰερουσαλήμ.

Jerusalem and is assured he will create chaos and accomplish nothing. The upshot is, Jerusalem will be a disaster for everyone.

Jerusalem (21:15–17)

Paul finally arrives in Jerusalem. This destination, however, is a detour in the divine itinerary. Paul *should* be in Rome right now (19:21).

The host is Mnason of Cyprus (21:16). Mnason is given two details. He is an "early disciple," which should remind the reader of the beginning of the Hellenist movement, the very matter that now is at stake. Also, he is from Cyprus, which is kind of ironic. Barnabas was from Cyprus too (4:36). Barnabas had been the great Pentecost facilitator for Saul's early work, and the reason Saul even became a leader in Antioch in the first place. Cyprus also was the first target of the 1MJ

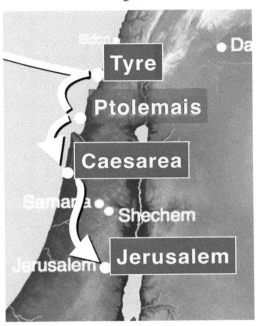

FIGURE 12.48. 3MJ—Return: Jerusalem.

and became a source of contention about John Mark's departure after Cyprus. Finally, Saul's suggestion to revisit churches of the 1MJ included those of Cyprus, which had been bypassed on the return back to Antioch ("every city," 15:36). Thus, Cyprus brings to mind another time Paul was off track from God's will and that characteristic stubbornness that had split the Antioch mission team. That same stubbornness is in play again.

When they arrive in Jerusalem, "the brothers welcomed us warmly," says Luke (21:17). The chaos, however, begins immediately the next day. The group will meet with James and the elders, and the crisis Paul's unexpected presence instantly has created is painfully obvious. James formulates an ill-conceived scheme in a desperate effort at damage control. He will fail. After trying to advise Paul in Caesarea but being rebuffed, then witnessing the half-baked idea being concocted in desperation by Jerusalem church leaders, Luke takes himself out of the inevitable Jerusalem debacle he can surmise is about to unfold. Note that the second "we section" ends abruptly after Luke's joint audience with James the next day after arriving in Jerusalem (21:18).

SUMMARY

Once again, journey highlights are summarized as bullet points. The following are significant features of the 3MJ.

(1) Mute points in Luke's account
- Corinthian crisis Paul endured (potential loss of church)
- Extent of dangers Paul faced in Ephesus
- Symbolic collection Paul gathered for Jerusalem
- Spanish mission Paul planned for the future

(2) The Ephesian crown jewel
- Paul is at the zenith of his gentile mission
- Story vignettes illustrate apologetics, Spirit, preaching, miracles, reputation, and impact

(3) Satellite churches are established
- Associates establish Pauline churches in surrounding regions
- Epaphras in Colossae is one example

(4) Crisis of ministry collapse
- Announcement of going to Jerusalem
- Silversmiths' riot suddenly ends Ephesian ministry

(5) Ambiguity of Macedonian/Greece movement
- Movement through Macedonia, rendezvous with Titus
- Context for 2 Corinthians
- Illyricum work at this time (Rom 15:19)?
- Winter in Corinth; context for Romans
- Macedonia, Corinth movement all for Jerusalem collection, but Luke says not a word of this, suppresses collection reason

(6) Crisis of Jerusalem journey
- Plot on life forces overland route back through Macedonia
- Second "we section" begins again at Philippi (where first one left off), but drops suddenly after arrival in Jerusalem
- Companion list explodes without explanation (collection)
- Miletus sermon (third example, church audience)

(7) The issue of God's will
- Critical texts: 19:21; 20:22; 21:4, 12
- Rome is God's will after Ephesus
- Jerusalem is Paul's obstinate detour

(8) Pauline correspondence
- Ephesus: Corinthian letters ("previous," 1 Cor, "harsh")
- Macedonia: 2 Cor
- Corinth: Romans

We have arrived at another major transition in the Acts narrative. The second half of Acts is the Holy Spirit empowering world mission. This story is told in two parts. The first part is world mission journeys the Spirit generates within the Hellenist movement in the impulse to gentile mission. These journeys originate in the Antioch church but transition to Paul's mission mandates. The second part is the divine destiny of Rome, obstructed by Paul, but achieved by God.

ACTS: A NEW VISION OF THE PEOPLE OF GOD

I. THE SPIRIT EMPOWERS MESSIANIC ISRAEL (ACTS 1–12)
   A. *The Spirit Empowers Messianic Israel's Renewal (1–5)*
      1. Renewal Beginnings (1)
      2. Renewal Empowerment (2)
      3. Renewal Witness (3–5)
   B. *The Spirit Empowers Messianic Israel's Hellenists (6–12)*
      1. Hellenist Leaders Emerge (6–7)
      2. Hellenist Mission Advances (8–10)
      3. Hellenist Center Shifts (11–12)

II. THE SPIRIT EMPOWERS WORLD MISSION (13–28)
   A. *The Spirit Empowers World Mission Journeys (13:1—21:17)*
      1. 1MJ: From Cyprus to Conference (13–15)
      2. 2MJ: From Asia to Europe (16–18)
      3. 3MJ: Ephesus (18:23—21:17)
   B. *The Spirit Empowers World Mission Destiny (21:18—28:31)*
      1. Destiny Denied: Jerusalem Disaster (21:18—23:32)
      2. Destiny Delayed: Caesarean Custody (23:33—26:32)
      3. Destiny Achieved: Journey to Rome (27–28)

13

Destiny Denied

Jerusalem Disaster (Acts 21–23)

DESTINY DENIED IS THE JERUSALEM disaster that ensues as a direct result of Paul's arrival in Jerusalem. Paul was supposed to be in Rome (19:21). On his own recognizance he has insisted on a Jerusalem detour first, against God's will. The reader needs not to forget, as far as the narrative of Acts has developed to this point, that every day Paul spends on the road to Jerusalem, and every day Paul spends in Jerusalem, is a day out of God's will. Further, the reader has to remember that, to this point, Luke *still* has not even insinuated *why* Paul insisted on going to Jerusalem. Only a knowledge of the Pauline letters makes us as readers omniscient to the narrative of Acts.

If all one had, however, were Acts itself, one would have to remember that Jerusalem would be one huge mystery. The reader would be acutely aware that the Spirit had told Paul directly and explicitly not to go to Jerusalem (21:4), and then God through one of his faithful prophets had warned Paul of imprisonment and tribulations if Paul disobeyed (21:11). God would not *spring* Paul out of prison; instead, God promised he deliberately would *put* Paul in prison. The reader of Acts, then, reading only Acts, has nothing but a huge question mark over the narrative: Why in the world did Paul feel like he *had* to go to Jerusalem? Why does Paul act so confident, behaving as if his idea was better than God's, as if he himself could convince God at some point of the wisdom of his going to Jerusalem if he kept insisting on this itinerary? This idea of trying to convince God his idea was better than God's idea Luke actually will use soon in a stunning plot device to come.

451

CHURCH DISASTER

Church Crisis (21:18–25)

James and the Elders (21:18)

The figures of James and "all the elders" represents a decided leadership shift in Jerusalem (21:18). Note that the apostles are completely absent. The story in Acts starts off with the apostles exclusively as the leaders of messianic Israel. They number Twelve for this very reason of their representative value, a new vision of the people of God. These apostles function exclusively as leaders into Acts 11. Elders, however, show up abruptly in the famine relief delivered by Barnabas and Saul, which is sent to the "elders" in Jerusalem, not to the apostles, who were still there (11:1 vs. 11:30). This development notably occurs after Peter's Cornelius affair that was opposed by conservative elements in the Jerusalem church (11:2). After Acts 11 and the Cornelius affair, the next time reference is made to leadership in Jerusalem, the Jerusalem Conference provoked by the 1MJ, one hears only of the combination of "apostles and elders." That is, throughout Acts 15 the apostles at the conference never are referred to exclusively as an independent entity, "the apostles," but always as "the apostles and the elders." After this conference, we never hear of the apostles again in Acts. So crucial at the beginning of the story, so symbolic, so important, they simply ride off into the sunset after Acts 15 without a word. Given their symbolic role in Luke-Acts as the ongoing story of Jesus out of the Gospel of Luke by continuing the same story of all that "Jesus began to do" (1:1) into all that Jesus continued to do, the narrative fade is so poignant. Without them, no apostolic church, no apostolic doctrine, no story of what Jesus continued to do. The

FIGURE 13.1. The Symbolic Twelve.

church now has taken a decidedly conservative turn in the road. Both internal and external pressure must have been intense.

"We Section" Ends (21:18)

Luke's silence is deafening. He never says *why* Paul is in Jerusalem (i.e., the collection). Luke is buffering Paul in this account. After the audience with James (21:18), Luke's "we section" that has been running continuously since Philippi (20:6) abruptly ends. Luke takes himself out of the Jerusalem picture. He did not agree with Paul going and told Paul so (21:12). Now in Jerusalem, disobedient to God, Paul no longer has Luke's support. Paul also no longer has wise counsel. That is why Paul agrees with the bad advice James is about to give.

Paul's Audience (21:18–22)

Paul's gentile mission is praised (21:20), no doubt because of the substantial sum of money Paul has just put in their hands, but Luke does not say a word about the collection Paul has been gathering for years. Luke had said Paul was trying to get to Jerusalem for the festival of Pentecost (20:16). Luke does not indicate whether Paul achieved this goal. Perhaps he does not say because what happens in Jerusalem will render the symbolic point of harvest fullness in messianic Israel rather meaningless. Barnabas and Saul's famine relief visit to Jerusalem earlier in the story did play into that theme. This Jerusalem visit has an entirely different character.

While his mission is praised, Paul's presence is problematic and has created an immediate crisis. Conservative believers react negatively. No matter the money, Paul is still a problem. That reality is what Paul never understood, or at least seemed unwilling to admit. When the matter was Jerusalem, Paul simply did not "get it." The situation now was like showing up to the church in Jerusalem immediately after the Damascus Road thinking everyone would be so delighted to see him (9:26). James puts the quandary succinctly.

> "You see, brother, how many thousands of believers there are among the Jews, and they are all zealous for the law. They have been told about you, that you teach all the Jews living among the gentiles to forsake Moses, and that you tell them not to circumcise their children or observe the customs. What then is to be done? They will certainly hear that you have come (21:20–22).

We have two problems here. The first problem is basic teaching and practice: "thousands of believers . . . all zealous for the law" (21:20). Law-observant Jews would be one matter, but "zealous" for the law?

What about the Jesus tradition should make one "zealous" for the law? Such zeal could mean only one truth: Stephen has not been heard in the Jerusalem church, or, if heard, dismissed. Stephen had made clear Jesus transcended Moses by cutting a new covenant that rendered the law and temple obsolete. If what James says is true, then the essence of the Jesus tradition never has been grasped fully in Jerusalem or has been seriously distorted. The Jerusalem church has a fundamental problem bigger than Paul. The absence of the voice of the apostles in Jerusalem may be beginning to show in what is taught and practiced. This first problem they do not seem to recognize.

The second problem is Paul: "They will certainly hear that you have come." That reality is their immediate and pressing problem—simply Paul's presence, nothing more. No matter if everything being said about Paul is untrue or grossly misconstrued. Notice how Luke's account already has falsified Jerusalem rumors about Paul, as in "not to circumcise their children," with not a word about Paul having Timothy circumcised in Lystra (16:3), or "not to observe the customs" with not a word about Paul shaving his head to keep a Jewish vow in Cenchreae (18:18). Rumors, however, always seem more powerful than the truth. Human gullibility virtually guarantees that vulnerability.

James's Plan (21:23–25)

James concocts a half-baked idea. He wants Paul to join four Jews in a Jewish vow. The vow has two insurmountable problems. First, *the vow has no mention of the Holy Spirit's guidance.* When Luke wants to say the Holy Spirit is involved, he will say so. Second, the vow requires the very action that God in his heavenly wisdom has been keen to avoid—*any connection between Paul and the temple.* For a *Hellenist* such as Paul, that prospect simply will not do! The reader never should forget the impact of the Stephen speech on the Sanhedrin and on Jerusalem. Stephen was stoned. Ever since the Damascus Road, Paul has become the epitome of the Hellenist movement for which Stephen died, the very voice of that movement. Somehow, Paul simply did not "get it." God did. Paul has no business in Jerusalem. Now that Paul is out of God's will, Paul will spiral ever downward. Paul's acceptance of James's ill-conceived and guaranteed-to-fail plot is the first sign of an increasingly debilitated Paul in this whole Jerusalem ordeal.

Strategy Failure (21:26–30)

In any case, the moment Paul arrives in Jerusalem, disaster ensues. The first disaster is for James and the church with this doomed plan. Paul had shaved his head at Cenchreae, so paying the fees for the shaving of the heads of four men certainly would not have been onerous to Paul as a Jew. The act was supposed to demonstrate that Paul "guarded the law" (21:24). However, for a public already convinced Paul does not guard the law, then the pro forma performance is in vain.

That public prejudice immediately kicks into gear the moment Paul is spied in the temple by "Jews from Asia" (21:27). Mention of the specific group is no accident by Luke. "Asia" likely means Ephesus. Ephesus likely means Jews who witnessed the silversmiths' riot over Paul. Paul avoided Ephesus on the trip to Jerusalem probably for the very reason of what now was transpiring in Jerusalem—public agitation. Paul just cannot catch a break with this "Ephesian factor" in his life. Ever since he made that fateful decision at Ephesus to detour to Jerusalem before taking up the mission mandate to Rome, the entire superstructure has been coming down around him. The charge they make compares to the charge against Stephen: "against our people, our law, and this place" (21:28). With this charge, Luke makes clear that Paul is seen as another Hellenist in the vein of Stephen in the eyes of the Jews of Jerusalem.

To strike a match to the gasoline they have poured, they further claim that "he has actually brought Greeks into the temple and has defiled this holy place" (21:28). That type of accusation would close the case. In-

FIGURE 13.2. Jerusalem Temple Inscription. Inscription posted on the temple wall warning of death for trespassing: "No foreigner may enter within the balustrade around the sanctuary and the enclosure. Whoever is caught, on himself shall be placed the blame for the death to follow" (IAM). Credit: oncenawhile/CC-BY-SA-3.0.

scriptions on the outer wall of the temple warned gentiles of the penalty of death for violating the temple precincts. Josephus tells of the slabs that were in Greek and Roman characters distributed at equal intervals on the wall to warn trespassing was on pain of death.[1] Luke gives the reason for their deduction that Paul had violated the temple: "For they had previously seen Trophimus the Ephesian with him in the city, and they supposed that Paul had brought him into the temple" (21:29). This deduction is what reveals that the more general expression "Jews from Asia" actually means Ephesians. These Jews know Trophimus of Ephesus. Thus, the Ephesian crisis still dogs Paul. A life-threatening riot ensues. Notice how a theme of riot begins to define the story of Paul in Jerusalem—nothing but riot ever results from his presence or of his attempts to speak (21:30–31).

James's idea explodes in a city riot. So much for suggesting Paul should go to the temple. Such a city riot is a public relations disaster for the church. Once Paul's reception by James is public knowledge, the damage is done to the reputation of James and the church. Paul, insisting on accompanying the collection to Jerusalem, thinking by doing so he was doing great good, now has done great harm. The money has become a moot point. What James would not give to buy back good reputation right about now.

MISSION DISASTER (21:31—23:22)

Paul's arrival in Jerusalem becomes a disaster for his own mission as well, as Paul goes into Roman custody at this moment and stays in custody for the rest of Acts. Agabus was right. The reader of Luke's Jerusalem narrative needs to attend to Luke's characterization of actors and action.

FIGURE 13.3. Ivory Panel Relief. Military scene depicting tribune flanked by his centurions on the left. (EMS).

[1] *J.W.* 5.5.2 (193–94). Archeologists have discovered several of these inscriptions.

Tribune's Intervention (21:31–39)

The Jerusalem tribune intervenes (21:31–34). Rome tolerated no public disturbance, most especially in Jerusalem related to the temple. If Pentecost was near, Jerusalem's population may have swelled, putting Romans on edge. Tribunes commanded centurions and were under a regional legate, who himself was under higher magistrates, such as consuls, praetors, and promagistrates. A legion typically had six tribunes, drawn from senatorial or equestrian families. Each commanded a cohort, ostensibly about a thousand troops, but less on occasion. A tribune might have political ambitions; military service was one track toward becoming a senator.[2] Since "all Jerusalem was in an uproar," the tribune had to act quickly and decisively (21:31).

The tribune put Paul in chains (21:32). Roman custody is now a subordinate sovereignty over Paul's life, allowed by God. Paul's movements from this point on no longer are his own. From this perspective, fulfilling God's will now seems impossible. Agabus had said Paul would be bound by gentiles, and so he is. Thus, the tribune's chains are another spiral downward out of control for Paul.

FIGURE 13.4. Antonia Fortress. Jerusalem temple mount model shows the four towers of the Antonia Fortress military barracks immediately adjacent to the temple walls where legionnaires were stationed for quick access to quell any disturbances (IMJ).

The tribune investigated, but the agitated crowd made getting the facts difficult (21:33). He ordered the prisoner transferred to the Antonia military barracks for safety and further questioning. Pressure on the tribune abides unabated, the crowd wanting Paul executed (21:34–36).

---

[2] On social rank, Suetonius *Aug.* 38; *Otho* 10. On general history, cf. Ferguson, *Backgrounds*, 28–29; 56–57; Liberati and Bourbon, *Ancient Rome*, 36; 40–41.

Paul makes his ignorant move again, like at Ephesus. He seeks to address a riotous mob (21:37). The evocation of the silversmiths' riot at Ephesus could not be stronger. Back then, Paul also had wanted to address the riotous mob, and only barely was dissuaded by his own associates and personal friends among the Asiarchs (19:30–31). The wisdom of that kind of counter-advice is precisely what Paul does not have now. Paul has no friends to restrain him as at Ephesus. Wanting to address a mob is an idea worse than James's half-baked vow proposal. All the tribune has to clarify is whether Paul is the reappearance of a recent Egyptian insurrectionist that had caused a commotion.[3] The Egyptian false prophet and his band were surprised at their camp on the Mount of Olives by governor Felix and Roman heavy infantry. Many followers were killed, but the Egyptian false prophet escaped. Paul assures the tribune that Paul's origin is in the province of Cilicia, the opposite direction from Egypt. Paul's fluent Greek also does not fit the profile of an uneducated commoner as the Egyptian probably was. Therefore, the tribune lets Paul address the mob (22:37–39).

Paul's Defense (21:40—22:21)

Paul addresses the crowd in their own Hebrew dialect, so immediately gains their close attention (21:40—22:2). He insists that he is a Jew, (22:3), but the real question for this crowd is whether he is an observant Jew. That more pertinent issue is why he delves into his Pharisaic training. Few would be willing to question a Pharisee's commitment to Moses. In

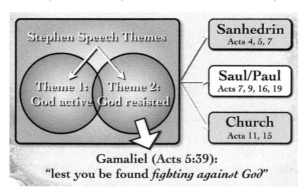

FIGURE 13.5. Stephen Speech Themes: Acts 22.

the process, Paul refers to being a student of Gamaliel ("at the feet of," 22:3). This reference to Gamaliel is a deliberate literary tie-in by Luke.

[3]Josephus *J.W.* 2.13.5 (261–63) gives details, some embellished, such as the size of the following (30,000 versus 4,000 in Acts).

Gamaliel's name occurs only twice in Acts. The first time is when Gamaliel addresses the Sanhedrin warning them to beware lest they find themselves "fighting against God" (5:39). Now, here is Gamaliel's prize student fighting against God and fulfilling his own Pharisaic teacher's warning in this Jerusalem debacle. Clearly, the student is *not* following his teacher. In fact, Paul is fulfilling all warnings that he has been given, including those from the disciples at Tyre and from Agabus at Caesarea. He even admits his persecuting zeal (22:4–5).

Damascus Road #2 (22:6–16)

Luke uses Paul's defense before the Jerusalem crowd as a second opportunity to tell the Damascus Road. The differences from the first account in Acts 9 generally show Paul shaping the story to emphasize its Jewish elements, appropriate for this Jewish audience. Jewish elements include:

- The descriptor "of Nazareth" added to Jesus's name (22:8)
- The emphasis on Ananias's Jewishness (22:12)
- The expression "God of our fathers" in the call report (22:14)
- The title "Righteous One" used of Jesus (22:14)

The point of rehearsing the Damascus Road for Luke is to emphasize that what changed Paul's life was *listening* to God, not ignoring God. The reader needs to be reminded that God temporarily had to blind Paul to get his attention. Paul's zeal had blinded Paul to God's will.

Paul's Temple Vision (22:17–21)

Paul's account here of his temple vision immediately after the Damascus Road is a stunning *tour de force* by Luke. The reader only now is discovering that, in fact, *Saul had two visions proximate in time to the Damascus Road*. Luke deliberately delayed reporting the second vision for dramatic effect, and does he ever drop a narrative bomb. Where was this vision? In Jerusalem in the temple—precisely where Paul has provoked this mob reaction he now is attempting to address! Paul's account of the words spoken to him *by Jesus himself in the temple* is a masterful stroke by Luke. Saul's Damascus Road revelation was, "I am Jesus *whom you are persecuting*" (emphasis added, 9:5). The persecution of Jesus's disciples includes a zeal hurting Jesus. Luke has shown that Saul's blinding zeal did not suddenly vanish on the Damascus Road.

Here is Paul's report of his mystery temple vision. Notice what is communicated directly by Jesus in no uncertain terms.

> "After I had returned to Jerusalem and while I was praying in the temple, I fell into a trance and saw Jesus saying to me, 'Hurry! Get out of Jerusalem quickly, because they will not accept your testimony about me.' And I said, 'Lord, they themselves know that in every synagogue I imprisoned and beat those who believed in you. And while the blood of your witness Stephen was shed, I myself was standing by, approving and keeping the coats of those who killed him.' Then he said to me, 'Go! For I will send you far away to the gentiles.'" (22:17–21).

Paul's admission here is extraordinary. Jesus told Paul in no uncertain terms to get out of Jerusalem. Jesus also went to the trouble to explain why, which he was not obligated to do. The reason was simple and one whose very nature would determine that this reason would be forever true: "they will not accept your testimony about me." One would think a direct command from Jesus himself would be honored with direct and immediate obedience on the part of the disciple. No, not Paul.

Paul has a better idea. Basically, Paul argues with Jesus. (Let that thought simmer for a moment.) He tries to argue on what he thinks is obvious about his story. Paraphrased, basically he says, "I have such a great testimony, they *have* to listen to me!" Jesus does not hesitate a second to respond to Paul's obtuseness. Jesus immediately commands Paul *a second time*, "Go!" Note carefully that Jesus then commissions Paul *far away*. Wherever Paul is supposed to be, that place is to be "far away" from Jerusalem, among gentiles, not among Jerusalemites. One could wonder if Rome might qualify for "far away"?

What we have in this exchange is God's abiding word to Paul on Jerusalem. This abiding word is made clear at the *beginning* of Paul's ministry. Jerusalem is no mystery to Paul. Paul has known from the beginning that his call is to the gentiles and that God never wanted him in Jerusalem. Now the reader suddenly realizes that Paul's seemingly innocent announcement in 19:21 of going to Jerusalem is *direct rebellion against God, and Paul knew that at the time*. Even more shocking, the incriminating evidence for this rebellion *has come from Paul's own lips*! Paul as obstinate Saul has come home to roost. Paul in insisting on going to Jerusalem has been too zealous—again.

At this point, Paul makes a strategic rhetorical blunder (22:21). Paul uses the word "gentiles." The issue of gentiles is the whole point of the riot. That one word reignites the explosive crowd. *The crowd's explosive reaction to Paul fulfills the words of Jesus in the temple vision:* "they will not accept your testimony about me." Paul's so-called "defense" before the Jerusalem crowds is a total failure and no defense at all. The riotous mob simply moves from mad to murderous. Trying to address the crowd collapses into crowd chaos again, where we started.

Paul's Citizenship Claim (22:22–29)

The tribune cannot ignore the rioting crowd. He decides to examine the prisoner by flogging (*flagellum*), a military procedure to get at the truth (22:24). Flogging can be a life-threatening event. Indeed, some died from the procedure. This threat will be Paul's first opportunity to fulfill his promise that he was ready to die in Jerusalem in his response to the Agabus prophecy (21:13). Paul, however, conveniently seems to have forgotten that promise he made in Caesarea. Paul avoids flogging by claiming Roman citizenship (22:25). Such a claim at this juncture is inconsistent, because such action is precisely what Paul did *not* do in Philippi to avoid a beating with rods (16:22–23). Further, this behavior does not match that of Jesus and the apostles. Flogging is what Jesus himself had to endure in Jerusalem from Pontius Pilate (Luke 23:22); flogging also is what the apostles themselves had to endure in Jerusalem from the Sanhedrin. Not only that, the apostles even praised God that they were counted worthy to be flogged (Acts 5:40)! In the context of the whole narrative of Luke-Acts, then, why Paul thought he should be exempt from the same fate of Jesus and the apostles in Jerusalem is not clear. Paul's assertion of Roman citizenship to avoid flogging shows Paul continues his spiral downward. His behavior is nothing to emulate, nothing bold, nothing courageous, nothing praiseworthy.

The tribune is notified of a claim to Roman citizenship by one of his centurions (22:26). If the matter is true, he has committed a critical military blunder that could cost him his future political career. He interrogates Paul on the claim, and Paul affirms its truth (22:27). The tribune challenges that such privilege usually came at great cost, which is how he himself obtained his citizenship. Paul socially "one-ups" the tribune with more honorable social status—inherited citizenship (22:28).

So Paul socially outclasses the tribune. The tribune suddenly is thrust into a precarious place both legally and socially. Now, he will have to depend on the Sanhedrin to adjudicate the charge.

Paul's Sanhedrin Appearance (22:30—23:10)

Paul is released but called to appear before the Sanhedrin to settle the matter (22:30). This appearance is back to the beginning, because this group was the authority in whose name Saul had left Jerusalem with letters in hand for Damascus (9:1–2). Paul has an altercation with the high priest that has ambiguity in the behavior and words. Paul claims a clear conscience before God, but for that the high priest orders him struck (23:1–2). This high priest would be Ananias who began to rule in AD 47. The greed of Ananias is legendary in the Jewish Talmud. Between the death of the procurator Festus and before his replacement, Albinus, could arrive on the scene, Ananias seized opportunity to have James the brother of Jesus killed.[4] Later, Ananias himself eventually was killed by Jewish zealots in the First Jewish War (66–70).[5] Paul is indignant that he has been struck before even formally being accused of anything, so he reacts to the high priest for this illegal and unethical action, "God will strike you, you whitewashed wall!" (23:3). Others who hear Paul are amazed that God's high priest is insulted so impudently and exclaim so to Paul (23:4). Paul then either makes an intentionally enigmatic statement, or Luke is not clear about what Paul meant: "I did not realize, brothers, that he was high priest" (23:5). Did Paul not actually recognize the high priest personally? He would not have to. The high priest was distinguished by his robes (even if this meeting was informal). Did Paul mean to speak ironically? That is, did he admit a person was wearing the robes of the high priest, but was not acting properly as the high priest, so was a religious imposter? Hard to know.

To throw the proceedings off, Paul pulls a manipulative ploy out of his Pharisee bag: "Brothers, I am a Pharisee, a son of Pharisees. I am on trial concerning the hope of the resurrection of the dead" (23:6). Paul here deliberately exploits Pharisee versus Sadducee doctrinal debate. Paul instantly creates council chaos, which was his true intent. Thrusting resurrection doctrine into the deliberation was not really an effort

---

[4] Josephus *Ant.* 20.9.1 (200).
[5] Josephus *J.W.* 2.17.9 (441).

to witness, because Paul said nothing about Jesus. Such shouting about resurrection in the Sanhedrin full of Sadducees is simply Paul in his continuing spiral downward. Nothing but chaos shadows his every move in Jerusalem. "Fearing they would tear Paul to pieces," the tribune retrieves Paul back into the Antonia fortress barracks (23:10).

Paul's Antonia Vision (23:11)

In Acts, Paul usually gets a vision when he is off track from God's will. That purpose is behind the Damascus Road vision, the temple vision immediately after the Damascus Road, and the Troas vision. This Antonia vision in the military barracks falls into the same category. The vision is the beginning of a long process of getting Paul back on track. This vision is a reminder of God's sovereignty over Paul's life. Paul is exhorted to keep up his courage, a word he desperately needs since he is spiraling completely out of control.

The present situation is described in characteristic Lukan double entendre: "Just as you have testified for me in Jerusalem." To read this statement as commendation, even more as praise, simply ignores completely what *actually* has been narrated in the last two chapters. Paul really has done nothing but instigate riot by every word that comes out of his mouth, whether in the streets of Jerusalem or the halls of the Sanhedrin. In Jerusalem, no miracles are performed. No one is saved. No one receives the Spirit. No one speaks in tongues. No churches are established. No magical books are burned. In such a narrative context, the "as" in "as you have testified" is *ironic*. The "as" is reference to the surrounding conditions, which would be "in chains." Further, when God finally gets Paul to Rome, he is going to leave Paul in chains as a reminder of this Jerusalem episode of Paul's zealous pursuit of his own plans over God's purposes. In a way, "in chains" will function as *another* thorn in the flesh that God will refuse to remove from Paul (2 Cor 12:7).

Paul now is reminded of the divine destiny he royally has frustrated by insisting on this Jerusalem detour—Rome. The Lord tells Paul, "you *must* bear witness also in Rome" (emphasis added, 23:11). Luke uses his special verb of divine necessity in Luke-Acts, "must" (*dei*, δεῖ). This word is precisely the divine directive Paul already had received in Ephesus (19:21). God in his sovereignty will get Paul to Rome, because Rome is the divine destiny of the Hellenist movement.

Paul's Endangered Life (23:12–32)

Now that Paul is in Jerusalem only one thing can be on his Jewish opponents' mind, seeking Paul's death, just as Saul had agreed with the death of Stephen and sought the death of followers of Jesus. Jesus's admonishment to Saul, "they will not accept your testimony," in the temple vision comes to consummation in a plot on Paul's life. Forty men vow to kill Paul and conspire with the Sanhedrin to feign another audience of Paul on pretense of further examination and murder Paul on the way before he even arrives (23:14–15). The plot became known to Paul's nephew, son of Paul's sister apparently living in Jerusalem. This nephew gains entrance to the Antonia where Paul is barracked, not an easy matter to achieve, and tells Paul. Paul instructs a centurion to have the young man taken to the tribune for an important word. The centurion probably complies because of the previous citizenship contest that had revealed Paul held higher social status than even the tribune (23:16–17).

The nephew is taken to the tribune and relates the story in detail of the plot on Paul's life (23:18–22). The nephew's news forces the tribune's hand. The death of a Roman citizen in his custody would be an egregious failure of military duty. The tribune will contravene the plot by a clandestine move of the prisoner that very night from Jerusalem to Caesarea with the incumbent change of legal venue from tribune to governor.

The tribune first sets up the transfer detail. A heavy guard is set, because a plot of forty men is a significant challenge to circumvent, and the entire city has been in uproar. Further, the countryside could prove unpredictable in such a volatile province as Judea, and robbers thrived in the darkness of night. Two centurions with their hundred-soldier centuries, seventy horsemen, and two hundred spearmen are called to duty, almost a third of the garrison's forces. Paul is to have mounts to ride, which indicates speed and a forced march (23:23–24).

The tribune then has to write a letter of formal transfer. From the letter, we first learn the tribune's name, Claudius Lysias (23:26). He had purchased his citizenship during the time Claudius was emperor. The letter is self-serving and exonerates Lysias by how he characterizes the nature of his intervention. He falsifies the actual sequence of learning about Paul's Roman citizenship. He says not a word about almost flogging Paul. So, Lysias here "saves" a Roman citizen from a Jewish mob.

Lysias's letter exonerates Paul. Lysias declares Paul was "charged with nothing deserving death or imprisonment" (23:29). Lukan apologetic on the innocence of Christianity is in play. Luke also anticipates Felix's malfeasance of office by holding Paul for two years. With Lysias's letter as a narrative precursor to Paul's imprisonment, Felix inherently is condemned even in Roman eyes.[6]

The military detail reached Antipatris that night, a little over halfway at about thirty-five miles from Jerusalem and about twenty-five miles south of Caesarea. (Soldiers were trained to do all night marches for surprise attack stratagems). Fortunately for this detail, the march was downhill out of mountains into the foothills and then coastal plain. The next day the cavalry completed the course to Caesarea while the rest of the detachment returned to the Antonia fortress back in Jerusalem to return the garrison to full

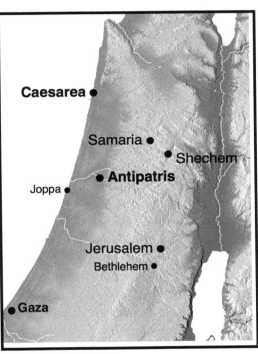

FIGURE 13.6. Antipatris. Paul's extradition to Caesarea was in two stages, with a stop in Antipatris.

strength, except for the cavalry detail (23:31–32). Paul's gentile mission now is in shambles. Jerusalem is a mission disaster.

SUMMARY

By the time Paul arrives in Jerusalem at the end of the 3MJ, leadership of the mother church has completed the shift from the distinct group of the apostles at the beginning to the Jewish pattern of synagogue elders.

[6]Roman and Jewish historians alike condemned Felix as ruthless, corrupt, heavy-handed, instigating bloody massacres; Tacitus *Annals* 12.54; Josephus *Ant.* 20.8.5.

The apostles represented a direct historical link to Jesus himself and the ongoing story of Jesus after the ascension. This leadership shift away from the apostles runs parallel to the more conservative complexion of the church. This church had difficulty with its Hellenist wing from the beginning, noted in the daily distribution blatantly ignoring Hellenist widows. The Hellenist Stephen brings the matter to a head with his (in)famous speech to the Sanhedrin about their idolatry regarding the temple monument to the Davidic monarchy. Persecution arose, scattering Hellenists out of Jerusalem. Hellenists thereafter begin moving the gospel into uncharted territory for Jewish preaching, Samaritans for one, then an Ethiopian "God-fearer" for another, which opened the door for the "God-fearer" Cornelius in Caesarea, stamped with the imprimatur of approval by the apostle Peter. Peter tied the Jerusalem church's hand on the matter of gentiles being accepted into messianic Israel, but did not answer their question on Moses and the law, even though Stephen implicitly already had indicated the answer. Thus, the suspicion and animosity of the conservative element of the Jerusalem church toward the Hellenist movement and its gentile work ran unabated until breaking out in full force after the stunning gentile results of the 1MJ forced the issue. A decision was made that settled the matter for Diaspora Judaism in the Jerusalem Conference, but that decision also left the conservative element in the Jerusalem church unaffected. This conservative bent runs hand-in-glove with the historical observation that Jerusalem never corporately sponsored a missionary journey of anyone anywhere. Therefore, whereas an *official* reception of Paul in Jerusalem might be expressed as "warmly," any representative of the Hellenist movement back in Jerusalem surely would raise the hackles of the "thousands" zealous for Jewish ancestral traditions—which is precisely what Paul, the premier voice of the Hellenist movement, did when he showed up in Jerusalem. The moment Paul arrived, James immediately spelled out that blunt truth to Paul.

Luke has been writing in a "we section" mode ever since joining Paul's Jerusalem group in Philippi. His purpose is to confirm that he is an eyewitness to the truth that the divine will was that Paul *not* go to Jerusalem. He himself even urged Paul not to go. Paul, however, in his personal zeal, ignored both the Spirit's direct communication as well as all the good advice around him. As soon as Luke hears James's half-baked idea suggesting Paul go into the Jerusalem temple, Luke knows the volatile situation in Jerusalem will explode and takes himself out of the equation. He has done all he could do. Paul is officially out of control. Only God can handle him. Therefore, the "we section" ends after the audience with James.

Paul's mission is praised, but his presence is problematic. Thousands of believers zealous for the law (hiding an essential problem in the Jerusalem church's teaching) make impossible any good result from Paul's unexpected and frankly unwanted arrival. James concocts a plan for Paul to pacify zealous believers about Paul's commitment to Jewish traditions. James wants Paul to underwrite the expenses of four men undergoing a Jewish vow. The plan, however, requires Paul to show up in the temple, a proposal flirting with irrationality. James's reasoning is simplistic, naïve, and dangerous. Further, the Holy Spirit does not inspire this action. When Paul accepts the plan, the fuse on the powder keg is lit.

The explosion is violent. Paul is spotted in the temple, assumed to be with the gentile Trophimus, and he nearly is killed by the mob. The tribune intervenes, allows Paul to address the violent crowd, and Paul retells the Damascus Road for its second time in Acts. The emphasis this time is on Jewish elements. The narrative bomb for the reader is learning Saul actually had *two* visions proximate to Damascus. The second one was a vision of Jesus in the temple in Jerusalem telling Paul to leave Jerusalem, because Jerusalemites would not accept his testimony, no matter how dramatic. Jesus told Saul his work was "far away," that is, never in Jerusalem. The temple vision makes clear that Paul's decision to go to Jerusalem while in Ephesus was knowing disobedience to the standing divine command not to try to minister on his own in that city.

Paul mentions gentiles again, a strategic blunder, and the crowd goes from mad to murderous. The tribune takes Paul to the barracks and almost has him flogged to get information, but Paul appeals to his Roman citizenship, denying the earlier promise he made to Agabus in Caesarea that he was ready to die in Jerusalem. A vain appearance before the Sanhedrin the next day also ends without resolution. Paul plays the Pharisee resurrection card to agitate the Sadducean majority and throw the proceedings into chaos deliberately.

Paul has another vision. Most of Paul's visions in Acts are when he is off track from God's will. This Antonia vision affirms the divine destiny of Rome but promises Paul will remain in Roman custody for this testimony, precisely how he has "testified" in Jerusalem. The word about testifying is euphemistic. Paul in reality has created nothing but chaos and riot and has temporarily frustrated the divine will. Paul's gentile mission is damaged seriously. Jerusalem has become one royal mess, for James and the church, as well as for Paul.

A plot on Paul's life forces the tribune to extradite his detainee to Caesarea and remand Paul's case to the governor of Judea. The trip to the coast requires an emergency forced march by night. Lysias's letter to Felix exonerates Paul as deserving nothing of death or imprisonment, a conclusion that implicitly indicts governor Felix for holding Paul for the next two years in Caesarea.

14

Destiny Delayed

Caesarean Custody (Acts 24–26)

ELIX KEPT PAUL TWO YEARS in Caesarea because he was looking for a bribe (24:26). Perhaps he had gotten wind that this prisoner had brought a large sum of money to Jerusalem, but that is just speculation. Everyone knew Felix was corrupt, so seeking a bribe could have been simply his standard *modus operandi*. Note Luke's narrative sequence is bounded by the city of Caesarea. Caesarea for the reader is Agabus déjà vu. Paul's extradition to Caesarea under Roman guard moves the story full circle back to the point of origination—Agabus's prophecy. Agabus had predicted that Paul by insisting on going to Jerusalem would wind up bound by gentiles. Now, Paul is back exactly where the prophecy was spoken, bound by gentile Romans. Prophecy fulfilled.

CAESAREAN ARRIVAL

Initial Audience (23:33–35)

Paul arrived in Caesarea safely (23:33). The governor's initial question of provenance was political protocol (23:34). If the subject of a client king were involved, diplomatic courtesy would require consultation of the client king about his subject. The province of Cilicia was united administratively with Syria, whose governor was Felix's supervisor, so Felix was free to proceed straightway with the accused. Felix agrees to hear the case, but he must wait for Paul's accusers from Jerusalem (23:35). In Roman law, if no accusers appeared on the day of court, the case was dismissed. Paul was accommodated in "Herod's quarters," which would be some arrangement in the palace quarters that Herod the Great had built for himself when he originally built the port of Caesarea, which served as his capital and permanent residence.

FIGURE 14.1. Caesarea Drawing. Theater is far left and Herod's Palace on the promontory jut out above, with stadium nearby. Harbor and warehouses right.

FIGURE 14.2. Caesarea: Herod's Palace. On a promontory was Herod's Palace that became the Roman governor's residence and administrative center.

FIGURE 14.3. Caesarea: Administrative Center. Administrative area of the governor's residence at Caesarea. In this area Paul would have met the governor Felix, and later Festus and king Agrippa II.

FIGURE 14.4. Caesarea: Herod's Palace Pool. Herod's palace complex even was graced with a fresh water pool right at the ocean's edge.

FIGURE 14.5. Pontius Pilate Inscription. This inscription is a replica of the inscription found at Caesarea naming the prefect Pontius Pilate, our only extant evidence of Pilate's existence outside the Gospels. Pilate's name is in the second line in Latin, PILATVS, "Pilatus."

FIGURE 14.6. Caesarea: Hippodrome. The stadium at Caesarea is near the Herod Palace complex and was built right alongside the ocean's edge to catch the sea breezes.

FIGURE 14.7. Caesarea: Augustus Temple Foundation. Greeting all mariners at the harbor entrance was a temple Herod the Great dedicated to his patron, the emperor Augustus. Herod's capital city was named for the emperor.

FIGURE 14.8. Caesarea: Harbor Warehouses, North. Products and supplies coming into the harbor were stored in large warehouses within the harbor complex.

FIGURE 14.9. Caesarea: Harbor Warehouses, South. The view of the warehouse area from the southern end.

FIGURE 14.10. Caesarea: Harbor Boat Ring. The large trading vessels would anchor in the harbor's manmade lagoon, and skiffs would bring the goods to the dock. The boat rings are for tying up the skiffs at dockside.

FIGURE 14.11. Caesarea: Harbor Dock Steps. These steps would have allowed passengers to board the skiffs to be ferried out to their ship of passage.

FIGURE 14.12. Caesarea: Harbor Mosaic. Mosaic floor within the harbor warehouse district.

FIGURE 14.13. Caesarea Aqueduct. Aqueduct bringing fresh water to Herod the Great's Caesarea Maritima ("Caesarea by the Sea").

Paul is in a genuine quandary. Which city should he desire for the adjudication of his case, Jerusalem or Caesarea? Jerusalem spells chaos. Caesarea spells corruption. In Jerusalem Paul now knows all he can expect is disturbance, riot, and death threats. Neither his return nor his presence in that city is feasible. On the other hand, Felix is an infamously corrupt procurator riding on the coattails of his brother Pallus in Rome, who has the emperor's ear. Roman jurisdiction in Judea is a roll of the dice. Paul is on the horns of a dilemma.

Further, Paul's true disaster is the loss of his gentile mission, which is dead in its tracks. The irony is going to be that Paul will wind up as long in Caesarea as he was in Ephesus. Paul has no one to blame but himself. He is responsible for this mess. His own rebellion against God (19:21; 21:4) was not innocent and not without consequences. The divine itinerary after Ephesus was Rome. Paul's itinerary, in bold contrast, included a detour to Jerusalem first God did not approve. The result is a costly, two-year delay in getting to Rome.

Paul's Plans: Summary

Now that Paul is in Roman custody in Caesarea, we can review the business of Paul's journey to Jerusalem at the end of the 3MJ. Luke simply does not intend this trip as parallel to Jesus's own journey to Jerusalem, which is a major motif of the Gospel (9:51—19:27).[1] Commentators trying to parallel Jesus and Paul on a "journey to Jerusalem" scheme are trying to hammer a narrative square peg into a round hole, almost like reading with narrative cataracts. Some even propose a hermeneutic of denial. Such readings dramatically miss Luke's point.[2] Luke actually is straightforward, and perhaps just more bluntly honest about Paul than we want him to be after centuries of painting a halo on Paul's head.

- Luke is blunt that Jerusalem was *not* God's will for Paul. The evidence of 21:4 is unimpeachable.

- Any explicit statement that Jerusalem is God's will is only from the mouth of Paul himself—and he continually is contradicted all the way to Jerusalem, even by Luke himself (21:12).

- The divine necessity verb, *dei* (δεῖ, "must"), Luke never uses with Jerusalem, only with Rome (19:21; 23:11).

- Luke carefully balances Paul's insistence (*etheto*, ἔθετο, imperfect, 19:21) with the determined objection of the Holy Spirit (*elegon*, ἔλεγον, imperfect, 21:4).

- What the Spirit does say to Paul about Jerusalem always is negative, including prophetic judgment, with no promise of protection, rather, only bonds and affliction.

- In a brilliant literary move, Luke delays telling the reader a vision Paul had *in the temple* just after the Damascus Road that communicated clearly to Paul that *Paul always was going to be a problem for God in Jerusalem*, so Paul should get out and stay out (go "far away").

[1]For Jesus's own journey as a major Gospel motif, see "Preliminaries," 8–10.

[2]Polhill, *Acts*, 498, is typical. His "parallels to the passion of Christ" scheme from Acts 21 on is labored and tendentious. More recently, the "twelve similarities" Keener details (*Acts*, 4:3448–49) fall apart on the failure to acknowledge inevitable common denominators inherent to closely similar contexts. Whereas Luke does have narrative parallels between the Gospel and Acts, *the journey to Jerusalem is not one of them*. Jesus going to Jerusalem was in the center of God's will—Paul most certainly was not.

- Paul's troubles with the will of God at the beginning of the 2MJ are Luke's premonition for the reader of the Jerusalem disaster caused by Paul's stubbornness and zeal, just as in the fight with Barnabas.

- The themes of the Stephen speech find their most stunning and tragic illustration in all of Acts in the life of Paul himself in the Ephesian ministry immediately followed by this trip to Jerusalem.

- Luke never indicates *why* Paul is going to Jerusalem. Paul's own letters at this time make clear this trip is to deliver the collection from Paul's gentile churches for the church in Jerusalem. Luke, however, intentionally is suppressing any connection of this trip with the collection. Why?

We can summarize Luke's view on Paul's plans for Jerusalem:

1. *Unintended detour.* Luke viewed Paul's trip to Jerusalem as an unintended detour in the divine itinerary west to Rome after Ephesus.

2. *Unfortunate decision.* Luke viewed Paul's trip to Jerusalem as an unfortunate decision by Paul in the matter of the collection that destroyed its impact.

Paul's Plans

✤ Paul's Plans: Luke's View

✤ 1. *Unintended detour:* Luke viewed Paul's trip to Jerusalem as an unintended detour in the divine itinerary west to Rome after Ephesus.

✤ 2. *Unfortunate decision:* Luke viewed Paul's trip to Jerusalem as an unfortunate decision by Paul in the matter of the collection that destroyed its impact.

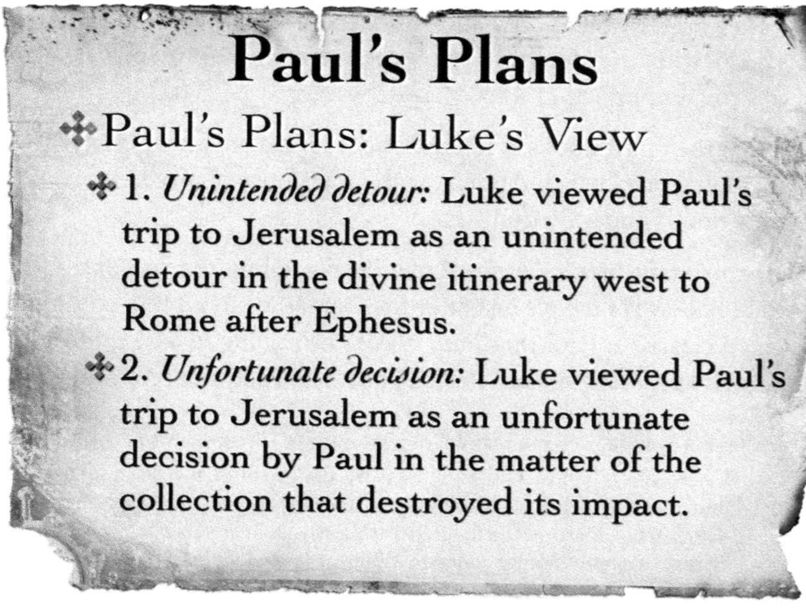

FIGURE 14.14. Luke's View on Paul's Plans for Jerusalem.

Thus, Luke shields the glory of Paul's most brilliant idea, the collection, from the shame of his most baneful idea, that is, that Paul concluded he personally should deliver the collection to Jerusalem, *against God's known will about his presence in Jerusalem*. The result was an unmitigated disaster for James and the Jerusalem church and for Paul and the gentile mission. From Ephesus to Jerusalem is quite a journey for Paul. The catastrophic collapse of his Ephesian mission and the uncontrolled chaos of the following Jerusalem disaster means Paul's entire mission program is in grave peril due to sudden storm. His mission is foundering like a storm-battered ship. The peril only increases for all on board as the captain insists on pushing on rather than take his passengers' advice to put into safe harbor.

PAUL AND FELIX

Paul is in a real pickle now. Not only does his gentile mission lie shipwrecked on his own self-will. Worse still, Paul here gets snakebit by the injustice of a Roman provincial governor whose administration was so corrupt that he wound up being recalled to Rome.

Marcus Antonius Felix (52–58) was part of a family of freedmen of the imperial family, which means this family had low social status. Though of low social status, they managed to exert some power due to the influence Pallus, Felix's brother, had in emperor Claudius's court as secretary of the treasury. Thus, the power broker in Felix's family was his brother Pallus in Rome. After emperor Claudius came Nero, who deposed Pallus (AD 55), which weakened Felix's office in Judea. Increasing turmoil over Roman occupation in Judea also threatened the stability of Felix's governorship. The rising tide of Jewish nationalism put great pressure on Felix. To aggravate an already precarious situation in Judea, Felix himself was arbitrary in his governance and insensitive in his administration. Felix was smitten by the beautiful Herodian princess, Drusilla, sister to Agrippa II, and talked her into marrying him. They both had to divorce spouses in order to marry. Thus, married to a Jewish princess, Felix had an inside understanding of Jewish matters. Felix and Drusilla had a son, named Marcus Antonius Agrippa III. Tragically, Drusilla and her son Agrippa III died in the eruption of Mount Vesuvius that destroyed Herculaneum and Pompeii in AD 79 while vacationing at their villa in Pompeii.

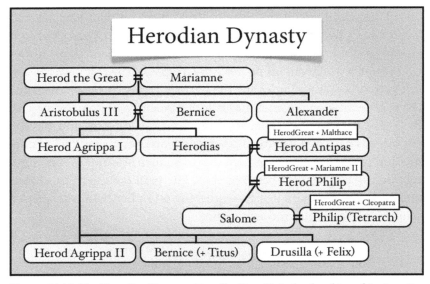

FIGURE 14.15. The Herodian Dynasty: Drusilla. Drusilla is the daughter of Agrippa I, the Jewish king who was taken mortally ill suddenly in the theater at Caesarea.

FIGURE 14.16. Mount Vesuvius. Ancient Herculaneum foregrounds Vesuvius, one-third of its dome missing after the AD 79 explosion that destroyed surrounding cities.

Sanhedrin's Case (24:1–9)

Paul's accusers arrive from Jerusalem, including the high priest, Ananias, his retinue, and their lawyer, Tertullus. Their strategy is to use Felix's problems in Judea. The flattery is obsequious and false. Saying Fe-

Figure 14.17. Aristocratic Cosmetic Box. Beautiful ivory and rare wood jewelry box from Pompeii. Ivory plates on front depict caryatids, and on either side winged Eros figures, with ivory lid top. In the box were found a mirror, wooden case, bone comb, ring, items of gold, two silver buckles, jar, bone needle, spatula, and hair pins. This cosmetic box of an elite Roman woman illustrates what could have been part of princess Drusilla's boudoir during her final days vacationing in Pompeii (NNAM).

lix has "long enjoyed peace" (24:2) is an outright lie, and talk of "reforms" made "for this people because of your foresight" is a broad stretch by any Jewish imagination among the common folk. To try to trigger the Roman hot button, Paul is presented as a "perfect pest," an "agitator," and a "ringleader" (24:5), all of which translates as general lawbreaker. So, Paul is accused of fomenting uprisings in provinces, but where are the witnesses for this accusation? Almost comically, Paul is accused of being a Nazarene sect ringleader, but where are the witnesses for this? This accusation is belied by public knowledge: the truly outstanding leader and quite well known in Jerusalem is James.

The Jewish hot button is presented next. "He even tried to profane the temple" (24:6). Of course, the irony here is, laws already were on the books about the sanctity of the Jewish temple in Jerusalem, and that did not require the Roman governor's involvement. Had the charge really been true, the tribune Lysias never would have remanded the detainee to Caesarea in the first place. What will complicate the matter is that Lysias is implicated as interfering with their own police action ("so we seized him," 24:6). All the Jews present then joined in to agree with the accusations (24:9).

Paul's Rebuttal (24:10–23)

Felix gives Paul a chance to respond. Rebuttal one is that all his activities were private, not public, so the "perfect pest" slander is impossible. Paul further points out he has been in Jerusalem only twelve days (24:11), not even a smidgen of the time required to pull off all that has been accused. Paul was not disputing with anyone nor stirring up a crowd in the synagogues or elsewhere in the city (24:12). Paul admits to being a follower of "the Way" (24:14), that he has hope in God for resurrection (24:15), and that he lives with a clear conscience (24:16). He was in Jerusalem to bring alms to the nation (24:17), which would be the only subtle allusion Luke ever makes to the collection. These alms, in fact, were the real reason Paul was in Jerusalem. The reference here may have been what could have given Felix the idea of asking for a bribe later. What they found him actually doing in the temple was performing rites of a standard Jewish vow, and that without crowd or disturbance (24:18).

Rebuttal two is no witnesses. Jews from Asia made the fuss, but they are strangely absent from the court (24:19). If actual witnesses are produced, their testimony will be the opposite of the charges. With this rebuttal Paul already has trumped his accusers. Felix well knows that no witnesses means the entire proceeding is illegal in Roman law, and Felix should dismiss the case immediately.

Rebuttal three Paul himself did not make. This rebuttal would be Lysias's letter the tribune himself wrote to accompany the detainee to Caesarea. Lysias in his letter already had testified that the prisoner was "not guilty." He had written to Felix flatly that Paul was "charged with nothing deserving of death or imprisonment" (23:29).

Felix vacillates. The "case" should have been dismissed. (Contrast the action of Gallio!) Felix pretends to wait to hear from the tribune on the implication of Tertullus of interference (24:22). This reason is a sham. Luke carefully tells the reader that Felix is "rather well informed about the Way" (24:22). This information likely is the result of his marriage to Drusilla, the Herodian princess fully acquainted with the Jewish affairs of her nation. From a Jewish perspective, Felix knows that Romans could care less for Sanhedrin religious disputes, such as the resurrection doctrine that Paul professed (24:21; compare Gallio). So, the religious case is bogus. From a Roman perspective, Felix knows that no witnesses means the case has no legal standing in Roman law whatsoever. Luke insinuates Felix's procrastination is a miscarriage of Roman justice and that Paul should have been released immediately. Felix, however, orders Paul kept in custody. The procurator allows some liberty and visits from friends to see to Paul's needs (24:23). Felix clearly is no Gallio!

Private Conference (24:24–25)

Paul is summoned for a private audience with governor Felix, who is accompanied by his wife, Drusilla. Felix hears Paul speak about "faith in Messiah Jesus" (24:24). Felix possibly may

Paul's Message to Felix	
"justice"	Felix's *court*
"self-control"	Felix's *administration*
"future judgment"	Felix's *career*

FIGURE 14.18. Paul's Message to Felix. Paul pulls no punches.

have been entertaining his wife, Drusilla, by playing sport with this prisoner. Paul, however, pulled no punches. Speaking about "justice" was about the problem in this Roman court. Speaking about "self-control" was the problem in this Roman administration. Speaking about "future judgment" was about the problem for this Roman career, both with Rome and with God, a savvy double entendre by Paul (24:25).

Felix is frightened, and sends Paul away (24:25). Luke spells out he delays for two reasons. The first reason is looking for a bribe from Paul (24:26). Luke here actually is charging Felix with malfeasance of office. Perhaps Felix was thinking of the "alms" Paul had said he had brought to Jerusalem (24:17). Felix sends for Paul often to "converse with him" (24:26). Paul is snakebit by provincial corruption and now stuck in an infinite loop—no charges, no case, no release. This chicanery went on for a full two years (24:27a).

The second reason for delay was to do the Jews a favor at the end of his term. Felix was recalled to Rome. His replacement was Porcius Festus (24:27). Felix was in a weakened condition in Rome with his brother Pallus falling out of favor, and he had powerful opposition in Judea. Thus, Festus inherited a prisoner with no charges and no case. Luke is at great pains to point out that the only time Paul ever was detained by a provincial Roman administration for an extended period of time, he was held without legal cause through the corruption of a local, Roman provincial official.

PAUL AND FESTUS

Little is known of Festus's political background. Even his time of office cannot be determined with certainty.[3] He seems to have fared better than Felix in his administrative policies in Judea, as he never seemed to have developed the kind of bad reputation that Felix did among Roman historians. He died in office from illness.

Complaint Resumption (25:1–5)

With the arrival of a new and unseasoned procurator, Paul's opponents see a possible opening for jump-starting their case again. When the procurator pays a courtesy call on Jewish leaders in Jerusalem, they seek a new advantage to resume legal efforts with this inexperienced official fresh on the job (25:1–2). All of this court activity, however, is a pretense just to get Paul to Jerusalem in order to kill him by ambush along the way (25:3).

Festus is unseasoned but not dumb. Transfer of a prisoner would be costly and completely unnecessary. Further, his itinerary would have him in Caesarea shortly anyway (25:4). The Jewish leaders could come to him at Caesarea and make their case (25:5). The offer to hear the case was a new lease on life for their designs. This new procurator changes the equation. He shows himself ready to resume the trial, and as new on the job, he needs to curry favor with Jerusalem's leaders. So, he offers a retrial back in Caesarea. With that offer, the Sanhedrin's case suddenly revives after being on life support for two years. All around, this unexpected change in political scenery portends bad news for Paul.

Festus's Tribunal (25:6–12)

A little over a week later, Festus goes to Caesarea, and, true to his word, orders Paul to be brought the next day (25:6). Paul is surrounded by many accusers who have traveled with Festus to Caesarea, but they run

---

[3]Traditionally, about AD 59–62 on numismatic evidence (Bruce, *Acts*, 345–46; AD 60 for Conybeare and Howson, *Life and Epistles of St. Paul*, 899–900). However, as early as AD 55 actually is possible. See Keener, *Acts*, 4:3444–46.

into the same legal problem as before, "bringing many serious charges against him, which they could not prove" (25:7). They could not prove these changes, because, exactly as before, they had no witnesses. The case is illegitimate in Roman law, which Festus should have cognized immediately.

In response, Paul fundamentally denies all charges. He asserts he has given no offense to the law, the temple, nor to the emperor (25:8). Festus is in an awkward spot with no witnesses. He most likely did not anticipate that scenario, since that situation would be extraordinarily humiliating for Paul's accusers, and Festus would not have expected them to be caught in so simple a predicament. Festus, however, is new to the job, and does need to get off on the right foot with Jewish leadership in Jerusalem. So, "wishing to do the Jews a favor" (25:9), Festus proposes a change of venue to Jerusalem (25:9). Perhaps Festus hopes witnesses are there.

Paul for his part probably is stunned. Moving the case back to Jerusalem is the nuclear option. This change of venue proposal has been the Sanhedrin's goal for the last two years. The anticipated move would make Paul's future prospects very dim indeed. The effort of his nephew to save his uncle will have gone completely in vain. Here is Paul's second chance to keep the promise he made of willingness to die for Jesus (21:13).[4] Paul had boasted this claim of "willingness to die in Jerusalem" to Agabus, to Luke, and all the other believers witnessing that prophetic moment in Paul's life *in this very city of Caesarea*. When his martyr moment arrives, however, unlike Stephen, Paul completely capitulates.

> Paul said, "I am appealing to the emperor's tribunal; this is where I should be tried. I have done no wrong to the Jews, as you very well know. Now if I am in the wrong and have committed something for which I deserve to die, I am not trying to escape death; but if there is nothing to their charges against me, no one can turn me over to them. I appeal to the emperor (25:10–11).

As Paul frames his appeal to Caesar, the reader of Acts needs to ask, "What's wrong with this picture?" Several matters are egregiously wrong. First, note carefully Paul's flimsy rationalization. Paul says he is willing to die only if he is "in the wrong" and has done something for

---

[4]The first was avoiding flogging by claiming Roman citizenship (22:25).

which he "deserves to die." Pray tell, which Christian martyr "deserved" to die? Did Jesus deserve to die? The Roman centurion, in fact, seeing the death Jesus died, confessed, "Surely this man was innocent" (23:47). Did Stephen deserve to die when Saul was holding the cloaks of those stoning Stephen? Did the apostle James, the brother of John, deserve to die? No. Paul's rationalization here will not do, not even for one moment. The reasoning is self-serving. Paul in no way has justified the action he is about to take.

Second, note careful-ly what Paul opts to do at this point. He opts to ap-peal to Caesar. *The appeal to Caesar is the appeal to another lord.* This Caesar is Nero. When Festus dic-tates his memorandum to Nero, Festus will address the emperor as "my lord Caesar." Instead of bear-ing letters about him from the Sanhedrin to the syna-gogues of Damascus, now Paul will go with a letter about him from a provin-cial governor to the Roman emperor, lord Nero. With

FIGURE 14.19. Nero Sestertius Coin. NERO CAE-SAR AVG GERM IM[P], "Nero Caesar Augustus Germanicus Imperator." Reverse of imperial coins often depicts a god enthroned (MCF).

Festus's proposal for a change of venue back to Jerusalem, Paul played what he probably at the time considered his Roman citizenship trump card, his appeal to the protection of lord Caesar's tribunal. What readers might ignore here is that God *as Lord already had promised his own protection for Paul* in the Antonia vision ("you must bear witness also in Rome," 23:11). Note that in the vision description Luke is careful to make clear that Paul saw the "Lord" standing by him. The elephant in the room almost universally overlooked by readers of Acts in Paul's ap-peal to Caesar *is this issue of lordship.*

The appeal will tie Festus's hands, and Paul knows this. Thus, the note of Festus conferring with his council has a perfunctory character. The result of the conferral is expected: "You have appealed to the emperor; to the emperor you will go" (25:12). Paul's case soon will be leaving Caesarea and Judea altogether. Paul has escalated the matter to the point of no return. He has appealed to another sovereign.

Paul now has made three different appeals to avoid life-threatening moments in Jerusalem and Caesarea:

- Roman citizenship to escape Roman flogging (22:25)
- Resurrection doctrine to escape inevitable Sanhedrin verdict (23:6)
- Caesar's tribunal to escape deposition, retrial in Jerusalem (25:11)

From losing the Ephesian mission, to accepting the half-baked vow proposal of James and the Jerusalem church, to wanting to address a murderous mob, to being forced to make three desperate appeals to escape life-threatening moments—these are all the moves of a life careening out of control. Paul's tragic spiral downward after announcing his decision in Ephesus to go to Jerusalem is complete. With this appeal to the protection of lord Caesar, Paul has hit rock bottom.

PAUL AND AGRIPPA II

Herod Agrippa II was a pro-Roman client king his entire political career. The emperor Claudius (41–54) considered Agrippa II too young to succeed his father, Agrippa I, as king of Judea in AD 44. Soon after, though, Agrippa II began receiving his first appointments. In AD 48, he received Herod's kingdom of Chalcis and was granted authority to appoint the high priest in Jerusalem. Five years later in AD 53, he exchanged Chalcis for other regions, including Philip's two territories of Iturea and Trachonitus and Lysanias's Abilene. Under emperor Nero (54–68), Agrippa II continued his steady advance. In AD 56, Agrippa II added the Sea of Galilee region and towns in Perea. The territorial gains included the cities of Tiberius, Caesarea Philippi, and Tarichea, as well as Julias and its fourteen surrounding villages.

As everything else in Judea, Agrippa II's political career was stymied by the outbreak of the First Jewish War in AD 66. Agrippa II was loyal to Rome and opposed the war and lobbied hard to try to prevent its outbreak. After the war, Agrippa II, as did many of the aristocrats of Judea loyal to empire, immigrated to Rome. In AD 70, he gained more territories, and in AD 75, he was promoted to praetorian rank.

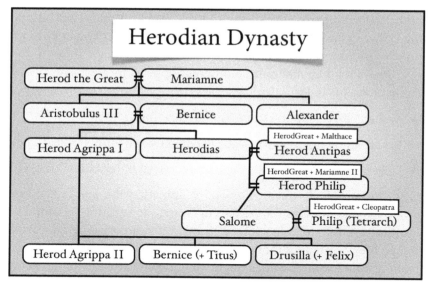

FIGURE 14.20. The Herodian Dynasty: Agrippa II. Agrippa II was considered by the Romans too young to rule when his father died unexpectedly in Caesarea.

In his final years, Agrippa II played a role about AD 77 as a consultant for Josephus's research for the *Jewish War*. The last word we have of Agrippa II is his death about AD 100. Agrippa II left no heirs. As a result, he sometimes is referred to as the "last of the Herods."

Agrippa II's personal life is intertwined with that of his sister, Bernice. Her first marriage was to her uncle, Herod of Chalcis. When Herod of Chalcis died in AD 48, Bernice moved in with her brother. She accompanied Agrippa II everywhere, which raised rumors of an incestuous relationship between her and her brother. This period with Agrippa II is the time of Paul's audience with Agrippa II. Thus, Bernice accompanies Agrippa II to greet Festus, the new governor of Judea (25:13). In AD 63, Bernice married for the second time, this time to Polemon of Cilicia. The marriage did not last long. The idea was whispered that the marriage was arranged in order to attempt to suppress the rumormongering about her and her brother. After the First Jewish War, Bernice also immigrated to Rome. In Rome, Bernice became the mistress of emperor Titus.

Agrippa II's post-war career in Rome allows him to serve as a reference and authority on Jewish matters for Josephus's *Jewish War*. Likewise, anyone wishing to check Luke's presentation of Paul's audience with the Jewish king *could ask Agrippa II personally as an eyewitness*, fulfilling Luke's eyewitness promise in his Gospel prologue.

Paul's Defense (25:13—26:32)

Agrippa II, accompanied by his sister, Bernice, arrive in Caesarea calling upon the new procurator (25:13). Their appearance is a boon for Festus due to access to their expert, local advice. Festus seizes his opportunity. He explains Paul's case, but ingeniously hides his political motives and casts himself in a favorable light as judicious.

Case History (25:14–22)

Festus explains the problem is not his but inherited from Felix (25:14). The chief priests and elders leaned on the new procurator for an immediate sentence (25:15), but Festus appealed to Roman jurisprudence and proper procedure of meeting accusers face to face and making a defense (25:16). Festus conducted a tribunal with dispatch (25:17), but the charges took him by surprise, since they had nothing to do with the typical charges on a procurator's docket (25:18). The charges concerned their own internal religious affairs, and other disputes about a Jesus who had died, "but whom Paul asserted was alive" (25:19). Obviously, all this was Jerusalem's affair, not Caesarea, and Festus was quite unprepared to insert himself into such disputes, so Festus asked the prisoner if he wished to go to Jerusalem for more proper adjudication of the case (25:20). The prisoner, however, Festus explains, unexpectedly appealed to the imperial sovereign, which has put Festus in a real dilemma of needing to transfer a prisoner to the emperor, but not understanding what case to describe, since all the charges are religious disputes (25:21).[5]

Agrippa II takes the bait and agrees to "hear the man myself," that is, act as a political consultant for Festus (25:22). Agrippa II's accommodation is Festus's ticket for writing up the case to the emperor. Festus needs this help because the prisoner is innocent in Roman law, and the procurator novice on Jewish issues. A bogus *provocatio* report to the

---

[5]Here, "imperial sovereign" translates *Sebastou* (Σεβαστοῦ), which itself is a translation of the Latin *augustus*, "revered one," "august," from which the name Augustus derives, given to Octavian for establishing the Roman Empire after winning the battle of Actium in 31 BC. The name became part of the official title of the Roman emperor.

emperor could harm this procurator's career. To have king Agrippa II as a "ghost writer" would be a political landfall. So, Agrippa II's role is as an expert on Jewish matters engaged as a court consultant. He first needs a case review, though, in order to help the procurator word the *provocatio* document to emperor Nero.

Festus's Preamble (25:23–27)

Pomp and circumstance attends the next day's audience hall assembly. Agrippa and Bernice are accompanied by military tribunes and "the prominent men of the city" (25:23). This assemblage of notables is extraordinary. Caesarea had five cohorts, so five tribunes attend, whose roles are similar to the one tribune, Lysias, in Jerusalem. The procurator apparently considers the matter of some military import, since Jerusalem temple disturbances are on the record with this case. The vague category of "prominent men" perhaps are Jewish leaders in Caesarea invited by Festus, as well as others, since the matter seems entirely of Jewish concern to Festus, and some even in Caesarea have accused Paul ("the whole Jewish community petitioned me, both in Jerusalem and here," 25:24).

Festus makes a stunning, public admission: "But I found that he had done nothing deserving death" (25:25). With the admission of Paul's innocence in the earlier letter of the tribune Lysias to Felix, now part of court records, Paul's innocence now is repeated for the second time by Festus. Festus tacitly faults Felix's procrastination. In essence, Festus asserts that Paul's *provocatio* appeal is unnecessary, but the legal gears already have been engaged by the prisoner. So, Festus is blaming Paul. However, Festus is misstating the case. If Paul has done "nothing deserving of death," why is he still in Roman custody in the first place? Festus is trying to abdicate judicial responsibility, but not successfully. Festus should have released Paul immediately. After all, even in Festus's own hearing of the case, *no witnesses were produced*. Legally, the case has no grounds whatsoever, and should have been dismissed without delay, but Festus conveniently skirts around this crucial legal point.

A case that is no case is the problem. That strange profile is why Festus admits that he has "nothing definite to write" (25:26). No joke. Festus now already is publicly committed to Paul's innocence. This revelation of the procurator's admission of the prisoner's innocence in his preamble statement probably catches Agrippa II totally off guard.

The nature of the report to Caesar is prejudiced already to have to be composed in terms of the prisoner's innocence. Such a report will be awkward to write indeed. Agrippa II now knows he *really* has his work cut out for him. This consultation will not be as easy as he first might have thought. Thus, Festus's closing word is an astute note of dark humor by Luke: "for to send a prisoner without indicating the charges against him seems to me unreasonable" (25:27). You think?

Note to whom Festus clearly indicates he is addressing his report, "to our Lord" (25:26).[6] Now is when Luke makes clear how appeal to Caesar by Paul the Roman citizen should be contextualized. Appeal to Caesar is *not* to be commended facilely as a cunning dodge of local, provincial administration by Paul. Appeal to Caesar is an exchange of sovereignty, of Paul putting more faith in Rome than in God.

Paul's Presentation (26:1–23)

The judge has to give the prisoner permission to speak before the defense can begin, which Agrippa does (26:1). In stretching forth his hand, Paul shows customary rhetorical style of making a speech with proper gestures. Agrippa II with his intimate acquaintance of Jewish matters without personal involvement in the matter at hand is Paul's best chance for a positive result in this entire two-year affair. Paul probably takes this presentation seriously and not perfunctorily. Polhill notes how Paul's defense before Agrippa II fulfills Jesus's Damascus Road prediction that Paul would witness to kings (9:15), as well as Jesus's earlier promise to his disciples (Luke 21:12–15).[7]

Acknowledgment (26:2–3). Paul speaks well in this address. He has appropriate gravity and cultured expression, complimenting without perjuring himself for hypocrisy. He first acknowledges Agrippa II's role, "because you are especially familiar with all the customs and controversies of the Jews" (26:3), which is a genuine appreciation by Paul, given that he has had no help at all from Roman procurators.

Assertion (26:4–8). Paul then asserts Jewish faithfulness. He has spent his life among his people and in Jerusalem, so he is no outside imposter. He excelled at his Jewishness more than others as a devoted

---

[6]Greek: *tōi kyriōi* (τῷ κυρίῳ). The article stands in for the adjectival possessive pronoun, clear in this context of a Roman addressing Romans.

[7]Polhill, *Acts*, 498; Keener, *Acts*, 4:3429.

Pharisee, "the strictest sect of our religion" (26:5). Paul smartly frames his trial in terms of *faithfulness*, not unfaithfulness, turning the cart upside down on the Sanhedrin, because he is living out his testimony "on account of my hope in the promise God made to our ancestors" (26:6). Not only this, but this hope in the promise is universal to all "twelve tribes," so is not really accurately described as a sect (26:7). Paul's Pharisaic belief in resurrection then overwhelms the rationale of his argument: "Why is God raising the dead judged by you as unbelievable?" (26:8).

Admission (26:9–11). After acknowledging Agrippa II's role and asserting his own Jewish faithfulness, Paul then admits his persecution of believers. He frames this persecution as under divine necessity; that is, Paul uses Luke's divine necessity verb "must" (*dei*, δεῖ) to describe persecution of believers. That tacit admission by Paul that in his zealousness he could confuse his actions with God's will *is the very issue of this trip to Jerusalem* that has triggered all his present troubles and predicament. Luke's narrative characterization of Saul of Tarsus has been consistent since first introducing Saul into the narrative. Luke is clear: "Paul" never totally quit being "Saul." To grasp this character in Acts properly, then, one needs to think about him always as Saul-Paul.

Paul admits not only his role in hunting down and imprisoning followers of Jesus of Nazareth, but also that he "cast my vote against them when they were being condemned to death" (26:10).[8] Now, he is innocent, just like believers he falsely condemned, and having death urged on him by his own opponents. Yet, ironically, Paul is appealing to be exempt from what he himself inflicted—innocent, to be sure, just like all the rest—but still seeking exemption from the fate he decreed.

Paul tried to force followers of Jesus to blaspheme by "punishing them often in all the synagogues" (26:11), which makes sense from the standpoint that this institution was the Pharisee's own special domain. Paul further admits that "being furiously enraged" (*emmainomenos*, ἐμμαινόμενος), he pushed the matter outside Judea. What is communicated in "furiously enraged" is the piety of Pharisaic zeal, not a modern concept of loss of self-control. Zeal was a virtue for a Pharisee, not

---

[8]The statement in 22:4 (*achri thanatou*, ἄχρι θανάτου) is slightly ambiguous as to whether death actually was the result.

a vice. Paul thus continues to hammer home how *faithful* he was to his religious traditions—*more* faithful than most Jews, zealous even.

Commission (26:12–21). Paul next shares his experience—what changed his direction and commitment (but not his zeal)—his divine commission and his obedience (faithfulness) on the Damascus Road. This telling is the *third* time the Damascus Road has been presented in Acts. Three passes by this narrative event indicates its importance to Luke about church mission.[9] But why tell *three* times in Acts? Does the *reader* actually need this narrative redundancy to get the point about mission? Who not yet has appreciated and assimilated fully the meaning of the Damascus Road? Saul-Paul. In this retelling, what Saul-Paul needs to focus on surfaces, and that is why this account differs from the other two. God will have Paul go back to the Damascus Road eventually to get him back on track. The three Damascus Road accounts are placed specifically where they are to develop the full character of Saul-Paul according to the two driving themes of the Stephen speech of God active, God resisted. Paul in his own personal zeal constantly and unknowingly presents himself to God as a problem—a resistant, reluctant witness— but Luke in the three Damascus Road accounts shows how God in his sovereignty is able to transform Paul's character into actual usefulness to the kingdom and to messianic Israel.[10]

In this third account of the Damascus Road, three new emphases become apparent. The first new emphasis is the theme of "light" (26:13). This light is associated with the commission account. The focus is on the core essence of Paul's call, to bring light. The Damascus Road is a divine commissioning, and that is why the account is reminiscent of Old Testament commissionings. The call is to a steward to perform a servant role with witness function, echoing Acts 1:8. Such themes reflect Isaiah's "Servant Songs," particularly Isa 42:6 and 49:6: "to open their eyes and turn them from darkness to light." Thus, Saul's own Damascus Road blindness is paradigmatic of his own divine commis-

---

[9]Emphasis is one obvious use of repetition, as noted by Haenchen, *Acts*, 327, and this emphasis as mission has been noted by many. All, including Haenchen, basically are following von Dobschütz in this analysis. What none of them do is explain specific literary *placement* of the three accounts. Cf. discussion in Shipp, *Reluctant Witness*, 11–13.

[10]For a formal presentation of Luke's use of the three Damascus Road accounts for the character development of Saul-Paul, see Shipp, *Reluctant Witness*.

sion, what he will be doing among the gentiles. We have arrived again at the light theme Luke has developed with Simeon's prophecy (Luke 2:32), Philip's Ethiopian eunuch (Acts 8:32), Saul's Damascus Road (Acts 9:3), Jesus's commission (Acts 9:15), and

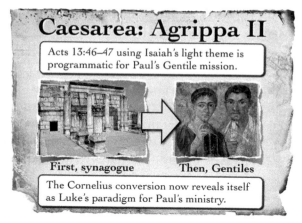

Caesarea: Agrippa II

Acts 13:46–47 using Isaiah's light theme is programmatic for Paul's Gentile mission.

First, synagogue   Then, Gentiles

The Cornelius conversion now reveals itself as Luke's paradigm for Paul's ministry.

FIGURE 14.21. Light for the Gentiles: Caesarea.

Paul's sermon at Pisidian Antioch (Acts 13:47).[11] Clear from Acts is that early Christian leaders were guided by Isaiah's Servant songs outlining Israel's intended destiny as God's witness to the nations. This destiny they saw fulfilled in the Servant-Messiah, Jesus, and those now proclaiming him. Most likely this Isaiah tradition comes from Jesus himself. This hermeneutic of Isaiah's Servant songs probably was part of what Jesus shared about the kingdom with the Emmaus disciples (Luke 24:25–27), with his disciples after the resurrection (Luke 24:44–47), and during the forty days that begins Acts (Acts 1:3).

The second new emphasis in this third account of the Damascus Road is on Paul's companions (26:13–14). They are objective validation and confirmation that the experience Paul had was more than just an "internal psychological process." The Damascus Road was an event.

The third new emphasis in this third account of the Damascus Road is a new word of Jesus: "hard for you to kick against the goads" (26:14). This saying is proverbial for resisting one's destiny or fighting the will of the gods. Luke finds this saying ironically pertinent to Paul's current situation. Saul of yesterday insisting on going "to Damascus" thinking he is serving God but really fighting God is equivalent to the Paul of today insisting on going "to Jerusalem"! Paul eventually will have to come to this realization for himself to get back on track with the will of God. Getting back on track will be the literary burden of the story of the journey to Rome—with Luke back on board (final "we section").

---

[11]For discussion of the light theme in the sermon at Pisidian Antioch, cf. p. 314.

Conclusion (26:22–23). Paul skillfully concludes with an *inclusio* on the light theme with which he started. The interpretation of the abstraction of darkness and light he already has provided. Dark to light is framed as a transition from the "power of Satan to God" and provides "forgiveness of sins" and "a place among those who are sanctified by faith" (26:18). Paul insists that his preaching of Jesus is fulfillment of what the prophets and Moses all testified (26:22). Their testimony was "that the Messiah must suffer, and that, by being the first to rise from the dead, he would proclaim light both to our people and to the gentiles" (26:23).

Festus's Famous Interruption (26:24)

Resurrection was not an irrational belief for many Jews. All Pharisees taught resurrection. However, no Pharisee taught a solo resurrection without anyone else at the same time. Further, no Pharisee taught resurrection without an end time and final judgment immediately consequent. Paul's assertion that Jesus has risen from the dead, but no one else has, obviously, and with time continuing to click on, was too much probably even for the seasoned Agrippa II. However, Festus the Roman could not restrain himself. He interrupted Paul with the obvious pagan objection to such nonsense, "You are mad, Paul!" (26:24). Then, he throws in the old academic envy jab, "Too much learning is driving you insane!" Festus responds stereotypically as any educated Roman would to such strange and foreign religious ideas.

The political problem here is that Festus's outburst publicly constrains Agrippa II. If the procurator just had declared he thought Paul was crazy, the king politically would be crazy himself to agree openly with Paul, even if he wanted to, when Paul later put the question directly to Agrippa II. Thus, when Paul does ask Agrippa II, his subsequent reply to Paul of necessity is polite but non-committal.

Paul's Appeal to Agrippa II (26:25–29)

Paul masterfully uses the outburst to his advantage as a way to transition back to Agrippa II. Paul stays focused on his target like a red-dot laser sighting device. Paul insists he is not out of his mind; rather, he is speaking "sober truth" (26:25). Paul then sneaks in his transition by saying, "Indeed the king knows about these things" (26:26). What Paul is alluding to by "these things" has two levels. The first level is common public knowledge. Even Agrippa II's own subjects would know about the reports from Jerusalem of the claimed resurrection of Jesus, as well as all the power and miracles that were manifest in the messianic community in Jerusalem, and that thousands of Jews, even of the most conservative Jews, were now followers of this Jesus. Those phenomena were easily available to common public knowledge, and plenty of time had transpired to suffuse the information throughout Judea and surrounding territories. The second level in the reference to "these things" is personal. Paul makes subtle allusion to the personal family tradition in which this Herodian ruler stood. Agrippa II's own father, Agrippa I, had begun executing leaders of this movement in Jerusalem itself, which Luke had detailed in Acts 12. So, Paul's artful turns of phrase in "not escaped his notice" and "not done in a corner" are powerful tongue-in-cheek, rhetorical devices implicating Agrippa II himself through his father without ever saying his father's name or even dishonoring his father's memory.

Paul has Agrippa II in the rhetorical crosshairs and now pulls the trigger. "Do you believe the prophets?" Paul asks directly (26:27). The question is whether Agrippa II believes in the coming of Messiah. That question for a Jew has only one answer, and that reality is why Paul without pause insists, "I know that you believe." Paul is not prescient nor presumptuous. Most Jews believed in the coming of a messiah. Of course, if the true Messiah actually has arrived as Paul has claimed, Agrippa II is out of a job. Agrippa II's famous response is revelatory: "In so short a time do you persuade me to become a Christian?" (26:28). Agrippa's words, "so short a time," in that culture rhetorically are definite refusal, but politely phrased.

What is more revealing is Agrippa's insertion of a term Paul has not used, "Christian." Use of "Christian" by Agrippa II is only the second and last time this term occurs in Acts and takes the reader back to its first occurrence in Antioch as the first time the name is used for followers of Jesus (11:26). As has been argued, the designation likely arose in the pagan population at Antioch as description of a subgroup in the synagogue beginning to distinguish itself as a social unit, almost as a fictive family, likely due to the impact of Saul's preaching of Jesus as "Christ" (Messiah) at the time, with inclusion of gentiles into this fictive family group.[12] Luke uses "Christian" to round out the Pauline story back to the beginnings of the Hellenist movement and its origins in Antioch. A slight touch of nostalgia or "Camelot" might even be present for Luke. God has been able to use Paul as the voice of the Hellenist movement even in this most cantankerous time. Further, Agrippa II in his use of this technical term provides evidence that the Hellenist movement even has impacted the vocabulary of the upper echelons of Jewish royalty and society.

Paul responds to Agrippa's polite rebuff with the perfect touch of light humor. He prays to God that all hearing him in that audience hall "might become such as I am—except for these chains" (26:29), and he probably raised his hands to rattle them gently at that moment. That was a "good one," as the famous Inspector Clouseau would say.

Innocence Declaration (26:30–32)

When the king stands, the meeting formally is over (26:30). Luke says they "say to one another," indicating they all come to the same conclusion; the decision is unanimous. Paul has not experienced unanimous agreement with him about anything in his ministry ever in Acts. Mark this agreement down, a first. All conclude, "This man is doing nothing deserving death or imprisonment" (26:31). The first word concerning death is a rejection of the Sanhedrin's case against Paul. The second word about imprisonment is an indictment of Felix's corrupt treatment of the prisoner over the last two years. In other words, Paul here receives total exoneration, both in the Jewish arena and in the Roman arena. This unanimous opinion is the *fourth* time in Acts Paul has been declared innocent: once by the tribune Lysias in his letter to Felix (23:29), twice by Festus himself (25:18, 25), and now by all the civic and military elite of Caesarea, as well as Judean royalty (26:31). Luke may intend some irony in king Agrippa II's pronouncement of Paul's innocence when Agrippa's own father, Agrippa I, earlier in Acts had sought the death of Christian leaders in Jerusalem. Thus, the death of James, the brother of John, at the hands of Agrippa I (12:2) eventually is vindicated in the storyline by the pronouncement of innocence by Agrippa I's own son for a later leader of the same movement.

[12]The argument is developed fully in chapter 2, "Hellenists and Antioch," 81–82.

One would think a declaration of innocence would be a time for great celebration. Normally, that would be the case. Paul's legal situation, however, is anything but normal. The wheels of Roman jurisprudence inevitably turn. The tragedy and pathos comes in the follow up admission that Agrippa makes to Festus: "This man could have been set free if he had not appealed to the emperor" (26:32). Here is the ironic final word, "had he not appealed to Caesar." Paul's senseless appeal to Caesar has cooked his own goose. Innocent though he might be, Paul will go to Nero. Imagine Festus and Agrippa II trying to compose that letter!

Why highlight Paul's appearance before Agrippa II? Luke's highlighting of Paul's appearance before Agrippa II is because, if we are correct on dating Acts in the first century not the second, then *Agrippa II was still alive when Acts was published*. This Jewish king held a high reputation among Romans in Rome after the First Jewish War. As Josephus had consulted Agrippa II on Jewish matters for his *Jewish War*, Luke is pointing the same direction for anyone wishing to check out the accuracy of his portrayal of Paul in Caesarea after the apostle's tragic death under Nero, to whom Paul had appealed.

SUMMARY

Paul has lost all momentum on the gentile mission. He has only himself to blame. Jerusalem was not God's will for Paul. All statements to the contrary are begging the question by Paul. Paul has known this divine will about Jerusalem ever since the Damascus Road. Luke views the journey to Jerusalem as an unintended detour on the divine itinerary west to Rome and an unfortunate decision by Paul that destroyed the impact of the collection for Jerusalem.

Paul has to appear before three rulers in Caesarea over the space of two years, two Roman governors and a Jewish king. Felix presents the challenge of a corrupt administration. No witnesses are produced by the Sanhedrin, but Felix still detains Paul in custody in Caesarea. Felix has a private audience with Paul, along with his Herodian princess wife, Drusilla, but Paul pulls no punches on justice, self-control, and future judgment, all allusions to Felix's court, administration, and career. For two years, Felix looked for a bribe from Paul, and when recalled to Rome, left Paul in prison as a favor to the Jews.

The Sanhedrin tries to re-crank the case with the new procurator. However, they fail to prove charges. Festus wishes to ingratiate himself and do the Jews a favor. He suggests moving the case to Jerusalem, as accusations are religious, and Jerusalem probably is where witnesses might be located to testify. For Paul, Festus's suggestion is the nuclear option. Paul appeals to lord Nero's tribunal, even though the Lord God already had promised his own protection for Paul in the Antonia vision. Paul now has made three appeals to avoid life-threatening moments in Jerusalem and Caesarea, belying his braggart promise of willingness to die in Jerusalem he earlier had made to Agabus, Luke, and the rest in Caesarea.

The appeal to Caesar by a Roman citizen takes the matter out of Festus's hands, but he still has to compose a letter to the emperor describing a case for which no witnesses exist. The arrival of Agrippa II and his sister-consort, Bernice, to Caesarea making a political courtesy call on the new governor is Festus's ticket. Agrippa II agrees to hear the case as political consultant to Festus. In his preamble to Paul's defense, Festus admits he found nothing deserving of death, so has nothing to write to "our lord," a phrasing Luke deliberately uses to put Paul's appeal into its proper context as an exchange of lordship.

Paul's defense before Agrippa II is well constructed. He acknowledges without obsequious flattery Agrippa II's Jewish expertise, which Paul genuinely hopes will help his case. Paul asserts his fundamental Jewish faithfulness, as a zealous and strict Pharisee, more faithful than most of those accusing him. Pharisee hope for resurrection is what Paul finds answered in Jesus. Paul admits to persecuting believers, but, in an odd way, that too illustrates his zealous faithfulness to Jewish traditions. What changed his direction and commitment, but not his zeal, was his commission by Jesus on the Damascus Road to bring light for the gentiles. This third retelling of the Damascus Road does more than simply emphasize the event and gentile mission. Luke's placement and integration of the three accounts together serve the purpose of showing the transformation of the character of Saul-Paul into actual usefulness for the kingdom and to messianic Israel.

The companions of Paul show this experience to be objective reality, not just a totally subjective, one person story. The new word for Paul about "kicking against the goads" has double entendre not only for what Saul was doing then, but what Paul is doing now, insisting on having to come to Jerusalem, zealously getting in God's way, actually resisting God in the process.

When Paul mentions Messiah being raised from the dead as a part of this new reality of the Damascus Road, Festus blurts out Paul has gone mad. The outburst restricts Agrippa II's ability to respond positively to Paul when Paul puts the direct question to Agrippa II about belief in Moses and the prophets about the coming of a messiah and Jesus being that Messiah. Such events were not accomplished in the dark nor in a corner, nor had they escaped Agrippa II's attention, Paul insists. Paul in this way subtly alludes to the action of Agrippa II's own father, Agrippa I, who had his own interaction with Jesus followers by putting to death one leader of the Jesus movement in Jerusalem.

Agrippa II politely refuses to answer Paul, and in the process uses the rare term "Christian" for only the second and last time in Acts. This term links Paul's defense before king Agrippa II with memory of Antioch, the mother church of the Hellenist mission. The impact of the Hellenist movement includes aristocratic Jewish royalty and even their vocabulary. Paul responds to Agrippa II's gentle rebuff with a touch of humor about wishing all were like him, except for his chains.

The decision among the august crowd of civic, political, religious, and military elite of Caesarea is unanimous: Paul is innocent. The Sanhedrin's case is fabricated, and Felix was wrong to detain Paul in Roman custody without a viable case for the last two years. Tragically, had Paul not appealed to Caesar, he could have been released. Paul's appearance before Agrippa II serves to fulfill Luke's promise in the prologue to the Gospel that he provides eyewitness testimony. Since the Herodian king was still alive when Acts was written, Agrippa II himself was one of those eyewitnesses anyone could ask if they wished.

Paul eventually will have to come to grips with Jerusalem as an act of raw hubris, of fighting God in his own self-assured zeal. Paul's rebellion is no more poignantly revealed than by his desperate appeal to another lord, Nero, the emperor of Rome. The journey to Rome is a journey back into God's will, and Luke rejoins him when Paul finally begins moving at last toward his divinely appointed destiny.

15

Destiny Achieved

Journey to Rome (Acts 27–28)

ROME IS THE DESTINY OF THE Hellenist movement of Acts. Paul knew this in Ephesus, but had a better idea (19:21). His insistence on personally delivering the collection to the Jerusalem church when God had told him from the beginning of his ministry to stay out of Jerusalem was a catastrophe for the Jerusalem church and the gentile mission. In going to Jerusalem, Paul was going the opposite direction from Rome, so effectively denied the divine mission mandate to Rome and precipitated a two-year delay in launching that mandate.

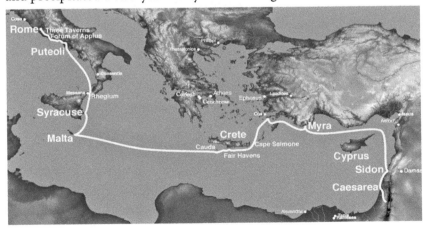

FIGURE 15.1. Journey to Rome: Overview.

Now that we are off to Rome, one would think everything is fine. Not really. Paul still does not have his head on straight. Of his own vo-

499

lition Paul has placed himself under the protection of another lordship by appealing to Nero. Not until Paul recommits to the protection of the Lord God will he truly be back on track.

Getting Paul to Rome, then, is the story of God overcoming at all odds Paul's unfortunate decision to detour to Jerusalem before going to Rome. The point is that "Lord" Jesus not "Lord" Caesar is Paul's true protector even as Jesus had promised in the Antonia vision in Jerusalem (23:11). Paul's journey to Rome is a journey back into God's will. In the real life story of the captain and his crew and the storm at sea, Paul vicariously will experience what he himself has generated for his own companions in Jerusalem. He will watch a metaphorical rerun of his own life since Ephesus through the eyes of his Roman centurion guard and the decisions of a grain ship captain—and a hurricane. As the reader could suspect by now in Acts, since Paul is off track, a vision will mark the supreme moment of divine mandate for Saul-Paul. The vision at sea assures Paul of his date with destiny in Rome.

FIGURE 15.2. Roman Merchant Ship. Model of typical corn galley bound for Rome, 90 feet long, hauling 250 tons. The mainsail is the main power, but steering is by headsail on heavy spar raking overextending the bow (Science and Society Picture Library).

VOYAGE AND SHIPWRECK

Caesarea to Myra (27:1–5)

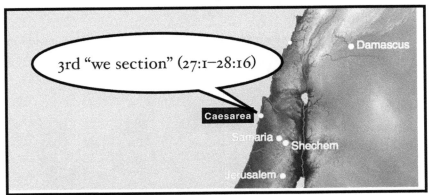

3rd "we section" (27:1–28:16)

Damascus

Caesarea

Samaria ● ●Shechem

Jerusalem ●

FIGURE 15.3. Third "We Section" of Acts. Luke uses the third "we section" of Acts to affirm Rome as the divine will for Paul's mission.

The third and final "we section" launches the voyage to Rome. Luke has been out of the picture ever since the audience with James and the elders upon first arriving in Jerusalem. Suddenly, when Paul is on his way to Rome, Luke rejoins. Once again, by using this "we section" technique, Luke is adding his own imprimatur on the Rome itinerary. Luke affirms by his personal presence that Rome is God's will and Paul's true mission mandate.

Paul and the other prisoners were delivered over to the custody of Julius, a centurion of the Augustan Cohort (27:1), which recalls the story of Cornelius. His commander would have been one of the five tribunes that had heard Paul's defense before king Agrippa II (25:23). Thus, the tribune of this cohort would have appraised his centurion of this particular prisoner. He probably told Julius that all present in the august assembly that day had

FIGURE 15.4. Mounted Centurion Relief. Depicted, sword drawn, charging (YMY).

agreed Paul was innocent. To establish this likely channel of inside information about Paul to Julius is why Luke mentions in particular that five tribunes attended Paul's audience with king Agrippa II. This connection also would explain why Julius straightway is inclined to extend Paul favors before Julius hardly has gotten to know him at their very first stop in Sidon.

Their first ship was a smaller vessel that worked the coastal ports along the way to a final destination, which, in this case was the port of Adramyttium, not too far from Troas in Mysia. Passengers were carried as extras to the cargo vessels. Most of the time a port

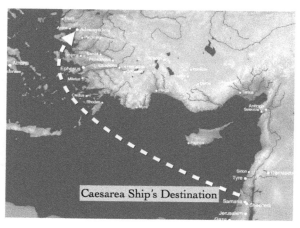

FIGURE 15.5. Port of Adramyttium in Mysia.

could be reached each day to allow overnight on land. Passengers were out on the main deck all the time, rain or shine, day or night. Luke's "we" possibly could mean just three, Paul, Luke, and Aristarchus, a Macedonian from Thessalonica who had been caught up in the riot in Ephesus and was part of the entourage to Jerusalem accompanying the collection (27:2; 19:29; 20:4).

Sidon (27:3)

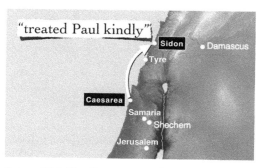

FIGURE 15.6. JR—Caesarea to Sidon.

The next day, as was normal, the ship ports at Sidon, having passed up Tyre (27:3). Notable is Julius's kind treatment of Paul by allowing Paul to be cared for by friends. Luke notes this behavior by Julius to Paul on several occasions. Showing unusual courtesy to a prisoner under normal military protocol would not be likely. The action suggests those in charge of Paul know he is innocent, just as already acknowledged repeatedly by Lysias, Festus, and Agrippa II.

FIGURE 15.7. Sidon Inscription. Roman, 1st cent. AD, about the time Paul was in Sidon. Votive text: "Heliodorus, the grandson of Apollophanes, the son of Apollonius, the ruler of the cutlers, [has dedicated] to the holy gods for Koinos" (IAM).

Who Paul's "friends" in Sidon were Luke does not say, but the Hellenist movement reached the area after the persecution of Stephen (11:19), and Barnabas and Paul passed through this region of Phoenicia on the way to the Jerusalem Conference (15:3). The report of gentile conversion "brought great joy to all the believers" at that time (15:3). Likely, those communities were still part of Paul's Hellenist contacts. The region was quite pagan, so evidence of viable Christian communities is notable. "To be cared for" has a sense of "give close or diligent attention to," but the inference is not clear.[1]

FIGURE 15.8. Girne Port. Modern Girne on the north side of Cyprus is ancient Kyrenia, a busy harbor that Luke and company would have passed by as they sailed on the leeward side of the island due to contrary winds late in the sailing season.

Myra (27:4–5)

From Sidon they put to sea, but have to pass under the lee of Cyprus, which means putting the island between the ship and open seas as a buffer, "because the winds were against us" (27:4). This note is the first chord of the storm symphony.[2] The problem is the lateness of the

---

[1]Greek: *epimeleias tychein* (ἐπιμελείας τυχεῖν); that is, whether Paul might have been ill is simply unknown.

[2]The first two notes of the approach of the great white shark.

sailing season, as winds shift more westerly, making progress to the west more difficult due to constant tacking of the ship and sails.

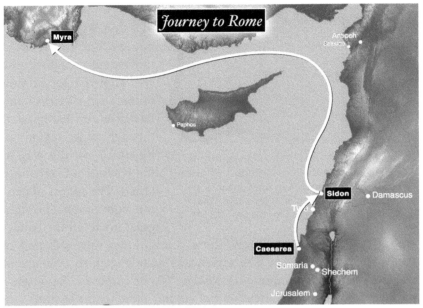

FIGURE 15.9. JR—Sidon to Myra.

They followed the shoreline of the two provinces of Cilicia and Pamphylia, and finally arrived at Myra in the province of Lycia (27:5). The trip unexpectedly took several days, so they had to bunk a few nights out on the open deck. Myra actually was two miles inland from the harbor, so if the crew and passengers had shore leave, they had to walk to reach town. Myra would be the last port with the present ship, as their paths from here diverged. The Adramyttium ship will turn northward to ply the coast of Asia. Julius and his group needed to strike out due west for Rome. Myra was a good port for transfer as the first stop of the gigantic grain ships departing Alexandria for Rome be-

FIGURE 15.10. Alexandrian Grain Ship's Destination.

fore striking out west across dangerous open waters. These grain ships were almost three times larger than the coasting vessel Julius had been on, with a cargo of eight-hundred tons. They were one of the most important assets of the Roman empire, for they fed the capital of a million people. Grain merchants, though low in social status, were some of the wealthiest Romans. How much time Julius took to book passage on another vessel to Rome is unknown, perhaps soon.[3]

FIGURE 15.11. Alexandrian Grain Ship Mosaic. The Ostia port at the mouth of the Tiber River on the coast of Italy sixteen miles from Rome overtook Puteoli as the major port of the empire later in the first century, avoiding the longer overland route. Ostia merchants advertised their names and occupations with illustrative floor mosaics. This shop owner was a merchant of the lucrative Alexandrian grain trade.

FIGURE 15.12. Ostia Wheat Warehouse. Near the port docks of Ostia were large warehouses supporting the commerce of Rome, such as this wheat warehouse.

[3] An excellent resource on these grain ships is Hirschfeld, "The Ship of Saint Paul."

Myra to Malta (27:6–44)

Cape Salmone (27:6–7)

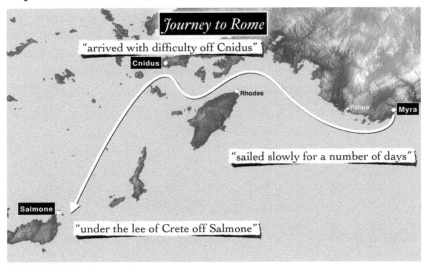

FIGURE 15.13. JR—Myra to Cape Salmone.

The centurion has his company board an Alexandrian ship bound for Italy, which means Rome (27:6). Later on, Luke will number the ship's crew and passengers as two-hundred and seventy-six (27:37). Thus, this vessel is one of the behemoth grain supply ships feeding Rome.

These ships were part of a special fleet especially designed by Rome to move grain from the breadbasket of Egypt to Italy.[4] Josephus rode one of these ships, but his ship had six hundred passengers on board. Like Paul, he was bound for Rome. He was to plead the case of priests that the procurator Felix had imprisoned over a trifling matter and sent to Caesar's tribunal. Again, like Paul, the historian's ship also sank in the Adriatic Sea. Josephus spent all night in the sea, and was rescued the next day by a another ship from Cyrene.[5]

Grain ships were maximized for cargo, which means minimized for safety. They had rather flat hulls, so lateral stability was not strong. The cross-lateral wave action of storms could fatally weaken structural integrity. Further, weatherproofing the cargo was imperative. Cargo

[4]See the remarks of Seneca *Epistulae* 77.1–2.
[5]Josephus *Life* 3.13–15.

holds had to stay dry. Wet grain swells, putting pressure on the beams of a ship, breaking the watertight seams. Better to lose the cargo than the ship. Thus, grain ships always had a difficult time in storms at sea.

The symphony begins its darker tones in a minor key after Myra. After casting off, Luke says they "sailed slowly for a number of days" (27:7). The contrary autumnal winds are unyielding. Luke continues, "and arrived with difficulty off Cnidus." "With difficulty" summarizes much maneuvering and counter-tacking the winds. This constant effort working the sails, tackle, and gear is demanding,

FIGURE 15.14. Grave Relief: Ship in Rough Seas. Fish and dolphin struggle as a helmsman with frightened passengers also fights to save his ship, 2nd cent. AD (HAMC).

unrelenting, and tiresome. The mariners are trying to use the islands and shoreline to buffer the winds. Eventually, however, they have to head into open waters to move west. Cnidus is about that point. Their strategy is to strike out for the island of Crete to use as a wind buffer. They tack southwest into open waters toward the lee side of the island of Crete, hoping for relief from the vexing winds, beginning at the eastern most point of Cape Salmone (27:7).

FIGURE 15.15. Cape Sideros, Crete. Luke's Cape Salmone is modern Cape Sideros. Its lighthouse is positioned on the hill in the far distance to the right. The cape is almost an island itself, connected to Crete only by a narrow isthmus with seas on either side. Cape Sideros today is a restricted military installation, so cannot be accessed.

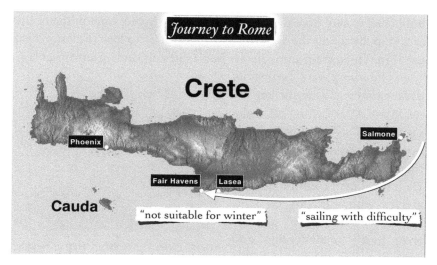

FIGURE 15.16. JR—Cape Salmone to Fair Havens.

Fair Havens (27:8–12)

The island of Crete is too parallel to the winds to provide the help they needed. Once again, Luke indicates the wear and tear on the crew, as he notes that they sail past Cape Salmone only "with difficulty" (27:8). They crawl westward along the southern side of the island to about the midway point, arriving at a small harbor called Fair Havens near the city of Lasea. Its problem was, Fair Havens was small and fully unprepared to host nearly three hundred people for an entire winter.

FIGURE 15.17. Fair Havens Harbor, Crete. The harbor at Fair Havens even today is minimal, without deep water, and the town itself (Kaloi Limenes) rather small.

They have reached a decision point. The island shoreline cuts up in a sharp northwest turn at Fair Havens, which exposes the ship to the full force of the westerly winds that have been working against them unrelentingly ever since their departure from Myra. Further, Luke notes that already "much time had been lost" (27:9). They probably are making a third or less of their normal transit times. Even "the Fast had gone by" (27:9). This fast was the Day of Atonement, falling from September to October. Mediterranean shipping closed down completely from mid-November to mid-March, as the winter storms were much too frequent and dangerous. The safe shipping window already was closing, since September to November, though possible, was risky at best for sailing. With the delay already incurred, they cannot possibly make Rome now before shipping lanes have closed for the season. Thus, the ship's captain has to make a difficult decision. Stay in Fair Havens with its inadequate wintering facilities, or fight northward up the coastline to make the better port of Phoenix on the western end of the island for wintering there?

Paul speaks up, the nautical expert that all Pharisees are. Surely the burley captain of a mighty Roman grain ship is anxious to hear the advice of a Jewish prisoner bound for Caesar's tribunal.

> "Men, I perceive that with injury and much loss not only of the cargo and the ship but even our lives this voyage is going to be" (27:10).

Paul's words spell out the likely prospects, given season and weather, more on the basis of common stories well known to all, such as told by Josephus, than any prophetic knowledge of the future. Luke does not present Paul speaking as a prophet. (Luke says nothing about the Holy Spirit.) Luke catches the incredible irony in Paul's words, and thought that irony worth preserving. In anticipating the likely outcome of the present course of action on the part of this captain and his ship, Paul here incriminates his own recent decisions. *These words of advice Paul is offering to this ship's captain are words of advice he himself had been offered multiple times as he insisted on pushing on to Jerusalem.* With Paul's advice to the ship captain here, Luke begins to develop the story of Paul's voyage and shipwreck as a narrative metaphor of Paul's journey to Jerusalem. Thus, Luke's storm at sea is more than just another storm at sea story. This storm is a metaphor of Paul's recent life story, particularly his fateful decision to go to Jerusalem against God's will. The parallel is striking: a leader refusing sensible advice not to push on, sailing straight into a disastrous storm, imperiling all on board.

FIGURE 15.18. Loutro Double Harbor, Crete. A peninsula jut-out into the sea with deep water inlets on either side creates the double harbor Luke references as Phoenix.

FIGURE 15.19. Loutro Harbor, Crete. The left harbor has developed as a resort area.

FIGURE 15.20. Phoenix Harbor, Crete. The right harbor is called Old Phoenix.

The centurion military officer is in preemptive charge on board a vessel of the Roman imperial service. He heeds the ship captain more than Paul, naturally (27:11). The majority opt for reaching the better wintering port of Phoenix, which had a dual inlet harbor that faced two directions, Luke points out (27:12). This deepwater harbor better suited the large, Alexandrian grain ships, and its community could winter the passengers with more suitable accommodations.

Euroquilo and Cauda (27:13–20)

A "moderate south wind" portends being able to push on to Phoenix, so they strike anchor intending to hug the shoreline of Crete (27:13). Even large ships under full sail could cover fifty nautical miles (fifty-seven statute miles) a day; thus, Phoenix should have been only a few hours sail. Fortune was not theirs this day. The symbols crash; the violins race; the high decibels of furious, brass-section chords let loose.

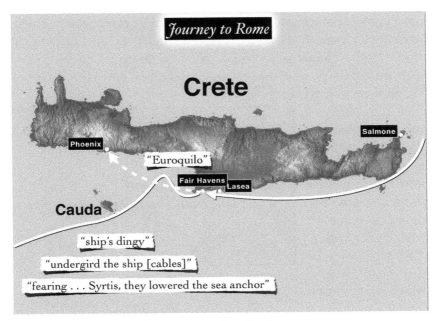

FIGURE 15.21. JR—Euroquilo Storm Drives Past Cauda.

A northeaster, called a Euroquilo, is something like a hurricane at sea. These storms can grow suddenly on Crete due to the mountain topography forming channels funneling wind currents like downtown skyscrapers, enhanced by sharp gradients in upper and lower level air temperatures. The winds sweep down from the mountains of Crete onto the sea surface, where latent air moisture creates storms (27:14). Turning "head-on" into the wind was normal nautical procedure for fighting storms to prevent the ship from rolling over. However, caught unprepared to turn the ship around, they had to be driven in whatever direction storm winds blew, which was the case for this ship (27:15). Storm winds drive the vessel away from the island of Crete out toward open ocean. The ship's dingy was towed behind the main vessel, used for directional control into harbors and transfer of persons or goods. The dingy was filling with water, putting serious stress on the stern. Running under the lee of Cauda, a small island twenty-six nautical miles (thirty statute miles) off Crete, provides barely enough wind buffer to pull the ship's dingy onto deck with great difficulty (27:16).

The grain ship's weakest structural element was its lateral stability due to the flat hulls for maximizing grain cargo, but rendering the ship most vulnerable to storms. Apparently, some technique had been developed to try to compensate the lateral weakness by running either ropes or cables underneath and around the ship's hull, thus "undergirding the ship" (27:17). The actual process is unknown. Perhaps one could slip a loop around the point of the bow and run the loop down the ship's hull and then tighten in place.

The specter of running aground on the Syrtis sands, a large shoal off the north African coast in the modern Gulf of Sidra, began to frighten the sailors. The sand bars of this shoal can shift, which renders map-

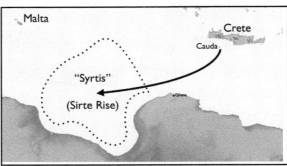

FIGURE 15.22. JR—Syrtis (Sirte Rise). In the modern Gulf of Sidra off north Africa is a famous shifting sand rise.

ping the seafloor and its depth most difficult and undependable. This shoal had been the graveyard of many ancient ships, and is feared even today.[6] They let down the ship's sea anchor to try to slow their forward progress if they were heading in the direction of this shoal.[7]

The storm raged on. Usually, storms could be ridden out in a day or two. Not this time. The ship continues violently storm-tossed even throughout the second day. Constant pounding of the waves outside and inevitable shifting of cargo inside meant the ship's hull integrity was taking a battering. Watertight seams would start giving way. They eventually have no choice but to throw cargo overboard, which is the ship captain's livelihood (27:18). The trip now is a business loss. On the third day, they throw "gear" overboard (exact meaning unclear), trying to lighten the ship's stress load in desperation (27:19).[8]

[6]See Josephus *J. W.* 2.16.4 (831) in reference to fear even of the name Syrtis itself.

[7]The exact action is ambiguous because the Greek is vague: *chalasantes to skeuos* (χαλάσαντες τὸ σκεῦος, "they lowered the instrument"). Louw and Nida interpret 27:17 as "generally understood to be the mainsail," which makes little sense at this late stage (*Semantic Domains* 6.1). Lowering the mainsail would have been immediate action upon the storm's onslaught. More likely, Luke describes lowering the kedge, or drag anchor (for which Luke knew not the technical term, so used the general *skeuos*).

[8]Luke's term, again, is ambiguous; perhaps the translation should not be "rigging" or "tackle," which is nautical terminology for the equipment for working the sails, since the mainsail is still operational later in the beaching narrative in 27:40.

FIGURE 15.23. Kyrenia Shipwreck. Owen Gander, expedition diver, checks scientific measurements for the famous shipwreck now preserved in Girne Castle, Cyprus that has revealed much about ancient shipbuilding, and tackle and gear (ASMK).

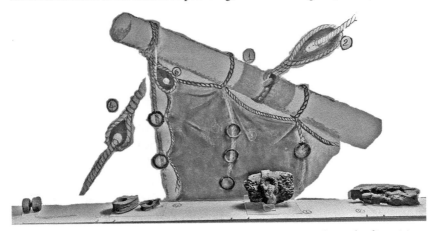

FIGURE 15.24. Kyrenia Shipwreck Tackle. An artist's illustration shows the disposition and use of surviving tackle of the Kyrenia shipwreck for working the sails (ASMK).

This monster storm is of an altogether different character than typical storms at sea, which do not last for "many days" (27:20). Something unusual is going on. If neither sun nor stars appeared during this time, all navigational reckoning is lost, and the ship's captain and crew have not a clue where they are. Helpless and lost, "all hope of our being saved was at last abandoned," Luke says, probably because they figure they have been pushed far out of shipping lanes, and, even if still in a shipping lane, the late season would mean hardly any ship could be expected to be passing nearby, or to have survived the storm themselves to pick up survivors bobbing in the ocean within a day or two before succumbing to cold or drowning (27:20).

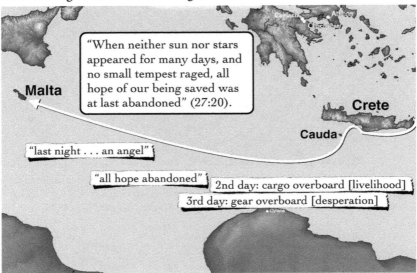

FIGURE 15.25. JR—All Hope Abandoned.

Paul's Sea Vision (27:21–26)

"All hope abandoned" is the key transition point in the story. The word of loss of all hope is critical to establishing that *any salvation now must be divine.* This word of genuine desperation leads the reader to conclude nothing less than that any salvation for this ship and its passengers is divine providence alone. The reader should ask why the storm lasted so unusually long. Luke seems to infer that God in his sovereignty was crushing reliance on any other claim to sovereignty, ability, or power. The lords of the sea for the sailors, the Dioscuri (28:11), or the Egyptian goddess of the sea for most passengers, Isis, have no power at all. *All* hope is lost, Luke says flatly. By now, *everyone* had quit praying to their pagan gods. Most importantly for this narrative, the *lord Caesar has no sovereignty* to command these seas, nor any power or ability to hold a ship together. Paul's appeal to Caesar at this moment is

FIGURE 15.26. Isis-Persephone (HAMC).

revealed to be the worthless hot air of human hubris. Bluntly clear now is that by appealing to Caesar, Paul has cast his hope on the wrong lord.

All on board had gone without food for a "long time" (27:21). Salt water draining throughout the ship had ruined most stores, and serious seasickness had prevented others from eating anyway. Passengers and crew were famished. The situation is thus marked as truly desperate.

Suddenly, in this dire and desperate moment, Paul receives yet another vision. The reader of Acts now well knows what Paul having a vision means—he is off track from the will of God. We have one more occasion for Saul-Paul, the reluctant witness, to be overcome again by the power of God and recommissioned by the grace of God. Paul stands up and addresses the group around him.

> "Men, you should have heeded me not to set sail from Crete to avoid incurring this injury and loss. And these things I now urge you: Take courage, for no loss of life will be for anyone among you, except for the ship. For on this night an angel of the God whose I am and whom I worship stood by me, and he said, 'Stop being afraid, Paul; you must stand before Caesar; and behold, God has granted to you the safety of all those who are sailing with you.' Therefore, be encouraged, men, for I believe God that exactly as has been spoken to me will be. But onto some certain island we must run aground" (27:21–26).

Were the situation not so desperate, Paul's admonition would be humorous. "You should have heeded me" (27:21) is straight out of the horse's mouth. Luke's narrative strategy regularly in Acts we have seen is to use Paul's own words and actions as self-incriminating testimony on Paul's own story, as in the temple vision, the Antonia vision, and the third Damascus Road account before Agrippa II. Luke's climactic placement of Paul's last vision in Acts ties the knot on the Stephen speech themes. All Paul's visions in Acts that are life changing are to redeem a man fighting against God. This sea vision appeals to faith when all hope is lost. Not even lord Caesar can help. "I have faith in God," Paul avers. Paul here is returning to ground zero, his personal encounter with God in Jesus Christ on the Damascus Road, blind, helpless, and hopeless. If the reader recalls, Paul had asked on the Damascus Road, "Who are you, Lord?" (9:5). That question is a question of sovereignty. Paul coming to terms with God's sovereignty always had been his problem, whether one would like to speak about before or after the

Damascus Road.[9] God's best emissary also could be God's worst adversary—God active, God resisted, Stephen themes to the end.

The storm has gotten Paul's attention. Paul has gotten the point. Paul should have listened to God about not going to Jerusalem like the sailors should have listened to him about not setting sail to Phoenix. Paul now knows where to put the "must" verb in his itinerary, not Jerusalem, as he had insisted, but Rome. During this stormy period of Paul's life, God graciously has granted two visions to hammer home where the "must" in his mission mandate lies, in the Antonia vision (23:11) and the sea vision (27:23–24). Both assure Paul he will fulfill his mission mandate. The "must" of God's will for Paul is Rome.

Not all the consequences of disobedience, however, will be abrogated. Because of the present situation, Paul is told he "must" appear before Caesar in chains. Custody and chains are precisely what God had promised in the Antonia vision, and Paul himself had sealed that fate by his own faithless appeal to Caesar. Now, custody and chains forever will constrain Paul's witness in Rome. Paul will not arrive in Rome now as he would have back then in Ephesus had he done God's will and gone directly from Ephesus to Rome in the power of the Spirit that had supercharged the Paul of the Ephesian crown jewel who was firing on all pistons. Christianity never will know what could have been, what God originally had in mind in sending Paul directly to Rome right at the spiritual apex of Pauline persuasion and power.

Shipwreck (27:27–44)

After this amount of time, they figure they are drifting somewhere in the large Adriatic sea. About midnight on the fourteenth night (!), the sailors suspect land is near, probably meaning breakers could be heard crashing against an unseen shore. Unknowingly, they have neared the small island of Malta, perhaps rounding Koura point, the southeastern promontory into Saint Paul's Bay. Calculating known currents and the expected drift rate, Smith had estimated the movement from Cauda to Malta would take exactly fourteen days, and surmised a landing at Saint Paul's Bay, the most likely, but other sites have been argued.[10]

[9]Many parents know the problem of the strong-willed child. They never are wrong.

[10]Smith, *Voyage and Shipwreck of St. Paul*, 121–24. Cornuke, *The Lost Shipwreck of Paul*, recently attempted unsuccessfully to revitalize the Saint Thomas Bay theory.

FIGURE 15.27. JR—Koura Point, Saint Paul's Bay. The low, southeastern promontory.

FIGURE 15.28. First-Century Grain Ship Anchor. Anchor of the grain ship Hera with preserved petrified wood beam still in the center block (MANRC).

Taking soundings contributes to deciding how to work the ship if land is near and running aground a possibility. The rapid change from twenty fathoms (120 feet) to fifteen fathoms (90 feet) is alarming, because the ship's draw reduces the depth, and the minimum ten feet between ship and seafloor nautical wisdom required would be reached. The strategy is to slow the drifting into more and more shallow water. Four anchors are let down from the stern to slow the ship's movement landward (27:29).[11] Remnants of these massive grain ship anchors recently have been discovered. One anchor discovered in 2005 off Koura Point near Salina Bay is displayed in the Malta Maritime Museum in Vittoriosa.[12] Another anchor is displayed in the Museo Archeologico Nazionale di Reggio Calabria, Italy. The ship's name was "Hera," seen in the letters and seal stamped in reverse on one of the blades of the almost nine-foot long anchor. A piece of the wooden center beam that

[11]Most ancient ships had multiple anchors for various uses, sometimes as many as fifteen to twenty.

[12]Gatt, *PAVLVS: The Shipwreck 60 AD*, 46–63.

had copper-tipped arms even is preserved in petrified form. Obvious from this artifact is that maneuvering four of these massive anchors would have taken no small amount of time and effort.

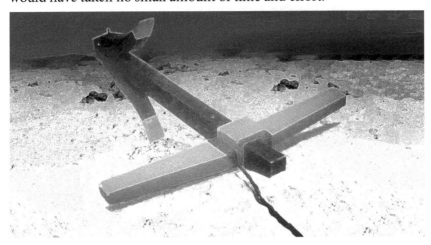

FIGURE 15.29. JR—Roman Anchor on Seafloor. The wooden beam inserted into the lead stock would have copper-tipped arms held in correct orientation by the lead stock in order to dig into the seafloor. A clay bed would provide strong retention.

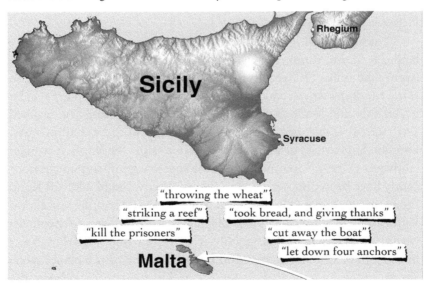

FIGURE 15.30. JR—Approaching Malta and Shipwreck.

They anxiously await daylight, because they know the ship is going to founder or crash onto the shore, and they need to be able to see their exact location and disposition with regard to cliffs, beaches, reefs, or sandbars to try to maximize their chances for survival, if possible. Parts of Saint Paul's Bay have steep and threatening cliffs.

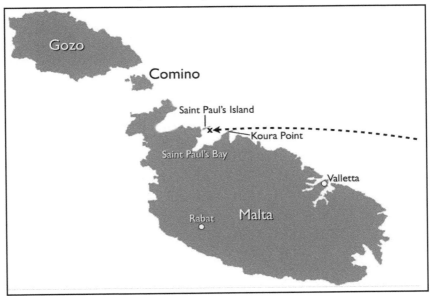

FIGURE 15.31. Map of Saint Paul's Bay, Malta.

FIGURE 15.32. Saint Paul's Bay, Malta. This view is looking toward Saint Paul's Island.

Luke now begins to turn the narrative toward a positive direction for Paul. Notice how as soon as Paul has voiced "I have faith in God," *Paul immediately begins to make positive contributions to the story for the first time since Ephesus.* The narrative device to begin making this turn is the devious plot of some sailors to abandon their post and escape the ship. Their plan was to use the dingy that had been hauled aboard the first day. Their subterfuge for lowering the dingy was supposedly to put out anchors from the bow. Such bow anchors, however, were not necessary, and they actually would disrupt directing the ship landward (27:30).

FIGURE 15.33. Saint Paul's Island, Malta. A statue commemorates Paul's shipwreck.

FIGURE 15.34. Smith Illustration. "Situation of the Ship on the Fifteenth Morning," painted by H. Smartly, is accurate in its details and orientation in Saint Paul's Bay.

Paul is not fooled by their ruse and warns the centurion, "Unless these men stay in the ship, you cannot be saved" (27:31). For this centurion, Paul is trustworthy; Julius already has granted Paul favor in Sidon, and Paul's wisdom was confirmed in the validation of his advice about not attempting to make the crossing to Phoenix from Fair Havens. Hence, the centurion takes Paul's advice to heart immediately this time, and orders his soldiers to cut away the ropes retaining the dingy and let the boat drift away (27:32). The loss is unfortunate, since had the ship survived, the dingy could have ferried those who could not swim to the shore, if possible to reach shore that way.

Daybreak on the fifteenth morning was the zero hour for action. Paul again intervenes positively. He urges all to take food as nourishment that would give needed strength to make the shore, some wise and timely advice (27:33). Again emphasizing his faith in the vision God had granted, he repeats that no soul would be lost (27:34). In effect, this repetition makes clear to all that when they survive, they will know to which divinity to give thanks. Paul "took bread, and giving thanks to God

FIGURE 15.35. Kyrenia Shipwreck Grape Seeds. Diet at sea included bread, caught fish for meat, and preserved fruits and nuts (ASMK).

in the presence of all, he broke it and began to eat" (27:35). While this action has a Eucharistic sound, the action also is quite traditional for the head of a Jewish household. The setting is not really ecclesial nor of the community of the saved, so probably not meant by Luke to evoke the Eucharist meal. Paul's advice is well received, as all were encouraged at the possibility of survival, so they took food to this end (27:36). Here is where Luke notes the total number on the ship, two-hundred seventy-six persons (27:37). He does this not out of arcane interest in details but to emphasize the full force of the miracle about to take place. For not one soul to be lost from such a significant number, especially as many could not swim, is a notable miracle.

The next goal was to prepare the ship for grounding. This preparation included lightening the weight to lower the draw. Some wheat is still on board because some cargo was needed for ballast to control the wild rolling and violent movement of the ship during the storm. They now threw their remaining ballast wheat into the sea (27:38).

At the light of daybreak, they cannot recognize the land to which they have arrived. Immediately, however, they spot a bay with a sandy beach, which, if the channel depth allowed, would facilitate running the ship aground in a controlled beaching, from which then passengers could disembark by climbing down ropes thrown along the side (27:39). They now have a workable plan of action.

They take three cooperative actions, probably simultaneously. They release four stern anchors into the sea and also loosen the twin steering paddles to minimize any undesired counter steering to the intended beaching spot. Another part of the crew hoists the foresail to the wind. Through these three

FIGURE 15.36. Kyrenia Shipwreck Sail Tackle. Preserved wood tackle for working the main sail and rigging (ASMK).

mutual maneuvers, they hope to gain as much quick speed as possible in order to run the ship aground with sufficient momentum to secure the vessel onto the beach (27:40).

Unfortunately, they did not see the mud reef between their present position and shore. They grounded deeply into the mud bar, but still out at sea. Now, because of the reef, they are stuck right where sea breakers are crashing. This result is the worst possible. Because of their increasing speed, they rammed the reef with some force, so never would be able to get loose. Yet, because they now are stuck right where the sea waves are breaking, the stern of the boat begins to take the brunt of the crashing waves flowing toward the shoreline. The stern quickly begins breaking apart, having been weakened severely already by two weeks of storm (27:41). Worse, they are too far from shore to jump out and wade safely. At this point with these conditions, no one should survive.

Luke curiously indicates this place of getting stuck as "between the seas," or, "between two seas."[13] This rather strange expression is clarified by the topography at the entrance to Saint Paul's Bay. The shoreline of Malta is separated from nearby Saint Paul's island by a small cut

---

[13]Acts 27:41, *eis topon dithalasson*, εἰς τόπον διθάλασσον. *Not* a sandbar or reef (see English translations). The well-known words for sandbar and reef Luke did not use.

about three hundred yards wide. Through this cut one has a simultaneous view of "two seas" on either side of the land break. Here, near this cut, is likely where Paul shipwrecked.

FIGURE 15.37. Between Two Seas. Luke's curious expression in Acts 27:41 is explained by the unusual topography of a close island at the entrance to Saint Paul's Bay.

In such a chaotic and catastrophic scene, prisoners easily could escape. Loss of prisoners could result in death for the soldiers, as happened to Agrippa I's soldiers who guarded Peter when Peter escaped (12:19). These Roman soldiers counsel together to act preemptively by killing all the prisoners first to prevent any from escaping (27:42). Paul passively intervenes. First, the incident with the dingy, then the advice to take food for energy, and now Paul has his third positive impact on the story because of the centurion's regard for Paul. "But the centurion, wishing to save Paul, kept them from carrying out their plan" (27:43). The close bond that has developed over this journey between Paul and Julius pays dividends. Paul is responsible for saving the lives of every prisoner on board that ship. We are witnessing Paul's character transformation before our very eyes. And to think, all this simply because Paul said "I believe God" rather than "I appeal to Caesar."

The centurion takes charge to insure the orderly evacuation of the ship. He orders those who can swim to jump overboard first and swim to land, so as not to overwhelm in frantic flight those who cannot swim (27:43). He then methodically gets the rest who cannot swim to follow using available flotsam from the disintegrating vessel (27:44). Then, Luke states the miraculous with a rather mundane air, "And so it was that all were brought safely to land" (27:44). From a ship that had run aground far from shore and broken apart against the force of large sea breakers, two hundred and seventy-six persons were saved. Not one soul lost. As understated a miracle as in all of Acts. God kept his word to Paul. God demonstrated his true lordship over land, sea, and lives.

Due to Luke's extensive weather, time, and nautical notations, combined with accurate knowledge of sea currents and other nautical information, the location of Paul's actual shipwreck can be determined with a fairly high degree of certainty. In fact, the traditional St. Paul's Bay on the island of Malta is where the ship foundered.[14] This location is one of the rare times that a traditional religious site has high claim to veracity. Even the slightest adjustment south, and they would have missed the island altogether and drifted several more days until finally reaching the north African coastline of modern Tunisia.

MISSION DESTINY

Winter in Malta (28:1–10)

After they got to land safely, they learned they were on the island of Malta with its two other islets of Comino and Gozo (28:1). Natives on the island had been watching this drama unfolding on their shoreline. A winter rain had set in for the morning, creating a cold, dreary day. The natives had gone to the trouble to prepare a warming fire to greet any fortunate survivors. Luke distinctly notes their "unusual kindness" (28:2). The exact nature of what marked their kindness as "unusual" is not known. Perhaps this description alludes to other actions also taken that Luke leaves unspecified, as in providing food and dry clothes.

Snakebite Justice (28:3–6)

Paul, apparently in good condition even after making his way through open, wave-crashing waters onto the beach, was helping kindle the fire with brush. Some viper[15] stirred by the heat came out and latched onto

[14]The brilliant, detailed, and thorough-going research of James Smith, *The Voyage and Shipwreck of St. Paul* (1856), never has been surpassed.

[15]The term *echidna* (ἔχιδνα) is generic for "snake" and not differentiated enough to identify specific species, but regularly is used in contexts of poisonous varieties, hence, a translation of "viper" seems justified in the context of the reaction of the natives. Malta today, however, has no poisonous snakes.

Paul's hand (28:3). One common theme of survival stories is the gods insuring a balance of justice when a criminal who thinks to have survived one disaster is struck down soon after by another. Seeing the viper latch onto Paul, the natives conclude Paul is a murderer (life for life) and that their god "Justice" has decreed the fated destiny (28:4).[16] Paul, however, dislodged the snake into the fire, and suffered no harm immediately (28:5). The natives, however, imagined time would tell the truth, and Paul soon would swell up or drop dead. They waited a long time for this denouement, but the expected fate never occurred. They then had to adjust their narrative to fit the facts before them. Within their worldview, the only other conclusion was Paul was a god yet unknown to them (28:6), like the unknown god of the Athenians (17:23).

FIGURE 15.38. The Shipwreck of Saint Paul Mural. Saint Paul's Cathedral, Mdina on Malta has a magnificent mural of Paul's shipwreck in the semidome of the altar apse by the 1600s Italian Baroque master, Mattia Preti. The focal point is on God in his sovereignty, even as Luke was keen to communicate through the snakebite story.

Luke tells this story neither to entertain nor to aggrandize Paul.[17] Luke tells the story because his focus is divine destiny, and the natives' narrative is divine destiny. Luke has put unswerving emphasis on the divine mission mandate of Rome ever since Acts 19:21. That destiny

[16]Translations not capitalizing "Justice" do not capture the indigenous reference by these natives to their own divine hierarchy, which is clear in the context.

[17]After following Luke's carefully constructed narrative of Paul's downward spiral fighting God for the last eight chapters, the idea that he would feel a need to polish the halo on Paul's head seems completely out of touch with the actual Acts narrative.

will be achieved by divine sovereignty, even as in the false storyline the natives have invented. So, inadvertently and unknowingly, the natives actually have told the story of Paul: not personal self-will, murderous mob, scheming council, conniving procurator, faithless appeal, violent storm, disastrous shipwreck, nor poisonous snakebite can keep God from getting Paul to Rome. Rome is Paul's divine destiny. Even though wrong that Paul is a god, the natives are right that Paul is under divine destiny. Even island natives can perceive that divine destiny is integral to Paul's story.

FIGURE 15.39. Roman Domus: Claudius Statue. Imperial image prominently displayed in the tablinum next to the triclinium dining area (DRM).

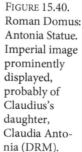

FIGURE 15.40. Roman Domus: Antonia Statue. Imperial image prominently displayed, probably of Claudius's daughter, Claudia Antonia (DRM).

FIGURE 15.41. Roman Domus: Peristyle Courtyard. Classic colonnaded courtyard with beautifully preserved, complete mosaic floor as fine as from Pompeii or elsewhere. Centerpiece follows often copied style, the "Drinking Doves of Sosus," the famous mosaic artist of Pergamum (DRM).

Malta Miracles (28:7–9)

Paul's snakebite survival story likely spread across the island. No wonder the chief person of the island,[18] Publius, received and entertained
hospitably Paul and his companions[19] over a three-day period (28:7).
Such hospitality likely included the centurion, ship captain, and a few
others as well. In effect, Publius established himself as Paul's patron, a
political, social move as much as personal. We should not think of this
arrangement as islanders in palm-branched bungalows by the beach.

A first-century Roman domus[20] in Rabat, Malta provides a context for understanding better the administrative and social construct of
Publius's life as Roman governor of the island. This large and lux-
urious complex with its unusual emphasis on imperial portrait statuary, common in public spaces but rare for private estates, all speak to
an aristocrat emphasizing connections to imperial Rome. If this first-
century domus coincides with the first-century governorship of Publius, then the residence would be that of a Roman nobleman on the
island with whom Publius socially and politically inevitably interacted.

Publius's estate, probably looking similar to the domus in Rabat,
provides a new scene from which to narrate the recovery of miracle
working power on Paul's part, not heard of since Ephesus. Publius's
father lies sick with fever and dysentery. The particular illness cannot
be identified. Paul visits and cures the man by "praying and putting his
hands on him" (28:8). Good news spreads quickly, as good news always
does, and the rest of the sick islanders came to Paul and also were cured
(28:9). This type of miracle working power by Paul's hand has not been
heard since Ephesus. In all Paul's time in Jerusalem and Caesarea,
which was almost as long as he was in Ephesus, not once do we hear of
any miracle performed by Paul. Suddenly, however, after the shipwreck,
the miracle flood gates are thrown open wide.

The time on the island of Malta to the inattentive reader could
seem simple happenstance in the aftermath of a storm at sea. Luke,
however, artfully chooses the episodes he tells. He is compressing and

[18]The expression, "the first of the island" (*tōi prōtōi tēs nēsou*, τῷ πρώτῳ τῆς νήσου),
probably is meant as the official island governor designated by Rome.

[19]Luke specifically uses the plural, "received us and entertained us."

[20]A domus was the urban home of elite Romans constricted by city buildings. The
Roman villa was the country home with more spacious layouts in the countryside.

summarizing his narrative. The stories he incorporates make a point. So, why Malta? Here on the island of Malta for the first time since the aborted Ephesian ministry, Paul shows power (snakebite) and miracles (healings). Alert readers will note these Malta events happen *immediately after Paul's faith response to the sea vision*. Luke's Malta narrative shows Paul finally regaining mission momentum after the implosion of his Ephesian ministry, which was of his own brash doing.

FIGURE 15.42. Valletta Harbor. Mouth of the harbor of densely populated Valletta.

Malta Departure (28:10)

After passing three months of winter on the island, the hardy shipwreck survivors prepare to leave the island as the spring sailing season has reopened the sea lanes. The port of departure is unknown, but a principal eastern port today is Valletta.

Luke indicates that the islanders "bestowed many honors on us," which, in light

FIGURE 15.43. Map of Harbor City of Valletta.

of the tremendous benefits they had derived from Paul, is appropriate. The islanders also stocked the ship with the needed provisions, since the shipwreck survivors had lost everything in their misfortune. These actions show genuine respect for Paul and company, and likely Publius in his proper role as Roman patron to these Roman citizens.

Malta to Rome (28:11–16)

"Three months" on Malta means through the winter when sailing was impossible (28:11). Ironically, another Alexandrian grain ship also had wintered on Malta, so, once again, a grain ship becomes their new transport on to Italy, almost as if the storm was just a bad dream. Luke notes the ship's figurehead is the mythological "Twin Brothers" (*Dioskourois*, Διοσκούροις). The narrative irony is that the Twin Brothers were the fabled Castor and Pollux, sons of Zeus, portrayed in myths as protectors of

FIGURE 15.44. Nautical Fresco. Pompeii fresco with painted eyes bow decoration. Decorating ship bows is a centuries old maritime tradition (NNAM).

ships at sea, so the object of mariners' prayers when facing storms at sea. Luke's shipwreck sea vision belies worship of these pagan gods.

Syracuse to Puteoli (28:12–14)

FIGURE 15.45. Altar of Hieron II. At 653 by 75 feet, this Syracuse altar featured the longest altar base ever built, 3rd cent. BC.

FIGURE 15.46. Syracuse Greek Theater. This huge 5rd cent. BC theater likely saw productions of Aeschylus's plays.

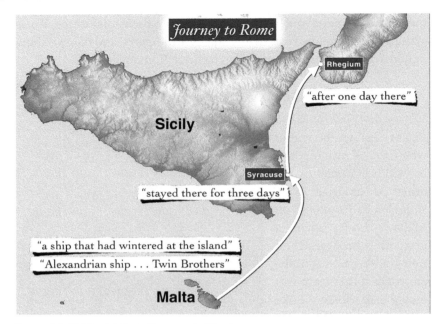

FIGURE 15.47. JR—Malta to Syracuse to Rhegium.

FIGURE 15.48. Syracuse Harbor. Syracuse is the setting of the historical drama of the Roman siege (214–212 BC) featuring the famous Archimedes of Syracuse.

The Alexandrian grain ship takes the normal route along the island of Sicily up to the toe of Italy and through the straits of Messina into the Tyrrhenian Sea west of the Italian mainland. The first stop is a brief three-day stay at the port at Syracuse, probably a holding pattern to obtain the best winds (28:12). Syracuse was the principal city of Sicily, famous in history and rich in Greek and Roman culture. The famous Greek mathematician, physicist, engineer, and inventor, Archimedes, was a native of Syracuse. He is regarded as the greatest mathematician of all time, and one of the greatest scientists of classical antiquity. He died right at the end of the Roman siege of Syracuse (214–212 BC).

FIGURE 15.49. Taormina View. The eastern coastline of Sicily offers dramatic mountain vistas, as this one from the top of the theater at Taormina.

Winds turned favorable soon, since their stay was only three days. They weighed anchor from Syracuse and sailed on up the beautiful, dramatic eastern coast of Sicily to the port of ancient Rhegium on Italy's toe. Rhegium was a staging port for ships preparing to negotiate the difficult and often contrary winds of the narrow straits of Messina on into the Tyrrhenian Sea (28:13).

FIGURE 15.50. Straits of Messina, Messina. View of the straits from Messina, Sicily across to Italy.

FIGURE 15.51. Straits of Messina, Reggio Calabria. View of the straits from the beach at Reggio Calabria (ancient Rhegium) back towards Messina on the coast of Sicily.

FIGURE 15.52. Millennium Monument to San Paolo. This montage bronze work in Reggio Calabria celebrates the second millennium of Paul's arrival to Italy.

Reggio Calabria (ancient Rhegium) has celebrated the second millennium of Paul's arrival to the shores of Italy at Rhegium via the Malta shipwreck with a richly symbolic bronze work on display near the seaside. The ship is represented in the mangled sails and broken ship timbers. Roman custody is symbolized by the Roman military standard, centurion helmet, and chains along the right side. Survival on Malta's shore is seen in the seagulls. The fire and Greek column to the left relate to a local legend of the miracle of fire burning a column as Paul preached to worshippers of Diana in the temple of Artemis at Rhegium.

Rhegium proved an even shorter stop than Syracuse. The perfect south wind needed for passage through the Straits of Messina came up the very next day. Their destination was Puteoli, final port of call for the massive Alexandrian grain ships supplying Rome. Leaving Rhegium one day, they made the port of Puteoli sometime the next day, which was no small feat. Given the distance overall, they averaged about ninety miles a day, when fifty miles a day was considered normal. The winds must have been incredibly strong and perfectly directed. This feat Luke will weave subtly into his point.

Ancient Puteoli (modern Pozzuoli), actually is in the center of a volcanic caldera called Campi Flegrei. Puteoli's deepwater port long had served as the emporium for the great Alexandrian grain ships and many other goods imported to Italy from around the world.[21] The added expense and time of ground transportation to Rome is why the closer port of Ostia at the mouth of the Tiber river eventually overtook Puteoli in preeminence as the premier Roman port in the first century AD.

[21]Strabo *Geog.* 17; Suetonius *Aug.* 98; Seneca *Epistulae* 77.

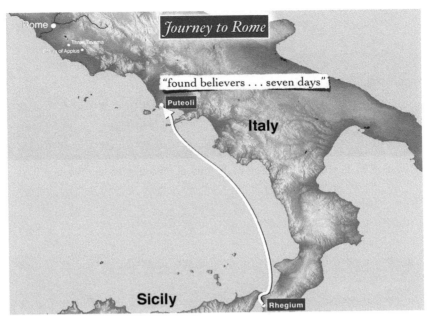

FIGURE 15.53. JR—Rhegium to Puteoli.

The port at Puteoli was not the only famous port in this area. The naval base at the nearby port of Misenum in the same bay was home to the largest naval fleet in the world. Pliny the Elder was the prefect in charge of the naval fleet at Misenum when he perished tragically pursuing the massive eruption of Mount Vesuvius, in a story told by his nephew, Pliny the Younger.

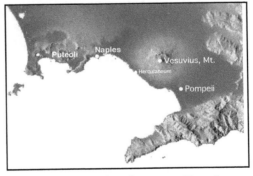

FIGURE 15.54. Gulf of Naples: Mount Vesuvius.

Another famous city nearby was Neapolis (Naples), only seven miles east, situated on the Gulf of Naples. Only twenty-eight miles away from Puteoli was Mount Vesuvius. The mountain had not erupted in living memory, so inhabitants in surrounding regions were not aware the volcano actually was active. The violent AD 79 eruption was catastrophic for Pompeii and Herculaneum, completely burying these vibrant, first-century Roman towns for centuries only about twenty years after Paul spent his brief time in the port city of Puteoli on his way to Rome.

FIGURE 15.55. Pozzuoli Harbor Approach. Ancient Puteoli is modern Pozzuoli.

FIGURE 15.56. Pozzuoli Harbor. A large tanker slowly pushes its way past the long breakwater wall to steer left out into the open waters of the Tyrrhenian Sea.

Paul and company find believers in Puteoli and are invited to stay for a week. This group of believers in Puteoli confirms what is known; that is, that thriving Christian congregations are established in Italy. Paul previously met Aquila and Priscilla of Rome in Corinth,

FIGURE 15.57. Macellum of Puteoli. The Puteoli meat market, late 1st cent. AD, has suffered bradyseism (slow earthquakes) of the Campi Flegrei volcanic caldera raising and lowering the site above and below sea level over the centuries, leaving the borings of marine mollusks, visible on the three columns still left standing.

Christian leaders evicted from Rome by the edict of Claudius (18:2). He also already had written the letter of Romans, in which he acknowledged their long-standing faith and his need for their assistance to support his Spanish mission.[22] Thus, Rome as Paul's destiny in Acts cannot be because Christian communities do not yet exist there. Readers already have their clue that Paul's Roman destiny has some other narrative reason than evangelism in virgin territory.

FIGURE 15.58. Flavian Amphitheater of Puteoli. The third largest in Italy, built by the architects of the Colosseum in Rome, this amphitheater was financed by Vespasian and his son, Titus, as was the Colosseum, and hosted similar spectacles.

FIGURE 15.59. Subterranean Structures. Unlike the Roman Colosseum, visitors to this amphitheater can tour underground structures to see how spectacles worked, with elevators to raise men, animals, and props to the arena floor.

In Puteoli, Luke states, "and in this manner we came to Rome" (28:14). This statement of arrival in Rome seems repeated redundantly again only two verses later in 28:16. Further, since they are yet only in Puteoli, the statement of a Rome arrival in 28:14 seems premature. Commentators have speculated Luke here carelessly has combined two sources without smoothing out the redundancy of noting arrival in Rome twice. Such a low evaluation of Luke's literary skills does not correspond with the facts of the narrative we have been engaging, so is a most unlikely explanation for the phenomenon of "two arrival statements." Luke does not show himself to be that clumsy a writer.

[22]Rom 1:12; 15:20, 24.

Closely observed, the two statements in 28:14 and 28:16 are not actually grammatically the same. They carefully are distinguished. The statement in 28:14 is an *adverb of manner*, "in this way" (*outōs*, οὕτως). In contrast, the statement in 28:16 is a *temporal conjunction*, "when" (*ote*, ὅτε). Thus, in 28:14 the emphasis is on the *way* in which they came to Rome, but in 28:16 the emphasis is on the *time* when they came to Rome. We will address the matter of the *way* Paul came to Rome in the next section.

Puteoli Observations

Now that Paul has arrived safely on Italian soil at the imperial port of Puteoli, several observations need to be made revealing Luke's perspective. Some points should help answer what seem to be perennial questions about the Acts account of Paul's journey to Rome.

Narrative Time. Add the time up, and the entire trip from Malta to Puteoli, over five hundred miles, took only seven to eight days sailing. The impression almost is unavoidable that suddenly Paul is on a fast track to Rome. Attention to narrative time supports the observation that once Paul is back on board the will of God and affirming personal faith in God's own sovereignty as a result of the storm at sea, Rome not only is inevitable, Rome is a roller coaster rush. The rush of narrative time contributes to the theme of Rome as Paul's destiny.

Characters and Plot. Note the abrupt change at Puteoli regarding Roman characters and Paul's Roman appeal. After Puteoli, important Roman characters such as the centurion, Julius, quietly fade out of the narrative. Paul has been dependent upon these Romans ever since his arrival in Jerusalem. Suddenly, however, with Paul's arrival in Puteoli, Roman characters quietly fade out of the story with hardly a whisper. Why? Further, Paul's appeal has consumed two and a half chapters of the narrative. Why do we not hear another word about Paul's appeal to Caesar? Why fade the Roman characters and silence Paul's appeal? Because, for Luke, *Paul's Roman custody was a detour in the story, not the main event, and Paul's appeal to Caesar was a mistake, a failure of faith, and not the point of the story at all.* Therefore, after Puteoli, Luke has no further narrative interest in following Roman characters such as Julius nor in narrating any appearance of Paul before Nero.

Divine Sovereignty. Another crucial point about this journey to Rome needs to be emphasized from Luke's perspective: *Paul's appeal to*

Caesar did not get Paul to Rome. The journey to Rome that results from Paul's appeal is fraught with its two-week hurricane at sea, near starvation, life-threatening shipwreck, murderous Roman soldiers, and finally, venomous snakebite. *Had Jesus not protected Paul every mile, Paul never would have made Rome in the first place.* Lord Jesus got Paul to Rome, not lord Caesar. Paul was just three years late getting there by the circuitous route of his own self-will. In his story, Luke never would credit Paul's appeal to Caesar as getting Paul to Rome. In reality, that appeal almost killed Paul several times along the way had God not directly intervened. God's sovereignty is the whole lesson of Paul's experience of the storm at sea combined with its interpretive sea vision.

Puteoli Reception. So, what was the *way* in which they "came to Rome" that Luke wants to emphasize with his "in this way" in 28:14? The "way" in which they "came to Rome" is *typified by the hospitable response they all received in Puteoli.* This hospitality actually should be unexpected. Residents of Puteoli never have met Paul, Luke, and Aristarchus, and this alien group carries no letters of recommendation for prospective hosts.[23] That is, by the expression, "in this way we came to Rome," Luke means that how Paul and companions were treated by believers in Puteoli with warm hospitality hosting them and seeing to their needs for an entire week. With the adverbial "in this way," Luke intends to make the positive Puteoli reception a literary paradigm of their entire treatment by Italian believers all the way along the Via Appia before they even reach Rome—and is to be presumed also in Rome after they arrived. This Roman reception is important to Luke, not simply because hospitality was a premier Christian virtue in the early church, but because Luke already is establishing the point of *why Rome was God's destiny for Paul.* As will become clear as the narrative follows Paul into Rome, Luke is establishing *Roman believers already accept Paul's message and are ready to sponsor Paul's mission. That* is why God wanted Paul to go directly from Ephesus to Rome three years earlier—to begin the initiative in earnest to propagate the gospel to the "uttermost parts of the earth," the project announced in Acts 1:8. What could have been. Of course, as matters fell out, we never will know. The pathos that is Saul-Paul in Acts leaves a longing for the history of early Christianity that could have been written.

---

[23] As did Phoebe, bearing the letter of Romans (Rom 16:1). Cf. 2 Cor. 3:1.

Puteoli to Rome (28:15–16)

FIGURE 15.60. JR—Puteoli to Rome.

FIGURE 15.61. Capua: Laturno River. Flows through Capua out to the Tyrrhenian Sea.

The journey from Puteoli to Rome takes Paul up the Via Appia highway that the group would have to pick up by walking the thirty miles up to its junction near Puteoli at Capua. The Via Appia was one of the oldest and most famous highways of the empire, originally built from Rome to Capua in 312 BC by the censor Appius Claudius Caecus as a military highway to facilitate Roman troops making their way to the front lines of Rome's Samnite Wars past the barrier between Rome and Capua of the Pontine Marshes, nineteen miles of stagnant, foul swamps blocked from the sea by sand dunes and rife with malaria. In 162 BC, Marcus Cornelius Cathegus added a canal along the road in this marshy

area, because the road often was under repair in this difficult to maintain, marshy area. Romans preferred taking the canal.[24] As did many
Romans, Paul and company likely took the canal from Terracina on the
coast the eighteen miles up to the Forum of Appius.

FIGURE 15.62. Terracina Shoreline. As did most Romans, Paul likely picked up the
canal here at Terracina to travel this part of the Via Appia from the coast up to the
Forum of Appius through the unpleasant Pontine Marshes.

FIGURE 15.63. Canal Alongside the Via Appia Highway. A canal still runs alongside
the modern Via Appia (SS7) up to the Forum of Appius.

[24]See Hill, *Ancient Rome*, 60–61; 197–98; Liberati and Bourbon, *Ancient Rome*, 130.

The Forum of Appius can be established as somewhere within a mile or so of the ancient Roman mile marker 43.[25] This milestone with the mile indicated by the Roman numerals XLIII used to stand along the actual Via Appia highway very near the little Italian village of Borgo Faiti. Sadly, this crucial Roman artifact helping document the Acts story recently has been destroyed.[26] Fortunately,

FIGURE 15.64. Ancient Mile Marker 43. Only the bottom third of the base of this important Roman artifact documenting the precise location of the Forum of Appius is left after the top two-thirds was broken off and apparently destroyed.

two other ancient Roman inscriptions near this Forum of Appius location still stand and help document the general area and its history. Paul is met by a delegation of Roman believers here at the Forum of Appius. The significance of this entourage will be discussed shortly.

FIGURE 15.65. Forum of Appius Inscriptions. Two ancient Roman inscriptions stand near the ancient location of the Forum of Appius and help document the site.

A point of interest as one follows the Via Appia from the Forum of Appius to Three Taverns is Tor Tre Ponti. An inscription still stands at this location right alongside the modern SS7 road on the sidewalk. This inscription documents Trajan's efforts to build bridges and generally improve the roads along this section of the Via Appia. The Roman artifact indicates that the topography of the Via Appia through the Pontine Marshes always presented difficulties to maintain. One

FIGURE 15.66. Tor Tre Ponti Inscription.

[25]Horace *Satires* 1.5; Cicero *Epis. Att.* 2.10; 2.2.12; 2.2.13; Pliny the Elder *Nat. Hist.* 14.8.61; Tacitus *Annals* 3.2.

[26]Sometime between 2010–2015 according to documented site visits.

perennial idea in ancient times to overcome the problem was to drain the marshes. However, attempts to drain the marshes regularly failed over time; the sea and extensive lowlands always reclaimed the land.

A pithy description of traveling these regions putting concrete images to the nature of Paul's journey in this stretch of the road comes from the lines of Horace.[27] Horace provides colorful depictions of his own passage along this part of the Via Appia, including his stomach ailments, sleepless nights, and characters encountered who were about as foul in Horace's experience as the stagnant marsh waters. His tale of the lazy boatman who let out his mule to graze, leaving sleeping passengers to discover themselves in the same spot the next morning after waking up, is priceless.

> Leaving mighty Rome, I found shelter in a modest inn at Aricia, having for companion Heliodorus the rhetorician, far most learned of all Greeks. Next came Appii Forum, crammed with boatmen and stingy tavern-keepers. This stretch, we lazily cut in two, though smarter travelers make it in a single day: the Appian Way is less tiring, if taken slowly. Here owing to the water, for it was villainous, I declare war against my stomach, and wait impatiently while my companions dine.

> Already night was beginning to draw her curtain over the earth and to sprinkle the sky with stars. Then slaves loudly rail at boatmen, boatmen at slaves: "Bring to here!" "You're packing in hundreds!" "Stay, that's enough!" What with collecting fares and harnessing the mule a whole hour slips away. Cursed gnats and frogs of the fens drive off sleep, the boatman, soaked in sour wine, singing the while of the girl he left behind, and a passenger taking up the refrain. The passenger at last tires and falls asleep, and the lazy boatman turns his mule out to graze, ties the reins to a stone, and drops a-snoring on his back. Day was now dawning when we find that our craft was not under way, until one hot-headed fellow jumps out, and with willow cudgel bangs mule and boatman on back and head.

> At last, by ten o'clock we are barely landed, and wash face and hands in thy stream, Feronia. Then we breakfast, and crawling on three miles climb up to Anxur, perched on her far-gleaming rocks.

---

[27]Horace *Satires* 1.5. "Aricia" is today's Ariccia in the Alban hills, sixteen miles outside of Rome. "Anxur" is the modern, seaside resort city of Terracina just south of the Pontine Marshes.

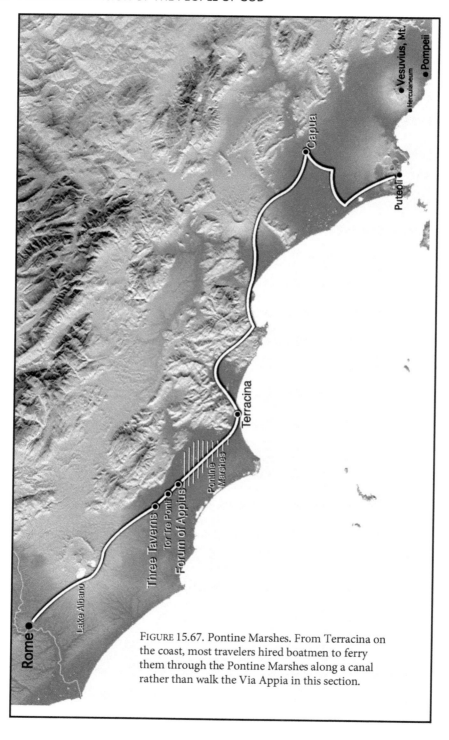

FIGURE 15.67. Pontine Marshes. From Terracina on the coast, most travelers hired boatmen to ferry them through the Pontine Marshes along a canal rather than walk the Via Appia in this section.

Paul himself traveled the nine miles on up the Via Appia to the intersection known as the Three Taverns. The name is misleading, as the location is not actually about three taverns but about three shops that serviced travelers at the first way station along the Via Appia after leaving Rome. Here at thirty or so miles from Rome was a junction of three roads from Tusculum, Alba Longa, and Antium—a long day's journey from Rome, if not trying to push on to the Forum of Appius. Here Paul was met by a second delegation from the churches in Rome. Nothing remains today of the likely location just south of Cisterna di Latina, except for some archeological surface work that has exposed the outlines of various buildings. From the Three Taverns, the ancient Via Appia cut through the Alban hills with steep grades but past several beautiful lakes and then ended on the outskirts of Rome.

FIGURE 15.68. Via Appia Highway at Three Taverns. This spot is in the likely general area of the ancient location of the Three Taverns by triangulating descriptions in various sources ancient and modern.

FIGURE 15.69. Archeological Work Near Three Taverns. The fenced off area on the western side of the Via Appia identifies archeological surface work exposing the outlines of ancient buildings in the likely vicinity of the Three Taverns.

FIGURE 15.70. Lake Albano. Beautiful lake vista in the Alban hills just south of Rome.

These last one hundred seventy miles of Paul's journey to Rome from Puteoli along the Appian Way is rushed along by Luke in only two verses (28:15–16). He has one main point to make: how Paul is received. That is, Luke's exclusive focus in this Via Appia narrative of Paul's journey to Rome is on the positive reception by Roman believers before Paul even gets to Rome.

Somehow Roman believers have gotten wind of Paul's imminent arrival to Rome. Luke does not specify how. Perhaps Paul's full week spent in Puteoli afforded an encounter with a Roman believer on the way back to Rome. In any case, Roman believers decide to journey out to intersect Paul and his entourage along the way. They rendezvous with Paul at the Forum of Appius, forty-three miles from Rome, and, apparently, by another group at the Three Taverns, thirty-one miles from Rome (28:15). These distances are one to two days walking. Both groups, then, would have to make preparations for overnight lodging and food, plus the days spent waiting for Paul and company to arrive at these intersections. Their plans also would include the expense of a return trip. *Such action never would be taken on a whim.* This action means Roman believers have a clear message to communicate to Paul. These two delegations represent a decided effort on the part of Roman congregations to welcome Paul and communicate a strong filial bond that already exists. No wonder Luke notes that "Paul thanked God and took courage" (28:15). A finely nuanced statement, to be sure. One of these congregations represented either by the delegation at the Forum of Appius or the other delegation at Three Taverns even could have been in the affiliation of Prisca and Aquila, Paul's longtime associates in Corinth, who would have returned to Rome by now after the edict of Claudius was rescinded upon his assassination in AD 54.[28]

Paul's positive reception by the Roman churches, made emphatic by repetition (Forum of Appius, Three Taverns), is unrivaled in any other city. This positive reception is Luke's clear signal of what could have been for Paul three years earlier after Ephesus: Rome as Paul's immediate and new mission base west. That truth is the whole point of the Jerusalem debacle. By insisting on the Jerusalem detour, Paul already is three years behind the divine itinerary west.[29]

---

[28]Which seems suggested already in the greetings in Rom 16:3.

[29]This narrative analysis is working from the Acts text, so Pauline correspondence is not made constitutive for its conclusions. Still, one could speculate at the historical level that Paul's letter to the Romans, written years before from Corinth, also played a formative role in this positive Roman reception.

FIGURE 15.71. Appia Antica. Ancient Via Appia just outside the outskirts of Rome.

FIGURE 15.72. Appia Antica Paving. Mortar has eroded from these finishing blocks. Romans leveled dirt, adding a layer of small stones in mortar, upon which gravel was laid, then this finishing layer of tight-fitting, finely cut cubes precisely placed. The road was middle cambered for water runoff, with side ditches and retaining walls.

The centuries-old terminus of the Via Appia is its junction with the Porta San Sebastiano, or Saint Sebastian Gate. This gate was built as a part of the expansion of the city walls of Rome by the emperors Aurelius and Probus in AD 271–275. The older Servian wall built during the Republic had been in place since the fourth century BC, but Rome had prided herself on not needing defenses due to the *Pax Romana* after the city grew in the early empire. Third-century incursions by Germanic tribes convinced Romans otherwise.

FIGURE 15.73. Porta San Sebastiano. The Via Appia's junction in Rome in the AD 275 Aurelian Walls expansion of the Porta Capena gate of the 4th cent. BC Servian Wall.

FIGURE 15.74. Via Appia from Porta San Sebastiano. View of the Via Appia intersection at its junction with the San Sebastiano Gate into Rome.

Luke indicates Paul arrives in Rome (28:16). Paul himself would have entered at the older Porta Capena gate of the Servian wall near the Caelian Hill. The meaning of the gate's name is uncertain; a reasonable suggestion is the name relates to Capua, the original terminus of the Via Appia. From this gate, Julius and his prisoners would have made their way to the soldier barracks to complete the official transfer of prisoner custody. Each prisoner's case and jurisdiction then would be established to determine housing (usually prison) and other arrangements.

Paul's own accommodations are lenient. He is allowed to live by himself, probably renting an upper level insula apartment, but he is accompanied by a Roman soldier. Paul's appeal to Caesar infers this soldier likely is from Caesar's own Praetorian Guard, that elite group of nine to twelve cohorts in Rome serving as the emperor's personal body guard. The guard commander was the prefect, quite a powerful position in Rome. At the time of Paul's imprisonment, this Praetorian prefect was Sextus Afranius Burrus, specially chosen by Nero's mother, Agrippina the Younger, to insure young Nero's advance to be emperor. Agrippina constituted Burrus and the Stoic philosopher, Seneca the Younger, to advise sixteen year old Nero. Seneca was the brother of the proconsul Gallio before whom Paul appeared in Corinth. Burrus died

FIGURE 15.75. Legionnaires. From a triumphal arch celebrating Trajan's victory over the Dacians, AD 98–117 (IAM).

FIGURE 15.76. Insula Second-Floor Steps. These steps led to the second level of insula apartments at the Ostia Antica port.

in AD 62 only a few years after Paul's arrival in Rome, allegedly poisoned on Nero's order.[30] Paul is lightly chained to his guard (28:20). Paul likely is cared for by members of the congregations who had greeted him along the way at the Forum of Appius and later the Three Taverns, for even then they were well aware he was a prisoner.

Paul has reached his mission destiny—finally. In terms of Luke's subtle narrative, picking up all the clues from Acts 19:21 forward, as well as working to interpret the extraordinary detail and time spent on the voyage and shipwreck, the most reasonable conclusion is that Luke intended us to read this journey to Rome as much a spiritual one for Paul personally as a geographical one for Julius professionally.

[30]For an excellent historical resource, see Bingham, *The Praetorian Guard.*

FIGURE 15.77. Medical Instruments. First-century medical tools from Pompeii. Scalpel with bronze handles and interchangeable blades of iron. One handle has the features of Hercules (NNAM).

Luke's third "we section" ends with this "when we came to Rome" noted in 28:16. These are Luke's last words in first person that kicked in with Paul's custodial departure from Caesarea bound for Rome. Now that Paul finally has achieved the destiny God commissioned, Luke considers his narrative role as a witness to God's will in Paul's life complete. So, what Luke had promised about providing eyewitness testimony in the prologue to his Gospel has been delivered. Luke, "the beloved physician" (Col 4:14) quietly walks off the stage of Acts. His Hellenist story, however, is not finished.

Paul's Roman imprisonment, dated about AD 60–62, would be the generally accepted timeframe for writing the Prison Epistles. Three of the letters (Colossians, Philemon, and Ephesians) show close connections of addressee, greetings, content, and biography. So, they often are taken together as written

Acts	Letter	From	Date
JC	Galatians	?	?
2MJ	1 Thess 2 Thess	Corinth	50
3MJ	"Previous Letter" 1 Corinthians "Harsh Letter" 2 Corinthians Romans	Ephesus Ephesus Ephesus Macedonia Corinth	55 55 56 56 57
Rome	Colossians Philemon Ephesians Philippians	Rome Rome Rome Rome	60 60 60 62

FIGURE 15.78. Pauline Correspondence: Prison Epistles.

within the same general timeframe. Philippians, on the other hand, is separated out usually as written more toward the latter period of the imprisonment, since Paul shows some expectation in the letter of a possible, but not guaranteed, release (Phil 1:25).

FIGURE 15.79. Roman Colosseum. Vespasian financed the project with First Jewish War spoils and Jewish slave labor. Symbolizes the ideology and power of imperial Rome not long after Paul wrote his Prison Epistles.

Jewish Leaders (28:17–28)

Paul takes initiative to assemble Jewish leaders in Rome. He wants to advise them of his case. Jews in the Diaspora did not have one governing body over the entire community in a given location. Instead, each synagogue operated independently. Numerous leaders came.

FIGURE 15.80. Jewish Synagogue at Ostia Antica. Oldest known synagogue in Europe and one of the oldest in the world. While the building itself dates from the reign of Claudius (41–54), its first-century use as a synagogue is argued (Levine, *The Ancient Synagogue*, 274–76). Ostia was the major port city of Rome in the later first century.

Case Summary (28:17–22)

Paul summarizes that his case had originated in Jerusalem, was conspired by the Sanhedrin, resulted in Roman custody, and included a charge of death (28:17). Roman authorities validated his innocence, but Jerusalem Jews still objected, forcing Paul to appeal to Caesar, so he now is in Rome, but is not here to make a charge against his nation (28:18–19). Paul continues to insist that he is bound with the chains of custody "for the sake of the hope of Israel," and that is why he wants to address Jewish leaders in Rome (28:20). Paul believed, and the early church continued to preach, that the God who worked in Jesus is the God who called Israel out of Egypt and promised a future deliverer.

Jewish leaders in Rome indicate they have no knowledge of Paul's case (28:21). This situation probably is because of the lack of travel for the last three months of winter in the first place. Further, Paul had a head start to Rome from the island of Malta when sailing season reopened. Finally, when Paul did reembark from Malta, the winds were favorable, and the grain ship cut the waters

FIGURE 15.81. Jewish Menorah Relief. Menorah relief on one of the support columns in the Ostia synagogue. Paul claims he is in chains "for the sake of the hope of Israel" (28:20).

of the Tyrrhenian Sea with amazing speed. Thus, no formal letters from the Sanhedrin in Judea, like the ones Saul had in hand when he went to Damascus (9:2), would have had the chance to preempt Paul's arrival in Rome, and verbal reports about Paul from Judea likewise would be scarce at this time.

The Jewish leaders, however, are interested, if Paul is a leader in the sect that "everywhere is spoken against" (28:22). They probably mean their "neck of the woods," that is, Rome and its surrounding regions. This bad Roman reputation likely is the result of the edict of Claudius in AD 49. This edict expelled Jews from Rome related to synagogue disturbances regarding one called by the Roman historians "Chrestus." This edict had propelled Prisca and Aquila to Corinth as refuges of Rome, where they met Paul and joined his mission there (18:2). Thus, an apparent leader of this sect from Jerusalem itself[31] might be able to offer direct insight into the sect and its teachings.

Paul's presentation to synagogue leaders in Rome will be Luke's last narrative word about Jews and their nation. The message is mixed.

---

[31]Yes, subtle irony that Paul is regarded as a Jerusalem leader of this sect apparently because his case originated in Jerusalem.

Paul's Presentation (28:23)

A formal, all-day audition is arranged. Visiting all of Rome's synagogues in his detainment status was both impractical and inefficient (would take too much time), so synagogue leaders come to Paul in his quarters "in great numbers" (28:23). Interest is high. Two main ideas surface in Luke's condensed summary of Paul's presentation.[32]

First, Paul explains the matter by "testifying to the kingdom of God." Here in this term is Luke's literary *inclusio* over his entire Acts narrative—from the kingdom of God reference in Acts 1 to the kingdom of God reference in Acts 28. The actual expression "kingdom of God," while rare in Acts, is placed prominently and strategically at the beginning and at the end. This bounding and prominent placement suggests Luke in Acts intends to redefine "kingdom of God" according to his new vision of the people of God, that is, according to the story of the Acts narrative. The key element of this vision is the transformed people of God, the new *laos* the prophet Amos had anticipated, even as James made clear in his address to the assembled Christian leaders at the Jerusalem Conference.[33] This new people is not defined by ethnicity and Moses, but by faith and Jesus. Thus, gentiles are included by the purifying power of the Pentecost Spirit. Israel still is defined by clean and unclean, but the transforming process to move from unclean to clean has been

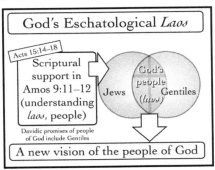

FIGURE 15.82. God's Eschatological *Laos*.

reconstituted by the new covenant of Jesus's death and resurrection. In the last days, historical Israel once defined nationally has transformed into the eschatological reality of messianic Israel now defined socially across national boundaries.

Second, Luke summarizes that throughout this assembly, Paul is "trying to convince them about Jesus" (28:23). We know from the Acts

---

[32]Paul spoke all day ("from morning until evening," 28:23). Clearly, Luke has condensed, which infers he loads each phrase with significance contextualized by the entire scope of the Acts narrative.

[33]See the discussion on p. 333.

account what this persuasion looks like. This persuasion looks like the sermon Paul preached to the Jewish synagogue in Antioch of Pisidia, the first of Luke's three paradigm sermons of Paul.[34] Paul would be using messianic texts from the law and prophets that anticipate the nature and mission of Jesus as Messiah. From a chosen nation to a chosen Son, Paul uses the royal house of David as the Old Testament jumping off place to preach Jesus. He then concludes with

Paul's Paradigm Sermons			
MJ	Place	Context	Audience
1MJ	Antioch	Synagogue	Jewish
2MJ	Athens	Market	Gentile
3MJ	Miletus	Church	Christian

FIGURE 15.83. Paul's Paradigm Sermons.

Habakkuk's warning to the nation on the eve of the rise of Babylon as a world power that God eventually would use to judge Israel.[35]

Response and Pronouncement (28:24–28)

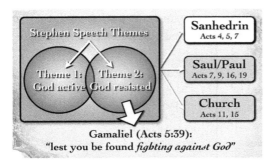

FIGURE 15.84. Stephen Speech Themes.

The response of the Jewish synagogue leaders is predictable. Add up all the synagogue encounters in Acts, and they can be summarized by this response of Jewish synagogue leaders in Rome: "Some were convinced by what he had said, while others refused to believe" (28:24). This mixed reaction is the synagogue pattern throughout Acts, so the reader is not surprised at all. The leaders debate the matter among themselves as they leave. Witnessing the obstinance of some, Paul observes how right was the Holy Spirit to pronounce a judgment oracle through Isaiah the prophet on Jewish ancestors who behaved similarly (28:25). The quote is from Isa 6:9–10. Isaiah's ironic word is about listening but not understanding, looking but not perceiving, because hearts are dull and ears deaf; without understanding, Israel cannot turn and be healed (28:26–27). This quote summarizes Acts, so

[34]Acts 13:16–41.

[35]See the discussion on pp. 312–13.

this quote also summarizes the Stephen speech themes. The theme of God resisted we have seen has become paradigmatic for all of Acts. "Go to this people and say" is a word of indictment for rejection and rebellion played out repeatedly in the Acts narrative:

- Jewish leaders in Jerusalem (4:17; 5:33)

- 1MJ: Antioch of Pisidia (13:40, 45–46); Iconium (14:5); Lystra (14:19)

- Jerusalem Conference (15:10; cf. 5:9)

- 2MJ: Paul himself (15:39; 16:6, 7); Thessalonica (17:5); Berea (17:13); Corinth (18:6)

- 3MJ: Ephesus (19:9); Corinth (20:3); Paul himself again (21:4, 12)

- Jerusalem again: inhabitants (21:27); Sanhedrin (22:30; 23:12; 25:2)

- Jewish leaders in Rome (28:24)

FIGURE 15.85. Arch of Titus. Celebrating Titus's victories, most especially defeat of the Jews in the First Jewish War. Jerusalem temple items fill the interior reliefs. Paul was right at the end of Acts: the Jewish nation soon would face judgment.

The upside will be that *some* do listen, respond, and find healing. This positive response is the other theme of the Stephen speech, God active. The dominant number of those responding to what God has done in Christ are gentiles. To this phenomenon Paul now turns. Once the synagogues equally have had a chance to hear the gospel presented clearly and powerfully and have rejected the message, then the same local pronouncement is made in Rome that has been made before in other localities, such as Antioch Pisidia (13:51) and Corinth (18:6): "Therefore, let this be known to you, that to the gentiles this salvation of God is sent; they themselves will listen" (28:28). This pronouncement, like the others in the Acts narrative, is local, that is, for Rome itself, not a final rejection of the Jewish people nor shuttering of a gospel mission to synagogues in the rest of the Diaspora throughout the world.

Paul is saying in Rome only what he has said repeatedly as a given synagogue in a given locale rejects the gospel message. If Jews refuse to listen, Paul is obligated by the gospel itself to go to gentiles in that region, because Scripture prophesies "they will listen."

The transition from 28:28 to 28:30 must have seemed abrupt to Byzantine copyists. They added verse 28:29 to compensate. This added verse repeats redundantly the information already given in 28:25 that the reaction was mixed and argument ensued as the synagogue leaders departed. This spurious verse redundantly reads, "And when he had said these words, the Jews departed and had great reasoning among themselves." The KJV and NKJV include this verse, quite simply because the knowledge of Greek manuscripts five-hundred years ago was extremely limited, they had only a few to translate from to begin with, and the few they had were all late Byzantine productions.[36]

ACTS CONCLUSION

Luke concludes Acts with an amazing economy of words in just two verses summarizing Paul in Rome (28:30–31). He marshals only three verbs for this purpose: lived, welcomed, proclaimed. Paul lived in Rome two whole years at his own expense. He welcomed all who came to him. He proclaimed the kingdom of God. Concise, but calculated. The glitter on the surface hides a gold mine underneath.

Paul in Rome

Residence in Rome

Paul's Residence. First, Luke says Paul lived in Rome. The entire narrative for the last nine chapters has been driving to be able to write this one sentence! That Paul takes up residence in Rome is a miracle of God and an illustration of divine grace. God overcame all obstacles to get Paul to Rome, including Paul himself.

Further, Luke infers with verb choice Paul conducts himself with the focus of a man on a mission, not a vacationer on a Roman holiday. The verb "lived" is a compound form of the verb for "abide," *emmenō*

---

[36] A number of commentators do not even remark on the verse, since its spurious nature is so obvious. For a brief discussion, see Peterson, *Acts*, 719–20.

(ἐμμένω), which form occurs only one other time in Acts (14:22). This other passage refers to believers continually persisting in the faith, so *emmenō* suggests for Luke staying on task, making determined effort. Luke prefers a different compound of this verb, *epimenō* (ἐπιμένω), when his thought is on the simple passing of time.[37] With this choice of verb in 28:30, Luke seems to infer a resoluteness to Paul's activity in Rome. Paul intently managed his time and activity with purpose and resolve. Paul was not twiddling his thumbs wondering how to pass the time waiting on Nero's judicial docket. Paul had a mission mandate to fulfill, and, even restrained, he was intent on fulfilling the mandate.

This time was not like incarceration. Paul's conditions were lenient. Though in custody, Paul had his own apartment, and he could move about. For example, he likely ate at the local thermopolium.

FIGURE 15.86. Ostia Thermopolium. A thermopolium is a ready-to-eat hot food restaurant. The selling counter open to the street on the left was near to the "menu," displayed in an illustrative fresco above and food dishes displayed on shelves below (center column). Despite typical artistic representations, Paul's custody in Rome would not have been bereft of access to these normal daily Roman activities.

Paul's Two Years. Luke indicates Paul stays two whole years. Interpreters try to divine the delimitation. Technically, one does not know if this time indication is meant to mark a terminus or simply to mark a continuing interval yet uninterrupted. Interpreters of Acts are compelled by curiosity to speculate the meaning of the two years.

[37]Acts 10:48; 12:16; 21:4, 10; 28:12, 14. Neither compound occurs in the Gospel, but the compound *diamenō* (διαμένω) occurs twice (Luke 1:22; 22:28).

One could speculate that a specific time frame indicates precisely where Luke is chronologically when writing Acts: Paul is still in prison, around AD 62, and the outcome of his appearance before Nero yet unknown. Or, one could speculate that Luke writes long after AD 62, and the result of Paul's appearance, for ill or for good, is well known to Luke's readers, so they can fill in the blank for themselves. Along these lines, those that assume a negative outcome try to bolster the argument with Paul's enigmatic statement causing great grief to the Ephesian elders that "no longer will you see my face" (20:25). The idea is that Luke has buried within this ominous word an inference of Paul's death as the outcome of Caesar's tribunal. Variations and other speculative schemes can be multiplied. They all are equally right (because they all are based equally on speculation). Luke simply does not explicitly say what any of these proposals suggest.

From a narrative point of view, the angel's statement in 27:24 is probably a more certain indicator about Caesar's tribunal than the entirely ambiguous and admittedly enigmatic comment Paul makes in 20:25. That is, Luke does infer in the angel's declaration to Paul that an appearance before Nero will happen, because he uses his verb of divine necessity (*dei*, δεῖ) to this effect in Paul's sea vision. In that sea vision, the angel tells Paul that he "must" stand before the emperor (27:24). Thus, standing before Caesar is a divine necessity, so Paul's destiny. However, whether the "two years" in 28:30 marks a terminus on that destiny or an interim still moving to that destiny is not clear. Thus, even knowing from the narrative that Paul assuredly will stand before Caesar, we still cannot definitively conclude that Paul already has appeared (or is about to appear) before Caesar at the end of Acts.

The problem in all these interpretive schemes is focusing on that which Luke does not focus—Paul's appeal. Outside the one reference in resignation by Agrippa II (26:32), and one brief mention by Paul himself in his own case summary to synagogue leaders in Rome (28:19), Luke himself never says another word about Paul's appeal to Caesar the moment the appeal is uttered. Thus, speculation that the exegetical significance of Luke's reference to two years is related to Paul's appeal to Caesar ignores the details of the actual story Luke composed.

Luke's reference to the two-year stay in Rome is *plot symmetry related to the divine will.* The narrative itself reveals the significance of a two year period: Paul was in Ephesus for two years (19:10); Paul was in Caesarea for two years (24:27); and Paul was in Rome for two years (28:30). *All of these two-year locations are directly related to the issue of Paul and God's will.* Nowhere else are specific, two-year periods thus marked in all of Acts: Ephesus, Caesarea, Rome. *The two year period is used to mark a plot summary of the struggle over God's will.* These two-year periods specifically trace Paul being in the center of God's will, to moving off-center from God's will, to returning to the center of God's will. The crown jewel of the Pauline missionary enterprise is Ephesus. Here, Paul is at the apex of his ministry and in the center of God's will. From Ephesus, Paul was supposed to go to Rome; Paul, however, impudently detoured to Jerusalem first, like Moses impudently striking the rock in the wilderness (Num 20:8–12). So, Jerusalem is the nadir of Paul's ministry and decidedly off-center from God's will. Finally, Paul gets to Rome, with a renewed sense of mission and returns back to the center of God's will.

All this information Luke has provided in the narrative—the incredible obstacles God had to overcome to get Paul here, Luke's verb choice to describe Paul's residence here, and Luke's two-year marking of the period in Rome to connect back to Caesarea and Ephesus—the narrative wheelbarrow is full enough to tell us Rome is Paul's destiny. Paul's destiny is achieved. Fundamentally, the story is complete.

Paul's Purpose. But why does Luke invest Paul in Rome with such narrative significance? After all, Jerusalem is hugely important to the story of Christianity, and where would we be without trend-setting Antioch, the paradigm? The answer is threefold, and found in Acts 1:8, the Puteoli narrative, and Stephen's Hellenist movement.

Acts 1:8. First, God wanted Paul in Rome *to establish Paul's Hellenist mission in the heart of the empire to facilitate the harvest of Acts 1:8.* We can note how Luke has constructed Rome to be the supreme destiny of Paul's mission. In truth, Rome is the mission base to which the successful Ephesian ministry was supposed to point. God had intended Ephesus to be Paul's preliminary qualifying heat for the final race of Rome. Unlike any other Pauline base, Rome always from the beginning was the critical key to achieving "the uttermost parts of the earth" of Acts 1:8. So, the first reason for why Rome is Rome is the key location for the fulfillment of Acts 1:8.

Puteoli Narrative. Second, God wanted Paul in Rome because the Puteoli narrative shows that *Roman believers were ready for Paul and his gospel mission whenever he could get there.* The positive reception in Puteoli demonstrated this truth. How did this positive reception come about historically before Paul even gets to Italy? Luke does not say. He only narratively harnesses the known positive reception and moves on.

The narrative, however, may have left us an implicit clue, if we venture outside of Acts. Paul already had help on this matter of getting the Pauline gospel established in Rome due to what God did for Paul in Corinth. In Corinth, God immediately introduced Paul to Prisca and Aquila, gifted Christian leaders from Rome. This powerful couple had worked closely with Paul in Corinth for a year and a half, and then helped Paul set up the Ephesian mission. As a result, this pair absorbed the Pauline gospel thoroughly and proved themselves faithful and long time co-laborers in Paul's ministry. This Roman couple, after working with Paul at length in Corinth and Ephesus, likely returned to Rome at the death of Claudius after his edicts were rescinded.[38] Thus, because we could surmise that leaders such as Prisca and Aquila had returned to Rome, a reasonable assumption would be that Paul's distinctive gospel message already was impacting Roman believers. If so, Paul meeting Prisca and Aquila on the 2MJ in Corinth already would be God sovereignly moving to prepare Rome for Paul's arrival and thus facilitating the situation expressed in these last two verses of Acts. In any case—for whatever reason—Puteoli makes clear the Romans are ready for Paul.

Hellenist Movement. Third, God wanted Paul in Rome because *Paul represented the voice of the Hellenist movement, and the Hellenist movement always was where God was going in Acts.* God wanted the Hellenist movement transplanted from Antioch to Rome to establish firmly this voice of the gospel message as a permanent heritage for all believers of all time expressing the core of Christian teaching, the consummation of God active, and the culmination of the story of Jesus. From another angle, one might say God wanted Paul in Rome to redeem the martyr blood of Stephen, one of the greatest leaders of the Jerusalem church.

The last words of Acts leave us with Paul proclaiming and teaching "with all boldness," which indicates a powerful messenger, and "without hindrance," which indicates a powerful message (28:31). Luke's thought

---

[38]They are greeted as in Rome again in the letter of Romans (Rom 16:3). Admittedly, their return to Rome is precisely what Acts leaves unmentioned, as well as that Paul wrote a letter to Rome from Corinth a few years before Paul arrived in Rome.

is an incredible point on its own. Yet, readers never should forget that in these final words concluding Acts, we are hearing Luke's clarion proclamation of the supreme success of the Hellenist movement. In these concluding words we hear the *premier Hellenist* leader preaching and teaching in the *preeminent heart* of the empire. Paul in Rome is the whole point of Acts tracing the Hellenist movement beginning in Acts 6. This crucial Hellenist tradition for which Stephen paid with his life, was early church tradition apparently no one else in the church was emphasizing to the degree Luke felt essential to making clear the true ongoing story of Jesus and its full theological and social implications for all believing communities gathering "in one accord" in the name of Jesus and around the world.

So, that Paul "lived in Rome," that he achieved his divine destiny, that he unleashed the Pentecostal fullness promised in Acts 1:8 and permanently established the Hellenist movement in the heart of the empire as the key legacy of Christianity, stands on its own as a significant exegetical point within the global plot of the Acts narrative. In this context, the appeal to Caesar is absolutely meaningless. The plot of Acts, bluntly, does not require any resolution of the misdirected and faithless appeal to Caesar. In typical fashion as we have seen before, Luke suppresses that which is distracting or does not advance his plot. Luke was not following Paul's errant appeal. Luke was following the divine will launching the Hellenist movement into the whole world.

So, the first golden nugget of the three verbs in the Acts 28:30–31 conclusion is Paul's *residence* in Rome. His "abiding" teaches the nature of that residence, the significance of its two-year time frame, and the purpose for Paul's presence in Rome. The second golden nugget in the concluding two verses is the verb that Paul was *welcoming* all who came to him.

Hospitality in Rome

Second, Paul welcomed all who visited him. Visitors is a word of good news. Paul is in custody. Potentially, he could have been shunned in his socially shamed condition. Without life experience in a world strongly impacted by honor-shame codes, understanding that Paul "rattles a chain every time he moves"[39] simply does not compute for modern readers.

---

[39]A rhetorical flourish perhaps overdone, but the sociological point is still pertinent.

That *anyone* comes would be good news in Paul's first-century world!
Yet, by adding the next verse, Luke intends to say more.

From Puteoli and the Forum of Appius and the Three Taverns, we
already know that Roman believers accept Paul. These believers probably are seeing to his needs
while he is in Rome. They
would represent all levels of
society, even as in Paul's missionary journeys. Some were
elite, probably similar to the
impression generated by a
Pompeii portrait of Terentius Neo and his elite wife.[40]
Prisca and Aquila may have
been of this number. They
are all important to Paul and
to Luke's narrative as well.

Such well-to-do believ-
ers, however, would not ex-
haust the meaning of those
"visitors" whom Luke references, as the very next verse

FIGURE 15.87. Terentius Neo Portrait. A Pompeii
portrait of a lawyer and his wife, AD 62–79. Paul
would have contacted some social elites similar
to this couple. Prisca and Aquila may have been
in this category (NNAM).

makes clear. The next verse indicates the content of the conversations
Paul was having. The content of the conversations is the "kingdom of
God" and "the things concerning the Lord Jesus, the Messiah" (28:31).
No accident that this phrasing repeats exactly the content of the conversation Paul had with Jewish synagogue leaders in the all day workshop
on Messiah (28:23). Thus, by specifying the conversation content in
28:31 as an echo of the previous conversation with synagogue leaders,
in his "visitors" Luke infers Paul *still is attracting Jewish interest from the*

---

[40]The portrait is social commentary. His rolled papyrus scroll could be a wedding con-
tract, so the painting a wedding portrait in a realistic, not idealized, style. He wears a toga,
but has cropped hair style, brow creases, scraggly moustache and beard, big ears and bony
features, and is tanned; clearly, not flattering features. She, in contrast, is sophisticated.
Her fair skin denotes the culturally elite (not a field hand). Her fine and delicate hair curls
took hours for a slave to accomplish in the dressing room. Her stylish head band, fine lips,
manicured nails, wealthy scarlet robe, and writing stylus with wax tablet all are signs of
significant wealth. They seem socially unmatched, but pleasantly paired. Cf. http://www.
kaptured.com/classicsy12/12classics/Pompeii_-_Terentius_Neo.html.

synagogues of Rome. Further, from the Acts narrative itself, one could surmise that another element among these inquiring "visitors" seeking to understand the kingdom of God and the story of Jesus would be gentiles, both "God-fearers" from within the synagogue on the pattern of the Cornelius paradigm, as well as from the general multicultural populations of Rome. Thus, knowing Luke's narrative, one reasonably could deduce that reference to "visitors" in this context means Paul is evangelizing—even though he is in chains. Again, by presenting Paul in chains as successful manifests another miracle of God's grace in Paul's life. So, a second golden nugget in the concluding two verses of Acts 28:30–31 is the verb that Paul *welcomed* all who came to him.

Proclamation in Rome

Third, Paul is proclaiming. Luke's last narrative nugget is the verb about Paul proclaiming, because proclamation is what the Roman empire was all about—the imperial propaganda codified across the empire in the *Res Gestae* inscriptions of Augustus's will and pushed on the world's population by all subsequent Julio-Claudian emperors in images on coins, buildings, statuary, inscriptions, literature and every other conceivable venue of propagation of a world kingdom with divine rights to rule all of humankind and whose heart was in Rome.[41] Temples to Augustus were already across the empire, including the nearby port city of Ostia but also in far away provincial cities Paul missionized, such as Antioch of Pisidia on the 1MJ, with its elaborate Augustan temple complex at the very top of the city.[42] The Pala-

FIGURE 15.88. Ostia: Temple of Augustus. Ostia had a large and commanding temple to Roma and Augustus before Augustus died, served by the flamines of the imperial cult in Ostia.

tine hill in the city of Rome already was on its way to becoming the centerpiece of imperial palace luxury overlooking the Forum of Rome

---

[41]Consult Zanker, *The Power of Images in the Age of Augustus*; Galinsky, *Augustan Culture*. For illustrations from Aphrodisias, see Stevens, *Revelation*, 212–27.

[42]For Antioch of Pisidia, see Fig. 10.32.

below, and Nero, to whom Paul had appealed, would soon launch a palace building project after the fire of Rome that would dwarf anything conceived previously after draining the marsh below the Forum to facilitate this immense monument to his reign.

FIGURE 15.89. Rome: The Palatine Hill. One of the "seven hills of Rome," the Palatine hill was the residence of the emperor of Rome overlooking the Forum below. Here lived the ruler of the world.

Roman emperors asserted divine right to rule the world. Their own narrative, however, disguised a perfidious lie. The "peace" of the Augustan Age was no true peace but only defeat by brute force, violent conquest—a submission at the hands of an overwhelming military might. A perverse ideology of violence and dominance was legitimated as divine right to rule and then reinforced by violent, brutal, and bloody gladia-

FIGURE 15.90. Grave Relief: Amazon Warrior Motif. Homer's *Iliad* began the myth of a race of Amazon warrior women fierce in battle, which became a martial motif into the Roman empire, as epitomized in this grave relief of a Roman soldier to honor his courage in battle (OAM).

torial combat in amphitheaters across the empire. Rome even told its beginnings as the legendary story of two violent brothers, Romulus and

Remus, twins conceived by Mars, god of war, abandoned, suckled by a she wolf. Romulus later murdered Remus over where to found Rome. This empire began in violence, breathed violence, bread violence, and baptized violence to the world in her legends and her legions—a kingdom aggrandizing force, dominance, and intimidation.

FIGURE 15.91. Cuirass of Hadrian. The legend of Rome's origins in the she wolf that suckled twin brothers Romulus and Remus is the centerpiece of this military cuirass of emperor Hadrian (117–138) standing in the ancient Agora of Athens. Nike, or Victory, is supported on the back of the she wolf. The she wolf legend tacitly codes the foundational truth that Rome even in its imperial ideology acknowledges its fundamental wild, aggressive, and violent DNA.

The Ara Pacis Augustae monument in Rome celebrates this Roman gospel and its kingdom. The Roman Senate in 13 BC commissioned a new altar in Rome dedicated to the goddess Peace to honor Augustus after his conquests of Gaul and Spain. Short wall reliefs depict scenes of peace and Roman ritual. Long wall reliefs depict the imperial family in sacrificial attire and procession. All the common motifs that would become foundational imperial ideology, including the imperial cult, already manifest in these reliefs. Lower register reliefs depict a harmonious intertwining of vines and nature to symbolize the "harmony and peace" Augustus has forged with its inevitable abundance and prosperity. The Ara Pacis is the greatest surviving monument propagating the grand themes of the Roman empire, preserving for generations to come the Roman gospel about the Augustan dynasty, its divine right to rule, and the benefits to the world of this glorious empire.

FIGURE 15.92. Ara Pacis Augustae. The Altar of Augustan Peace was commissioned by the Roman Senate in 13 BC to honor Augustus after his victories subduing Gaul and Spain. Reliefs promote the imperial cult and family and sacrifice to the goddess Peace.

We already have demonstrated with Luke's notation of "visitors" that Paul's proclamation in context is evangelistic. His proclamation is about another kingdom, God's, and his Messiah, Jesus, new realities transcending the Jewish nation and the law of Moses, as well as the imperial gospel already being proclaimed in Rome. In a way, for Luke, gospel proclamation *is* the kingdom of God. The confessional titles Paul uses in 28:31 echo his earliest proclamation in Damascus after the Damascus Road. "Lord" nuances Son of God (9:20) in the context of Caesar, and "Christ" nuances the promised Messiah (9:22) in the context of Moses. God's kingdom is centered on the new people of God. Paul's gospel is non-imperial, non-national—the multicultural *laos* of Amos's dreams, and the realization of James's message in Acts 15:16–18 of Jews and gentiles united by faith in Jesus the Messiah to become the eschatological messianic Israel of the last days—a new vision of the people of God and good news for the world. Thus, the third and last verb that is a golden nugget exegetically at the end of Acts in 28:30–31 is the most potent and challenging of all to Luke's Greco-Roman readers. Proclamation involves espousing a life philosophy. Proclamation reveals what drives a person, motivates their every thought and action, even sends them around the world—their Damascus Road.

Paul's proclamation in Rome at the end of Acts is Luke's way of narratively walking his readers around the Ara Pacis to reconsider the message of its reliefs. Not lost on Luke is that Paul traveled to Rome on an Alexandrian grain ship; Luke even noted the irony of the ship's figurehead (28:11). This ship belonged to the imperial fleet constantly cutting the seas to supply plebian Rome free bread. Bread, however, fundamentally comes from God, and acknowledging that truth is the essence of Israel's Pentecost celebration. Herod Agrippa I had tried to ignore this Pentecost truth in his dispute over food supply to Tyre and Sidon (12:20). Herod also threatened the famine-distressed Jerusalem church by attacking its leaders (12:1). The story of Herod's death is enveloped by the story of Antioch fulfilling the Pentecost promise of harvest abundance in messianic Israel by its famine relief effort to Jerusalem (11:29; 12:25). Now, we find that another Pentecost usurper is Rome, who falsely promised conquered peoples nature's abundant harvest, as in the reliefs of the Ara Pacis, but ravaged world wealth and resources in her own insatiable appetite for luxury.

An imperial gospel already was being proclaimed in Rome long before Paul arrived with his own: the good news of Caesar versus the good news of Christ. Rome told its story in the legend of Aeneas, divinely conceived of the goddess Aphrodite, escaping Troy's destruction by the Greeks, his son Lulus on his back, and arriving in Italy to become the progenitors of the imperial families of Julius and Augustus. Augustus is hailed by

FIGURE 15.93. Roman Aeneas Legend. Aeneas, son of divine Aphrodite, escapes Troy to become progenitor in Italy of the imperial families ruling Rome (AMA).

the Roman poet Virgil as Rome's peace and the world's savior, reconciler of enemy forces of a war-torn, dying Republic disintegrating away for two hundred years, herald of a new golden age of human history promising security and nature's profuse abundance.[43] Among Gospel writers, only Luke carefully times Jesus's birth, the true son of divinity, during the reign of Augustus (Luke 2:1). Luke asserts that Jesus's kingdom is the true good news, that Jesus's salvation is the true redemption of the world, and that Jesus's reign is the true peace and Pentecost abundance.[44]

The choice between these two gospels was stark, dramatic, and life changing. Paul was challenged to reaffirm his own choice by the divinely orchestrated storm that caused him to reassess trusting his appeal to Caesar to a renewed reliance upon Christ alone. A person considering Paul's gospel for the first time also would have to anticipate similarly moving from Caesar to the Christ. The beginning of such a decision would involve—as for Paul on the Damascus Road—a total shift, a courageous passage into a new worldview and associating with a new community of faithful followers of God's Messiah. This new life in God's messianic community would require nothing less than complete transformation of the mind through the infilling power of the Pentecost Spirit. Paul's gospel, then, had a dynamic power that Rome's did not. Paul's gospel reached into the depths of a person's soul, recognizing the quintessential truth that man does not live by bread alone—not even in Rome.

These last two verses of Acts with their three verbs summarizing Paul's activity as abiding, welcoming, and proclaiming tell us that Paul in Rome is the beginning of the realization of what Luke meant that they first were called Christians in Antioch (11:26). By this word Luke pointed to that Spirit-inspired Hellenist movement creating a cohesive spiritual family that transcends imperial, national, religious, and social boundaries. Being Christian in Antioch is defined as the messianic Israel of the last days in the fullness of God with enough bread for all and a message for the world. That story now is transplanted to Rome, threshold to the world. Paul in Rome is the Hellenist movement consummated, the heart of Luke-Acts, the essence of church destiny. Luke knows his readers now can write the rest of the story of the church on their own.

---

[43]Virgil *Ecl.* 4. The *Kaisaros hilasteriou* (Καίσαρος ἱλαστηρίου) inscription from Metropolis near Ephesus calls Augustus "reconciler" (dated after the defeat of Antony at Actium in 31 BC), suggesting Augustan imperial rhetoric might shed light on Paul's use of ἱλαστήριον in Rom 3:25. Cf. Wilson, "Hilasterion and Imperial Rhetoric."

[44]Luke 2:10, 11, 14; Acts 2:1; cf. six summaries (6:7; 9:31; 12:24; 16:5; 19:20; 28:31).

Last Points

FIGURE 15.94. Basilica of San Clemente. This basilica's history traces back to the earliest days of Christianity in Rome and Clement I, bishop of Rome (92–99). For a closer view of the central apse, see Fig. P8, p. 14.

To pull together some of the points above about Paul in Rome but synthesized with other issues, we note that the ending of Acts means:

- Paul is back on track. The journey to Rome is a journey back into God's will. Acts reaches its narrative climax with Paul in Rome. The appeal to Caesar is pointless to Luke's narrative strategy.

- Christianity is innocent. Christian messengers do not purpose to instigate riots, insurgency, or rebellion. Believers, however, do have another Lord and proclaim another gospel.

- Acts 1:8 is on the way to fulfillment. The program of gospel expansion to the ends of the earth reaches critical mass in Rome. This gospel message is epitomized in the Hellenist movement.

- National Israel is not God's people. The errant question of 1:6 finally is answered: Israel is not national. Messiah has transformed Israel into the eschatological messianic Israel, the people of God as non-national and multicultural—the core of the Hellenist gospel.

- Jewish rejection of the Messiah seems incorrigible. This rejection is widespread, from Jerusalem's Sanhedrin to Diaspora synagogues. The Jewish nation seems set on a collision course with divine judgment.

- The church's center is shifting to Rome. This impetus for the shift is Antioch's gentile mission with its fulfillment of Acts 1:8. Luke was prescient about the future direction of the story of Jesus.

Luke's narrative has run full circle back to Acts 1. Some issues are left without resolution. Yet, his story has arrived where he is confident the future of Christian history will be written.

FIGURE 15.95. Below San Clemente. A governmental building destroyed in the AD 64 fire of Rome with distinctive first-century herringbone floor and *opera reticulata* wall. A Roman estate built on this structure later was used as a church.

Acts in Retrospect

Ascension Again

With Paul in Rome, preaching and teaching "unhindered," Luke has reached his purposes for writing. He has defended Christianity, defined messianic Israel, clarified the church, nuanced the kingdom of God, demonstrated Pentecost fulfillment, vali-

FIGURE 15.96. Rome: Church Destiny.

dated the Hellenist movement, and knighted the apostle Paul. Now, the church has been appraised of its divine mission and destiny to realize a Pentecost harvest to the ends of the earth until Jesus comes.

FIGURE 15.97. The Message of the Ascension. The glorification of Jesus is a process taking place now between ascension and return—the Hellenist gospel expansion.

With the idea of Jesus's return, we are back to Luke's ascension message. We remember how Luke connects the ascension to the return of Jesus. Luke is the only Gospel writer to include the story of the ascension, and in a doublet fashion at the end of the Gospel of Luke and at the beginning of Acts. He intentionally creates this doublet in order to tie the resurrection of Jesus in the Gospel theologically to the outpouring of the Spirit at Pentecost in Acts. Thus, if the ascension is Jesus's glorification, and the ascension points to Pentecost, then what truly glorifies Jesus is not so much his being in heaven as his resurrection power manifest in the outpoured Spirit on earth. This outpoured Spirit is messianic Israel's quantum leap spiritually from national Israel. The Spirit cleanses like the law of Moses never could. Luke's ascension means the church has a mission obligation to bring Pentecost to the world in order for Jesus fully to be glorified. Theologically, Luke's tying ascension to the return of Jesus in effect establishes the job description of the church. The sequence in Acts 1 is clear:

- Jesus's command: "wait for what the Father promised" (1:4)

- Jesus's commission: "you will be my witnesses" (1:8)

- Angels' question: "why do you stand looking into the sky?" (1:11)

That is, between ascension and return is the commission in Acts 1:8. The new vision of the people of God is a people on Pentecost mission bringing Jesus into his fullest glory for his glorious return. That, for Luke, is the essence of the kingdom of God in this church age.

Damascus Road Again

What are the consequences of Paul's disobedience for the story of Christianity in Rome? We first should remind ourselves that Paul was hardly any different than Moses on this score. Not even the venerable Moses got to see the promised land because of his disobedience. Paul's intransigent insistence on going to Jerusalem first before Rome caused the Ephesian mission to collapse and Rome to be delayed seriously. Luke's story of Paul's Ephesian success presumes an unchained Paul. What would the story of Rome have been if Paul were *not* in chains, more on the pattern of Ephesus (28:20)? How *then* would the last chapter of Acts been written? Of course, we cannot know. In any case, Simeon's prophecy of Joseph and Mary's child being a "light for revelation to the gentiles and glory to your people Israel" (Luke 2:32) remains. The Damascus Road is a journey still to be walked. Something to ponder the next time the Spirit prompts a word of witness.

SUMMARY

Paul has appealed to Caesar, and he is on his way to Rome. Not all is well, though. Paul still has not seen the light about the disaster in Jerusalem he has caused. Getting Paul to Rome is the story of God overcoming all odds after this unfortunate detour to Jerusalem. The story of the captain and his crew and the storm at sea becomes a metaphor for Paul's own life. Since Paul is on his way to his divine destiny, Luke rejoins the story as they embark from Caesarea, his third "we section." Luke affirms by his personal presence that Rome is God's will.

Paul's guard is the centurion, Julius, who most likely has been appraised by his commander, the tribune, of this prisoner's innocence, since the tribune heard Paul's defense before Agrippa II. Thus, the very first stop at Sidon reveals Julius already showing Paul kindness. This relationship will be important later in the story as Julius has to trust Paul at a critical moment in the shipwreck story when some of the ship's crew serendipitously attempt to escape on their own.

The winds are contrary constantly, and that is the dark tone that will build the storm symphony. They catch an Alexandrian grain ship at Myra, but catch no favorable winds. They fight for even a little progress every hour. They have to leave the coast of Asia at Cnidus and try to gain relief from the island of Crete, but to no avail. They finally reach Fair Havens, but its port is too little for wintering, so they strike out for the better port of Phoenix on the western end of Crete. Paul's unsolicited words of advice to the captain and crew about injury and loss if they try to proceed to Phoenix is ironic for what Paul himself has been doing since insisting on going to Jerusalem. Advice is refused, and they sail right into a disastrous storm, imperiling all on board. One just could not have a better script for Paul's own life story.

The storm symphony now reaches its triple fortissimo chords as a Euroquilo hurricane sweeps down violently upon the grain ship after pulling up anchor from Fair Havens. The mariners are totally unprepared. They are swept past Cauda, a tiny island southwest of Crete. They struggle to pull the dingy on board before it tears apart the stern, and then have to throw cargo overboard to lessen the lateral stress on the ship, which means the ship captain's livelihood is lost. Finally, all hope of being saved is abandoned, marking the key transition point in the story. Loss of all hope means that no pagan god has responded to their prayers, and no divine sovereignty has intervened over the storm.

Right at this dire point of no hope, Paul has a vision. Paul having a vision in Acts means he is off track from God's will, and God is working graciously to restore him to kingdom service. Paul now comprehends that his errant appeal to Caesar was an appeal to the wrong lord. Caesar has no sovereignty that can help Paul now. Paul's "you should have heeded me" to the mariners is almost humorous, since God could be saying the exact same words back to Paul. Luke often has used Paul's own words in Acts as self-incriminating. This storm at sea finally has gotten Paul's attention like the storm in Jerusalem never did. Paul believes God and affirms the mission mandate of Rome. Paul's disobedience, however, still has consequences, since Paul, though he will go to Rome, will be in chains, and these chains diminish the impact.

Immediately after the sea vision and Paul's expression of faith in God, the narrative turns positive for Paul for the first time since Ephesus. After two weeks drifting, they hear breakers, so know they are near land. Paul, however, sees sailors attempting to escape with the dingy, tells the centurion, and the centurion immediately responds by cutting away the dingy and retaining all sailors, who will be needed to work the tackle of the ship to hoist the mainsail. Another positive action by Paul is encouragement to take food for strength for the final effort to get to shore. Luke notes the full number on the ship to emphasize the size of the miracle in that not a soul is lost.

They prepare the ship for grounding at daylight after spotting a bay and its beach. They did not see the reef into which they dug the ship's bow trying to run ashore. The ship begins breaking apart from crashing waves at the stern, but all get to shore safely. Island natives welcome with a fire, but Paul is bit by a viper as Paul tries to put more brush on the fire. The natives think their god "Justice" has decreed this criminal's just deserts after wrongfully escaping the storm, but Paul does not die. Luke uses the natives' narrative to emphasize the divine destiny that controls Paul's life. What gets Paul to Rome is not an appeal to Caesar but the sovereignty of God.

Paul does miracles on Malta. The last we heard of Paul working miracles was Ephesus. These miracles continue the theme that Paul is back on track with God's will.

After wintering in Malta, they find another Alexandrian grain ship heading to Rome. They board this vessel and make the port of Puteoli in Olympic record time. Again, the notable speed they accomplish enhances the theme that Paul's divine destiny is Rome. Once Paul is on the Italian mainland, Roman characters such as the centurion Julius that have dominated the story ever since Paul's arrival in Jerusalem quietly fade away. Luke also leaves Paul's appeal to Caesar completely unremarked. Luke has not forgotten the appeal. He simply does not care. The appeal to Caesar never was the narrative point in the first place. For Luke, that appeal was a serious mistake by Paul opting for the wrong lord. Only God and his divine protection got Paul to Rome. Paul was just three years late on the divine itinerary. The positive reception of Paul and his company at Puteoli intimates why God wanted Paul in Rome. Roman believers long had been ready for Paul and his mission. This focus by Luke on the positive reception of Paul by these Roman believers at Puteoli is reinforced in the narrative by stories of double delegations from Christian congregations coming out to greet Paul on his route at the Forum of Appius and the Three Taverns well before he even arrives in Rome.

Paul arrives in Rome. His mission destiny is achieved. Luke's role as witness to this divine will for Paul is complete, and so the third "we section" ends. The Roman imprisonment at the end of Acts is the likely time of Paul's Prison Epistles.

Paul establishes contact with synagogue leaders to appraise them of his case and to present the gospel. Luke summarizes an all-day affair. Two important concepts in his summary are the kingdom of God and persuasion about Jesus. The kingdom of God is envisioned as the new *laos* Amos predicted God would create in the last days. This new people of God no longer would be defined by ethnicity and Moses but by faith and Jesus. Jesus is the Messiah. Messianic Israel is the result.

The response to Paul's presentation is predictable from the Acts account—mixed. That is, some believe, but others refuse to believe. In response to those not believing, Paul quotes Isa 6:9–10 about deficiency in understanding, refusing to see or hear, so missing the opportunity. This negative response fulfills the God resisted theme of the Stephen speech that has driven the entire plot of Acts. The upside is that some do listen. Most of these happen to be gentiles, so that receptive audience is where Paul now will focus his attention while in Rome.

Acts concludes with three verbs about Paul that are crucial to an interpretation of the Acts narrative ending. First, Acts concludes with Paul's Roman residence, which is the point, not the appeal to Caesar. Paul is a man on a mission—to be sure, in chains—but still on a mission. A two-year time frame intratextually marks Luke's plot summary of Paul's struggle over God's will with the only notations of two-year time frames in Acts: Ephesus, Caesarea, Rome. Rome is divine destiny, and that destiny has been achieved, against all odds. But why Rome? God's purpose for Paul in Rome was threefold. First, God put Paul's mission in the heart of the empire to begin to fulfill Acts 1:8. Second, God put Paul in Rome because Roman believers were ready to function as his mission base. Third, God put Paul in Rome because Paul was the voice of the Hellenist movement God had been guiding along ever since Stephen spilled his blood for the truth of the Hellenist understanding of the story of Jesus.

Second, Acts concludes with Paul showing hospitality to many visitors. These visitors are more than just those taking care of Paul. They come from Jewish synagogues, as well as the general populations of Rome. Paul is evangelizing. Paul cannot move, but the gospel Paul preaches moves throughout Rome, perhaps even beyond.

Lastly, Acts concludes with Paul proclaiming and teaching. The content is the kingdom of God and Jesus. The term kingdom of God is not frequent in Acts, but Luke uses the expression as an *inclusio* over the entire narrative thereby redefining what constitutes the kingdom in the messianic age of the last days. Jesus reconstitutes the kingdom. This kingdom now is the age of the Spirit of Jesus outpoured, bringing salvation and a word to the world of that promised divine abundance inherent in the Jewish Pentecost festival. Pentecost is to be realized to the uttermost parts of the earth—why they first were called Christians in Antioch, because they first fully understood and sought to realize in earnest the Pentecost vision.

Acts in retrospect requires reflecting again on the meaning of the ascension, a story only Luke records. The ascension ties resurrection to Pentecost. Luke highlights Pentecost as Jesus's resurrection power un-leashed on the church. Pentecost realized in the lives of believers is what glorifies Jesus for his return, not simply a transit to heaven. What happens on earth in the church is his glory, not what happens in heaven.

Finally, Luke ends Luke-Acts with Paul's proclamation in Rome, not the appeal to Caesar, because the Hellenist gospel —Messiah Jesus, world Savior—countered Rome's gospel. The imperial false gospel was Luke's point in the end. Jesus is the true ruler with divine heritage and mandate to rule all nations to the uttermost parts of the earth, not Rome. Augustus is no messiah, and his empire no golden age. True Pentecost abundance for all humankind is Jesus (Luke 2:11; Acts 28:31).

Luke's story complete, we cannot help but speculate. What if Paul had not disobeyed God and gone straight from Ephesus to Rome? What would have been the Christian story? Obviously, we cannot say, but one does wonder the plot that would have ensued.

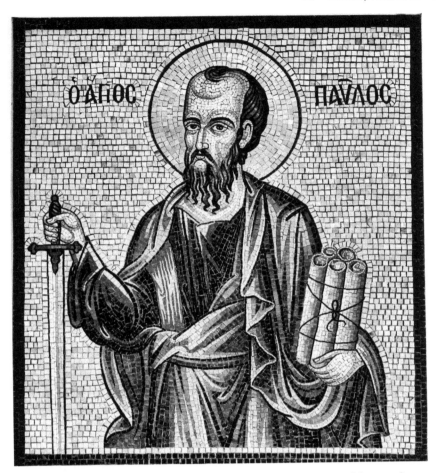

FIGURE 15.98. Apostle Paul Mosaic. One of two outstanding mosaics of the apostle Paul at the Saint Paul Monument in Berea, the imagery evokes Paul's apostolic office of preaching the gospel through the powerful sword of the Spirit in one hand and his apostolic office of teaching the churches through his powerful pastoral letters in the other hand. His amazing legacy reverberates across two millennia of church history. Luke seemed to have had a premonition when he wrote that that would be so. Note the thin face, high and furrowed forehead, and pointed beard—stereotypical features in the depiction of Paul in ancient church art. (See the catacomb portrait of Paul discussion in the Epilogue, p. 597.)

FIGURE 15.99. Peter's Crucifixion Upside Down (NMB). This bold marble relief is by the famed Florentine sculptor Luca Della Robbia, c. 1409. The martyrdom of Peter tradition is that Peter asked not to be crucified in the same manner as his Lord, so he was crucified upside down. The story is told in the apocryphal account of the *Acts of Peter and Paul* (ca. 180–200). See *APeterPaul* 81.1–3 (Tucker, *Apocryphal Acts*). For a discussion of the church traditions related to Paul's death and burial, see the following Epilogue.

Epilogue

Intimations of Mortality:
On Conjuring Paul's Death and Burial

F OR SOMEONE WE FEEL LIKE we know really well from his letters, knowing little about Paul's death and burial comes as a surprise. We feel pressed to say at least something. Certainly he died under some particular circumstances, and surely eyewitnesses shared the story after the event. But that is the rub. Apparently, whatever information could be gathered from eyewitnesses never was written down at the time. Oral tradition was all that remained, and oral tradition in later generations among those not eyewitnesses in popular imagination can take on a life of its own, building up and accumulating extraneous material around the center, like a snowball rolling downhill. Worse still, oral tradition can be the devil to document and validate to the satisfaction of historical inquiry. Thus, any discussion of Paul's death and burial is confronted with significant historical problems.[1]

Historically, neither the primary material (Paul's letters) nor close secondary material (Acts) offer sufficient details about what happened

---

[1]Only recently have earlier, scattered and brief treatments in essays, journal articles, dictionaries, and encyclopedias found more extensive coverage with provisions of actual texts and translations. As a sample of both earlier and recent works, cf. Duchesne, *Liber Pontificalis*; Bonnet, *Acta Apostolorum Apocrypha*; Macpherson, "Was There a Second Imprisonment of Paul in Rome?"; Edmundson, *The Church in Rome in the First Century*; Lipsius and Turner, "Actus Petri cum Simone (Vercellenses)"; Chadwick, "St. Peter and St. Paul in Rome"; MacDonald, "Apocryphal and Canonical Narratives about Paul"; Hennecke and Schneemelcher, *New Testament Apocrypha*; Elliot, *The Apocryphal New Testament*; Tajra, *The Martyrdom of St. Paul*; Bakirtzis and Koester, *Philippi at the Time of Paul and after His Death*; Cooper, "The martyr, the matrona and the bishop"; Eastman, *The Ancient Martyrdom Accounts of Peter and Paul*; Döhler, *Acta Petri*.

after the imprisonment narrated at the end of Acts or assumed in the Prison Epistles to be helpful.[2] Church tradition, scarce at best, set out to fill this historical void, but simply dumped legendary information in the form of a pseudo-biography of Paul beginning where Luke left off creating a story of release, Spanish mission, second imprisonment, and death under Nero after the fire of Rome—an invented pseudo-biography too often assumed fact. What church traditions we have offering actual details about Paul's death and burial do not show up until the martyrological period beginning in the second century. The rise of martyrdom in the second and third centuries of the church inspired the publication of martyrologies designed to encourage the faithful. These writings gave new impetus to focus on the deaths of Peter and Paul. Unfortunately, by then historical memory already had languished at least a century, with no traceable trail of oral tradition, and no written account offering specific details beyond what easily could be mined in Acts or the Prison Epistles.[3] Further inducement for the second- and third-century focus on Peter and Paul particularly was that church centers in the East (Jerusalem and Antioch) and West (Rome) were contesting their supremacy over the Christian faith and the faithful. The East argued that they were founded first by the apostles, but Rome to great effect was able to harness the place of martyrdom for both Peter and Paul to their advantage. How trustworthy is this second- and third-century martyrological material, produced for other purposes in the designs of the church, for producing an historical biography of Paul's death and burial? That is the abiding and vexing question.

In short, Paul's death and burial are undocumented. We often do not make sufficiently clear to our lay audiences that we mostly are just speculating or guessing when we make statements suggesting any kind of specificity of knowledge about Paul post Acts. Three historical problems for discussing this question involve complex interrelationships of the exact literary settings of our New Testament sources, the late date or unreliability of other historical sources, and legendary church traditions speculated from thin evidence. In the following discussion, we provide a brief overview of these three, interrelated problems, a proposed solution, and a conclusion.

---

[2]Issues of authorship, date, and authenticity of New Testament documents are not essential to discussion of their use by the church fathers in tracing traditions on Paul.

[3]We will deal with Clement of Rome shortly.

PROBLEM OF NEW TESTAMENT SOURCES

The first problem to establishing information on Paul's death and burial are the historical settings of our potential New Testament sources. Three sources in particular have been invoked: Acts, the Pastoral Epistles (1–2 Timothy, Titus), and Philippians. The setting and applicability of each is argued.

The Historical Setting of Acts

The problem of Acts is that the ending is thoroughly ambiguous about either an actual appearance of Paul before Caesar or its outcome. Tradition abhors a vacuum, so an invented church tradition of release and second imprisonment rushed in to fill the Acts void.[4] The legend then became an interpretive tsunami so powerful as to flood out every attempt at historical discussion of Paul's death and burial. Significant problems with the entrenched tradition are ignored or downplayed to the detriment of historical inquiry. Often unremarked is how flimsy is the actual evidence for this invented history, unless one presumptively begs the question with the Pastorals themselves. Disparate pieces of texts in Acts and the Pastorals are cobbled together to fit only one interpretation that flows into later church tradition to create a pseudo-biography of Paul post Acts as if certified history. Examples of such disconnected pieces contributing to this highly dubious legendary wave include:

- Paul's anticipated mission to Spain[5]

- Paul's ambiguous statement to the Ephesian elders of "seeing his face no more"[6]

---

[4]Church tradition of release and second imprisonment actually may have developed more to solve the problem presented by the Pastoral Epistles than the riddle of Paul's death. Another solution to deal with the Pastorals is pseudonymity. Tajra assumed the Pastorals were the work of a "sincere Paulinist" author writing for the needs of the later Pauline churches after Paul's martyrdom (*The Martyrdom of St. Paul*, 84). The Pastorals, then, for Tajra do not apply to the question of how Paul died, but just to attempts to leverage Paul's martyrdom for later ecclesial purposes on the two themes of abandonment and Paul's death as sacrifice (pp. 86–98).

[5]Rom 15:24, 28.

[6]Acts 20:25, 28.

- Clement of Rome saying Paul had preached "to the farthest bounds of the West"[7]

- late church tradition claiming Peter and Paul together founded the church in Rome[8]

- late church tradition that Peter and Paul suffered martyrdom together in Rome[9]

- late Muratorian Canon tradition guessing why Spain goes unmentioned by Luke in Acts[10]

- late apocryphal tradition of Roman believers' angst over Paul's departure for Spain[11]

That is pretty much the bulk of what we have for developing the release and second imprisonment legend outside the Pastoral Epistles themselves (see below).

Obvious even in this short list is how all this snowball of tradition traces back to total dependency upon one comment by Paul at the end of Romans of an intended mission to Spain (Rom 15:24, 28). Intention,

---

[7]*1 Clem.* 5:7: ἐπὶ τὸ τέρμα τῆς δύσεως, *epi to terma tēs dyseōs*. About AD 88–99.

[8]Irenaeus *Adv. Haer.* 3, (AD 175); Gaius of Rome (2nd–3rd cent.) in Eusebius *H.E.* 2.28.

[9]Dionysius of Corinth (AD 170) in Eusebius *H.E.* 2.28, inferring Paul's death is later than Acts.

[10]On the false supposition that Luke wrote only about what he had witnessed (2nd–3rd cent.).

[11]*Actus Petri Vercellenses* 1–3 (AD 180–200). In *Vercellenses*, Paul is so bound to Roman believers that he needs the Lord commanding him in a vision to pry him out of Rome: "Paul, rise up and become a physician by your presence to those who live in Spain" (*Paule, surge et qui in Spania sunt corpore tuo medicus esto*), *Acta Petri* 1. In this text, Paul's departure for Spain is what requires Peter to go to Rome (also by vision) to confront the magician Simon Magus, who has arisen in Rome to destroy the church Paul had established; cf. *Acta Petri* 4. The *Vercellenses Acts* is a Latin version of the *Acts of Peter and Paul*. For earlier work on this text, see Lipsius and Turner, "Actus Petri cum Simone (Vercellenses)." More recently, Hilhorst, "The Text of the Actus Vercellenses." For a theory on origins, cf. Baldwin, *Whose Acts of Peter?* For the most recent overview of research, with translation and commentary, see Döhler, *Acta Petri*. Döhler summarized the scholarly consensus that this text's origin is indecisive between Rome and Asia Minor but that the date is late second century, with some hedging to early third century (*Acta Petri*, 35–48).

however, is not history. The only other possible piece of evidence for a mission West is Clement of Rome (AD 88–99), but Clement's statement is no slam-dunk, as often assumed, for proving Paul had a mission West. In interpreting Clement's "having reached the farthest bounds of the West" (ἐπὶ τὸ τέρμα τῆς δύσεως) we should remember that the point of this summary of Paul's life work by Clement is to climax with Paul's martyrdom, characterized as Paul giving his "testimony" (μαρτυρία, *martyria*) before the rulers of the world. Admittedly, the word "testimony" does not yet have the immediate meaning of death as in the later martyr period of church history,[12] but Clement could be read with this sense in the context of speaking of the climax of Paul's career. Such a climatic "testimony" at the end of a series of clauses summarizing Paul's life work could mean Paul's death, though this inference is debatable. If by using "testimony" Clement metaphorically is speaking of Paul's death, note that Clement assumes Paul's death happened in Rome. No, a resident of Rome such as Clement probably would not themselves refer to Rome as τέρμα ("limit," "end," "farthest bounds"), but Clement's rhetoric is assuming Paul's ethos in speaking for Paul, not Clement's ethos, as is proper in ancient rhetorical conventions, and Paul most certainly could refer to Rome as τέρμα.[13] Finally, one should note that no early church father one might presume to have known *1 Clement* (e.g., Peter of Alexandria, Pseudo-Clementine Epistle to James, Origin, Cyril of Jerusalem, Eusebius) ever appealed to *1 Clem.* 5:7 to argue a Spanish mission for Paul.[14]

[12]See Stoops, "If I Suffer . . . Epistolary Authority in Ignatius of Antioch." Cf. Ignatius *Eph.* 12.1–2.

[13]Cf. Macpherson, "Was There a Second Imprisonment of Paul in Rome?" 33–35. Also, note, "Whether or not Paul ever made it to Spain . . . , it is this Roman appearance that signaled for him the end of his course and the successful discharge of his apostolic responsibilities. Rome was for Paul the symbolic cosmopolitan center of 'the nations (Acts 23:11),'" Towner, "1,2 Tim, Titus," NICNT, 643. Clement's phrase secondarily might shed light on Luke's own famous phrase at the beginning of his narrative, "to the ends of the earth" (ἕως ἐσχάτου τῆς γῆς, *heōs eschatou tēs gēs*, Acts 1:8). Since Acts ends in Rome, that ending by default seems to be Luke's own implicit hermeneutic of Acts 1:8. That is, Luke intends to show Acts 1:8 as fulfilled *within* the storyline, not outside the storyline. So, whether Luke's "to the ends of the earth" or Clement's "farthest bounds of the West," in both the meaning *in context* is Rome.

[14]So Macpherson, 36.

Not even Eusebius appealed to Clement's statement as testimony for Paul's supposed mission West. Instead, Eusebius simply repeated the church tradition of release and second imprisonment, appealing to no authority for support. After leaving the text of Acts, Eusebius said, "the word is that the apostle was sent again on the ministry of preaching."[15] The deliberately vague "the word is" (λόγος ἔχει, *logos echei*) is a dead giveaway Eusebius is referring to no authority. Also note his deliberately vague "ministry of preaching." Eusebius here is suspiciously ambiguous about what exactly Paul did after release, suggesting he had no church tradition giving any details. The Pauline documentation to which he does appeal in his argument, the Pastorals, have not a word about Spain, but also have no clear itinerary. The Spain tradition is clear, however, in later martyrologies.[16] Eusebius indirectly provides evidence that Spain is not an essential component for inventing a post-release biography of Paul. Indeed, since the Pastorals themselves so clearly contradict the Spain motif, how this Spain motif got so entrenched in later martyrological material is a mystery outside of the luxury of having a blank whiteboard upon which to write any story with no historical accountability.

After suggesting some type of a post-release ministry of Paul with only the vaguest of information, Eusebius then proceeded to pick back up the church myth again, "upon coming to the same city a second time, he suffered martyrdom." He then offered his own take on 2 Timothy, emphasizing the tradition that the letter was composed during Paul's second imprisonment, since Paul mentions a "first defense" (2 Tim 4:16) but now impending death. Eusebius interpreted Paul's reference to the "heavenly kingdom" (2 Tim 4:18) as Paul's metaphor for martyrdom, and closed the case for martyrdom with Paul's "For I already am being

---

[15]Eusebius *H.E.* 2.22.2, αὖθις ἐπὶ τὴν τοῦ κηρύγματος διακονίαν λόγος ἔχει στείλασθαι τὸν Ἀπόστολον, *authis epi tēn tou kērygmatos diakonian logos echei steilasthai ton Apostolon.*

[16]See *MPeterPaul* 1.1; 3.1 (Tucker, *Apocryphal Acts*). Paul's mission in Spain is the backdrop to the third-century apocryphal romance novel, *The Acts of Xanthippe, Polyxena, and Rebecca.* In the sixth or seventh century, we have the detail that Paul spent a whole decade in Spain, although how that timing works with his reported death under Nero never is pondered; cf. *History of the Holy Apostle My Lord Paul* 9 (Eastman, *The Ancient Martyrdom Accounts*, 195).

poured out, and the time of my departure has arrived" (2 Tim 4:6).[17] Eusebius then added a note on Luke's biography to tie up a Lukan loose end on this post-Acts myth. Eusebius asserted that Luke had to have been absent in the first defense, because Paul said so (2 Tim 4:16, "no one came to my support")—hence, the ending of Acts without mention of tribunal result reveals that Luke was writing only down to the period he was with Paul.[18] Eusebius concluded with the moral of his story: "But these things have been adduced by us to show that Paul's martyrdom did not take place at the time of the Roman sojourn which Luke records."[19] Basically, strip away the church myth, for which Eusebius offers not one bit of substantiation, and Eusebius's entire presentation boils down to a tendentious reading of only three verses in Paul. Challenge only one assumption, that the Pastorals are after Acts, and the whole superstructure immediately falls. If Paul's story ended soon after Acts, a possibility Eusebius simply refused to entertain due to church myth, 2 Timothy could fit that setting just as easily as long after Acts. We should be reminded that a presumed setting for the Pastoral Epistles is just that—presupposition—not historical fact.[20]

Conveniently ignored in all this superstructure raised upon the myth of Paul's mission in the West after Acts is that almost no church west of Rome relates its founding to Paul.[21] Almost all churches west of Rome relate their founding to Peter. Macpherson noted that Sepp, *History of the Apostles*, in a detailed study found only four churches with traditions even *loosely* associated with Paul.[22] Adding insult to historical

---

[17]Eusebius *H.E.* 2.22.3–5.

[18]Ibid., 2.22.6.

[19]Ibid., 2.22.7.

[20]Take, for example, "first defense" (Ἐν τῇ πρώτῃ μου ἀπολογίᾳ, *En tēi prōtēi mou apologiai*, 2 Tim 4:16). The expression does not have to mean two different court cases. Such a "defense" (*apologia*) could be part of one continuous legal case; the first action, *prima actio*, would be the preliminary hearing to determine the legal viability of charges before troubling to conduct the main hearing to adjudicate the case. For a careful and balanced discussion of this issue as well as this passage in context, see Towner, "1,2 Tim, Titus," NICNT, 635–49. Also, even if "first defense" were an allusion to a separate court case, nothing demands an interval of years between them. Finally, 2 Timothy's "Paul abandoned" idea might clue in something radical, rapid, and unexpected after Acts 28.

[21]Macpherson, 42.

[22]Ibid.

injury, not one ecclesial inscription of any kind ever has been found documenting Paul's presence anywhere west of Rome.[23] Even the simple question *why* Paul would want to go to Spain in the first place is thoroughly without agreement among scholars.[24]

---

[23]Tajra's attempt to argue that Paul was in Spain offered no improvement on this dearth of data. His *only* evidence was the claim made on a 1963 modern statue of Paul in the city of Tarragona. The statue's inscription celebrates the nineteenth centenary of Paul's coming to Spain (1963) and the city's tradition of Paul's supposed stay at Tarragona. Tajra tried to prop up support for this modern claim of Paul in Tarragona by appealing to the third-century martyrdom of the Spanish bishop Fructuosus and his two deacons in the Valerian persecutions of 258, as well as some third-century Christian graves at Tarragona (*The Martyrdom of St. Paul*, 104). Somehow, third-century data jumps automatically to the first, and a modern statue erected nineteen centuries later seals the deal. So famous a missionary as Paul, whose presence supposedly bedazzled all of Rome and roused such notable opposition almost immediately, could not cast even the faintest historical shadow in Spain, nor could such a prolific letter-writing pastor compose even one short letter like the single sheet of papyrus that contained Philemon to send to one Spanish believer or congregation that they would value and preserve. To speak of a mission pastor who in the New Testament leaves the decided impression that he hardly went anywhere without trailing letters behind him—including known letters he wrote but we do not have (cf. 2 Thess 2:2, 15; 1 Cor 5:9; 2 Cor 2:3, 4, 9; 7:8, 12; Col 4:16)—then we have dug a deep historical hole to claim this mission pastor ministered in Spain and left hardly a trace, whether actual congregations, traditions, or letters. Yes, we are saying the king has no clothes. (Cf. Hans Christian Anderson, "The Emperor's New Clothes").

[24]Numerous theories have floated, but the three main ones are: attraction of Jewish *populations*, completion of Isaiah's prophetic circle of the gentiles and thereby inaugurating the *parousia*, and counter-*proclamation* within territories of imperial strength. **(1) Population.** The assumption of Jewish populations and synagogues in Spain attracting Paul like a bee to flowers was common among an older generation of classic commentaries on Romans (cf. Käsemann, 383). Bowers argued the assumption was all wrong, that Spain had few Jews and few, if any, synagogues (Bowers, "Jewish Communities in Spain," 395–402). Thornton in the same year added how archeological evidence was sparse (Thornton, "St. Paul's Missionary Intention in Spain," 120). Citing Bowers and Thornton, Jewett argued that Spain was not anywhere in the same league of mission feasibility as Asia Minor, Macedonia, or Greece; all of Rome's three Spanish provinces presented immense logistical and tactical problems (*Romans*, 74–79). However, Wright here did not agree with Jewett, and argued the opposite, that is, for a significant Jewish presence in Spain. Wright offered as rebuttal comments about the ubiquity of Jews around the world by Strabo, Seneca, Josephus, and Philo (*Paul and the Faithfulness of God*, 4999, n. 55). Wright's *literary* argument, however, fundamentally is flawed; the argument appeals to obvious, hyperbolic rhetoric on the part of these writers, so simply is not persuasive; archeological evidence speaks stronger to this point. Thus, to conclude, "We may therefore take it that Paul at least believed that there were significant Jewish communities in Spain" (*Paul and the Faithfulness of God*, 1500) is not based on evidence of the right kind. **(2) Parousia.** Johannes Munck popularized the

The Historical Setting of the Pastorals

The Pastoral Epistles (1–2 Timothy, Titus) long have been presumed by those who assume their authenticity as the de facto evidence of Paul's mission work after Acts. Yet, even if these epistles are assumed as from the hand of Paul, we still have two significant problems in the presumed historical setting. First, the biographical notations in the Pastorals themselves have nothing to do particularly with Spain or, even more generally, work in the West. So, we are appealing to documents as if supporting the church legend of a release, work in the West, and second imprisonment of Paul that themselves internally contradict the core operating thesis of that legend (Spanish mission achieved). Second, and even more problematic, is the precarious assumption regularly made that all three epistles were composed around the same time. Nothing exegetically, however, actually demands an assumption of close compositional setting.

If one separates these epistles, then another thesis that argues that two of the epistles (1 Timothy, Titus) can be situated *within* the Acts narrative gains exegetical traction.[25] If an Acts setting for two of the Pastoral

---

theory that Paul's mission strategy was inspired by the prophetic idea of Messiah and the circle of the gentiles laid out by Isa 66:19, but which required Munck to interpret Isaiah's "Tarshish" as Spain (*Paul and the Salvation of Mankind*). Munck particularly associated this prophetic fulfillment scheme with Paul thinking he thereby would provoke the *parousia*. The theory continues to attract attention, as in Dunn, *Romans*, 2:872. **(3) Proclamation.** Wright, however, as noted above, unsuccessfully attempted to reject the lack of Jewish population argument. He also rejected rather summarily Munck's circle of the gentiles theory. Wright offered his own theory of an intentional imperial critique by Paul in which Paul deliberately chose imperial strongholds for counter-proclamation of the gospel to demonstrate that the gospel's power combined with the glory of God could conquer the conqueror (*Paul and the Faithfulness of God*, 1502). The proposal seems similar in thought to the apocryphal prediction Paul makes to Nero who, Paul says, thinks himself the conqueror, but will know he has been conquered by Paul's unconquered King when Paul appears in a vision to Nero after Paul's execution; cf. Pseudo-Linus *Martyrdom of the Blessed Apostle Paul* 8 (Eastman, *The Ancient Martyrdom Accounts*, 155).

[25]Situating 1 Timothy and Titus with their biographical notations within the narrative of Acts is a sustainable hypothesis. Macpherson already demonstrated this feasibility, if only briefly, at the beginning of the twentieth century ("Was There a Second Imprisonment of Paul in Rome?" 45–48). More fully developed is the posthumous publication of the work of Bo Reicke, *Re-examining Paul's Letters*. Reicke built a case for 1 Timothy being composed at the end of the Ephesian ministry, Paul leaving Timothy behind in Ephesus to provide leadership while Paul went on to Troas and Macedonia (1 Tim 1:1–3). Timothy later rejoined Paul in Macedonia to be co-author of 2 Corinthians (2 Cor 1:1); *Re-examining Paul's Letters*, 51–59. Titus was sent by Paul to Corinth

Epistles is viable, then the last epistle, 2 Timothy, universally agreed to have been written close to the end of Paul's life, still could be situated after the two-year imprisonment concluding Acts. Under this interpretive scheme, the Pastoral Epistles would concord with the idea that the end of Acts is the end of Paul.

Tajra argued differently. He said Luke intentionally dropped plenty of hints to lead the reader to assume Paul was released at the end of Acts.[26] We would not disagree with such a reading as probably correct. Tajra, however, loses his historical compass about what this possible reading of Acts infers. He can be unexpectedly uncritical about church tradition at important junctures in his argument.[27] One crucial dependence on church tradition is a post-Acts mission of Paul.[28] Further, Paul

to help prepare the collection before Paul arrived (2 Cor 8:6, 17). Yet, Titus notably is absent from those sending greetings to Rome at the end Paul's letter to the Romans written during Paul's winter residence in Corinth (Rom 16:21–23). Similar to Paul sending Titus to Corinth on his behalf, Paul apparently sent Titus from Corinth to Crete on his behalf. Paul later composed the letter of Titus on his way to Jerusalem, sent from one of the ports that would have regular contacts with Crete, such as the famous double-port at Miletus; *Re-examining Paul's Letters*, 68–73. Luke's information on Corinth (Greece) is sparse, having only one cursory verse (Acts 20:3), because Luke was not in Corinth, but rather in Macedonia (Acts 20:4). Thus, Luke does not provide any details about Corinth or, therefore, Titus's movements. The unusual style of both epistles conforms to the Asianic rhetoric of which Paul as a citizen of Tarsus would have been aware and to which he could conform, including the required and expected use of appropriate personal notices; *Re-examining Paul's Letters*, 54–55. For difficulties relating the Pastorals to Acts, see Keener's helpful excursus and table (*Acts*, 3:3023–26). Keener, however, does not include or interact with Reicke on this point.

[26]As examples, Paul's previous favorable appearances in Roman courts in Acts (*The Martyrdom of St. Paul*, pp. 33–36); the Miletus speech as pointing to a later martyrdom, not the Acts custody in Rome (p. 37), Paul's lenient custodial arrangements in Rome (p. 44), Paul's open preaching permitted as the prerogative of a Roman citizen and demonstrating no threat perceivable by Roman authorities (p. 50).

[27]Such as, "Tradition uniformly cites decapitation as the mode of Paul's martyrdom" (*The Martyrdom of St. Paul*, 23). Univocal tradition is no historical guarantee: Every instance here could be based on simple deduction from Acts (Luke's claim of Roman citizenship for Paul > Roman citizens were beheaded > Paul was beheaded). That Paul was beheaded is not *testimonium oculatus*, especially when all so-called "witnesses" are no earlier than late second century. We already have dealt with Tajra's ineffective invocation of Spanish tradition for Paul's supposed mission West.

[28]Tajra, of course, must appeal foremost to the statement in *1 Clement*, since that alone is our singular literary reference closest in time, but still distanced by thirty years. He reveals how dependent he is on this one piece of evidence by escalating the argu-

obviously had a post-Acts mission, Tajra insisted, since Paul himself so implied.[29]

What Tajra did not seem to consider is an alternate historical scenario. We can agree with Tajra that Paul's case probably defaulted by failure of Sanhedrin representatives to appear in Rome to make the case in the legally required timeframe.[30] We also can agree that Paul's enemies in Rome became increasingly aware during Paul's two-year detention that his "doctrine" was subversive to their understanding of a law-observant lifestyle. As Tajra noted, "Paul's stay in Rome had not conciliated the Judeo-Christians, ever under the influence of the synagogal authorities; rather it had augmented the malice aimed at him."[31] What we would disagree with Tajra about is *when* enemies[32] of Paul would have gone into action against Paul after the Sanhedrin case from Jerusalem, upon which they were depending, had defaulted and been dismissed. Tajra assumed they acted *after* further mission activity by Paul post

---

ment beyond credulity. He asserted, "Clement was an eyewitness to the events to which he alludes in his composition" (*The Martyrdom of St. Paul*, 108). This assertion is clearly specious: Clement himself never once even insinuated such. Further, such an assertion actually works against Tajra, because he thereby presents Clement as rhetorically inept. In all Clement's apologetic in his letters, for persuasive purposes alone, Clement should have been appealing constantly to his personal knowledge of Paul. He never does so. He appeals only to Paul's letters.

[29]Tajra asserted, "It is unlikely that Paul ever returned to the Hellenistic East" (*The Martyrdom of St. Paul*, 102). Tajra for substantiation pointed to Paul's "fully preached" comment in Rom 15:19. Once again, intention is not history. He also appealed to the enigmatic "see my face no more" in Acts 20:25 (p. 103), and statements in Acts 13:47 ("uttermost parts of the earth," p. 106) and in Rom 1:5 ("among all the nations," p. 107), and Rom 15:20–21 ("not building on another's foundation," p. 107). In all of this, though, Tajra never acknowledged that his only appeal here is to statements by Paul of *general mission strategy, not* statements by Paul of *specific life biography.*

[30]Tajra, *The Martyrdom of St. Paul*, 31.

[31]Ibid., 65.

[32]We strongly disagree with Tajra's insinuation that law-observant *believers* in the church at Rome ("Judeo-Christians") were the root source, Phil 1:17 notwithstanding. Paul there addressed preaching with ill motive, not seeking to cause his death (Phil 1:18). Even the trajectory suggested by Acts is that law-observant believers in Jerusalem tried to work out a compromise with Paul, not that they slyly conspired to murder him (Acts 21:20–25). All plots against Paul's life in Acts (Damascus, 9:24; Greece, 20:3; Jerusalem, 23:12, 14) always are by Jews or Jewish leadership. Finally, the root source of bringing a *legal* complaint to be heard by Roman authorities to be effective would need to come from synagogue authorities in Rome.

Acts, setting up the so-called second Roman imprisonment of Paul. However, just as easily, one could assume that Paul's enemies in Rome would go into action *immediately*, worried this agitator now freed from the restraints of legal custody would be set loose on Rome to do even greater damage. Why would they wait? Why would they not go into legal action immediately? If Tajra reads the Acts narrative as suggesting Paul was released from custody, he conveniently ignores hints from that same narrative that Jews did not hesitate to go into action against Paul as soon as his preaching of Jesus as Messiah was encountered.[33] Paul himself implies similarly when he chronicles suffering the supreme penalty of "forty lashes minus one" from synagogue authorities no less than five times.[34] Even more importantly, in terms of Paul's preaching Jesus as Messiah, Jewish synagogue authorities in Rome would have a potent legal and political precedent over the Jerusalem Sanhedrin. The recent turmoil over the "Chrestus" preaching in the synagogues of Rome that had provoked the Edict of Claudius[35] only thirteen or fourteen years earlier[36] would present an entirely different complexion to the issue of a complaint raised against Paul in Rome by synagogal leadership in the early 60s. The immediate threat of a freed Paul's increasing presence and preaching in Rome to the peace of Rome against the vivid backdrop of recent Jewish-Roman imperial history would be readily grasped by both synagogue and Roman authorities.

Thus, presuming the Pastoral Epistles *demonstrate* a release and renewed incarceration is a classic begging the question. Setting two Pastoral Epistles within Acts *before* Paul got to Rome, with 2 Timothy situated soon after the end of Acts, actually would be a neater, cleaner historical solution than inventing an entire fictional legend of pseudo-biography perilously tottering on Paul's brief and exclusive reference to *intended* plans for Spain in Romans. Whether Clement's "farthest limit" means

---

[33]Cf. early at Damascus, Acts 9:24; Greece, Acts 20:3; Jerusalem, Acts 23:12, 14.

[34]2 Cor 11:24; cf. Deut 25:2–3. Cf. Levine, *The Ancient Synagogue*, 131–32; Runesson, Binder, and Olsson, *The Ancient Synagogue*, 230–37.

[35]Suetonius *Claud.* 25. "Chrestus" could be mistaking the common Roman name for the Greek term "Christos," i.e., "Christ" ("messiah"). Presumably, then, preaching Jesus as Messiah caused disturbances in Roman synagogues. Tiberius expelled Jews in AD 19 (Josephus *Ant.* 18.3.5; Tacitus *Annals* 2.85; Suetonius *Tib.* 36), but the circumstances were entirely different (social offense to a Roman matron, not synagogue disturbances). Cf. Merrill, "The Expulsion of Jews from Rome under Tiberius."

[36]Supposing AD 49; the date is debated.

"Rome" or "Spain" (or just assumes Romans), the absence of confirming historical artifacts mitigates Clement's weight. Occam's razor.

One safely may conclude that the existence of the Pastoral Epistles as evidence for the legend of the release and second imprisonment of Paul is equivocal. In no way do the Pastorals actually *demand* a release, trans-Rome mission work, and second imprisonment presumption (e.g., Eusebius).[37] Further, internal biographical notations in the Pastorals *actually contradict the core assumption* of the legend that Paul had a mission in the West, the typical interpretation of Clement of Rome. Arguing both simultaneously (Pastorals/Clement) is simply illogical.

The Historical Setting of Philippians

One might be surprised to hear that Paul was not martyred in Rome but in Philippi. This provocative thesis has been proposed by Koester and Callahan in their two essays within a volume on archeological work at Philippi.[38] The controversial proposal attempts to interpret the significance of an unusual octagonal structure revealed in archeological work at Philippi. The complex argument, however, depends upon a combination of several debatable theories. The problems include the tendentious use of Acts, a conjectured Ephesian imprisonment, and dubious source-critical theories of the letter of Philippians. In the end, the argument is unpersuasive.[39] In any case, both proposed contexts for martyrdom,

---

[37]Certainly a moot point if the Pastorals are non-Pauline, as assumed, for example, by Tajra, who quickly displaces the historical weight of the Pastorals in this way. We are not arguing for or against Pauline authorship of the Pastorals. We simply would like to demonstrate for consideration of those who argue Pauline authorship that they are not compelled simultaneously and inevitably to assume fictitious church legend as history in order to background their exegesis of these epistles.

[38]Bakirtzis and Koester, eds., *Philippi at the Time of Paul and after His Death.*

[39]The first two of the book's four essays by Koukouli-Chrysantaki and Bakirtzis give an update on archeology at Philippi that is informative and helpful. The last two essays by Koester and Callahan are not so helpful. They attempt, unsuccessfully, to develop a theory of Paul's supposed martyrdom in Philippi. The unconvincing arguments depend upon Duncan's old 1929 theory of an Ephesian imprisonment of Paul compounded by even more dubious source-critical assertions about the letter of Philippians depending on Michaelis's 1925 theory of multi-fragment forms of the canonical Philippians (that in no instance have textual critical support). Further, tendentious methodological inconsistency is patently evident by using Acts when agreeable to the theory (Acts 16, 20, etc.) but arbitrarily rejecting Acts when not (Acts 21–28).

whether Rome or Philippi, still have at least one common denominator. They both suffer historically as arguments from silence.

PROBLEM OF OTHER SOURCES

The second major problem in discussing Paul's death is one of the date and quality of the other historical sources outside the New Testament. We have next to nothing documenting Paul's actual death or his burial within the New Testament, and our sources outside the New Testament offer precious little more, being either ambiguous, or inconveniently centuries removed in time, or of questionable reliability. We will mention a few of these sources to illustrate these problems. Some traditions cannot even be traced to a source. Such legends represent popular martyr imagination in the first centuries of the church demanding invention of *some* story in order to provide details, even if completely mythical, of the famous apostle's martyr death to succor the faithful during the martyr period of the church.

Tertullian (200)—Martyrdom

As indicated previously, Clement spoke of Paul having given his "testimony" in Rome.[40] Since this testimony was "before rulers," Clement might be alluding to Paul's death in Rome, but the meaning is ambiguous. The Latin church father, Tertullian, however, seems to offer our first literary evidence to mention that Paul, in fact, was regarded to have been martyred. Of both Peter and Paul, Tertullian said, "bequeathed the gospel even sealed with their own blood."[41] One obviously would have to interpret the expression "sealed with their own blood" as a metaphor for martyrdom, but that reading seems likely. If so, Tertullian's remark would be the first *clear* reference in early Christian literature to Paul's martyrdom.[42] Given his second-century date, Tertullian as our first clear

---

[40] *1 Clem.* 5.7.

[41] Tertullian *Adv. Mar.* 4.5.

[42] Our problem is wording. For example, we have references to Paul's "departure" (Irenaeus *Adv. Her.* 3.1.1), or Paul being "well-attested" (Ignatius *Eph.* 12.1–2, μαρτυρέω), but the meaning in each context is not clear cut. For an illustrative compilation of possible early Christian and patristic references to the deaths of Peter and Paul, cf. Eastman, *The Ancient Martyrdom Accounts*, 389–443.

reference illustrates how the literary evidence for Paul's martyrdom hardly penetrates a second-century wall of ambiguity.

Eusebius (265–340)—Rome, Nero, Beheading

The most often quoted tradition on Paul's death comes from the church historian, Eusebius. His record, however, is several centuries removed from the event. As a result, Eusebius is difficult to evaluate in terms of historical accuracy or his own sources.

Eusebius said that Paul was beheaded in Rome by Nero, and that the names of both martyrs Peter and Paul "are preserved in the cemeteries of that place [Rome] even to the present day."[43] Eusebius then enlists the testimony of the presbyter Gaius (ca. AD 200) that these burial trophies (τρόπαια) were in place at the Vatican (Peter) and along the Ostian Way (Paul) at least back to Gaius's time.[44] This data certainly sounds specific, but Eusebius's comments actually might not get us very far down the historical road. Under which emperor Paul died is easy to guess just from following the storyline in Acts. The method of execution also would not be that hard to deduce from information in Acts. Execution by beheading would be congruent with Paul's reputed Roman citizenship.[45] A Roman citizen by law could not be executed by a tortured or lingering death, of which one example would be crucifixion. Instead, a swift death either by a lictor's axe or military sword was administered (*honestiores capite puniantur*). The lictor's axe was not without brutality, since the victim would be tied to a stake and scourged with rods first.[46] Death by military sword would be considered more honorable and involve a praetorian guard executioner overseen by a centurion. If Paul, in fact, were executed as a Roman citizen, then the process likely would be either of these two methods. According to Luke,

---

[43]*H. E.* 2.25.5.

[44]Ibid., 2.25.6–7, in Gaius's published disputation with Proclus, leader of a Phrygian heresy.

[45]Acts 21:39; 22:25–29; 23:27. Note that beheading as a Roman citizen is the deduction easily picked up in the apocryphal martyrdom traditions: "And when Caesar heard that, he commanded all the prisoners to be burned with fire, but Paul to be beheaded after the law of the Romans," *MPaul* 3:7 (Tucker, *Apocryphal Acts*).

[46]Livy 2.5.8.

Paul made direct appeal to Caesar as a Roman citizen.[47] Such appeal would put Paul under imperial house arrest, which means the soldier Luke mentions guarding Paul in Rome infers one from Caesar's own praetorian guard.[48] Assuming Acts information, proposing execution under Nero by beheading would be a reasonable deduction. Traditional burial monuments (*trophoea*) of Peter and Paul in Rome help establish *later traditional* sites of veneration, but the tradition to which Eusebius appeals in Gaius *still is no earlier than late second century.*

Therefore, the information in Eusebius when examined briefly is seen actually not to advance the discussion that much beyond the Acts account.[49] The impression that second-century literary evidence is not that compelling simply is hard to avoid.

Acts of Peter and Paul (180–200)

Beheading, Three Miles, Aquae Salviae

The apocryphal *Acts of Peter and Paul* from the second or third century purports to narrate the shared preaching ministry of Peter and Paul in Rome, the principal story being refutation of the sorcerer Simon. While this apocryphal document suggests Peter was crucified upside down, the location of Paul's death by beheading was said to be three miles out of the city at a place called Aquae Salviae, which was near the third milestone of the Ostian Way, the Roman road to the port city of Ostia.[50] This Aquae Salviae site, known more commonly as the Three Fountains, eventually saw the building of the Abbey of Three Fountains and later the monumental imperial cathedrals and the modern Saint Paul's cathedral of today. This evidence is late second century.[51]

---

[47] Acts 25:11.

[48] Acts 28:16, 20.

[49] Patristic traditions themselves could be based on pure deduction from trajectories already launched in the Acts account. A similar problem is inherent to the *Apocryphal Acts.*

[50] *APeterPaul* 80.2, 8; for Peter's martyrdom, cf. 81.1–3 (Tucker, *Apocryphal Acts*). For a marble relief depicting Peter's crucifixion, see Fig. 15.99 (p. 576).

[51] About the burial details in this apocryphal document, Edmundson claimed, "This tradition has not been seriously disputed" (*The Church in Rome in the First Century*, 262). This claim is quite hard to comprehend, however, being at once transparently plea bargaining. One cannot dispute a matter only one document documents, since no other

Superstitious local legend associated with the Aquae Salviae location added that, when cut off, Paul's severed head bounced three times, and three fountains spontaneously sprang up at those spots.[52] The Abbey of Three Fountains was built at that traditional execution location for the veneration of Paul.

Outside the City, Notoriety

Roman officials often executed notable Roman prisoners some distance outside the city of Rome to prevent public disturbance.[53] The famous case of Calpernius Galerianus, the central figure in the Pisonian plot against Nero in AD 65, is typical. Tacitus explained about the conspirator, "Lest his execution in the capital should excite too much notice, they conducted him to the fortieth milestone from Rome on the Appian Road, and there put him to death by opening his veins."[54] Thus, a notable prisoner could be executed "outside the city" (*extra ciuitatem duxerunt*) for security reasons.

The *Acts of Peter and Paul* preserves the tradition that Paul's execution took place "outside the city."[55] Martyrdom accounts of other individuals follow this lead as well.[56] These documents, however, are no earlier than late second century, some as late at fifth to sixth century,

---

evidence for confirmation or disconfirmation exists. Further, ignored completely by Edmundson is that the evidence has little weight in the first place due to its late date.

[52]The source of this local legend is undocumented. Curious how this story completely ignores that the existence of these natural springs was known long before the arrival of the apostles to Rome—demonstrating, once again, that if you simply repeat something enough times, fact inevitably emerges.

[53]Livy 4.49; Tacitus *Annals* 14.42, 45; *Histories* 1.59.

[54]Tacitus *Histories* 4.11.

[55]*APeterPaul* 80.2 (Tucker, *Apocryphal Acts*): "about three miles away from the city" (ἀπὸ τῆς πόλεως ἄχρι μιλίον τριῶν, *apo tēs poleiōs achri milion triōn*).

[56]Cf. *AThomas* 164.1 (Tucker, *Apocryphal Acts*): "for he was afraid because of the crowd standing around, for many had believed on him, even some officials; and rising up, he took Judas outside of the city; and a few soldiers with weapons followed along with him." This "outside the city" tradition had become commonplace by the fifth- to sixth-century martyrologies. Cf. "leading to the outside of the city" (*ut illum extra urbem ducentes*) in Pseudo-Linus, *Martyrdom of the Blessed Apostle Paul* 7 (Eastman, *The Ancient Martyrdom Accounts*, 153); note Pseudo-Abdias, *Passion of Saint Paul* 8: "the soldiers came and led him bound outside and out of the city" (Eastman, *Ancient Martyrdom Accounts*, 185); Pseudo-Abdias likely traces to sixth-century Gaul (cf. p. 172).

so, problematic historically. What might be the apologetic point? Perhaps the "outside the city" tradition arose to infer Paul's ministry in Rome had become so famous as to merit execution as a Roman citizen in this manner.

Whether Paul actually would fall into this category of being notable, whose execution therefore would arouse a possible disturbance, is debatable. One might assume such a process could have taken place in Paul's case. However, to make this case for Paul being executed outside Rome because he was famous and, hence, dangerous publicly often involves tendentiously overstating the success of Paul's preaching in Rome, which is about the only way to make Paul famous in Rome.[57] Indeed, exaggerating Paul's popularity in Rome is precisely the tendency in the apocryphal Acts material: "And he became well-known, and many souls were added to the Lord, so that there was a rumor throughout all Rome, and a great multitude came to him from the household of Caesar, believing, and there was great joy."[58] The "popular preacher Paul" supposition of these apocryphal traditions (or today) requires tendentiously exaggerating the significance of certain comments in Acts or in the Prison Epistles related to Paul's preaching in Rome.[59] Paul's preaching in Rome had some success, no doubt. This result clearly is the impression Luke intends to leave the reader in Acts 28:30–31. But painting a picture of all of Rome as swamped with gospel goodness because of Paul's bold preaching overstates the case in the effort to build a case supporting the

[57]Paul has no political, military, or aristocratic connections to invoke—the typical signatures of notoriety in Rome. Note how in later martyrologies we have complaints like that of the prefect Tertullus to Caesar, "Paul had made all of Rome into Christians," *History of the Holy Apostle My Lord Paul* 10 (Eastman, *The Ancient Martyrdom Accounts*, 195).

[58]*MPaul* 1.3 (Tucker, *Apocryphal Acts*). Note the "great crowds" that respond to Paul in repentance and lamentation in Pseudo-Linus *Martyrdom of the Blessed Apostle Paul* 12 (Eastman, *The Ancient Martyrdom Accounts*, 161). Another common thread is that the soldiers leading Paul to his execution are converted, but how many, their names, and the exact circumstances are all quite confused and contradictory; see the summary in Eastman, *The Ancient Martyrdom Accounts*, 307, n. 160.

[59]Examples of such exaggerations would include presuming to know the exact circumstances of Paul's house arrest (Acts 28:16–20), or interpreting a more extensive meaning than Paul intends for "whole praetorium" in terms of awareness of the gospel (Phil 1:13), or refusing to acknowledge that as few as two or three individuals fully could satisfy the plural pronoun of "those of Caesar's household" sending greetings (Phil 4:22).

church tradition that Paul was executed outside the walls of Rome. Such a picture is fanciful imagination and patently ignores entirely that Paul goes unmentioned in any Roman source of his time.[60] Paul could have been executed "outside the city" as a notorious prisoner, but exaggerated interpretations of his fame to support this idea speculatively based on overstressing a few Lukan and Pauline texts in no way moves the historical argument from possible to probable.

PROBLEM OF BURIAL TRADITIONS

The third major problem in discussing Paul's death is that confusion reigns in the burial traditions related to both Peter and Paul. Three memorial shrines to Peter and Paul in Rome suggest two different burial places for each of these apostles that emerged in the late second- and third-century traditions of the church. One shrine is a mid-third century double memorial suggesting both apostles initially were buried along the Via Appia. The second shrine is to Peter on Vatican hill. The third shrine is to Paul on the Via Ostia. If the Via Appia double shrine indicated the initial interment, the other two shrines consequentially would be transfer shrines. In the favor of all three locations, no tradition asserts that any one of the other two is flat out wrong. However, saddled with the obvious problem of multiple shrines, burial traditions always are under burden to provide an explanatory narrative, sometimes as dramatic as an earthquake omen, that supports any transfer scenario proposed to accommodate the existence of multiple shrines.[61]

---

[60]Josephus, who lived three decades in Rome after the Jewish war, would be one. However, this point could be mitigated by Asiedu's argument in *Josephus, Paul, and the Fate of Early Christianity* that Josephus *intentionally* wrote Paul out of his post-war version of Jewish history. The evidence, however, is more inferred than explicit, so debatable.

[61]As in the apocryphal *MPeterPaul* 59:2; 63.2–66.4; and in *APeterPaul* 87.1–3 (Tucker, *Apocryphal Acts*). In the various sources, the common denominator is two principal burial locations involving an initial burial and a transfer burial (whether temporary or permanent). The locations consistently are just three: (1) three miles down the Via Appia (Peter and Paul together), or (2) three miles down the Via Ostia (Paul), or (3) the Vatican hill (Peter). The issue is whether the Via Appia site is initial burial or temporary transfer burial. Chadwick attempted to argue, without success, that the Via Appia as the initial burial site needed more consideration; "St. Peter and St. Paul in Rome," 31–52. Most hold the Via Appia as a temporary transfer burial tradition.

Via Appia

Memoria Apostolorum ad Catacumbas (mid-3rd cent.)

The Memoria Apostolorum ad Catacumbas is a double shrine memorial to both Peter and Paul at the third milestone on the Via Appia that was discovered in 1915 beneath the Saint Sebastian church.[62] The likely date of this shrine is the mid-third century. Chadwick argued local graffiti at the church, as well as the famous metrical inscription of Pope Damasus, support a strong belief in popular piety that this site was the original burial site of both apostles; after all, Chadwick wryly noted, "No body, no cult."[63] However, Chadwick failed to weigh properly that this "Ad Catacumbas" tradition is later than other burial traditions.

Passion and Acts of the Holy Apostles Peter and Paul (5th–6th cent.)

In this account, likely dated fifth to sixth century, people from the East conspire to dig up the bodies of Peter and Paul to take them back East. An earthquake rouses the people of Rome, who discover the plot of those from the East, and the Romans intercept those attempting to carry off the bodies of the apostles about three miles outside the city on the Via Appia. After repossessing the apostolic remains, Romans then temporarily place the bodies in the catacombs along the Via Appia until the remains can be moved back to their original locations.[64]

Via Ostia

Presbyter Gaius (AD 200)

Already mentioned is the earliest attestation to memorial trophies of both Peter and Paul from the presbyter Gaius, according to Eusebius,

---

[62]Tolotti, *Memorie degli Apostoli in Catacumbas.*

[63]Chadwick, "St. Peter and St. Paul in Rome," 33–34; for the quote, 44.

[64]*Passion and Acts of the Holy Apostles* 87 (Eastman, *The Ancient Martyrdom Accounts*, 313). As noted, Chadwick tried to argue the *Via Appia* was the *original* burial place. However, the preponderance of martyrdom traditions, as here, regularly tend the other way, that is, framing the Via Appia location as part of a secondary and temporary burial.

about the end of the second century or beginning of the third century. Gaius said the memorial to the burial site of Paul was on the Via Ostia. Eusebius added that these memorials still were standing a century later in his day.[65] The statement by Gaius, however, fails to provide a crucial piece of information. Gaius fails to indicate exactly how long the Petrine and Pauline memorials in Rome of which he is aware actually had been standing by his time. Thus, with our martyr and burial traditions we keep encountering that almost impenetrable second-century wall.

Catacomb Portrait of Paul (4th cent.)

Catacomb burials by Christians were facilitated by the soft tufa rock under the city of Rome that allowed easily carving rectangular niches in the walls to hold bones of the deceased. Catacomb walls often were decorated with Christian art and graffiti. Potentially the oldest known portrait of Paul dating to the fourth century was discovered in 2009 during Vatican restoration procedures in the Catacomb of St. Thecla on the Ostian Way near the Basilica of St. Paul Outside the Walls.[66] Laser technology helped remove layers of clay and limestone from the fresco to reveal its bright colors. The circular portrait shows a man with a thin face, black, pointed, beard, and a high and furrowed forehead—traditional elements for imaging the apostle Paul (see Fig. 15.98, p. 575). Paul's face is set against a dramatic red background and encircled with a bright yellow ring. This portrait documents that veneration of the apostles, including Paul, began earlier than previously thought. That this discovery was made in a catacomb in the vicinity of the Basilica of Saint Paul Outside the Walls seems a fitting touch for the on-going traditions surrounding the death and burial of Paul.

Matrona Lucina (6th cent.)

Another Via Ostia burial tradition is at a spot supposedly donated by Matrona Lucina, a purported believer and Roman noblewoman, about a mile or two further down from the traditional Abbey of Three Fountains execution spot along the Ostian Way. The burial supposedly was in Lucina's own family property within an existing Roman necropolis. This Lucina tradition is very late, however, with first documentation

---

[65]*H. E.* 2.25.5–7.
[66]Pullelia, "Roman archeologists find oldest image of Apostles in a catacomb."

not until the sixth century.[67] In this source, Lucina is said to have helped the pope move the bodies of both Peter and Paul from the catacombs to her family crypt. Another Lucina tradition, apparently confused, has the opposite story, that is, that Paul's remains were dug up *from* this original Lucina family tomb and moved to be hidden for safe-keeping to the Catacombs of San Sebastian during Vespasian's reign and later returned to the original Lucina tomb. This particular transfer tradition makes no sense, both in its association of Lucina with the first century and of associating emperor Vespasian as having any connection to Paul. A cottage industry of legends grew up around a Lucina matron active in the burial of martyr saints dating all the way from the first through the third centuries—pious but fanciful imagination during the Christian martyr period. The total sources about Lucina may number as many as eleven, but most seem quite confused, even contradictory, about this matron and her setting, so whether such a Lucina even existed cannot be established.[68] In any case, these Lucina traditions at least illustrate that the Abby of Three Fountains near the supposed site of Paul's execution on the Ostian Way continued to be venerated as Paul's traditional burial site, offering a place of especial comfort and encouragement during the later imperial persecutions and even into later centuries.

Saint Paul Outside the Walls

Imperial Basilica (4th–19th cent.). Imperial persecution finally came to an end with Constantine. Paul's traditional burial location then began to be adorned with famous cathedrals. Constantine built the monumental

---

[67] *Liber Pontificalis* 22 within its biography of Pope Cornelius (251–253); the *Liber Pontificalis* is a document providing details for each of the popes of Rome in sequence, published by Louis Duchesne as *Liber Pontificalis I*, (Paris, 1886); see p. 150. For easier access to the Latin text of the pertinent Cornelius material in the *Liber Pontificalis*, see *Chadwick: Selected Writings*, 135, n. 31. Compare the similar statement in Pseudo-Abdias, *Passion of Saint Paul* 8: "Lucina, a servant of Christ, packed his body with spices and buried it at the second milestone from the city on the Ostian Road on her own estate" (Eastman, *Ancient Martyrdom Accounts*, 185).

[68] For Lucina as a conventional figure spanning centuries, see *Chadwick: Selected Writings*, 136. For political analysis of late martyr traditions, and those of the patroness Lucina, see Cooper, "The martyr, the matrona and the bishop." For any appearance of a Lucina figure in these martyrdom accounts as a signature of hagiography, cf. Eastman, *Paul the Martyr*, 107–110.

Basilica of Saint Paul Outside the Walls (San Paolo Fuori Le Mura) in AD 320 close to the Abbey of Three Fountains to venerate the apostle at the traditional site of both execution and burial (i.e., along the Via Ostia). This cathedral was consecrated by Pope Sylvester in AD 324.[69] Theodosius enlarged Constantine's original basilica in AD 390. At this time, the supposed remains of Paul were placed in a sarcophagus that was integral to the foundation wall inside the Theodosian basilica. Unfortunately, an earthquake soon after in AD 433 collapsed parts of Theodosius's basilica, and the renovations required raising up the floor level to the top of the immovable sarcophagus, which then was marked from above with a marble tombstone slab over the top of the sarcophagus location. The repaired Theodosian basilica stood for centuries as a site for the veneration of Paul's burial until catastrophically destroyed by fire on the night of July 15, 1823.

Modern Basilica (19th–21st cent.). A new basilica soon was built on top of the ancient imperial basilica ruins with generous donations from around the world in the decades that followed the tragic fire. The plan followed the imperial building closely, and was consecrated in 1840 by Pope Gregory XVI. The main altar of the new structure was oriented immediately over the known location of the ancient crypt. The modern basilica, however, no longer allowed pilgrims access to view or touch any of the ancient artifacts related to the veneration of Paul.

Vatican Excavations (2002–2006). During the Jubilee 2000 millennial celebration of Saint Paul by the Roman Catholic Church, Christian pilgrims to Rome reportedly were disappointed by the lack of access to Pauline artifacts at the basilica. This disappointment among the faithful is said to have motivated the Vatican to conduct excavations under the basilica's main altar from 2002–2006 to expose the crypt and related area.[70] The excavations raised great excitement when a marble slab was uncovered with the Latin inscription "Paulo Apostolo Mart" ("Apostle Paul, Martyr"). This marble slab likely is the one associated with the renovations of Theodosius from the fourth century. Carbon 14 dating by experts of bone fragments taken from inside the sarcophagus

---

[69]The cathedral was placed a little over a mile outside the Aurelian wall of Rome. The following information in the paragraph is from the Vatican description accessed at http://www.vatican.va/ various/basiliche/sanpaolo/en/basilica/storia.htm.

[70]Valsecchi, "St. Paul's Tomb Unearthed in Rome."

under the marble slab date to the first or second century AD. No way exists to determine whether these bone fragments actually belong to Paul, of course, but the carbon 14 dating definitively affirms that the veneration associated with this crypt and sarcophagus indeed is ancient, even possibly back to the first century. The scientifically executed carbon 14 dating of artifacts within the sarcophagus would be the first time documented veneration associated with the apostle Paul has broken through the second-century historical barrier hobbling all literary traditions. The dating results leave open the possibility that the remains inside the sarcophagus could be those of the apostle.

Archeological Park (2007–2013). After the Vatican excavations under the altar, further archeological work next to the basilica has revealed the vibrant history of the site as an ancient center of Christian veneration. Funds were raised for an archeological park in this area for the benefit of tourists and the faithful, which was constructed from 2007–2013.[71] The archeological park displays development and expansion of the veneration site into its own bustling city, especially from the fifth to eighth centuries, but then eventually going into decline after the tenth century.

PROPOSED SOLUTION

That Paul did not survive the tumultuous decade of the 60s seems evident from the lack of any epistolary activity past the 60s ascribed to him.[72] What weight should we assign to church tradition of martyrdom in Rome? Probably significant weight. Early and later church traditions are unanimous, and nothing in canonical literature would lead us to think otherwise.

When Is the Question

While we would not argue *where* Paul was martyred, we would argue *when*. Most certainly, the church legend of an assumed release post Acts, western mission, second Roman imprisonment, and death under Nero's tribunal the second time is simply that—assumed and speculated. A

---

[71]Glatz, "Shining a light on St. Paul: Archeological site renovated."
[72]That is, beyond the Prison Epistles and the Pastorals (speculated as after Acts).

presumptive superstructure of a church myth has been raised on the meager foundation of one statement of intention noted by Paul enhanced with known fault lines in the Rome-Paul relationship to be inferred from Acts and insinuated in the Prison and Pastoral Epistles. Further, literary martyr traditions add little beyond the implications to be gathered from the New Testament itself, dead-ending in a second-century historical wall nearly impossible to penetrate. Tellingly, we have no corroborating archeological or inscriptional evidence and near silent church-founding tradition to establish the point. Thus, we are left always begging the literature that itself begs the question.

Acts Is the Answer

Instead, a historically simpler and more viable solution than speculating further missionary activity after Acts is speculating that the end of Acts is the end of Paul. We need to be clear that Luke had no narrative need to conclude Paul's appeal to Caesar, especially since Luke drops any mention of the appeal like a lead balloon immediately after Paul arrives on Italian soil at the port of Puteoli. The story Luke was plotting out—insinuated in Acts 1 (a mission) and getting into gear in Acts 6 (a movement)—never was about a tribunal appearance before Caesar in the first place. When Luke has Paul in Rome, he has him right where he wants him, because the original Hellenist movement so key to Luke's plot and preeminently represented in the character of Saul-Paul now clearly is seen as destined to become the future of the church and the consummation of the story of Jesus that opens the first volume and the story of the church that fills the second volume. Acts 1:8 has Rome in mind, because Rome has the world in mind.

Thus, Luke has no concern whatsoever to avoid speaking of the death of Paul, as if Paul's death would destroy his point. Not at all, and, in fact, the opposite. Careful attention to Luke's actual narrative would indicate quickly that Paul's martyr death only would invoke the same message as the martyr death of Stephen—that nothing hinders the unrelenting advance of the gospel, not even the death of a famous leader preaching a powerful message. Indeed, "unhindered" is Luke's very last word of his very last verse.[73]

A Plausible End

So what happened to Paul after Acts 28? We speculate that Paul *did* have a second tribunal before Nero, but *sooner* rather than later. Immediately on the heels of the defaulted Sanhedrin case, as allowed by the imperial docket, Jewish synagogue authorities in Rome instigated another procedure before Nero. Synagogue authorities likely had been formulating their plans for some time. They had watched with increasing concern the unexpected effectiveness of Paul's preaching in Rome even in chains, not only among gentiles, but particularly among their own synagogue proselytes, as well as gentiles of Rome already attracted to the synagogue. Paul over the two-year period that ends Acts had become sufficiently known to traditional synagogue life and teaching in Rome as to become too dangerous to ignore. Against this backdrop of the effective Pauline mission in Rome, these synagogue leaders also had watched with increasing alarm how the Sanhedrin in Jerusalem over a two-year period was making clear as the months went by that Jerusalem had no genuine intention of pursuing their case in Rome, that is, that the Sanhedrin already had decided to default on their own case by a no show in Rome.[74] Local synagogue authorities, therefore, had calculated that were Paul to be released, they probably had a brushfire on their hands too hard to extinguish before engulfing too many Roman synagogues in contentious debate hazardous to the peace of Rome and evoking memory of the recent Edict of Claudius. They decided, therefore, in the event the troublemaker Paul were set loose on Rome, they would need immediately to initiate their own legal action against him to neutralize the perceived danger before their fears materialized so rapidly as to frustrate decisive and effective response. They, however,

---

[73] Acts 28:31, the adverb ἀκωλύτως, *akōlytōs*, "unhindered." Cf. Frank Stagg, *The Book of Acts: The Early Struggle for an Unhindered Gospel.*

[74] Real chance of controlling the outcome was in a Jewish court in Judea, not a gentile court in Rome. That Roman synagogues as independent entities had no central authority (cf. Jeffers, *Conflict at Rome*, 40) should not be considered any impediment to their leaders mutually responding in concert to a perceived threat (cf. Acts 28:17–24).

would prosecute with much more vigor, earnestness, and effectiveness than had the Sanhedrin.

Luke's own narrative suggests the plausibility of such a negative, rapid, and strong synagogue response to this liberated Paul.[75] The legal strategy already was set in the trial of Jesus. Jesus too was slandered as a troublemaker to the Jewish nation and a threat to imperial policies.[76] The antagonism echoes forward in the arrest of Peter and John in the temple, the arrest of the apostles by the Sanhedrin, the martyrdom of Stephen, Agrippa I murdering James of Zebedee and then intending the same for Peter, and forward into the mission work of Paul.[77] Paul's end in Rome, then, ironically would reflect his beginning in Jerusalem. He died victim to the same Jewish antagonism to the Christian movement he himself had expressed.[78] What was intended by Jerusalem authorities for Paul, we could note, was similar to the High Priest Ananus, who had James, the brother of Jesus and leader of the Jerusalem church, killed in AD 62 during the brief interregnum after the death of Festus before the new procurator, Albinus, arrived to take control over Judea.[79]

Thus, shortly after Acts, a second tribunal against Paul was initiated quickly and prosecuted vigorously by Roman synagogue authorities. As legal strategy, they likely worked into their case with potent effectiveness a reminder of the recent imperial action in the Edict of Claudius spurred by disruptive, alien preaching in Roman synagogues only a few years before. The new synagogue case against Paul, therefore,

---

[75]Negative and quick synagogue and Jewish reaction to Paul's preaching is constant, consistent, and ubiquitous throughout Paul's story in Acts. Cf. Damascus (Acts 9:23–25); early Jerusalem (Acts 9:29); Antioch of Pisidia (Acts 13:40–46); Thessalonica (Acts 15:5); Berea (Acts 17:13); Corinth (Acts 18:6); Ephesus (Acts 19:9); Corinth again (Acts 20:3); Jerusalem again (Acts 21:27–31); Rome (Acts 28:24). On Paul's own admission of receiving severe synagogue discipline in 2 Cor 11:24, see note 34. Also, note the bad press for the Jesus sect among Roman synagogues admitted to Paul: "on the other hand concerning this sect it is known to us that everywhere it is spoken against" (Acts 28:22). As Fine noted, "with all the varied responses to Christianity in Rabbinic literature, not a single text reflects any positive attitude toward this religion or its founders" ("Non-Jews in the Synagogues of Late-Antique Palestine," 233).

[76]The verb is "misleading" or "perverting" (διαστρέφω, *diastrephō*), Luke 23:2.

[77]Acts 4:1; 5:17; 7:52; 12:2–4. For Paul, cf. note 75.

[78]Acts 8:1–3; 22:3, 19 ("I imprisoned and beat those who believed"); 26:9–11 ("cast my vote against them when they were being condemned to death"). Cf. Rom 10:2.

[79]Josephus *Ant.* 20.9; Eusebius *H. E.* 2.23.

unlike the Sanhedrin's, had an inherent Roman logic, so was successful.[80] Paul was convicted and executed by Nero about AD 62–64, but
before the fire of Rome. So, how did the church obscure or confuse its
memory of the events surrounding Paul's death?

The reason for confusion is the fire of Rome. The fire had a devastating impact on Rome's Christian community coming shortly thereafter, perhaps a year or less. In this scenario, the fire of Rome was not
the reason for Paul's death. The devastating destruction of Rome, which
engulfed practically the whole city,[81] was the reason for the quick loss of
the details of Paul's actual story, a voice choked off within the atmosphere
of Rome's ruinous smoke and rubble. Rome's catastrophic conflagration came so quickly on the heels of Paul's execution as to overwhelm
and absorb the actual story of Paul's death into the story of Rome's fire.
In short order, among the traumatized, victimized Roman believers, the
story soon was told by those who were not there that Paul died as a
martyr, not at the hands of synagogue officials but at the whims of a
notoriously infamous emperor after the fire. This version of events had
the great story-telling advantage and high satisfaction quotient of con-
forming the famous apostle's fate to the fate of so many of the believers
in Rome. Now, that is the beginning of a legend that could succor the
future faithful in their grievous hour of martyr trial. Tacitus makes clear
that "multitudes" of Christians were killed after the fire of Rome, and
this action most certainly would have targeted Christian leadership in
particular.[82] Paul's actual end occurring in such close proximity to this
devastation to the Christian community in Rome is what obscured so
quickly the exact circumstances of Paul's death in oral memory among

[80]Rajak noted how ancient synagogues operate "precisely as miniature versions of the
city of which they are a part" in terms of underlying social assumptions and symbols,
so that even their structure reflects "what goes on in the city" ("The Synagogue Within
the Greco-Roman City," 164–65); further, a strict monotheistic faith was no impediment
to a "capacity for integration" (165). Thus, suggesting close social and political ties between synagogue leadership and imperial politics in Rome as above is reasonable.

[81]Tacitus said only four of Rome's fourteen districts escaped destruction or damage
(*Annals* 15.38–41). Three districts were leveled completely, and seven others had left
only smoldering relics here or there. Many inhabitants of Rome also were killed.

[82]*Annals* 15.44. Roman historians often exaggerated numbers for effect, but the point
does not depend on actual figures. "Multitudes" by any count Tacitus meant to be read to
indicate a significant component of the total population of Christians in Rome.

Roman believers in particular. Thus, the general chaos and confusion in the Christian community after the fire of Rome, the consequent loss of Christian leaders, and the weakened ability of the church as a result to preserve stable, reliable Christian tradition in Rome in the aftermath, all combined together in a perfect historical storm to sink the ship of facts about Paul's demise.

CONCLUSION

In this scenario, a pre-fire execution instigated by synagogue leadership immediately after the defaulted Sanhedrin case whose details were lost in the proximate fire of Rome with its devastating persecution of the Christian community seems to be a much more likely historical reason why we hardly have a clue of Paul's death and burial today, and probably never will. This explanation is simpler than the plea bargaining and begging the question maneuvers that are even more speculative with even less evidence. Such myth-making efforts to narrate Paul's story after Acts inexplicably ignore the questions why, if Paul traveled and worked rather extensively and for some time after a first Roman imprisonment:

- the church literally has no direct memory of his movements and activities whatsoever

- no known or unknown Pauline associate ever thought to share any knowledge of this post-first Roman imprisonment activity

- no church anywhere claimed any clear, early, church-founding tradition of any kind directly reflective of this so-called post-Roman imprisonment mission East or West

- no Paulinist close in time ever saw fit to pass on any details of this mythically exonerated and triumphant Paul for apologetic purposes

- no church offered any cherished and authoritative letters from Paul from this period for general edification of all believers or to validate claims to their own apostolic origins

- the church, ever protective of authoritative tradition, had no effective response to Spanish mission myths rampant in later martyrologies when the lack of historical artifacts clearly said no

Church memory of Paul's death in Rome at the tribunal of Nero likely is on the mark. Significant travel and mission activity post Nero's tribunal, however, clearly is legend. Even Eusebius had nothing more than the Pastorals for that. No one has any substantiated, known biography. Eusebius was plea bargaining his case, as do all who appeal to the Pastorals to invent a supposed post-Acts story of Paul, but only by ignoring the elephant in Rome: not a historical whisper. So the end of Acts is the end of Paul.

Under the current proposal, perhaps Paul's ominous words to the Ephesian elders in Acts 20:25 should be read with historical weight. While narrative trajectories do suggest Paul was released after the tribunal anticipated in Acts 28, other trajectories in Acts at the same time also suggest the story still ended tragically and quickly. The Sanhedrin's death plot, then, simply was forestalled. The synagogue's prosecution in Rome finished the job. If this scenario is plausible, one implication probably would be that Luke, in fact, *did* intend Acts 20:25 to be read at face value.

In conclusion, Paul might be buried "outside the walls," but we always hit a wall literarily trying to get there.[83] No matter how hard we try, without some type of conjecture, we simply cannot conjure Paul's death and burial. Sadly, all this discussion leaves an inevitable sense that the silence of Luke on the matter forever seems to have sealed the fate of ever answering definitively the question of the actual circumstances surrounding the end of Paul's life, but most especially that of his death and burial, even if we have his bones. In the end, all we probably ever will have are intimations of mortality.[84]

---

[83] As Chadwick mused, "the Christians of Rome during the second and early third centuries had no reason to be much more certain about the true sites of the apostolic graves than we are today" ("St. Peter and St. Paul in Rome," 51).

[84] Cf. the title of the famous poem, "Ode: Intimations of Immortality from Recollections of Early Childhood," by William Wordsworth. On this poem as perhaps Wordsworth's best, cf. Sisman, *The Friendship: Wordsworth and Coleridge*, 342.

Appendix

Video Resources

These links to online videos illustrate the story of Acts and a study of its text. On-location visits by the author following the travels of Paul include images, maps, and museum resources that make the historical, social, and political world of Acts come alive. For video catalog content description, cf. https://drkoine.com/paul/ActsVideoCatalog.pdf.

PAUL'S MISSIONARY JOURNEYS

Home: https://drkoine.com/paul/index.html
Site navigation: https://drkoine.com/paul/journeys/index.html

First Missionary Journey

Cyprus

https://drkoine.com/paul/journeys/1mj/cyprus/index.html

South Galatia

https://drkoine.com/paul/journeys/1mj/south-galatia/index.html

Second Missionary Journey

Asia

https://drkoine.com/paul/journeys/2mj/asia/index.html

Europe

https://drkoine.com/paul/journeys/2mj/europe/index.html

Third Missionary Journey

Ephesus

https://drkoine.com/paul/journeys/3mj/ephesus/index.html

Macedonia

https://drkoine.com/paul/journeys/3mj/macedonia/index.html

Greece

https://drkoine.com/paul/journeys/3mj/greece/index.html

Asia

https://drkoine.com/paul/journeys/3mj/asia/index.html

Jerusalem

https://drkoine.com/paul/journeys/3mj/jerusalem/index.html

PAUL'S JOURNEY TO ROME

Site navigation: https://drkoine.com/paul/rome/index.html

Caesarea

https://drkoine.com/paul/rome/caesarea/index.html

Crete

https://drkoine.com/paul/rome/crete/index.html

Malta

https://drkoine.com/paul/rome/malta/index.html

Sicily

https://drkoine.com/paul/rome/sicily/index.html

Italy

https://drkoine.com/paul/rome/italy/index.html

Bibliography

Abbott, Frank Frost. *The Common People of Ancient Rome: Studies in Roman Life and Literature.* New York: Biblo and Tannen, 1965.

Accordance, Version 11.1. OakTree Software Specialists, Altamonte Springs, Fla., 2013.

Achtemeier, Paul J. *1 Peter: A Commentary on 1 Peter,* Hermeneia—A Critical and Historical Commentary on the Bible. Ed. Eldon J. Epp. Minneapolis: Fortress, 1996.

A. D.: The Bible Continues, Prod. Roma Downey, Mark Burnett, and Richard Bedser. Dir. Ciaran Donnelly. Tel. mini-series. United Artists Media Group, 2015.

Aland, Barbara, Kurt Aland, Johannes Karavidopoulos, Carlo M. Martini, and Bruce M. Metzger, eds. *The Greek New Testament.* 5th Rev. ed. Stuttgart: United Bible Societies, 2014.

Aland, Barbara, Kurt Aland, Johannes Karavidopoulos, Carlo M. Martini, and Bruce M. Metzger, eds. *Novum Testamentum Graece.* 28th ed. Stuttgart: German Bible Society, 2012.

Aland, Kurt and Barbara Aland. *The Text of the New Testament.* 2nd ed. Translated by Erroll F. Rhodes. Grand Rapids: Eerdmans, 1989.

Aland, Kurt, ed. *Kurzgefasste Liste der griechischen Handschriften des neuen Testaments.* 2nd ed. Arbeiten zur neutestamentlichen Textforschung 1. Berlin: Walter de Gruyter, 1994.

Anderson, Hans Christian. "The Emperor's New Clothes." *Fairy Tales Told for Children.* Copenhagen: C. A. Reitzel, 1837.

Aratus, *Phaenomena.* John Hopkins New Translations from Antiquity. Aaron Poochigian, trans. Baltimore, Md.: The John Hopkins University Press, 2010.

Ariel, Israel and Chaim Richman. *Carta's Illustrated Encyclopedia of the Holy Temple in Jerusalem.* Trans. Yehoshua Wertheimer. Jerusalem: The Temple Institute and Carta, 2005.

Aristeas. *The Old Testament Pseudepigrapha.* Accordance, Version 10.1.7. 2013. Print ed.: In vol. 1 of *Old Testament Pseudepigrapha,* ed. R. H. Charles. 1913. 3 vols. Oxford: Clarendon.

Aristides, Aelius. *The Complete Works: Orations 1–16.* Leiden, The Netherlands: Brill, 1997.

Aristotle. *Ars Rhetorica.* Ed. W. D. Ross. Oxford: Clarendon, 1959.

_____. *On Rhetoric: A Theory of Civic Discourse.* Trans. George A. Kennedy. Oxford: Oxford University Press, 1991.

Arnold, Clinton E. *Acts.* Zondervan Illustrated Bible Backgrounds Commentary. Grand Rapids: Zondervan, 2007.

Asiedu, F. B. A. *Josephus, Paul, and the Fate of Early Christianity.* Minneapolis: Fortress Academic, 2019.

Athenagoras. *The Ante-Nicene Fathers* on CD-ROM. Logos Research Systems Version 2.0. 1997. Print ed.: Athenagoras. In vol. 2 of *The Ante-Nicene Fathers,* ed. Alexander Roberts, James Donaldson, and A. Cleveland Coxe. 1885–1896. 10 vols. New York: Christian Literature Company.

Augustine. *The Nicene and Post-Nicene Fathers of the Christian Church* on CD-ROM. Accordance Bible Software Version 10.1.5, 2013. Print ed.: Augustine. In vol. 1 of *The Nicene and Post-Nicene Fathers of the Christian Church.* Series 2. 1886–1889, ed. Philip Schaff and Henry Wace. 14 vols. New York: Christian Literature Company.

Augustus. *Res Gestae Divi Augusti: The Achievements of the Divine Augustus,* with an introduction and commentary by P. A. Brunt and J. M. Moore. Oxford, New York: Oxford University Press, 1967.

Aune, David E. "The Influence of Roman Imperial Court Ceremonial on the Apocalypse of John." Biblical Research 28 (1983): 5–26.

———. *Revelation.* WBC, Vols. 52a, 52b, 52c. Dallas: Word, 1997, 1998.

Bakirtzis, Charalambos and Helmut Koester, eds. *Philippi at the Time of Paul and after His Death.* Harrisburg, Penn.: Trinity, 1998.

Baldwin, Matthew C. *Whose Acts of Peter? Text and Historical Context of the Actus Vercellenses.* Tübingen: Mohr Siebeck, 2005.

Barclay, John M. G. "Deviance and Apostasy: Some Applications of Deviance Theory to First-Century Judaism and Christianity." Pages 110–23 in *Modeling Early Christianity: Social-Scientific Studies of the New Testament,* ed. Philip Esler, New York: Routledge, 1995.

———. *Jews In The Mediterranean Diaspora: From Alexander to Trajan (323 BCE–117 CE).* Edinburgh: T&T Clark,1996.

Barrett, C. K. *A Critical and Exegetical Commentary on The Acts of the Apostles,* The International Critical Commentary on the Holy Scriptures of the Old and New Testaments. Gen. eds. J. A. Emerton, C. E. B. Cranfield, and G. N. Stanton, 2 vols. Edinburgh: T&T Clark, 1994, 1998.

Bartchy, S. Scott. "Slavery (Greco-Roman)." *The Anchor Bible Dictionary,* ed. David Noel Freedman. 6 vols. New York: Doubleday & Co., 1992. 6:66–67.

Beard, Mary. *The Parthenon.* Cambridge: Harvard University Press, 2002.

Beard, Mary, et al. *Religions of Rome.* Vol. 1: *A History.* Cambridge: Cambridge University Press, 1998.

Best, Ernest.*1 Peter,* New Century Bible. Ed. Ernest Best. London: Oliphants; Marshall, Morgan, and Scott, Ltd., 1971.

Bieber, Margarete. *The History of the Greek and Roman Theater.* Princeton: Princeton University Press, 1961.

Bingham, Sandra. *The Praetorian Guard: A History of Rome's Elite Special Forces.* Waco, Tex.: Baylor University Press, 2013.

Bock, Darrell L. *Acts.* Baker Exegetical Commentary on the New Testament. Robert W. Yarbrough and Robert H. Stein, gen. eds. Grand Rapids: Baker Academic, 2007.

———. *A Theology of Luke and Acts: God's Promised Program, Realized for All Nations.* Biblical Theology of the New Testament. Andreas J. Köstenberger, gen. ed. Grand Rapids: Zondervan, 2012.

Bonnet, Maximilian, ed. *Acta Apostolorum Apocrypha*, 3 Vols. Leipzig: 1891–1903. Electronic text by James M. Tucker, *Apocryphal Acts* (English) in *Accordance*. Altamonte Springs, Fla.: OakTree Software, 2011.

Boyle, Anthony James. *An Introduction to Roman Tragedy*. New York: Routledge, 2006.

Bowers, W. P. "Jewish Communities in Spain in the Time of Paul the Apostle." *Journal of Theological Studies*. N. S. 26(2)(1975): 395–402.

Braginton, Mary V. "Exile under the Roman Emperors." CJ. Vol. 39, No. 7 (Apr., 1944), 391–407.

Brouskari, Maria. *The Monuments of the Acropolis*. 3rd ed. Athens: Ministry of Culture, Archaeological Receipts Fund, 2006.

Bruce, F. F. *The Book of Acts: Revised Edition*. The New International Commentary on the New Testament, F. F. Bruce, Gen. ed. Grand Rapids: Eerdmans, 1988.

Burge, Gary M. *Jesus and the Land: The New Testament Challenge to "Holy Land" Theology*. Grand Rapids: Baker Academic, 2010.

Burkett, Delbert. *The Son of Man Debate: A History and Evaluation*. SNTSMS, Vol. 107. Cambridge: University Press, 1999.

Burridge, W. *Seeking the Site of St. Paul's Shipwreck*. Valletta, Malta: Progress, 1952.

Camp, John M. *The Archaeology of Athens*. New Haven: Yale University Press, 2001.

Carter, Warren. "Roman Imperial Power: A New Testament Perspective." *Rome and Religion: A Cross-Disciplinary Dialogue on the Imperial Cult*, 137–51, ed. Jeffrey Brodd and Jonathan L. Reed. WGRWSS, No. 5. Atlanta: Society of Biblical Literature, 2011.

Cary, M. and H. H. Scullard. *A History of Rome: Down to the Reign of Constantine*. 3rd ed. Bedford: St. Martin's, 1976.

Casey, Maurice. *The Solution to the 'Son of Man' Problem*. New York: T&T Clark, 2009.

Chadwick, Henry. "St. Peter and St. Paul in Rome: The Problem of the Memoria Apostolorum ad Catacumbas." *The Journal of Theological Studies*, Vol. 8, Issue 1 (April 1957), 31–52.

_____. *Chadwick: Selected Writings*, Edited by William G. Rusch. Grand Rapids: Eerdmans, 2017)

Chaniotis, Angelos. "The Jews of Aphrodisias: New Evidence and Old Problems." *Scripta Classica Israelica* 21 (2002): 209–42.

Chrysostom, John. *John Chrysostom: On the Priesthood, Ascetic Treatises, Homilies and Letters*. Ed. Philip Schaff. Grand Rapids: Eerdmans, 1975.

Cicero, M. Tullius. *Tusculan Disputations*. Translated by J. E. King. LCL 141. 1927. Cambridge, Mass.: Harvard University Press, 1960.

_____. *Epistulae ad familiares*; URL: http://www.perseus.tufts.edu/hopper/text?doc= Cic.+Fam.+2.8.1&fromdoc=Perseus%3Atext%3A1999.02.0009; accessed 08 April 2015.

Clarke, Andrew D. *Secular and Christian Leadership in Corinth: A Socio-Historical and Exegetical Study of 1 Corinthians 1–6*. In Arbeiten Zur Geschichte Des Antiken, 18. Leiden: Brill Academic, 1993.

Clement of Alexandria. *The Ante-Nicene Fathers* on CD-ROM. Accordance Bible Software Version 10.1.5, 2013. Print ed.: Clement of Alexandria. In vol. 2 of *The Ante-Nicene Fathers*, ed. Alexander Roberts, James Donaldson, and A. Cleveland Coxe. 1885–1896. 10 vols. New York: Christian Literature Company.

Clement of Rome. *The Ante-Nicene Fathers* on CD-ROM. Logos Research Systems Version 2.0. 1997. Print ed.: Clement of Rome. In vol. 1 of *The Ante-Nicene Fathers*, ed. Alexander Roberts, James Donaldson, and A. Cleveland Coxe. 1885–1896. 10 vols. New York: Christian Literature Company.

Collingwood, R. G. and J. N. L. Myres. *Roman Britain and the English Settlements*. 2nd ed. OHE. Oxford: Oxford University Press, 1937.

Conybeare, W. J. and J. S. Howson. *The Life and Epistles of St. Paul*. Hartford: S. S. Scranton Company, 1893.

Cooper, Kate. "The martyr, the matrona and the bishop: the matron Lucina and the politics of martyr cult in fifth- and sixth-century Rome." *Early Medieval Europe*. Vol. 8, Issue 3 (November, 1999): 297–317.

Cornuke, Robert. *The Lost Shipwreck of Paul*. Bend, OR: Global Publishing Service, 2003.

Cyril of Jerusalem. *The Nicene and Post-Nicene Fathers of the Christian Church* on CD-ROM. Accordance Bible Software Version 10.1.5, 2013. Print ed.: Cyril of Jerusalem. In vol. 7 of *The Nicene and Post-Nicene Fathers of the Christian Church*. Series 2. 1886–1889, ed. Philip Schaff and Henry Wace. 14 vols. New York: Christian Literature Company.

Davids, Peter H. *The First Epistle of Peter*, The New International Commentary on the New Testament. Gen. ed. Gordon D. Fee. Grand Rapids: Eerdmans, 1990.

Deissmann, Adolf. *Light from the Ancient East: The New Testament Illustrated by Recently Discovered Texts of the Graeco Roman World*. Lionel R. M. Strachan, trans. Eugene, Ore.: Wipf and Stock, 2004.

deSilva, David A. "The Social Setting of the Revelation to John: Conflicts Within, Fears Without," *Westminster Theological Journal* 54, 1992.

_____. *Honor, Patronage, Kinship, and Purity: Unlocking New Testament Culture*. Downers Grove: InterVarsity, 2000.

_____. *An Introduction to the New Testament: Contexts, Methods and Ministry Formation*. Downers Grove: Intervarsity, 2004.

Destro, Adriana, and Mauro Pesce. "Father and Householders in the Jesus Movement: The Perspective of the Gospel of Luke." *Biblical Interpretation* 11.2 (2003): 211–38.

Dicke, John. "Christian," in *The International Standard Bible Encyclopedia, Fully Revised, Illustrated, in Four Volumes*. Gen. ed. Geoffrey W. Bromiley. Vol. 1. Grand Rapids: Eerdmans, 1979.

Dio Cassius. *Roman History*. Trans. Ernest Carey, LCL. Vol. 3. Cambridge: Harvard University Press; London: William Heinemann, 1914.

Diogenes Laertius. *Delphi Complete Works of Diogenes Laertius (Illustrated)*. R. D. Hicks, trans. Delphi ancient Classics, Vol. 47. Delphi Classics, Kindle Edition, 2015.

Dodd, Charles H. *The Apostolic Preaching and Its Development*. New York: Harper-Collins, 1936.

Döhler, Marietheres, ed. *Acta Petri: Text, Übersetzung und Kommentar zu den Actus Vercellenses*. In Texte und Untersuchungen zur Geschichte der altchristlichen Literatur (TU), ed. O. von Gebhardt and A. von Harnack. Vol. 171. Berlin: De Gruyter, 2018.

Douglas, Mary. *Purity and Danger: An Analysis of the Concepts of Pollution and Taboo*. New York: Routledge and Kegan Paul, 1966.

_____. *Natural Symbols: Explorations in Cosmology*, 3d ed. (New York: Pantheon, 1982).

Downey, Glanville. *Ancient Antioch*. Princeton: Princeton University Press, 1963.

Duchesne, Louis. *Liber Pontificalis I*. Paris: 1886.

Dunn, James D. G. *Romans*. In WBC, Vols. 38a, 38b. Dallas: Word, 1988.

_____. "Pentecost, Feast of," *The New International Dictionary of New Testament Theology*. Gen. ed. Colin Brown, 3 vols. Grand Rapids: Zondervan, 1976.

_____. *The Partings of the Ways: Between Christianity and Judaism and Their Significance for Christianity*. Norwich, UK: SCM, 1991.

_____. *The Acts of the Apostles*. Narrative Commentaries, Ivor H. Jones, Gen. ed. Valley Forge, Penn.: Trinity Press International, 1996.

Eastman, David L. *Paul the Martyr: The Cult of the Apostle in the Latin West*, WGRW-Sup 4. Atlanta: Society of Biblical Literature, 2011.

_____. *The Ancient Martyrdom Accounts of Peter and Paul*. In Writings from the Greco-Roman World, Vol. 39. Atlanta: SBL Press, 2015.

Edmundson, George. *The Church in Rome in the First Century: An Examination of Various Controverted Questions Relating to Its History, Chronology, Literature, and Traditions; Eight Lectures Preached before the University of Oxford in the Year 1913 on the Foundation of the Late Rev. John Bampton*. Oxford, 1913; reprint, CreateSpace Independent Publishing Platform, 2016.

Elliot, J. K. *The Apocryphal New Testament*. Oxford: Clarendon, 1993.

Elliott, John H. *1 Peter: A New Translation with Introduction and Commentary*, The Anchor Bible. Ed. William Foxwell Albright and David Noel Freedman, Vol. 37B. New York: Doubleday, 2000.

Elliott, Neil. *The Arrogance of Nations: Reading Romans in the Shadow of Empire*. PCCS. Minneapolis: Fortress, 2008.

Epictetus. *The Discourses as Reported by Arrian, the Manual and Fragments*. Vol. 2. Translated by W. A. Oldfather. LCL 218. 1926–28. Cambridge, Mass.: Harvard University Press, 1969.

Epiphanius. *The Panarion of Epiphanius of Salamis, Book I (Sects 1–46)*. 2nd Rev. Exp. Ed. Trans. by Frank Williams. Nag Hammadi and Manichean Studies (Book 63). Leiden: Brill Academic, 2008.

Eusebius. *The Nicene and Post-Nicene Fathers of the Christian Church* on CD-ROM. Accordance Bible Software Version 10.1.5, 2013. Print ed.: Eusebius. Vol. 1, *The Nicene and Post-Nicene Fathers of the Christian Church*. Series 2. 1886–1889, ed. Philip Schaff and Henry Wace. 14 vols. New York: Christian Literature Company.

Falk, Daniel K. "Jewish Prayer Literature and the Jerusalem Church in Acts," *The Book of Acts in its First Century Setting*. Ed. Bruce W. Winter, *Volume 4: Palestinian Setting*. Ed. Richard Bauckham. Grand Rapids: Eerdmans; Carlisle: The Paternoster, 1995.

Fanning, Bruce M. *Verbal Aspect in New Testament Greek*. Oxford: Clarendon, 1990.

Fee, Gordon D. and Douglas Stuart. *How to Read the Bible for All Its Worth*. Grand Rapids: Zondervan, 2003.

Feldman, Louis H. "Financing the Colosseum," *Biblical Archeology Review*, July-August 2001.

Ferguson, Everett. *Backgrounds of Early Christianity*. 3rd ed. Grand Rapids: Eerdmans, 2003.

Fine, Steven. "Non-Jews in the Synagogues of Late-Antique Palestine: Rabbinic and Archeological Evidence." *Jews, Christians, and Polytheists in the Ancient Synagogue: Cultural Interaction during the Greco-Roman Period*, 224–42, ed. Steven Fine. Baltimore Studies in the History of Judaism. London, New York: Routledge, 1999.

Fitzgerald, Michael. "The Ship of Saint Paul, Part II: Comparative Archeology." *Biblical Archeologist* 53/1 (March 1990): 31–39.

Fitzmyer, Joseph A. *The Acts of the Apostles: A New Translation with Introduction and Commentary.* The Anchor Bible, Vol. 31. Gen. eds. William Foxwell Albright and David Noel Freedman. New York: Doubleday, 1998.

Fox, Robert Lane. *Pagans and Christians.* New York: HarperCollins, 1986.

Freeman, D. "Pentecost, Feast of." *The Illustrated Bible Dictionary.* Revision ed. N. Hillyer, 3 Vols. Leicester, Eng.: InterVarsity, 1980.

Futral, Jr., James Robert. "The Rhetorical Value of *City* as a Sociological Symbol in the Book of Revelation." PhD diss., New Orleans Baptist Theological Seminary, 2002.

Galinsky, Karl. *Augustan Culture: An Interpretive Introduction.* Princeton: Princeton University Press, 1996.

———. "The Cult of the Roman Emperor: Uniter or Divider?" *Rome and Religion: A Cross-Disciplinary Dialogue on the Imperial Cult,* 1–21, ed. Jeffrey Brodd and Jonathan L. Reed. WGRWSS, No. 5. Atlanta: Society of Biblical Literature, 2011.

Gamble, Harry Jr. *The Textual History of the Letter to the Romans.* Studies and Documents 42, ed. Irving Alan Sparks. Grand Rapids: Eerdmans, 1977.

Gaster, Theodor H. *Festivals of the Jewish Year: A Modern Interpretation and Guide* (New York: William Morrow & Co., Inc., 1952, 1953).

Gates, Charles. *Ancient Cities: The Archaeology of Urban Life in the Ancient Near East and Egypt, Greece, and Rome.* London: Routledge, 2003.

Gatt, Mark. *PAVLVS: The Shipwreck 60 AD.* Valletta, Malta: Allied Publications, 2009.

Gaventa, Beverly Roberts. *Acts.* Abingdon New Testament Commentaries. Nashville: Abingdon, 2003.

Glatz, Carol. "Shining a light on St. Paul: Archeological site renovated." *Catholic News Service* (Sept. 6, 2018). Accessed at https://www.vaticannews.va/en/vatican-city/news/2018-07/vatican-saint-paul-basilica-archeology-monks-orchard.html.

Gonis, N., J. Chapa, W. E. H. Cockle, and Dirk Obbink, eds. *The Oxyrhynchus Papyri.* Vol. 66. London: Egypt Exploration Society, 1999.

Greek Drama: From Ritual to Theater. DVD. Princeton: Films for the Humanities and Sciences, 2005.

Griffin, Miriam. "Urbs Roma, Plebs, and Princeps," in *Images of Empire.* Ed. Loveday Alexander. Sheffield: Sheffield Academic, 1991.

Gruber, Daniel. *Rabbi Akiba's Messiah: The Origins of Rabbinic Authority.* Kindle Edition. Elijah Publishing, 2012. ASIN: B00ACVN8MO.

Grudem, Wayne. *Bible Doctrine: Essential Teachings of the Christian Faith,* ed. Jeff Purswell. Grand Rapids: Zondervan, 1999.

Grundmann, Walter. "Χρίω κτλ." in *Theological Dictionary of the New Testament.* Ed. Gerhard Kittel and Gerhard Friedrich. Trans. Geoffrey W. Bromiley. Vol. 9. Grand Rapids: Eerdmans, 1974.

Haenchen, Ernst. *The Acts of the Apostles: A Commentary.* Trans. Bernard Noble and Gerald Shinn, rev. R. McL. Wilson. Philadelphia: Westminster, 1971.

Hanson, Kenneth C. and Douglas E. Oakman, *Palestine in the Time of Jesus: Social Structures and Social Conflicts.* Minneapolis: Augsburg Fortress, 1998.

Harril, J. Albert. *Slaves in the New Testament: Literary, Social, and Moral Dimensions.* Minneapolis: Fortress, 2006.

Harris, J. Rendel. "Cretans Always Liars." *The Expositor* (October 1906): 305–17. Seventh Series, No. 10. London: Hodder & Stoughton.

Hastings, James, Ann Wilson Hastings, and Edward Hastings. eds. "Notes of Recent Exposition." *The Expository Times.* Vol. 18, No. 3 (Dec 1906): 97–103.

Heemstra, Marius. *How Rome's Administration of the Fiscus Judaicus Accelerated the Parting of the Ways Between Judaism and Christianity: Rereading 1 Peter, Revelation, the Letter to the Hebrews, and the Gospel of John in Their Roman and Jewish Contexts*. Doctoral Dissertation, September 2009, Rijksuniversiteit Groningen. Veenendal, the Netherlands: Universal, 2009.

Hengel, Martin. *Judaism and Hellenism: Studies in Their Encounter in Palestine in the Early Hellenistic Period*. Trans. John Bowden, *2 vols*. Grand Rapids: Fortress, 1981.

Hennecke, Edgar and William Schneemelcher, eds. *New Testament Apocrypha*. Trans. R. McL. Wilson. 5th Ed. Vol. 2. Louisville: Westminster John Knox, 1992.

Herbert, A. S. *Historical Catalogue of Printed Editions of the English Bible 1525–1961*. Rev. and exp. ed. London: British and Foreign Bible Society, 1968.

Herodotus. *The Persian Wars*. Translated by A. D. Godley. 2 vols. LCL. Cambridge: Harvard University Press, 1921–1925.

Hilhorst, A. "The Text of the Actus Vercellenses." *The Apocryphal Acts of Peter*, ed. J. N. Bremmer. Leuven: Peters, 1998, 148–60.

Hill, Duncan. *Ancient Rome: From the Republic to the Empire*. Bath, UK: Parragon, 2007.

Hillyer, Norman. *1 and 2 Peter, Jude*, New International Commentary, New Testament Series. Ed. W. Ward Gasque. Peabody: Hendrickson, 1992.

Hippocrates. *On the Sacred Disease*. In *The Law, The Oath of Hippocrates, and On the Sacred Disease*. Translated by Francis Adams. Gloucestershire, UK: Dodo, 2009.

Hirschfeld, Nicolle. "The Ship of Saint Paul, Part I: Historical Background." *Biblical Archeologist* 53/1 (March 1990): 25–30.

Hobart, William Kirk. *The Medical Language of St. Luke*. Dublin: Hodges, Figgis, 1882. Repr., Eugene, Ore.: Wipf and Stock, 2004.

Holmes, Michael W. *The Apostolic Fathers : Greek Texts and English Translations*. Updated ed. Grand Rapids: Baker, 1999.

Hood, Renate Viveen. "A Socio-Anthropological Analysis of Gentile-Jew Relationships in Rome and Antioch." Ph.D. diss., New Orleans Baptist Theological Seminary, 2002.

Horace. *Satires, Epistles, and Ars poetica*. Trans. by H. Rushton Fairclough, LCL 194. Cambridge, Mass.: Harvard University Press, 1926, 1960.

Horsley, Richard A., ed. *Paul and the Roman Imperial Order*. Harrisburg, PA: Trinity Press International, 2004.

Huttner, Ulrich. *Early Christianity in the Lycus Valley*. David Green, trans. Ancient Judaism and Early Christianity. Leiden: Brill, 2013.

Ignatius. *Apostolic Fathers: English Translation* on CD-ROM. Accordance Bible Software Version 10.1.5, 2013. Print ed.: Ignatius. *The Apostolic Fathers: English Translation*. Translated by Michael W. Holmes. Grand Rapids: Baker, 1992, 1999.

Irenaeus. *The Ante-Nicene Fathers* in *Accordance Bible Software*, Version 10.1.5. 2013. Print ed.: Irenaeus. In vol. 1 of *The Ante-Nicene Fathers*, ed. Alexander Roberts, James Donaldson, and A. Cleveland Coxe. 1885–1896. 10 vols. New York: Christian Literature Company.

Jacobus, Lee A. *The Bedford Introduction to Drama*. 6th ed. New York: Bedford/St. Martin's, 2009.

Järvinen, Arto. "The Son of Man and His Followers: A Q Portrait of Jesus." *Characterization in the Gospels*, 180–222. David Rhoads and Kari Syreeni, eds. JSNT-Sup 184. Sheffield: Sheffield Academic, 1999.

Jeffers, James S. *Conflict at Rome: Social Order and Hierarchy in Early Christianity*. Minneapolis: Fortress, 1991.

Jerusalem Talmud. *The Jerusalem Talmud: A Translation and Commentary on CD*, ed. Jacob Neusner. Trans. by Jacob Neusner and Tzvee Zahavy. Peabody, Mass.: Hendrickson, 2010. ISBN: 1598565281.

Jewett, Robert. *Romans: A Commentary*. Hermeneia: A Critical and Historical Commentary on the Bible. Minneapolis: Fortress, 2006.

Jones, Brian W. *The Emperor Domitian*. Reprint edition. London: Routledge, 1993.

_____. *Suetonius: Domitian*. Bristol: Bristol Classic, 1996.

Josephus. Modules on CD-ROM. Accordance Bible Software. OakTree Software, Inc., Altamonte Springs, Fla. Greek text, ver. 1.5. 2005. Based on 1890 Niese edition, public domain. English text, ver. 1.3. 2005. Print ed.: *The Works of Flavius Josephus, Complete and Unabridged*. Updated edition. Translated by William Whiston. Peabody, Mass.: Hendrickson, 1987.

_____. Translated by H. St. J. Thackeray et al. 10 vols. LCL. Cambridge: Harvard University Press, 1926–1965; reprint 1968.

_____. *The Works of Josephus: Complete and Unabridged*. Updated edition. Translated by William Whiston. Peabody: Hendrickson, 1987.

Justin Martyr. *The Ante-Nicene Fathers* on CD-ROM. in *Accordance Bible Software*, Version 10.1.5. 2013. Print ed.: Justin Martyr. In vol. 1 of *The Ante-Nicene Fathers*, ed. Alexander Roberts, James Donaldson, and A. Cleveland Coxe. 1885–1896. 10 vols. New York: Christian Literature Company.

Justin's History of the World. In *Justin's Epitome of The History of Pompeius Trogus, Literally Translated, with Notes and a General Index*. Translated by John Selby Watson. London: George Bell and Sons, 1886.

Käsemann, Ernest. *Commentary on Romans*. Translated and edited by Geoffrey W. Bromiley. Grand Rapids: Eerdmans, 1980.

Kasher, Aryeh. *Jews, Idumeans, and Ancient Arabs*. Tübingen: J. C. B. Mohr, 1988.

Katzev, Susan W. and Michael L. Katzev. "Last Harbor for the Oldest Ship." National Geographic 146 (1974): 618–25. Accessible online at: http://www.kyrenia-collection.org/resources/PDF_Files/NGS-Nov.-1974.pdf.

Kee, Howard Clark. *To Every Nation Under Heaven: The Acts of the Apostles*. The New Testament In Context, Howard Clark Kee and J. Andrew Overman, eds. Harrisburg: Penn.: Trinity Press International, 1997.

Keener, Craig S. *IVP Bible Background Commentary: New Testament*. Downer's Grove: InterVarsity, 1993.

_____. *Acts: An Exegetical Commentary*. Vol. 1: Introduction and 1:1—2:47; Vol. 2: 3:1—14:28; Vol. 3: 15:1—23:35; Vol. 4: 24:1—28:31. Grand Rapids: Baker Aca-demic, 2012–2015.

Kelly, John N. D. *The Epistles of Peter and of Jude*, Black's New Testament Commen-tary (London: A. and C. Black, Ltd., 1969.

Klaus, Carl H., Miriam Gilbert, and Bradford S. Field Jr., eds. *Stages of Drama: Classical to Contemporary Theater*, 5th ed. Boston: Bedford/St. Martin's, 2003.

Klein, William, Craig Blomberg, and Robert Hubbard. *Introduction to Biblical Interpretation*. Rev. ed. Downers Grove: InterVarsity, 2004.

Koester, Helmut. *Introduction to the New Testament. Volume 1: History, Culture, and Religion of the Hellenistic Age*, 2d ed. 2 Vols. New York: Walter de Gruyter, 1995.

Kraemer, Ross S. "Typical and Atypical Jewish Family Dynamics: The Cases of Babatha and Berenice," in *Early Christian Families in Context: An Interdisciplinary Dialogue*. Ed. David L. Balch and Carolyn Osiek, Religion, Marriage, and Family, ed. Don S. Browning and David Clairmont. Grand Rapids: Eerdmans, 2003.

Lactantius. *The Ante-Nicene Fathers* in *Accordance Bible Software*, Version 10.1.5. 2013. Print ed.: Lactantius. In vol. 7 of *The Ante-Nicene Fathers*, ed. Alexander Roberts, James Donaldson, and A. Cleveland Coxe. 1885–1896. 10 vols. New York: Christian Literature Company.

Lau, Rabbi Binyamin. *The Second Temple Period: Character, Context & Creativity*. Vol. 1 of *The Sages*. Translated by Michael Prawer. Jerusalem: Maggid, 2010.

Lawlor, H. J. "St. Paul's Quotations from Epimenides." *The Irish Church Quarterly*. Vol. 9, No. 35 (July 1916): 180–93.

Leeman, A. D. *Orationis Ratio: The Stylistic Theories and Practice of the Roman Orators Historians and Philosophers, Vols. 1–2*, in one vol. Amsterdam: Adolf M. Hakkert, 2001; reprint of the 1963 edition.

Lennon, John and Paul McCartney. *Nowhere Man*. London: Capitol Records, 1965.

Levine, Lee I. *The Ancient Synagogue: The First Thousand Years*. 2d ed. New Haven, CT: Yale University Press, 2005.

Levinskaya, Irina A. "The Inscription from Aphrodisias and the Problem of God-Fearers." *Tyndale Bulletin* 41.2 (1990): 312–18.

Liberati, Anna Maria and Fabio Bourbon. *Ancient Rome: History of a Civilization that Ruled the World*. New York: Barnes and Noble, 2000, arrangement with original publishers, White Star, Vercelli, Italy, 1996.

Lightfoot, J. B. *The Acts of the Apostles: A Newly Discovered Commentary*. The Lightfoot Legacy Set, Vol. 1, ed. Ben Witherington III and Todd D. Still. Downers Grove, IL: InterVarsity, 2014.

Lipsius, R. A. and C. H. Turner. "Actus Petri cum Simone (Vercellenses)," *The Journal of Theological Studies*. Vol. 32, No. 126 (Jan 1931): 119–33

Livy. *History of Rome*. Translated by Frank Gardner Moore et al. 14 vols. LCL. Cambridge: Harvard University Press, 1919–1959; reprint 1965.

Lohse, Eduard. "πεντηκοστή," *Theological Dictionary of the New Testament*. Ed. Gerhard Friedrich, Trans. and ed., Geoffrey W. Bromiley, 10 vols. Grand Rapids: Eerdmans, 1968.

Longenecker, Richard N. "Antioch of Syria," in *Major Cities of the Biblical World*. Ed. R. K. Harrison. Nashville: Thomas Nelson, 1985.

Louw, Johannes P. and Eugene A. Nida, eds., Rondal B. Smith, part-time ed., Karen A. Munson, assoc. ed., *Greek English Lexicon of the New Testament Based on Semantic Domains, Second Edition*. Vol. 1: Introduction and Domains. New York: United Bible Societies, 1988, 1989.

MacDonald, Dennis R. "Apocryphal and Canonical Narratives about Paul." *Paul and the Legacies of Paul*, 55–70, ed. William S. Babcock. Dallas: Southern Methodist University Press, 1990.

MacMullan, Ramsay. *Enemies of the Roman Order: Treason, Unrest, and Alienation in the Empire*. Cambridge: Harvard University Press, 1966.

Macpherson, John. "Was There a Second Imprisonment of Paul in Rome?" *The American Journal of Theology*, Vol. 4, No 1 (Jan 1900): 33–35.

Malina, Bruce J. *Christian Origins and Cultural Anthropology: Practical Models for Biblical Interpretation*. Louisville: Westminster John Knox, 1986.

_____. *The New Jerusalem in the Revelation of John: The City as Symbol of Life with God*. Collegeville, Minn.: Liturgical, 2000.

_____. *The New Testament World: Insights from Cultural Anthropology*. 3rd ed. Louisville: Westminster John Knox, 2001.

Marshak, Adam Kolman. *The Many Faces of Herod the Great*. Grand Rapids: Eerdmans, 2015.

Marshall, I. Howard. *Acts*, TNTC. Leicester: InterVarsity, 1980.

_____. *1 Peter*, The IVP New Testament Commentary Series. Ed. Grant R. Osborne. Downers Grove: InterVarsity, 1991.

_____. *New Testament Theology: Many Witnesses, One Gospel*. Downers Grove: InterVarsity, 2004.

Martyrdom of Polycarp. Apostolic Fathers: English Translation on CD-ROM. Accordance Bible Software Version 10.1.5, 2013. Print ed.: Martyrdom of Polycarp. *The Apostolic Fathers: English Translation*. Translated by Michael W. Holmes. Grand Rapids: Baker, 1992, 1999.

McGrath, Alister E. *Christian Theology: An Introduction*. Oxford, U. K.; Cambridge, Mass.: Blackwell, 1994.

McKay, K. L. *A New Syntax of the Verb in New Testament Greek: An Aspectual Approach*. SBG, Vol. 5. New York: Peter Lang, 1994.

Meinardus, Otto F. A. "St. Paul shipwrecked in Dalmatia." *Biblical Archeologist*, 39/4 (December 1976): 145–47.

Merrill, Elmer Truesdell. "The Expulsion of Jews from Rome under Tiberius." *Classical Philology* 14/4 (October 1919): 365–72.

Metzger, Bruce M. *A Textual Commentary on the Greek New Testament: A Companion Volume to the United Bible Societies' Greek New Testament (Fourth Revised Edition)*. 2nd ed. Stuttgart: German Bible Society, 1994.

Michaels, J. Ramsey. *1 Peter*. Word Biblical Commentary. Ed. David A. Hubbard and Glenn W. Barker. Vol. 49. Waco: Word, 1988.

The Mishnah, Translated from the Hebrew with Introduction and Brief Explanatory Notes. Trans. Herbert Danby. Oxford: Oxford University Press, 1933.

Moessner, David P. *Lord of the Banquet: The Literary and Theological Significance of the Lukan Travel Narrative*. Minneapolis: Fortress, 1989.

Moxnes, Halvor. "Honor and Shame." *The Social Sciences and New Testament Interpretation*, 19–40, ed. Richard Rohrbaugh. Peabody: Hendrickson, 1996.

Müller, Mogens. *The Expression 'Son of Man' and the Development of Christology: A History of Interpretation*. CIS, ed. Thomas L. Thompson. London, Oakville: Equinox, 2008.

Munck, Johannes. *Paulus und die Heilsgeschichte*. Acta Jutlandica 26:1; Tellogisk serie 6. Aarhus: Aarhus University Press, 1954. See *Paul and the Salvation of Mankind*. Translated by Frank Clarke. Atlanta: John Knox, 1959; paperback, 1997.

Musgrave, George. *Friendly Refuge*. Heathfield, Sussex: Heathfield, 1979.

My Fair Lady, Prod. Jack L. Warner. Dir. George Cukor, 170 min., Warner Bros. Pictures, 1964. DVD release, Paramount, 2009.

Neyrey, Jerome H. *The Social World of Luke-Acts: Models for Interpretation*. Peabody, Mass.: Hendrickson, 1991.

_____. "The Idea and the System of Purity." *The Social Sciences and New Testament Interpretation*, 80–106, ed. Richard Rohrbaugh. Peabody, Mass.: Hendrickson, 1996.

Oden, Thomas C. *The Rebirth of Orthodoxy: Signs of New Life in Christianity*. New York: HarperSanFrancisco, 2003.

Olson, Mark J. "Pentecost," *The Anchor Bible Dictionary*, ed. David Noel Freedman. Nashville: Fortress, 1995.

Pao, David W. *Acts and the Isaianic New Exodus*. Grand Rapids: Baker Academic, 2002; reprint of J. C. B. Mohr, 2000.

Parker, Robert. *Miasma: Pollution and Purification in Early Greek Religion*. New York: Oxford University Press, 1983.

Parsons, Mikeal C. *Acts*. Paideia Commentaries on the New Testament. Mikeal C. Parsons and Charles H. Talbert, gen. eds. Grand Rapids: Baker Academic, 2008.

Perriman, Andrew. *The Coming of the Son of Man: New Testament Eschatology for an Emerging Church*. Bletchley, Milton Keynes, UK: Paternoster, 2005.

Pervo, Richard I. *Acts: A Commentary*. Hermeneia. Minneapolis: Fortress, 2009.

Peterson, David G. *The Acts of the Apostles*. Pillar New Testament Commentary. Grand Rapids: Eerdmans, 2009.

Petronius. Translated by W. H. D. Rouse and E. H. Warmington. LCL. Cambridge: Harvard University Press, 1913; updated by Michael Heseltine 1987.

Philo. *The Works of Philo, Completed and Unabridged*. New Updated Edition. Trans. by C. D. Yonge. (Peabody: Hendrickson, 1993). Oaktree Software module, ver. 1.2.

_____. *Philo, With an English Translation by F. H. Colson*, 9 vols. LCL. London: William Heinemann Ltd.; Cambridge, MA: Harvard University Press, 1937.

Plevnik, Joseph. "Honor/Shame." *Handbook of Biblical Social Values*, 106–15, ed. John J. Pilch and Bruce J. Malina. Peabody: Hendrickson, 1998.

Pliny the Younger. Translated by Betty Radice. 2 vols. LCL. Cambridge: Harvard University Press, 1969.

Plutarch. *The Parallel Lives*. Translated by Bernadotte Perrin et al. 28 vols. LCL. Cambridge: Harvard University Press, 1914–1969.

Polhill, John B. *Acts, The New American Commentary*, Vol. 26. Gen. ed. David S. Dockery. Nashville: Broadman, 1992.

Polybius. *The Histories*. Trans. W. R. Paton, LCL. Vol. 6. Cambridge: Harvard University Press; London: William Heinemann, 1925; reprinted 1954.

Polycarp. *Apostolic Fathers: English Translation* on CD-ROM. Accordance Bible Software Version 10.1.5, 2013. Print ed.: Polycarp. *The Apostolic Fathers: English Translation*. Translated by Michael W. Holmes. Grand Rapids: Baker, 1992, 1999.

Porter, Stanley E. *Verbal Aspect in the Greek of the New Testament, with Reference to Tense and Mood*. SBG. Vol. 1. New York: Peter Lang, 1989, 1993.

Price, S. R. F. *Rituals and Power: The Roman Imperial Cult in Asia Minor*. Cambridge: Cambridge University Press, 1984.

Pullelia, Philip. "Roman archeologists find oldest image of Apostles in a catacomb." Reuters (June 22, 2010). Accessed at http://blogs.reuters.com/faithworld/2010/06/22/roman-arch-aeologists-find-oldest-images-of-apostles-in-a-catacomb/.

Pummer, Reinhard. *The Samaritans: A Profile*. Grand Rapids: Eerdmans, 2016.

Quintilian. *The Orator's Education*, Ed. and trans. Donald A. Russell, LCL Vol. 3. Cambridge: Harvard University Press, 2001.

Rajak, Tessa. "The Synagogue within the Greco-Roman City," *Jews, Christians, and Polytheists in the Ancient Synagogue: Cultural Interaction during the Greco-Roman Period*, 161–73, ed. Steven Fine. Baltimore Studies in the History of Judaism. London, New York: Routledge, 1999.

Rapsky, Brian. *The Book of Acts and Paul in Roman Custody*. Vol. 3 in The Book of Acts in Its First-Century Setting. Ed. Bruce W. Winter. Consulting eds. I. Howard Marshal and David W. J. Gill. Grand Rapids: Eerdmans; Carisle; Paternoster, 1994.

Reicke, Bo. *Re-examining Paul's Letters: The History of the Pauline Correspondence*, ed. David P. Moessner and Ingalisa Reicke. Harrisburg, Penn: Trinity Press International, 2001.

Reinhardt, Wolfgang. "The Population Size of Jerusalem and the Numerical Growth of the Jerusalem Church," *The Book of Acts in its First Century Setting*, ed. Bruce W. Winter, *Volume 4: Palestinian Setting*, ed. Richard Bauckham. Grand Rapids: Eerdmans; Carisle: Paternoster, 1995.

Reynolds, J. and R. Tannenbaum, *Jews and God-fearers at Aphrodisias: Greek Inscriptions with Commentary*, Proceedings of the Cambridge Philological Association Supp. 12. Cambridge Philological Society 1987.

Rhoads, David M. *Reading Mark, Engaging the Gospel*. Minneapolis: Fortress, 2004.

Richardson, Peter. *Herod: King of the Jews and Friend of the Romans*. SPNT, ed. D. Moody Smith. Columbia, S.C.: University of South Carolina Press, 1996.

Rosenberg, Irene Merker and Yale L. Rosenberg. "Of God's Mercy and the Four Biblical Methods of Capital Punishment: Stoning, Burning, Beheading, and Strangulation." *Tul. L. Rev.* 79 (March 2004).

Rubén, R. Dupertuis and Todd Penner, eds. *Engaging Early Christian History: Reading Acts in the Second Century*. Durham: Acumen, 2013.

Runesson, Anders, Donald D. Binder, and Birger Olsson. *The Ancient Synagogue from its Origins to 200 C.E.: A Source Book*. Ancient Judaism and Early Christianity 72. Leiden: Brill, 2008.

Sanders, E. P. *Judaism: Practice and Belief, 63 BCE–66 C*. London: SCM; Philadelphia: Trinity Press International, 1992.

Schillebeeckx, Edward. *The Church: The Human Story of God*. London: SCM, 1990.

Schreiner, Thomas R. *1, 2 Peter, Jude*, The New American Commentary. Gen. ed. E. Ray Clendenen. Nashville: Broadman and Holman, 2003.

Scrivener, Frederick H. A. *A Plain Introduction to the Criticism of the New Testament: For the Use of Biblical Students*. 4th ed. 2 vols., ed. Edward Miller. London: George Bell & Sons, 1894.

Seneca, Lucius Annaeus. *Epistolae morales ad Lucilium. Seneca: Epistles 66–92*. LCL, 3 vols. Tichard M. Gummere, trans. Cambridge, Mass.: Harvard University Press, 1920.

Septuaginta. Ed. Alfred Rahlfs. Editio altera by Robert Hanhart. Stuttgart: Deutsche Bibelgesellschaft, 2006. Accordance module, Ver. 11, Oaktree Software.

Shear, Theodore L. "Excavations in the Theatre District and Tombs of Corinth in 1929." *American Journal of Archeology* 33.4 (1929): 515–46.

Shipp, David Blake. *Paul the Reluctant Witness: Power and Weakness in Luke's Portrayal*. Eugene, Ore.: Wipf and Stock, 2005.

Sibylline Oracles. *The Sibylline Oracles: Translated from the Greek into English Blank Verse*. Trans. by Terry Milton. Geneva: IPA, 2008.

Sifre: A Tannaitic Commentary on the Book of Deuteronomy, Translated from the Hebrew with Introduction and Notes by Reuven Hammer, Yale Judaica Series, Ed. Leon Nemoy, Vol. XXIV: Sifre on Deuteronomy. London: Yale University Press, 1986.

Sisman, Adam. *The Friendship: Wordsworth and Coleridge*. New York: Viking, 2007.

Smith, Dennis E. and Joseph B. Tyson, eds. *Acts and Christian Beginnings: The Acts Seminar Report*. Salem, Ore.: Polebridge, 2013.

Smith, James. *The Voyage and Shipwreck of St. Paul: With Dissertations on the Life and Writings of St. Luke, and the Ships and Navigation of the Antients*. 2d ed. London: Longman, Brown, Green, Longmans, & Roberts, 1856. Nabu Public Domain Reprints, n.d.

Spencer, F. Scott. *Journeying Through Acts: A Literary-Cultural Reading*. Peabody, Mass.: Hendrickson, 2004.

Stagg, Frank. *The Book of Acts: The Early Struggle for an Unhindered Gospel*. Nashville: Broadman, 1955.

Stevens, Gerald L. "The Literary Background and Theological Significance of ΟΡΓΗ ΘΕΟΥ in the Pauline Epistles." Unpublished PhD dissertation. New Orleans Baptist Theological Seminary, 1981.

_____. "Capital Crimes in the Roman Empire" *Biblical Illustrator*. Vol. 26, No. 2, (Winter 1999–2000), 60–63.

_____. Review Article: A Theology of Luke and Acts: God's Promised Program Realized for All Nations by Darrell L. Bock. *Journal for Baptist Theology and Ministry*, Fall 2013, Vol. 10, No. 2, 74–82.

_____. *Revelation: The Past and Future of John's Apocalypse*. Eugene, OR: Pickwick Publications, 2014.

Stoops, Robert F. "If I Suffer . . . Epistolary Authority in Ignatius of Antioch." *Harvard Theological Review* 80 (1987): 165–67.

Stowers, Stanley K. "On the Comparison of Blood in Greek and Israelite Ritual." *Hesed Ve-Emet: Studies in Honor of Ernest S. Frerichs*, 179–96. BJS. Jodi Magness and Seymour Gitin, eds. Atlanta: Scholars, 1998.

Strabo. *The Geography of Strabo*. Vol. 2. Translated by Horace Leonard Jones. LCL 50, 1923. Cambridge, Mass.: Harvard University Press, 1988.

Strange, W. A. *The Problem of the Text of Acts*. Society for New Testament Studies, Monograph Series Vol. 71, gen. ed. G. N. Stanton. Cambridge: Cambridge University Press, 1992.

Suetonius. *The Lives of the Caesars*. Translated by J. C. Rolfe. 2 vols. LCL. Cambridge: Harvard University Press, 1914; reprint 1965.

Tacitus. Translated by M. Hutton et al. 5 vols. LCL. Cambridge: Harvard University Press, 1914–1937.

Tajra, Harry W. *The Martyrdom of St. Paul: Historical and Judicial Context, Traditions, and Legends*. WUNT 2/67. Tübingen: Mohr, 1994; reprint, Wipf and Stock, 2010.

Tannehill, Robert C. *The Narrative Unity of Luke-Acts: A Literary Interpretation*, vol. 2: The Acts of the Apostles. Minneapolis: Fortress, 1990.

Taplin, Oliver. *Greek Tragedy in Action*. Berkeley: University of California Press, 1978.

Tàrrech, Armand Puig i. "Les Voyages à Jerusalem (Lc 9,51; Ac 19,21)," *The Unity of Luke-Acts*, 493–505, ed. J. Verheyden. Bibliotheca Ephemeridum Theologicarum Lov Aniensium, Vol. 142. Leuven: Leuven University Press, 1999.

The Terminator. Prod. Gale Anne Hurd. Dir. James Cameron, 107 min., Orion Pictures, 1984. DVD release, Image Entertainment, 1997.

Tertullian. *The Ante-Nicene Fathers* on CD-ROM. Accordance Bible Software Version 10.1.5, 2013. Print ed.: Tertullian. In vol. 3 of *The Ante-Nicene Fathers*. 1885–1896. 10 vols., ed. Alexander Roberts, James Donaldson, and A. Cleveland Coxe. New York: Christian Literature Company.

Theophilus. *Ad Autolycum*. Trans. and ed. Robert M. Grant, Oxford Early Christian Texts. New York: Oxford University Press, 1970.

Thompson, Leonard L. *The Book of Revelation: Apocalypse and Empire*. Oxford: Oxford University Press, 1990.

Thornton, T. C. G. "St. Paul's Missionary Intention in Spain." *Expository Times* 86(4) (1975): 120.

Thucydides. *History of the Peloponnesian War*. Translated by Charles Forster Smith, LCL, Vol. 1. Cambridge: Harvard University Press, 1923, rev. and reprinted 1935.

Tödt, Heinz Eduard. *The Son of Man in the Synoptic Tradition*. NTL. Alan Richardson, ed. London: SCM, 1965.

Tolotti, Francesco. *Memorie degli Apostoli in Catacumbas*. Vatican City, 1953.

Towner, Philip H. "1,2 Tim, Titus." NICNT. Grand Rapids: Eerdmans, 2006.

Trebilco, Paul. *The Early Christians in Ephesus from Paul to Ignatius*. Grand Rapids: Eerdmans, 2007.

Troeltsch, Ernst. *The Christian Faith*. Fortress Texts in Modern Theology. Minneapolis: Fortress, 1991.

Troy. Prod. Wolfgang Petersen, Diana Rathbun, and Colin Wilson. Dir. Wolfgang Petersen, 165 min., Warner Bros. Pictures, 2004, DVD.

Valsecchi, Maria Christina. "St. Paul's Tomb Unearthed in Rome," *National Geographic Online* (Dec. 31, 2006). Accessed at https://www.nationalgeographic.com/science/2006/12/news-st-paul-tomb-found-rome/.

Vermes, Geza. *The True Herod*. London, New York: Bloomsbury T&T Clark, 2014.

Virgil. Translated by H. Rushton Fairclough. 2 vols. LCL. Cambridge: Harvard University Press, 1916.

Walton, Steve. *Acts*. Word Biblical Commentary 37A. Dallas: Word, 2008.

White, L. Michael. "Capitalizing on the Imperial Cult: Some Jewish Perspectives." *Rome and Religion: A Cross-Disciplinary Dialogue on the Imperial Cult*, 173–214, ed. Jeffrey Brodd and Jonathan L. Reed. WGRWSS, No. 5. Atlanta: Society of Biblical Literature, 2011.

Wilson, Mark. "Hilasterion and Imperial Rhetoric: A Possible New Reading of Romans 3:25." Paper presentation. Society of Biblical Literature, Atlanta, 2015.

Winter, Bruce W. "Acts and Food Shortages," *The Book of Acts in Its Graeco-Roman Setting*. Ed. David W. J. Gill and Conrad Gempf, The Book of Acts in Its First-Century Setting. Ed. Bruce W. Winter. Vol. 2. Grand Rapids: Eerdmans; Carlisle: Paternoster, 1995.

Witherington, III, Ben. *The Acts of the Apostles: A Social-Rhetorical Commentary*. Grand Rapids: Eerdmans, 1998.

Wright, Nicholas Thomas. *The New Testament and the People of God* in Christian Origins and the Question of God, Vol. 1. Minneapolis: Fortress, 1992.

———. *Surprised by Hope: Rethinking Heaven, the Resurrection, and the Mission of the Church*. New York: HarperCollins, 2008.

———. *Paul and the Faithfulness of God*. Christian Origins and the Faithfulness of God, Vol. 4. Minneapolis: Fortress, 2013.

Zanker, Paul. *The Power of Images in the Age of Augustus*. Ann Arbor, Mich.: University of Michigan Press, 1990.

Scripture Index

Ancient Documents Index

Modern Authors Index

639

Subject Index

CPSIA information can be obtained
at www.ICGtesting.com
Printed in the USA
LVHW111615171121
703615LV00005B/208

9 781532 693243